# The First Three
# Years of Life

# The Early Childhood Development Center's Parenting Series

## The First Three Years of Life

Nina R. Lief, M.C.,
with Mary Ellen Fahs
and Rebecca M. Thomas

SMITHMARK

For Victor Filler Lief,
whose early encouragement,
perceptive criticism, and loving support
made this effort possible
("The First Year of Life")

For Amanda Lief Schuster
and Thomas Reade Fahs
("The Second Year of Life")

For Brooke and Austin Thomas, and all the children
who have participated in the
Early Childhood Development Center's
program and all the children to come
("The Third Year of Life")

Materials in this book were drawn from:
*The First Year of Life* © 1991 by the Early Childhood Development Center
*The Second Year of Life* © 1991 by the Early Childhood Development Center
*The Third Year of Life* © 1991 by the Early Childhood Development Center

This edition published in 1997 by
SMITHMARK Publishers
A division of U.S. Media Holdings, Inc.
16 East 32nd Street, New York, NY 10016

SMITHMARK books are available for bulk purchase for sales,
promotion and premium use. For details, write or call the
manager of special sales, SMITHMARK Publishers,
16 East 32nd Street, New York, NY 10016; (212) 532-6600.

Printed in the United States of America

ISBN: 0-7651-9657-3

10  9  8  7  6  5  4  3  2  1

# Contents

## *The Second Year of Life* 259

## *The Third Year of Life* 501

### SECTION I
### AGE TWENTY-FOUR TO THIRTY MONTHS  503

### SECTION II
### AGE THIRTY TO THIRTY-SIX MONTHS  599

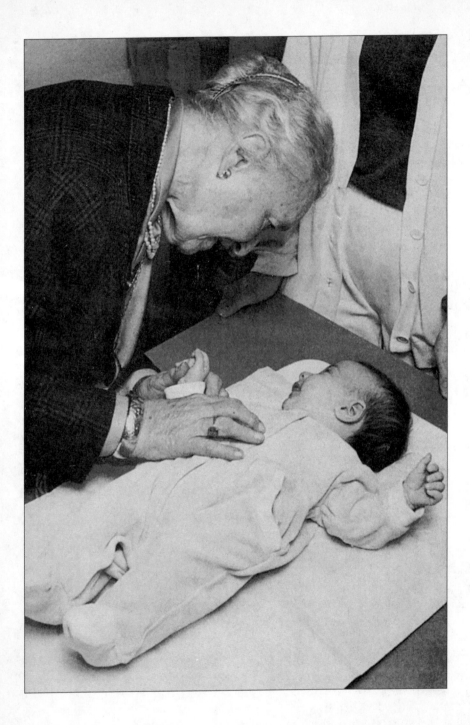

# *Introduction*

Much research has been done on the crucial importance of a child's earliest years, but little of the knowledge and understanding derived from this research reaches the parents, who have primary responsibility for the child's care and development. To provide parents with this information as well as with support and encouragement in their roles as parents, New York Medical College and the New York Junior League established the Early Childhood Development Center in 1974.

At the Center, small groups of parents (usually from eight to ten adults) and their children meet with a trained group leader in weekly discussion sessions. The curriculum for the discussions is based on the best current information regarding a child's emotional, social, and cognitive development, as well as on the real-life concerns of parents, as expressed in their questions. The links between appropriate child-rearing methods and developmental theory are continually demonstrated, thereby enabling parents to see how child-rearing techniques directly influence the child's cognitive, social, and emotional development.

The major aims of the Center's program are to assist parents in guiding their children toward healthy personality development and to help mothers and fathers derive enjoyment and satisfaction from their roles as parents. While other programs have emphasized the physical and cognitive aspects of a child's development, the Center is more concerned with helping the parent understand the emotional and social side of that development and the importance of parent-child interaction in this process. The Center recognizes the uniqueness of each child and each family's situation. It adheres to the belief that the most effective child-rearing results from the parents' understanding of their own child's needs, temperament, and level of development as well as knowledge of appropriate child-rearing options. Parents come to understand and follow the child-rearing practices appropriate for their own child through the discussions at the parenting sessions rather than from specific directions, as no one method suits all children.

In *The First Three Years of Life*, the curriculum used at the Early Childhood Development Center has been divided into segments that span a child's first three years of life. The first segment, entitled "The First Year of Life" (Chapters 1 through 12), covers the first year of life in five-week intervals, beginning with week four. "The Second Year of Life," Chapters 13 through 16, covers the second year in three-month intervals. And "The

Third Year of Life," Chapters 17 through 28, covers the third year of life in six-month intervals. Each of the chapters focuses on developmental highlights, followed by discussions—as they took place with parents at the Early Childhood Development Center—on a series of topics relating to child development and child-rearing issues, as well as the parents' feelings.

Every effort has been made to avoid sexist use of pronouns in referring to the gender of the children who form the subject of this book. This explains why the pronoun referring to the child is sometimes masculine and sometimes feminine, and why the gender of the pronoun appears to change arbitrarily from section to section.

Similarly, throughout the text the parent is more often referred to as the mother, rather than the father. This is not due to any sexist orientation but simply to the fact that the great majority of the parents who provide the major amount of care during the child's earliest years are mothers. It is our belief that parenting is a shared male-female responsibility, and the word *father* may be substituted for the word *mother* in most cases.

Further, a growing number of mothers of children under three years of age are working outside the home. Because the child's needs regarding nutrition, attention, and discipline are similar whether his or her parents work, topics throughout the book discuss the variety of ways that parents in differing circumstances may meet their children's needs. The purpose of this book is to foster the healthiest possible growth and development of the child and to make parenting less stressful and more enjoyable. This is important and possible, whether parents work outside the home or not.

# The First Year
## of Life

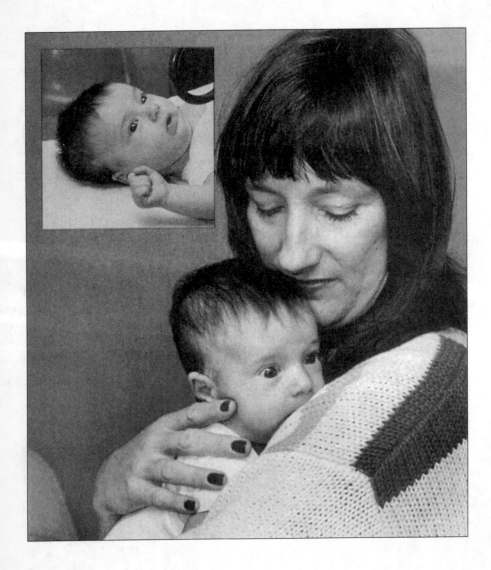

## *Highlights of Development—Four Weeks*

For most parents, the newborn infant seems to be doing very little; but a closer look reveals that the baby is engaged in small but exciting activities. In the earliest weeks of life, the baby holds himself with hands fisted, one above his head and the other outstretched. His legs are pulled up under him, so that his posture is asymmetrical. The baby is sensitive to touch all over and is aware of how he is being held.

Intellectual development and learning begin with eye contact and visual tracking. This ability can be encouraged by dangling a red ring on a string about eight inches in front of the baby to see if she will look at it briefly. In the coming weeks, the baby will begin to follow the ring with her eyes. (A red ring is one of the most useful toys a baby can have. The red color attracts the baby's attention more than the usual pastel shades of nursery toys.) When a rattle is placed in the baby's palm, she may grasp it reflexively before dropping it. If the grasp is maintained, this is an indication of more advanced motor development. If one makes a sudden noise, like ringing a bell, near the baby's head, the baby generally reacts by either a diminution of activity, a startle of the whole body, a change of expression, or by crying.

At this age, a baby's face is impassive, and a seemingly vacant, indirect stare at surroundings is normal. This stare becomes focused with maturation and stimulation. Looking at a parent's face, staring at surroundings, and listening to sounds are all early signs of socialization.

## *Mothers' Feelings About Having a Child*

Most mothers have special feelings about having a child, and these feelings differ from mother to mother. Some mothers want children very much.

Some feel that their children arrived at the wrong time; they wanted them earlier or later in life. Some never had experience with babies; others are very confident because they have had experience with younger members of their own families. Some may have wanted a girl and others a boy.

How did you feel about having a baby? Did you feel ready?

*"We were just so delighted when she came. We had wanted a baby for such a long time. We feel she is more important than anything else in our lives, and she makes us happier than any of the other experiences we have ever had. But, still, I always wonder if I'm doing the right thing."*

*"I certainly wanted the baby, but I feel I'm a little too old and have had no experience with children. When my husband left me the first morning and I realized I was alone with the baby and he was my responsibility, I just panicked. I guess that's why I'm here."*

This feeling of being responsible for another human being who is small, helpless, and utterly dependent on the parents is often frightening, especially if a person has never had any experience with newborns. One has endless questions. This is one of the reasons for this program.

*"Well, I am a trained nurse used to infants, but this one is mine, and it's a different feeling. I need help too. I feel I know about the physical part, but I want to learn about the baby's feelings and how I should treat him."*

That is a very good point of view. We will become more concerned with emotional development as the physical problems of child care become less pressing.

Did most of you immediately feel a sense of love for the baby, or has this feeling been developing gradually?

*"My baby is a month old and, much as I wanted him, he still seems like a stranger to me. I can't believe he's mine . . . maybe because he just cries and sleeps a lot, and doesn't seem to respond as though I meant something to him. He leaves me with kind of a 'blah' feeling."*

This is a very apt description of how many mothers and fathers feel about a new baby. Not all parents have an immediate feeling of love and affection, and they find the baby unresponsive. Few new parents know what to expect of a newborn baby. I know from asking this question many times that frequently a parent's mental picture of a newborn baby is actually that of a four- or five-month-old infant smiling in an endearing way from the cover of *Parents* magazine. This is surely the picture of a baby anyone would fall in love with at first sight. But don't worry. Your baby will appear this way when he is older, and your feelings for each other will develop in time.

*"I am so glad you said that . . . because I was having some of the same feelings, and I thought that there was something wrong with me—maybe I wasn't cut out to be a mother, or maybe my baby wasn't all right. I just didn't dare say it to anybody."*

■                                                                                    ■

It is good that you are finally able to express these feelings. You know now that others have had the same experience, and that there is nothing wrong with you or the baby. The feeling of having the baby belong to you, and you to him, is a process that takes time to develop. One of the topics that we will be discussing throughout this program is how parents can move through this process with understanding and enjoyment.

## *Mother's Need for Help—Father's Role*

Having a new baby and accomplishing as much as you did before the baby came is difficult. Are you finding this hard? How are you managing?

*"My big problem is how to get the shopping done. I don't have a carriage yet, so it's a little hard. I've resorted to calling the stores on the phone, but that always turns out to be more expensive."*

In some families the father can help with the shopping. Often a friend or relative is willing to lend a hand. However, there are some families without relatives or friends in their neighborhoods, and these people do have to rely on the telephone until they get organized.

*"My problem is that I haven't adjusted to being awakened at night to feed the baby. I never get any sleep during the day when the baby is asleep because I try to get the housework done. What I wouldn't give for a full night's sleep!"*

This kind of fatigue is very common among new mothers. Some mothers feel it more than others. It is quite an adjustment, but there are ways of coping. One good solution is to have a nap during the day when the baby is asleep. That way you will be able to enjoy the baby more and accomplish more. Another solution is to have father take over for a while, so that you can have a rest. The father will feel more needed and will get to know his baby better as well.

*"Those are good ideas, and I have used them, but still I can't get the laundry done, the house cleaned, and the meals cooked because the baby takes so much time. Sometimes it's only two hours between feedings, and each one takes time. So, some days I never get anything done, and my husband just can't understand why things don't run just the way they used to."*

No one should expect a household to be run exactly as it was before the baby came. There must be some changes and accommodations to the baby's needs. The mother's and baby's health should be the top priority. To make matters even more difficult, the baby's schedule is very variable at first, before a pattern is established.

# *The Baby's Neurological Development and Rhythm of Activities*

*"When do babies begin to see and hear?"*

The development of the baby's central nervous system begins with the head. The mouth is the first organ for sensation and exploration. Hearing is fairly well developed at birth; even a premature baby in an incubator responds to a soothing voice. A baby's vision is blurred at first, but soon he can see the parent's face and distinct patterns. His attention can be drawn momentarily to brightly colored objects within a range of about eight inches.

*"When will my baby be able to lift her head up?"*

As babies respond to sound and sight, the first movement of the head is from side to side. At about four weeks they begin to lift their heads. Then gradually they begin to use their hands, slowly becoming competent with them. Next they master the arts of sitting, crawling, standing, and finally walking. Thus, development proceeds from the head down to the arms and hands and finally to the legs and feet by about one year of age.

Parents seem to like to encourage their children to walk, but most children will develop this motor ability unaided. Development of visual attention and speech, however, need parental encouragement. Parents can stimulate visual attention with mobiles and other visually attractive toys. They can encourage the abilities of listening and speech by talking to their children.

*"At what age will these developments occur?"*

Development generally follows this neurological sequence from the head down to the legs and feet. Parents will be reassured to know that each child has his own maturational timetable and develops various abilities during different weeks and months of life. Some children walk earlier; others talk earlier. Each child is a unique individual. We should not compare children to see who is ahead of whom. Instead, we should watch their development and note the unique and marvelous differences among them.

Each child also has her own genetic endowment, her own inherited characteristics, her own rhythm of activity. This cannot be changed, but parents can assist the infant in achieving her or his potential, so that there will be the maximum possible growth and a happy interaction between child and parents—and fulfillment for all.

## *Sleeping; Waking for Feeding*

Most of us have had a pattern and rhythm to our lives. Each of us has a biological clock; we don't each get hungry at the same times or need the same amount of sleep. Much as we knew things would be different after the baby came, few of us could foresee just how it would affect us. This is partly because we were not aware that each baby has his or her own biological clock and rhythm, which may or may not coincide with our notions of what this clock or rhythm should be. Yet parents have to adapt to their baby's rhythm because the baby, with her immature nervous system, cannot adapt to her parents' time schedule. At first, the baby takes a great deal of time. As the baby gets older, however, patterns are established according to the baby's particular biological clock. You will come to understand your baby's needs better; child care will take less time and be more enjoyable.

Child-care books tell us that infants sleep most of the time and wake only for feedings. While this may hold true for some babies, many do not follow this pattern. They seem to sleep for shorter intervals and need to be changed or fed more frequently. Also, some babies have certain periods when they take long naps, while at other times they take short naps. Gradually, the parents will be able to adjust their housekeeping and resting to coincide with their baby's napping patterns.

I wonder how you have adapted to your baby's rhythm and kept up with his needs.

*"He has changed our lives completely. We can't count on his sleeping when we want to eat. In fact, dinnertime, when my husband comes home, is the most difficult time to get the baby to sleep."*

It is very difficult in the beginning to meet your baby's needs in such a way that you can continue your own routines. The problem of management is difficult, and some compromises have to be made. Each family must select for itself which personal and social activities are important, and which can be given lower priority.

*"I'm having a different concern: it's not that my baby won't sleep or wakes too soon, but that she sleeps past her feeding times, sometimes for five or six hours. Then I get worried and go in to look at her to see if she is breathing. I don't know if I should wake her or let her sleep."*

All parents get anxious when babies sleep too long. All of us have heard stories that make us worry. It is natural and right to go in and check on the baby at intervals, whether she is sleeping overtime or not. You have to get to know your baby. From the start some babies begin to wake and sleep at predictable intervals, so parents can plan their days accordingly. Others remain unpredictable for months. We no longer believe in fixing "time-clock" schedules for babies—waking them to be fed or forcing them to wait if they are hungry. There is a good body of experience now which indicates that the baby who is fed on her own time schedule, according to her own needs, will eventually have fewer feedings and get into a schedule more easily than the baby who is fed according to a fixed schedule set by the clock. We have also found that if the baby is awakened for a feeding when she is not hungry, she may not take the feeding well, thus frustrating the parents as well as the baby. There are even some babies who wake so hungry that they take the feeding too fast and become gassy and uncomfortable.

Parents have to get to know which system works best for their baby. You have to experiment and use your own judgment. This takes a little time and patience, but it can be achieved. Some parents manage to do this in the first weeks; for others it may take as long as three months. As the baby's pattern is established, parents are able to reestablish a pattern of their own, and life takes on a more satisfactory tempo.

## Burping—The Anatomy of the Stomach

Parents also have to learn when the baby is crying for a feeding and when the cry means there is a burp that must come up. Indeed, the whole technique of how to burp your infant has to be learned by trial and error.

Just lifting some babies to a sitting position on the parent's lap and rubbing the baby's back gently brings up the burp. Other babies need to be held high on the parent's shoulder, which acts as a support for the baby's abdomen. Still other babies do better being patted as they lie across the mother's lap. Some babies burp quickly; some take a long time. Some have to be burped during a feeding; others only afterward.

In any case, burping is an important part of the feeding procedure and if done patiently and consistently, can help prevent crying after feedings and difficulty in sleeping—situations that are frustrating to baby and parent alike.

Babies often spit up with a burp. Some do a great deal of this, and sometimes most of the feeding is lost. When a lot of spitting occurs, the baby may need a little more food before settling down, or may wake earlier for the next feeding. Mothers soon get to know which is the better method for burping their baby.

Are any of you having difficulty with the baby's burping and spitting up?

*"My baby takes forever to burp. I have tried holding him over my shoulder and patting his back. I have also tried sitting him up, but nothing helps much."*

The important thing is not to try to hurry the burp. Take plenty of time. The parent's tenseness and desire to hurry communicate themselves to the baby and keep the baby from relaxing to bring up the air. Perhaps you are not giving your baby enough time.

*"I have the same experience. Waiting for a burp may take fifteen minutes. Then the bottle has to be warmed again, and the entire feeding and changing routine takes most of the morning or afternoon. There is no time to get anything done between feedings!"*

■                                                                            ■

Most parents are not prepared for the amount of time it takes to perform the ordinary tasks of feeding, burping, and changing a baby. It comes as a shock. Sometimes parents think there is something wrong with the baby, but there is nothing wrong. This period in the baby's life will not last forever. It may be shortened by taking it easy and not feeling rushed by the need to get housework done. At first, some things may have to be postponed until the baby and mother develop a pattern for burping, and until the mother becomes more adept at baby care. It all comes with practice.

Knowing a little about the anatomy of the stomach may help you to deal better with burping. The stomach looks like a bottle with the neck at the top that contains an air bubble. If the baby is lying down when she is fed, the bubble will be at the bottom of the stomach under the food the baby has eaten, and will need time to work its way to the top for emission of the burp. Sometimes this air bubble pushes some of the food ahead of it, and spitting up occurs. If the baby is held at the proper angle—almost sitting in the mothers' arms during feeding—the bubble will come toward the top of the food, and the emission will be easier. Sometimes, even with these precautions, some of the air is trapped, and the burp needs to be expelled at a later time. It's a good idea to hold the baby after a feeding for a long enough time to allow a final burp to occur. Sometimes this final burp occurs only when the baby is on her stomach in the crib. Each mother gets to know very soon how to cope with burping her baby.

*"I was always told that putting a baby on her stomach was dangerous, that she might choke if she burped and spat up a little food."*

Actually, it is safer for the baby to be on her stomach because the force of gravity will cause the milk to flow right out of the baby's mouth. If she is on her back, there is more chance to aspirate the milk that comes up. Most healthy babies can lift their heads away from the wet spot by themselves unless they have actually vomited the whole feeding. In any event, it is a good practice to look in on the baby occasionally after she is put to bed to be sure that all is well.

## *Wetting and Bowel Movements*

There are other reasons for crying. Some babies cry when they are wet or have had a bowel movement and are uncomfortable.

Many mothers are annoyed at the number of necessary diaper changes. This varies from day to day and does not last forever. Mothers soon learn to tell the cry that signals a diaper change from other kinds of cries.

Breast-fed babies usually have more frequent bowel movements and looser stools with more variation in color than do bottle-fed babies. Some babies have only one or two bowel movements a day. Some babies do not have movements every day and are comfortable without them. If they are

■                                                                      ■

uncomfortable without them, seek medical advice. If the movements become too frequent, or if the stools become loose, or large and foamy, also seek medical advice.

Do any of you have concerns about the many changes of diapers?

*"For one thing, it's got to be quite a problem having enough diapers on hand so as not to run short. I don't mind the crying when he is wet. I just didn't have any idea a baby could use so many diapers in a week. I just wonder what mothers did when they had to wash them by hand."*

It does come as a surprise to find out how frequently a baby wets, but this frequency is perfectly normal. After all, a baby's total intake at first is purely liquid, the bladder capacity is small, and sphincter control has not developed yet. This is just another item about babies that may not have been emphasized sufficiently in your prenatal classes.

*"I don't use synthetic diapers because my baby got a rash, and my pediatrician advised using regular diapers. I do them in the washing machine at home. There are about fifteen to eighteen a day. It's not difficult to do, and the rash has cleared up."*

It's good that you have found a solution to your problem and can now cope so comfortably. Your experience shows again that each baby is different and may need special ways of handling.

*"Does a baby have to be changed every time she is wet? Should you wake a baby to change her?"*

It is best to change a baby as frequently as she wets, especially if the wet diaper annoys her. It is not necessary to wake a baby from a daytime nap to change her, unless the baby has sensitive skin or the doctor has advised you to do so. Sometimes it is a good practice to change a baby before you go to bed at night, so that she won't spend such a long time in a wet diaper and run the risk of developing an annoying diaper rash. There are many creams now that are used to protect against this kind of discomfort. Again, each mother has to find out for herself what system works best for her baby.

*"There is one other question that bothers me, and that is how many bowel movements are normal for a baby. Also, does the color matter? I've heard so much about diarrhea and how dangerous it is. My baby has a soft greenish movement after almost every feeding. Sometimes it's curdy, so I worry even though my doctor tells me not to."*

Breast-fed babies usually have more frequent bowel movements, and these are often green and "curdy," as you say. This is perfectly normal. If that is the usual occurrence with your baby, there is no need to worry. However, if there is a change to more frequency and a watery consistency, then you should consult your doctor.

Formula-fed babies usually have less frequent bowel movements, and these are apt to be smoother and more yellow in color. The color simply indicates how rapidly the stool has moved through the digestive tract. Green stool shows most rapid movement; yellow slower. Darker brown may indicate constipation. Most formula-fed babies have one or two movements a day. However, there are some babies that may skip a day without a movement and are perfectly comfortable. If the baby seems uncomfortable, then the doctor should be consulted for a change in formula or another remedy. Each baby is different, and, here again, parents have to learn what is normal and usual for their baby.

## Semisolid Food

Ideas of the age at which to introduce semisolid foods (such as cereal, fruits, strained meat or vegetables) vary among pediatricians. There may also be a difference in which food they suggest first and the order of introduction. These differences are really not important. What is important is that the feeding experience should be a pleasant one for both baby and mother.

We have found that most babies accept a cereal feeding when it is introduced at the second morning feeding, either before the bottle or after the first pause in the bottle feeding. At that time, offer the baby a little loose cereal off the tip of a spoon. Let her sip it as though she were drinking it. After rolling it around in her mouth, the baby may swallow it. If she likes it, try another sip. If not, continue with the bottle or breast feeding, and try again in the same way the next morning.

Do not expect to feed half a jar of semisolid food to your baby the first time. If you have such expectations, you are likely to be disappointed. Infants rarely respond immediately to change. You should not expect your baby to get a major part of her nourishment from the spoon at this stage in her life. You should only try to make taking food from a spoon a new and happy experience. It is a learning process. When your baby has learned to eat semisolids, and this may take several weeks, you can then make spoon feeding a longer part of the meal. In no instance is forcing worthwhile, because it can set up the beginning of an eating problem that may later carry over into oppositional behavior in other areas.

Babies usually have an innate sense of their own capacity and what foods agree with them. Babies with allergies usually prefer foods that agree with them or make them feel the most comfortable. At the onset of an illness as yet unrecognized by the parents, babies often refuse to eat. Parents should respect and think about their baby's eating preferences.

*"My pediatrician is opposed to starting semisolid feeding too early, but all my friends with babies of the same age as mine have already begun to do it, and that bothers me."*

Your pediatrician may be very wise in his advice because he knows that most of the nourishment a baby receives at this age is still from milk, and he may feel your baby is not ready for spoon feeding. Early spoon feeding is the vogue at present, but it is not necessarily best for all babies.

*"My baby spits the cereal out. Should I keep trying?"*

It sounds as though your baby is not ready or does not like the food you introduced. Give up spoon feeding for now, and try again later. If it still doesn't work, ask your pediatrician about another food, but do not force your baby to eat from a spoon. There is no rush.

One procedure some parents follow in trying to spoon-feed their babies is to insert the full spoon into the baby's mouth, so that no food spills on the outside of the mouth. The mother gets every drop in, but the baby may find this shoveling technique a most unpleasant sensation. Indeed, the baby may respond by clamping her mouth shut when the next spoonful is offered. This response indicates that the mother has set up a resistance to spoon feeding. Often, the mother compounds this error by attempting to force the food in if the baby resists.

Another habit some mothers develop is to wipe the baby's mouth after every spoonful to avoid messiness. Babies usually find this annoying, and it may make them uninterested or irritable at feeding time.

*"That's just how I've seen mothers feed their babies, and I thought that was the correct way!"*

It is not a question of whether this technique is "correct" or not, but a question of whether the technique allows both mother and baby to derive pleasure from the eating experience. Clearly, in most cases, it does not. Some babies may accept the shoveling type of feeding, and the mothers are satisfied because the food gets down. However, later eating problems may be related to this early form of feeding.

## Stimulation: Overstimulation and Soothing

Playing is a pleasant way of stimulating the baby. It can produce pleasure for both baby and parent. Indeed, it is such fun that sometimes the parent overdoes it. Usually when the baby tires, he will no longer pay attention, and the parent gets the signal that it's time to stop. However, we have all been bombarded lately with newspaper and magazine articles about the deleterious effects of understimulation and the resulting slowing down of development. While this is a correct observation, it may make some parents a little overzealous and cause them to overlook their baby's fatigue signals. It is important to be able to gauge how much stimulation a baby can tolerate.

Overstimulated babies "tune out" visual stimuli and will not respond to adults who are too overwhelming in their approach. They can be upset by overstimulation and become restless and fussy. Also, a lot of activity sometimes makes them cry and fret before going to sleep.

Sometimes we may interpret the baby's need as stimulation when he really needs soothing. Each baby needs to be soothed in his own way. Some simply require holding; some a little gentle rocking or patting; some singing or soft talking; some only a change of position; some feeding. Parents soon learn to recognize how best to soothe their baby.

What experiences have you had in playing with your babies?

*"Well, the baby would respond to play for only a short time some days, and that upset me. Now he seems to respond more, but the other day we were getting on fine when all of a sudden he began to cry. I thought he had a cramp or a burp. Now I'm beginning to think I just wore him out."*

Until you have had enough time to get to know your baby's responses to play, you may misinterpret the fussiness of overstimulation. Sometimes parents become annoyed when they don't understand the situation. If they are showing the baby off to friends and he becomes fussy, it may cause embarrassment.

*"That happened to us last Sunday when my husband's parents came to visit. We showed them how the baby holds the rattle once or twice. Then Grandpa tried, and that was okay. But when Grandma tried, the baby just dropped the rattle and began to cry. Grandma thought he didn't like her, and that upset her. Maybe he was tired from overstimulation. I'll tell her; she will be so glad to hear it. Now we'll look out for that."*

In addition to avoiding overstimulation, it is also important not to expect too much of babies. They don't like being "shown off" any more than adults do.

*"What about the danger of having a baby near a color television because of radiation?"*

That is a valid concern. It is important to keep the baby at least four to five feet from the set. In addition, television may be overstimulating. As a result, it may not be a good baby-sitter, although we have come to use it as such. A recent university experiment has found that babies respond to visual stimuli earlier than first thought. If overdone, however, this stimulation produces fussiness.

# Development of Basic Trust

## Patterning and Sequencing

We have discussed the need to understand a baby's rhythm or biological clock. We will now turn to the need to establish a schedule for the baby. We do not mean a precise hourly schedule, such as feedings or six, ten, or two o'clock, but a sequence of activities in a regular order. This kind of sequenced schedule not only makes life easier for the parents but also has a beneficial effect on the baby. It helps organize the baby's understanding of the life he is to lead. When the activities on the schedule are done in

■                                                                                          ■

the same sequence each day, the baby will acquire a sense of knowing and remembering what comes next. For example, at the first waking in the morning, the mother may change the baby, feed and burp him, and then put him down in his favorite sleeping position for another nap. At the next waking, she may bathe and then feed him. It is good if these activities continue in this order each day. Determining the sequence is especially important for working mothers, who need to instruct caretakers so they will adhere to the established program.

When the daily activities are repeated with this kind of regularity, the baby can begin to remember the events of his day and can then begin to anticipate these events. This gives him a sense of security and trust in the world around him and the people in it. This sense of trust is a very important cornerstone in personality development. It gives the baby a feeling that he will be cared for in a predictable way and that he can rely on his parents for this care. If basic trust is not established early, the baby may become an anxious, insecure, suspicious person. Parents, therefore, play a vital role in their baby's personality development beginning at an early age. An orderly life pattern also contributes to the development of memory and logical thought. We will discuss the intellectual aspects of this topic later.

Have you begun to get the baby's day to follow some regular sequence?

*"My pediatrician gave me a schedule to follow. It gives the feeding time for the formula. I've been trying to follow it, but it just doesn't come out right. Doing things one after the other without watching the clock will make it easier for me. I won't be feeling that there is something wrong with my way of taking care of the baby. Not being able to keep up with the clock made me so uneasy. Maybe that made the baby uneasy too."*

Trying to live by the clock on the wall rather than by responding to the baby's biological clock often leads to an unsatisfactory relationship between mother and baby. One becomes tempted to force the baby to eat when he is not hungry and then not to respond when he is. Establishing a sequence for the day, rather than a time for everything in the day, will help both mother and baby make easy transitions in the daily routine.

*"I began trying to do things 'on time' but found it made me tense and always off schedule. Now I go along with the baby, and we are all happier. Is that what is called 'feeding on demand'?"*

Yes, you could call it that. I would prefer to think of it, however, as responding to the baby according to his needs. It will be easier for you in the long run because when the baby's biological clock takes over, a definite pattern, which you will recognize, will be established. It may interest all of you to know that studies have shown that babies fed this way often require fewer feedings and are more comfortable than babies kept to a strict timetable. At first the baby's schedule will be unpredictable, but when the mother becomes familiar with the baby's needs, the baby soon settles into a fairly predictable rhythm. He will become comfortable as his needs are met; and the groundwork for basic trust is being established.

*"I guess I was lucky. My baby seemed to respond to the schedule started in the hospital, and she continued it at home. She just eats and sleeps at the same times—eight, twelve, four, eight, twelve, and three or four in the morning. It just happens that is good for us because my husband gets home at seven* P.M. *and can give her the eight* P.M. *bottle while I fix dinner."*

You are lucky that your needs and the baby's coincide so well. This is the arrangement most parents expect, and they are, therefore, disappointed when it doesn't occur quickly. If, however, the parents are properly "cued in" to the baby's needs, a schedule that suits both parents and child usually does come about in time.

## Crying, Spoiling, and Picking Up

There is another way in which the parents give the baby a sense of trust— a feeling that someone will help him when he needs it—and that is by responding when the baby cries as quickly as possible. This is an important subject, over which there has always been controversy. Many people think attending to a baby's cry "spoils" the baby.

How do each of you feel about this? I am sure you have all been concerned about your baby's crying and whether to respond promptly or not. Perhaps you've been advised about what to do by someone in the family, a neighbor, or friends. What do you do when your baby cries?

*"It seems to me that everything you have been saying is what my mother and other relatives think is catering to the baby. They say if I pick him up every time he cries, he will always cry, and that I will become a slave to him. They think he has to learn early that crying doesn't pay."*

And what do you feel about that?

*"My instincts tell me to pick him up, and that's what I do when we are alone. I get along fine, but when my mother comes over, well, then I get very tense and don't know what to do."*

This is a very common situation. There is such a misconception about "spoiling" children and what to do about crying. A great deal of study has gone into clarifying this important subject.

In the past, recognized scientists and many lay people advocated picking up babies when they stopped crying to teach them that crying didn't pay off in getting attention. To be sure, a baby will eventually give up and stop crying, but we think this may have deleterious effects on character development. It may produce either a child who has no hope or trust in his surroundings and becomes passive and submissive, or one who stores up much frustration and anger and becomes very demanding.

■                                               ■

Crying is the only language babies have. They are saying something is needed, perhaps only a change in position or a soothing word. Perhaps they need a change in diaper or another burp, and they should get a response from the caretaker—be it mother, father, or baby-sitter.

Research has been done about the relationship between crying and mother's response, notably by Dr. Ainsworth at Johns Hopkins University. She has shown that babies who are picked up when they cry are those who eventually cry least, while those whose cries have not been heeded become the "cry babies." What really "spoils" a child is inconsistency in handling. Responding to a baby's cries part of the time and ignoring them the rest of the time is confusing to the baby. He may become irritable— and you feel you have a "spoiled" child. What has really happened is that your child has become insecure because of inconsistent handling.

You will find that as you tune in to your baby's needs and give the appropriate responses, the baby will become less anxious, more comfortable, and more easily satisfied. Your relationship will become mutually satisfying and set the basis for attachment and affection.

*"How can you get this across to parents and relatives who criticize you?"*

I would say very sweetly and politely that this is your baby. You know they brought up their children the way they thought was best. More is known about babies and their emotional development now, so you would like to use this information and do what you feel is best for your baby. If you make a mistake, it's your problem—you are the one who is with him most of the time. Child psychologists believe it is best to pick up the baby and find out what he wants. Because he is so young, crying is his only language. When you explain your behavior that way, there may be a better acceptance of your way of doing things. You have to be your baby's advocate to protect his immature nervous system from unnecessary stress.

## Physicians and Pediatricians

It is important to make arrangements for regular pediatric care for your baby. We feel that the pediatrician will be available to answer any questions about diet and health that are of concern to you: what to do for a cold, loose or hard stools, vomiting, fever, rashes, and the baby's reaction to new foods.

Often doctors are very busy with sick children. However, most pediatricians do have a telephone time for answering questions. Naturally, they would prefer not to be called during busy office hours unless the call is really urgent.

*"That's true, but often what I think is urgent, the doctor dismisses as of no importance."*

To a new parent many things that are not very urgent may seem so. As you develop experience, however, you will be able to recognize what is really important. Perhaps we can help you do this.

# Stimulation: Ways to Spend Time with the Baby

## Language

Now that the baby is getting older, staying awake longer, and becoming more curious about surroundings, you, as parents, can utilize this time for appropriate stimulation. One of the most important forms of stimulation is talking to the baby. Babies respond to voices around them, particularly the mother's voice. Many people think babies can't understand and that language stimulation can come later. Do any of you feel this way?

*"I do feel that way, but sometimes I just can't help talking to the baby, and then if others are around, I feel a little silly. I know she can't understand what I say, but she turns and looks at me very hard when I talk to her and sometimes seems to have a little glimmer in her eye."*

It is true, babies do not understand what you are saying, but they can tell intuitively from your tone and the expression on your face if you are pleased and happy or angry and upset. They respond best to musical, rhythmically modulated speech. The human voice can be very soothing to babies. Even a premature infant in an incubator can be soothed by hearing the comforting voice of a nurse. Responding to the human voice seems to be one of the infant's very early abilities and should be encouraged. All babies who are healthy and not confined will learn to walk according to their own timetables. While they make sounds spontaneously, babies do not learn to speak a language without being spoken to; they must have speech models.

Some parents talk to their babies as they care for them or as they move about the baby's room cleaning and arranging things. The baby listens to the mother and, when she pauses, tries to respond by making some gurgling sounds. It is important to repeat these sounds back to the baby; the baby soon gets the idea that the sounds she makes evoke a response. This is communication and the beginning of conversation, another link in establishing trust and attachment.

Very often talking to the baby evokes a smile rather than a vocal response. Smiling is also communication. The first smile is a great moment for all parents.

*"At what age do babies begin to smile? I thought my baby smiled at me, but my mother said it was only gas."*

Babies begin to smile responsively at varying ages. The responsive smile is generally preceded by a glimmer in the eye. It is sometimes possible to evoke a smile at about eight weeks, but a spontaneous social smile comes at about four months. The more a baby is spoken to and the more she sees her parents' smiling faces, the earlier she is apt to respond.

■ ■

*"My baby just looks at me very seriously when I talk to her. I haven't been able to make her smile, but she seems to be intently watching my mouth move. She looks as though she wants to say something."*

Babies usually make some responsive gesture. They may give a little grunt or coo, purse their lips, move their tongues a little, or just look at you intently. All of these responses should be viewed as communication. Some parents poke the baby's face to stimulate a response. In this case, the baby is responding more to touch than to speech. Babies get tactile stimulation from being held, dressed, burped, and comforted. Parents must make a conscious effort to give early speech stimulation.

## Visual and Tactile Stimulation: Games and Toys

Another form of stimulation for this age is visual. Dangle a bright toy about eight to ten inches from the baby's eye level. (A red ring is one of the best toys for this purpose.) When the toy is in the baby's line of vision, move it back and forth saying some special phrase like, "See, see" or "Look, look." Approve and smile as the baby follows the toy with her eyes. At first the baby's visual range will be very limited, but at about three months she will be able to follow an object through 180 degrees.

Babies can also be stimulated to grasp a dumbbell-shaped rattle when it is placed in one of their hands. They may reflexively grasp the rattle without as yet recognizing that they are holding it. They may wave it up and down. This stimulation should be offered daily at playtime. Both parents should participate in it. They can get a good deal of pleasure noticing how the amount of time the rattle is held in each hand slowly increases, which hand is stronger, how much the baby waves the rattle, and how happy the baby is with the parents' attention.

How have you been trying to play with your baby?

*"I talk to the baby and hug him, but I haven't tried playing with the ring or rattle. I thought he was too young. My husband talks to him too and chucks him on the chin or cheek to try to get a response, but there isn't much reaction yet. He just stares into space. Sometimes he seems to watch me but for only a couple of seconds."*

The responses you can expect now are visual tracking and grasping. As the baby's nervous system gradually matures, you will see more and more response. This development is fun to watch.

*"I'm glad to hear that. My husband and I try once in a while, but the baby doesn't often respond. So my husband has decided he has a dumb child. I guess we don't know what to expect."*

There is nothing wrong with your baby. It does help, however, to know what to expect. If you continue to play with the ring and the rattle and to stimulate with speech and smiling, you will see the baby's responses develop. Each baby has a different timetable. Some babies respond earlier than others to visual or vocal stimulation. Don't worry about what other babies are doing. It's fun to keep tabs on your *own* baby—she's the only one that counts for you.

## Motor Stimulation; Large-Muscle Stimulation

Parents can also give babies physical stimulation or exercise. Here are a few exercises you might want to try: (a) While the baby is lying flat on her back, grasp the baby's hands and gently extend the baby's arms toward you until they are straight and you feel a little tension. This will stimulate the baby to flex her neck and lift her head slightly off the surface. This exercise is a good way not only to strengthen the baby's neck by practice in flexing the neck muscles, but also to strengthen the abdominal muscles that contract as the baby lifts her head. Our only caution is that the parent should not pull the baby's arms so that the baby's shoulders are lifted up, leaving the baby's head on the surface. The whole point of the exercise is to get the baby to lift *her own* head up. If the baby does not respond by flexing her neck muscles and lifting her head, the parent should discontinue the exercise and try it again in a few days. (b) Place the baby on her stomach and see how well she can lift her head. Call to her from above her eye level, so she will try to look up. Then call to her from below eye level, so she tries to look below the level of the surface she is lying on. By the time babies are four months old, they can do this well. The exercise can be developed into the game of "Peekaboo," which both parents and child will enjoy—and which will also help strengthen the feelings of attachment. (c) Draw the opposite knees and elbows of the baby together a few times. Each knee can be flexed toward the abdomen, and each arm and elbow toward the chest and back out.

None of these exercises is essential, because babies squirm, kick, and move about if given the freedom to do so. However, they are a way of playing with the baby, a way of interacting and having fun with the baby. This is important for both parents and child.

How many of you have tried any games or exercise with your babies?

*"I have seen you do the one where you extend the baby's hands toward you and the baby begins to pull his head up. My mother says a baby's head always has to be supported, and I could damage his neck if I do this exercise. I didn't dare try it."*

In general, people are worried about injuring a baby's neck. The baby's neck and head are attached by very strong muscles, and the head won't fall off. You will notice, however, that we don't jerk or pull the baby's head up. We simply put a little tension on the extended arms, and this stimulates the baby to lift her head herself. With practice and growth, the baby is able to lift her head higher and higher. By five or six months, babies can pull themselves to a sitting posture if someone gives them support by holding their hands. It is fun to see this ability develop. If you do this exercise the way we have described it, no harm will come to your baby.

■                                                                                             ■

*"We do push his legs on his abdomen and have found that he is able to expel his bowel movement more easily. He is happier and more comfortable."*

I am glad you discovered that. All of the little exercises we have been discussing help to build up the muscle tone, so that the baby can take care of normal physiological functions more easily. In addition, these exercises are fun for you and the baby.

## Stimulation from the Outdoors

Being taken out of doors in the carriage is stimulating because of the change of air temperature, the motion, the new sights and sounds. The baby is often soothed to sleep by the motion or by the fatigue produced by the stimulation. The seemingly simple activity of dressing for the outdoors can be both stimulating and fatiguing for mother and child.

Have you been taking the baby out regularly?

*"I can't seem to manage it every day. By the time I get the baby all bundled up, my clothes on, the diaper changes and bottle together, and the carriage out, it's almost time to come back."*

It does take organization. The first few times are hard, especially if it is cold, and there is so much to get ready. But once you get a routine set, you will find it easier. It will be helpful for the baby to be in a different environment, and taking the baby for a stroll will permit you to get out of the house.

*"I go out as often as the weather permits. The fresh air helps the baby sleep. I get my shopping done and meet people. Everyone says, 'What a cute baby,' and whether they really mean it or not, that makes me feel great."*

Mothers often enjoy dressing children up, and babies get a feeling that others are pleased with their appearance. At first, preparing for a stroll with the baby seems like a lot of trouble, but as you become adept at infant care, it will become less difficult.

*"On the whole, I think I'm doing pretty well. Certain days are bad. The baby cries a lot, and I don't catch on quickly to what's bothering her. When I do finally figure it out, I feel good."*

As you get to know your baby better, you'll "catch on" faster. Your ability to respond quickly and appropriately will lessen the amount of crying. Most young babies cry a good deal more than one unfamiliar with infants would expect. Babies cry to make adults understand what they need. The important thing is not to think that there is something seriously wrong with you or the baby if the baby cries. You'll soon be able to tell whether the baby's cry means hunger, wetness, gas, fatigue, or simply the need for entertainment or loving.

It is important to realize that the loudness of a young baby's cry is not always proportionate to her need. At this stage, babies cry just as loud for a small discomfort as for a big pain. Because of the immaturity of their nervous systems, they do not have the capacity to modulate the cry in proportion to the need. Their reactions are all or nothing. The intensity of the cry may not, therefore, mean anything. It is important, however, to calm the baby to see what specific attention is needed.

## Caretaking and Attachment

Some of you who have not planned to devote all of your time to your babies may be beginning to wonder about the appropriate time to resume your jobs. You have given the babies a good start with your undivided attention, and the babies are getting more settled in their routines. Some of you may be wondering if your baby will be just as well off with another caretaker, such as a maid, neighbor, grandmother, or other relative. Others of you may be deciding that you are enjoying child rearing and that the quality of caretaking is more important than you realized. You are probably also aware that the question of who should take primary care of the baby is widely discussed among professionals and parents alike. Each of you will have to decide what is best for your baby and your family according to your own circumstances. We will all share our thinking on this subject so that you will understand all aspects of it.

Some believe that a baby should get used to being taken care of by several people. However, there is now a large body of research and experience that points up the baby's need to form an *early* one-to-one attachment to the mother, the father, or other caretaker, so that later in life the baby will be able to form attachments and relate well to other people. In order to form this attachment, a baby needs to see the same face as she feeds, to feel the same arms hold her, so that she gets a sense of familiarity with that particular hold, face, voice, and smile. This familiarity establishes the baby's sense of security and attachment. If the relationship is primarily with the mother, a baby can also get used to the father at certain feeding times, or diaper changes, or playing times. However, one person should remain the primary caretaker at first.

We talked earlier about the surprise mothers felt when they didn't have a sense of closeness to their babies when they were first born. Are you now beginning to feel that sense of attachment more than you thought you were going to at the beginning? Do the babies seem less like strangers now?

*"Oh, yes. It's an entirely different feeling. I'm really getting to know the baby and love him—not just deriving pride and fun out of dressing him up like a doll, the way it was before. Now I think he is getting to know me. His eyes follow me around the room, and he kicks and smiles when I come in. It's different."*

■                                                                    ■

That's a very important awareness that you just described, and it's what makes child rearing fun.

*"When you first talked of feeling attached to the baby, I just didn't think that would happen to me. I didn't think I liked babies. But now I can't wait for my baby to wake. I miss him when he is asleep, and tiptoe in to look at him. I'm not the same me."*

So you are really having a whole new enriching experience that you didn't know you could have. You can't get that out of a book. It has to be experienced to be understood.

*"We've had a hard time with our baby. He has had a digestion problem and cries a lot, so I have to hold him. At first I resented the baby because I didn't want him in the first place. I wanted to go to graduate school, but the pregnancy was too far along for an abortion, and I had to give up school. But now when I get him comforted, it gives me a sense of being needed and close to him, and I like that. What happens when babies are taken care of by different people?"*

The sense of attachment that we are discussing is lacking in the development of many children in their own homes when care is divided and inconsistent. In children's institutions where there are three eight-hour shifts, care is even more inconsistent. Often attendants cannot be assigned the same babies to care for each day. It is difficult to replicate the consistency of parental care. Institutionalized babies grow up trying to make attachments to anyone and everyone; they have difficulty in making permanent attachments later on.

We consider early binding attachments important because of their relationship to later attachments to spouse and children. Good early attachments also prepare the child for coping in learning and school situations. The child's early relationships are important for future healthy personality development. Though much of early caretaking is time-consuming and tedious, the attachment that develops at the same time is vitally important. Parents can gain satisfaction from caretaking when they understand what they are doing and why it is important. We are not trained to be parents, but it is an achievement as important as, if not more important than, any other career. When we know how to do a job well, we enjoy it more. The same holds true for parenting.

*"You talk more about attachment to the mother. Isn't the father just as important?"*

The child's attachment to the father is, of course, important. We talk more about the attachment to the mother because in our society it is still, usually, the mother who takes primary care of the baby in the first years. The father is home only at night and on weekends, so that his contact with the baby is not as consistent. However, with planning it can be made consistent. The father can always take over a specific feeding or bathing

■                                                                                        ■

or playtime, so that the attachment to him can be developing simultaneously with that to the mother. There are some families in which the mother is the one who goes to work, and the father is the primary caretaker. In such cases, the primary attachment is to the father, and the mother arranges specific contacts with the baby. In other families, both parents have to work and the baby may be left with a grandmother or other caretaker, who becomes the primary caretaker.

We will talk further about how to manage if both parents must or want to work. There are stages in the baby's life when it is more appropriate for the mother to resume work. Most people have thought that the ideal time for this is when the baby is six months old. Actually, this may be the most difficult time for the baby because by the age of six months she has begun to form a binding attachment to the mother. Also, at about five to seven months comes an awareness of the difference between mother and others. This is, therefore, a difficult time to leave the baby with a new caretaker. If a mother must return to full-time work in the baby's first year, it is better, in our opinion, to do it when the baby is about three months old. In this way, the baby begins to form an attachment to the other caretaker. The mother will then need to set up her own particular routines with the baby, so that attachment forms with her as well, much in the same way it does with the father.

Each of you will have to decide what is best for your family. The important issue to understand is that a child needs the consistency of the same caretaker—mother, father, or other person—so that a binding relationship, which is the foundation of healthy personality development, can be established.

■

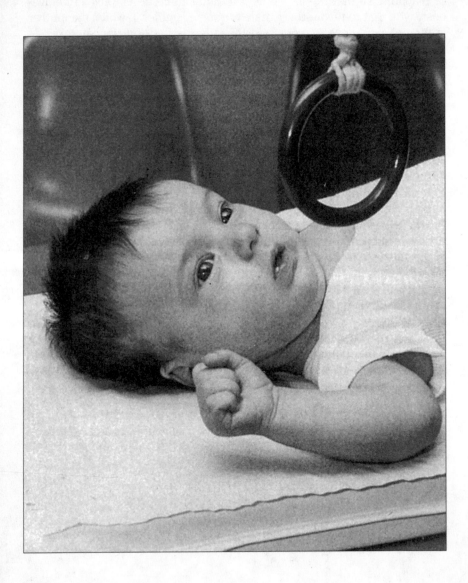

# 2

## *Highlights of Development—Eight Weeks*

By eight weeks, the baby can control her head much better. When on her stomach, she can lift her chin farther off the surface on which she is lying and may even look around. During the exercise described on page 19, in which tension is placed on the baby's extended arms as she lies on her back, the baby will be able to lift her head farther off the surface as well.

The baby is much more attentive to the red ring dangled about eight inches above his head. He may even be able to follow it briefly. The baby can hold the rattle or red ring much longer in each hand. The strength of the baby's grip with each hand may be tested by gently pulling the toy away. This may give some early indication of handedness, which will be of interest to parents.

Now when the baby hears a loud noise near her, she may not react with her entire body, as at four weeks, but there should be a change in facial expression. The baby is more alert and expressive, and may have begun to smile. The baby looks much more directly and definitely at the parent and at others.

The baby may begin making sounds in response to the parent's smiling and talking. The baby's lip and tongue movements are his first attempt to reply. The baby's facial expression now changes in response to contact with adults and surroundings. The baby is gaining the ability to visually track the parents as they come and go around him. By now, some babies have progressed to only one night feeding. (Any feedings after the early-evening feeding and before the first morning feeding are considered night feedings.)

# *Parents' Feelings and Expectations*

Your babies are now about two months old. Are you beginning to understand their needs better? Are you becoming less worried?

*"I think I'm getting better at burping the baby, and she is less fussy. The feedings are taking just as long, maybe longer, because I'm allowing more time for burping and getting settled, but her sleep time is getting longer, too."*

That sounds like a great deal of progress. What else are you noticing?

*"I think the baby is a little more responsive. I think she is at last beginning to smile."*

Many of you expected the baby to smile, return your hug, and seem pleased to be your baby right away. You were prepared to give so much, and the baby seemed unresponsive. Now you are beginning to have different feelings.

Are you beginning to feel that the baby is more of a person, not just a "chore"?

*"I can't say yet child care is not a chore, but I'm beginning to understand the kind of response a baby can make, so I'm getting more satisfaction."*

*"It seems to me that the baby always had a personality, but he wasn't reachable. Now he is beginning to follow me with his eyes and to smile. I've learned to talk to him and can see his mouth move as though he were trying to answer. I'm getting a real feeling for him, and the fun of having a baby is beginning to come true for me."*

## *Baby Talk*

*"The baby still takes too much time, but some of the routines are becoming more automatic and less burdensome. I'm beginning to take time to talk to the baby too. I was wondering about 'baby talk' and if that was all right."*

We have been encouraging you to talk to your babies, responding to their sounds, repeating them, and letting the babies respond to you. Some of you may consider this "baby talk," but it is actually appropriate speech stimulation. We encourage you to make cooing and other pleasing sounds to the baby that the baby may imitate. The baby feels the warmth and pleasure you convey and responds. This vocal interaction results in speech stimulation, communication, and strengthening of the ties of attachment. When we offer a bottle to a baby and say "baa' tle" with the proper inflection, that distinguishes the sounds for the baby and is still good English. If a mother says "lé che," that is still good Spanish, but it is easier for the baby to distinguish the sounds. There is nothing fatally wrong if a mother says "baa' tle," provided she says "bottle" later on when the baby's development is more advanced.

Do you have other ideas about this?

*"I have always said before I had a baby that I would never use baby talk, but now I realize that what turned me off was the "itsy-bitsy-baby' way some parents spoke to older children who could already talk."*

Your point is a good one. There is a difference between infantilizing an older child and responding appropriately to an infant. The former retards the child's speech; the latter enhances the establishment of communication and attachment. The parent's response has to be appropriate for the child's age and level of development.

## Fathers' Feelings About Parenthood

Fathers have an important role in providing stimulation for the infants. Often they need encouragement, however, because they feel that babies are fragile and they are afraid of hurting them. Sometimes they are concerned about disturbing the babies.

The mothers have been telling us in the past weeks about the changes their babies have made in their feelings and their lives. Fathers, too, must be having new experiences and feelings, and we would like to discuss that with you.

Is the experience what you expected, or different?

*"We went to Lamaze classes, and I was very involved in the whole delivery process. But I didn't know, and I don't think anyone ever discussed, how much time and effort babies take. It all appears so easy—they just eat, sleep, and have to be changed. Well, you can forget that right away. Even if they are on a schedule from the start, just one feeding from start to finish can take an hour and a half sometimes."*

*"Our baby really hasn't been more trouble than we thought, but I would have liked to come to these sessions sooner because I feel so involved and want to be sure my wife and I understand things the same way."*

*"I don't think it's a father's job to care for such a small baby. It's a job for mothers. When our son is older, say a year or so, then I think I'll be able to do more. I'm just not good around small babies."*

We seem to have a variety of feelings—from wanting to be more involved or involved earlier to feeling out of place with a small baby. These are all natural responses. One feeling that seems to prevail is the lack of preparation for the time and energy it takes to care for an infant. Though you may have heard it, it doesn't fully sink in until you experience it personally. Fortunately, this is not a permanent situation. As the baby matures and the parents come to understand the baby's needs and how to satisfy those needs, the baby takes less time and her schedule becomes more routine. The parents and the baby get to know one another, and some of the ways the parents related to one another before the baby was born begin to return. Gradually some of the social activities that the parents used to enjoy—having friends over for dinner or going out—can be planned again.

*"When do the night feedings stop? That's the hardest part. My wife is knocked out at the end of the day, so she is asleep by nine. I stay up for the late-night feeding at eleven or twelve. She gets up for the four or six o'clock feeding so I can sleep to seven to have some energy to go to work."*

■      ■

When night feedings stop varies with each infant. Usually it occurs when the baby is between three and six months old. It depends on each child's metabolism, weight, and biological clock. The early-morning feedings will gradually come later as well.

*"The part of having a baby that bothers me most is the spitting up. How long will that last?"*

Spitting up may last until the baby is about a year old, but she will do it less and less as time goes on. The reason a baby spits up is that she has a gas bubble underneath the food. The tummy is shaped like a bottle, and the gas bubble is at the bottom. When you hold the baby up, this bubble comes to the top and pushes out the food in front of it. The reason we adults are better able to keep food down, although our stomachs are also bottle-shaped, is that the nerve controlling the muscles is matured and can keep the muscle closed. But with the babies, these are not developed yet and the maturation time varies with each child.

We have been mentioning the difficulties with a new baby. What aspect of having a baby is fun?

*"My big kick comes from giving the baby a bath. That's our thing together. I seem to be less afraid of dropping the baby, so my wife is glad to have me give the baby her bath."*

*"I have a good feeling when I feed the baby and hold him. He relaxes in my arms and takes his feeding well. And if he burps well, I feel I have it made."*

*"So far, there doesn't seem to be much to crow about. He opens his eyes and stares once in a while. That's about all. He doesn't seem like anything to me. I just don't feel he is anybody yet."*

*"I can't wait to get home from the office and look at her. Just seeing that she is alive and well and has made it through another day is fine with me. Then my wife tells me how well she ate and burped, and how her bowel movements were. While we are talking, I chuck her under the chin, and I think she likes it. There is a kind of a smile. That's great!"*

Different aspects of the baby's development affect each of you, very much as the mothers have been affected. Each parent responds to the baby differently, and each baby responds to her parents and her surroundings differently. There is a great deal of difference in parents and their babies. Each one of us is unique. We need to remember this about the baby, so that we don't try to fit the baby into a stereotype.

## Fathers' Roles in Stimulation

It used to be considered that a quiet baby was a good baby. The thing to do was to leave a baby alone and let her sleep. Visitors might peek into the crib, but the baby couldn't be touched or upset. The object was peace and quiet at any price. Now, however, we have learned through observation and experimen-

■                                                              ■

tal studies that babies need stimulation. They need body contact, auditory and visual stimulation. But they need stimulation timed to their level of development, so that it is appropriate for the baby and rewarding for the parent. We use our knowledge about how the nervous system matures from the head down and from the center out in the way we stimulate the baby.

The infant is born able to hear, so we can stimulate her hearing response by ringing a bell farther away and then nearer her ear. The baby's earliest response will be the startled reaction of throwing the head back and arms out, or blinking the eyes, or even crying. We can also stimulate babies with a music-box type of toy placed in or above the crib.

The best stimulus is the parent's voice. However, the baby can sense at a very early age whether that voice is loving and approving or harsh and critical. Even a premature infant crying in an incubator can respond to a caretaker's voice and be soothed. So, even though a baby cannot understand what you are saying, the tone in which you talk to the baby is very important.

How have you fathers been trying to stimulate your babies?

*"I know so little about babies. I am really afraid to touch him. If he is quiet, I don't want to upset him. If he is crying, forget it. He's my wife's then."*

*"I guess my contact is just to chuck her under the chin a little to see if I can get a response of some kind. There isn't much yet."*

*"Sometimes when I put my finger into his hand, he curls his fingers around my finger. I pull on it a little, and then he seems to look at me. But that's about it."*

You all seem to be trying to get a response from the baby, so let's talk a little about what the baby can do and what you can do to experience more fun with the baby. When you talk to your babies, you will see them work their mouths trying to respond. They may even break into a smile when you do this. Although the baby doesn't understand what you say, she knows if you are pleased and responds to your tone and expression. This kind of exchange between parent and child is very important for early language stimulation.

Have you noticed this response?

*"To tell the truth, I feel like an idiot talking to such a little baby, so I guess I don't do it enough and think the baby is unresponsive. But from now on I'll try. It doesn't have to be baby talk, does it?"*

No, it doesn't have to be baby talk. Warmth and friendliness need to be conveyed. What you say doesn't matter, just how you say it.

*"Well, I'm one of those 'idiots' that loves to talk to the baby, and it gives me a great thrill when he curls up his mouth and acts as if he wants to answer back."*

*"I thought it was too early, so I never tried."*

*"I do talk to the baby, and I noticed the motions or grunts he made. But it never occurred to me that it was a kind of reply. That's really great!"*

A baby's visual development also needs stimulation. Visual ability develops a little later than hearing. At first the baby has a random kind of gaze. She sees

■                                                                              ■

objects in front of her, but the outlines are hazy. When the baby is about a month old, if a brightly colored object (such as a red ring) is dangled at the right distance and angle, the baby may glance at it momentarily. In the next month, with stimulation and maturation of the nervous system, the baby begins to follow the ring a little way. By three months, she may follow it through 180 degrees. The baby also begins to follow the parents as they move about the room. The sequence of visual development is fun to observe and is enhanced by parental stimulation.

How many of you have been noticing this change in your babies?

*"We haven't been able to get much response with the red ring. In watching you here, I think we were holding it too far away. It makes us anxious when she doesn't follow quickly, so we avoid doing it. We are anxious about her vision because both of us have such poor eyesight."*

It is easy to understand your feelings and your protection against anxiety, but it is much better for the baby to have visual stimulation. One study has shown that the babies near the nurses' station in a large infant ward, where there was much movement, had better visual responses and general development than did the babies at the far end of the ward, where there was less opportunity for stimulation.

*"When we first noticed that the baby followed us when we moved around the room, it was a great thrill. Now we use it as a game."*

*"Won't the baby develop vision anyway, whether we stimulate her or not?"*

Yes, she will, but you can enhance the development by stimulation. More important, the parent can use visual stimulation to develop an avenue of communication and interaction that is pleasing to both parent and child. This pleasant interaction is the beginning of a good relationship.

You may have also noticed that a very young baby keeps her fingers clenched in a tight fist most of the time. Later the baby's hands unclench, and her position becomes more symmetrical. This is an important sign of development.

The babies can now flail their arms around and kick, but they can't reach. However, they can hold a rattle in their hand if it is put there. At first they hold it momentarily, but as their grip strengthens, they hold it longer. At this stage, parents should be putting things into their baby's hands. This activity demonstrates the maturation of the central nervous system from the head to the hand.

Have you been playing in this way with your babies?

*"Actually, no. I couldn't say I was making a game of it because she drops the rattle right away. I thought it was too soon and I'd just be picking up the rattle over and over again."*

Certainly, that is the situation now, but you can watch the development of the hand coordination by regularly stimulating the baby to grasp the toy. One day you will notice that the baby will hold it a longer time. Soon she will hold it by intention instead of reflex, and that will be quite a thrill.

*"How long does that take?"*

For each baby it is different. Each baby has his or her own maturational timetable. One baby's grip will be slow in developing. Another baby will grasp the rattle very quickly and fling it about occasionally, even hitting herself with it. Each baby will reach that stage. It is fun to observe how babies arrive at it. The red ring is a good object to use, and so is a small dumbbell-shaped rattle, which the baby can grasp easily.

*"How long should you play like that with a baby of this age?"*

The length of time varies with each baby. There should be at least one special time set aside in the day to engage in visual, auditory, and tactile stimulation. One can also do this at each changing before putting the baby back to sleep after feeding. Sometimes the baby will show signs of overstimulation. She will turn away, cease to pay attention, or get fussy. As parents get to know the baby better, they can tell what is enough. Sometimes there needs to be a quiet soothing period after stimulating play, so the baby can relax and go off to sleep. Sometimes the baby just goes off to sleep on her own. Parents soon get to know what their baby's style is.

## *Patterning and Sequencing in Relation to Basic Trust: A Review*

We have been discussing consistent stimulation, and this activity fits into another very important topic. We will talk now about patterning and sequencing. We do not mean a rigid time schedule, such as feedings at six, ten, and twelve o'clock, bath at five, and bed at six. That used to be considered the correct way to set up the daily pattern. We are not so rigid now. What we do consider important is that each procedure come in a regular sequence. If the first activities in the morning are changing, feeding, burping, and then sleeping, this sequence should be followed each day. If the next activity is a bath, then a feeding, and then going outdoors, this sequence should be followed regularly. Soon the baby begins to remember the sequence and comes to rely on it. This pattern helps to organize her life and, by consistent repetition, she develops a sense of trust in the parent and an awareness that her needs will be taken care of in a dependable way. This consistency is the beginning of basic trust.

This sense of trust in the parents is one of the essential elements in healthy character formation. Having a regular pattern also helps the mother to organize her day. She does not impose a schedule on the baby, but she responds to the baby's needs. She soon learns whether the baby is apt to take a longer nap in the afternoon or morning, and she can arrange to do her housework or rest during those periods.

Sometimes other relatives become impatient. They often urge that a regular time schedule be followed and that the baby be allowed to cry so she learns to conform to her parents' time schedule. The impression is that the parent is spoiling the child by accommodating to the baby's pattern. They think the baby is spoiled if she is picked up and tended when she cries.

How have you been dealing with the patterning and sequencing of the baby's activities during the day?

*"Establishing a pattern—is that one of the purposes of these discussions?"*

Our overall purpose is to help the babies establish the kind of personality that will help them to reach their maximum potential with the endowment that they have, for each baby is differently endowed. Some children will be more interested in muscular activities, some more interested in visual things, some more interested in academic work. We hope to help them to reach their maximum development. We have learned from experience that there are certain important items that help them along that way. Patterning and sequencing is one of them.

It is important because it helps both parents and baby in organizing their lives and, in so doing, gives the baby a sense of knowing what to expect. This helps the baby develop a sense of trust in her caretaker.

## Spoiling

*"In our family we are having some discussion and disagreement. My wife picks the baby up when he cries. I don't see how she can ever get him to fit into any kind of schedule if she does that. If the baby is left to cry it out, he will know crying won't get him anywhere. My wife is just too softhearted."*

*"We began with the same idea, but as we experimented and got more experience, we found out that our baby cried for something. Now that we have sort of caught on, he cries less and less, and there is more peace around the house."*

It seems one of your major concerns is about "spoiling" the baby. Although the first weeks may be more difficult for the parents because the baby's timing may be unpredictable, studies have shown that as parents begin to tune in to their baby's timing, the baby is more contented, requires fewer feedings, and is easier to take care of. As to spoiling, it has been shown that the babies who are picked up when they cry become the babies who eventually cry least. The babies who have sometimes been picked up and sometimes left to cry, or those who have always been left to cry, are the ones who become clinging, whining children.

Always picking up the baby when she cries gives the baby the sense that her parents are reliable and available to help. Crying is the baby's first language and her only way of conveying her needs to the world around her. Crying may mean the baby needs to be turned over, or cuddled, to be fed or changed, or wants a little attention.

■                                                                                                    ■

*"I think our baby often cries just to get attention. Right now it seems she wants undivided attention."*

That's right. As she gets older and can do things for herself, she will not need undivided attention. Now she needs it, and lots of people think that if you pick up the baby every time she cries, you are spoiling her.

*"When she started to teethe, she began screaming so much that we couldn't understand what was wrong. The only thing we could imagine was teething. So we took her to the doctor, and he said to give her all the nursing she wants, and sure enough that's what it was."*

That's right. You might have taken the attitude that she needed discipline. I am glad you didn't feel that way, but there are parents who do.

The behaviorist school of psychology believes that you should condition babies in that way; it used to be very popular years ago. The baby will finally stop crying, but that baby may become an unhappy, cranky person, not trusting anyone around her. Another baby might become inhibited, without the drive to achieve all that she could achieve. We have people in our clinics who have been brought up that way and are having problems that are not easy to solve. Because we have had those experiences and because it has been so hard to treat those patients, we recognize that the problems begin very early. We are trying in this program to prevent such personality problems.

*"Are there no occasions when you should let a baby cry?"*

Such occasions are rare. When you get to know your baby, you may find that if the baby is overtired, she sometimes needs to cry a little to settle down to sleep. That's her way of doing things. Once the parents know their baby well enough, they get to understand and respond to the baby's needs, and the baby cries less and less. "Cuing in" to the baby enhances this process, as does the baby's growing trust in her parents.

*"After a whole day with the baby, I get very tired and angry."*

That's why it's very important sometimes for Papa to help when he comes home. It's very important for mothers to have some time away from the baby.

*"Sometimes I yell at him, and then I feel terrible for the rest of the day. I feel I did something to his personality."*

It may be difficult for the baby to understand why his usually pleasant mother suddenly lost her temper. We are all human, and occasionally we all lose our tempers. Problems arise when our responses to the baby are unpredictable and inconsistent *most* of the time. If a mother feels she is having a bad day with the baby, she should call for help from a neighbor. Perhaps she should take the baby out to change the scenery and mood. There are days when babies are hard to comfort. It may help you to know that babies behave rather badly on days just before there is a change in their development. As they are reaching a new stage, they have a feeling that things are not in equilibrium.

The important thing to remember is that the baby is not going to behave like this forever. As you learn to cue in to the baby, there will be fewer days when you yell or feel like yelling. Parenting should be fun most of the time, and we are trying to help you get fun out of the experience.

*"I understand that it's a good idea to come here. But I am amazed when I tell somebody about it at the office. They laugh. They think it's a big joke."*

They think you don't need to train to be a parent?

*"That's it exactly."*

In years gone by, most people had large families. These relatives could hand on knowledge of child rearing from generation to generation. Now, we live in smaller quarters and there are no extra hands to help and no one to verify that what we are doing is right. So there's a need now for this kind of program, especially when the population of this country is very mobile and has lost many of its family ties.

Our purpose is to try to supply the missing support that young parents used to have. In addition, we are making available to parents the experience and new information gleaned from recent research on child development in the critical first three years of a child's life.

# Playtime

## Playtime with Parents

We have already mentioned how parents can stimulate their babies by playing with them. As the babies grow older and sleep less, they will need more playtime. There should be at least one time each day for play when there is a real face-to-face interchange of cooing and talking, a period for dangling a red ring with a smiling interchange, a time to watch the parent move around the room. For some babies, play becomes the routine after certain feedings. Often this is the early-afternoon feeling. In some families it is the evening feeding when Daddy comes home, so he can participate. After a playtime, there may be a need for a simmering-down period when the baby is changed. Sometimes another sip of the bottle or breast is needed before the baby is put back to bed. Each family has to establish this playtime in a way that works best for it.

## Playing Alone with Toys

Some of you are beginning to introduce toys for your babies to hold. At present, the babies do not realize that the toys are in their hands, but it is good for them to have practice gripping the toy and flinging it. Some of you have reported that they are beginning to notice their cradle gyms. Some have even banged them accidentally with their hands or feet. Because they are beginning to coordinate more, this accidental contact will soon be purposeful.

Have you been noticing this?

■                                                                        ■

*"Yes, that's the new thing, but it amuses him for only a few minutes. Then he gets tired and wants to be picked up. Then I get his musical mobile going, and that entertains him another few minutes. Perhaps he's alone for five minutes. Shouldn't it be longer? It hardly seems like any concentration at all."*

Five minutes of concentration is a very long time for a baby of this age. A mother would like to have the baby amuse himself longer because she needs more time to get things done, but for the baby five minutes is a long time. Sometimes the baby's play can be prolonged if the parent plays a little, introduces another toy, or recognizes the baby's pleasure with a pleasant remark. The baby can then follow his own interests for another brief period of time.

Periodic communication with the baby gives him a sense of pleasure and enhances his trust that his parents are available in good times as well as bad. All of this helps create a good reciprocal relationship between infant and parent. It's one of the fun parts of parenting. Gradually the baby's concentration span increases, and he can play alone longer because he has experienced the frequent return of his mother or father to cheer him on.

How many of you have been trying to do this?

*"I've been noticing how excited our baby gets when he hits his cradle gym. He likes to see it move when I hit it for him. It takes the monotony out of baby care now that there is more play. It's fun to watch."*

*"By talking, coming back to the crib and putting another toy in, or banging the cradle gym, I've managed to get the baby's room cleaned up or the laundry sorted. The day is going better. I don't mean such devices always work, but he entertains himself more than he used to."*

*"My baby still likes to watch his mobile or communicate with a red doll I put in the crib. He hasn't discovered the cradle gym yet."*

Each baby responds somewhat differently. Each baby's timetable for responding is different, and each response is different. That's what makes getting to know your own baby so interesting. Each discovery is a milestone. The parents' overt recognition of each new activity enhances the baby's development.

## Fingers in the Mouth

Although the babies are only between eight and ten weeks old, one will occasionally get his fingers in his mouth and suck on them. When the baby's hand lands near his mouth, it is accidental, not purposeful, behavior. In the next month this hand-to-mouth activity will become more frequent and purposeful. Most parents have negative feelings about babies sucking their fingers, especially their thumbs.

How do you feel about it?

*"I don't want my baby to suck his thumb. I think it's a bad habit. So I put a pacifier in his mouth instead, but he spits it right out. Then I don't know what to do."*

■       ■

Most mothers don't recognize that the baby's ability to put his hand to his mouth is an achievement representing increasing coordination. The baby's hand is the first pacifier he can control. He may put his hand to his mouth repeatedly when he first becomes aware he can do this wonderful thing. This annoys parents, but it is a natural development and shows progress. Babies usually acquire this skill between three and four months of age, but there is a great deal of variation from baby to baby.

When the baby can put his hand in his mouth purposefully, he can also hold a teething ring, the red ring that you have for play stimulation, or another firm toy. He will suck or chew on these toys as he does with his fingers. If the baby is teething, this activity will be comforting.

## Pacifiers

*"Is the pacifier a bad thing to use? You hear so much pro and con about it now. What do you think?"*

We think the hand is a better object for teething than the pacifier. The pacifier has another function. It is good for babies who do not get enough sucking. Often bottle-fed babies take their feedings too fast and need more sucking. Breast-fed babies usually stay at the breast long enough so that they do not need extra sucking. When a pacifier is placed in a baby's mouth, it is not a stimulus for hand-to-mouth coordination, nor is it a good teething ring. There is another drawback: Pacifiers are often dropped on the floor or street, and keeping them reasonably clean becomes an extra chore.

*"Then you are not absolutely against pacifiers?"*

Pacifiers are useful for babies who need more sucking time. One often sees parents taking the baby's hand out of his mouth. This is very frustrating for the baby because this hand-to-mouth activity is a natural part of his motor and cognitive development. It is also one of the first ways a baby learns about his own body. A baby sucks his fingers less when he is able to hold other things and put them into his mouth. Parents can assist this process of exploration by putting appropriate things in the baby's hand.

Babies who need more sucking may need the pacifier. A pacifier should not, however, be used to stop the baby from crying every time she opens her mouth. She may be signaling that she is hungry or thirsty or that she needs to be held or comforted. As parents get to know their baby, they learn what this finger sucking means and can respond appropriately. The more parents tune in to the baby's needs, the more secure the baby becomes. This helps establish a happy relationship between parents and child.

*"What about those two- and three-year-olds who walk around with a pacifier?"*

One needs to know what the past history of that child is, what kind of need is being satisfied, and what sort of deprivation this child may have had earlier in order to answer this question. What these children are doing has some

■                                                                              ■

meaning that the parents may or may not understand. Many children seem to need a bottle or pacifier, or to suck their thumbs, in order to go to sleep. There is some reason why they need to do that.

*"But isn't it more natural for a mother to pull the baby's hand out of his mouth than to let him suck his fingers?"*

I think it is the most common adult response, but that doesn't mean it is correct. We must remember that this activity is comforting to the baby and provides a means for the baby to begin to understand that these fingers belong to him. This is the beginning of his realization of the extent of his body.

## Conflict Between Parents and Baby

Constantly pulling the baby's thumb out of his mouth is very frustrating for the baby. It is an unnecessary kind of frustration. Frustration leads to anger, which babies express by being fussy. A conflict develops between parent and baby that is unproductive and can lead to an oppositional relationship. The development in a child's personality structure of a feeling that he has to battle his parents can begin early, often on this kind of seemingly innocent little issue.

*"Do you think that you always have to give in to the baby?"*

I would not call it "giving in to the baby." In my view, it is understanding the baby's needs and trying to satisfy them appropriately. If the baby sucks his thumb, I feel that this signifies something. The baby either needs an object to bite on or suck, or he needs other diversion. The parent must try to determine what the baby needs, and supply a teething object for teething needs and longer breast or bottle feedings for sucking needs. A pacifier should be used only as a last resort. If the baby needs diversion, the parent can offer a toy or talk or sing to him. Parents will learn what the right thing is as they come to understand their baby's needs. Instead of a conflict, a reciprocal relationship develops, which not only gives pleasure to both baby and parents but contributes to the baby's sense of basic trust. Parents also feel satisfaction from being able to "tune in" correctly to their baby.

In general, we get too concerned about how long a baby has a bottle or a pacifier or is breast-fed. The tendency has been to wean babies too early and too abruptly—that is, when the mother, not when the baby, is ready. It may be appropriate for children to continue with at least one bottle until they are two or three years old.

## Babies' Individual Differences

All of this reemphasizes that our job is to understand and "tune in" to the child's needs at each stage of development. In addition, each child has his own individual style. Some babies are frightened when they are given a bath and cry throughout the whole process. Others may not sleep well in their cribs but will sleep in their carriages.

Have you noticed any preferences that your babies have?

*"I find the bath the most difficult thing to handle. I've tried everything—warmer or cooler water, sponges and washcloths. I've tried a little plastic tub and the sink. I've tried having a toy that he likes in the tub. I've tried changing the time of day. I even had my mother give him a bath, because I thought it was my inexperience, but he still was terrified. So now I just give up, but I feel badly because I know a baby should be bathed daily. Now I just hold him and sponge him off, which he doesn't like either, but it has to be done. Then after the bath is over, he is very happy, and that puzzles me."*

There are some babies who take a very long time to get used to their baths. Most parents are a little tense themselves when they begin to bathe a baby. This tension communicates itself to the baby. Some babies are sensitive to exposure. You can begin by first sponging off each part, covering that part, and then going on to the next so the baby does not feel exposed. Then, when the baby seems used to that, you can try submerging one leg at a time in the tub, then finally more of the baby till the baby is in the tub. As we've discussed before, the intensity of a baby's cry does not necessarily signify the amount of discomfort. Babies still cannot modulate their cries. For the babies who do not like baths, it helps to give the bath as quickly as possible. Sometimes a baby can be distracted by talking or singing in a soothing tone.

The important thing is to find the most suitable way for your baby and then repeat it in the same sequence each day. When a pattern is established, the baby begins to respond to the procedure and gains a sense of security and eventually pleasure. In some families, bath time is a fun time, and the whole family likes to participate. Fathers often enjoy bathing the baby and look forward to it.

*"My baby is the kind that loves his bath and hates his crib. If I put him in his crib at night, he will cry and won't go to sleep. The minute I put him in his carriage in his room, he quiets down and goes off to sleep."*

For some reason he may feel more secure in his carriage. Perhaps it is smaller than the crib and he feels less exposed. As you can see, each baby has his own individual likes and dislikes. It isn't always easy to tell why, but it is important for each parent to respond to the baby's individual needs. Each baby needs to be treated differently. We adults make a mistake in expecting all babies to be alike. We are not all alike, so how can they be?

*"I understand that we are all different, but it seems to me that you are recommending that we cater to our child's every wish. There are some things that we all have to learn to do in life. Why not start young?"*

What needs to be started young is the feeling that parents can be trusted to give comfort and security. The child who has this feeling of basic trust will be ready when he is older to cope with the difficulties and hardships of life. At

■                                                                                    ■

this age, he needs attention. If he gets appropriate attention now, he won't crave it later when it is not appropriate. He will be able to cope later if he is helped now to feel secure.

## Sleep

### Establishing a Pattern

By now, some of the babies have established a sleeping pattern that suits the parents' way of life and all is well. Some babies had what seemed to be a pattern, but some development like the onset of teething has disturbed this pattern.

Have any of you encountered this situation?

*"That's just what I wanted to talk about. My baby was a good sleeper until a week ago, but now she wakes once or twice during the night. At first I didn't mind this, but now I'm getting tired of it."*

Usually a baby who has had a good sleep pattern will return to that pattern when the discomfort is over. Most prospective and new parents worry a great deal whether a baby will sleep or not and whether they will be up all night.

How many of you anticipated this?

*"That was the first thing my friends warned us about when they found out we were having a baby. But, so far, our baby has not kept us up much. Each time there has been a good reason, such as a cold or a tooth or a tummy ache when a new food disagreed with her."*

Some parents are needlessly frightened ahead of time. Other parents never anticipated anything but a quiet, sleeping baby; it's a shock for them when the baby cries. New parents who are called on to be up day and night really have difficulty coping and need help. All feelings of affection for the baby may be driven away by sheer fatigue. This situation is hard to deal with in our nuclear families where there are often no relatives nearby to help the new parents. Also, in a large, impersonal city we often have no friendly neighbors to lend a hand. A father who has been working all day comes home to find the household in an uproar—no dinner ready and a distraught mother with a crying baby. Some fathers can size up the situation and lend a hand. Some, in fact, like the role of rescuer and want to help. Others become angry and feel that their wives are giving too much attention to the infant and not enough to managing the house.

How are you managing?

*"My husband was an only child and was very indulged, so he just couldn't cope with my not being available to have his dinner ready on time. Now he is getting to know and like the baby, so the situation is not so bad. But I still think deep down he resents the attention the baby gets."*

■ ■

That is quite a common situation and makes it hard for both parents. If you can talk about the problem, it is easier to deal with. It may help your husband to understand that you are also having to make a lot of adjustments.

*"My trouble is not that the baby wakes so much, but that I have difficulty getting back to sleep. I just can't do all the things I need to because I have to nap during the day. The situation's better now, but I was lucky because my husband understood and really helped a lot."*

The majority of infants do eventually sleep at regular intervals, waking only for changing and feeding. A few do this from the start. Others get into a pattern if their parents follow a regular sequence for the day's activities in a patient and relaxed way. You may bathe the baby regularly either morning or evening. You may take her out after the second morning feeding or the first afternoon feeding. If you do all of these things in a regular sequence that suits both parents and baby, gradually the baby's life will get into a pattern. This pattern will give the baby a sense of security and trust in her parents because she gets a feeling for what comes next. This pattern also gives some organization to the parents' lives. Then, the mother can gradually get to do more of the neglected tasks.

Each of you has to find the best way of settling your baby for sleep. If she fusses a bit, you tolerate it; but if she cries, you try to discover the reason and comfort her. You may need to hold the baby for a while or rock her a little.

You know there was a reason for those antique cradles: babies need some rocking. In primitive societies, they are carried on the mother's back or hung in a swing fixed to a tree branch, where they are lulled to sleep by swaying in the breeze. It is only in our scientific, mechanized world that babies are supposed to go to sleep without some sort of soothing motion.

We can, however, develop familiar patterns of activities that lead up to sleep. For example, the parent can sit in a relaxed frame of mind, feeding the baby, patiently getting up the burps, and playing with the baby if she seems inclined. Then the baby may be changed again and put on her side or stomach to sleep. Most babies prefer a certain posture for sleeping, and just putting them in this position cues them in to the sleeping situation after the routine of feeding, burping, and playing.

Are you beginning a pattern of the sequence of events leading up to sleep?

*"Well, the sequence that seems to work best for us is to give the baby his evening bath, then a bottle, and put him in his crib on his stomach with his pet toy, a calico cat, in the corner where he can see it. He squirms around and moves his hands and feet. Then he settles his head in a comfortable position, sometimes with a little whimper, and goes to sleep."*

That's the idea. You seem to have found a good pattern for your baby.

*"Do you think bathing the baby is better at night than in the morning? Does it help the baby to get to sleep?"*

■                  ■

For some babies bathing at night helps them get off to sleep more easily. Each mother has to decide what is the best way for her and her baby.

## Parental Roles in Establishing a Sleep Pattern

What we have been discussing is the usual manner of establishing a pattern, and this is intimately connected with establishing basic trust. The father should also become part of this process, so that the baby counts on him and he becomes a part of the process of developing basic trust. There should be a certain feeding, or perhaps the bath, that the father regularly takes over. He can also help with the bedtime routine.

Sometimes, particularly at night when he comes home and the mother and baby are overtired, a father may step in and soothe both by his reassuring presence. Often the father, who hasn't seen the baby all day, wants to play with the baby. When he has had enough, the father puts the baby down. But the baby has enjoyed the play and refuses to go to sleep or is too stimulated to settle down. In either case, it is necessary to have a quiet period with the baby, giving her time to simmer down and relax. Then repeat your normal bedtime routine very quietly with no unnecessary stimulation. Babies often find it soothing when parents pat them a little, hum a lullaby, or turn on a music box or record. Sometimes babies may need an extra pat or an extra burp. If a regular bedtime routine is followed, the baby eventually cues in and gets into a sleeping pattern.

## Colic and Parental Anxiety

If a baby cries a great deal, pulls her legs up on her abdomen, flails about, and won't sleep, she may be having colic. She may also sleep for a very short time and then wake up crying. If this is the situation, the baby's doctor should be called. The doctor is the one to decide whether the feedings need to be changed, whether there is an allergic reaction to some food, or whether some medication is needed. Fewer babies seem to suffer from colic than used to be the case, but there is always a small group of them who have a real problem.

There are also babies who appear colicky but are only a little uneasy because they sense the tenseness and anxiety of the parent. As parents become more certain of their roles and begin to cue in better to the baby, the so-called colic ceases.

Is this happening to some of you now?

*"I'm glad to say my baby is responding better. I think it is because I feel more secure as I see him progress from day to day. Knowing that this is something that we have to learn together, that it doesn't just happen to some and not to others, helps me keep trying. It's like practicing a sport. The more you do it, the better you get at it."*

## Other Upsets to Sleep Patterns

There are some babies who are very light sleepers, and families tiptoe around whispering when the baby is asleep. But this is rarely necessary. Usually a baby who is sleeping can sleep through the usual household noises like those made by the washing machine, cleaning, the radio, the television set, or conversation. The baby gets used to these household sounds. However, they do startle and often wake if there is a sudden loud noise—a car backfiring, a fire engine, a clap of thunder. Then the baby may become frightened and need comforting. Sometimes a single such episode breaks up a sleep pattern, and the pattern has to be patiently established again. This is upsetting to parents, but the interruption will not last long if handled appropriately.

Has this happened to any of you?

*"Yes, we went to visit my mother, and there is a firehouse next door. The engines woke the baby for several days while we were there. When we were about to leave, he began to sleep through the noise."*

*"We have a dog that barks when the doorbell rings, and that wakes up the baby. I'm hoping the baby will get used to it. I put a sign on the door asking people not to ring the bell because the baby is sleeping, but sometimes that doesn't help either. We may have to get rid of the dog."*

That would be a sacrifice, I'm sure, but you may have to do just that if the baby doesn't eventually learn to ignore the dog's barking.

*"How long should a baby sleep in a day? I've heard that they should sleep about twenty out of the twenty-four hours. Mine doesn't do that."*

Many mothers ask that question. It may come as a shock that a minimum of fourteen hours out of the twenty-four is average for many babies.

## Do Dreams Upset Babies?

Occasionally babies will also be upset by their dreams. Recent research on sleep has involved a device that registers rapid eye movements (REM). Rapid eye movements are interpreted as indicating dreaming and have been found in infants. What babies dream about is, of course, speculation. Because they often startle during sleep, it has been suggested that babies may be dreaming of falling or floating. As they grow older, they dream of events that have occurred during the day. Sometimes, if you watch sleeping babies, you will see them making sucking movements. It's conjectured that they are dreaming of nursing. The subject of babies' dreams requires much more exploration.

## Traveling with a Baby

*"I'd like to ask about traveling. We've been going away weekends to a farm. What is the baby aware of?"*

She is certainly aware of the change. How was she during the trip?

*"The first time she cried and didn't sleep at all. The second time I took the carriage toys that detach, and she slept on the trip, but when we were at the farm, she didn't sleep well."*

Your baby was certainly aware of the change in surroundings. Sleep disturbances will be a common indication of this awareness. Babies feel comfortable
with sameness—the same room, the same pictures, the same toy in the crib.
This is the consistency that they need to develop a sense of security and trust.
Babies do not respond well to constant shifts. If a family decides to go away
on a long trip, say for the summer, the baby has time to adjust. It is hard for a
baby to adjust to a new place each weekend. However, if you are going to your
farm regularly, the baby will begin to feel at home there in time, especially if
you bring along enough of her favorite things.

We're not advocating that parents should stay home every weekend, but
you do have to realize that the baby may not adjust readily, and you should
not be too disappointed if she doesn't. If you find your baby is a good traveler,
you can take advantage of it.

Again, there are individual differences, and each parent has to tune in to
his or her child.

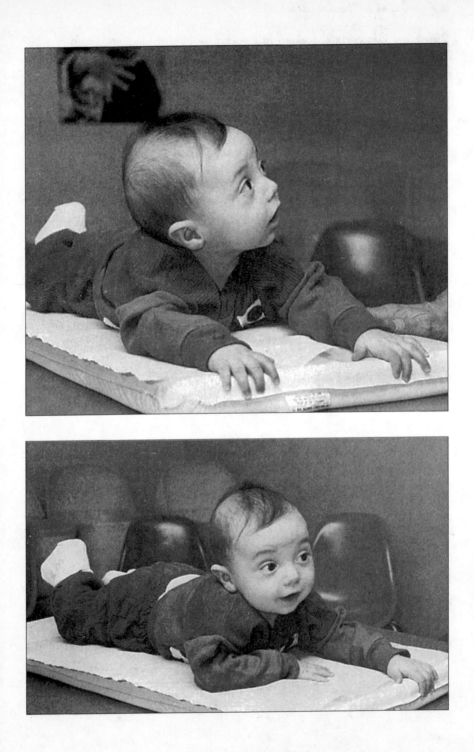

# 3

## Age Twelve to Sixteen Weeks

## Highlights of Development—Twelve Weeks

Parents will notice more developmental changes at this age. When the baby is lying on her back, she holds her head so that her face is more straight up, rather than to the side. Now the hands are not held as tightly clenched and are open more often. When supported in a standing position, the baby lifts one foot momentarily. When turned on her stomach, she braces herself on her forearms and holds up her head to look around, keeping her hips on the table.

Most babies can now follow the red ring through an arc of 180 degrees when it is dangled above their heads as they are lying on their backs. This is a skill that improves with practice and may be used as a play activity that enhances parent-child interaction.

The baby now holds the rattle or ring placed in his hand more firmly and may even glance at the toy. Glancing at the toy is a big step forward in development. If the parent holds up two objects, such as a cup and a small block (preferably a one-inch red cube), the baby may glance at each of them, showing that he can attend to two things of different sizes at the same time.

When a parent talks to the baby, the baby may observe the parent very intently and then smile, coo, or chuckle. Her vocal response may be accompanied by some physical activity such as waving the arms and legs.

The babies may also be looking at their hands now and pulling blankets or clothes over their faces. Parents can utilize the latter develop-

ment in a beginning "Peekaboo" game. (Some parents may worry that babies will smother if they cover their faces, but there is no need for worry because the babies will do this only momentarily and plenty of air can get through baby clothes and bedding. Thin plastic materials such as cleaning bags are, however, *exceedingly dangerous* and should be kept away from the baby.)

## Central Nervous System Development: From Head to Hands

In one of our earlier sessions, we mentioned that the central nervous system matures from the head down. We pointed out that the baby first hears and then sees. She learns to turn her head from side to side. Gradually she lifts her head by herself when she is facedown, and with her parents' help when she is on her back. She is becoming more successful at these activities. She is lifting her head higher from both positions. Parents can now observe these achievements, and show the baby more emphatically how pleased they are.

Have any of you begun to experience this?

*"My baby is able to get her head up ever so much more. Each night, her father watches to see if she has made any progress. He gets a big kick out of it—as much as the baby does, I think."*

This is a very good way to engage father and baby in an interaction. Most babies are ready to play the "I See" game—an early form of "Peekaboo." When the baby is on her stomach, the parent gets below eye level, encouraging the baby to look down, and then slowly gets up again while calling to the baby so she will look up. The baby will not be too good at this at first, but this is a good time to start the activity. It is good for both parents and baby. Aside from stimulating motor and sensory development, it has other results that are as important. The parents get a sense of pleasure and achievement from the baby's response. The baby gets a sense of recognition and approval, which she may show by smiling or activating her hands and feet in a sort of swimming motion. Parental recognition of this achievement helps the baby establish a good self-image. Beginning to acquire a good self-image early is very important to personality development.

*"Do you mean that the baby understands so young that she is doing something great? When she gets excited like that, I just worry that she'll strain herself. Everybody has been telling me we get the baby too worked up."*

Of course, one has to use judgment and not get the baby overtired. However, stimulating the baby and giving her the feeling that she is doing something that you like are very important. This is the beginning of her positive awareness of herself. It is a small but very important beginning.

As we discussed earlier, the ability of babies to get their hands to their mouths is an achievement. Some of the babies may be putting toys that have been placed in their hands into their mouths. At first, the baby will not look at the toy in her hand and will not be aware that it is there. As the development of the nervous system progresses from head to hand, however, she will begin to look at her hand and what it is holding. She will also begin to play with her fingers, hold up her hands, look at them, and clench her hands together. For some babies this begins in the third month and is fairly well established by the fourth. When the baby drops the toy, she obviously can't retrieve it. Picking up and handing back a lost toy is another game parents can play with babies.

Have you been having this experience?

*"My baby is just beginning to do that, but as soon as he loses the rattle, he cries. It's getting to be a great nuisance."*

It is too bad that you see the situation that way. It sounds as though you were giving your baby the toy to silence him, so you can leave him alone. It is better, however, to sit with him and retrieve the toy with a positive comment like "Here's your rattle" or "Here you are." When the parent becomes tired or bored, a different activity should be started. It may be easier for parents to make this activity a positive experience by thinking of it as a game. It is important to realize that this game enhances spatial exploration.

## Early Exploration and Play

As the baby develops the use of her hands, she can bring things to her mouth to explore their taste and texture. She may hold them up and look at them momentarily, thus getting some idea of size and shape. Then she will probably put them back into her mouth.

If the baby is propped up in a sitting position for a few minutes several times a day, she can explore her surroundings better visually. It is important for the parent to make available small toys such as rattles, inch blocks, and small stuffed animals that the baby can hold and manipulate.

Many parents, as we may have mentioned before, are disturbed when babies put things in their mouths and often inhibit this form of exploration. If you inhibit oral exploration, however, you deprive the baby of one of the ways she learns about the world, a way that is appropriate for her age and level of development. Of course, not everything should go in the mouth. Appropriate objects should be clean—but not necessarily surgically sterile—and nontoxic. They should have no sharp edges or parts that can be pulled off and aspirated or swallowed. There are many objects that meet these safety qualifications, such as small blocks, empty thread spools, small terry-cloth stuffed toys, and small wooden shapes.

We have noticed over the years that oral exploration is one of the more difficult areas of a baby's development for parents to cope with. It seems to arouse anxieties concerning cleanliness and safety.

How many of your babies have reached this stage, and how do you feel about oral exploration?

■                                                                              ■

*"I'm afraid my reaction is the wrong one. I can't bear to have the baby put things into his mouth, salivate over them, and then drop them. Usually they fall on the floor. Then I have to wash them."*

If you sit by your baby when he is experimenting with a toy, you can often intercept it before it falls on the floor. You could also have a supply of several rattles or rings and wash them all at one time. When you realize the importance of this activity to the baby's development and observe the growth of the baby's coordination, then perhaps you will get some pleasure and satisfaction out of it.

*"I don't mind picking up the toy and washing it over and over again, but the baby gets her clothes so wet with the saliva. That's what I mind."*

That's why bibs were invented. If your baby does a lot of salivating and chewing on toys, a bib will help you keep her clothes dry and fresh. You don't have to use a fancy bib, either; a small hand towel or diaper tied around the baby's neck will do.

*"Why is it so important to let them do this now? I hate to see my baby messy."*

The importance lies in the fact that this early exploration is the precursor of the drive to explore and learn later on in school. If this early form of the drive to explore is inhibited by the parent's attitude, the baby may not try, or be afraid, to explore later.

*"This is a point of view I never heard before. I'm sure my husband will be quite surprised. He is so fussy! He won't come near the baby if the baby is even a little messy."*

## Teething

Some of the hand-to-mouth activity that you are noticing may not be entirely exploration. Sometimes a baby inserts her hand into her mouth to chew because she is teething. For some infants, teething begins very early. Some of you have noticed an increase in drooling. This is a sign of teething. The need to bite on something may be another sign. The usual time for a first tooth to erupt (usually the lower middle incisor) is at six months, but this is very variable. Teething is not always accompanied by great distress, but it can be. Some infants have very thick gums and the teeth have difficulty in penetrating. There may be swelling and inflammation of the gum that make sucking and eating painful.

*"Do babies get sick and have a fever with teething? I told my doctor I thought my baby's fever was due to teething, and she said it couldn't be."*

Doctors do not agree on this. Some think the inflammatory reaction may cause fever. Other doctors believe fever during teething is caused by an accompanying upper respiratory or other infection. Whatever the theory, the baby is apt to be irritable and need soothing, emotionally and also locally on her gums.

*"What should one do to comfort the baby if holding and rocking him isn't enough and he won't take a bottle?"*

In our experience, rubbing the gums with a little ice or using a commercial refrigerated teething ring often helps temporarily so that the baby may be fed. Each pediatrician has his own approach to meeting the baby's and the parents' needs. Some use medication; some do not. It is best to consult your doctors about this.

Teething is often apt to upset the patterning and sequencing we have been discussing, particularly the sleeping pattern. Often a sleeping baby will bite down on a sore gum. This causes pain and the baby awakens. Sometimes it is hard to get the baby back to sleep again. At other times, just opening the mouth to cry relieves the pressure on the gums, and the baby quickly goes back to sleep by herself. Many parents find this irregular sleep pattern one of the harder problems to cope with and fear it will become permanent. Usually it is transitory, and as soon as the bothersome tooth has erupted, the usual pattern of sleeping will be reestablished.

Are any of you encountering much difficulty yet?

*"My baby is drooling a lot. Aside from its being a nuisance to change bibs. I have had no trouble. I was wondering if the drooling meant teething because there is no whiteness in her gums and I can't feel any bumps."*

Very often there is little evidence except increased drooling for a long time. Sometimes the gums are very swollen for weeks or months before there is any sign of a tooth. Sometimes there is no evidence of anything different until a mother hears a click on the spoon in the baby's mouth. When she investigates, she feels the sharp edges of a new tooth. What an exciting moment that is! Each baby teethes differently, and there is often a family pattern.

*"My baby has been having a very runny nose and drooling but no fever. My pediatrician says she may be teething."*

*"My baby seems to cry for no reason that I can find out. I was beginning to feel she was just bad-tempered at times. Maybe there is a reason after all. It never occurred to me that she could be starting to teethe so young."*

Some parents misinterpret an infant's bona fide need for comforting as malevolence, especially if the incident happens at night. They think the baby just wants to get them out of bed. Actually, a baby has no way of expressing her need except to cry; that is her language. As we have said before, the sooner the parent tries to meet the need, the less the baby will cry. To be held and consoled when she needs it gives the baby a sense of trust that the parent is available and trying to help.

■                                                                                    ■

*"My first baby was cranky and had loose green stools for two days. It happened each time a tooth was coming. It seemed as though it would never end, but it did. I hope this baby doesn't teethe the same way."*

It may be different. In any case, you now know that this period is intermittent. It is bad for a day or two, and then the baby goes back to her normal routine.

## Visual Exploration and Stimulation

Until the last fifteen years not much was known about infants' visual acuity and it was assumed they couldn't see too much. It is now known that the baby's visual system, though immature, is functional at birth. From the earliest days, babies are able to orient toward visual stimulation and have the necessary muscular control to focus with both eyes. There is, however, an optimal focus distance for babies of about eight inches. It is interesting to realize that a nursing baby's face is approximately eight inches from the mother's face. Objects nearer or farther than eight inches appear blurred to the baby for the first few weeks, but then there is rapid development of visual ability. By now, you will probably notice your babies' fixing on small, distinct patterns like those on the bumper of the crib or on mother's dress.

*"At first, I was worried that my baby seemed to pay so little attention; his stare seemed so blank. In the last week or so, I have noticed that he really seems to look at me and see me."*

Parents are often concerned about the baby's early blank stare; they expect more and often worry needlessly about the baby's visual ability. Babies look intently at the mother or other caretaker during feeding. This is the beginning of visual exploration at the optimal focus distance for the baby. Babies also may stare at patterns or objects in their cribs that happen to be at the appropriate distance. Soon they begin to follow or track the parent visually as he or she moves around the room.

It is believed that babies pay most attention to bright colors, particularly red. This is why we encourage you to dangle the red ring in front of them to stimulate visual response. It is also why we encourage you to get toys that are bright, with marked color contrasts, so they will be visually attractive to the babies. It is fun for parents to play with their baby in this way, and it helps visual development.

Babies become attached to these bright toys and feel more secure if these objects are nearby in their usual places. For that reason, it is a good idea to bring a familiar toy or two with you when you come here. These toys will help the babies make the transition from a familiar to an unfamiliar place.

By three months, most of the babies will follow the ring through 180 degrees and begin to see across a room. Around four months, they begin to develop depth perception, and their vision becomes more like ours.

They continue to need visual stimulation, and we'll talk more about that in the coming weeks.

*"What if the baby is a little cross-eyed? Should that be corrected right away, or will it improve by itself?"*

Very often an infant's eyes do not focus on an object well because there may be an imbalance in the immature musculature. The muscle pulling the eye in one direction may be stronger than the muscle pulling the eye in the opposite direction, and this gives the baby a squint or cross-eyed look. This muscle imbalance may be present in one or both eyes and may correct itself as the baby matures. Stimulating the baby to use his eyes to follow a moving object may help to exercise the lagging muscle. If this condition persists beyond the first year, however, the baby's eyes should be examined by an ophthalmologist.

## *Handedness*

*"How can you tell if a baby is going to be right- or left-handed?"*

It's not easy at first. At this age, the hand on the side that the baby turns toward—the one that is held up clenched—may be the dominant hand. Also, the hand that holds the rattle more firmly and longer may become dominant. At this age, parents should begin observing these signs. If a parent is left-handed, that is sometimes a clue. When the babies are five or six months old and begin to reach for things, they show the hand of preference.

*"When can you finally decide?"*

Some children are definitely left- or right-handed, and that is obvious very early. With other children you may not know until they are five or six years old. They may have mixed dominance and even reverse letters in school until that time. It is a good idea to hand something to a child in a way that will allow the child to decide for himself which hand to accept it with— that is, offer an object to a spot between the child's hands rather than directly to one of them. Sometimes right-handed parents unconsciously hand things to the right hand of a child. Then we discover later in school that the child is left-handed and is using his right hand, left eye, and left foot, exhibiting mixed dominance.

*"Does handing things to a particular hand cause any harm? I hand things to the baby's left because he seems to hold them best in that hand. My mother says not to do that. She says that I am making the baby left-handed and I must train him to use his right hand. Is that right?"*

I am sorry to say your mother does not seem to be correct. If the baby has a preference for using his left hand, it should not be discouraged. Recently we have found that it was not a good idea to force use of the right hand

■                                                                    ■

because the nervous system is designed so that we are dominant on one side. Some people are meant to be right-handed and some left-handed.

*"It does harm, then, to change the handedness?"*

Often it does. At least, it may hold up the development of reading and writing skills because the eye-hand coordination isn't as smooth as it might be. In the old days everyone had to use his right hand in school. If a child had a preference for the left hand, he was trained to use his right hand. It is now recognized that some reading problems are related to this change in handedness. This practice has been abandoned, but some grandparents may not be aware of the change. I think they will be less insistent if you explain the change in practice to them.

## Feeding Solid Foods

Mothers are usually concerned about the quantity and variety of food that the babies are consuming. There seems to be more and more of a trend toward starting solids early and increasing their variety and quantity quickly.

*"Oh, I began trying to give the baby cereal from a spoon when he was a month old, but he didn't seem to like it, so I put it into the bottle and make the holes in the nipple larger."*

Did your doctor feel the baby needed solid food?

*"No, I just thought the baby would be more filled-up and sleep better, so I did it on my own. He is sleeping longer, but I don't know if that's because he's getting the solid food or just because he's getting older."*

*"I tried a new food, lamb and vegetables, but the baby was very cranky the whole weekend. I don't know if it was the food or not."*

In that case it is better to begin with small amounts for a week and slowly increase the amount over a two-week period. Beginning slowly and introducing a new food every two weeks gives you an opportunity to notice any food allergies, particularly if you have a history of them in your family. There is no need to rush into a variety of foods. It's best to be sure that each new food agrees with the baby and that the baby likes it. If the baby doesn't like a certain food, there is no need to force it on the baby. There are many alternative foods of equal nutritional value. Maybe, when you try the rejected food several weeks later, it will be accepted. Taste for different flavors develops at different times, and often a baby with a well-established habit of eating from a spoon will eat whatever is given.

Actually, at this age most of the valuable nutrition still comes from milk. The ability to eat solids well does not develop until after about six months. What you are doing now is getting your babies used to the sensation of spoon feeding and swallowing solids. The variety and quantity is not important yet. There is more chance your baby will be a good eater if food is not forced or shoveled in. Feeding is another area where an early conflict between parent and baby may develop. Feeding time should be a pleasurable encounter. It can be made unnecessarily difficult if the parent is anxious to get the food in, no matter how the baby responds.

*"It upsets me when the baby doesn't finish every morsel. I know it shouldn't, but it does."*

The baby's life doesn't depend on spoon feeding at this stage. He is just learning to eat, and not eating doesn't mean he is naughty or doesn't love you. Often, feeding a baby is equated with love. Giving the baby food means you love him; accepting it means he loves you in return. Actually, you will show your love more by respecting his level of development and need. Then you do not become a controlling, but a patient and understanding, mother. Good care of a child used to be measured largely by weight. We feel differently now.

*"That's just the way my mother still feels. For her a fat baby is a healthy baby."*

Recent studies show that longevity is enhanced by being thin. Obesity causes multiple health problems and shortening of the life span. Present knowledge indicates that if the cells of the body become accustomed to an increased fat content in infancy, they carry on this need through life, and it is difficult to get over obesity. Therefore, it is best not to overfeed infants.

*"How much is enough, then?"*

The baby will accept what he needs unless there is some special nutritional problem, which should be discussed with your doctor. Most babies' capacity for food is very much less than adults think. It varies with each baby. Some are well fed on a teaspoon or two; others require half a jar of food at a time. The amount also varies from feeding to feeding and from day to day.

We also have to remember that some babies, particularly those in families with a history of allergies, seem to have an innate sense that certain foods disagree with them and will refuse to eat them. It is, therefore, safer not to coax a baby to eat a food that he persistently refuses.

## Attachment and Its Relation to Basic Trust

### Parents' Fears About Babies' Unresponsiveness

We have talked in previous sessions, especially in our first sessions, about the sense of disappointment new parents may feel because the newborn infant seems so unresponsive. The parents may have spent months dream-ing about the new baby—how they are going to cuddle her and how she is going to respond and return the loving they give. Instead, at the beginning, the infant only occasionally opens her eyes long enough to glance about, perhaps not even in the direction of the adoring parent who is talking, cooing, or even rocking the baby. Sometimes the baby just yawns and goes off to sleep, or she may cry and show discomfort, much to the parents' consternation. Initially, parents have to be satisfied if the baby takes her feeding, burps, and goes off to sleep.

Do you remember that period? Do you remember some of you said you regarded the baby as a stranger and, much as you had wanted the baby, you were surprised that you didn't have the feelings you expected? That the baby didn't respond as you expected?

*"I remember that quite well. I was feeling very upset at the time because the baby was so unresponsive—by my standards. I was even worried the baby might be retarded. Now I know better."*

*"The thought that the baby might be mentally retarded or impaired in some other way bothered me all the time during my pregnancy. Now I watch every movement secretly, because I still have that fear."*

This is a very common worry, and the infant's limited responses keep parents in suspense for a long time. Learning what normal or appropriate responses are for the babies' age should be of some help in allaying the anxiety. There is a very wide range of reactions that are considered "normal." No two babies begin to smile, sit, stand, or talk at exactly the same age. However, the developmental sequence is usually the same: Babies look around first, then smile, then turn over, then sit, then stand. Children in the same family may be very different; even identical twins do not mature in the same areas at exactly the same age.

*"Well, that makes me more comfortable. I remember that my brother was a fast walker and a slow talker, but he is a lawyer now."*

*"I wasn't afraid that the baby was retarded, but I thought there must be something wrong with me because I just didn't feel close to the baby. I was disappointed."*

## Mutual Attachments

By now there is beginning to be a change in the baby's responses. All of these weeks, you have been trying to set up routines of feeding, sleeping, going out regularly, stimulating with toys, talking, cuddling, and comfort-ing the baby. You have been advised to try to arrange the events of the baby's day in a more predictable sequence, so that she will get to know what is coming next.

We emphasize this sequencing because it helps the baby begin to develop memory. Also, by this repetition she will begin to develop a sense of trust in her parents and a feeling that things will be done in a dependable sequence. As the baby begins to develop this sense of trust, she begins to form a primary attachment to the person who has been taking most care of her. By now, the parents are forming the attachment to the baby that they expected to feel the very first day.

On the baby's part, attachment is a feeling that develops over time, with the gradual maturing of the baby's central nervous system and the growing understanding that there is a reliable person always ready to try to respond to her needs—perhaps even anticipate some of them. For the parents, attachment develops as they find they can satisfy the baby's needs and that the baby is thriving and beginning to recognize them. They respond as the baby watches them move about the room, gives them a special smile, coos, gurgles, flails her arms, and kicks her feet when they approach. Some babies can even manage to reach up when held to explore the parent's face or pull the parent's hair.

Have any of you begun to notice this? Do you think your baby is beginning to know you?

*"I'm not sure my baby really knows me better than she knows the house-keeper, but she certainly responds with her eyes and flops her hands when I come into the room. If that's attachment, we are there!"*

*"My baby may not be as attached to me as I am to him. Now I can't go out even for a little while without missing him. Earlier I just couldn't wait to get out; now, I can't wait to get back!"*

## Attachment to the Father

*"I know my baby knows me. He kicks and smiles and gurgles as soon as I get near his crib. That makes everything worthwhile—the diaper changing, the lack of sleep, the messy house, the confinement. I was wondering if babies have the same feeling for the father, and how they can develop it when their fathers are away as much as my husband is?"*

We talked earlier about the father's role in establishing patterning and in developing basic trust. The earliest strong attachment is usually to the mother, because she spends the most time with the baby. The father, who is away much of the day, often has less chance to relate to the baby. However, this does not mean that he cannot have a role or place in the baby's day. There can be a feeding, playing time, bath, or bedtime routine that the father handles each day. In this way, the baby and father develop an attachment for each other. Soon the baby begins to know when her father is coming home and what the sound of the key in the latch means. Often the baby shows a great deal of excitement and enjoyment at the sound and sight of Daddy. Sometimes, the mother may have feelings of jealousy about the baby's interest in Daddy or feel "left out" when the father is engrossed with the baby. It is good to remember that fathers may often have had the same "left-out" feeling when the mother concentrated all her attention on the baby.

In what way or ways are you arranging for Daddy to get to know his baby? How much is he talking to the baby and playing with her? Do you think the baby is beginning to recognize her father?

*"My husband said the baby doesn't know who he is, so he spent the whole evening talking to her."*

It is very important that the fathers talk and play with their babies, even if it means the babies go to bed later. The babies need to know both parents.

*"If I didn't keep the baby up a little later, my husband wouldn't see him at all. I wait to give him a bath until my husband is there. He enjoys watching the baby bathed and has even done it a few times. He likes to give the baby the bedtime bottle. Then we both tuck him in. I think they are beginning to have a real feeling for each other."*

*"My mother says my father never touched us when we were babies and he never really learned how to deal with us. I decided early that I would see to it that my husband got to know his child. As a matter of fact, we both decided that before the baby was born. So my husband gives the first morning bottle while I make breakfast."*

*"My husband is home during the day, so the baby gets to see him a good deal. However, I don't think the baby can tell the difference between us yet. Is that all right?"*

That may be so now, but the baby is forming an impression of both of you as you care for her and play with her. Soon you will begin to see evidence of this recognition and attachment.

*"My husband doesn't do any feeding or bathing, but he spends a lot of time talking and playing with the baby. Although our baby seems to respond to all the members of the family, I think the response to my husband and me is a little different; she just seems more animated."*

The development of an attachment to the mother, father, or other caretaker, and then to more people, is associated with basic trust, and is one of the most important beginnings of personality development. If a parent gives the baby a chance to develop this basic trust, the baby will have one of the most important gifts she will ever get in her life. Those children who have not developed an early attachment and trust may not be able to form appropriate and close relationships with others later in life. Their relationships remain superficial. Sometimes they are apt to be suspicious when it is not appropriate to be so. Children in institutions where caretakers work in eight-hour shifts and change frequently often have such problems. Parents who work must be careful that baby-sitters are not constantly changed.

We think this trust and attachment relates later in life to the ability to be involved with the teacher in school and with a drive for learning. A sense of attachment is a precursor to cognitive development.

*"Are you saying that it is best for the same person always to take care of the baby, so she can form this attachment? Do you mean that only the mother should be responsible for child care?"*

The baby needs to have a constant, consistent caretaker. That person doesn't necessarily have to be the mother, although in our society it usually is the mother. In some families, the mother works and the father is at home, so he's the caretaker. Sometimes, it's the grandmother or an aunt. The caretaker, however, should be constant. The baby needs to establish a feeling of security and relationship with one person. She will be forming attachments to her father and other family members as well, though these attachments may be less intense at first.

*"Then what about day care?"*

*One of the drawbacks of the day-care system is that the personnel, no matter how good, shifts. No employed person keeps the hours that are required for a baby's care. Also, it is very expensive to replicate the one-to-one relationship needed by infants. Most day care as we know it is more appropriate as the children get older.*

## Mothers' Feelings of Being "Trapped"

*"So the mother is always trapped!"*

Parents often do not realize how important they are to their child's healthy development or how much time child care takes. *Someone* must make the commitment to create a special bond or attachment with the infant. The mother has traditionally done this, but increasingly in the future, families may decide that the role of primary caretaker will be taken by the father or another person. The baby needs consistent care in the early developmental period. Once basic trust is established, the baby can begin to relate to other members of the family, to close friends, and then to neighbors. Finally, the baby becomes a secure, social person. This development takes time, but the baby has to have a chance to form the first close relationship with his parents or a substitute caretaker to be able to make other social relationships later in life.

Most of you have worked and been very free to come and go. Your lives are very changed now; a lot of adjustments are necessary. Our society needs to be more supportive of and more sensitive to the concerns of young parents. Then there would be less inclination to feel "trapped."

Some parents may already be experiencing some aspects of attachment, such as when the baby will not let you out of her sight, even to go to the bathroom. This may intensify your feeling of being "trapped" and be annoying. This is, however, a normal stage in the development of attachment and lasts until the baby has had sufficient maturation and experience to know you will return. At this stage of her development, the baby does not know that you still exist if she cannot see you. She does not have that comprehension; she knows only what she sees. Therefore, it is best for the baby to be able to see the parent in the same room or through a doorway. You can reassure her by getting into her line of vision, calling to her, or, better yet, taking her with you. Primitive people recognized this need and kept their babies close to them in papoose boards or slings. Now some mothers are adopting this custom by wearing carriers, and it works. When you disappear from sight, the baby thinks it is forever, just as you think it is forever when she won't let you out of sight. It is a stage in good, healthy development. In fact, we are concerned if a baby doesn't care if her parents come or go, because this may indicate that the baby is not forming an attachment.

Have you begun to have this experience yet? How have you been dealing with the experience, and how do you feel about it?

*"I noticed my baby cried when I walked out of the room. I thought I had spoiled her by being with her too much. But I just couldn't let her cry, so I'd pick her up and carry her with me. I thought I was doing the wrong thing, but now I see that she needs that kind of attention."*

If the baby cries when you leave, it is a sign of her attachment, and that is good. It shows normal, healthy development and progress. At times it may, of course, be inconvenient. If you understand that the baby's crying is her way of saying. "Please don't leave me; I can't do without you," then you won't feel as angry or trapped. Some crying is inevitable; we can't be "superparents" all the time.

*"My mother says I must let the baby cry, or the baby will be 'spoiled' and always cry for me."*

We hear the comment all the time that responding to a baby's cry will "spoil" him. What we are dealing with here is the old concept that good children should be "seen but not heard." This is a misconception. A quiet child may be depressed, understimulated, or even autistic.

This is such an important issue that extensive research has been done on it. Many of these studies show that the babies who were attended to when they cried come to cry less and were able to relinquish their mothers earlier, while those that were allowed to cry without attention remained "cry babies" and were more reluctant to separate from their mothers later. We are concerned with the development of healthy personalities. The child whose needs are responded to will trust the people around her and have confidence in herself; she will not be a spoiled child.

# Sensory-Motor Developments

## Turning Over

At the same time that you have been noticing the development of the baby's attachment to you, the baby has been displaying new motor activity.

■                                                                                                      ■

The effect of the baby's new motor development on parents is different for each family and often for each parent. Now that the babies are beginning to turn over, some parents are very pleased. They regard this skill as an achievement. Other parents are not so happy because it's no longer safe to leave the baby alone on a changing table or bed. The new skill puts a new pressure on parents to guard the baby's safety. Perhaps some mothers feel this makes life more difficult and causes them more anxiety. Though this is indeed true, the development of the new skill is also a milestone in the baby's life.

This motor achievement is one of which fathers are often more proud than mothers. Mothers, however, often observe the developmental change first. It is fun to display this new ability to the father. It gets him involved, and he can help in safety precautions.

How do you and your husbands feel about your babies' greater activity?

*"All the time I saw the baby struggling to turn over, I felt like helping him. Now that he can do it by himself, I'm glad, but it makes me nervous. I always double-check to be sure I have pulled up the crib side and never leave him on our bed anymore."*

*"My husband is very proud of this new achievement. But right away he ordered carpeting for the baby's room, so a fall would be softened a little. We also put heavy, shaggy rugs beside the crib and by our bed, and a heavier pad in the playpen."*

All of those are good precautions because a parent can't be as quick as the baby sometimes. From now on, the babies have to be watched more carefully. At first it is difficult to keep an eye on the baby all the time, but in time doing so gets to be second nature.

## Eye-Hand Coordination

In addition to the large motor advance of turning over, babies are now beginning to play with their hands, perhaps clasping them or just staring at their fingers.

The babies are becoming much more observant and can now enjoy more play with a toy. Now, when a toy is placed in the baby's hand, he may look at it or look from the toy to his hand. He is gradually getting the notion that he is holding the toy in his hand, that he extends to the end of those fingers holding the toy. This, too, is a milestone in development; it is the beginning of eye-hand coordination, a skill that becomes very important later on in school.

Have you been noticing this in your babies?

*"My baby holds the rattle and bangs it, but I haven't seen her look at it yet."*

■                                                                                    ■

Each baby does that on his own individual timetable. Some babies look at their hands before they look at objects. It's great fun to see their concentration when they finally do notice their own hands.

*"My baby began last week. My husband and I get such a kick out of watching her look at her fingers. She screws up her face and looks at them very seriously."*

When the baby begins to look at his fingers, it is very good to put a toy in his hand. That way, he can begin to explore new objects as well.

## Sitting Propped Up

Are you beginning to prop the babies up to sit for a short time?

*"I've found the greatest infant seat. It is part of a walker, and the seat goes on at different heights. It's all padded like a chaise lounge. The baby can't tip over, and you can regulate the angle of the back. We feed our baby in this seat. So she is propped up and we have our hands free. She is also free and has a certain amount of independence."*

The seat is one way to prop the baby up. You can also use a pillow in the carriage or the corner of the living room sofa, carefully watched, of course. The baby needs to begin to see the world from this angle and learn that there is more to observe than what he views lying on his back.

Of course, the view from his back is more stimulating if he can see a mobile. If the mobile also plays music, the baby will be more interested. The baby will watch for a few minutes while the parent does something else. However, it is tempting if the baby is quiet to leave him flat on his back too long. Now is the time to think about a little propped sitting—for five minutes or so at a time.

Some of you may find that sitting up also helps your babies burp and get rid of gas bubbles. They often burp on their own while sitting. Some may cry, and you may interpret this as not wanting to sit, but it may mean the gas bubble is hurting, and a change of position is necessary to help release it.

# Stimulation Through Play Activities

## Toys for Eye-Hand Coordination

Toys are very useful in stimulating eye-hand coordination. A red ring or a red dumbbell-shaped rattle is especially helpful. Red is more attractive to babies than are the pale pastel colors used on most toys.

The baby's attention span may not be long. He may soon drop the toy. He may even look for it momentarily. Then mother or father can retrieve the toy, and continue the game for as long as baby seems interested in

■                                                                    ■

holding the toy, looking at it, putting it into his mouth, waving it in the air, or banging it against the crib or playpen.

Have you begun to play this way with your babies?

*"I thought the baby was too young because he didn't seem to pay much attention to the rattle."*

Babies may not pay much attention at first, but if you keep stimulating them with the toy as they mature, they will pay more and more attention to it. It is fun to watch this happen.

*"My husband does this with the baby while I'm getting dinner ready. That's his thing with the baby."*

That's good interaction between father and baby. Now that the babies are beginning to play with toys, it is important to have appropriate ones. The best toys for children are those that they can manipulate. For babies, in addition to the rattle and ring, small one-inch cube blocks, empty spools of thread, and small toys with projections that can be gripped (such as a small rag doll) are best. It is always a temptation to buy a big teddy bear, an enormous fire engine, a large doll. These are more fun for the parents than the baby. The baby can look at these large things, but he can't really play with them. He needs small things that stimulate his eye-hand coordination, toys whose manipulation he can master.

## Attention Span and Playtime

The babies are now at an age when they can pay more attention to cradle gyms and mobiles of colorful, simple shapes. These should be arranged over the crib, so that the baby may hit or kick them accidentally. Later on, as his ability increases and his central nervous system matures, he will intentionally put them into motion. The babies are now beginning to have a longer concentration span and may be able to amuse themselves alone for about ten minutes while exploring a toy or cradle gym. Ten minutes is a long time for a baby. Then new stimulus has to be introduced, or the old one moved to a different position, like the other side of the crib. Babies soon tire, and you must let them rest. Turn them over for sleep, change, or feed them according to their daily pattern. As we have said before, playtime should be a part of their daily schedule; it is part of their education.

Are you enjoying your playtime with the baby? Is the father entering into this?

*"I'm so busy I can't say I really play with the baby if by 'play' you mean sitting by him and continually picking up a toy he has dropped. If I happen to have a little time, I do. Otherwise, I just go to him when he cries."*

You should, of course, go to him when he cries, but the baby also needs stimulating play. A baby learns through play. You don't have to sit beside the baby constantly; he can't concentrate for long periods. There should, however, be two or three short play periods with you or the father each day as a regular part of the baby's program. It can really be fun for both parent and child.

*"My husband and I take turns. I do most of the playing during the week. He does it over the weekend. Sometimes we do it together. That's the best way for us, I think."*

*"My husband says he has no patience for playing with the baby with a rattle or a ring. When the baby is big enough to ride a bike or play baseball, then my husband says he'll play with him, but not now."*

There are some parents who have difficulty relating to very young babies and are better with older children. However, a baby needs to have contact with both parents from infancy. Once the mother can demonstrate to the father the changes in the baby's development and their importance, the father may become more interested in the baby and find it easier to play with him with these simple toys.

## Baby's Sense of Mastery

In addition to playing with the baby, you need to show approval of him. Your approval should be verbal and physical. Your tone of voice and facial expression should show that you are pleased, even delighted, with the baby's achievements. The baby then gets a sense of pleasure at mastery and a feeling of approval. If parents are quiet, objective observers, noting the achievement but not conveying their satisfaction, the baby does not feel approval or develop a sense of pleasure at mastery, which is necessary for a positive self-image. This approval is the earliest way in which parents can help a child establish the inner drive toward achievement that is necessary later on for school achievement. This is the time for the parent to begin to look for achievement and recognize it. The baby thrives on this recognition. It may mean the difference between a self-confident person who strives for achievement and one who doesn't try because he never experienced recognition while his personality was developing.

How do you signal to your babies that you have noticed what the baby is doing and like it?

*"Oh, I pick him up and kiss and hug him."*

*"I don't say anything; I just watch. I guess I should say something. I thought he would not understand. But his father says 'Marvelous.' "*

Many mothers say, "I pick him up and kiss and hug him," or "I say, 'You're the most wonderful baby in the world,' " or "I tell him that he's marvelous," and so forth. The response does not have to be vigorous body contact or lavish praise, but it does need to be recognizable approval. For young babies, clapping or saying "Good" is enough. They understand tone of voice and facial expression, if not your exact words. Later, as they grow older, a nod, a smile, or a little pat—some signal the child understands—is all that is necessary. Even young children seem to understand that lavish praise is uncalled for and often insincere.

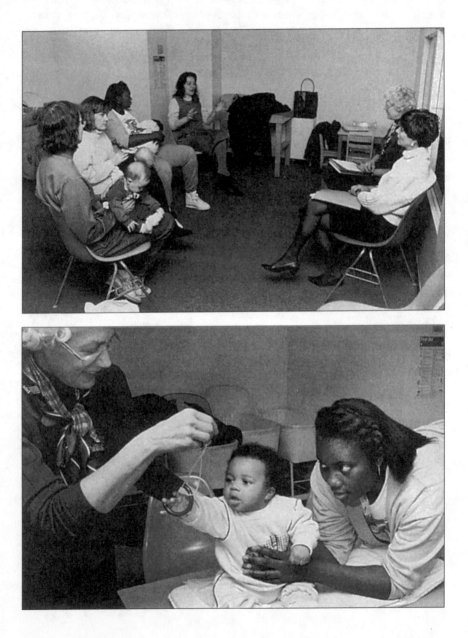

# 4

# *Age Sixteen to Twenty Weeks*

## *Highlights of Development—Sixteen Weeks*

When the baby is lying on his back, his posture is now symmetrical, with his head facing straight up instead of to the side as formerly. The activity of his arms is more parallel and he may clasp his hands together. When the baby pulls himself toward the sitting position while his arms are supported by the parent (*see exercise described on page 19*), he is now able to hold his head steadily forward without bobbing. When placed on his stomach, he can now lift his head well off the surface to about a 45-degree angle. In this position, he is also on the verge of rolling over. (Parents should be on the lookout for this development because the baby may roll off the bed or table.)

The baby now looks immediately at the red ring or rattle when it is offered and her arms activate at the sight of the toy. When the baby is holding the ring, she looks at her hand, showing that she is beginning to know that her hand is part of her person. She will try to bring the ring to her mouth and her free hand to the middle of her body. She may look from hand to object. She may also begin playing with her fingers. The baby's attention can now be engaged by something as small as a marble, especially if it is a bright color, demonstrating her increasing visual acuity and ability.

At this age, excited heavy breathing represents a form of expression and the beginning of language. The babies are also beginning to laugh. They often vocalize and laugh in interactions with their parents. They are likely to exhibit a spontaneous social smile when approached by the parent or another familiar person. Babies are now ready to view the world from a more upright position; they can sit propped up for ten to fifteen minutes, two or three times a day. When the mother approaches with the bottle or other food, or goes through the routines preparatory to breast feeding, the baby may exhibit anticipatory behavior, such as sucking or mouthing motions or waving of the arms.

## Cuing In: Response to the Baby's Needs

We have discussed the new levels of development and how to utilize them to enhance the baby's progress. What we are suggesting is that you pick up "cues" from the baby. For example, when the baby is ready (that is, has reached the appropriate maturational level) to hold a rattle, the parent should be ready to supply it. In other words, the parent is patterning activities around the baby's demonstrated needs and developmental level.

Another example of this "cuing in" to the baby's needs, which you are all doing, is feeding. When the baby is hungry, she signals to you by crying or sucking her fingers. You then feed her either with the breast or the bottle. You respond to her need. This is sometimes called "demand feeding," but we prefer to think of it as a response or "cuing in" to the baby's need. "Demand" has a negative connotation. One can quibble about semantics, but a mother who feels she is *responding* to a need feels more positive about the baby than if she feels a *demand* is being made upon her.

How does your baby let you know she is hungry?

*"My baby whimpers a little, then sucks her index and middle fingers. When I hear her, I get ready for the feeding."*

*"My baby never cries; he just looks around and kicks. Then I change him while I'm warming the bottle. The bottle is ready before he gets a chance to cry. I just can't bear to have him cry."*

*"My baby wakes with a loud, piercing cry, and nothing I do soothes him until he gets his feeding. There is never a warning. I'm in a panic, and I guess he is too until he gets at the breast. I've tried to change him first. If he is just wet, I feed him first. If he has soiled, I usually change him first, but his crying upsets me. I just wish he could wait a little."*

You have all noted cues that you use to get the feeding ready and satisfy your babies' needs. Some of you have pointed out with some distress that the baby wants an immediate response. She puts you under intense pressure with her crying. Sometimes the baby even makes you a little angry because she can't wait.

### Need for Gratification

It's natural to be upset when the baby cries violently and can't wait. However, parents must understand that not being able to wait is part of the baby's lack of neurological development. To be able to wait your turn is part of maturity. A parent can wait, but a baby cannot.

As baby's nervous system matures and as her needs are met, she learns to wait because she has established a sense of trust that her parent will meet her needs. The more often the baby experiences this gratification of her needs, the more secure she will become and the more she will develop a sense of trust.

If, on the other hand, a mother is inconsistent in her responses, the baby gets no sense of what actions on her part produce dependable responses, and she does not develop basic trust. This does not mean that the mother needs to sit with a bottle in hand, ready in case the baby cries. It does mean that the mother has to have some idea of the baby's pattern and must arrange her day to suit it. For example, if you know the baby usually wakes for a feeding at 11:00 A.M., you should not plan to go shopping, visiting, or to the doctor's at that time without providing for the baby's feeding.

How do you feel about a baby's inability to wait? Does knowing that this is the result of immaturity of the baby's nervous system help you cope any better with this behavior?

*"I hate to hear my baby cry, but isn't always getting what he wants at once going to lead to a spoiled baby that always cries?"*

*"My husband thinks that babies need to cry to develop their lungs and that it's bad to give in to them right away."*

*"I think a baby cries because he needs something, and it's my job to find out what he needs. Letting him cry just isn't our style. Luckily, my husband and I feel the same way, so if one of us is busy with something or tired, the other goes to the baby."*

## Different Types of Cries

As we have said, crying, in the beginning, is the baby's only language. We have to learn, therefore, what each cry means and how to respond to it.

Are you beginning to catch on better to what your baby is trying to communicate?

*"I think I have learned the meaning of a new kind of cry. It's not because the baby is hungry or uncomfortable, but because he wants to play with a certain thing. The other day, my baby screamed until the dog came over so that he could pet it."*

That's exactly it. People are social beings; we like to interact with others. Babies have this same desire. Now you know that your baby is interested in the dog. The next time he cries when the dog is around, you can take him to the dog and not wait until the dog decides to come over.

Other babies may get bored and fussy, and just want to be picked up for a "chat" with you or for the opportunity to look at something with you. As the babies grow, your repertoire of things to do to interest them and calm the fussiness will increase. Sometimes you will have to go through a sequence of holding, walking, talking, playing, feeding, and changing the diaper. By this age, your babies are old enough to be amused with an object to hold and play with. The object may only be the cover of the Vaseline jar or the pull cord on the shade or a favorite toy. Sometimes they respond to music. These are small things, but an understanding response on the part of the parent is very important in giving the baby the feeling that there is someone who tries to satisfy his needs. With practice, you will "tune in" better to your baby's needs and moods. As they develop, the babies' interests will change and enlarge, and you will be changing with them.

*"But what if you can't tune in to the cries every time? Sometimes I get it right; sometimes it's my husband who does."*

The fact that you are now beginning to know the different cries is very important. When the baby understands that you understand what he wants—even fifty percent of the time—it gives him the sense of trust and security that we have talked about. That basic trust is the earliest building block of character development. It forms the basis for all the baby's future relationships with people.

None of us can be perfect parents—I certainly was not one myself. We are not trying to make you into perfect parents with perfect children. We are trying to help you understand your children better so that you can enjoy each other more. You know that in your adult relationships, the more a friend understands what you are saying, the more comfortable you feel. If you have had *some* conversations in which there was complete understanding, your relationship can survive a few misunderstandings. It is the same with the relationship between you and your baby. Sometimes, even if you don't understand what the baby wants but are physically there and comforting, the baby will be comforted and satisfied. We do the best we can to understand our babies. Our ability grows with practice, and the baby's sense of basic trust grows as well.

## Spoiling and the Development of Basic Trust

We have talked a great deal about picking up the babies when they cry and its relation to the development of basic trust. We are all aware, however, that the idea that you will spoil a baby if you pick him up when he cries is very ingrained in traditional child-rearing attitudes. We worry about "spoiling" our children by attending to them. Actually, what we're really doing is spoiling our children by *not* paying attention to them. This is an awfully hard idea for lots of people to understand. Maybe you think we dwell on it too much, but it comes up over and over again in various ways at different ages.

*"I would just like to go over the idea again to see if I got it right. If you pick up a baby whenever he needs it, he looks for that satisfaction. You feed him or comfort him so when you put him back to bed, he is satisfied. He gets*

*what he needs; he doesn't get spoiled. When you pick up a baby that much, it's because he needs it that much, and that's not spoiling."*

That's right. It is supplying the baby's need when he needs it. The baby who doesn't get what he needs when he needs it is the one who lacks trust and is never satisfied. It is very hard to reshape this kind of basic character structure. You have seen older children who are never satisfied, no matter what you give them. If you could go back in their life history, you would probably find that these were the babies who didn't get what they needed when they were very, very young.

You see it also in adults. For some people nothing is quite enough. If they have one kind of camera, they've got to have another and another—nothing is quite sufficient. These adults are really trying to satisfy with material things a need that wasn't satisfied in early infancy. These material things do not replace what was needed, so they are never totally satisfying.

Parents often buy their children enormous presents but spend no time with them. They don't give of themselves at all. They think they are giving to the child, and they can't understand why the child is not satisfied. Such parents are only substituting material things for themselves, for spending time with their children. Nothing should be given *instead* of sharing feelings and time with a child. There is no substitute for filling important emotional needs. Actually, children often enjoy small things—a spool, an eraser, or a small box—if it is something that the parents are sharing *with* them.

*"But my mother says it will spoil the baby to pick her up when she cries."*

This topic comes up over and over again as relations and neighbors criticize parents for responding to babies' cries. There seems to be little understanding that until a baby is verbal, crying is his language, the way he brings attention to his needs. Trying to find out what the baby needs is the parents' job. As the parents become more accustomed to the type of cry, they begin to understand what the baby means and can satisfy him more quickly.

Consistent response to a child's needs enhances his sense of basic trust. The way a baby is spoiled is by inconsistency. When a need is satisfied sometimes and ignored other times, it makes a baby insecure. He doesn't get gratification consistently, and so he becomes very demanding in order to get a response. He learns that he must cry louder in order to be heard. This leads to a very aggressive, angry relationship between mother and baby, and the baby's personality will generally remain angry and aggressive. Other babies may only whine and cry. Still others give up easily and stop expressing their needs. These children will have little drive for success later on because they have had no experience of achieving satisfaction. None of these traits leads to healthy personality development. The babies who have been responded to appropriately are more likely to be pleasant, secure, and effective children and adults.

■                                                                              ■

*"You have been stressing the words 'appropriate response.' Does that mean that what is appropriate now may not be when the children are older?"*

That is absolutely right. Since little babies can only cry, we must try to figure out what their cries mean. Toddlers can say a few words, and we need to learn to interpret them. A four-year-old can sometimes express himself very accurately. A baby must learn to trust the people around him. Delay causes him great anxiety and teaches mistrust. An older child who has developed basic trust in his parents will believe them when they say "in a little while."

As the babies get older, we will talk about teaching the babies to delay, to learn that they cannot always have everything they want immediately. This process of delaying gratification must also be learned and is a part of healthy personality development. But it is the second step. The first step is to learn trust because one's needs have been responded to and gratified.

Have you noticed any difference in your babies when you respond to them quickly and when you let them cry?

*"Well, I came from a family that believes it will spoil a baby if he is picked up any time he cries. But since I came here, I've been listening to you, and now my baby is a little doll. He is not a crybaby."*

*"My instinct is to pick up the baby. When I do, I'm happy and so is the baby. But when my mother-in-law is there, she gives me the business, and, although I still pick the baby up, I feel umcomfortable."*

*"You know, I get this from my mother too, about how she raised five children and she never picked them up when they cried. I don't say anything. I just can't tell her three of her children are in therapy, but it's true."*

You are all in a difficult position. Perhaps you should tell your families that you understand that they mean well for the baby, and that you know they did the best they knew how in raising their children. But point out that new things have been found out about babies' development, and that you are trying to follow what you think is best for your baby. Tell them you mean no disrespect to them, and ask them to give you a chance to see if your way works.

Many people expect children to be able to do things that are beyond their emotional maturity and beyond the maturity of their central nervous systems. Explain that when the baby is older, you will be teaching him to be more self-reliant and less demanding. But also point out that you won't try to do this until the baby has reached the appropriate stage of emotional and physical development for it.

## Fathers' Attitudes Toward Crying and Spoiling

In the last sessions, we have been talking with the mothers about different kinds of crying. Some cries mean the babies are hungry; others mean they need a diaper change; still others mean they are bored. The baby may just want a little company and change of scene. Each kind of cry needs a different kind of parental response. The mothers feel that they are beginning to understand these cries and how to respond to them.

We have also been talking about the importance to the babies' personality development of getting their needs satisfied appropriately as soon as possible.

How do fathers feel about this? Are you beginning to tell the difference between the various kinds of crying your baby does? How do you feel about attending to your baby's cries? Do you think this causes spoiling?

*"When I get home, sometimes everything is calm. Other times I can tell from my wife's expression and the baby's crankiness that it's been a bad day. I decide right then that my wife needs a break. I play with the baby. You know, I think he really likes to see a new face. He laughs, no matter what I do. But other times, in the night, I can't do anything, and it takes a long time to quiet him. Then I think I have spoiled him."*

*"Yes, those are the times that drive me crazy. Sometimes my wife and I pace around all night, it seems, and the baby keeps fretting. Then if we put her down, she screams."*

*"I was brought up in a large family. I remember that one of my younger brothers was always crying when I came home from school. For that reason, a crying baby seems a natural thing to me. I know that period will pass. I don't think of the baby as spoiled. I can see now that a large family has its advantages."*

*"My mother says those are the times to let the baby cry it out, but my wife can't stand it. She says you think it's bad for the baby, and then I have two miserable people on my hands. So I get up and pace around with the baby. I'm sure she's going to end up a spoiled brat."*

Crying is the baby's only language at this age. She is telling you she is uncomfortable and needs something. If you respond to her cries and try to help—if only by being a warm human presence—she will begin to feel that the people around her can be trusted to help. Answering the baby's needs is not "spoiling" the baby. We do not "spoil" our children by attending to them; we spoil our children by *not* paying attention to them consistently.

Inconsistency is also hard on the baby. She can't understand why sometimes you help her and sometimes you don't. This confuses the baby—a spoiled baby is a confused baby. It is important for parents to be consistent in the way they handle the baby and for both parents to try to act the same. If it is always the mother who attends to the baby's needs and never the father, the baby may grow up feeling that only women are comforting. It is important for children to see both parents as loving and caring, so that later on they can also accept both parents as limiting and disciplining without resentment.

*"Now I can see that all the little things a mother does are important and that my response can mean a lot to the baby."*

## More on Attachment

### Attachment to Parents and Other Caretakers

While you are satisfying your babies' needs and establishing their trust in you, something else is happening. As the baby is beginning to have faith in you, she is also becoming more and more attached to you. She watches you as you move around the room; perhaps she cries now if you leave or smiles and coos when you return. If the mother is the main caretaker, she will be the first to experience this special recognition from the baby. But fathers can also have this experience if their attentions to the baby are as frequent and consistent as the mothers'.

How many of you have already noticed this special kind of response in your baby? Is the response to different members of your family different or the same? What evidence that the baby recognizes and is attached to you have you seen so far?

*"My wife and I both work. The baby is not really attached to anyone yet. How can we help her form attachments to us and the baby-sitter?"*

As we discussed earlier (*see Chapter I*), I think your wife returned to work at the right time—before the baby was attached *only* to her. Now you have to make sure that your caretaking is consistent, that you have one consistent baby-sitter, and that each of you has special times with the baby. For example, when you get home, you might play with the baby while your wife fixes dinner (or vice versa, if you are the cook). Then your wife might have her special quiet playtime with the baby before the baby goes to bed. Your wife might also give your baby the evening and morning bottles. It would also be good if you were both around most of the time on weekends. The routines of care are important; then the baby learns which adult fills which part of the daily caretaking.

*"It sounds as though we'll be doing nothing but taking care of the baby and working at our jobs."*

It is important that you give your baby as much attention as you can. Whatever sacrifices you and your wife make now will pay off later. After a while, you will be able to do more for yourselves; the baby will not always need so much attention. If you are consistent with your attention now, I think you will soon begin to notice signs of attachment. It may take longer, but it will happen.

*"My baby is mostly attached to me, but she is also beginning to become attached to my husband. He gets home early in the evening, and they play*

*together. She really sees and reacts favorably to about six people because all of our parents are around a lot, too."*

But you noticed some difference in her behavior toward you? What did you especially notice?

*"Yes, she has begun to cry when I leave the room, and she kicks and laughs when I come back."*

The baby's strongest attachment is to the person who takes most care of her. She is most comfortable with that person because she is familiar with the way that person handles her and she feels secure.

*"Our baby is also mostly attached to me. She looks for me just to be sure I'm there. She'll respond to some people and not to others, as you said. We are moving soon. I wonder if it will bother the baby?"*

## Attachment to Places

Babies become attached not only to people but also to favorite toys and familiar surroundings. You may find that there will be a change in your baby, that she'll recognize the difference in the room. So it's a good idea to put the same things in her crib. Try to arrange her new room as nearly like the old room as possible. Babies like familiar things more than they like change. We introduce change to stimulate them and keep them interested, but they do not welcome complete or abrupt changes in their environment, such as a move to a new house entails.

Have you noticed that your baby is especially attached to some of her toys or to her surroundings?

*"We noticed that when we moved. Our baby was terribly interested in two green pictures that were in her room, and she kept looking for them. So we put them up right away. We were surprised that she seemed to miss them."*

It was very sensitive of you to recognize that. It is always a good idea when one moves to get the baby's room settled first and make it as nearly like the old room as possible, with special things that have meaning for the baby in place.

*"We often go away for weekends, and I find that the baby doesn't do as well in a strange place. Now, to make her comfortable, I have to take all her crib toys and some other things with us, and arrange them as similarly as possible to the way they are at home."*

Having her toys in their familiar places makes your baby feel more secure. It is important to understand that this sense of security is easily upset just when it is beginning to develop. This attachment that we are talking about is as important as basic trust in a child's development. The baby who establishes an attachment and feels secure with one person and place will then be able to relate to other people and other places as well. Our experience has been that children who don't make close attachments do

■                                                                                                    ■

not grow up to be adults who can. One must experience attachment early in life. First comes attachment to one person, the primary caretaker. Sometimes, if parents share caretaking duties, the early attachment is to both parents almost equally or, in the case of working parents, to the baby-sitter and the parents. Later, the attachment enlarges to include relatives and friends and, in later life, to one's mate and children.

We will discuss the whole sequence of attachment much more fully in the future. An awareness and understanding of the child's emotional as well as physical development makes parenting interesting and exciting.

*"Yes, and scary when you think how many mistakes you can make."*

You will make some mistakes, and other people with influence over your children's lives will make mistakes. No one is perfect; we all make mistakes. All of us have a certain tolerance and plasticity; we can recover from some mistakes. But you are correct in feeling that parenthood is a great responsibility. We agree with you. That is why our program exists: to give you support, and help you get more pleasure out of bringing up your babies.

## *More on Exploration*

### *From Oral to Visual Exploration*

Now the babies are getting more mobile. They are beginning to spend more time sitting up. Some of them can even turn over. They are still interested in exploring things with their mouths, but now they are beginning to be more interested in looking at them. They peer closely at them, wave them in the air, and bang them against other objects. Soon, they will lose the toy over the side of the table or carriage. This will be more or less accidental at first; later it will be more purposeful. If the babies' central nervous systems have developed sufficiently, they will momentarily notice the disappearance of the toy and look for it. After a second or two, they will lose interest and explore something else. "Out of sight, out of mind" literally explains this stage of development. Some babies are also able to hold one small toy while trying to reach for another.

Have you noticed your baby beginning to explore visually? Have you noticed an increased interest in touching things or trying to manipulate them?

*"My baby tries to put everything in her mouth. As I'm about to pull it out, she takes it out herself. Then the object is all wet with saliva. She looks at it and puts it back in her mouth, then takes it out again. Finally she begins to bang it on her table or whatever is near. She makes such a mess!"*

Perhaps it is a mess, but this exploration is your baby's earliest form of intellectual curiosity and should not be discouraged. Just try to have the baby do this in her play area, high chair, or playpen, where she can't make too much of a mess. Babies are not fastidious; they're not supposed to be. They will learn not to make a mess when they are older. Now is the time to be messy.

*"My baby gets so excited when he holds the rattle, looks at it, and then makes a noise by banging it on the tray. He seems to be trying to see if he is the one that is causing the noise."*

You are right, and it is a great discovery for him. He should feel that you both recognize his achievement, too.

## New Ways to Play

*"Our baby seems to take great pleasure in dropping his toys and seeing us pick them up. I think he is trying to get our goat."*

Parents can utilize this level of development by playing the game of "Where Is It?" When the baby drops something, pick it up and say, "Here it is!" or "Here is your block or ball or doll," mentioning the name of the object. This game has many advantages. It utilizes the baby's level of development in motor and visual coordination. It also provides language stimulation, both in the words the parents use and in the child's communication of pleasure at finding the lost toy. It can be a happy encounter with the parents. Later on, the baby will become more adept and retrieve the toy herself if she can reach it, but, at present, it is the parents' job to retrieve the object.

Some parents begin to feel that the baby is dropping things purposely just to make them pick them up, just to "get your goat." This is a common adult interpretation of what the baby is doing, but it is mistaken. The baby is merely exploring space. She is only trying to solve the mystery of why a block placed on a table disappears when it is moved a little bit.

Have you noticed your baby trying to explore space? How do you feel about this new experience?

*"My baby has just begun to drop toys, and I have tried to stop her because I have a bad back and can't be constantly bending down to pick things up."*

That is unfortunate because the baby needs to be able to explore. Perhaps you can attach a string to her toy and tie the string to the chair or carriage. That way you can return the toy by pulling on the string without bending down. That will also enhance the play a little because the baby will be able to watch the toy reappear. Or you can arrange for someone else to be around for this playtime. The game could be saved for the time father is home. It could be father's special game with the baby.

*"Why shouldn't we stop our babies from throwing things down and making a mess?"*

We feel that this early exploration should not be thwarted because studies indicate that babies who have been thwarted at this age may give up and lose the drive to explore and study that is so important when they are in school. This early curiosity is the precursor of the curiosity and drive to explore that is so necessary to success in later learning.

This is not the first exploratory effort the baby has made. We have encouraged you to allow her to touch your face, your hair, your clothes. These were the beginning exploratory gestures. Now the babies are beginning to explore space.

Another game that enhances the baby's concept of space and language is "Up and Down." When the toy falls, the parent says, "Down." When the parent picks the toy up, he says, "Up." In this way, the baby learns the concepts of up and down. No one says that this kind of game is not tiring or that the parent will want to repeat the game as many times as the baby may need to repeat it in order to understand the ideas of solid space, empty space, and up and down. When you get tired, just give the baby a new activity; pick her up and take her to another part of the home, go out for a walk, or play another game. Incidentally, another good game for a child this age is "Clap Hands."

The whole idea is to understand that the baby is not malevolent. She is not trying to upset you; she is merely trying to understand the world around her, and she needs her parents' help to do this. This can really be one of the aspects of parenthood that gives parents the most fun and satisfaction. It is also fun when both parents share in these play experiences.

*"The baby is much more interesting to me now. I hold things up for him, and he reaches for things more now. He seems so happy when he gets hold of them, when he drops them and I give them back. It is fun. When I get tired or he gets tired, we do something else. It's no big deal to do that."*

*"Our baby takes her rattle and smashes it against the wall. Sometimes she flings a toy, and it breaks."*

This flinging she's doing is also experimenting, but the toys used in this experimenting should be sturdy, so that they don't break when they're dropped or thrown. Babies should be able to drop or throw things. Say "Up" when you pick the object up, and "Down" when she throws it down. The baby's really trying to explore space. That is a stage of development all babies must go through. It is a learning experience.

*"I thought maybe she was enjoying breaking it."*

She doesn't know it's going to break; she just enjoys banging it. You have to give her things that are substantial, that are not going to break. It is a pity that so many toys are plastic because plastic toys tend to be fragile. Once all toys were made of wood and were durable. Plastic toys gained popularity because they were less expensive than the wooden ones. I don't think you can say that your baby is being destructive; it's just that the toys you've been providing break easily.

■                                                              ■

*"If we let her do this now, won't she grow up hitting things against the wall?"*

No, this is just a phase of development. If you don't want your baby to hit the toy against the wall, move her away from the wall, and give her something she can bang her toys on. Demonstrate for her what she may do. It is the job of the parents to arrange the baby's environment so that it is not dangerous for baby, parents, or property, while at the same time allowing the baby the opportunity for exploration.

## *Mothers' Conflicts About Working*

Most mothers have concerns relating to when and whether to return to work. Often conflicts develop between husband and wife over this issue.

*"Because we talk so much about the importance of the baby's forming an early attachment to one person, my husband said to me: 'That's it; you've got to stay home. No job is as important as giving our baby a good start.' I feel totally trapped."*

*"As you know, I have to work. I feel guilty about not being at home, but your suggestions about how I can help my baby make me feel better."*

It is very important that all of you have the opportunity to express your feelings about this subject. Our society is changing rapidly. It is widely thought today that the only meaningful work is outside the home. Society places little value on homemaking and child rearing. Many older women suddenly feel that they've wasted their lives; younger women are determined not to follow in their mothers' footsteps. This attitude ignores children's needs; it often ignores women's needs as well. The child needs a consistent caretaker in order to develop the appropriate attachment or bond for healthy personality development. Being a good mother is as important and worthwhile a job as being a good lawyer or a good doctor. We encourage those of you who can or want to stay home with your children to do so—and enjoy it.

At the same time, we know that some of you must work and that others of you will be happier if you work. A child will be better off with a good mother substitute and a happy part-time mother than a full-time mother who is unhappy or angry about being stuck at home. We are ready to help all of you, whether you work or not, to foster your babies' attachment and security and to meet your babies' needs.

Each of you must decide what is best for yourselves and your families; we are here to give you help and support.

## *Feeding*

### *Feeding Techniques; Avoiding Eating Problems*

By now most of you have begun introducing solid foods. The babies' main nourishment, particularly protein, however, still comes from milk and will continue to do so for some time. The purpose of beginning solid foods now—cereal, fruits, vegetables, and meat—is mainly to get the baby used to eating from a spoon. By the time the babies are nine or ten months old, when more nourishment is derived from solids, they will have learned to eat from a spoon and will be able to do it well. By patiently introducing new foods, you will help them develop a taste for a variety of different foods.

Not all babies like a wide variety of foods. Some will enjoy only one or two cereals, one or two fruits or vegetables, and one or two kinds of meat. Some babies will eat no vegetables—only fruit. Others like only vegetables and not fruit. This should not be a cause for concern. The important thing is not to force food so that feeding becomes a struggle and a battleground. A food that is refused at six months may be "adored" at nine months. If at first the baby does not like a particular food, a mother can always try to introduce it again later.

*"Some days my baby will eat all her meals well. Other days she will eat only one meal, or not at all. Usually, if she takes her first feeding well, I know it will probably be a good eating day."*

*"Well, I'm not sure how the baby's going to eat until lunchtime."*

Experiments have shown that, over time, a baby generally learns to take a sufficient amount of the right foods. In any one day, or at any one meal, he may not have a balanced diet, but in the long run he gets a balanced diet if this is what is offered to him. There are some who overeat and need some limitation. There are some that may eat well for a day or two and then have a day or two when they do not eat well at all.

Each mother has to learn her own baby's style and accommodate to it. It is important not to force a child of any age to eat. The best way to create an eating problem is to try to force a child to eat. When the baby eats, make a favorable comment like "Good" or "All gone." If he doesn't eat, remove the food without comment. The baby will know when you are pleased and when you are not. The important thing is not to make a big issue of eating.

*"I know that is right. I have heard it before, but somehow I feel so upset when the baby doesn't eat well."*

You are worried about his health, but perhaps you also feel you are failing as a mother. In giving food to the baby, you feel you are giving love. When the baby doesn't eat, you feel that he is rejecting your love.

*"That's absolutely right. How did you know?"*

That's a very usual feeling for mothers to have. It's one of the universal attitudes. But as we've said before, good care is not measured by the child's weight. A baby that doesn't eat a great deal can still thrive and

■                                                                    ■

make progress. Each child grows physically at a different rate and needs a different amount of food for healthy growth.

Different doctors recommend that mothers begin spoon-feeding their babies at different times with different foods. Some advise starting with fruit; some with cereal. The doctor has reasons for his recommendations, and they should be followed, even if your neighbor is doing it differently. It is not important which food is started first; what is important is whether the baby is ready for it. The mother should realize that the introduction of each new food is an experiment. Her reputation as a mother and the baby's future do not depend on the baby's acceptance of each new food on the first try.

*"Aren't there some babies who have special problems with eating? My neighbor's baby is on a special diet because he has celiac disease."*

Yes, and there are babies that are allergic to certain foods, even to milk, but we are talking about the average baby. There are some babies who do have specific problems in food digestion, and the babies' doctors should be consulted. When there is vomiting of an explosive kind, not just spitting up, or when the stools are loose and frequent, or the baby is colicky, the doctor should be consulted. But these situations are not relevant here because we are talking about ways of starting good eating habits and avoiding emotional problems centered on eating.

There have been reports recently concerning the deleterious effects of various additives, particularly coloring, in prepared baby foods. While there isn't complete agreement on this subject, it is a concern. For that reason, it is a good idea to read all labels on baby-food containers carefully and make sure of the ingredients. If you study baby food labels carefully, you will see that a large part of any given baby food is water with some thickening substance added to give the food bulk. It may occur to some of you that you would prefer to prepare the food at home with a blender. You can always freeze some for use as needed. In this way, you will be more certain of the contents.

*"My baby is one of those allergic ones. She breaks out in a rash from some mixed baby foods. So I can give her only simple foods, like pears alone or applesauce alone."*

*"I have something of the same problem. My baby doesn't get a rash; he gets cramps and sometimes loose stools from new foods. So I can't give him mixed foods, and I've started to give him homemade food. I just steam the vegetable, say carrots, and put it through a food processor. You can use a blender if you have one, I guess. I make enough for several days, freeze it in the ice-cube tray, and warm one compartment when I'm ready to feed him that food. It sounds like a lot of work, but it really isn't. I find it cheaper, and the baby likes the food better."*

*"It may be better because you know exactly what went into it. If it disagrees with the baby, you know just what to eliminate from his diet, and you're not stuck with a lot of jars of food you can't use."*

After consulting the doctor, each mother has to do what is most convenient for her and agrees best with her baby. We get into set patterns of doing things sometimes and overlook the possibility of sensible changes.

*"My mother saw a kind of straw that fits in a bottle. Do you know the gadget I'm talking about? It's a straw inside of the nipple, so a baby can hold the bottle upright. At what age should babies be using this device, or should they use it at all?"*

Yes, I know what you mean. This gadget is designed to hasten the baby's holding the bottle for himself, because he does not have to hold the bottle up to drink. It is also supposed to assist in diminishing the amount of air swallowed. It may do both of these things, but there are other considerations. One is that the baby does not have to be held for his feedings; he can feed himself. While this may relieve the mother, the baby may still need the closeness of being held. So one has to be sure the baby is ready for this independence. Second, it makes sucking easier and faster. Cutting down the sucking time may not be an advantage if the baby then needs supplemental sucking time with a pacifier. In some cases, therefore, it may force independence on the baby before he is ready for it. In others, it may make the mother feel that the baby has accomplished something he really hasn't. Some babies may enjoy the independence when they are older. Each mother has to evaluate the situation for her baby and his needs.

*"I had the feeling that my mother thought the gadget was great."*

It may be great for children who dawdle and need the help, but it would not seem to be particularly necessary for children who take their bottles well.

## Effect of Teething and Hot Weather on Appetite

*"What makes babies' appetites so erratic? One day my baby eats so well, and the next almost nothing but some liquid."*

Many factors alter a baby's appetite. One of the most frequent of these is teething. Teething may make food intake painful. Another is temperature; some babies eat poorly in hot weather. Actually, babies respond very much as adults do. They too may prefer liquids to solid foods in hot weather or want only certain types of food. This should cause no concern if the babies continue to take in adequate amounts of liquid in their formulas, water, or juice, and get enough vitamins. On a cool day their appetites will return, and they will eat more if they need it.

Have others of you been noticing these changes in diet and amount of food eaten?

*"I notice a change in hot weather; my baby only wants to drink."*

Milk is still the most important food for babies of this age. That's the food their digestive tracts can handle best. Usually, during the summer months there will be days when babies won't eat very much. If this condition lasts for weeks, or if the babies don't take their milk, then the doctor should be consulted. If they are taking their milk, some fruit juice, weak tea, or plain water with some sugar in it, then you don't really have to worry as long as the baby is active, contented, and developing well.

## Exposure to the Sun

*"In the hot weather I don't take my baby out for long. I'd rather keep her in the shade. I heard from some mothers that it wasn't good to keep the baby exposed to the sun for any length of time, only two minutes or so."*

That is necessary especially with blond or redheaded babies. Their skin is more sensitive to strong sunlight or even reflected light. In general, it is right not to expose the baby to hot sun for a long time. It is better to increase the baby's tolerance to sun gradually, in two- to three-minute increments each day. The baby does need to have some sunlight in contact with his skin because the sun's rays help produce the natural vitamin D that prevents rickets. When the skin is tanned, it no longer permits the sun's penetration. The tan acts as a shield, preventing the production of vitamin D. That is why it is a good practice to expose only a small part of the baby's skin at a time, so there will always be some untanned parts. We've all become "sun worshipers" and want to be suntanned. It is not the best thing for us. Blistering from a sunburn is very painful for a baby and can be toxic like any other burn. This is another reason for cautious exposure to the sun.

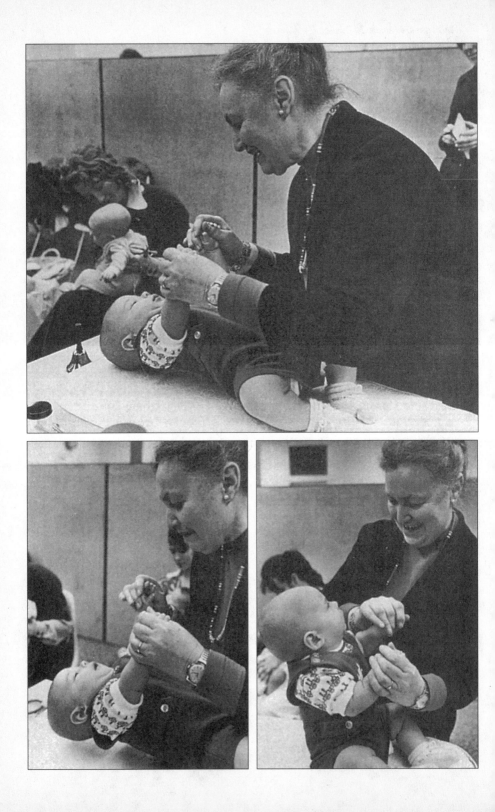

## *Highlights of Development—Twenty Weeks*

At the age of twenty weeks, the baby seems suddenly to make quite a leap ahead in development. She seems much more alert and competent. As the baby pulls herself to a sitting position (*see exercise, page 19*), there should now be no head lag. Once in the sitting position, the baby's head should be held steady and erect, not forward as a month ago.

 When the baby is seated in a high chair, or on his parent's lap near a table, he may scratch the tray or tabletop. This is the beginning of manual exploration. The baby is also becoming more adept with his hands. When the baby is offered a small block close to his hand, he may make a sweeping gesture with his hand that may enclose the block. Parents may be surprised at the tentativeness of this grasp; but this is normal for this age. Practice with small blocks or empty spools of thread increases this beginning manual skill. If a second block is offered to the baby, he may look at it but will probably make no effort to grasp it.

When a rattle is held close to the baby, she may make a two-handed attempt to get hold of it. The same phenomenon may be observed if the parent dangles the red ring near the baby. The baby may now look momentarily for the block or the rattle when she drops either of them. All of these activities are indications of important developmental advances.

The baby's great achievement in language at this age is squealing. Some parents may be disturbed by squealing because they think it is a form of crying; but, in actuality, it is an important new vocal ability.

If the parent places a mirror in front of the baby, after a little staring, he will smile at his image. During the feeding, the baby begins now to pat the bottle, which he will be able to hold in several months. (Breast-fed babies will do this when given a bottle of water or juice.)

About this age, some of the babies may recognize that there is a difference between their parents and others, particularly strangers. This "stranger anxiety" may cause them to stare or cry. This ability to discriminate familiar from unfamiliar people is a big developmental milestone (*see following discussion*).

Because so many important developments take place at about twenty weeks, there may be significant differences between babies of this age. Some babies may be turning over completely, some not at all. Some may have already discovered their feet and are putting them in their mouths. Some may grasp objects well; others are not yet able to do so. It is important for parents to remember that each baby develops in her or his own way and at his or her own rate. Often a baby will advance in one area faster than in another; eventually, development evens out.

## Stranger Anxiety

Some of you may now be noticing that your baby is aware of strangers and seems to cling more to you when they are around, or she may freeze up and look apprehensive at the stranger. Most of you are pleased that your babies have been very friendly and have not objected to being held by a visiting relative or friend. Now all of a sudden, for no apparent reason, the baby cries and won't leave mother. If you are not prepared for this stage of development, it comes as a great shock and may even be embarrassing if the visitor happens to be the baby's grandmother or the boss's wife. Have any of you had this experience yet?

*"It happened with my husband's mother. She lives on the West Coast, and she came to visit us for the first time. She was so anxious to hold the baby and hug her, but the baby just took one look and let out a scream. Poor Grandmother looked as though she would cry, so I had to comfort the baby and assure Grandmother it happened because the baby didn't know her. But it was upsetting. It took about half an hour of eyeing Grandmother and just sitting next to her till the baby finally let Grandmother touch her. Now they are friends. But it was tough there for a while."*

*"Well, that happened to us with a visitor who claimed to know all about children. She practically grabbed the baby from my arms, and he cried, really yelled and kicked. She told me in no uncertain terms that there must be something wrong with my baby or the way I was bringing him up."*

Yes, some people who do not really understand babies regard this behavior as an expression of an unpleasant disposition, crabbiness, or parents' failure to bring up the baby properly. However, this display of wariness toward strangers really shows that the baby has advanced in her development. She is beginning to know the difference between her mother and a stranger. She has just recently learned that the appendage that holds the toy is her hand. She is just beginning to get a sense of *self* and a sense of *others,* a real milestone in her development. The problem is most apt to occur when the visitor rushes up to the baby, speaking loudly and overenthusiastically. The baby feels threatened and clings to "Mommy" or bursts out crying. Of course, if the visitor is a grandmother who is seeing the baby for the first time, or after a long interval, one must understand her enthusiasm and disappointment that her warm greeting is met with such a negative reaction. It is generally a good idea to warn visitors, especially someone like a grandmother who is meeting the baby for the first time, to go about making friends with the baby slowly. That way, the baby will have a chance to get used to the new person, and her initial reaction will not be negative. Tense social situations can often be avoided in this way.

*"What is the best thing to do? It's been a problem for me because my son behaves that way with his grandpa."*

The best thing to do is to hold the baby close to comfort him and ask the grandfather to sit down a little bit away. Inform Grandpa that the baby is at a stage in which he is just beginning to recognize the difference between mother and other people, and that he needs a little time to get used to a visitor. Assure Grandpa that he is not at fault, that the baby's fearfulness or outburst of crying does not mean that he does not like him. Later, the baby may reach toward Grandpa and make his own overtures. The best thing is not to place too much emphasis on the whole episode. It is especially important not to communicate to the baby that you are displeased with him.

*"What if there is a certain person the baby just can't take? Mine doesn't cry with anyone else but her grandmother, who comes quite often."*

There are instances in which babies don't like certain people. For some reason, that person arouses some anxiety in the baby. It may be the quality of voice, the facial expression, the person's size, the vigor of the approach, some characteristic that upsets the baby. The baby's reaction may last for some time, even several weeks or months. This is a difficult situation both for the baby and the other person, especially if the other person is a close relative. Sometimes it may even happen to the father, if he has been away for a while. It is painful for all concerned, but the baby needs to be comforted and exposed gradually to the other person from the safe vantage point of mother's arms or lap, or his carriage or crib, anywhere the baby feels safe on his own ground. When the baby feels secure, he will show interest in the new person.

*"You answered my question. Grandfather is a very large, tall man, and he has a loud, booming voice. He's very jolly and vigorous. I think that's just what frightens the baby. Just what all of us like about Grandpa is upsetting the baby. I never thought of it that way. None of us did. That's why we couldn't understand why the baby cries every time he sees Grandfather!"*

Most problems occur because we don't understand things from a baby's point of view, only from our own.

*"My baby goes to everyone. He doesn't seem to have any fear of anyone. Should I be expecting this to change?"*

Yes, most babies pass through this stage at around five to seven months. Here again it is important to remember that each child is different. They will all pass through this stage on their own timetables.

## Separation Anxiety

This brings us to another situation in which baby cries and the mother is puzzled and annoyed. That's when mother leaves the baby alone for a moment to answer the doorbell or telephone, go to the bathroom, or attend to some chore in the house. The baby cries; the mother can't understand why. This happens because the baby has not reached that stage of development when she can separate from the mother; she can't bear to have her mother out of sight. We know that mothers are ready to separate from their babies long before the babies are ready to separate from them. We all know about the physical stages that lead to walking; we know the baby has to turn over, sit, crawl, stand, and then walk. We accept this gradual process. However, the stages in separation and individuation are not as well known. Our understanding of this area of development has been acquired rather recently, largely due to the research of Dr. Margaret Mahler in which she was able to delineate the process of separation in normal children.

*"That is something I never heard of, and I have been upset because I can't leave the baby alone a minute. As soon as he realizes I am not there, he cries, and it's driving me up the wall. What are the stages we should expect?"*

The baby needs to be in very close proximity to the mother (or to caretaker). As the baby's central nervous system matures, she begins to become aware of her own body. You have seen this begin to happen in the way the babies are now looking at the toys they are holding and at their hands. Gradually, when the baby drops her toys, she begins to look to see where they went. Later, she finds her feet and puts them in her mouth. There are signs that the baby is becoming aware of the extent of her own body. Then the baby realizes that she is not near her mother and is very much in need of her. Shortly after this, she begins to recognize that strangers are different from her mother. She may even feel that a stranger will take her from her mother. When the baby has reached this level of development, she cries when her mother leaves, even for a minute.

For mothers this may be a great nuisance. It is annoying if it is regarded as improper or naughty behavior on the infant's part. Instead, if you understand that this behavior is a stage in development that will pass as the baby matures, you will find it less annoying. For the baby, it is very frightening when she cannot see her parent because what cannot be seen does not exist as far as the baby is concerned. This is also why babies of this age do not look very long for toys they drop. Their central nervous systems have not yet developed to this level of understanding. They must learn from positive experience that their mothers will return. At this age, babies do not yet have the capacity to remember people or objects. This comes with experience. The pathways carrying messages to their brains have to be developed so that these events will register.

*"How much time does all this take?"*

It will probably come as a stunning surprise to most of you that it may take some babies until they are three years old to separate fully from their mothers. Some can do it earlier; others take even longer. The average age is around three years.

When babies first begin to crawl and walk, they leave their mothers momentarily but come right back when they discover how far away they have gotten. As they get older, they travel farther. Studies have shown that the distance is proportional to the baby's age. Mothers say, "Well, she runs away from *me.* Why can't I leave *her?*" The baby knows she is coming back to you, but she doesn't yet know you will come back to her, and she can't get along without you. When the baby is more competent in her motor skills, and when she is verbal, she will begin to understand that you will come back, and that you do exist even if she can't see you. When a child can say "Mama" and talk about "Mama," this helps her hold the image and memory of mother, and mother continues to exist. When the baby has achieved this understanding, then separation and individuation can take place. So you see, separation has its stages, just as physical development has. If a parent understands these stages, coping with them is easier. Then, the baby's crying is not interpreted as "bad behavior" but as part of her immaturity, her "babiness." This understanding can help the parent have less of a feeling of being "trapped" by a demanding child and more of a feeling of being needed. Understanding that you are fulfilling such a need is one of the satisfactions of parenthood.

What have you been doing if the babies cry when you leave them? How do you feel about the baby's crying in this kind of situation?

*"I just decided I couldn't stand the crying, so I usually turn on music, carry the baby with me, or put him in the back sling as I do my work. He seems to enjoy that much more than being in his crib, and I'm happier too."*

*"Everyone used to tell me to leave her alone and let her cry. They said I was spoiling her by carrying her with me. But I don't leave her alone or with anybody who would let her cry. I thought it was interesting when you said that at this age babies cannot separate. It frightens them when they can't see or hear you."*

That's right, it frightens them because they don't know you're somewhere else and that you will come back. That's why what you're both doing is just fine. Taking the babies with you so that they can see you is the best way to cope with this problem.

*"Oh, you hear so many different things. I guess you have to decide: 'This is the way I'm going to do it.' Everyone went through that business about 'Don't pick the baby up because it'll spoil him!' I'm going through it now. All my friends say, 'Let him cry, and he'll get strong lungs.' "*

There was a time when the baby needed to cry to inflate her lungs, but that was when she was first born. She had to cry to get her lungs to function and, in the first few weeks of life, to keep all of the lung expanded. But that is not needed at this age. The advice you've been given is a misapplication of what was *physiologically* important early in infancy but is not *psychologically* correct now.

*"The hardest thing is the fact that my baby always needs to be where she can see me."*

Yes, that's hard. It means that she needs to learn that you will come back. She has to have the repeated experience of your going and returning. She will then begin to develop trust in your returning. That takes time. Everyone knows the babies are not going to walk or talk the day they are born, but everyone thinks the babies know that you're coming back. Babies simply do not know this; it is something they have to learn by repeated experience.

*"I think one of the hardest things initially is to learn to put your own needs second and to adjust to the baby's needs. The baby just cannot adjust to us."*

It is very important for parents to understand their baby's helplessness and needs. When you realize that you are doing all these things because of your baby's needs, parenting becomes easier and can be more gratifying because it stops a battle for control.

## Mother's Needs in Relation to Baby's Needs

### Mother's Time for Herself

Mothers in primitive societies seemed to be able to cope with their babies' separation problems in a more natural way than we in our complex society can. They carried their babies on their backs, on papoose boards, or wrapped in shawls or slings. When they worked in the fields, they put the babies down alongside them or, at least, near them. Whatever they were doing, the baby was close by. If the baby was not close to his own mother, then he was close to a mother substitute in the extended family or tribe.

In our society, the baby's need for close contact comes as a surprise and is an unwelcome aspect of parenting. However, the baby's needs have not changed. We are just beginning again to recognize these needs. What should we, in our society, do? How can we keep our talented, educated, independent, sophisticated mothers from feeling that the baby is a burden and not a joy, and that they are "trapped" by their baby's needs?

Perhaps all this discussion about the baby's needs has given you a feeling that you are in for a long siege and that you are really trapped, and there is no way for your own needs to be met.

*"Yes, that is just what I've been thinking. You talk about the babies' needs, but what about time off for the mothers?"*

It is absolutely essential now that the babies have a more predictable pattern that each mother has time off. She may not be able to go off when the spirit moves her, but she can work out a system for having a regular afternoon or day a week when she can go out by herself or with her husband or friends. Besides being a parent, she is also an adult with needs that have to be met. Parenting does not have to be servitude if one organizes one's life. There should be some arrangement made with an aunt, a grandmother, or a regular baby-sitter. Then the mother feels, "This is my time." Mothers can have time for themselves and still remain the primary caretaker of the baby.

*"I do think that's terribly important, at least one day a week, and you can dream about what you're going to do on your day off. Sometimes it can be a whole day, sometimes it can be an hour or half an hour or half a day, but you must have that time, and taking it doesn't mean that you don't love your baby. I know I love mine, but still I need time off."*

Doctors, lawyers, and carpenters all have to have time off. No one can do a good job twenty-four hours a day, seven days a week. There has to be some change of pace. Each mother has to know she can have a specific time when she can do what she wants.

Gradually, as the baby gets older, it is possible to include the baby in some of the things that a mother wants to do. Also as the baby gets older, the mother gets more time off because the baby begins to develop an interest in playing with his toys and exploring his world. He becomes less constantly demanding.

*"I notice that the baby falls asleep after her bottle, so that's a fine time to read the paper. Then I know the baby's going to be up for a time, and I'm going to be entirely devoted to her. If I go down to the laundry or go marketing, I take the baby. If I'm going to the beauty parlor, I leave her with a neighbor or with her grandmother. That's every Thursday, and I don't feel like a prisoner. I really enjoy the time I'm with the baby much more."*

*"I just keep wondering if there is something wrong with me. I waited a long*

*time to have this baby. I've always wanted to be a mother, so I don't want to be away from my baby. If my baby needs me, that is what I am there for. That's very satisfying to me. When we go out, we always take our baby with us. We don't find that a burden or confining."*

That is how you feel, and that is right for you and your baby. Some mothers have waited a long time to have a baby and are very happy to stay home with the baby all the time. They are also happy to go everywhere with the baby. If there is a place where the baby can't go, the mother doesn't go, and she doesn't mind. However, there are other mothers who need to have some time of their own—perhaps a short time each day when the baby can be left with a neighbor or relative, or a longer period once or twice a week when they can do things on their own like shopping, going to the beauty parlor, lunching with friends, or going to a movie, or when they can do something that was an important part of their lives before the baby came. They still feel they need this free time in order to be more patient with the baby and the baby's needs.

*"If you are the kind of mother who needs time off, how can you make your time off fit in with the baby's needs?"*

That has to be worked out carefully. It is important to have the baby cared for in the mother's absence by the same person on a regular basis, so that this substitute care becomes part of the baby's pattern of life. It is best to have the caretaker come to your house, rather than leave the baby in the caretaker's house, unless it is a house the baby has become very familiar with, like Grandma's or a neighbor's. The baby needs to get to know the person who takes care of him in the mother's absence. He needs to adjust to this person before the mother leaves. She can then leave the baby confident that he and the caretaker will get along.

*"Every time I leave, my baby cries, even when I leave him with my husband. So I have to sneak out. I hate to do that. Is it the right thing to do?"*

Very often parents feel it is best to sneak out, but this will bring about a lack of trust on the baby's part. He will cling more to mother because he will be afraid she will sneak off again. It is best to say a formal good-bye quickly and casually and then to make the return greeting prolonged, happy, and enthusiastic. After sufficient experience with a happy return, the baby will be less upset when you leave. His protest at your leaving indicates his attachment, and that is good. It is appropriate for his age. He can soon be distracted by the caretaker.

## Returning to Work

*"What about a mother's returning to work? When is the best time for that?"*

In one of our earlier sessions, we talked about this and the difficulty of returning to work at this period of developing attachment. Some of you are already back at work and have told us about your routines for establishing your baby's attachment to both you and the baby-sitter. This is a good time to discuss it further.

In view of the stages in a baby's ability to cope with separation, the baby needs a consistent caretaker until he can achieve his own separate and individual existence. For some babies, this may not occur until around three years of age. Other babies may be able to separate at two and a half or earlier, and some will take longer. One must judge the right time for one's own child. The stages in the process are the same for all babies, but the timing—the maturational timetable—is unique for each child. A mother should feel that giving her baby this secure start in life is a worthy and important job, and society should support her in this undertaking.

*"What if the mother has to return to work and just can't put it off until the baby is ready?"*

This is a very serious question, and many families have had to make this decision. If the mother must return to work for financial reasons, or has a profession she can't or doesn't want to give up, then she has to make a serious choice regarding the baby's separation needs. As we have said, it is better for a mother to return to work before the baby is attached mainly to her. In this way, the baby forms an attachment to the caretaker, who should be a constant person in the baby's life. Secondly, the mother has to arrange her time so that when she is home, she really spends meaningful time with her baby. Just being at home or in the same room while she is doing admittedly necessary housework is not adequate for the baby's need. There have to be playtimes and caretaking activities that are done exclusively by the mother. This can in part make up for the time she is not there. The problem arises when the mother comes home tired and expects the baby to appreciate how hard she has been working and not bother her. Obviously, the baby cannot be expected to do that. He needs the mother's attention when she returns. If parents are aware of this, then the necessary adjustments can be made. When the mother understands the baby's needs, she will feel less irritation with the baby's clinging demands for attention. Remember: It's a good sign if the baby demands your attention; such behavior means that the baby is attached to you.

*"Very soon I may have to go back to work. Is there something special in the baby's behavior I should be prepared for?"*

A baby who has become accustomed to his mother's care and attached to her will protest at her leaving. After being without her all day, no matter how good the substitute care, this child will be fussy, his sleeping and eating schedules may be disrupted, and he may want to be held more. The mother needs to expect this and plan to spend a lot of time with him when she comes home. Children who have experienced too early separation won't let their parents out of sight for a moment without crying when the parents return. Parents should recognize this behavior as an expression of the child's need and not get angry.

*"Is there some way to help the baby separate without excess anxiety?"*

The most important thing is that the introduction of a new caretaker be gradual. The caretaker, whether it be a relative or a hired baby-sitter, should come to your home for a few days to watch your way of caring for your baby and then gradually take over some of your functions. In this way, the baby gets to know her and becomes accustomed to her way of doing things with him. During this time, you can absent yourself for short periods, then longer periods, until the baby accepts your leaving without too much agitation and begins to learn that you will return.

Many parents may not be able to find an appropriate person to come to their homes to care for their children. Another solution for children of this age is called "family day care." This means care given by a qualified person in her own home. Regulations vary in different states, but generally, licensed family day care strictly limits the number of children who may be cared for by one person and assures a certain level of competence. Care in a day-care center is also a possibility, but we feel it is the least desirable alternative for babies of this age (actually, center care is rarely an alternative, as few centers take children under two years of age). If you leave your child with another mother or in a family day care, the process of separation should also be gradual so that the child becomes familiar with the new caretaker, the new routines, and the new environment while the parent is still available for support. To make the transition, it is necessary to bring a few of the child's toys from home, especially favorite ones such as his blanket or teddy bear. In the long run, extra time spent at the beginning of different care is time well spent in maintaining the child's sense of security and well-being.

*"But that may take a long time, a week or more."*

Yes, it may, but the question was, "Is there some way to help the baby separate without excess anxiety?" This is just the way to do it. For each child, the time it takes for such an adjustment varies.

*"Does child care have to be all the mother's job? Can't the father help a little too? I'm not thinking of a fifty-fifty arrangement, but just sharing a little of the responsibility."*

Naturally, the father can help and share in filling the gap. Some fathers work at home and can do a great deal. Some like to take over the baby's bedtime routine when they come home. Some can play patiently and happily with the baby. Some help with the household chores. Some mothers and fathers naturally and spontaneously can be very cooperative;

■                                                                              ■

others have to make formal and explicit assignments of roles and obligations. Actually, all of this ought to be discussed and agreed upon well before the baby arrives. But even if it has been, new parents find it very hard to comprehend and how many time-consuming jobs taking care of a baby entails, even under the best circumstances, with the most contented baby in the world.

Therefore, some reasonable adjustments have to be made. It is not an impossible situation. A little understanding of the baby's and the parents' needs will make it easier.

*"Until I had the baby, I thought I'd go right back to my job. But since it is not a financial necessity, and it can mean so much to the baby to have me home, I've decided to stay home."*

*"I never for a moment thought of going back to work until my baby was in school. I have had enough of the business world."*

*"Well, we need the money, and I've been planning to return to work. I am a teacher, and I like my work, but I am going to postpone returning to my job as long as I can. The baby needs me, and I enjoy taking care of her."*

*"I had to go back to work because my husband lost his job. I'm a nurse. My husband took care of the baby in the morning. In the afternoon when he went to school, he left him at the baby-sitter's house. I took him home at six. He cried a long time, and for a few weeks he would not eat at the baby-sitter's house—only when I took him home. It was very hard. Now my husband is working again, and I am home. It is much better that way."*

Your baby had already become attached to you, so that leaving him with someone else created a trauma for him. Sometimes one cannot avoid that but I am glad that things are better now for your baby and your family.

*"I went back to work when the baby was about three months old. It's tough. My husband and I devote all our time to nothing but the baby and our jobs. But I think the baby is forming an attachment to us and the baby-sitter."*

It is hard work to meet the demands of both a baby and a job successfully. The development of attachment takes time. The baby's attachment to a full-time baby-sitter is different from his attachment to his parents, but it can supply the security and feeling of trust so important to healthy development. The most important thing is to have a consistent caretaker that you and the baby like. It is not always easy to find such a person, especially one who shares your ideas of child rearing. If you work part-time, it is sometimes easier to find a good caretaker. A grandparent or other relative may be available to baby-sit on a regular basis. Sometimes one can arrange something with a neighbor who also needs a similar service on a regular schedule.

## Baby-sitters

*"I don't work, but I like to get out one or two afternoons a week. Do I need the same baby-sitter, someone the baby knows, each time?"*

It is important that the baby-sitter be known to the baby and come regularly. It is very difficult for the baby if there is a different baby-sitter each time. Some mothers put the baby to bed before the baby-sitter comes and then leave. If the baby wakes to find a stranger, this can set up a long period of difficulty in getting the baby to sleep on subsequent nights. The baby is anxious that Mother may be away again when he wakes. This sort of interference with the development of a baby's basic trust and separation is avoidable. But once it has occurred, it takes a long time to undo. How are you all managing?

*"Well, I'm lucky. My mother lives nearby, and she loves to baby-sit. The baby is quite happy with her. She knows his whole routine."*

*"I have to take our son to my mother-in-law's house. There are other people there, so he is entertained. But when I get him home, he is irritable. I think he gets overexcited, and my mother-in-law doesn't handle him the way I do. She knows how to take care of children. She has had plenty of experience. But it's just different."*

*"I have a neighbor across the hall with a baby our baby's age. We are in each other's apartments all the time, so my baby knows her and her baby. We both need to economize, so we exchange baby-sitting services. If it's at night, either my husband or I sit in her apartment, and she does the same for us. It works out okay."*

*"The landlady is my lifesaver. She is fond of the baby and has had nine of her own, so she is glad to help me out. She seems to know just how to handle my baby, too."*

*"I've tried using the student nurses at the hospital across the street. Their schedules vary so much that now I have two sitters. That gives me a 'backup,' and the baby likes them both."*

*"I just haven't been able to find anyone, and I don't think the sitters available are worth the money. Besides, we like taking the baby with us."*

Each of you seems to have found the solution that suits your needs. But each solution is different, and that is to be expected because each baby and each family situation is a little different.

## TV as a Baby-sitter and Stimulus

Nowadays we have another type of baby-sitter available to us. This baby-sitter is not human; it's electronic. I'm talking, of course, about the TV, and we should take some time now to review its advantages and disadvantages as a baby-sitter and stimulus.

Many parents have reported that their babies are just fascinated by the TV screen. With babies this age, TV provides the stimulation of exciting movement and sound, and it's fine for a few minutes. But it is not good as a constant diet. It is not something to put the baby in front of while you do chores, no matter how quiet it keeps the baby. The quieter the baby, the better mother likes it. But the electronic companion is not a substitute for human contact and stimulation. If the baby is exposed to TV for too long a time, either he is bombarded with too much stimulation, or he gets bored with the device, turns away from it, and is alone in the room without mother's stimulation of speech, touch, and involvement.

One also must think about program selection. The tone of voice, manner, and gestures used by some of the characters in television and videos are frequently imitated by young children. Constant exposure may give a speech model that is not the one you may wish to foster in your child. It is true that children can parrot letters and numbers earlier after seeing *Sesame Street,* but whether this really helps them to learn concepts is still in question.

Also, a mother may leave her child watching a pleasant, harmless program, stay away a bit too long, and return to find the child looking at something frightening, unpleasant, or violent. There have been no reliable studies of the effects of violent programs on children, but violent programs clearly are bad models of life. For the older child who is verbal, there is, in some children's programs, a very subtle but definite teaching of deception. One need only watch these programs occasionally to see that much of what is supposed to be humorous is really detrimental to the teaching of reality in life and the difference between right and wrong.

*"Then what options are left to the mother? What relief can she have for a few minutes while she tends to something urgent?"*

There may be short intervals of judicious use of TV. The mother's intervals of time for herself come as the baby begins to be stimulated by appropriate toys that he can manipulate himself in a safe place close to mother. Of course, she can always use nap time and after the baby's bedtime for things she needs to do. Mothers must understand that "bad" days, when the baby is restless and needs her undivided attention, are not going to last forever. On some days, the baby is striving to reach a new and more mature level of development. Trying to do this gives him a feeling of disequilibrium. Being understanding and patient are a big help to the baby. This attitude will make it easier for the mother as well because she will not be adding her agitation to the baby's.

## Approval

### Recognition of Approved Behavior

Now that the babies are more competent and can do more sitting, reaching, and holding, they need to be given the message that their progress is being noted and approved. It is common practice for parents to take approved behavior for granted and to comment only if they disapprove. The most important thing, however, is to let the baby know when you approve of her behavior. The human animal has a built-in need for recognition. This need should be fulfilled early in the baby's life. The baby understands approval very well. For example, when a baby takes her bottle well or takes a mouthful of cereal, and the mother acknowledges this by saying "Good," a smile spreads over the baby's face.

When the baby plays with a toy appropriately (for example, shakes her rattle), responds when her mother enters the room, pulls herself to a sitting position, or turns over, the parent should recognize this accomplishment in a clear, positive way.

Human beings learn best when they receive approval. Most of us would agree with this statement. Our experiences with children tend to verify it, but it has also been demonstrated scientifically. Experiments have shown that children who have been doing poorly in school begin to do better and behave better when given appropriate approval.

Have you begun to show approval of your babies' accomplishments, and how do you do it?

*"Well, there are lots of things the baby does that please us, but I thought she was too young to have our approval really mean anything to her. I noticed that she grinned when I smiled at something she did, but I didn't attach any significance to it."*

*"I think my ideas are a little like that too. When I told some of my friends my reactions to what my baby did, they said that I was making too much of her achievements because all babies do similar things. So now I just kind of keep quiet."*

It seems that some of you have been inhibited in your natural expression of appreciation of the baby's accomplishments by comments of people whose notions about babies are not in keeping with what is best for the baby. But the point you should bear in mind is that you want to let your baby, not other people, know you like what she is doing.

There are also many parents who are pleased by their baby's developments and proudly point them out to someone else, but make no comment to the baby. The baby needs positive reinforcement for her successes. That's how she learns that she is successful. She needs to know that her achievements please you. Then she will be pleased with herself and will try to evoke this response from you again. She will have an incentive to work for success.

The drive to achieve is a very important element in personality development. If a baby does not get positive response, she loses incentive for success and gets no sense of satisfaction from achievement. If this lack of recognition persists, this child will have difficulty in working to achieve during the school years. Such a child will have passed a critical period when she could have acquired this drive for achievement. That is why it is so important to recognize all the little bits of developmental progress. The baby learns the feeling of success, and the foundation for further incentive to achieve is established.

You may notice that no mention has been made of praise or adulation; all we have been concerned with is simple recognition. It is not necessary to "go into ecstasy," unless you feel that way, and it's natural for you to express yourself in such terms. One doesn't have to say, "Oh, you marvelous baby!" Just "Good" and a smile or pat will do.

*"Well, I try to show my approval by a smile; my husband does, too. I think the baby is getting the message because he tries to repeat whatever we smiled at."*

*"I pick my baby up and hug and kiss her whenever she does anything I think is cute and makes me happy. Is that wrong?"*

There is nothing wrong in hugging the baby if you feel moved to do that. However, it should not be the only way of showing recognition for what the baby does. A smile or a "Good" will be enough. The baby will get the message that you approve from your facial expression and tone of voice.

*"Some people tell me the baby will be spoiled by being praised. He'll think he always has to be praised."*

We are not talking about praise, we are talking about recognizing the baby's accomplishments so that the baby will get the feeling of approval for achievement.

*"Won't a baby need to be reassured all her life, then? Won't she grow accustomed to such recognition and need it all the time?"*

That is what happens to the baby who doesn't get consistent reassurance. The baby who gets consistent reassurance develops self-esteem and doesn't require constant reinforcement. She gives it to herself. The baby who has never had consistent recognition is never certain of herself and is constantly seeking recognition from others. Perhaps you know adults who constantly need to be told that they are doing a good job. No matter how well they perform, they never feel that what they have done is good enough.

*"Well, I always thought that kind of reaction was just modesty and good manners, but sometimes it has seemed a bit much."*

Such behavior is more likely to be caused by insecurity, which has its origin in a nonresponsive, nonapproving atmosphere during infancy.

## Discipline: Setting Limits

Just as it is important for the baby to know that you approve of certain things, she must also learn what is not acceptable. She must be protected from danger. The baby must learn not to touch electric outlets, the hot stove, or a plant that may fall on her. To teach what is unacceptable, the parent should consistently and firmly say, "No," remove the baby from the forbidden activity, and immediately give an alternate activity from which the baby can derive loud and clear approval. This must be done consistently and firmly, but not angrily. In this way you are teaching "limitations." Do not expect that the baby will get the message the first time. There will have to be countless repetitions of the situation before the baby learns. Each baby has a different learning rate. Some may learn in a month; others only after several months.

Has your baby reached the stage of development where she is ready to learn some discipline? How have you been handling the problem? Have you found that instead of approving of your baby's activities, you are saying "No" more often?

*"I guess I do emphasize the 'No's.' If the baby is doing something that I don't like but that isn't harmful or dangerous, I just let it go. For example, when he is touching something like a cup of hot coffee, I say 'No' or something to stop him. But if he bangs a spoon—well, I just let it go."*

*"It bothers me when my baby bangs with a spoon; it makes too much noise, and I say 'No.' "*

Actually, banging against the table with the spoon is an accomplishment for this age. If the baby is making too much noise, you can put a napkin or mat on the table. That will cut down on the noise considerably. Also, the change in surface will produce a change in sound that will be of interest to the baby.

*"I thought the baby banged because it bothered me, so I say 'No!' "*

That is a common misconception. The baby does not intend to annoy you. In most cases, she is just showing off a new achievement.

*"Well, how will she learn to stop? What is the way to teach her?"*

The process of learning limitations goes through stages just as learning to walk goes through stages. We all know about the stages connected with learning to walk and accept them. The stages of internalizing limitations and restrictions are not so well known. The baby should be limited and given an alternate, acceptable outlet for her activity. However, at first, she may persist in going back to the forbidden activity and look to see if mother will stop her again. At this stage, the baby should not be expected to have learned. She may smile coyly and try to evoke a smile from her mother. Mother, however, should unsmilingly and firmly remove the baby from the forbidden object or activity. In the next stage, the baby may go up to the object, say "No" to herself, but still touch it. However, she still relies on the mother to remove her because she still needs the parent's help in learning what behavior is acceptable. Finally, the baby will get to the stage when she can go up to the object, say "No," and not touch it. At this point, the baby should get recognition for her achievement in self-control. She is then at a stage when she can also sometimes find an alternate, acceptable activity for herself. A few children can achieve this by three years; others may take longer. Also, it will depend on the attraction of the object in each given case.

*"It seems that this is not an easy process. Does it come naturally with age?"*

This is a process that develops only with parental help. No one says it is easy. But once the process has been achieved, the baby is on the road to establishing conscience mechanisms. The growing child will be able to discipline herself according to the standards set by her parents and the cultural values her family holds. Helping the baby develop self-discipline is one of the big jobs and great opportunities of parenthood. When the child has learned this, it is a tremendous satisfaction to both parents and child, and sets the pattern for all self-discipline later in life.

*"I never realized there was so much to it. My husband and mother think if you tell the baby to stop, she should—and right there and then, too!"*

*"That's the way I was brought up. When someone said, 'No' to a child, it meant 'No right now, this minute.' The child was supposed to do as she was told immediately."*

Some parents have been brought up to think that if you say "Stop" or "No" to a child, she should do so immediately. If she doesn't, she is a bad baby. In fact, the younger the child, the less she is able to respond at once because her central nervous system has not matured sufficiently. Responding to verbal instructions is learned behavior. The message must go to the brain, be processed and understood, and then directed back to the arms and legs involved in the activity. It's a more complicated process than most of us realize. It takes time for a child to develop the appropriate pathways in the brain.

This process is not completely developed in some children until they are seven or eight or nine years old. Something stimulates a baby to want to reach for something, and that message goes to the brain. That stimulus has to be discharged by some activity; it can't just stop. That is why the baby should be given an alternate outlet or activity until she learns how to deal with such situations. The child's response is not a matter of being good or bad, obeying or disobeying. It is a matter of anatomical and physiological development—that is, maturation of the central nervous system. This is not generally understood, and that lack of understanding gets in the way of establishing good parent-child relations and good character structure.

*"When I limit my baby in any way, my mother says: 'Let him be! He is only a baby. When he is bigger, he will learn to behave. Now let him be!' Is she right? Is that what you mean? Is that the thing to do?"*

It does not help to let a baby do anything she wants for a long time and then begin to set limits. It is better for the baby to learn to cope with limitations gradually, according to her development capacity. There are many parents who for some time let a baby do anything she pleases. Then one day, the parents decide they have had enough and come down on the baby like a ton of bricks. This is not logical or effective. In fact, it is counterproductive.

These two areas of child rearing—appropriate recognition and consistent appropriate limitation—are vital to the development of a healthy, responsible personality. When these areas are not handled properly beginning in early life, they may become the nucleus around which develops a maladjusted personality who becomes the school dropout or delinquent. That is why we make such a point of these two topics in our discussions, and why we will be discussing them again in many frames of reference.

*"Well, what stage are our babies in right now?"*

It varies with each one, as you know, but in general your babies are or will be soon at the stage where they recognize your approval by your smile or tone of voice. They are beginning to recognize, too, what you mean when you frown or use a disapproving voice. In other words, they are beginning to recognize the difference between these two kinds of behavior on your part, but they are much too young to control their actions.

*"Are they really beginning to tell the difference already?"*

Yes, they are just beginning this process and they need your help: first to learn what is approved and disapproved, and then how to control and adjust their own actions. They also need your help in learning to accept alternate outlets when what they want is not acceptable. You will help them along this pathway, and finally they will be able to say "No" to themselves and find another activity or plaything. You will find, however, that children sometimes need help in selecting alternate activities, even as teenagers. Learning self-discipline goes through many stages of development during the whole period of childhood.

*"At what age can a child look at something she knows is not allowed and say 'No'?"*

That may take what seems a very long time to you. It varies with each child. A few babies begin to get some understanding by eighteen months; most take until three years or longer. If you are consistent and patient, your child will be a bit closer each day to achieving that level of development, the beginning of conscience. When she has arrived at that level, she will begin to internalize "No"—and your values.

*"How long does it take to teach a child not to touch just one thing she shouldn't?"*

That depends on the individual child and how consistently the parent handles the situation. With some children the learning process must be repeated a hundred times before the lesson becomes fixed in the child's mind; with other children it need be repeated only ten times. How long the process must go on varies with each child and each situation. Every child has his or her own maturational timetable, and learning what not to do depends on that.

*"How do you indicate to a child that you don't approve of what she's doing but still love her?"*

When a child is older and more verbal, you can make the distinction between the child's actions and the child herself. You say, in effect, "I don't like what you're doing, but I like you." Your babies, however, are too young to understand this verbal distinction.

Your babies are now at the very beginning stage of this understanding. The biggest clue your babies now have to your attitude is your voice. They sense the attitude inherent in a particular tone of voice—that is, the "meaning" of the tone, as distinct from the words spoken. Also, as you hold them, they can sense whether you're angry or comforting, soothing, and pleased—and they can feel the difference between the two attitudes. In the same way, you comunicate your state of mind—whether you're tense or relaxed—when you feed your baby.

At this age, the babies are also beginning to be more visually discriminating. They are able to see that your eyes are set back and that your nose protrudes. They are also beginning to see your facial expression, and they can sense your approval or disapproval from it.

In addition, the baby can detect your attitudes from what you do. For example, when you are feeding the baby and she spits the food out, you wipe it off and let her know you don't like what she's done. Then, when she takes her food well, you say, "Mmmmm, good." These small actions and others like them give the baby a clear idea of how you feel about what she's doing.

## The "Angry Alliance"

### How Babies and Parents Upset Each Other

We have tried on the whole to emphasize the positive things that parents can do to help the babies develop healthy personalities. There are times, however, when things do not run smoothly, and you get angry at the baby. You lose patience and scold the baby or handle him roughly. This often happens when you have planned to do something while the baby is napping. Then, for some reason, the baby does not want to nap. Maybe you were in a bit of a hurry to get something done, and you put the baby down a little bit too soon. The baby protests. You get angry, go to the baby, and scold him. Then you put him down firmly and leave. The baby protests again, and you repeat your previous responses—only this time a little more forcefully. If you "win," and the baby finally goes to sleep because he is tired by this time, you remain upset. The hassle has diminished your satisfaction in your own planned activity. The baby's basic trust in a loving, need-satisfying mother has been damaged a little as well.

On another day, the baby is teething or some food has upset him or he is entering a new developmental stage, and his physiological equilibrium is disturbed. For that reason, he is fussy and hard to soothe. You want him to play quietly with a toy or sit quietly in his high chair while you do something in the kitchen. But he cries and constantly interrupts you. Your voice and your way of holding him show your annoyance. The baby senses mother's anger and disapproval. The baby gets worse, and the mother gets more tense. Pretty soon both mother and child are angry.

When this kind of interaction becomes frequent, it may become the pattern of the parent-child relationship. This we call an "angry alliance." Does this sound familiar to you? What experiences of this kind have you had? How have you reacted during them?

*"I consider my baby very good, but I must confess we do have some 'bad days,' especially if I am expecting company and want to get a little more time in the kitchen. I guess I do hurry a little, and the baby feels the difference and gets fussy. When I simmer down, she responds better."*

*"That's happened to me a lot, especially if I'm hurrying to get the baby down for a nap so I can keep an appointment. I have a feeling that he just gets fussy in order to keep me with him. I feel myself getting angry, and I begin to wonder: 'Gee, why did I want this baby so much? Life was so simple before he arrived.' Then when I'm away for a while, I miss the baby so much that I can't wait to get back home."*

## The Baby's Need for Gratification

*"Most of the days were like that at the beginning. I just hated to be with the baby. Then we got a routine going, and things have been going along pretty well, except for some days. On those days my husband comes home and finds me in tears and the baby crabby. My husband is more patient than I am. He gets us both calmed down."*

Interestingly enough, the parents' needs are the same as the babies', but parents rarely recognize this fact. The adults' central nervous systems work just the same as the babies'. If the parent plans to do something special while the baby is asleep, and the baby interferes with the plan, the parent is frustrated. All the messages going up to the brain ("bake a cake," "do the laundry," "read the newspaper," "pay the bills") are stopped by the baby, and the parent has no outlet but anger at the baby because the baby has frustrated the parent's plan.

When the baby has a need for some activity (to touch some forbidden object, put his hands in the cereal, or touch a TV dial), the parent stops him. He is frustrated and persists or cries until the parent diverts the baby's stimulus for activity toward a substitute, acceptable activity. The baby needs a substitute outlet for the stimulus to his central nervous system. His need to complete the planned activity is just the same as his parent's need to carry out his or her plans. The difference is that the baby is an infant. The pathways for postponement in his central nervous system are not yet developed. He needs an immediate outlet; the parent has to find the substitute gratification for him.

The adult, however, should have matured enough so that his or her postponing mechanisms are developed. Thus, the adult, not the baby, is the one who has to postpone gratification of a plan and find an acceptable substitute. A mother can do this, for instance, by comforting and diverting her baby. Sometimes if she relaxes and realizes that she can always carry out her other plans later, the baby relaxes and goes off to sleep. She will find that adaptability pays off in the long run.

Have you ever thought that you and the baby share the same feelings and react in the same way to frustration?

*"No, I never thought that. I find I'm too concerned with how the baby makes me feel and not concerned enough about how the baby feels."*

*"Maybe what we are trying to do is make the baby fit in with our own needs rather than trying to meet the baby's needs."*

*"Sure, that's it. When I was going to have the baby, everyone said: 'Now just don't let the baby run your life. Get back to your normal routine as soon as you can.' I guess I'm trying to do that, and the baby is too young to be ready for it."*

Part of the difficulty that some mothers have with postponing their own gratification may go back to their own childhood and upbringing. It may be that they were brought up with the philosophy that immediate gratification of an infant's needs meant "spoiling." So these mothers did not get satisfaction at the appropriate time and are still striving for it. Also, they have been so thoroughly indoctrinated with the idea of not "spoiling" a child that they are having a hard time unlearning that lesson.

## Teaching Delay of Gratification

*"That's exactly it. I'm petrified of bringing up a spoiled brat. I'm determined that mine won't be one."*

Some mothers think that a baby whose needs have always been met quickly will expect such a reaction all his life and will never be able to tolerate anything but instantaneous gratification. That would be true if we did not also teach the baby to tolerate delay. However, this teaching of delay must come at the appropriate time, when the baby's central nervous system has matured sufficiently. The baby must have had enough satisfactory experience with his environment to trust that his needs will get attention before he can learn to tolerate delay.

*"Well, how does one arrange to have a baby tolerate delay?"*

Let's take the feeding situation as an example. At first, the baby cries violently when hungry and quiets down when the bottle is thrust into his mouth. That is his first form of gratification. His crying gives the new mother a sense of urgency, and she responds quickly. As he gets older, the baby may whimper a little and can wait a bit before starting to howl. He is maturing, and he is less insistent; he is learning to wait. Later, he may begin to cry for his feeding, hear his mother making certain familiar noises that he has come to associate with the arrival of his food, and quiet down and wait. If she takes too long, or his hunger pains become very strong, he may cry again. The mother can also try to soothe the baby with her voice as she prepares his food. He learns that her soothing words precede the feeding, and that his needs will be met. This is the beginning of postponing gratification. It must come gradually in accordance with the baby's developmental level. Later, when the baby is sitting up in the kitchen and can watch his mother prepare his food, he learns to wait a little longer. Then as the baby becomes more verbal, one can say, "Just a minute, I'm coming," in a friendly, assuring manner. As the baby gets older, that "minute" can be extended. Each mother learns what her baby's level of tolerance is, and she gradually teaches him to wait a little longer before she satisfies his need.

*"How long does it take a baby to get to the stage when he can tolerate delay?"*

The timetable for this level of maturity is different for each baby. Some learn early. They have good experience with their parents. They know their parents keep their word, and they trust them. Some babies are apprehensive; they do not develop trust as quickly. This apprehension may be due to their particular endowment, or it may be the result of inconsistent responses on the part of the parents. Some days the parents respond immediately, and other days they take a while to respond. It takes these children longer to learn to trust their parents and, consequently, longer to tolerate delay.

*"What happens to the baby whose mother does not respond to him when he needs it?"*

The baby whose needs have hardly ever been responded to promptly is the one who grows up impatient and unable to wait for gratification. This is the person who can't wait to be served in a restaurant, can't wait in traffic, or can't wait for solutions to problems. In some cases, people who cannot tolerate any delay of gratification become "sitting ducks" for the kinds of doubtful enjoyments that seem to afford a large degree of instant gratification—for example, alcohol or drugs. These people, of course, constitute extreme examples of what happens to the baby whose needs are hardly ever met promptly; there are many degrees of reaction up to that point.

*"At what stage do you think our babies are now in their ability to wait for a bottle?"*

They are about ready to recognize some of the sounds you make in preparing food for them. If they can see you, they are beginning to know what you are doing. They can be quieted by your voice when you say, "Here comes your lunch," or "I'm getting your bottle," or "Here comes Mommy." They don't exactly understand the words you are saying, but they do understand that food is coming.

Have you noticed your baby behaving in a way that indicates that he is waiting for you or that he understands what is going on?

*"Yes, I think the baby isn't as shrill in her cry, and she seems to be able to give me a warning cry and then wait a little."*

*"Mine isn't up to that yet. He shrieks till I get there, and sometimes he can't quiet down right away. He needs a good bit of soothing."*

*"Well, mine can wait what seems like a few seconds—maybe even a minute—if I talk to her all the time while I'm on the way over to her. The waiting time is very short, though."*

Infants and children have no real sense of time, and a minute may seem very long to them. Adults have to be aware of that. A child does not really learn to wait and postpone, in the sense that adults understand those ideas, until he is verbal, usually around three years of age or later. One of the measures of our maturity is how long we can postpone gratification. One of the first things children are taught in nursery school is taking turns, waiting to get what one wants. Entry into nursery school coincides with the maturational level at which most children develop the ability to learn to wait.

*"Well, I guess adults' expectations are a little out of line. I'll have to explain this at home because everyone gets on me when I say, 'The baby can't wait and must be tended to first.' "*

*"Do these babies really know when we are angry with them?"*

Yes, they can feel the displeasure of the parent, and it can create the same angry reaction in them as it does in you. If such an "angry alliance" gets to be the pattern of the relationship between parent and child, the seeds have been sown for the development of an individual who responds with anger all the time. A crabby, angry baby may grow into a crabby, angry adult. This is what all parents want to avoid.

Except for those few children who seem to have a genetic endowment for hyperirritability, most babies respond to patient and consistent attention. It may be harder with those few children who seem to have a genetic disposition for hyperirritability, but even they can be helped to overcome their innate tendency.

*"If you get into this angry pattern with your child, can it be overcome?"*

The longer it goes on, the harder it is to undo. It takes many hours of therapy and great expense to undo what need never have happened if the parents understood their children's developmental needs.

*"I've noticed that if I am patient, my baby relaxes, and neither of us gets upset."*

*"Well, I've had that feeling of frustration once in a while, and my husband has too. I guess both of us want things to go on just as they did before the baby arrived, and we have had trouble adapting. Being able to see what's behind our reaction makes it easier to cope."*

We must recognize what is happening. Instead of being childish ourselves, we must wait that little bit extra and show that we are more grown up than the baby. The whole process of growing up is developing the ability to delay gratification. We help the baby develop that capacity by teaching him to tolerate more and more delay, according to his maturational level.

*"My baby cries as soon as he wakes from a nap. It's happening more and more every day."*

He cries when he wakes up because he is hungry, and he wants something to eat. He's trying to tell you that he wants something. There are some babies who want the bottle or breast immediately, just as some people want coffee immediately on waking and others are able to shower and dress first. We all have certain innate tendencies. Each mother has to know how to adapt to her baby's style. She can't expect the baby to adapt to her; the baby is not adequately developed for that. We are not taught enough about child development. We think, "We're going to get married and have children, and the children are going to do just what we want them to do, just like dolls." And, when the babies are very, very tiny, mothers can do just what they want to with them. But as soon as the baby begins to develop and to assert himself, the mother is surprised and disappointed.

*"Yes, that is exactly the way I'm beginning to feel. I'm beginning to wonder, 'What happened to my sweet little baby?' He cries, and he's not as quiet as he was. He is not minding. There is something wrong with him."*

He is crying only because he can't say: "Mother, please come here. I'm lonesome; play with me," or "I'm hungry," or whatever his message is. Crying is his only way of speaking.

▪                                                                    ▪

*"My baby always cries so loud even when there isn't anything much wrong. Why is that?"*

Babies of this age are not yet able to modulate their cry in proportion to their feelings or needs. A mother must remember that the volume of the cry—and some babies cry more lustily than others—is not necessarily in proportion to the need. Loud crying should not be viewed as a crisis or as a fit of anger.

*"You think a mother should get to the baby at once anyway, even if she knows that?"*

Yes, she should respond to the baby as quickly as she can. But, if she understands the meaning of the cry, she doesn't have to race to the baby with her heart pounding as though a catastrophe had occurred.

*"Well, I'm still doing that. I'm almost in a cold sweat till I see that the baby is okay."*

Most parents go through that to some degree, but in time they get to know their baby and they become more secure. So does the baby.

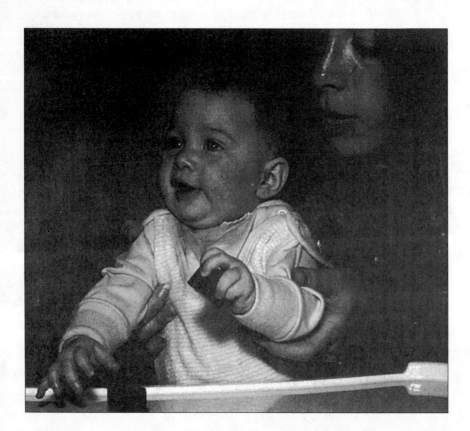

# Age Twenty-four to Twenty-eight Weeks

## Highlights of Development—
## Twenty-four Weeks

When the baby is lying on his back, he holds his legs up and extended. He is more likely to roll over on his stomach by himself. When the baby pulls himself to the sitting position (*see exercise, page 19*), he lifts his head higher and sits much straighter. Most babies should be able to sit propped up for about thirty minutes at a time now and some babies may enjoy doing it even longer.

When seated in an infant seat or high chair, the baby may now begin to grasp a block or cube in a *palmer grasp* (cupping an object against the palm of the hand and then closing the fingers around it) and will hold it longer. While holding one block or spool, the baby will reach for a second and will also look at a third, if it is presented. This shows the baby's greater awareness of several objects presented at the same time.

Babies will now hold on to a rattle or ring for a long time and will usually bring these objects to their mouths. This kind of oral exploration is of developmental value and should not be discouraged by the parents, unless the object is dirty or dangerous. When the babies drop the rattle or block now, most will look for it momentarily.

Babies should be beginning to make sounds and spontaneous vocalizations in response to parents' conversation. They should respond to loud noises or a bell being rung near their heads by turning toward the sound.

(If the baby consistently shows no response to such activity, the parent should consult the baby's physician to make sure there is no hearing deficit and that this lack of response is due only to lack of attention or immaturity. After colds, the baby's ears should be examined to make sure there has been no infection that can cause hearing impairment.)

Many babies of this age now recognize that there is a difference between their parents and strangers. This is age-appropriate "stranger anxiety."

By now, most babies are beginning to grasp their feet; they are, therefore, beginning to become aware of how far their bodies extend. When a mirror is placed in front of the baby, he is likely to smile or vocalize, although he does not yet really recognize the image as himself.

## *Comforting*

### *"Tuning In" to the Baby's Needs*

We've been talking for a while about mother's feelings of frustration. Part of this frustration results from the baby's need for comforting, which the baby expresses by crying. If a mother "tunes in" quickly to the baby's need and makes the baby happy, the mother is satisfied and gets a sense of accomplishment. If she can't comfort the baby, then both mother and baby are unhappy and frustrated.

In the early stages of infancy, the babies' needs were simpler. They needed to be fed, changed, burped, put into a more comfortable position, or rocked. If you fed or rocked them, they settled down. Now the babies are older, and their need for comforting is more varied and complex.

Have you noticed that your babies need different kinds of comforting now?

*"My baby needs more than just to be picked up. She wants to do something, like look out the window."*

Some mothers feel that feeding is the biggest comfort there is. How do you feel about that?

*"It depends on what's bothering my baby. Sometimes she's hungry, sometimes she has gas, sometimes I think she's bored. She wants someone to talk to or a little music. There's no one answer."*

*"There's a special game I play with my baby. I hold his feet and push his legs; he bends his knees until his legs are over his abdomen. This game seems to comfort him a lot. Even if he is angry and I do that, he calms down."*

*"My baby likes motion. We jog around a bit. Then I put him in the infant seat, and he watches what I'm doing."*

You are finding new things that you can do with your babies. It is good that you are finding other diversions besides food. The need to comfort or entertain oneself by eating can get started at this early period. Thinking of other diversions for your babies is important to their development and can make caretaking more interesting as well.

Now that the babies are older, they should be spending more time

■                                                                    ■

propped up in a sitting position. In this position they can see the world about them instead of just the ceiling and the mobiles over their heads. At first babies will be comforted and satisfied by sitting up alone. As it becomes less novel an experience, they will want something more.

They are also becoming interested in the things around them and are beginning to reach for objects. If they can't reach the object, they cry to have it put in their hands. They may also cry when a toy falls out of sight and become calm again when it is retrieved.

Some of the babies are teething and put things in their mouths to soothe sore gums. Others put things in their mouths to explore them orally. The babies are also at the stage when they may just stare at a toy, looking at it from various angles. The act of holding on to something is satisfying; small dolls and stuffed toys or toys with projections to hold on to are good for this purpose.

Some babies like vocal comforting—being talked to or sung to. Some still need to be held closely and walked or rocked. Others need to be taken outdoors where the air and the variety of sights and sounds keep them from being restless, sometimes even soothes them to sleep.

Some like squeaky toys or jangling keys or music boxes. Others like toys that produce noise when moved. Babies seem to derive a great deal of satisfaction from moving and controlling such a toy. A cradle gym put up across a crib or playpen can also be very stimulating and satisfying. Here again, the baby's satisfaction is derived from her ability to manipulate the device.

The introduction of these new devices for comforting your baby does not mean that the babies are through with the stage of being comforted by feeding, changing, burping, and rocking. It does mean, however, that something new is often needed. This need for more variety is a sign of progress and shows an advance in development.

*"Sometimes trying to comfort the baby becomes a burden. For instance, he often wakes up crying. Instead of taking the bottle I bring him, we have to walk around a bit or go look in a mirror."*

Now the baby's need for comforting is making more of a demand on Mother, but discovering new stages in the baby's development also adds interest to mothering. Finding new ways to comfort the baby gives the mother the satisfaction of knowing that she understands her baby's needs. As we have said before, you will not be able to understand and respond perfectly every time. The important thing for the baby is that her parents are available, paying attention, and trying to satisfy her need. This responsiveness increases the sense of trust and attachment, which are still the fundamental issues of personality development.

## Toys and Play

Most of the babies have been given many toys, some of which may now be just right for their age. A brightly colored cradle gym, suspended across the crib or playpen, can be very pleasing to the baby. A playpen is not essential; it is not useful very long and takes up a good deal of space. A blanket can be spread on the floor, and the baby can roll safetly on it and reach for toys. A playpen is, however, a safe place to put a baby. A mother can still see the baby, but the baby is out of the mother's way.

A baby who can sit up can be placed in a jump seat or high chair so she is out of Mother's way but still in sight. Too often a playpen is used as an isolation unit, and the baby is left unstimulated too long, especially if the child in question is a "quiet baby."

The way all pieces of equipment are used for the baby is important. The main objective should not be to isolate the baby, but to keep her safe, happy, and stimulated. They should also allow for development of motor and learning skills.

What toys does your baby enjoy playing with most now? Have you noticed that your baby is interested in some new kind of toy? What is it?

*"I have one of those balls that have hand grips. She holds on to it and also chews it."*

*"My baby plays in her playpen a lot. She can play in it for hours. She has a cradle gym with two yellow rings and a Humpty Dumpty. When she kicks the cradle gym, it makes a sound."*

Does she seem to get a sense of achievement out of playing with the cradle gym?

*"Yes, she does. She kicks it and plays with the rings."*

I see your baby has a sponge toy. What else does she like to play with, or does she just like to play with the one thing?

*"She also has a doll and an elephant. But the sponge toy is her favorite because she can squeeze it and get it to make a noise."*

She likes that because she can make a sound with very little effort. Many toys are hard to squeeze. She can also put it in her mouth and chew it. It is a very satisfying toy for her.

When the babies were little, we gave you a red ring. That's one of the best toys for the baby now. The baby can use it for teething; she can drop it and pick it up; and, if you hang it up, she can pull on it. It can also be attached to the side of the crib or the carriage so the baby can learn to pull it back after dropping it. Babies need little things they can play with and manipulate, and the red ring can be used for a long time.

*"My baby has a little toy with red feet. Every morning when I go in to him, he has the feet in his mouth. The toy keeps him company constantly."*

Well, he has already found a way to entertain himself.

*"What about those great big stuffed toys that everyone brings the baby as presents? Some scare my baby. One of them, a red clown, he really likes and looks and looks at."*

■                                                                        ■

Sometimes a baby becomes enamored of a large stuffed toy and likes to have it in his crib or playpen. At this age, it is more important for the baby to have small toys he can learn to hold and manipulate. A small rag doll, a squeaky toy with appendages that the baby can tug, poke, squeeze, and put safely in his mouth without having parts of it come off are best.

It is part of the fun of parenting to look for the right toys. Some mothers enjoy making wool or rag dolls themselves or cutting sponges into interesting shapes. Colored plastic measuring spoons make excellent toys. There are many things about the house that are fun for the baby. For example, an empty Vaseline jar with safety pins inside makes a satisfying toy for the baby to shake and make a sound which he can control. Make sure, of course, that the lid of the jar is screwed on tight.

*"I've tried that, and it has been more of a success than any expensive toy my baby has. He also loves to play with an old white sock of his father's that I stuffed and embroidered a face on."*

## The First Stage in Developing a Sense of Mastery

Now the babies are beginning to reach for things; they often miss what they're after, but by next month they will be more successful because their hand-eye coordination will have improved. Because they need the satisfaction of reaching for an object and getting it, they may need some help from the parent. This satisfaction in being able to reach out their hands and get what they want is the first stage in the development of a sense of mastery. This is a very important developmental step and should be recognized by parents with approving words and gestures.

### Parental Satisfaction from the Baby's Responses

By now the tremendous anxiety about feeding, burping, changing, and getting the schedule working should be diminishing. It should be possible to have more fun playing with the baby. The father can share in this. He may even be the one who finds new playthings for the baby or devises new ways in which both parents can enjoy the baby's progress together. Comforting and stimulating aren't just a mother's job.

*"I get a lot of satisfaction from finding the right thing to comfort the baby with, but my husband says I work too hard at that. It doesn't really make that much difference to the baby; if I leave him alone, he will quiet down."*

But it does indeed make a lot of difference! Your comforting the baby at this early stage helps the baby develop into a person who has a sense of security and trust in the people and the "world" around him.

A child who does not develop this sense of basic trust can become whining and cranky. He may also become very quiet. A quiet child, often mistaken for a "good child," may be depressed. Perhaps when the baby's father understands this, he will get more satisfaction out of finding ways to comfort the baby himself, and then he will form a closer relationship with his baby. If you both feel you are doing something important, then it isn't viewed as a nuisance. You are helping your child's personality development.

*"My baby is doing something now that I love: sometimes she will do something and look for my reaction, my approval. She does that naturally, and I get very excited. It makes me feel that I am important to her and that she trusts me and wants my approval."*

Your baby is beginning to look for your approval quite early, and it's very good that you noticed it.

*"I haven't noticed anything like that yet."*

Each baby develops on a different timetable. Your baby may be doing the same thing soon, or maybe she's doing it already and you haven't noticed. You have to be very, very perceptive to notice a baby's glance for approval at this age because it is quite subtle. Later on, it will be more easily noticed. It is very important to acknowledge this development and to reinforce it.

## Fathers' Feelings About the Babies' Development and Care

We have not met with the fathers for nearly two months, and you have probably noticed many changes in the babies during that period.

*"You are right. My baby has increased her activity considerably; she is much more interested in moving around and so on."*

And what do you think about that?

*"I was glad to see it, because I was concerned that she would end up as a halfback for the Giants. She eats so much; but if she exercises, she will gradually reach the right size. She is heavier, but she doesn't seem to be as sluggish."*

Some babies have a tendency to be heavier than others even without eating a great deal. Others remain tiny even if they eat more than most babies. Each baby is unique. Each starts out with certain endowments and an individual maturational timetable. The initially large child may turn out tall and thin, and the thin baby may become heavier as an adult. We can't tell in advance. Usually there is a family pattern, but this pattern is not always a reliable predictor of the future.

*"My baby is creeping, but he doesn't sit up. He is mostly doing physical things."*

■                                              ■

When you say he doesn't sit up, you mean he doesn't pull himself up to sitting? It is too soon for him to be doing this; most babies pull themselves into a sitting position around eight or nine months. However, your baby does maintain a sitting posture when you prop him up, and that is all that one should expect at this age.

*"I think my baby is stabilizing. She doesn't seem as nervous and insecure as she was. She's calming down. She does have occasional fits when she goes haywire and seems very angry."*

I am glad to hear that your baby seems less nervous. You have had a special problem because of her digestive disorders. She may still have periods of abdominal discomfort because of this. A baby like this needs more comforting than others—and much parental patience.

*"I don't think that's the problem. She just doesn't know how to behave. She just doesn't respond at times."*

Perhaps she is not responding as fast as you would like her to. There is a reason for that. All babies have a basic insecurity. We are all born with a basic anxiety because we don't know what's coming next and whether there will be anybody to take care of our needs. As babies, we are totally helpless. Our infancy and dependence on the parent last very much longer than they do for other animals. Maturity involves the development of a sense of security, and that takes a long time. So, if you expect a great deal from the baby now, you are bound to have disappointments because she can't make those quick responses. Some babies make more demands on their parents than others; it depends on what kind of nervous system they were born with. Some are very easygoing; others are more irritable and have a lower frustration tolerance. None of these babies is old enough— that is, their central nervous systems are not well enough developed—to make the instantaneous responses parents would like and expect. For example, you have seen me ring a bell at the side of the baby's head, and you have seen how long it takes for the baby to turn to the sound of the bell. She cannot turn at the fast rate of an older child.

*"When do they begin to make that quick response?"*

Children do not achieve those smooth, quick responses and reflexes until they are eight or nine years old. It takes a long time for the nerve endings to make all the proper connections in the central nervous system.

*"Oh, my goodness, that's a long time."*

You are all laughing with surprise. Just how long it takes this kind of maturity of the central nervous system to develop does usually come as a big surprise to most parents.

*"Okay. Even if her responses will develop slowly, will she always be querulous?"*

■                                                                                      ■

That goes away. You help the baby get over this querulous response by soothing her when she needs it, rather than being angry and impatient. It is not easy, but she is so much better that you must have been doing a good job.

*"Yes, she is better now. The trust is starting."*

Yes, it is, and that is very important. It is a good feeling for both parents and baby.

*"My baby's very active; he needs a man right now."*

Do you find this unpleasant, or are you pleased with it?

*"I'm very pleased, but I can see what a hard time my wife has all day."*

It's good that you realize this. Sometimes fathers have no idea how much a mother has to do to take care of a baby, and this sometimes makes mothers feel overburdened. It is good to let her know you understand this.

Do you all feel you are getting to know your babies better? Are you getting a feeling of attachment for them? Are they becoming attached to you?

*"I think that the longer you are exposed to the infant, the more you get to know her. That's the case with me. I spend most of my time with the baby on weekends because there is only about half an hour between the time I get home and the time she goes to sleep. I don't want to play too much then because she just gets hyper. Nonetheless, I feel that I know my baby and that she is attached to me. I don't have any yardstick to judge by, but I believe that's the case."*

Good! Some fathers don't feel attached to their babies at all because they are not with them very much. Other fathers do have a chance to do a great deal with their babies and enjoy doing it.

Is there any special function you perform for your baby that you especially like doing?

*"Yes, I gave her baths before she outgrew the sink. That was something I did regularly. I don't know if she associated it with me or not."*

Did you enjoy doing that?

*"Yes, I did. Now I give more general assistance: help out with certain feelings, help put her to bed, play with her. Playing is the main thing I do with her."*

Playing is an important way to relate to your babies. What kind of games do others play with their babies?

*"Mainly 'Boo, Who Are You?' and bouncing her on my lap or lifting her in the air—things that enable me to maintain my mental image of myself."*

Another version of that game is "Peekaboo." You know that when you play "Peekaboo" with a baby, you have to remain in view. Just covering one side of your face with your hand momentarily is enough at this stage. If you hide completely, the babies will think you've gone, and they will become upset. When you are both on the bed and you get down to hide, the baby has to be able to see enough of your body to know you are still there.

*"I push the carriage and the kiddie car around a lot. We get down on the floor together, and the baby watches TV in bed with us. I feed him in the mornings and at suppertime too."*

At this age, another game to play is "So Big." You play this game by raising the baby's hands way above her head and saying "So big." After a couple of months, the babies will follow the parents' demonstration of the game and will raise their own arms above their heads. In the meantime, they enjoy watching the parents do it.

Do any of the fathers have any special duties that you help your wives with, any special part of taking care of the baby that you take responsibility for?

*"We trade off on sleeping late on weekends, which we couldn't do when my wife was breast-feeding. I get up and give him a bottle on Saturday mornings so that my wife doesn't have to get up. The baby wakes up at six-thirty no matter what time he goes to bed."*

*"My wife is still breast-feeding, so it's hard to help in that way. I watch him for a couple of hours while my wife goes out."*

Have you been able to arrange your lives so that both of you can go out and leave the baby with somebody?

*"No, we don't have anyone to leave her with. We have to take her wherever we go."*

*"We are lucky. My father-in-law can sit for us now."*

*"We have neighbors across the hall, and we take care of their child when they go out. They do the same for us, but it's not often."*

Finding the right person to leave the baby with is difficult when there are no family members or close friends. Sometimes a student nurse can sit on her night off, or an older teenager who lives nearby. However, it is something that needs to be worked out. You see grown-ups, and there are some places that you want to go that are not appropriate for the baby. Besides, you do need time off *together* once in a while.

Sometimes, one or the other of the parents feels neglected because of the baby. Sometimes fathers feel that mothers are too wrapped up in the baby and are not paying any attention to their needs. Sometimes dinner is not ready or a shirt is not ironed. The wife may be worn out when the father gets home. Mothers, on the other hand, sometimes complain that fathers are so entranced by their babies that they ignore their wives. They never remember their birthdays, only the babies'.

Are any of you having these feelings?

*"To tell the truth, yes. That was the way it seemed to me at first. My wife was concerned only with the baby. But now that I'm getting more involved with the baby myself, I'm not so concerned about how much attention I get. Still, once in a while I'd like to feel I'm special too."*

*"I still feel my wife spends entirely too much time with the baby. We never have time to ourselves until after the baby is asleep for the night, and by then we are too tired ourselves."*

*"After my husband gets home, neither he nor the baby seems to know I'm around except if they need something."*

*"I don't mind that. It gives me time to get dinner. Then we put the baby to bed together and have dinner together. However, when I think about it, the baby seems to take up an awful lot more time and needs me more than I ever thought she would. It takes a lot of arranging for us to have time together."*

*"When will the baby be able to do without so much of my wife's time, our time?"*

What you are asking is when can parents expect the baby to be able to separate from them and not need so much attention and contact, so let's discuss that.

## Fathers' Feelings About Attachment and Separation

The mothers give us the impression that the fathers think that the babies should not still need to be so close to the parents and that the mothers are being too attentive, making the babies used to more attention than they really need. Is this a fair statement of how the fathers feel?

*"It is a fair statement, as far as I'm concerned. My wife and I are constantly battling about the attention the baby gets. My parents, who come often, also feel that we are, as they put it, too lenient with the baby."*

*"No, I have found that either I don't notice the crying as much, or the baby is crying less. She is happier and crying less—and needs less attention."*

*"How long does this whole period last? How do you hurry it along?"*

The babies need to have their parents available for a long time, and how long this "long time" will last will be different for each baby. Ideally, the parents should not separate from the baby before the baby is ready to separate from the parents. Parents get very annoyed if the baby cries when they go out of the room. Sometimes they scold the baby. But the baby does not know you are there if she cannot see you.

■        ■

*"But why is that? The baby sees us go into the other room. He must know we are there."*

His ability to integrate that experience has not matured in his central nervous system. Those associative tracts require use, experience, and the development of memory before the baby can understand that. This takes time, for some babies it takes until they are three years old.

That's why the "Peekaboo" game is important. It does two things: It shows the baby that when you disappear, you also come back; and it's the beginning of teaching a baby to be able to be without you, however momentarily.

But the whole process of learning to separate takes a long time. We all know about the babies' physical development—that first they learn to sit up, then to crawl, then to stand, and then to walk. We know that sequence, and we expect the babies to learn to walk in stages. Attachment and separation have a life history too. At first, the babies cannot separate from the parent or whoever is taking care of them. Then they need to be with the parent a great deal and can separate from their parents for only a short period of time. This is the stage the babies are in now.

*"That means you can't leave the baby at all?"*

That is not necessarily so. It does mean that the baby needs to get used to another person, the father or another caretaker, and to develop a sense of security with that person too.

## *Parent Substitutes: Baby-sitters*

If babies have a number of different people taking care of them (such as babies in an institution who have different attendants every eight hours and different caretakers for vacations and days off), the babies can never form the kind of attachment or relationship that will enable them to relate well to other people. That's why we stress the baby's need for a consistent caretaker, whether it is the mother, father, or someone else. That doesn't mean that you have to be tied to the baby for three years until the baby can separate, but you should leave the baby for short periods at the beginning and leave her only with someone with whom she is familiar, someone who is a good substitute for the parent.

*"Once we had an emergency and left the baby with a trained nurse who knew how to take care of babies. But the baby didn't know the nurse and was so weepy and hard to manage when we got back."*

Good parent substitutes are very hard to come by, and you're better off not leaving your baby with somebody who is a poor substitute and not a "mothering" person. By spending time with your baby during these early months, the baby's attachment to you is developing. By now the babies may also be used to the grandparents. Gradually they will get used to other people.

## More on Stranger Anxiety

*"Why do some babies seem to be able to go to other people at first, and then begin to cry at the sight of every stranger?"*

As we have already discussed with the mothers, some babies begin to show stranger anxiety when they are about six or seven months old. That's when they really begin to notice that other people are different from Mama and Papa. Sometimes Grandmother, who was a frequent visitor for the first six months, goes away for a week or two. When she comes back, she's regarded as a stranger. The baby cries, and Grandmother gets very upset. The same thing may happen with an aunt, a family friend who has not seen the baby for a while, or with a new friend. This reaction indicates that the babies have learned to tell the difference between the people who are close to them and those who are not. It shows a new level of development, which should please you but may need to be explained to the relative or friend.

*"My boss and his wife are coming for dinner next week. The baby was great the last time, but do you suppose he'll pull this 'stranger' bit this time? It will be hard to explain."*

I think now that you understand what is going on—that the reaction is a new stage in development—you will not have any difficulty explaining to your boss and his wife. Other people may feel that the baby is badly behaved. The parent has to be the baby's advocate and explain his situation to others. A parent who is sensitive at this stage helps instill basic trust in the baby by not scolding or handing the baby over to a stranger before the baby feels secure or shows an inclination to go to the stranger.

*"Well, what happens when parents don't understand or know about all this?"*

If the baby doesn't have basic trust in her parents, she won't develop basic trust in other people. That baby will be very difficult and may cry a great deal. If the baby establishes basic trust in the parents, then she looks upon other people with trust. Children are then able to separate from their parents much more easily. The process starts right here and now, and that's why we are talking about it. Just about now you are beginning to feel that you can leave the babies because they are older and should know that you are in the next room. But when you leave them, they don't know if you're coming back. That kind of separation is very difficult for them; many will be three years old before they are able to separate happily.

*"Well, what about the present trend of sending babies off to nursery groups earlier and earlier?"*

■                                                                 ■

We look upon nursery schools and day care as being rather difficult for children who are under three years old. You know it is even harder for children to separate from the parent in unfamiliar surroundings. This is quite different from being left at home with a familiar sitter. Some children are able to accomplish this at eighteen months; some not until they are three and a half, but the average age at which this happens is around three years. Then the child can walk away from the parent and stay in another room all by herself and not be upset. If, once in a while, you find a child crying all of a sudden because she doesn't know where you are, that shows that separation anxiety is still present. That's the reason we have to be careful about who takes care of the baby and when the change is introduced. A new caretaker has to be introduced gradually. I don't think parents should be made prisoners to their children, but, at the same time, parents should bear the baby's need in mind.

*"Well, what did our parents do? Did they stay with us all the time?"*

Some parents did stay with their children; others thought they were "liberated," so they didn't. I recall a common kind of incident years ago. A mother would go marketing and leave her baby sleeping in the carriage outside the store. When she came out, the baby would be screaming and frantic. The baby had awakened and felt deserted, a very traumatic experience for the baby. Some parents didn't realize how the baby felt and would be angry with the baby. Other parents would come out and soothe the baby. Then, as now, the parent's behavior depended upon whether she felt embarrassed because the baby was crying, or whether she was really sensitive to the baby's needs.

It is best to wait for the baby to separate from us rather than to attempt to separate from the baby. The process of separation goes through various stages, and one must handle it differently at each age. It comes up when a mother has to (or wants to) take a job. It comes up again when the parents want to take a vacation, and it comes up when you think the baby is ready to go off to nursery school. We'll discuss separation many times because it is such an important and sensitive topic.

## Mothers' Reactions to Fathers' Perceptions of Their Role

In our society, infants are cared for mainly by mothers or other female caretakers. The father's involvement has been minimal in the actual care of the baby. His role is mostly to be the provider of food and shelter for the family, and often this role leaves him little time to spend with a baby. In spite of this traditional concept of the father's role, some fathers look forward to coming home to feed, play with, teach, and help the development of a new baby.

In our group this seems true especially now that each baby is more competent, can sit up more, and is beginning to show more of his own personality. Some fathers come home with a desire to help in sterilizing bottles, doing the laundry, even marketing if mother has been unable to get out. This is probably the ideal father's response from the mother's point of view. That way, the mother can share the joys of child rearing as well as the more tedious tasks with the father. Other fathers may view their role differently. More involvement by the fathers is becoming necessary as more mothers return to the job market.

How does your husband view his role now that there is a baby in the family? Does he seem to have time to be a parent? Is the father's role in child raising causing any conflict between the parents?

*"My husband seems to make time for the baby. He was so anxious for a baby. He seems to come home only to see the baby. Sometimes he forgets to greet me, but I don't mind. The baby needs his attention too."*

*"My husband always calls to see if I've had time to go to market and if he can bring anything home. That's a big help."*

*"In our case, the situation's different. My husband works very late, and the baby is asleep when he gets home. The only time he has with the baby is early in the morning. Sometimes he gives the baby her first bottle."*

*"My husband works so hard at his job. He feels that's his part and it's enough. All the rest he leaves to me. He expects me to do everything, just as I did before the baby came."*

*"My husband says he can't handle babies. He feels that when the baby is five, he will start to become more involved."*

There are fathers who can't participate in caretaking and playing with their children. They see their role solely as providers and the mother's duty as child rearing. In addition, some want their wives to greet them at the door with a smile and with a well-prepared dinner ready on a beautifully set table. Even though there is a new baby in the household, they want everything just as it was before the baby was born. They cannot understand why their wives cannot function in the same way they used to. In fact, these men are often jealous of the attention that the baby gets and see a well-prepared dinner and neat house as attention to themselves. Sometimes these fathers, remembering usually their teenage years, recall homes in which their own mothers performed these almost-superhuman tasks, and they expect the same of their wives. Others come from homes where their mothers had a great deal of help and could wait on their fathers, even though there were small children in the family. This situation is not the usual one in our society now, but the memory of it is still there.

*"My husband couldn't care less if he comes home and finds the house in a mess and dinner not ready. He would just as soon go out and get us a*

*Chinese dinner. It makes me feel a little guilty, but I know that I will do better when I have the baby more settled. My husband comes from a family that's very easygoing."*

*"My husband is not like that; his situation is entirely different. He has two jobs, and I have to be sure that his dinner is ready when he gets home at five o'clock so that he can eat it quickly and go to his other job. He would be very angry if the dinner wasn't ready, and I understand that; but it does put a lot of pressure on me just around dinnertime when the baby begins to act up. But my husband is helpful, too, because he does the marketing on his way home. The only time he can play with the baby is for a little while before he eats."*

Yes, just around dinnertime is when most babies do begin to "act up." Now that they are able to sit up a little in an infant seat or high chair, they sometimes quiet down when they are watching you in the kitchen and you talk to them as you work. Then they don't have the sense of rejection. When you are not tense about the situation, they relax too. Babies are very sensitive to mothers' tensions. Some mothers resort to backpacks. In that way, their hands are free, but the baby is with them and doesn't feel isolated.

*"My husband came from a family where there was a great deal of help, and he expects everything to run just as smoothly in our family. His family was very autocratic, and that is the way that he understands child rearing. What can I do about that because that is not the way I want the baby to be brought up?"*

Different parental attitudes toward child rearing can be a source of much friction. We hope these sessions will be of some help to you both. Sometimes the conflict is difficult to resolve, and one must have special professional help with it.

It is important for both parents to try to talk objectively about their expectations of each other, now that there is a new baby in the household. Parental roles should have been discussed and settled before the baby came, but even if they had been, no parent really understands beforehand how much time and attention the baby will need or how difficult it becomes to take care of the baby and still do the household chores. Usually, the parents have to agree on a new set of priorities once the baby has arrived and they discover just how complicated meeting the demands of both baby and household can become.

There are also parents who have difficulty relating to infants but are able to assume the parental role more easily when the child is older and more verbal. When this is the case, it is difficult for the caretaking parent. It creates an added burden to try to explain and show off the baby's developmental achievements. Some parents, especially mothers, resent this attitude, and some of this resentment is reflected in their treatment of the baby. Some of the pleasure to be gained by sharing with the other parent is lacking. However, if the mother understands her husband's makeup (or vice versa), other helping roles can be found. It is also likely that a reluctant father will pick up some of the mother's enthusiasm for the baby's achievements. Most babies enjoy playing with their fathers, and this enjoyment usually becomes mutual, even before the baby is talking.

*"We can't wait until the time when the baby grows up and talks and does more things with us. We'll be more 'tuned in' then. We are both too old to cope with an infant."*

*"My husband is the patient one. He loves babies. Though I am enjoying the baby now, I'll be happier when she is older and can talk."*

Most of us develop our attitudes toward parental roles by the examples we have had as we grew up in our own families. There are some fathers who see their role as managing the family situation. Those men were brought up in an autocratic environment, and they are passing on that heritage in their own families. If such a man happens to marry a woman whose past experience has been the same, she will be able to cope with this situation. If, on the other hand, the mother comes from a less autocratic family, the situation can be painful. Adjustments will have to be made on both sides, but the problem is not insurmountable.

*"That sounds like us. By being patient and trying to understand, we are managing to cope. We did need help. Talking here helps, and then we go over things again ourselves."*

There are fathers who are much more "motherly" than some mothers. The mother may regard the father as much too fussy, much too anxious about the baby. She may feel that he interferes too much in her role as a mother and gives her the feeling that she is not taking good care of the baby. He is the one who jumps up first and attends to the baby during the night. Maybe it is just the father's nature to be anxious; maybe his father behaved in this way. Some fathers regard their wives as inefficient, so they try to take charge of the household. If fathers, however, do things for the baby naturally and uncritically, it is very helpful; but if they are critical, then they can cause friction and undermine the mother's self-esteem.

*"My husband is extremely fussy. He never seems to be happy with the way I do things, but he doesn't think that it is his role to help. He comes home at night with his work, and right after dinner he sits down to do it. If I need some help with the baby, he acts as though I were imposing on him."*

That attitude must seem unreasonable to you, and I can understand your feeling. But let's look at the matter from the father's point of view. If a father still has the pressure of work to do at night, one can perhaps understand how he may find it trivial and annoying to be asked to mind

■                                                                    ■

the baby, so that mother can get clean diapers from the laundry room. He may think, "Well, she's been home all day; she could have arranged to have her laundry ready for the night." The father is annoyed because he feels the mother is adding to the pressures on him.

But this is a situation that can be worked out. This same father may be happy to play with the baby when he is ready. Perhaps he could be encouraged to play with his child for a few minutes before dinner. That may be the moment for the mother to make a quick trip to the laundry room.

*"Oh, yes, on his own time my husband plays with the baby and shows her things, but he doesn't regard helping me as part of his role."*

Indeed, in most cases, it takes a lot of insight to find a successful way to interrupt someone who is absorbed in something. You have to learn what things antagonize the other person, and just how to behave to get the desired response.

*"What about the father who feels he has to have his exercise and outings, just as he used to before the baby came?"*

There are some fathers who stay little boys themselves, who feel that they should not be expected to assume the responsibilities of being fathers. They want to go on with their bowling, tennis, or sailing without making any accommodation for the fact that there is a new baby in the house. This can be very annoying to mothers who feel that they need more help and expect fathers to share the responsibility of child rearing.

On the other hand, it is necessary for most of us to have some exercise or playtime, which is relaxing and healthful. As men's health is statistically more vulnerable, it is probably best that their athletic activities be continued on a regular basis as a health measure. Perhaps men unconsciously feel the need for this exercise as a way to preserve their health, rather than as a way to get out of chores. Women may have to take a broader view of their husbands' needs. By the same token, mothers also need to arrange for some free time when they can do something that is relaxing for them. As a matter of fact, both parents come back to their parenting roles more able to cope with and enjoy the baby when they have some time for themselves.

*"That helps me understand my husband's point of view. I guess I should get out more myself."*

Perhaps we need to take a more objective view of what is going on. Few parents, whatever their antecedents or character structures, are unconcerned about their children, but each individual has a different way of showing this concern. All of us have preconceived notions of what to expect from a baby and what to do for a baby. No one realizes how time-consuming child rearing is. Most of us do not know what the timetable for the baby's development is and what the baby is going to need at each stage of development. As parents learn this together, they begin to get a great deal of pleasure in seeing the development of their baby. With knowledge and understanding, parents can enhance their baby's development.

Being a good parent takes patience, consistency, knowledge, and, above all, a sense of humor. Sometimes fathers who spend little time with their children do not consider things that mothers worry about as very serious. They sometimes joke about them or dismiss them as trivial. For some mothers, this is a great affront. They say, "Well, you haven't been with him all day." While this is true, the father has been putting up at work with a great many things that he has found very trying. When he discusses these problems with his wife, she looks at them differently and often makes some suggestions. To each, the other's job may seem easier; for each, the other's perspective can often be helpful.

## Adapting to Babies' Exploratory Behavior

Just as mothers have begun to feel comfortable about their babies' schedules and understand their behavior and needs, the babies go on to a new level of development. The new level at this age consists mainly of increased interest in exploration. The babies are now beginning to reach for things. They like to push things over the sides of their high chairs, and they are able to hold something in each hand. They sometimes grab hold of things that they shouldn't touch, such as the draperies, plants, or cups of hot coffee. This new exploratory behavior is also a sign of motor development and improved eye-hand coordination, which needs to be dealt with appropriately and not considered a nuisance.

The parents should make sure that the baby has small things that she can hold in her hand and explore by looking at them, by throwing them down, by tasting them. When she reaches for the thing that she should not have, the baby should be given something that she can hold so that her exploratory needs are met. When the baby is able to hold two small objects, one in each hand, and look from one to the other, she feels a sense of mastery. This activity should be recognized by the parent with some verbal comment such as "Good" or "Nice."

It is important that these early attempts at mastery be recognized because recognition helps the baby develop initiative and self-esteem. Parents should, therefore, get into the habit of reinforcing an infant's sense of mastery by recognizing the achievements no matter how small they may seem. While this advancement in development is harder on the parents, who must keep a closer watch on the baby, it should also give them pleasure. It is satisfying to see the smile of a baby who has reached out and grasped something that she wanted. If the parent then smiles and vocalizes something pleasant, the baby recognizes the approval and responds positively.

Have you noticed any of these developments in your baby? How have you been responding to them?

*"I have been noticing that I am more irritable with the baby. I guess I got used to having him sleep, and now he wants to play more. When I carry him around, he gets hold of the venetian blind cord or a plant. It has been making me angry. I think it is a nuisance—not an advance."*

I really think it helps parents to understand that this reaching and grabbing is an advance in development and a necessary step in maturation. Give the babies something to get hold of that won't be dangerous or annoying, so that they can use this newly developed behavior to advantage. From now on, child rearing will require more creative thinking and stimulation on the parents' part. It will demand more thought, but most parents will find that this produces more fun for them.

*"My baby reaches out and pulls my hair when I am feeding him. Sometimes that hurts."*

Babies often do reach for their mothers' hair; it is especially tempting to reach out and touch long hair. The babies do not know that they are hurting you. The baby should be allowed to explore his mother's hair and touch her face; this is how he gets to know who she is and what she looks and feels like. The mother can hold her hair so that the baby just gets the ends and pulls against her hand instead of against the hair in the scalp. Sometimes a baby uses a patting gesture to explore the mother's hair or face, and the mother likes this.

As parents, we must tolerate a few patterns of behavior that we don't particularly like because they fulfill a baby's need for development. Some of us may tolerate some of these better than others do. The important thing is to allow as much exploratory behavior as is possible and safe.

## Games: Challenge and Achievement

This new level of development makes new kinds of games possible. Parents can hold out toys that the baby can reach for and get hold of. It is important for the child to get a sense of achievement and parental approval. The toy should, therefore, be held so that the baby has to make a little effort to get it, but not so far away that the baby cannot reach it and gives up the effort. It is also important for cradle gyms and other such toys to be placed in a position that is conducive to appropriate challenge and achievement rather than to frustration. The baby will also enjoy holding a dumbbell-shaped rattle in his hand and shaking it while holding something else, such as a block, in the other hand. The baby enjoys the achievement of making noise by shaking or banging. Parents should take pleasure in this achievement as well and let the baby know they are pleased. To the adult the banging may be an unpleasant sound, but to the baby it is a great joy and achievement. Sometimes children make an unexpectedly loud sound with their toys and frighten themselves. Then they need to be soothed. Sometimes another object can be substituted, or a towel or diaper placed on the surface the baby is hitting to deaden the sound.

Babies of this age also enjoy the tinkling sound of a bell, which they are now able to grasp and bang but not actually ring in the normal sense of that word.

It is good to have a time each day in which either father or mother or both participate in this kind of play with the baby. This activity is fun for parents and also important for the babies' sense of achievement.

*"Our baby is starting to do these things. Now my husband, who had thought that the baby was just a lump and a chore, gets real pleasure in sitting by him and playing with him while I get supper."*

For babies, play is really learning. It is through play experiences that they learn most about the world around them. How do you feel about it when the baby drops something on the floor? We have talked before about how tiresome this was to many of you. Does it help at all to understand that the baby is exploring space?

*"Yes, it does. I've tried to do what you said. I say 'down' when the toy falls and 'up' when I pick it up. Yesterday she said 'uh, uh.' I like to think she was trying to say 'up.'"*

She probably was trying to say "up." Eventually the babies will learn these two words and the concepts that go with them. You are really teaching through play, and, as we have said before, the activity can always be changed when the parent gets tired. There's no need to get a backache!

*"I understand now that this kind of play is important, but my mother tells me that it's ridiculous. She thinks that I should teach the baby not to throw her toys on the floor by letting them stay there."*

It's hard to disagree with a grandmother, but sometimes it has to be done. We understand now that this exploratory behavior is important to healthy cognitive development. Research experiments have shown that this exploration becomes the stimulus for learning. If babies are thwarted at this age, they lose interest in exploration now and in learning later on in life.

■                                                                      ■

Therefore, what seems like a nuisance to parents now is really the very cornerstone of learning and intellectual growth. That is why we encourage you to enhance the baby's exploratory behavior. Perhaps if this were explained to the grandmother, she would understand our point of view.

## Vocalization: The Need for Reinforcement

At this time, in addition to greater development of manual ability, there is more vocalization. The baby is making more babbling sounds like "ah-ah," "mah-mah," or "dah-dah." The parents should repeat these babbling sounds so that the baby realizes the parents are pleased. This approval encourages the baby to try again. When he makes a sound and hears it repeated by the parent, he begins to have a sense of verbal communication because *his* sounds mean something to the parents. If the parent speaks to the baby so that he can pick out the sounds, the baby may try to make other sounds, too; this is the beginning of conversation. It is important also to speak with modulation in tone and rhythm. While the baby may not understand anything of what is said, he feels the pleasant tone of the parent's voice and has the sense of being attended to and recognized. Very often he will smile and gurgle in response to parental speech.

This kind of vocalizing back and forth should be done many times during the day. The mother can call to the baby from across the room, but sometimes she should be closer to the baby so that he can see her mouth move, meet her eyes, and respond to her smile. This activity is fun for fathers, too, and they should be encouraged to participate in it. Babies are very sensitive to sound, and they can tell by the tone of voice whether the parent is pleased or displeased. Sometimes a loud voice can make them cry. Parents have to be sensitive to this and learn how to talk to their babies.

*"You talk about having a conversation with the baby. When my friends hear me talking to the baby, they think I am silly because the baby can't understand me, and they make me feel self-conscious."*

We know now from research that the babies who are talked to and stimulated by speech are the ones who speak better and perhaps earlier. Speech is something that has to be taught. If a child were never spoken to, he could make sounds, but he would not learn to speak a language. The earlier one begins to stimulate a child with speech, the better it is for the baby; it doesn't matter if the baby understands the communication or not. Research has shown that babies babble in the same sounds in all cultures, but by six months they begin to make only the sounds of the language they hear around them. Communication through speech is necessary not only in itself but also as the foundation for learning to read. Children with limited vocabularies—and limited experience in verbal communication—have greater difficulty mastering reading and written communication.

*"After I say something, my baby looks at me for a long time, and then I see his mouth curl up as he tries to make sounds. Sometimes he does, and we smile at each other. It is great fun. Sometimes when I am in the corner of the room and I talk to him, I can see his arms and legs wave, and sometimes he makes a sound or two."*

This is just what we are talking about; that is the kind of stimulation we think the baby ought to be getting.

*"My husband is home very rarely, and he has a big, booming voice. Sometimes the baby cries when he talks to her, and that upsets him, of course."*

That is upsetting, but if you can explain to your husband that the baby is sensitive to sound, he will learn to use a softer tone with her. As she gets more used to him, she will then not be frightened by his usual voice. She needs to get better acquainted with her father and to develop a sense of trust in him. If a father is away for long periods of time, it is normal for the baby to be apprehensive. The father should be reassured that he is not doing anything wrong; the baby simply needs to get used to him.

*"In our family it is entirely different. The baby sometimes responds to me when I talk, but she responds much more to Daddy when he comes home. This makes me quite jealous. I talk to the baby all the time."*

Sometimes it's necessary to just say a little bit to the baby and give the baby a chance to talk back. Some mothers talk to their babies all the time; they talk at them without allowing the baby a chance to reply. Maybe this is what you were doing in your anxiety to get the baby to talk.

*"That may be so; I'll have to see if I do that."*

*"I have some of the same feelings. The baby responds more to my husband, whom he sees so little, while I'm home with the baby all day breaking my neck to take care of him."*

It's natural for a mother to want her baby to respond to her and to feel a little left out if she senses that the baby responds more to the father. Really, it is just a different response, not a better one. The father hasn't been there all day, so he brings some novelty and new stimulation to the scene. This is really a good thing because a baby needs to be attached to

■                                                                                    ■

both parents; but the baby should be allowed to respond to each in his own way.

Some babies take longer to respond than others. Each baby has his own timetable. All the babies will develop these abilities, but at different times. It is our job to understand that timetable. When we do, it is very satisfying to both parent and baby.

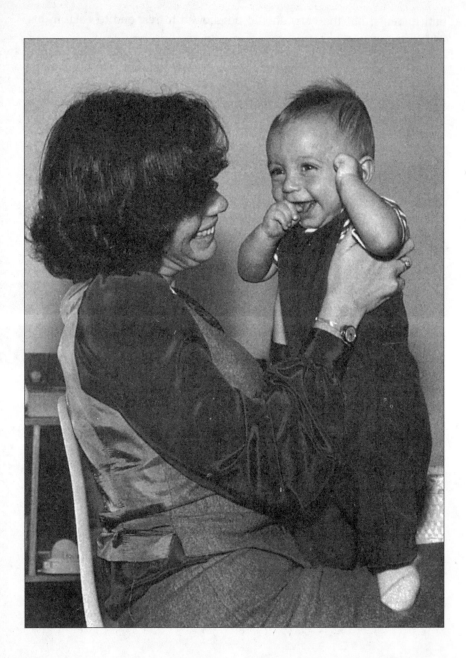

## Highlights of Development— Twenty-eight Weeks

When the baby pulls himself up from the supine position (holding on to the parent's hands), he is now able to maintain a sitting posture briefly by leaning forward. When placed in a sitting position, the baby may not need as much propping and can sit for longer periods. In this posture, he can begin to take solid foods more easily.

 When held in a standing position, the baby now has the ability to bounce a little. While fun for parents and child, the activity should not be overdone because babies should not stand until they can pull to a standing position by themselves. Some may be doing this on their own when on their parent's lap, which shows physical readiness for standing.

At this age, the increasing competence of the baby's hands is noticeable. Most babies now use a *palmer grasp*. They can grasp objects like a bell by the handle with one hand and bang it or shake a rattle. The baby can also hold a block and put it in her mouth while holding a second block in the other hand. She may even study the blocks a moment. This ability to hold two things at one time—more than momentarily—is a big developmental advance.

The baby may even transfer an object from one hand to the other. The baby's use of his hands should be encouraged and should be part of playtime—i.e., handing a small block or spool to the baby and recognizing his achievement of holding two blocks or transfering a spool from one hand to the other. Not all  babies will be able to do this at the beginning of the seventh month, but they should reach this stage by the end of the month. When the red ring is dangled beyond the baby's reach, he may try to grasp it. If he does not succeed, he will probably give up trying. Parents can stimulate these developments by engaging the baby in play with small blocks and the ring.

Vocalization is now progressing from the "mm-mm" sound in crying to babbling sounds like "ah-ah," "mah-mah," "dah-dah." Parents should listen for these sounds and repeat them to the baby. This is another area for playful interaction that stimulates speech and provides fun for the parent and child.

The baby may reach out and pat his image in the mirror. This is always a fun experience for baby and parents, though the baby does not yet recognize himself. The parent can say, "That's baby," or say the infant's name. Eventually, the baby will get to know his name and associate it with his image.

## Development in Relation to Feeding

### Exploration with the Hands

Now that the babies are taking semisolids and sitting up for their feedings, they are beginning to use their hands to intercept the spoon. For some mothers this poses a problem or becomes a nuisance, because it delays the feeding. Reaching for the spoon is normal behavior and is part of exploration. If it impedes the feeding, it is sometimes helpful to give the baby something else to hold in his hands, such as a toy or even another spoon to play with.

How do you feel about the baby doing this? How do you deal with it?

*"My baby is always putting his hands in his food, mooshing it around, and making a mess. He makes me very angry at feeding time. What should I do?"*

Well, you can see from what I have just said that exploration of food with the hands is a normal part of a baby's development. If it bothers you, hold the dish away from the baby so that he cannot touch it and give him something else to hold. If he still reaches for the food, help him to fill the spoon and get it to his mouth. A few babies may be ready for this. It may simply satisfy him to be able to experience this once or twice, and then he will gladly go back to banging the spoon or block on his high chair tray. The important thing is not to get upset or angry. Try to use each new stage of exploratory development constructively according to the baby's ability.

*"When can babies begin to feed themselves?"*

Some babies, even at this age, can assist the feeding by putting their hands around the spoon, which is guided to the mouth by the mother's hand. In this way, early self-feeding may be started with the infants who are ready for it. Each mother can find out on her own whether her baby is ready. No matter what technique is employed, the feeding should not become a battle between mother and child. The atmosphere at feeding time is much more important at this period than the quantity of food consumed. In the long run, the food consumption will be enhanced by a pleasant atmosphere at mealtime. Eating will become an enjoyable experience for the baby. He will not begin to use food to establish his autonomy. Eating problems can have their inception at this very early age.

*"If I let the baby help me feed him, it will take forever."*

It may seem forever, but actually it will only take a few minutes longer. The baby may then learn to feed himself early, and you will have more free time in the long run. Really, feeding time should be a relaxed, enjoyable period. It should not be rushed.

*"I just can't stand the mess the baby makes when he eats. I am sorry, I know I am wrong, but I just can't stand it."*

Mothers are often annoyed by the messiness caused by the child's attempts to grasp the spoon or food. Messiness, however, is a normal part of infant feeding; that is why we have bibs. It is not necessary that every drop should get into the child's mouth or that the child's mouth should be wiped after each insertion of the food. This is very annoying to the baby. A baby's mouth should be wiped at the end of the feeding.

*"These are some of the things that are so hard to get used to."*

There are some things about raising babies that are more difficult for parents to do than others. One must bear in mind how the baby feels about it. You seem to be concerned only with how *you* feel about it. Would you think it pleasant to have your mouth firmly wiped after each mouthful, to have your hands constrained while you were eating? It is important to try to understand how the baby feels and how things appear to the baby. Then it is possible for adults to modify some of their thinking.

## Nutritional Value of Different Solid Foods

Babies often show a preference for certain foods and refuse others. Some mothers are very upset when the baby refuses vegetables that the pediatrician has recommended. Some babies prefer fruit to vegetables, and some prefer vegetables to fruit. These foods are really interchangeable in their nutritional value, and it makes very little difference which is eaten. Other mothers become very upset if the baby will only take one kind of cereal. Some babies, now or perhaps a little later, will prefer to pick up dry cereal in their hands and feed themselves. Some babies prefer chicken to meat; others do not like either chicken or meat. Some like liver; some do not. Some like the commercial mixtures of meat, vegetables, and cereal; other babies prefer the single varieties. Some prefer food that is ground up and prepared by the mother herself. Some babies like cottage cheese, which is a good protein substitute if they do not like meat. The important thing is for the mother not to get tense and anxious about the variety and the quantity of solid food consumed at this period. As we have said before, the babies' main nutrition is still derived from milk; they do not need a wide assortment of food. What the baby is learning at this time is how to take solid foods from a spoon and to get pleasure in this achievement.

How do you feel you are getting along in helping the babies learn to eat food from a spoon?

*"My baby takes his milk well, but he takes only a very small amount of cereal and a few mouthfuls of fruit. Then he turns his head away and doesn't want any more. What should I do? My mother says I must make him eat, or else he will never be a good eater."*

This is your mother's point of view; maybe this is what she learned when she was bringing you up. It is our view, based on recent research, that whatever the baby takes, and takes willingly, is fine. He probably takes just what he needs.

As we have said, a baby's main nutrition still comes from his milk. If he is forced to eat, then he will resist even more, and a real feeding problem will be created. Feeding should not become a battleground between parent and child.

*"If a baby is allowed to eat only what she wants to eat, will she ever learn to eat other foods?"*

She will learn to eat other foods, but in her own time. Perhaps you are presenting foods that she doesn't particularly like now, but that doesn't mean she won't like them later. However, if the foods are forced on the baby now, she may despise them for life. There are many children who grow up liking very few foods until they are able to make their own choices. If they are healthy, and if no issue is made of their eating, they will turn out to be good eaters. I think all of us can think of a food that our parents tried to make us eat. They thought it was good for us or that it was good discipline to make us eat it even if we didn't like it. Some of us still don't like that food. What we are trying to do is prevent the child from developing that kind of attitude about food.

*"I still remember the spinach scenes—no spinach, no dessert. I vowed I'd never do that."*

*"Won't the babies get anemia if they drink only milk?"*

That used to be common before babies were given other foods in the first year. For those few infants who refuse solids, the baby's doctor can prescribe iron supplements and vitamins. That is a fairly unusual situation. We are talking about the gradual introduction of solid food and not forcing the baby to eat the foods he doesn't happen to like at first. We are stressing keeping the feeding period a pleasurable time and not making it a contest between parent and child.

*"I don't want my baby to get too fat. If you let a baby have just what he wants all the time, won't food become the main interest in his life?"*

If the parents show approval only when the baby eats his food, then he may indeed eat more to get approval. We are not advocating overdoing the approval if the child eats. Also, we are not recommending that a child be forced to eat something that he doesn't like. The parents have to respond to each stage or phase of development in an appropriate way.

## Changes in the Baby's Schedule

Most of the babies are getting onto a schedule, and mothers are getting used to the schedule. Then suddenly, the babies seem to go off schedule and seemingly inexplicable changes in routine occur. The baby who had been sleeping through the night now wakes once or twice. The baby who had been taking two-hour naps suddenly wakes after half an hour. Such changes are usually very disconcerting. At first, the mother may be angry because the change in routine interferes with her plans, or she may be alarmed and decide that she is failing, that all of her good work has been for naught. However, if the mother thinks the situation over, she will find that there is usually a reason for this change in schedule.

*"What makes these changes? I think the baby and I are going through such a period now."*

There are many causes for sudden changes in a baby's routine. Such changes occur most often when the baby has been taken on a visit, or when there are new people in the house. Sometimes such a change means that a tooth or an illness is coming. Perhaps the mother herself is under some stress and is unconsciously conveying that to the baby. Perhaps the baby is being overstimulated prior to a nap time or bedtime; perhaps the baby has arrived at a new stage and requires less sleep. As the length of the day changes with the seasons, there may also be changes in the babies' biological clock in response.

Sometimes a baby who has been eating well will suddenly manifest little interest in food. This is not occasion for alarm but for an assessment of the situation. Perhaps the baby has become tired of the menu. Perhaps the mother is a little hurried when she's feeding her.

Have any of your babies been changing their schedules? Has this bothered you? What have you done to help yourselves?

*"You just put your finger on what is bothering me. I had my baby on what seemed like a comfortable schedule for us. Then he started cutting teeth, and now he wakes at night. I don't know whether to go and comfort him or*

*let him cry it out, so he will know that he has to sleep at night. Some people tell me if I go into him when he cries, it will set up a bad habit and I'll never get him to sleep all night again."*

Waking in the night happens very often during teething. The baby cries because he is in pain. He may have clamped down on a painfully swollen gum. He needs to be soothed. When you go to him, he learns that you are reliable and will try to help him. That supports the baby's basic trust. At the same time, you are meeting his physical need by rubbing his gums, giving him something to bite on, or applying some medication if your doctor has advised it. A baby who has once established good sleeping patterns will return to them.

*"The same thing happened to me when our baby had a cold. He would wake when his nose was stuffy and he couldn't breathe. I went to him and wiped his nose, gave him some water to drink, and put the vaporizer on. When he was better, he gradually went back to his regular sleeping pattern."*

*"We've had trouble with eating. The baby was always a good eater, but now she takes some feedings better than others. What should I do?"*

If you do not try to force your baby to eat, she will eat well again when she is ready. She is passing through a phase of not being as hungry as before. Perhaps you have conveyed a bit of your anxiety to her, thus adding to her unwillingness to eat. Food should not be made a cause for conflict. If her nutrition suffers, your pediatrician will be able to tell you what supplements she may need. But such supplements are rarely needed.

*"My baby used to take two long naps during the day, and I looked forward to that because then I could get my work done, or rest, or read. Now he takes a long morning nap but a very short afternoon nap. Is that going to go on?"*

We have to remember that the babies are getting older, and that they do not now require as much sleep as they used to. This varies with each child, of course. Some will still need two long naps; some will drop the morning nap and continue with a long afternoon nap, or vice versa. Each mother has to adapt to her own baby's needs. Actually, the longer period of being awake allows more time for play and interaction with the parents. Now that they can sit propped up in their carriages for a longer time, they can be more stimulated by the sights around them. When they get tired, they can be put down flat for a nap. When the babies are taken out in their carriages, you can do your marketing and at the same time point out to the baby items of interest such as a car, a dog, another baby. These can be fun times, a growing amount of time to be enjoyed and used profitably.

*"I thought my baby was changing his sleep time when we came back from a week's vacation. He was at Grandma's and had a great deal of stimula-*

*tion, but after a few days at home alone with me, he soon went back to his old pattern."*

We can see from what has been said that most of these changes in patterns are temporary, but some signify a change in level of development. Now that the babies are beginning to move to new levels of competence, mothers need to adapt to these changes just when they have become comfortable with the previous patterns.

## Differences in Mothers' Enjoyment of Babies

Mothers usually disagree about which phases of mothering give them most pleasure. Some mothers have always looked forward to dressing the baby in pretty clothes and consider that the most pleasant part of mothering. Others are more satisfied if the baby takes her feedings well; this is especially true of nursing mothers. Still others enjoy bathing the baby; some even teach their babies the rudiments of swimming during bath time. Others find each new exploratory advance very exciting and try to antici- pate what is coming next. They proudly relate each one of the baby's exploratory achievements; they wait for the fathers to come home to show off the baby's achievements. Other mothers are most interested in the baby's speech development and make special efforts to get communication going and to help the baby make understandable sounds. Mothers can derive pleasure from progress in any one of these areas, but it is especially nice to be able to enjoy your baby in more than one way. Your pleasure communicates itself to the babies and enhances their self-esteem and sense of well-being.

What phase of taking care of your baby do you like best?

*"I had to laugh when you said that some mothers thought only about dressing a baby up in pretty clothes, because that's the way I visualized taking care of a baby. I didn't know there were such things as burping, bathing, cleaning up dirty diapers, entertaining and amusing a baby. I've learned a lot, and I now find that I am excited by other things. As a matter of fact, I am beginning to enjoy all of the things that I do for the baby. Does that mean I am not discriminating enough?"*

On the contrary, it would seem that you are learning how to enjoy all phases of mothering.

*"I am not like that. I really like taking the baby out all dressed up and having people say, 'Oh, what a pretty baby.' "*

That's a very normal attitude; there's nothing wrong with it. That's why we pointed out that different mothers get pleasure out of different aspects of baby care.

*"I guess my husband and I get most excited when the baby jumps up and down on our laps. You pointed out that the babies are able to hold a little*

*of their weight now and support it, but my baby seems to be ready to stand up and climb all over me. She doesn't want to sit down. Should I encourage this?"*

If the baby pulls herself up, you should not stop her, but you should not encourage it. This is something that the baby will develop on her own. You should, however, encourage her to play with small objects, such as a rattle or block. She will learn to stand on her own as her central nervous system develops. Fine motor coordination will not develop, however, if she is not encouraged to hold and manipulate small objects. She cannot do this on her own or without her parents' assistance.

*"Perhaps we are so pleased with this stage of development because we see it as a preliminary to walking, and we are anxious for her to walk—to be more active."*

You and your husband are active, athletic people, so you are pleased that the baby is becoming more like you. Just remember that she will learn to walk when she is ready, and that she should be allowed to achieve this on her own maturational timetable. You are lucky that your baby's natural endowments seem to be matching yours.

*"I can't wait for the baby to talk. That seems to me the most important part of being a parent, and each time she makes a noise that sounds like something, I get very excited. Do you think that I could be overstimulating her speech?"*

If you talk to her all the time and are never quiet so that she can reply, you may be hindering her speech development. However, if you imitate her sounds and give her a chance to respond with another sound, then you are stimulating the development. It is very good to talk to the baby as you dress her, feed her, and do your chores, but stop every once in a while to see if she will make some kind of reply to you.

*"That's really what I do, and it is such fun!"*

Several of you have expressed enjoyment of different aspects or phases of your babies' development. You probably recognize that the baby is beginning to exhibit traits that suit aspects of your own personalities. This is very nice. It is important to remember, however, that each baby is an individual, not just a duplicate of the mother or the father. Some aspects of the baby's personality may be very different and should be appreciated and respected. When there is a big difference, it can cause difficulties. An active, noisy toddler can be upsetting to a reflective, quiet mother; a shy, quiet baby can be a puzzle to a hearty, outgoing father. Differences or similarities in the temperaments of parents and children will become more apparent as the children get older. For that reason, we will talk more about the topic later. For now, it is good to recognize that different parents appreciate and enjoy different aspects of their baby's development. Everyone does not have to be the same.

## *Giving Instructions to Baby-sitters*

We have talked in previous sessions about a parent's need for some time off from child care, the use of baby-sitters, and the necessity of using the same substitute consistenly so as not to disrupt the baby's development of basic trust. But we have not really discussed the practical instructions the parents should leave with the sitter. Whether the sitter is a relative or not, a teenager or an older woman, she should have a phone number where the parents can be reached in case of emergency. The telephone number of the baby's pediatrician should also be readily available, as well as the address of the nearest hospital emergency room. It is also a good idea to leave some money tacked up where you have the list of emergency services, so that the baby-sitter has the taxi money to get to the hospital or the pediatrician without delay. Actually, it is a good idea to have taxi money available at all times, so you yourselves are not unprepared in an emergency.

Besides these emergency instructions, it is important to review that portion of the baby's daily routine that the sitter will have to cover. The baby-sitter should know which are the baby's favorite toys and which ones she goes to sleep with. The parent should also discuss the kinds of things that comfort the baby when she cries. The parents may want to ask the sitter to call them if there is any difficulty that the sitter doesn't quite know how to cope with. At that point the parents may be able to give the sitter advice, or they may wish to come home earlier.

Parents should not anticipate that there's always going to be trouble when they go out. Usually everything goes very smoothly. You must, however, be prepared for the unusual situation. Parents need to feel comfortable that the sitter can handle difficult situations as well as routine ones.

By making these suggestions, we hope to help you feel more comfortable when you leave the baby. Emergencies are rare, but it's better to be prepared.

*"I've been leaving a telephone number for the sitter, and that makes me feel easier. I hadn't thought of taxi money. That's a great idea."*

*"You talk about instructions for the baby-sitter. Suppose the sitter is your mother or mother-in-law? How can you tell her what to do, even if you know her way isn't yours?"*

That's a situation that requires tact. But you should use tact with all baby-sitters. You can remind your mother gently where you keep all the baby's things, in case she needs them, and leave her a list or schedule of the baby's routine, just as you would for an "ordinary" baby-sitter. I can't believe that she wouldn't want to know how to reach you or the doctor if she needed to. She will probably admire you for your forethought in providing this information. She won't necessarily take it to mean that you don't trust her. You'll get her cooperation if you remember to say and do things tactfully when she's involved.

*"My mother is very glad to have everything written down because she is just as much of a worrywart as I am."*

*"My mother-in-law thinks I'm 'kooky' anyway, so she expects me to write everything down."*

*"When you mention all the precautions to take before going out and leaving the baby with a baby-sitter, it frightens me. Do you think it is better to stay home with your baby all the time, or take him with you, or what?"*

Many parents have qualms about leaving their babies even with the best of baby-sitters and feel better when the baby is with them. For these parents, perhaps it's best to take the baby with them whenever it is possible. However, there are times when parents, no matter how devoted they are to their babies, must have time to do things together. Usually this involves going someplace where it is not appropriate to take the baby. It is important for a good marital relationship to arrange to do things together as frequently as possible, on a weekly or biweekly basis, depending on the family setup, and leave the baby home with a competent caretaker whom the baby knows and trusts.

## *Spacing of Children*

Spacing of children is a topic that arouses a great deal of discussion and evokes many different responses. For some people there are religious reasons why the spacing of children is not considered a matter of choice but something that should be accepted as nature provides. If one holds such views, we do not wish to interfere. It is a matter of the parents' personal lives and an issue that they face for themselves.

There are some parents who feel the issue should be decided entirely by the financial situation of the family. They want to give each child the very best they can. They feel they should not have more children when they can afford to have only one, or that the second child should not arrive until they can afford that child. This, too, is a valid consideration in spacing children.

Other parents feel that the physical health of the mother is endangered by having children too close together. In some cases, the mother's physical condition demands a long interval between children, or there may be physical reasons why the mother cannot have a second child.

Still other parents feel it was a mistake to have had their first child so early in their marriage. They feel that they were not prepared for raising the infant, so they want to postpone having a second one until they are better prepared. Some may even decide not to have any others at all.

There are parents who want to have their children very close together

■                                                                           ■

while they are young and vigorous and able to take care of them. They look forward to a long period of married life in which there are no new babies, so they will be able to have all the fun and do all the things they think they miss when they have babies to care for. On the other hand, some women who marry later in life may feel that they have only a limited amount of time in which to have healthy children.

Some parents feel that their living conditions are too crowded and they have no room for a second child. They do not feel prepared to make changes in their living arrangements, so they postpone having another child. All of these are valid solutions to the important question of spacing your children.

How do you feel about having another child? Perhaps you have other ideas.

*"The only thing that is stopping us from having another baby is that we cannot afford one. We are just managing now. We want to give this baby the very best start in life we can, and we feel that having another baby would detract from what we could provide for the child we already have. That's our only reason for putting off having another baby."*

*"I think that when babies come, at whatever time nature decrees, one can always manage to support them somehow and give them the very best one can. I don't think financial reasons are the only consideration."*

*"We were married a long time before we felt we were able to afford a baby. We wanted one very much. We had no idea how expensive a baby would be, how much time he would take, but we are loving every minute of the experience because we had many years of our own personal pleasures and are now ready to devote ourselves to our baby."*

*"I'm afraid our reason for not having another baby soon is purely materialistic. We have an apartment that we like, and there is just room for the three of us. Having another baby would mean moving. We are happy the way we are at the moment. We may change our minds later on, but this is the way we feel now."*

*"I always thought that I would like to have all of my babies close together so that, as you say, there would be many years when I would be free of child care and when my husband and I could lead the lives that we had planned. Now that I have my first baby, I see how much work babies are, and I'm not sure that I am ready to have another one right away."*

*"I feel just the opposite. I feel I'm just in the swing of learning how to take care of a baby and that I'd like to have another one while I still have all the equipment together and the routine fresh in my mind. That way I won't get rusty and have to learn all over again."*

*"I had to have a cesarean section, and I think I'd like to wait a while before going through that again."*

All of the considerations you have mentioned are important. Each family has to decide for itself what is right for it.

Perhaps we do need to ask, "Why have another child, anyway?"

*"Because that's a natural thing to do. Otherwise, why marry?"*

*"I wasn't anxious to have a baby, but my husband wanted one so badly that I thought that would be the right thing to do. Now, I'm not sorry. We might have another."*

*"We think we should have another child as a companion for our first one. That way, he will always have someone to play with later."*

*"Well, we had our baby because we wanted one, because both of us love children, and that is why we would have another."*

That is the best reason for having a baby—because you want one, you want to be a parent, and you love having children. To have a second child just for the sake of the first usually is not the best idea. One cannot ensure the compatability or companionship of siblings.

Assuming the timing can be controlled—and these days that's one of the things many parents wish to, and can, control—how much time should elapse before you have another child? Let's talk about that.

When birth control and planned parenthood were first practiced in this country, two years was considered a good interval between children. It was thought that two years gave the mother ample time to recover from the birth process and also provided a suitable breathing space in which to give the baby a good start in life.

Now we think that three years is the appropriate interval between children. Our reasons are not related to financial, physical, or religious considerations, but rather to the effect of a sibling on the first child and of the first child on the second.

When a baby is one year old, he still needs pretty constant attention from the mother. Having a new baby at this time would deprive the first child of the mother's very needed attention. Also, the needs of the first child would make it difficult for the mother to attend to the second child adequately.

At the age of two, the child is not yet verbal and is just beginning the process of separating from his mother. He is just beginning to understand and test his own autonomy. Also, he is not yet toilet trained. The period from two to three is very crucial to development in many areas—individuation and separation, toilet training, and speech. The child's development can be set back by the demands of a second child, especially if the parents are not aware of the first child's needs.

However, when the first child is about three years old, he has already achieved a certain mastery. He can express his feelings and understand communication. He has learned to eat by himself, he is almost completely toilet trained, and he is able to play in a separate room and even separate from his mother for part of the day at a nursery school or play group.

When a child is able to do this, he has become an individual with a sense of his own resources. At this point, it may be easier for the first child to adjust to a new baby. In addition, the mother has more time to devote to the second child without provoking intense sibling rivalry, although there is *always* some of this.

For these reasons, we feel that the most appropriate time to have a second child is when the first child is more able to accept the second child as a pleasant companion and a source of new interest. Three years is not an absolute age because some children mature more rapidly than others and may be ready for the new brother or sister at two and a half years of age. Other children may not be ready until three and a half years of age.

Some parents say, "I want to have another child soon because I want to have a playmate for my first child." This is not a good reason to have a second child quickly. Perhaps you can already see there are other considerations to be taken into account. You should have a second child, not as a companion for the first child, but because you want another child. The second child should be wanted as much as the first child and should be given as much attention as the first.

*"I want to have four children. If I waited three years between children, I would be very old by the time my fourth child arrived. Waiting such a long interval between children would make having four impossible."*

We are not saying that you *must* wait three years between children; we are saying three years is the ideal interval. There are certainly a number of circumstances that make a shorter interval desirable. However, if you know what is involved, especially how the first child can be affected by the second, you will be more understanding of the first child's needs. The mother who has children closer together must be prepared to have greater demands made on her than she expected with the first child. If one understands what is going to happen and does not become impatient, then one can deal with the situation. One must expect that at any given moment the children may have important yet conflicting needs. Handling this demands great patience, not to mention stamina.

*"I understand exactly what you are saying because there is only a year between my two children. My first child is very timid and clinging and never seems to have enough of me, while my second child seems to be able to manage much better. Perhaps I know how to handle her better than my first baby. Having them close together is very difficult physically and emotionally. Had I known more, I would have made a different choice."*

*"I want to return to my career. If I take three years between children, I will always be just getting back into the swing of things in my work when I have to take time out to have a baby. So I think I would like to have all of my children close together and have their care settled. Then I'll go back to my work and know that I can keep at it without taking time out for maternity leave."*

This is an entirely individual decision that a mother has to make for herself. What we are talking about is what would be ideal for each child.

We are concerned with each child's development and the parents' understanding of what is good for his development at different ages.

It is possible that if a mother understands what is involved, she could manage to have children closer together and raise them well, providing she had sufficient help. Mothers and fathers have to make these decisions for themselves. If they understand the effects close siblings can have on one another, parents can make the appropriate adjustments in order to provide the children with what is best for them.

*"If parents postpone having more children, by the time they have their second child or third they may be too old to be able to enjoy the children. They may find them a hindrance to their lives and resent them. Whereas, if they had the second child when they were younger, they might not feel that way."*

This is a serious decision for the father and mother to make. But we are talking about what is best for the individual child. Certainly, if parents are going to resent having a child, they shouldn't have one. Children are to be loved and enjoyed; they should not be considered a burden that has to be endured. The whole object of our sessions is to help parents get the most pleasure from their children's development and to understand how to enhance their development, so that they can profit by what they have learned and be proud of their achievement as parents.

*"I am enjoying every minute of my baby's waking time. I enjoy everything that I see him do, and I wouldn't want to give up any of these joys. If I had two children that were close together, I feel that the joy I am deriving from my first baby would be greatly diminished. As a matter of fact, both my husband and I so love this baby that we are wondering whether we could love another child as much, and whether it would be fair to this baby and to us to have another."*

This, too, is an individual decision. It is not a decision that other people can make for you. Many parents are often worried about loving the first child. Usually that love develops. It also develops in the same way for a second child, particularly if the parents do not feel strained and harassed and are able to enjoy the developing personalities.

## Increased Motor Development

### Use of the Legs

As you are well aware, your babies are getting much more active. They are turning over; some can get to the sitting position alone; they are using their hands much more competently. You will remember that months ago we described neurological development as progressing from the head to the feet. Now the development has reached the legs. The babies are beginning to use their legs. Therefore, they need more room to kick while on their stomachs. They need space in a playpen or on the floor to make the transition to crawling. They need space now to use their legs.

Many mothers keep the baby in a carrier or sling on their backs while doing the housework in order to keep the baby close to them but at the same time giving themselves the freedom to do their housework. This was useful when the babies were not mobile, but it may hamper the child's development if it is continued too long and interferes with her exploratory behavior and muscular development.

How much freedom of movement are you allowing your baby? How do you manage to give the baby room to move and still keep her safe? Are you still using slings?

*"I still use a sling when I'm in the kitchen or when I go marketing. I don't want the baby underfoot, but he still needs to be near me. At other times, he is on the floor or in his bed or in a high chair."*

The sling, or pack, still has its uses, but you must decide whether it is hampering the baby's development because he now needs more room for movement and exploration. Even in the kitchen, a corner can be fenced off so the baby can have more freedom of movement.

*"That's just what I did! You just get a flexible gate, stretch it, and fasten it across a corner of the room so that the baby has floor space, is in sight, and yet is out of danger. My husband set such gates up in the kitchen and living room."*

*"My baby's increased activity has been bothering me a lot because I'm afraid he'll fall off the bed. He doesn't like the playpen because he can't brace himself on the pad, and there just isn't that much space in my apartment to put a blanket on the floor or set up a gate. We're still in one room and haven't been able to get a larger place yet."*

The lack of space in city apartments does make providing the baby with ample room for exploration difficult, but babies must get the chance to use their legs and start to crawl. Would it be possible to rearrange the furniture in your apartment so that at some time each day your baby gets a chance to exercise his legs? It is a nuisance, but then you can return things to their usual places. Perhaps a friend or neighbor who has more space would not mind it if once in a while you spread a small blanket or pad on her floor to give the baby a chance to move about.

*"But isn't it dangerous to have the baby on a drafty floor? In my apartment the floor is so cold."*

Of course it is not good for the baby to be down on a cold floor. Wait until the room is warm enough, and place the baby on a thick rug or blanket. A bath mat will also do because the baby isn't going to go very far just yet. If the floor is always cold, place the baby on a firm bed, and watch her carefully.

■                                                                                    ■

*"I've been noticing that the baby moves around his crib a lot on his stomach, but I was afraid it was too early to put him down on the floor. Now I see that perhaps I was holding back his development."*

Yes, it is very easy to make that error. Some parents unconsciously do it because they want to keep the baby on their laps and under control. The more active the baby, the more work for the parent. Other parents make the mistake, as you say, because they don't realize the baby is ready for this stage of development. That's what these sessions are about, helping parents learn to "tune in" to the baby's devlopment at the right time. Sometimes babies get ahead of us and are doing things that were not anticipated for their chronological age. This happens because the babies' maturational timetables are more rapid than expected. Things like that keep us all on our toes. That's why we need to observe and interpret a baby's needs and level of development.

*"I guess I am the impatient kind that 'jumps the gun.' I have been putting my baby on my bed and on the floor, and he just remains in the same place on his stomach, like a lump."*

Don't be discouraged; you just happen to be ahead of his developmental timetable. One of these days if you put something interesting down in front of him, he may be able to make a move toward it by kicking his legs and waving his arms. He will do this when he is ready. We have said many times before that babies usually follow the same sequence of development, but each has his or her own timetable for maturation.

## Language and Communication

While it is important to allow the babies freedom to develop their legs, it is not necessary, at this age, to spend time helping the baby to stand or encouraging walking. The baby will develop the ability to walk when his central nervous system matures and he is ready.

What is important at this age is the stimulation of language. A baby will make sounds spontaneously; these sounds will not become language unless the baby hears language. We have all heard of children brought up in the wild, without human contact, who could make all kinds of sounds and could communicate pleasure and displeasure, but who could not speak a language.

As you know, crying is the baby's first language. Her cries differ to express different needs and moods. From the cry comes the first language sound of "m-m-m." In the next stage, the repeated babbling sounds like "ah-ah," "mah-mah," and "dah-dah" are produced. Some of the babies may now be progressing to single syllable sounds like "dah," "bah," "kah," and "mah." Production of these single-syllable sounds represents an advance in development because these sounds will later be used as the names for things, the first "words." Babbling shows the baby's experimentation with vocalization. The single-syllable sounds form the foundation for the baby's understanding of vocalization as language. For example, the baby will eventually be able to associate the particular sound "dah" with "Daddy" or "bah" with "bottle."

When you hear a syllable sound, you should face the baby and then repeat the sound. Perhaps at first the baby will only look at you intently and not make the sound again. The next time you hear the syllable, you should repeat it again and show your enjoyment by your voice and expression. Pretty soon the baby will begin to respond by repeating the syllable with varying intensity, and you must do the same. Then you can offer other distinct sounds for her to repeat. As we have said before, the parent's repetition of the baby's sounds gives them importance for the baby and forms the beginning of a conversation. This kind of communication is great fun and something that both parents can enjoy. Fathers like to participate with the baby in this way.

Have any of you begun doing this yet?

*"I find it very hard to repeat a syllable or talk to the baby at all, because sometimes he looks at me as if he is surprised, and I feel so silly when I don't get a response."*

Perhaps you are expecting a mature answer; looking at you is your baby's response. He is processing this contact with you. If you speak to him often and consistently, he will have sounds to process and store for future use. When that part of his central nervous system relating to speech production is sufficiently developed, he will make a response of some kind. This is a milestone in his speech development and a "red-letter day" for you because it was your stimulation that helped evoke the response.

Perhaps we all feel a little silly "gooing and aahing" to a baby. But if we realize that it serves a very important purpose in the teaching of language, we will lose some of the self-consciousness that causes us to feel silly.

*"I've been trying to talk to the baby, I think, since the day I brought her home from the hospital. I just can't wait to hear a sound back. Her father tries, too."*

You are on the right track, but, in your enthusiasm, you may be bombarding the baby with too much speech. Why don't you concentrate on just a few syllables like "ah," "dah," "mah," or "bah"? Say them in a lilting voice, and then wait for the baby to make a sound back. Or say, "Here's Dada" whenever Daddy comes in, so that the baby is not overwhelmed. Also, your baby's maturation may not yet have reached the level of making distinct sounds. Continue talking to the baby, and one day, when the baby is ready, you will hear a response that you can recognize.

■                                                                          ■

*"My husband is better at talking to the baby than I am. He seems more patient and isn't self-conscious, but I enjoy watching the interaction between them."*

It is nice when there is some area where the father has some special impact on the baby. Unfortunately, it does not happen often enough. It is good that you appreciate this, but it should not stop you from talking to the baby, even if your husband seems to get a better response. It is normal for babies to respond differently to father and mother because they do things in different ways.

*"Repeating syllables sounds to me like baby talk. I speak to my baby when I want to in the way I speak to adults. Is there anything wrong in that?"*

If there is enough speech, and you say the same thing repeatedly, the baby eventually will talk. Speaking in long sentences without reinforcing individual sounds is not in tune with the baby's level of development. If the baby is only able to say "Dada" and you respond by saying, "I can't understand you; speak more distinctly," there has been no reinforcement for the baby. She will not know that her speech experimenting has been recognized, and she will not be encouraged to try again. Thus, the process of learning to talk is slowed down. Some children like that may not speak until they can more closely imitate the adult. But why delay the process and lose the fun of helping the baby build up her ability to speak? Of course, the way a parent speaks to his or her baby will vary depending on the parent's personality. We are only suggesting ways in which speech and the parent's enjoyment of it may be enhanced.

*"I always wanted to say 'Dada' and 'Baba' back to the baby. It seemed the most natural thing for me to do, but I was afraid I was being too pushy with him and trying to move him ahead before it was time. Some friends made fun of me, too. It helps to know that speech should be stimulated and that my natural inclination in this area was right."*

Parents often have the right inclination but are, unfortunately, inhibited by the opinions and criticisms of less-informed people. It is a shame this happens so often. So, if you have feelings or ideas about a child-rearing topic that others disagree with, we want you to feel free to air them here.

## Need for New Toys

Up to this point, the baby's toys have consisted mostly of a stuffed cuddly toy, the red ring on a string, a cradle gym, and a rattle. They may be tiring of these toys and need more stimulation.

*"Yes, it seemed to me that the baby was bored with his cradle gym, so I just unstrung it and changed the position of the dangling balls and rings. Now he gets all excited when I put the gym across the crib."*

That was a very perceptive and ingenious thing to do. Something else you can do is use the ring on a string to stimulate reaching or pull it across the floor in front of the baby so he may be stimulated to try to wiggle after it.

*"My baby seemed uninterested too, so I brought out a lot of new things I had put away. I thought he would be very excited, but he seemed unhappy and didn't know what to make of them."*

It sounds as though you overwhelmed him with too many new things. He probably would have responded better if you had added only one new toy. Although the baby may not be as enthused as before about an old toy, he still has an attachment to it. Old toys should not be taken away entirely. If the new toy is right, it will be accepted and may even displace the old toy. The parent must keep the baby's level of interest and development in mind.

*"My baby used to be pleased with just looking at a stuffed toy in her crib. Now she struggles to reach it and wants to pull it or put it in her mouth. Isn't that unsanitary?"*

The baby needs to play with her toys in a familiar way. For the most part, at this stage that means putting them in her mouth. So it should be allowed. Try to get stuffed toys that can be washed; those made of terry cloth or a plastic that can be wiped clean are best. Babies become immune to the bacteria of their own homes. While toys need to be clean, they do not need to be surgically sterile. As you may have noticed, we wash all the testing materials after we test each child, but we do not sterilize them.

Babies need to be allowed to investigate the various aspects of their toys on their own. They need to touch, taste, throw, smell, pull, and manipulate them.

That brings us to the kind of new toys that may be good for your babies now. Soft toys that are small enough for them to manipulate, that have appendages and projections that they can hold on to—small rag dolls or animals, for instance—are eminently suitable right now. Babies the age of your children are also intrigued by a "roly-poly" that moves when touched.

## Highlights of Development— Thirty-two Weeks

The baby can now remain in a sitting position unsupported for long periods. Some babies may try to reach the sitting position on their own, although they may not fully succeed. The baby may be able to stand briefly when her hands are held, though standing should not be encouraged unless the baby can achieve the standing position on her own. Until she can stand on her own, she is not ready to bear her weight when supported. When allowed freedom in the prone position, the baby may pivot her body around in a rudimentary crawling motion.

The competence of the baby's hands is increasing. When presented with a marble-sized pellet, he may take it in using a modified *palmer grasp;* but he still is not capable of a *scissors grasp* (a grasp in which the thumb is opposed to the index and middle fingers). The baby can now hold a cube or block in each hand with a firmer grasp and retain both while observing a third cube. While holding a block, he may pay attention to a cup that is offered, although he may not reach for it.

The baby's vocalizations should now be clearer, and the baby may make single-syllable sounds, such as "dah," "bah," "kah," and "gah." Parents should repeat the syllables to the baby so she gets a sense of communication and approval from the parent.

The baby is now more playful. Most of his play consists of biting or chewing toys. To be safe, toys should be too large to swallow but small enough to be grasped by the baby. The baby will also be reaching for more toys. When the red ring is dangled from a string, the baby will persist in reaching to grasp it. Parents should hold the ring so that the baby is able to grasp it and gain a sense of mastery. This exercise can make a good game and provides an opportunity to express pleasure at the baby's achievement.

## *Exploration on the Floor*

Now that the babies are beginning to be placed on the floor, they are making preliminary crawling motions. Some are even able to cover some distance on the floor moving in this way. They are entering a new stage of development that leads to new ways of exploring. They are going to be noticing small objects on the floor. They will inspect the blanket or carpet on which they are placed. They will finger the design and texture and will invariably discover a crumb or particle that the mother was unaware of. They will most likely put this into their mouths. Because these activities require more vigilance, many mothers may be reluctant to allow the baby to make the transition from the lap, the sling, or the high chair, where they have more control, to the floor. This new developmental stage requires a new adjustment on the parents' part, and this adjustment may be difficult at first.

The baby should be allowed space to move about on the floor. The area on the rug, mat, or blanket should be circumscribed so that the mother is sure the baby will be safe from picking up pins, tacks, pills, or other dangerous items. Things that the parents themselves may not notice are often almost immediately discovered by a baby.

How do you feel about putting your baby on the floor? Have you done it yet, or are you already doing it consistently?

*"I'm afraid to put the baby down because the floor may not be clean and he may pick up dangerous things. As you said, having him on the floor makes me a little nervous."*

Putting the baby on the floor is a great concern to many mothers, but the dangers of doing it can be limited by keeping the baby on a blanket or mat. Of course you can't go away and leave the baby there; he requires watching. The baby should be put on the floor for short periods when the parent or other caretaker can devote undivided attention to the baby. Then the baby can be picked up and held or put in his high chair or carriage for another activity.

*"Our floor is always cold, so I let the baby crawl on the bed, but he gets to the edge in two seconds. Isn't this a good time to use a playpen? It's several inches above the floor, it's fenced in, and you can be sure the mat is clean before you put the baby in. You can leave him and feel he is safe."*

A playpen does have the advantage of being above the draft on the floor. The area of exploration is limited, and parents have a feeling of security about the baby when he is in the pen. However, it is a very confined space for the baby and takes a lot of room in a small apartment. Also, playpens are expensive and useful for only a very short period in the baby's life.

*"I agree that playpens are too confining. Also the mat rumples up, no matter how it's fastened, and hampers the baby's ability to crawl."*

As we have said before, playpens have an added disadvantage for a baby. Once she is in the playpen, a baby, especially a quiet baby, is apt to be left alone too

■                                    ■

long without parental stimulation. Making sure the baby doesn't develop the feeling that she's been left alone is really the most important consideration from our point of view. That consideration leads us to another aspect of exploration.

At this stage, the baby's locomotion may not get her very far, but she will wiggle and try to reach a toy placed a few inches from her. Now that the baby is moving, you should take care to provide stimulation for this ability. As the baby becomes more proficient at moving, the toy may be placed a little farther away, but never so far as to discourage her. When she has taken hold of the toy, she may utter a sound of glee, or smile and gurgle. The parent should reinforce this achievement with some kind of recognition—for example, smile or say "Good" or clap her hands, whatever comes naturally. However, the recognition must be obvious enough for the baby to understand that what she has done is an achievement.

In this way, the parent rewards the baby's exploratory effort and enhances her budding self-image as an achiever. As we have said before, this feeling of achievement and mastery is an important element in the baby's personality development and can have important implications for later achievement in school. Leaving the baby alone in a playpen does not give her this sense of mastery and recognition. Of course, if the parents sit by the playpen and attend to the baby, they can get excited with the baby over her accomplishments and enhance her sense of mastery. The playpen is useful as long as it is large enough not to limit movement, and as long as the baby is not isolated in it. For some families it may serve a need, but it is not a "must" for all families.

## Setting Limits and the Beginning of Conscience

Now that there is more exploration, babies will inevitably reach for things that are dangerous: the stove, a knife, or an expensive ornament. In the last instance the danger is, of course, probably more to the ornament than to the child. In any case, such exploratory attempts have to be limited for the sake of safety. Now is the time to begin teaching the baby to accept certain limitations. These limitations should be few but consistent. The parent should say a firm but kind "No" and give the baby another safe object to explore. This substitute should preferably be the baby's own toy or cup if she was reaching, for example, for the mother's cup of hot coffee.

Have you yet encountered any situations like the ones I just described? How have you been handling them?

*"This is very confusing for me because just a moment ago we were talking about allowing freedom for exploration and now you are saying we must begin limitation."*

How much exploration to permit and when to limit it is a difficult issue. The limitations are for the sake of safety, either for the baby or your possessions.

They should always be firm and consistent; a substitute object or activity that can be approved should be introduced quickly. For example, if the baby is on the floor and manages to get near the corner of a tablecloth and is about to pull it and the dishes on the table over, he must be stopped. You may say "No," pick the baby up, and give him a napkin or a spoon to explore. Say to the baby, "Yes, you may play with this," and by your tone of voice convey your approval.

*"When my baby touches something I don't want him to touch, I just move him away. Then he cries, and it gets me very upset. I feel so cruel, and yet I know it's not safe to let him touch certain things like a hot light bulb."*

You don't need to feel so guilty; you are doing something that mothers must do. It is part of a mother's job to set limits. However, give your baby another object that he can explore. You will find that that will stop the crying quickly. If you make the substitution fast enough, it may not even occur at all.

*"I find myself saying 'No' most of the day, and the baby doesn't pay attention. Sometimes I find myself screaming. I must be doing something wrong."*

Just saying "No" is not enough; a substitute object or activity must be offered. Also, it's not effective to say "No" too often. The "No's" have to be limited to a few things and then consistently applied. Too often we say "No" when no real danger is involved. We turn off normal, safe exploratory impulses, which is not really what we want to do.

*"I wonder whether the baby understands the meaning of 'No' now?"*

The babies really don't understand the meaning of "No" at this age. You are teaching it to them by repetition of the word and the simultaneous limitation and change in activity.

It takes a long time for the baby to associate "No" with the particular activity. The length of time varies with each child's capacity and level of development—and the parents' consistency in limiting the baby. For some babies it may take a week or two; for the others many weeks. For the baby, this is the beginning of learning to understand limitation. It is an important part of growing up and must be handled patiently and consistently.

## Father's Role in Recognizing Achievement and Setting Limits

Fathers, in our society, often have little time with their babies, but some time must be arranged so that they can enjoy the baby and participate in enhancing development.

Fathers enjoy watching children try to crawl and are very proud and pleased when they see this developing. Sometimes they may be a little impatient with the wiggling movements because they don't seem to get the baby very far. But if the father can be encouraged to spend some time watching the baby struggle to reach and finally get a toy, he too participates in the baby's achievement, and his approval adds to the baby's self-esteem.

Are the fathers beginning to spend more time playing with the babies and recognizing their achievements?

■                                                                                          ■

*"You are right about fathers having no time for babies. My husband leaves early and comes home when the baby is in bed. Only on weekends, if he is not working then too, he gets to see how far the baby has developed. He enjoys it when the baby sits in his lap and reaches for the rattle he is holding."*

*"My husband thinks there is something wrong with the baby because she isn't crawling yet. He doesn't recognize that the baby is in the beginning stage."*

*"My husband was like that too, but the other day the baby actually got to the doll he put down near her on the floor and was he so proud!"*

Some fathers are not aware of the stages in development, and it seems strange to them that each new achievement takes so long. However, once they get the idea, they can be helpful in the recognition of achievement.

How are the fathers responding to the need for limitations? Are the fathers saying "No" frequently to the babies?

*"My husband has a very loud voice. When he says 'No' to the baby, it frightens her and she cries. Then my husband becomes annoyed."*

Perhaps you can tell your husband that if he talks more softly to the baby and immediately gives her another object to play with, the baby will respond better and learn to accept limitations from him. It is very important to establish an acceptance of the father's limitations and for father to know how to limit.

*"My husband doesn't want to be the one to limit the baby. He sees the baby so little that he is afraid she won't like him if he says 'No.' "*

*"I am a working mother and I work outside the home, and when I come home I don't want to be the one who limits her either. I want her to love me. I want to make up for being away from her."*

That's a common attitude among parents. It makes for a great deal of confusion for the baby if only mother says "No" and father does not, or vice versa. Explain to the father that the baby will love him just as much and will develop, in time, a sense of security because both parents impose the same limitations. The baby will learn to accept limitations from both parents. If one parent limits and the other does not, it is a good way to set the stage for manipulative and delinquent behavior. It undermines the establishment of conscience development. Parents need to understand that babies will love them just as much and will develop a sense of security when parents and caretakers set the same limitations consistently, firmly, and kindly. We will talk about that in greater detail as the babies grow older.

*"I think my husband has a tendency to be harsh in setting limits. I think he hollers at the baby needlessly and gets impatient too quickly. He thinks I am too soft and that I spoil the baby."*

This is a frequent problem because men were often severely disciplined by their own fathers, and they repeat that pattern. Perhaps we can help you best by discussing this with the fathers on the next Fathers' Night.

We must realize, however, that mothers can be just as harsh and strict as fathers. I have seen many families in which the father was the gentle, soothing one and the mother the harsh disciplinarian. Much of our parenting style reflects our own upbringing. We hope to show parents alternate ways that we feel are more constructive for healthy personality development and better parent-child relations.

## Baby's Need to Explore and Maintaining an Orderly Household

We have been talking about the babies' increasing mobility and their need for space in which to develop the use of their legs through moving and crawling on the floor. At the same time that they need space to crawl, they also need freedom to explore an extended environment. They need the experience of getting around the room and exploring. It's not a good idea, therefore, to have them always fenced in, although for safety's sake this is occasionally necessary.

We do recognize, however, that as the babies get more mobile, they can reach for things and pull them from their proper places. Some can maneuver to reach the lower shelf of a bookcase and pull out books and strew them over the floor. The baby's toys are now left in odd places, and adults frequently stumble over them.

In other words, the babies are beginning to make a "mess." If the parents are usually very orderly, this disorder may become a source of annoyance. Other parents are more relaxed and are pleased that the baby has reached this level of development. Although they may complain a little about the extra work, they accept it as part of their baby's growing up.

*"My baby is not going after books, but we have a tall plant that he makes a beeline for whenever I put him on the floor. It's an expensive plant, and he is destroying it by pulling off the leaves. I know it's exploration, but I don't want the plant destroyed. I move him away, but he goes right back. It is a big tall plant that is too heavy to move and too large to be put up high. Besides the damage to the plant, I am afraid someday he will pull it over on himself."*

This is a difficult problem, but not an uncommon one. You want to save the baby and the plant. I would suggest that you never leave the baby unattended in that room. When he gets close to the plant and makes a gesture toward the leaves, indicate your disapproval by saying "No." Then, immediately give him some other way of discharging his impulse to touch the leaves. This will not only provide a distraction from the temptation of the plant, but an outlet for the baby's impulse to touch. The message "Reach out and touch" is already traveling along the pathways of the baby's central nervous system. You must help the baby find a substitute outlet. You might substitute a stuffed animal with long ears or tail that he could pull or touch. When he does that, the baby needs to be shown enthusiastic approval. By consistent repetition of this procedure, you will teach the baby to refrain from pulling the leaves on the plant. Your approval will become something pleasant, and he will prefer it to your disapproval.

*"How long will I have to keep this up?"*

That varies with each child. Some catch on very quickly; others need weeks of repetition. We began talking about this subject when the babies were approaching six months. At that time, they were just beginning to *recognize* the difference between approval and disapproval. Now they are more ready to respond. Most of the babies at this age will stop, however, briefly, when you say "No."

*"Since the baby is moving about on a blanket on the floor of the living room, which is also the dining room and our bedroom at night, our house always looks like a mess. I am resigned to this, but my husband really doesn't like it. We always took pride in the way we kept our home. We are not fanatics, but we do like to keep the place neat."*

It is very hard to keep a small apartment in the city neat when you have an active, curious baby who needs to explore and have room to play. When housing was less expensive and apartments larger, it was possible to have a playroom for the baby. The "parlor" or living room was kept sacrosanct. Some of us were brought up this way and feel frustrated when the baby interferes with our idea of a "well-kept house."

With a young baby, your priorities may have to change for a while. This period, however, will not last forever. If you look upon it as a period of advance in the baby's development, perhaps you will be less upset. We hope you will derive satisfaction from the baby's progress. Looking at the period in this light may also help your husband, relatives, and friends accept the situation more patiently.

*"At first I thought it was fun to see things strewn around. Then picking up after the baby all the time began to get to me. Now I leave things around until the baby is in bed. Then it takes just a few minutes to straighten up. I put everything in a box in the corner. Then we have our living room as we want it for ourselves and company for the rest of the evening. It's a little more effort, but it works. My husband now helps put things in order and doesn't mind the mess as much as he did at first. He knows now it can be cleaned in a jiffy. The worse it is, the more he laughs."*

*"I guess I'm lucky because we have a large bedroom that we made into the baby's room. I keep him there for playtime. I don't care what kind of a mess he makes there. When he is in the living room, I hold him or have him in a high chair. I know this can't last forever; sometime soon the baby will want to get down on the floor in the living room. I dread that day because my mother-in-law was a great housekeeper, and my husband thinks his home has to be kept the same way. To him anyone who can't keep a house like his mother did is incompetent."*

Each of you has to resolve this problem in a way that suits both the emotional and physical requirements of your family. However, everybody involved—and that includes your husband and your mother-in-law—will have to reorder some priorities to allow the baby to develop properly. Everybody has to remember that this is a stage that will pass. The length of time it takes to pass will, of course, vary depending on the baby's rate of development, but someday your home will be neat again.

## The Development of Conscience: A Review

### The Life History of "No"

Parents must realize that a baby's understanding of limitations and his ability to respond appropriately to "No" have a developmental sequence just as learning to walk does. Everyone accepts the fact that before a baby can walk alone, he has to turn over, sit up, crawl, stand, and walk with help. We also recognize that some babies walk by ten or eleven months while some do not until fourteen to sixteen months. Some of us may put a high premium on walking and try to coax a baby to walk earlier than he is ready to. In general, however, we know the sequence of the maturational levels that must be achieved before walking alone is accomplished, and we wait for the baby to achieve them in his own good time.

Understanding "No"—that is, internalizing limitations—also has a developmental sequence. Parents play a key role in helping this understanding to develop. The first step is to say "No" to the baby and remove him from the forbidden activity. It is equally important for the parent to provide another outlet for the baby's impulse by substituting an approved activity. This combined act of limitation and substitution has to be repeated consistently before it begins to take effect.

In the next stage of the baby's development, he stops and turns to look at his mother to see if she will say "No." The baby stops momentarily but will continue the activity unless the parent removes him and gives him an alternate acceptable outlet. Then he will go back and try again until he is certain his parent meant what he or she said. At first, the baby just can't believe that this loving parent who has provided so many good things will really deprive him of this gratification.

The third step of this sequence comes when the baby goes up to the object, says "No, no" to himself, and still pursues the activity unless stopped. He still needs help in stopping; he has not fully integrated the "No."

Finally, when the baby has matured sufficiently and developed more self-control, he is able to go up to the object, say "No" to himself, desist, and find his own substitute activity. He has integrated the "No." This is the beginning of his own conscience mechanism.

*"I never knew about that sequence or thought of conscience developing that way, but the process sounds like it is going to take a very long time."*

Yes, it does seem to take a very long time, just as learning to walk does, but the time it takes varies with each child's endowment and with the manner and consistency with which the parents respond. The process is usually accomplished when the child is about three years of age.

*"We have a special problem because my husband has his office in the house, and there are many things in the office that are tempting for the baby to touch. When the baby is in there, we are saying 'No' all the time, and I don't want to do that. Do you think it is better to put the whole room off limits or continue saying so many 'No's?"*

In such an instance, it would be less stressful to put the room "off limits." Keep the door closed and take the baby in for short visits. If one says "No" all the time, the baby soon begins to pay no attention. The "No's" have to be reserved for a few specific instances—situations that will be dangerous to the child or to your possessions—a hot stove or radiator, a sharp object, electric outlets (which should be covered), or lamps that can be overturned. Kitchen and bathroom cabinets should have safety locks. A special cabinet in the kitchen can be supplied with toys and pots and pans for the baby. Here he can explore and play safely.

Parents should decide together which things will be prohibited, and each parent should respond in the same way for the given situation. The number of prohibited things should be limited.

We will have further discussions about setting limits. What is important to understand at this point is that parents should start early, be consistent and kind, but firm in the way they say "No." Parents should not say "No" and smile because that gives the baby the idea that saying "No" is a game and that the "No" is not really meant. That way, the message is not clear, but ambivalent and confusing to the baby.

To be able to accept limitations is a very important part of a person's personality structure. The consistency with which the limitation is set and the mood in which it is done are very important.

*"It is very helpful to understand the stages the babies must pass through before they will be able to accept limits and control themselves. But I can see it's going to be quite a job."*

It is a difficult job; no one said it was easy. But it will be rewarding. We all want our children to develop good conscience mechanisms and self-control.

## *Encouraging Play Versus Setting Limits*

We have been talking a good deal about limitations. We must bear in mind that at this stage setting limits should not take up all of your energy. The main focus should be on helping the child use her newfound motor and mental development in a way that gives her a sense of mastery. Play is the child's "work," and the adult needs to assist in this "work."

We talked previously about new play activities and kinds of toys the babies will enjoy and that will enhance their development. Play is also a way in which parents can communicate with their baby and a way for the baby to learn about different personalities. Each parent has his or her own style of playing with the baby. The baby learns to enjoy and expect a different way of doing things with each parent. Mothers often think that the father plays with the child better and that the child finds playing with him more enjoyable. Actually the baby may enjoy the novelty of the father's presence because he has been away all day. It is not that the father plays *better; he plays differently.* Each parent is perceived differently by the child. It is important that the child makes this distinction and is able to make an attachment to both mother and father.

## *Father's Role in Play*

### *"Roughhousing" and Overstimulation*

Often fathers like "roughhousing" with the baby. This attitude seems to be rather universal, especially when baby boys are concerned. Fathers like to swing them by the arms and throw them in the air. Some babies chortle and seem to enjoy this activity, but most are frightened, and the chortle may not be a sign of joy. When the baby is swung by his arms, a dislocation of the shoulder joint may occur. Children should be lifted under the armpits to avoid this injury. When a baby is tossed into the air, he loses the feeling of support he needs. Loss of the feeling of support can be very devastating to the baby. In addition, there is always the danger that the parent will not catch the baby in time or without hurting him.

Instead of this way of playing, fathers need to be encouraged to utilize the babies' developmental level, their new motor and mental skills. The baby can watch the father toss and catch some of the baby's toys. The father can topple the toys from a table or bounce them off his own head. Babies like all of these surprise activities because they add a new dimension to their experience, and their laughter is genuine and enthusiastic.

How have your husbands been playing with the babies? Have they been "roughhousing" with them?

*"That's exactly what my husband does. He throws the baby up in the air so high that I'm scared to death. The baby squeals. I think it is a squeal of fright rather than an indication of pleasure, but my husband insists the baby likes it. Besides, he thinks that is the way to make a man of him. Life, my husband says, is rough, so the baby must get used to rough stuff."*

You will have to caution your husband as tactfully as you can against continuing this activity. Perhaps you can tell him that doctors do not advise this type of play with babies of this age. Frightening a baby early does not enhance his ability to cope with a "rough world." In fact, it may so impair his sense of basic trust that coping with life will become more difficult for him later on. This is a basic issue that we need to take up with the fathers on Fathers' Night.

*"My husband did something different. He hid behind the door and then came out with a big loud 'Boo.' The baby was startled and cried. He hasn't done it since. He learned his lesson, and now he plays 'Boo' very gently, just touching the baby's forehead to his and saying 'Boo.' "*

*"My husband is very gentle with the baby. Maybe because she is a girl and is petite. He is almost afraid to handle her. He thinks I'm tough with her."*

*"My husband does something the baby likes very much. When he is pushing the baby in the carriage, every once in a while he will give the carriage a hard shove so it will go a little faster. He is close to the carriage and in perfect control of it when he does this so that there is no danger."*

Again we see different types of engagement between father and baby. The important thing is for father and child to relate to each other on a level that is suitable for and not dangerous to the baby, yet in keeping with the father's personality and style.

All of our concerns seem to have been toward stimulating the babies. However, one must remember that babies can be overstimulated. This makes them fussy and irritable. They may have trouble eating and sleeping when they have been overstimulated.

Some babies become overstimulated by visits to friends or relatives; others by too many guests in the house. Even loving grandparents can overdo things. Parental play that is too vigorous can also be overstimulating, as we have just pointed out.

As you get to know your baby's tolerance, you will learn to stay short of the point of overstimulation. However, if overstimulation occurs, it is best to take the baby to another room, preferably his own room, where he can be quietly held and rocked until he settles down. Then one can proceed with mealtime or bedtime. For some babies a bath can be a very soothing activity. A baby needs time and help to "wind down" after a period of play or other excitement.

Have you observed periods of overstimulation in your baby? If so, how do you calm the baby down?

*"I have that problem with my baby. My husband comes home just as I am about to get the baby off to sleep. Of course he wants to play with the baby, and I feel he should, but the baby gets all excited. When my husband has had enough play and wants to put the baby down to sleep, the baby is not ready. We have a hard time getting her off to sleep. Our dinner has to wait, and my husband gets annoyed and blames me."*

It is right to let father have time with the baby. It needs to be pointed out, however, that the baby does get overexcited and needs time to wind down. Suggest to your husband that he could be the one who soothes and calms the baby while you prepare dinner. If you discuss this objectively without trying to assign blame, your husband will probably cooperate. You will have helped him to understand what is happening with the baby, and he will have an added role to play in the baby's day.

■      ■

*"Should a baby be played with before bedtime? I always thought it was wrong. I have the baby asleep before my husband comes home."*

It is easier to get the baby to sleep if there is no stimulation before bedtime. If that is the only time the father has to see the baby and they can enjoy each other, some accommodation has to be made. Some fathers play with their children for just a few minutes before they leave for work in the morning and then while they are home on weekends.

*"My husband wants the baby asleep when he comes home so we can eat in peace and quiet. He says he likes to play with her on weekends when he is not tired and can be patient and when the two of them can be more active."*

Parents have to adapt to the requirements of their own families. One needs to understand the basic principles and do the best one can. Parents can learn to recognize when the baby is overstimulated and what soothing measures are appropriate. It is important not to become frustrated and feel anger toward the baby or the person who is responsible for the overstimulation.

*"How can you tell grandparents what to do, even if you know they are upsetting the baby and you will have hours of extra work getting him quieted down when they have gone?"*

That's always hard. It depends a great deal on the grandparents' personalities and how well you get on with them. It is the baby's reaction that is really important. You can try to explain to the grandparents that the whole family will enjoy the visit more if they don't overdo the play. Any grandparent, reminded with tact, can recollect similar experiences with his or her own children. Overstimulation is not something new to this generation of babies. The nervous systems of our babies are responding to stimuli in the same way that the nervous systems of all babies have.

*"Now I understand why our baby behaves so badly when we come home from a visit or a shopping trip during which we have tried to show him all sorts of things. We were so disappointed that he wasn't enjoying the outing, but I guess we tried to do too much too long."*

Perhaps your baby is not yet ready for as much stimulation as you offered. It will be very satisfying to you when you learn just what is enough for him. In fact, this is part of knowing your baby. Knowing his capacity for stimulation is an important part of parenting, not only now but as your child grows and progresses.

## Standing in the Crib: Safety Precautions

Some of the babies may be beginning to stand up in their cribs. Others may not reach this stage until they are about a year old. A wide time range in this area is normal. At whatever age they accomplish this, however, the process is about the same. They stand momentarily and then fall down into the crib because they have not learned to sit down. Or else they cry to have someone help them get down.

Have any of your babies started doing this yet?

*"We are just going through that now. Last night he got up during the night and could not get down. I heard him crying. All he wanted was to be put back down."*

This is another stage of development: The baby can get up but can't get down. It usually is upsetting both for the parents and the baby. Sometimes babies fall down with quite a bump. This process may be repeated many times during the day, and unfortunately also at night. But this problem is of short duration because in the course of a week or two, babies master the procedure of getting up and sitting down. If you think about all of the muscle coordination needed in order to get up, release your grasp, and then sit down, you can be more sympathetic and supportive of the baby and control your impulse to get angry.

*"I think my baby is about to learn to sit down. He stands up, hangs on to the rail with one hand, looks behind him, and tries to size up the situation. Then he gives up and holds the rail with two hands again, bouncing just a little. I help him down before he cries. I can hardly wait for him to put it together and sit down. My husband likes to watch him and thinks it is very funny. We just couldn't imagine sitting was so hard to learn. I guess if he cries during the night because he can't sit down, I may not be so amused, but I don't think I'll get angry."*

There are many activities that adults take for granted but that babies must learn. If we watch our babies carefully, however, we will see how much difficulty a baby can experience in learning how to do some things. Later on, you will see what a complicated experience it is to learn to sit down on a small chair. Parenting involves a great deal of observation and understanding that you might not have anticipated; this is one small example. It is a great satisfaction both for parent and child when the skill has been mastered.

Once the babies begin to stand in their cribs, the bumpers may become a hazard rather than an asset. Bumpers are used as a protection so that the baby will not bump against the edge of the crib or get wedged between the rails. When babies can stand in the crib, they may stand on the bumper. Then they can lose their footing and fall back into bed. Some may even be able to elevate themselves sufficiently on the bumper to lean over the rail and fall out of bed. Parents need to watch for this new development and be ready to remove the bumpers if necessary. Whether the bumpers will become a problem depends on the baby's height, the height of the rail, and the baby's competence and temperament.

*"I took the bumper out because the baby was standing on it, but you know what she did? She used the crumpled blankets and quilt to stand on and was able to lean way over the crib rail."*

In that case, you have to be very careful to come in as soon as the baby wakes and take her out of the crib. Another possibility is to attach extenders to the crib rails to increase their height. But you have to be certain that they fit the crib firmly and are not made of flimsy plastic.

■                                                                                           ■

*"I asked about extenders in the furniture store and was told they were not safe. But I found good wooden ones in another store. I was worried because my sister's child fell out of the crib. I haven't bought them yet because the baby can't even pull himself to his knees."*

Perhaps you can give us the information about those extenders so that we can share it. Some cribs have rails that are quite high and won't need extenders, and some babies are not so venturesome and don't become "climbers." Each family must assess the situation for itself.

## Beginning Self-feeding

A short time ago, we talked about teaching the baby to accept food offered from a spoon. Now, most of the babies have learned to do this and are beginning to use their hands to put bits of food in their mouths by themselves. They often reach for the spoon the mother is holding and try to advance it to their mouths. Some babies are advanced enough to get the spoon to their mouths, though they will most often invert the spoon. It is important at this stage that the food be thick and pasty so that it clings to the spoon and the baby gets some food and also develops a sense of self-feeding. Even with spoons, babies are not neat eaters, and you should not expect them to be. In time, they will all learn to hold spoons right side up and get them into their mouths without mishap. Now, however, they are at the reaching, spilling, messy stage.

Besides reaching for the spoon, babies also put their hands into the dish to pick up the food by themselves, again producing quite a mess. Some are also becoming ready for food that they can hold in their hands—for example, crackers, zweiback, teething biscuits, hard crusts, or toast. These signs of progress may cause concern because they interfere with the mother's usual feeding routines.

How are you coping with your babies' advances in the area of feeding?

*"My baby takes some of his food when I feed him. Then he likes to mess around a little in the food that's left if I don't take it away fast enough. If some spills on the tray, he loves to pick at it and feed himself. He seems to enjoy cold and messy food. Is that all right?"*

Most babies of this age don't care if their food is the temperature and consistency that we think is enjoyable. Some may indeed prefer to eat it cold and messy. It is perfectly all right for him to feed himself bits of food left on the tray.

*"My baby seems to like only a few foods. It's very hard to introduce a new food. He prefers fruit to vegetables and likes his cereal cold and congealed."*

That's another example of a baby's individual preferences and should be respected. It is good that you recognize his tastes and don't force him to take

■                                                                                              ■

the food in a form he does not like. As we've said before, forcing the baby to eat something he does not like is a good way to initiate an eating problem that may be very hard to overcome.

*"My baby is so greedy for the cracker or toast that I give him that he puts too much in his mouth and almost chokes. I've almost decided not to give these things to him because I'm afraid he will choke."*

Babies don't have good judgment. Moreover, their ability to swallow solids may not be fully developed, so they do have a tendency to choke or cough at times. It is best not to let a baby eat crackers or toast without supervision and to monitor how much the baby puts in his mouth until he matures enough to manage on his own. Some teething biscuits are very firm and do not break off until well-softened by saliva. This helps cut down on difficulties in swallowing.

No matter how worried you are, you do have to give the babies a chance to learn to feed themselves as soon as they show signs of readiness. Each mother has to experiment with her baby to see when to do this and which foods are most suitable for this stage. Pediatricians usually suggest a proper time to start the baby on certain foods.

*"My baby reaches for his food and makes such a mess that I have swaddled him in a towel so he can't get his hands free until I have finished feeding him. He doesn't like it, but he eats."*

That seems like a rather drastic solution. If you keep it up over a long period of time, you may make the baby angry and inhibit his desire to feed himself when he is capable of it. It would seem to me that there are other alternatives. One (which I would consider third choice) is to hold him in your lap, cross your free arm over his chest to inhibit arm movements, and then feed him while talking to him and approving of his eating. Another technique is to sit the baby in his high chair and give him a spoon in one hand and a bottle cap or piece of bread in the other hand so he has something to do with his hands while you feed him. Or you could see if he was ready to hold the spoon himself after you have filled it and then help him guide it to his mouth. This is the best way for you to respond to this situation. If you find he is ready for self-feeding, progress has indeed been made.

*"My baby is getting tired of his cereals, and I don't know what to substitute. I've tried them all."*

Sometimes babies tire of the bland taste of cereal. If your baby likes fruit, mix some fruit with the cereal to enliven the taste. Also, toast and zwieback have the same food value as cereal and can be eaten as is or softened with milk. Oatmeal cookies are also a good substitute for cereal.

*"I had that problem, and I solved it by sometimes giving the baby French toast. He likes to pick it up with his hands and eat it."*

*"My baby sometimes won't eat cereal. When she sees me eating toast with cream cheese and jelly, she almost jumps from her chair to get it. So I give*

*some to her. She eats the jelly and cheese mostly. She seems happy and it agrees with her. My pediatrician says it's okay."*

There seem to be several alternatives. The babies are getting older, and we have to respond appropriately to their maturing tastes and changes in habit.

*"I'm introducing meat to my baby, and I give him a teaspoon from the jar. I continue with that same meat until the baby gets used to it. I finish one meat before I start another. Someone said, however, that I should vary the food more, so the baby won't get tired of just one kind."*

It is safer to introduce a small amount of a new food (a teaspoon or half a teaspoon at first) until one is sure the baby likes and can digest it. Then gradually increase the amount to a tablespoon or two, depending on the baby's appetite. There is too much concern about variety too early. It is better to be certain one food agrees with the baby before introducing another.

Some of you may wish to prepare your own baby food in the blender and freeze it in ice-cube trays, as one mother suggested earlier. One is then sure of the contents of the food. A large percentage of the commercially prepared food is water and thickening (that is, cereal). The advantage of these prepared foods is their convenience, not their nutritional content.

## Learning to Drink from a Cup

The babies are also now beginning to put their hands around their bottles to hold them themselves. This should not be a signal for mothers to stop holding the baby for the feeding. This is still a time for closeness. However, it does signal the time to introduce cup feeding. You need to offer only a little milk or juice from the cup, holding the cup for the baby, who may put his hands around it, helping the parent guide it to his mouth. This should be done regularly, so that the baby gets used to the experience of drinking from a cup. Parents should not expect that large amounts of liquid will be taken in this way at first. The introduction of the use of the cup needs to be systematic and gradual, just as spoon feeding was gradual. At first, the cup should be introduced at only one feeding a day, but its use may be increased as the baby becomes more accustomed to it.

Have you tried cup feeding yet? How are the babies doing?

*"Yes, I've started with the cup; I had to. He reached out for my cup whenever I was drinking tea or coffee, so I put a little of his milk in a cup, and he seemed to like it. Now he lets me drink from my cup. He can't really hold his cup, but I sit by him and hold his in one hand and mine in the other hand. It sounds hard, but it really isn't."*

Your description shows that you have found a way to respond to this new development that suits you. This is an excellent way to "cue in" to the babies' needs and move with their readiness.

*"My baby did the same thing with me, and I tried the cup. Most of the milk spilled down his front, so I stopped."*

■                                                                    ■

Of course there will be much spilling at first. That's the reason for bibs. But the baby needs the experience of drinking from a cup. There are special cups with lids and spouts to facilitate drinking and prevent spilling. They are useful at first for some babies. A cup with a curved lip that fits over the baby's lip often helps in drinking. Learning to drink from the cup is achieved slowly but should be started when the baby shows readiness.

*"I don't like to cup-feed because it takes so much longer. I just want to get finished."*

Feeding the babies and teaching them how to eat and drink takes time. Mealtime should not be rushed. It should be leisurely and pleasant for baby and parent. Too many adults gulp down their food in a rush, and want to set up this pattern for the babies now. In most cases, it is impossible to do because the babies' central nervous systems do not permit hurrying.

## The Baby's Intrusion on the Parents' Time Together

We have just been talking about the time to feed babies and to help them develop on their own timetable. Perhaps what some mothers are really complaining about is not that each event in the baby's day takes so much time but that so much time is spent in dealing with the babies' needs that the mothers have no time to spend with their husbands or with other adults.

As we have mentioned a number of times, parents have little idea of how much time baby care takes. No one who has not had a baby can quite envision just how much time, effort, and physical work is entailed, especially when baby care is combined with maintaining a household. This can sometimes become a real threat to enjoying the baby and may even endanger the marriage.

When the parents feel that the baby is taking too much time and begin to get angry about it, they need to communicate this annoyance to each other and see how they both can try to arrange for more time together. They should not harbor their feelings in silence but should deal with them openly so they can decide together how to cope sensibly and positively with the situation.

Do you find that your baby's taking too much time away from your relationship with your husband? How have you been coping with the situation?

*"In the beginning I felt the baby was taking too much time, but now that he goes to bed regularly at seven o'clock and doesn't get up till about seven in the morning, I don't feel that way anymore. I'm glad when I see him awake in his crib in the morning."*

*"My baby stays up too late in the evening. It's because my husband comes home late and needs to see her. By the time she is asleep, I'm too tired to even talk to my husband."*

Perhaps you should reorganize your life so that you take a rest when the baby naps. That way, you will have some reserve energy and will be able to spend time with your husband after the baby is in bed.

*"We wanted our baby so much. We went to classes before he was born, and we decided we would put in the time needed to care for the baby by sharing as much of the work as we could. That way, we would be together even though we knew the baby would make many demands on our time. Our plan has succeeded beyond our wildest expectations."*

Good for you! That is the ideal way to handle the situation and the way most of us would like to handle it, but some parents are not as well prepared as you were to cope with the changes in living patterns a new baby in the household entails. Most parents have to learn by trial and error after the baby is born. We think it is worthwhile to discuss problem situations because they can be resolved if the parents can communicate their feelings to each other and help each other to deal with them. If they cannot resolve a problem situation by themselves, they can always seek professional help.

Aside from being with the baby and relating to each other as caretakers, parents need time off by themselves as a couple to do the things they enjoyed before the baby came.

Have you begun to arrange time together for yourselves and your husbands? Have you been able to find the time to resume some of the activities you both enjoyed before the baby was born?

*"No, we haven't gone out by ourselves yet, because both of us are afraid no one else will take as good care of our baby as we do. We don't mind staying home, and when we go out, we take the baby. We visit friends with him. That was always our main way of relaxing anyway."*

That seems to suit your way of life now, but you do seem to be a bit too anxious about the baby. Perhaps you could get over your anxiety by starting to let a trusted friend or relative take some care of the baby while you are there to supervise. Then you will feel comfortable enough to leave the baby with her, for a short time at first and then for longer and longer periods. The length of time you leave the baby should increase gradually. It will be good for the baby, too, to learn to relate to another person, in addition to his parents. Of course, this should be done only when you feel ready for it.

*"We have tried to go out on a regular basis—one night a week—so that we can get the same baby-sitter. We use a student nurse. Unfortunately, her schedule is so irregular that sometimes we haven't been able to use her, but we keep trying. My husband used to get a little annoyed that I was so particular about the arrangements, but now that he plays with the baby more and is getting to feel that the baby is his too, he has become just as particular as I am."*

Your husband's response is very supportive. Fathers really care about their babies, and they care more as they take on more responsiblity for the babies' care and have more contact with them. Some fathers like infants and are very

■　　　　　　　　　　　　　　　　　　　　　　　　　■

handy with them; others are a little afraid to handle infants and do better with older babies or children.

*"We have neighbors with a baby. All of us have a problem with the cost of sitters, so we exchange baby-sitting services once every week or two. When our neighbors go out, we stay with their baby in their apartment; they do the same thing for us. It's working out well."*

That is a very good arrangement. It's a way of extending your social attachments and those of the babies, especially if the babies play together as well.

*"We are lucky because our families live nearby, and both sets of grandparents are pleased to sit for us. It gives them a chance to spend time alone with their grandchild, and the baby gets to know them better."*

You are lucky indeed to have your families so close by. It is a problem nowadays that families do not live near each other. Many children do not get to know their grandparents, and family socializing is sometimes limited. We will talk more about how babies begin to socialize in the next chapter.

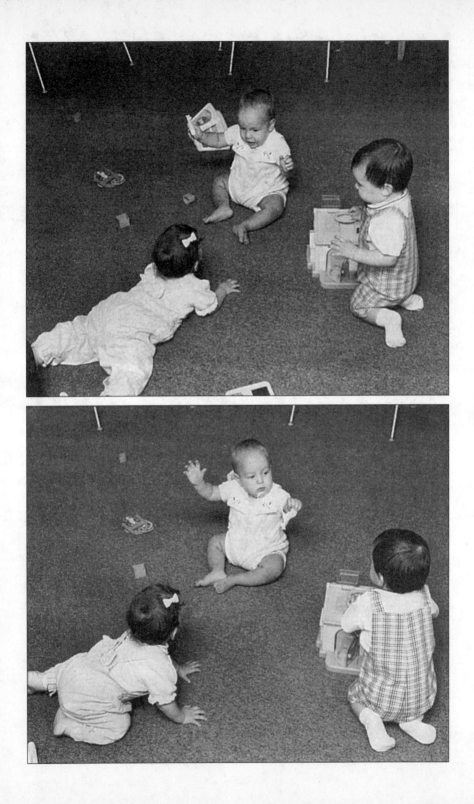

# Age Thirty-six to Forty Weeks

## Highlights of Development—Thirty-six Weeks

The baby is now sitting unsupported for a longer time and may be able to return to an erect sitting posture after leaning forward. Some babies may be able to maintain a standing position when holding on to the crib rail, although most cannot pull themselves to a standing position yet. This indicates further extension of the maturation of the central nervous system down to the legs.

The increasing competence of the baby's hands is evident in his attempt to pick up a marble-sized pellet with a *scissors grasp* (a grasp in which the thumb is opposed to the index and middle fingers). The baby can now grasp the third block while holding two others. He can also push one cube against another and touch a cube to the cup  when it is offered. The baby is now interested in manipulating the string instead of reaching only for the red ring. These advances indicate increased fine motor coordination as well as the exploration of the relationship of objects.

Babies should be demonstrating increased vocalization and making recognizable sounds such as "da-da" and single syllables like "dah," "bah," and "mah." Babies will begin to imitate sounds made by the parent, if they are carefully and slowly enunciated. Some differentiations may begin now; for example, "da-da" may become "da-dee." Babies may respond to their own names and may even respond to "No, no" momentarily. This is early evidence of the comprehension of language.

By this time, some of the babies may be able to clasp their hands around the bottle, but they still need help in holding the bottle for feeding. Emotionally, they still need to be held by the parent during feeding as well. The babies may be able to hold and eat a cracker or baby cookie, but they are still not able to feed themselves alone.

# The Beginning of Socialization

## Rough Play with Other Babies

Some of you have noticed that the babies are paying more attention to each other. When placed on the floor near each other, they look and smile at each other and make reaching gestures. Sometimes one baby reaches for the toy another is holding. Sometimes one lunges toward another, and the encounter seems rough and dangerous. Babies are not intentionally rough; they simply do not have the coordination, control, and social experience to regulate their approach. Often the awkward approach of one baby will frighten another. For that reason, the babies should be carefully watched.

Have you noticed that your baby has begun to socialize? How are you coping with your baby's actions and reactions?

*"I notice my baby gets very excited when she sees another baby sitting beside us in the park. She smiles and watches the older children playing for long periods of time. Does she really know that they are children?"*

The babies are beginning to recognize the difference in size between a grown-up and child. They seem to have the capacity for socialization earlier than we had been prepared to expect.

*"My baby is just the opposite. He screams and is frightened when a child comes near him in the park. What should I do?"*

When he seems frightened, he has to be held and comforted. For some reason, something connected with the children—perhaps the sounds they are making or their gestures—appears menacing to him. If you do not seem upset with the baby but comfort him and, if necessary, allow him to observe from a greater distance, he will eventually enjoy contact with other children. He should not be forced to engage in this activity, but should feel protected by you as long as he seems to need it.

*"I find that when babies touch each other, they are very rough. I get angry and pull my baby away when he is rough or when another baby is rough with him."*

Anger is spontaneous response on your part; it may be your way of dealing with your fear of possible negative consequences of the babies' socialization. It would be better for you to handle the situation by separating the children gently and demonstrating to children how they should play. For example, pat your baby gently with the other baby's hand and say "Nice and easy" or "Nice baby." Then pat the other baby gently with your baby's hand. Repeat the demonstration as often as necessary. Eventually both babies will begin to understand and get control of their movements.

■                                             ■

*"My baby is rough when she touches my face. She also pulls my hair and even pinches me sometimes. I get very angry and scream at her. That frightens her and she cries. Then I regret my reaction."*

It's only natural for you to cry out when the baby hurts you, but there is no point in being angry at the baby. She really meant no harm; she was only attempting affectionate or exploratory contact with you. In trying to find out what you feel like, she pinched you. In exploring your hair, she pulled it—but not to hurt you, just to find out how it felt to touch your hair. It may feel like a slap when the baby pats your face, but the baby does not know she is being rough. She must be shown how to touch and explore. When she reaches for your face, intercept her hand and guide it so she will not hurt you. Show approval of this approach, and gradually she will be able to understand what you are indicating and control her exploration. Roughness is all part of the baby's immaturity, and it's part of the parent's job to help the baby explore or express affection in a more acceptable way.

## *Visiting and Social Development*

Some time ago we discussed traveling with an infant and all that it entails. Many families do not have the means, opportunities, or time for long trips but do go visiting with their baby. Mothers often take their babies to a friend's house for an afternoon, especially if the friend has a baby of a similar or even somewhat older age. Some babies will sleep throughout the visit, allowing mothers to have some adult social exchange. If the babies are awake, they are often left in a playpen together or on the floor with toys, and the mothers stay nearby trying to exchange a few words. Usually this does not last for long because babies of this age do not have a repertoire of play activity that is extensive enough to allow for a prolonged visit. They look at each other, touch each other, perhaps even pull hair, poke at eyes, or reach for each other's toys. This is the beginning of their socialization.

The babies' actions are entirely exploratory at this age. No matter how dangerous the contacts they make may appear, they are not malevolent, just exploratory. But babies of this age need careful monitoring and managing by the mothers. This disappoints some mothers, perhaps because they have been looking forward to visiting with a friend and it seems that the babies are interfering. The truth of the matter is that the mothers' expectations of their babies' social ability are too high. If the babies can manage to amuse themselves in adjacent areas for a few minutes, or at closer range in a protected setting, such as on each mother's lap but within reach of each other, they can learn to touch and wave a toy at each other. That is all that can be expected in the way of play. The mothers may continue to hold them in their laps, feed them a bit of cookie or fruit, and try to finish their own refreshments. Then the mothers can play with the babies on the floor, rolling balls, pushing a toy to each, or playing "Peekaboo." At this age it is impossible to leave the babies to their own devices. The adults must participate in their play.

Because the adults have to participate so much, the visit may seem like a useless exercise, but it is the beginning of socializing. If repeated with compatible mothers and babies, with the mothers intent on developing the babies' social responses rather than on conversing with each other, it can be a good learning experience. As the babies grow older, the mothers can take pleasure in seeing the maturation of their babies' social development.

If there are older children present, they may enjoy entertaining the babies. Babies are often content for a long time merely watching older children at play. This is a good experience for them and a boon to both mothers.

Have you begun to take your babies on visits? How have these visits worked out?

*"I go visiting only on rainy days when we can't go to the park and it would be misery to be penned up all day. At first, my baby sits in my lap and plays with the spoon while I try to have coffee. My friend has a younger baby, who usually is asleep, and an older boy. The boy tries to play with my baby and does amuse him a little. But mostly I have to play with him if he doesn't want to sit on the floor by my chair and play with the toys I bring. We roll the ball back and forth while I get in a word or two with my friend. Sometimes it works well, and I feel refreshed by the visit. Sometimes her baby is cranky or her son is cross, and the visit doesn't work, so I go home. But the length of time I can stay at her house is getting longer."*

*"That's exactly my experience. I'm glad to know it's the same for someone else. I'm told by my mother-in-law that I 'give in' to the baby too much. She thinks I should let him cry while I have my coffee and not hold him and play with him. She thinks he should have 'visiting manners' at this age. She says her children behaved better."*

Members of the older generation forget at what ages their babies developed "social manners." Your mother-in-law is probably recalling her children at a later stage in their development. For this age you and your baby are "doing your thing" appropriately. "Manners" are not learned until a very much later stage and should not be the concern of parents of babies in this age.

*"I find that the best way for me to socialize is to go walking with my friends when the baby is in the carriage watching the scenery or sleeping and their babies are doing the same. When we are in each other's houses, we can't talk; we just have to tend to the babies. If we sit down for coffee with the children in our laps, they may reach for and spill something. Coffee is too much of a hassle now, so we just settle for a Coke. At least that is not hot and can't hurt the babies if it spills on them. It worked out all right if you*

*don't expect more. I know that babies grow fast and that this time will pass."*

That's a good compromise and a realistic attitude.

*"I just can't see taking the baby out visiting when the visit is likely to end up in disaster. First of all, there is so much gear to get ready—the diapers, the bottle, a change of clothes, the toys, the cookies. Then undressing the baby when you get there and redressing him to go home. It just doesn't seem worth the bother. I think I'm just going to wait till my baby is older and less is needed."*

It may seem like a great deal of work to go visiting with a baby. If you have enough company at home and you don't feel isolated and deprived, that is certainly a reasonable attitude to have. Each parent has to suit his or her own needs and personality. However, you should also recognize that socialization is an important part of growing up and some provision needs to be made for it.

## Entertaining at Home

Now that the babies are older, you should try to resume your social life. You might begin doing this by inviting a couple or two over for the evening when the baby is asleep.

Parents often think that the babies sense that something is going on and choose just that night not to go to sleep at the expected time. This may, in fact, happen. The mother may hurry the baby just a little because she is anxious to get the baby to bed. The baby senses this and reacts in the only way he can—by crying or being irritable. Or, when preparing for company, the mother may change the schedule a little; she may keep the baby waiting for something or let the baby get a bit overtired while she is preparing for her company. Then the baby makes his displeasure known by fussing and has more difficulty settling down to sleep.

These reactions by the babies do not mean parents ought not to entertain. You simply must take a more casual attitude to the company, or plan ahead, so that preparations are simplified. If the plans are not carried out as carefully as prior to the baby's arrival, no one will mind. The important thing is to be able to be together with friends—not whether the silver is polished or the table is set before your guests arrive. Good friends can always pitch in and help after they arrive if all is not ready in advance. Some such compromises may have to be made.

There are some parents who have been accustomed to entertaining a great deal by dividing the work. They can continue this after the baby comes. One parent attends to the baby's needs, and the other prepares for the company. After the baby has been taken care of, they both tackle what still remains to be done.

Sometimes one's guests have children, too, and know what to expect. They can be useful and not critical. They, too, are glad to get out again and value the adult companionship more than the decor or the kind of refreshments offered. Of course, there is always the shortcut of sending out for Chinese food, fried chicken, or pizza.

Have you begun to entertain company again? How have you been handling the situation?

*"It's funny that this should be brought up now, because last night for the first time since the baby came we asked my husband's boss and his wife over to see the baby and have dinner. We had been very friendly with them before the baby came, but I thought having them over would be a nice gesture. I cooked the night before and had everything ready. It only needed to be heated, and my husband brought home the dessert. So it really wasn't a big deal."*

*"They came a little earlier than expected, just as the baby was getting his bath, so I invited them to watch. They seemed to enjoy this, and the baby's schedule wasn't interrupted. They waited until I had fed him and put him to bed as usual. Everything went off well, but if I'd known they would get there before the baby was bathed and fed, I'd have been a bundle of nerves, and things would have been a mess."*

It really takes guts to ask the boss and his wife as your first guests, but you managed very well. What you describe is the kind of anxious state some people can get into by anticipating the worst. Just taking things as they come, and not worrying about the impression you make on the boss or any other guest, makes everything come out more comfortably.

*"She was very lucky the baby went off to sleep as usual. That isn't what happened to me when I invited some relatives over. I purposely invited them for after the baby's bedtime, but they came early, played with the baby, and got him overexcited. Then I had to hold the baby in my arms for almost half an hour to quiet him down. I guess I should have been glad my guests were so interested in the baby, but I was really concerned about not being ready for them."*

You may have been too concerned, and the baby may have sensed that. However, if visitors do come at bedtime, there is nothing wrong in telling them that the baby will be too stimulated to go to sleep if they play with him. Just ask them to look at him and leave the room, so the baby can be put to bed. You can say very pleasantly: "It's his bedtime now, so it's best just to have a 'look-see.' That way, he won't get too excited and not be able to go off to sleep." Very often, the father can say this as he leads the guests into the room in which the baby is being cared for, or the mother may say it if the father is taking care of the baby.

*"What can you do when visitors come during the day? Suppose the baby isn't napping, and they hop all over and upset him?"*

Some babies, depending on their stage of development and personality, take to strangers and can be amused by the visitors while you prepare something, provided you are close by and in sight. If the babies are going through the period of stranger anxiety, they may howl. In that case, the baby's interests have to be defended. The baby has to be held close and the visitors asked to pay no attention to the baby and allow him to get used to their presence. Later, the baby will respond to their advances if they are gentle and not intrusive.

The parent can ease the way a little by having the visitor offer the baby one of his favorite toys or a cookie or dangle some object, not too vigorously, to attract the baby's attention. When parents know their baby's temperament and stage of development, they can guide the visitor so that the encounter will be as pleasant as possible.

If all of this fails, just take the baby into another room, settle him down, and go on with his regular schedule. If the visit works, fine. If not, ask the friends back for another visit when the baby is asleep. There is no need to feel embarrassed or guilty if such visits aren't successful the first time.

*"Well, if you are always catering to the babies like that, how will they ever get to be sociable, and how will we ever get to have friends around during the day?"*

Adults who have no experience with babies have to be helped to understand their needs. The baby will learn gradually as he develops and is exposed to social situations with which he can cope. His coping repertoire increases as his successful encounters with visitors increase. It is important for the baby to have a sense of parental support and understanding rather than to feel their displeasure and disappointment at his social failures. This is not catering to the baby but moving with the baby's readiness to socialize.

*"What do you do if the baby fusses when you go visiting at a house where there are no children and the grown-ups make a big fuss over your baby? They are practically standing on their heads to entertain the baby, and still he responds to them so negatively."*

If you know from previous experience that the baby responds that way to strange people and places, warn the hosts. Tell them in advance that he is at the stage when he gets very upset if new people make advances to him, and that he needs to look the situation over and relax. Always take some of his favorite toys with you to distract him. Hold him yourself; don't let anyone take him from you. For example, the natural thing for the host to do is offer to hold the baby while you remove your coat. Don't let the host have the baby. Also, talk to the baby in a comforting, reassuring voice, and soon he will relax and be his usual self.

*"That's what happened to me on my first visit to old friends of the family. I was so embarrassed, and my husband was a little angry with the baby, which made matters worse. Finally I took the baby, held him, and walked*

*around the living room showing him things. He gradually settled down. Then I gave our host the baby's favorite rattle to hand to him, and he was all smiles. The rest of the visit was fine. My husband thought the baby was spoiled because he cried."*

That seems to be the usual interpretation adults make when the baby doesn't fulfill their expectations. The baby is not a "spoiled" baby because he is upset in a new situation which he does not understand. He expresses his anxiety in the only way he knows how—by crying. It is the parents' job to understand him and his need, and not to be so concerned with the reactions of other adults. The baby is not able to say: "I don't know you. I don't know if I can trust you. So just let me get used to you, please, and decide if I like you." That's what he is saying when he is crying. He is not spoiled; he is frightened.

The parents are a little frightened at first, too, because they think their visit is going to be disrupted. They are afraid that they won't have a good time, that their friends won't invite them again. They think: "We're doomed to having to stay home with the baby all the time. What a brat we are raising." That's not the case at all. Parents often feel that way because of their own inexperience. That's the reason for talking over such situations. The babies will gradually learn about socializing from happy visits, and visiting will get easier.

## Current Manifestations of Separation Anxiety

We have mentioned before the stage that a baby passes in learning to separate from the mother. At present, our babies are becoming much more active physically. They are beginning to crawl, stand, and adventure beyond Mother's lap. But they still need to see the parent. They still do not know the parent exists when the parent is out of sight.

For some babies, being put to bed at night causes separation anxiety. Some cry and need to be patted to sleep or have a parent by the bed until they fall asleep. Others cry when the parent leaves the room to answer the doorbell or go to the bathroom. This is distressing and annoying for mothers and fathers unless they understand the baby's need to keep them in sight. Parents need to learn to deal appropriately with the situation. Instead of getting angry or frustrated, you should call to the baby, return as quickly as possible, and reassure the baby. You might even take the baby with you on such errands.

What experiences with this stage of attachment and separation anxiety have you been having?

*"Well, I have had the bedtime problem. It just began recently when I thought my baby was getting more grown up."*

*"All my friends and relatives have said: 'Let him cry; he will get used to it.' The first night I did that. He sobbed and coughed and gagged up some*

*food, so I knew I wasn't doing the right thing. From then on, I stood by his crib and patted him a little. Now he knows that when I turn him over and pat him it is sleep time. He goes to sleep in a minute or two that way."*

You were very perceptive to catch on so quickly to his need. Some babies will need a little more soothing. They must have a great sense of trust to be able to relax that easily and go off to sleep quickly.

Some babies require rocking or singing. What do you suppose was the origin of lullabies that have come down to us through the centuries? Babies have always been the same, and mothers have intuitively known what was needed. It is a satisfaction for parents when they "cue in" to their baby's needs and get a good response.

*"Every time I have to answer the doorbell and don't take him, my baby cries. It's quite a nuisance."*

It is a nuisance to you, but it is agony to the baby because he doesn't know that you will come back. He has no sense of time or of how long you are away. He just knows his mother has disappeared, and he is not ready for that. Some babies, if they can crawl, follow their mothers to see where they are going. In that way, they can continue the attachment and feel in control of the situation.

*"The worst part for me is getting to the bathroom. It is a little better now since the baby can sit and crawl. I take her with me, and she sits on the floor or crawls around. Now she is satisfied just to sit near the doorway so she can see me through the open door. Still, when I pull the shower curtain, she comes right over and peeks in. It has to be a very quick shower."*

*"I have my baby in a walker, and he can follow me everywhere. He can even go away from me too. Sometimes he gets too far away and begins to cry, or he gets wedged into places and can't get back to me. But most of the time, he seems to like the walker, and it's easier for me."*

The walker seems to work for you, but we usually do not recommend walkers for two reasons. One is that it encourages a baby to walk before his central nervous system has matured enough for him to walk on his own. The second reason is that the walker permits babies to get farther away from their mothers sooner than they would on their own. The incidents that you describe when the baby cannot see you and can't get back to you may be interfering with the natural development of your baby's ability to separate from you and may be causing him more anxiety than satisfaction.

Walkers make very nice, low seats in which babies can bob up and down. They are best used as seats, with the wheels off, so the babies can't walk. Then the babies can enjoy the walkers as a new play situation.

There is another objection to using walkers: They have a tendency to tip over easily. Babies really need to be watched when they are using them.

This stage of the process of separation is tough for both parents and children. Accommodations need to be made. Babies learn to be independent individuals by separating gradually from their parents; yet parents need to get out together and renew some of their activities. We recognize the needs of both babies and parents. How can we satisfy everyone's needs?

One of the ways of solving this problem is to leave the baby with a relative the baby is familiar with. That used to be the commonest solution when there were large, extended families living together. It's not so easy to do now. Often we have to rely on friends the baby knows and likes.

If it is not possible to have the baby with familiar relatives or friends, you should arrange for a regular baby-sitter. We have discussed this before, but it is an important topic, and you may wish to discuss it further. Adequate substitute child care is one of the most frequent problems for parents.

*"I am lucky. My baby is very happy with her grandmother. I can take the baby to her grandmother's house, and she seems happy there. My mother comes to our house if we need her help at night. I thought the baby didn't notice when I left, but she does get excited when I come back and only wants me to hold her."*

She likes her grandmother, but she still needs you, as evidenced by her clinging when you come back. It's a good idea to make your departure brief and have the caretaker get the baby quickly involved in something interesting. Then, make your return enthusiastic by picking the baby up and holding her close. Emphasize your return, rather than your departure.

*"The other day I was out from 9:30 in the morning until 9:30 at night. The sitter said the baby did all right, but for the next few days he was clinging to me all the time and wanted to be held."*

Twelve hours was a very long time to leave a baby. He missed you in ways the baby-sitter did not recognize or report, but he let you know by his clinging. If you must leave for such a long time, it is a good idea to prepare the baby for such extended absences by leaving for a short time, an hour or two at first, and then gradually lengthening the time so the baby gets accustomed gradually to the longer separations.

*"My baby cries so when I put on my coat to go out that I have taken to sneaking out because I can't bear the crying. But when I come back, he cries and clings. It happens more and more each time, and it's annoying. We do have to go out some of the time."*

Sneaking out never pays off. It is better for the baby to see you go and then be engaged by the sitter in some pleasant activity. Sometimes the activity of going to the window and waving "Bye-bye" is engaging enough. Then make the homecoming the important event.

When a parent sneaks out and the baby suddenly finds the parent gone, he is usually very upset. He loses his sense of trust in the parent and does not let that parent out of sight again because he never knows when the parent may disappear. However, if the baby gets used to saying "good-bye" to you and then begins to remember that you do return, his basic trust is not undermined, and he can begin to deal with separation. Sneaking out is a common practice because it appears easier, but it starts the parent on the deplorable road of dealing with a child deceptively. We will be discussing the importance of dealing honestly with our children again, because it is so important for healthy character development.

## *Parents' Feelings About Their Changed Lives*

Now that the babies are older, they may be affecting parents' lives in different ways. The babies' level of development requires new attitudes on the part of the parents. What changes have you been noticing?

*"For one thing—and I think it affects me most—I can't get out as often. I think my husband feels the same, don't you?"*

*"Yes, if we want to go out at night we have to get a baby-sitter. So that means I can't come home and spontaneously suggest going to a movie, or visiting friends, or taking a walk. Such things become a project. It used to gripe me a little at first, but not so much now. Of course, it's more a problem for my wife; she's the one who has to make all the arrangements."*

*"When I come home at night, I'm tired. I'm glad that we are not going out the way we used to. I'm happy to play with the baby and help put him to bed. Then I watch TV. I guess that's dull for my wife. I'm more ready to go out weekends."*

*"I don't mind not going out during the week. I'm pooped at the end of the day. I do wish I could sleep late one morning once in a while on weekends. We go out shopping with the baby during the day or just walking or visiting. At night we get a sitter, or we exchange sitting services with a neighbor. But I do miss the morning sleep on weekends."*

*"Well, I like to play golf weekends. It's no fun for my wife to wait at the golf course with the baby, so she stays home. This has caused some hard feelings at times, so now I stop by noon or early afternoon. That way, we have some of the day together to do what she wants."*

*"It took me a while to adjust to my husband's golf, but then I figured that he's cooped up all week and needs exercise and unwinding. If I want to go out, I can go out with the baby. Sometimes I get a baby-sitter or leave the baby with my mother and go to the golf course too. I stopped feeling like a martyr, and we're all happier, but it took a little time. We both have had to give up a little for the baby. We're young. He'll grown up. We'll have time together later."*

*"What seemed to bother us most was dinnertime. That used to be the time that the baby cried most, and needed most attention, and was hardest to*

*handle. Sometimes we couldn't get him to bed so easily. When I came home, dinner was never ready, my wife was a wreck, and I got mad. Now the baby is older, he goes to bed more regularly and easily, and I enjoy putting him to bed while my wife gets dinner ready. We had to learn the right way to put him to bed. We developed a regular pattern as you and our pediatrician suggested, but it took time. We were, as you say, impatient, the way most parents are."*

*"The difference I mind most is that I can't bring friends home from work for dinner on the spur of the moment. I have to give my wife notice, and even then, if the baby's had a bad day, it doesn't work out. So I usually have to take my friends out to dinner, and my wife has to stay home. Sometimes she can get a baby-sitter and comes too, but that's rare."*

*"What I mind most is the mess of toys and baby junk around. Does a baby need so much? Why can't it all be picked up before I get home?"*

Each family seems to have had to make some adjustments to the baby's presence. Most of the problems were due to not understanding in advance that there would be changes. At first, parents think babies sleep all the time and wake only for feedings and changings. Some few babies are like that, but most have difficulty learning to develop a pattern of sleeping and eating. You learned to cope and helped the babies develop their physiologic rhythms. You have had to adjust your social lives a great deal. We must remember that we are dealing with a being who has to be helped from total dependence to independence, and that's a long process entailing a whole career of parenting. If parents understand this process, it can be interesting, fun, and very rewarding. It does seem that most of you have worked out your individual adjustments.

If fathers hate to see toys strewn around, they can get a toy chest or basket where all the toys could be gathered together quickly. Some fathers come from homes where their mothers waited on their fathers, and they expect the same of their wives. Some wives can manage to do that if the baby isn't too active and demanding; others cannot. There are certain things that adults have to be mature enough to accept. After all, putting a few toys away is no big deal, so whichever parent can get to the chore first should do it. Bringing up a baby is a job for both parents. Dad has to have some input, too. His share of responsibility for the baby can't always be just the fun part of playing with the baby.

*"Don't you think that taking care of the baby and the house is the wife's job if the husband spends all day working?"*

For most jobs outside the home, the working day lasts from 9:00 A.M. to 5:00 P.M. The job inside the home, usually lasts from 6:00 A.M. to 12:00 midnight, with occasional night duties. By any standard, this is a long workday! In our society, most children are cared for by their mothers, but this may be changing. The mother caring for an active child and a home rarely has time to rest during the day, although she should. So a mother is not being inefficient, lazy, or inconsiderate, if she needs some help from father by the end of the day. The more the father participates in the child's rearing, the better for the child—and the stronger the bond between the parents too. We know that many young couples are partners in the parenting effort, and we recommend whatever arrangement suits each family's lifestyle, desires, and needs. There are many different ways of sharing the duties and pleasures of rearing children.

# *Fathers' Observations on Babies' Development*

## *Acceptable Forms of Play*

We have been talking about the fathers' feelings about the babies and the demands a child places on parents' time and energies. We are also interested to learn what the fathers have observed about the babies' development and how these observations have affected their involvement and fun with the baby.

*"The things I notice most is that the baby is more fun. In the first weeks, it seemed to me that the baby was mostly pesty if he wasn't asleep or being held. There was no real play. Now he plays a lot."*

That certainly is a nice change. What kind of play do you do now that you weren't able to before?

*"I especially enjoy roughhousing. I get down on the floor, make funny sounds at him, and chase him as he crawls. Sometimes I let him go after me as though he were chasing me. He couldn't do that before because he couldn't crawl. We have a great time. Only, my wife says that that kind of activity is too strenuous before bedtime, and that I get the baby too excited and he won't go to sleep. Sometimes we have a hassle about it. That's bad, so I don't do it too often, but I miss it."*

*"My baby likes me to throw him in the air. I enjoy that and she seems to enjoy it too, but my wife goes into a panic and puts a damper on the fun."*

*"I noticed my wife was right about the baby's having difficulty getting to sleep after rough play. I think maybe the baby is too young and a little scared. So now we sit quietly on the floor. I place a toy a little distance from us and have him crawl to get it and bring it back to me. Then I put it a little farther away, and he brings it back. Then maybe I'll put several around, and he'll get them all. This way we are doing something together, and it's not too exciting before bed. Sometimes now he hands me a toy and wants me to put it somewhere so he can get it. He's learning."*

*"I play by handing my baby a toy—say a ball or an animal or something and right away it goes into her mouth. That bothers me."*

It seems that the fathers are playing more with the babies and deriving more pleasure, but there are certain aspects of play that seem to need some discussion. One is the "roughhousing" before bed. Some of you have noticed that it interferes with the baby's ability to go to sleep quickly. That is because the baby becomes overstimulated and has difficulty settling down. This is not a reason to stop a pleasant encounter with the baby, but the father then must help the baby "simmer down." He should engage the baby in some quiet activity for a while, such as looking at a book with the baby, walking around holding the baby and pointing out objects in the house or cars passing in the street, holding the baby and singing to him, or handing him a toy to place on a shelf or in a chest. If this pattern of play followed by a quiet period is carried out consistently, it can become a pleasant bedtime routine for the baby. While the father is getting the baby to bed in this way, the mother can be getting dinner ready.

We must also discuss throwing the baby in the air. Mothers do have some reason to worry because this kind of play can be dangerous. On more than one occasion a baby who has been thrown in the air has not been caught in time. Babies are not predictable; they can swing away from the parent and fall. Sometimes, while being caught, they can swing their heads back and then vigorously forward, producing a "whiplash" injury similar to the results of a car accident. This doesn't mean that the father must desist from vigorous play, but that such play should be done in a safer way. Instead of throwing the baby free into the air, hold the baby under the arms, and lift him overhead and down again. Babies may shriek as though in glee when thrown in the air, but they are usually more frightened than delighted. It is really best not to let go of them in the air.

Another thing that seems to cause concern is that some of the babies are still putting toys into their mouths. This response is appropriate for the baby, as the mouth is still one of the main avenues of exploration. It may still be the way the baby derives pleasure from that toy. The toy should, therefore, not be pulled abruptly out of the baby's mouth. Instead the parent can try to induce the baby to extend the toy toward the parent; the baby may even be able to give it to the father and then take it back. A nice game can develop from this activity.

*"Well, we are doing something like that. What I do is hand my baby a small block, and he dumps it into a box. Then I give him another. His interest is sustained for about two or three minutes. Then we dump the blocks out and start all over again. I enjoy this activity very much. I guess in time the baby will be able to sustain interest for longer and longer periods of time."*

That's a good game because, like the other games we have been discussing, it involves motion and stimulating the baby's motor skills.

Do any of you play games involving communication, such as talking to the babies, imitating their sounds, or naming things for them?

*"I never really considered talking to the baby. He makes a few sounds that seem to be the beginnings of speech—for example, 'ah-ah,' 'da-da,' and*

*'yiggy-yiggy,' which his mother thinks is the name of his toy bear—but I haven't really tried talking to him yet."*

*"Is it important to talk to the babies in their own 'language,' to say back to them what they seem to be saying? Or should we speak to them in real words?"*

When we speak to the babies, we should use real language. If you are pointing out an object—a doll, for instance—say the word "doll" or "dolly" in a lilting tone, so they will get the modulation and rhythm. This modulation helps them imitate what you are saying. If you are giving the baby a bottle, say "bottle" ("bah-tell") in a lilting voice, so the baby can distinguish the sounds.

However, when they vocalize, making a few syllables with their own distinctive inflection, you should make similar sounds back. In this way, the babies get the feeling that their vocalizing is important and that the parent is on their wavelength. Doing this consistently sets up a sort of conversation, which is a very pleasant and productive game to play with the baby.

*"My husband does that with the baby by the hour. She talks more with him than with me. It's their thing. He couldn't come tonight, or he would have told you. It's a joy to watch."*

## Saying "No" and Setting Limits

*"I don't say much to the baby, but I think he understands when I say 'No' to him in a loud voice. He stops what he is doing; sometimes he even cries. I feel badly then."*

It is possible to be too emphatic and frighten the baby. However, if the baby is doing something you don't want him to do—and this happens often during this period of increased mobility—the parents should say "No." As we have said previously, these "No's" should be consistent— always for the same things. Then the baby should be immediately provided with an approved activity, and the parent should indicate his or her approval of the substitute by saying "Good," "Nice," "That's fine," or whatever is the parents' natural and usual expression of approval.

*"Sometimes I say 'No' just to see if the baby will stop. Then he will reach for something else, and I'll stop him again, until saying 'No' becomes a kind of game. Somehow it didn't seem just right to me to make a game of it; yet the baby seemed to enjoy the activity."*

It is best not to make a game of saying "No" because the parent is now beginning to teach the baby limitations. There may be very real and very negative consequences if the baby doesn't learn that "No" is a serious prohibition and not a game. In limiting a baby, one doesn't have to use an angry voice, but a firm tone and a serious facial expression are necessary. No matter how endearing or cute the baby may be, you should not smile when you say "No" because you confuse the signal you are giving the baby. We have to remember that what is cute now may not be cute later on.

## Expecting Too Much

*"I've noticed that when I say 'No,' the baby stops for a minute but then goes right ahead. So what good does it do to say 'No'?"*

That's a very accurate and perceptive observation. At this stage of the baby's development, he can respond only briefly to "No." The parent must immediately substitute an alternate approved activity. The impulse to perform an act has gone out from the baby's brain, and the act has to be completed. The check mechanism that causes a person to stop and not finish an act is not yet developed in babies of this age. This development in the central nervous system comes at a much later time. That's why the parent has to give the baby a substitute way of discharging the impulse.

*"But how long will we have to wait for the babies to be able to obey a command instantly?"*

Their control mechanisms may not mature sufficiently until about eight or nine years of age or sometimes even later. Parents expect this self-control now, but it's not physiologically possible. All the babies can do now is stop momentarily when parents say "No." If the baby does that, he is doing very well.

If parents expect more than a baby—or child of any age—is capable of delivering, the parent becomes angry and disappointed. Overestimating the child's ability and misunderstanding his behavior may lower his self-esteem or make him angry. A series of such unhappy encounters between parent and child may mar their relations and endanger the child's healthy personality development.

That is why we feel it is so important for parents to understand their baby's development, so that they may avoid the consequences of expecting too much too soon.

*"That makes sense. I understand all that better now. My wife and I have discussed setting limits, and I felt she wasn't firm enough. That is why I yelled so loud and was a little annoyed when she tried to calm me down. But what do you do when you understand this, and others like grandparents or friends don't?"*

That is hard because it's natural for us to want to show our parents and friends how well our babies behave and what competent parents we are.

■                                         ■

However, there are some things that have been learned in recent years about child development that they may not know. It is quite in order for the parent to explain to the grandparents, other relatives, or friends about the baby's level of development and that the goal of so-called "obedience" is for the future when the baby's nervous system has matured. Explain that you are taking the first steps by limiting the baby and then giving him a substitute approved activity.

## *Exploration: "Baby-proofing" and Setting Consistent Limits*

We have talked about the increased mobility and exploration of our babies. We discussed the balance between housekeeping needs and the babies' need to explore and satisfy their curiosity, to learn from more interaction with their expanding environments.

Increased mobility is probably increasing the number of situations in which the parents have to restrict the baby and say "No." While this limitation of the babies is necessary for their own protection and the protection of your possessions, it is important that the babies not be confronted at every turn with parental "No's." Too much limitation can be highly frustrating to a healthy, curious baby.

Parents also have to be careful not to use too many "No's" because the admonition will lose its impact and be ignored.

A baby needs to explore and have outlets for his curiosity, a chance to learn about the world around him. Some "baby-proofing" therefore has to be done. The most valuable or dangerous objects in the house should be removed from the baby's reach; safety plugs should be put into electric outlets; poisonous cleansers, bleaches, paints, and medications should be put on high shelves and in cabinets with safety latches. Parents have to provide an environment that is reasonably safe so that the child's exploration does not have to be constantly limited.

*"If you take everything that's interesting away, there is nothing for the baby to explore."*

Only dangerous or valuable items should be removed, so that the number of objects that the baby cannot touch is limited. Then the number of times a parent has to say "No" can be tolerated by the baby and can provide a good learning situation instead of a source of friction between parent and child.

*"Our main problem is when we visit one of the baby's grandmothers. She is a very old lady and has a house full of antiques. Before we come to visit, she clears away as much as she can, and she assures us not to worry if something gets broken. But we find we are constantly running after the baby and saying 'No.' When we leave, we are all pooped, and yet we want to visit her."*

■                                                                                             ■

Visiting with an inquisitive ten-month-old baby is often a trying experience. You are probably more tense than you need to be and ought to accept the grandmother's assurance that she will be able to cope if something is damaged. If you make the visits short but frequent, the baby will begin to learn what is available for her to explore there, and she will have an enriching experience. You can hold the baby, show her some of the pretty things her grandmother has, and then give her special things to play with. Since you visit often, the grandmother can arrange a special toy corner or shelf for the baby. Things the baby is allowed to play with can be placed there.

*"When we go visiting, our friends have things that are breakable on their coffee tables, while the things we leave on our own coffee table the baby can touch. Isn't that confusing to the baby?"*

It is confusing to the baby when she can do certain things in one house and not in another. So the parent should try to regularize the situation by saying to the hostess, "Let's put this out of the baby's reach, so we won't have any problem." Put out the toys or things the baby can touch, and replace the objects you have removed when you leave. It will make the visit easier and happier, and the hostess will appreciate it, even if she says she doesn't mind if something is broken. Then you'll be welcome again.

*"We have a glass coffee table in our living room that has very sharp corners and is breakable. It's just the right height for the baby to pull himself up with, and then he bangs on it with whatever he has in his hand. The atmosphere becomes very tense when he is in the living room, and that tension is getting to us. Should we just wait it out, or move the table?"*

If possible, it is best not to prolong situations that frustrate both parents and child. It seems that you are taking too much of a chance with the baby's safety and the life of the table. It probably would be easier to put the table out of the way until the baby is older and has learned to respond to your limitations.

It is also a good idea to have a place in each room with toys, cloth books, or blocks—pots and pans in the kitchen—that the baby is allowed to touch and manipulate. If the baby goes where he shouldn't, say "No" firmly, pick him up, and take him to the area where he is allowed to touch everything, giving affirmative approval by the tone of voice and words ("This is for baby," "Good," "How nice").

Parents must realize that the "No-No" items are very tempting. The babies are not at the stage where they can remember the "No" yet and control their desires. The procedure of saying "No" and providing an approved substitute will take several months before it will finally yield results and the baby gets the idea. The length of time varies with each baby.

■                                                                      ■

*"I know it's important to be consistent with the 'No's,' but sometimes the baby is so cute I just have to laugh. Does this set back her learning?"*

Behavior you disapprove of may indeed be very cute and amusing, but what is amusing at this age may not be amusing at a later stage. The parent, therefore, has to be firm and consistent, and try to save the laugh or smile for emphasizing the achievement of approved behavior.

If parents smile when they say "No," babies get two conflicting messages. This confuses them. Parents must say "No" with their whole demeanor and facial expression. The message must be clear and immediate. A parent shouldn't test to see if a baby of this age can stop by himself without parental reinforcement.

## *Slapping and Spanking*

Some parents get very angry when a baby does not respond at once to their admonitions. They lose their "cool" and slap the baby to reinforce the "No" and to relieve their feelings. Most adults do not realize how long it takes for the baby to be able to respond to "No" and how often the admonition will have to be given before the baby learns what is meant. Parents sometimes feel the process will be hastened by slapping.

*"That's exactly the way my husband thinks. He thinks the baby should stop at once, and if she doesn't, she should get slapped. My husband sees no harm in it. That's the way he was brought up, and his mother agrees with him."*

That is indeed the way most of us were brought up, and some of us have lasting marks of it in our character structure. We are impatient with others, get angry easily, and use our hands to reinforce what should be conveyed only by words.

Such negative personality traits are usually the results of mishandling in childhood, and usually this mishandling comes about because there has been no understanding of the responses that the babies' immature nervous systems can make. There is a long lag before the message to stop gets to the appropriate centers of control in the baby's brain and is translated into action. Babies are not being naughty or stubborn when they don't respond promptly; it simply is not possible for them to do so. Slapping the baby just jams the overloaded nervous system more. In addition, it gives the baby a negative model of behavior. At some later time, the baby will try to slap the parent or another person.

*"If a baby slaps you, shouldn't you slap him back to teach him a lesson?"*

No, if you do that, you will be teaching the baby *to slap* rather than not to slap because you are providing and reinforcing a behavior model. Also, slapping the baby back will only aggravate an already tense situation and may seriously damage the parent-child relationship.

While we are talking about slapping, we might as well talk about spanking. Spanking an older child to "teach him a lesson" does indeed teach a lesson—that when one is bigger and more powerful, one can hit another person and get away with it. We have seen in our groups here that the children who were spanked tend to hit others to settle their differences. Those who have been restrained verbally, in a way appropriate to their age, tend to settle their differences verbally.

We are not saying that an occasional slap will create a violent or overly submissive child. None of us is perfect, and there are times when babies and children can be exceedingly trying, usually just at the times when we as adults are tired or upset ourselves. If we realize, however, the bad effect physical discipline can have, we can try to control our own actions. Those adults who cannot control their own actions can become child abusers. All of us have the potential to become that kind of parent. Sometimes if your child angers you, it is best to put him in his crib, call a friend or your husband, and *tell that person* of your anger. Or else, you could put the baby in the carriage and go for a walk, or put the baby to bed and wash the kitchen floor. All of us have to learn how to handle and dispel our own anger. No one should feel guilty about having angry feelings. They are a natural part of our human makeup, but we all need to help each other learn how to release our angry feelings appropriately.

*"That explanation helps me to understand my baby's behavior better. My mother said to slap the baby's hands. She was angry with me when I refused. She said: 'You and your new ideas. I brought up five and they are fine.' I just couldn't tell her how many of us have had or need psychiatric help."*

*"I am so relieved to hear that other parents get angry. It makes me feel less guilty. The next time that happens, I will try to remember this discussion."*

Being a parent is a full-time job and takes patience and ingenuity. It's not easy to keep your wits about you and act positively all the time, but it pays off in helping the child accept limitations with a minimum of stress for both parent and child. As in any other profession, parents need "time off." No one can be patient and positive twenty-four hours a day, seven days a week.

No one works efficiently if the work is continuous without any time off for rest and recreation. In industry, when people are overworked and overtired, the accident rate goes up. At home, when parents are overworked and overtired, yelling and hitting increase. Therefore, parents must have time off in order to do their job well. Then physical punishment will not become part of their interaction with their children and be perpetuated in the next generation as a model for parent-child interaction.

To summarize, then, it is best not to slap or spank the baby. It does not have a good effect. Say "No" and mean it. Then remove the baby from the undesirable activity and offer her an approved activity. Try to reinforce the good, not the bad. Make the good activity the one recognized by smiles, approving gestures, and voice.

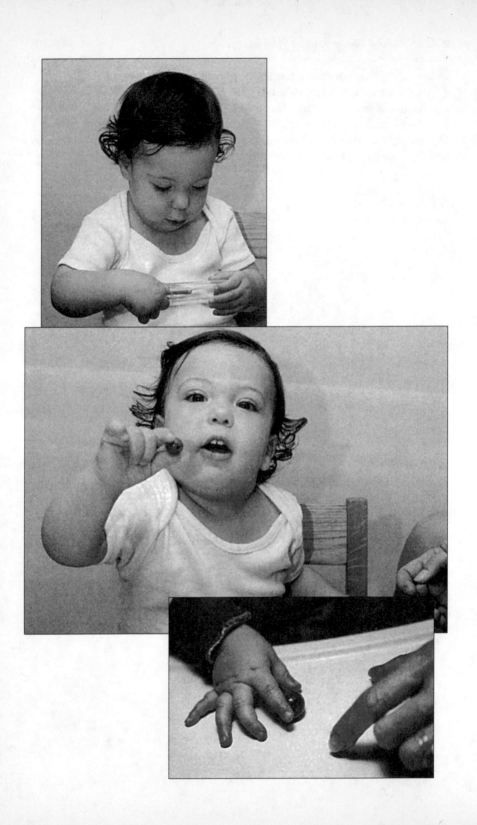

## *Highlights of Development—Forty Weeks*

The baby can now usually get to the sitting posture with a minimum of assistance or entirely on his own. Once sitting, he can maintain that posture indefinitely without falling over. He can also extend himself to the prone position and push himself back to a sitting position. The baby may now pull himself to a standing position. (The rail of the crib should, therefore, be up all the way from now on.) He may get down from a standing to a sitting position, and begin crawling movements.

The baby can now release a block by extending and releasing her fingers. She tries to pick up a marble-sized pellet with a beginning *pincers grasp* (opposing thumb and index finger) and can manage to pluck the string holding the red ring using the same grasp.

The baby is beginning to observe more carefully objects held in each hand and may try to match them together. When he notices a block in the

 cup, he may touch it but not yet be able to remove it. This is evidence that the baby is learning to understand the relationship of objects. When presented with a bell, the baby grasps the handle and may spontaneously wave or bang it. However, he is just as likely to suck or bite it. The baby may get pleasure from the sound he is making, but not understand its source.

The baby should be beginning to say "Mama" and "Dada" in a more recognizable way and even have one other single-syllable word in her vocabulary, such as "Hi," "Bye," the beginning of someone's name, or perhaps even "ba" for "bottle." (It is important for parents to repeat what they recognize of this rudimentary vocabulary; parents can foster the use of words by repetition and approval.)

Social play may have advanced to the point where the baby will respond to "Bye-bye" with a gesture of the arm or hand, if not yet a real wave. "Pat-a-

Cake" may be responded to by patting the table and finally opposing one hand against the other. At first, parents should demonstrate this game with their own hands. Then they can hold the babies' hands and show them how to do it. In time, with maturation and approval, the babies will begin to do it on their own. This game is great fun for both parent and child, as well as a profitable learning experience for the child.

# *Waking at Night*

## *Teething, Dreaming, and Other Discomforts*

During the first few weeks in caring for the baby, the pattern of sleep was of great concern to all of you. At first, the babies were waking frequently for feedings, not sleeping through the night, and getting up very early. You were not getting enough time to sleep, which made you a little edgy. Some of you were alarmed because you were afraid this was to be your way of life forever. We assured you that this period would pass in time.

By about four months most of the babies had, with the help of a regular sequence of daily activities, together with their own natural development, begun to settle into longer sleeping intervals. Many have now begun to sleep through the night, though a few continue to need a late-night bottle. In general, most of you have been getting more sleep and are more rested.

Now there is a new development: Some of the babies are waking during the night, again causing anxiety and loss of sleep to parents. This waking also will be temporary. Some of it is caused by teething. The gums become inflamed and sore. During sleep, the baby may clench down on his gums, causing pain. The pain wakes the baby momentarily and he cries. When he cries, he opens his mouth and is no longer biting down on the sore gum. But he is awake, so he has to be put back to sleep. To get to sleep, some babies may need to be changed and given some water; others may require a bottle; still others may only need to be comforted and patted back to sleep.

Have any of your babies awakened during the night because of teething problems?

*"That may be what's happening with us now. The baby's gums look very swollen. We can't see or feel any teeth yet, but she is drooling a lot and biting on everything. She wakes sometimes. It's not every night and not the same time each night. Do you think teething is what the problem could be?"*

Your description of the baby's drooling and swollen gums certainly indicates teething. What do you have to do to soothe her back to sleep when she wakes up at night crying?

*"I just pat her and cover her a little, and then she drops off to sleep. But I'm wide awake."*

It doesn't sound like you're having too bad a time of it. Now that you know that the problem is not so serious, maybe you won't awaken with such a start or stay so wide awake. You'll be able to relax and get back to sleep more easily. The crying periods come in spurts and subside until teething again becomes bothersome to the baby. Somehow parents usually get used to this periodic waking.

*"My baby has begun to wake too. At first I was very worried because I thought he had colic or appendicitis or something terrible. But he goes off to sleep again after I've changed his diaper and given him some water."*

*"You are all very lucky. When my baby wakes he is wide awake. He wants me to stay in the room with him and play. So I stay awhile. Then I get angry and say, 'You go to sleep,' and put him down firmly. But it doesn't help. He wants to play, and he cries."*

When you go in to him, do you turn on the light?

*"Yes, I do. I need to see what's going on."*

It's better not to put on the light in the baby's room but to do everything for him in the semidark of a night-light or a light from the hall. Speak very softly and give no encouragement for play. Put him down in the same position you do at bedtime and repeat whatever you say when you leave the room—"Nite, nite," "Sleep time." It will help you get the baby to sleep again if you repeat your pattern for getting him off to sleep at his normal bedtime.

The baby has no sense of time. He has been asleep for several hours; he is rested and ready for play. He has to get the message that this is not playtime but sleeptime. Sometimes the baby needs a little patting and comforting. Parents must be careful not to play or turn on the lights because then the baby thinks it's time to get up.

*"I found that out. When the baby cried a few weeks ago, I got all excited too and turned on the lights. After that I used a night-light. Since I've done that, things have been going better. But getting up in the middle of the night is murder, now that he is into everything all day. I need my eight hours sleep."*

It is hard to lose sleep. All of us can appreciate that, but losing sleep is unfortunately part of parenting. In most cases, however, the periods when you lose sleep are intermittent. Also, you and your husband can take turns getting up.

*"That's what we do, but not on a regular basis. Whichever of us hears the baby first or is less tired or not fast asleep, gets up to tend the baby."*

*"I don't mind getting up, but my husband is the light sleeper. He is the one out of bed first, and he gets the baby settled down pretty well."*

*"Well, I feel it's my job to get up at night because if my husband lost sleep, he would not be able to concentrate on his job. I can always nap in the daytime when the baby naps, or if I'm tired, I can let something go until another day. My husband can't do that."*

*"Our baby has been eating so poorly during the day that when he wakes at night, nothing satisfies him except a bottle. Now I have one ready. If he has a*

*bottle at night, sometimes he doesn't get up as early in the morning. It's a comfort to learn that the problem won't last forever, though sometimes that's hard to believe."*

All of you seem to be going through this phase in different ways. Each mother has to deal with her own child according to the child's needs and her understanding of those needs. Each mother learns what method works best.

*"Aren't there other things that wake babies besides teething? I have heard that they dream too, and that sometimes bad dreams wake them up."*

Babies do dream. Experiments show that babies have the same REM patterns found in dreaming adults. It is conceivable that babies have anxiety dreams that wake them. One of these, it has been postulated, is a dream of falling. Babies often seem to jump in their sleep as though bracing against a fall, much as adults do. Also, babies often make sucking motions during sleep, which suggests they are dreaming about feeding.

*"I'm very glad to hear that because I thought my baby was dreaming. When I come in, he seems frightened and needs a little cuddling. Then he goes right off to sleep. He doesn't seem in pain, and his gums are not swollen. I wondered about dreaming, but I thought he was too young to dream."*

There are other things too that cause babies to wake at night. Anything that changes the environment the baby is used to may cause poor sleep and awakening in the night. Such changes as going visiting, or on a trip, or moving to a new home are disturbing to the baby's routine.

Have you noticed whether a change of routine affects your baby's sleep pattern? How?

*"I go through that every weekend. We go to our country place because my husband likes to do some of his work there. Every weekend the baby wakes once or twice at night. At home he sleeps right through. I just didn't think the change could make such a difference because he is in the same kind of crib and I take his toys with him."*

First, there's the trip itself. Then, the baby knows the room is not the same: The pictures may be different; the light may come in in a different way. Babies are sensitive to such things, and they disturb their sleep patterns.

## Taking a Baby into the Parents' Bed

*"When we went away for the weekend with our baby, she wouldn't sleep in the crib the hotel provided. We had to take her into our bed. When we got home, I tried to put her into her own crib, and she would have none of it. She just cried and cried. So now we have to sleep with her in our bed if we want to get any sleep at all."*

Perhaps being in a hotel and not wanting to bother neighbors, parents feel justified in taking the baby into bed with them. However, it never proves to be a good solution. Sleeping with parents re-evokes the early feeling of closeness

■                                                                    ■

with the parent for which the baby always yearns. To be reunited and separated again is very hard for the baby. Of course, he will protest. Even in a hotel or at a friend's house, it is best to stay by the baby's crib, patting and comforting him until he falls asleep. You can always pull the crib close to you, but it is best for the baby to go to sleep in his own bed.

If visiting undoes an established sleep pattern, you should expect to have to go through the original routines you used to establish the pattern in the first place. Therefore, once you are home again, make the same preparations for bedtime as before going away. Keep repeating your routines until the baby resumes his normal sleep pattern.

This change of sleep pattern also happens after a baby has been ill. When the baby is well again, the old sleep pattern has to be reestablished.

Have you experienced any difficulties getting the baby to sleep after you have gone on a trip or the baby has been ill? Have they arisen because you took the baby into your bed?

*"We went to my in-laws for a week, and the baby just would not sleep until we took her into our bed. Then when we got home, she still wanted to sleep with us. My husband wouldn't put up with that. So I lay down on a sofa in her room and pretended to sleep, but that didn't work. So then I put her on our bed, and she fell asleep. When she was asleep, I moved her to her crib. She didn't seem to mind being in her own crib when she woke up. Now she is going to sleep again in her crib, but I'll never take her in my bed again."*

*"My baby had a bad cold, and he coughed and seemed to be choking. We got scared, and my husband said we should take the baby into our bed where we could watch him. When the cold was over, the baby made a terrible fuss about going back to his own bed. I won't try that again."*

When a baby is so ill that he must be watched during the night, it's better for the parents to take turns sitting up in the baby's room and really taking care of him. This is a rare situation and has to be met in a way that really deals effectively with the crisis. Just because the baby is in the parents' bed does not ensure that the parents will awaken and attend to the baby's needs.

*"I've heard that some houses get so cold at night that babies should be taken into the parents' bed to keep them warm."*

To take a baby into bed for that reason doesn't seem to have too much justification except in very unusual situations. Then one does what seems best and deals with the consequences later.

Most babies, if warmly covered, generate a great deal of heat under the covers, and often they perspire because they are too warmly wrapped. However, babies do have a way of moving about and getting uncovered. The covers need to be fastened under the mattress so that they cannot be pulled out. Also, the baby should wear warm outer pajamas in cold weather. Sometimes babies sleep better when the room is cooler.

*"Isn't there also the danger of rolling onto a baby and injuring her if she is sleeping in the same bed as her parents?"*

■                                                                                       ■

That is one of the reasons that having the baby sleep in his own crib became customary. There is also another reason. We now have better forms of birth control, so that the baby does not have to be kept between the parents to separate them from each other.

*"I've heard of that, too, and I guess some parents still resort to it. But isn't there any time that's all right to take the baby into bed with the parents?"*

There is no reason why, for a few minutes in the morning when the parents want to stay in bed a little longer, the baby can't be taken into bed to play with them. For some parents, this is a regular morning procedure; others do it only on weekends when there is no rush to get off to work. However, it is not a good idea to allow such an activity to develop into a prolonged morning nap with the parents because then the baby wants to sleep with his parents at night too.

## *Emergency Measures for Accidents*

### *Cuts, Bumps, and Other Accidents*

We have talked about some safety measures that are necessary now that the babies are more mobile. We suggested that plugs be inserted into electric outlets and that safety latches be put on cabinets containing pills or cleaning substances or that such items be moved to high shelves. It also helps to put gates by staircases. In spite of all these safety precautions, we can't prevent all the bumps, falls, scratches, and scrapes that babies experience. Because of their increased activity and lack of motor coordination, babies are bound sometimes to hurt themselves. If the injury causes bleeding, it is very alarming to parents. We will, therefore, talk a little about this type of accident and what first-aid measures are appropriate.

Have your babies had any accidents so far? How have you handled them?

*"My baby somehow fell this morning before we came here. I don't know how he did it. Fortunately, he just bumped his chin."*

Sometimes, if the babies have teeth, a tooth may cut through the lip or even the tongue when they fall. Usually just the application of pressure for a few minutes is sufficient to help the blood to clot and stop the bleeding. If the bleeding continues any longer than five minutes, the baby should be taken to the doctor or emergency room to be certain no stitches or other treatment is necessary.

A common mistake is to use a wet cloth to wash away the blood. This only encourages more bleeding because the natural clot is being continually washed away.

*"I thought you should wash the wound to be sure that it was clean, so that there will be no infection."*

■                                                                        ■

That is true if the injury occurs in a dirty area—a sandbox, for example. However, if the bleeding is very profuse, the blood usually washes the dirt away from the wound. This, however, has to be determined by careful inspection. For outdoor accidents and those that cause jagged dirty wounds, it is best to consult a physician.

*"My daughter fell, bit her mouth, and loosened a tooth. The gum was bleeding. I rushed to the neighbor, and she said the tooth would turn black. What should I do if that happens?"*

When teeth are injured, it is best to consult a dentist. Sometimes, when the tooth is loosened by a fall, it will heal by itself and become firm in the gum again. If the nerve is injured by the blow, the tooth may darken. In either case, a dentist should be consulted.

*"When a baby falls and gets a bump that swells but does not bleed, what should you do?"*

Usually a cold compress is soothing and helps the swelling go down. You must also determine whether the bump was severe. If in doubt, it is always best to consult a doctor. However, remember not to panic and scream because this only frightens the baby more. It is more important to soothe and comfort the baby first and then to pay attention to the actual wound. Sometimes a parent is so upset that, instead of comforting the child, she scolds him. This is particularly true if the child hurts himself by doing something that the parents had previously told him not to do.

*"I'm afraid that's just what I do. I get so excited I scold my baby. I remember that is what my parents did to me."*

We behave a certain way spontaneously and then often regret it. This is natural human behavior. It often takes a great deal of repatterning and learning new ways of controlling ourselves to get over this "reflex" behavior. We unconsciously imitate things our parents did. They may not have been perfect and we are not either, but we can try to improve. It's never too late to try to learn a better way of doing things.

*"When my baby hurts himself, he cries and holds his breath. This scares me, and I shake him to make him breathe again. It seems like hours before he does take a breath."*

The baby holds his breath because he is frightened, and shaking him will only frighten him more. It is a very scary experience for the parent. The quickest way to get the baby to stop holding his breath, however, is to soothe and comfort him. He will take another breath as the need for oxygen builds up. Natural physiological processes will take care of that, if the situation isn't intensified by the parents' alarm.

*"My mother said that when a baby or, I guess, anyone loses consciousness, the thing to do is to shake him and wake him up so he won't go into a coma."*

■                                                                                                             ■

If the injury is so severe that the baby loses consciousness, you couldn't do anything worse than shake him or try to keep him awake because you can injure him further by what you are doing. Instead, you should wrap the baby gently in a robe or blanket, keep him quiet, and take him at once to the nearest doctor or hospital.

Actually, serious accidents are not common. Most of you have taken precautions so that serious falls are prevented. We have suggested that you put carpets near cribs as your babies reach the climbing stage, so any fall will be cushioned. It is also good to keep staircases carpeted, with gates at the top and bottom. We also need to try to keep cords and protruding tables out of the way to prevent tripping and bumping.

Another type of injury that becomes more prevalent now that the babies are getting more active and moving faster is burns. Babies reach out and touch hot radiators or the oven and occasionally overturn a hot beverage. Sometimes these actions cause only small and superficial injuries with only a little redness occurring. If blisters form, however, the burn is more serious and needs medical attention. The blisters should not be broken or opened. A cold compress should be applied *at once* to *all* burns.

What precautions have you taken to prevent burns? What do you do if such an accident occurs?

*"I know prevention is the best policy, so when I'm cooking, I keep the baby in a high chair or in his playpen. But our radiators have no covers, and he likes to touch them. Yesterday, they were quite hot, and he put his hand on one before I could reach him. A big red line formed on the palm of his hand. He didn't seem to mind; he just cried a little. I didn't know what to do, so I just held it under cold water a little."*

Your instincts were right to put something cool and moist on the burn. What you have described sounds like a first-degree burn, which is superficial and will heal by itself when the initial sting is taken away by the application of a cold compress.

*"I always thought the thing to do was to apply butter or oil right away if you don't have a special burn salve. That's what my mother always did."*

That used to be the favorite remedy, but butter and oil are good culture media and invite infection in open wounds. You often can't tell immediately whether the burn is more than superficial and will blister. The best thing is to apply a clean, cold compress and, if in doubt, go to your doctor or a hospital emergency room. Even the commercial first-aid salves may not be the right thing to use, so it is best to have medical care as soon as possible.

The best approach to burns, of course, is to keep children away from something hot. Radiators should be covered, or a barrier should be put in front of them, so that they won't cause constant parent-child conflict and unnecessary anxiety.

■                                                                              ■

## *Choking*

*"I am very concerned that the baby will swallow or choke on something. What should we do if that happens?"*

If the baby actually swallows a small, smooth object, the most important thing to do is keep calm and not frighten the baby. Then, it is a good idea to give her something soft, like bread or thick cereal, to eat so that the object will be coated. If the object is sharp or jagged, and could cause a perforation, you should also give the child something soft to eat, and then get in touch with the baby's doctor immediately.

If the child is choking on an object or piece of food, again it is most important to keep calm and not frighten the baby. The first emergency procedure is to inspect quickly the baby's mouth to locate the object. If it can be reached, it should be pulled from the mouth immediately. If it is in the baby's throat, do not try to dislodge it with your fingers because you may just push it farther down and cause more difficulty. The best procedure is to make use of gravity by inverting the baby and slapping his back firmly. A good way to do this is on your lap or along your extended legs. If the object is not dislodged, place the baby facedown along your forearm (or, for a larger child, use your knee) so that his abdomen rests against your arm (or knee). Then press down with your clenched fist firmly and quickly three or four times on the baby's back. This usually causes the baby to cough up the object so that you can remove it from his mouth. (This procedure is known as the "Heimlich Maneuver.")

If these emergency measures fail, take the baby immediately to the nearest hospital emergency room. Even though an object is obstructing the baby's throat, enough air may be getting through to allow him to breathe. Soothing and calming the baby is important at this point, so that the spasms or crying are not intensified. Crying itself constricts the throat muscles, creating less air space.

We have talked about these emergency procedures to help you feel prepared. We want to reassure you that such serious accidents as we have been discussing are quite uncommon, and you probably will never need to use most of the information we have supplied.

*"If you always protect your children that way, how will they ever learn? Shouldn't they learn not to touch hot things by experience?"*

We are always in the process of teaching the babies what is forbidden. But until we are certain that the "No" has been firmly fixed in the baby's mind and that he has control enough to desist, we can't afford to take a chance. Until the babies mature and have the ability to exercise the necessary control, it is the adults who have to take the precautions. Parents have to get to know when their baby has reached that level. Each baby will reach that level of self-control at a different age. Some will learn "Hot, don't touch" quickly; others may learn not to pull down books first. It depends entirely on the individual baby's maturational level and the consistency with which the parents have pursued the training.

## Need for Exploration: Appropriate Toys

In taking precautions and safety measures, do not forget that the babies must explore. In our zeal to keep them safe, we must not inhibit safe exploration. As we have mentioned before, if exploration is turned off now, it may be difficult to restimulate it for formal learning in school. We have to arrange for safe areas for exploration and then encourage the babies to explore them.

Babies need to be able to play with small toys that they can manipulate and explore. Blocks that are small enough for babies to grasp but not small enough to be swallowed, such as the one-inch blocks we use in testing, make excellent toys. Another good kind of toy is a stuffed animal that has appendages that can be moved but not pulled off. It is also good if the eyes, nose, and mouth are embroidered on. At this age babies can pull button eyes off and swallow them or put them in their ears or noses. A rattle that can be banged against a firm metal or plastic cup and a small red ball that can be grasped and rolled are other toys that are good for exploration. There are also chains of big pop-out beads. As we cautioned earlier, the most important thing is to be certain that the toys the babies play with do not have parts that can be swallowed.

### Making Oral Exploration Safe and Clean

Now that the babies are exploring on the floor, they pick up things they find there. After some visual inspection, and sometimes without it, the babies put the things they find into their mouths, still their primary means of exploration. By putting things in their mouths, they test texture. They find out if the object is hard, soft, or just a little pliable, and whether its taste is pleasant or unpleasant. They also put things in their mouths as a reflex action because the hand-to-mouth reflex is still prominent.

Such behavior does not always meet with parental approval and often causes an unpleasant situation. This isn't totally unreasonable on the parents' part, of course, but it may seem so to the baby. He has just discovered this exciting object when suddenly mother or father pounces on him and removes it. Perhaps it is some small object that he could swallow or might aspirate and cause choking.

The parent is right to remove the object for the baby's safety. How the parent handles the situation, however, makes a great deal of difference. The parent can frighten the child by grabbing the object too suddenly. So it is best to offer a substitute as you remove the dangerous object from the child's grasp. It is important to try to make the situation a learning experience for the child, so that he comes to understand what he should not put in his mouth.

What experience with such situations have you had? How are you handling them?

■                                                                          ■

*"I am really afraid to let the baby crawl on the floor because we have a dog and it sheds all over the rug. I don't know just what the baby may pick up, so I only let him crawl in his own room. That has a limoleum floor I can keep clean. When the baby is in the living room, he has to stay in the playpen or his high chair."*

Limiting the child in this way for a short time may work, but soon it will seriously limit the variety of his experiences.

*"Why don't you vacuum the rug just before you put the baby on the floor? We don't have a dog or a cat, but I always vacuum the floor so it will be clean for the baby."*

*"Of course, it helps to vacuum, but, somehow or other, my baby always manages to find something I missed. He puts it right into his mouth, if I'm not watching. He especially likes to pick up cigarette butts and matches."*

These are items that should be kept out of the baby's reach. If he should get hold of something like that, it has to be taken away. Then it is important to give the baby something more suitable to play with. Babies like to play with tops of jars, cups, and sets of measuring spoons on a chain or string. It is well to keep a supply of suitable play objects handy wherever the baby is playing on the floor.

*"My baby is crazy about paper. He can spot the smallest piece before I do, and right into his mouth it goes. I scoop it out because I'm afraid he'll choke on it."*

*"My baby is wild about paper too—the newspaper, magazines, cellophane wrappers—all those things. At first he crumples them because he likes the sound and feel. Then he pulls a piece off and plops it into his mouth. I take it out. When he does it again, I just take the paper away."*

Babies go through a stage of enjoying playing with paper. At first it's the sound and feel that interests them, but everything ends up in their mouths. Babies are not very discriminating about their tastes, at least from our point of view. Babies also like the feeling of mastery involved in being able to tear the paper. Some exploration of paper needs to be allowed. Chewing on paper has to be limited because occasionally babies do gag or choke on it. They should never be left alone with paper; someone needs to keep a good watch on this part of their activities. This stage will also pass as the babies become more competent and have new interests.

*"What about toys that drop on the floor? Do they all have to be washed before giving them back to the baby? I was taught that it was unsanitary to let them play with things that had fallen on the floor, and at first I used to be running back and forth washing everything that fell. It got to be too much."*

*"I did that at first too, but now I just wipe off the toy a little and give it back."*

We used to make a big fuss about making sure the baby's things were sterile. We know now that the baby develops some immunity to the germs around his own home. It is sufficient to wash toys off once a day or more often if they get sticky or visibly dirty. It's impossible and unnecessary to try to keep everything about the baby as sterile as an operating room. The baby could not develop natural immunity that way. If you are outside, however, and the toy drops on the street or in the bus, it should be washed. When you are outside, it's a good idea to have some kind of toy that you can attach to the baby's jacket with a ribbon or string so that when he drops it, it doesn't fall to the ground. A set of measuring spoons or the red ring is good for this purpose.

When we take an educated guess about which is better for babies— constant restriction in the cause of cleanliness or exploration in the cause of learning—it's probably better to allow exploration—in most cases, anyway. Parents have to deal with their own backgrounds and inclinations and make the compromises that suit them best. However, some avenues of exploration must be left open to the baby. Much that parents often call "naughty" is really exploration and should be recognized as such.

*"I used to feel that the baby was 'naughty' or trying to test me when he dropped a toy on the floor. Then I would take it to the sink, wash it, and bring it back. Then he'd drop it again. I used to get angry until I understood he was exploring and wasn't doing it just to annoy me. Now I stop picking up when I'm tired of picking up and do something else with him. I don't get angry. It's a help to understand what he is trying to do."*

The babies need to have small toys to play with so that they can learn to manipulate them. Putting these objects in their mouths is a natural exploratory avenue for the baby. After putting the toy in her mouth, the baby tries to use it in other ways. She may bang it against something, push it along a table, or drop it. These are all experiences the baby needs to have to help her understand the world around her. This early understanding of space is essential to the later understanding of mathematics and other types of learning.

## More on Feeding

### Preparation and Temperature of Food

As the babies get older, their preferences for certain foods may become more pronounced. Besides trying to offer babies a nice variety of foods, most mothers are also very careful about the temperature of the food. They put the jars in hot water or put the portions to be eaten in a special hot plate. Then, much to their surprise, the baby doesn't want the food. If left in front of him, he may play with it, mushing it up all over his tray. This is very upsetting to mothers, who want the babies to eat the food when it is nice and warm.

Have you had this experience yet?

*"This happens to me at least once every day. I get the cereal ready. It's nice warm and appetizing. When I give it to the baby, he just clamps his mouth shut*

*and won't take it. So I take it away without a fuss. Then sometimes just before I throw it out when it's cold and congealed, I take a chance and offer it again. That's just the way he wants it."*

You were doing what you thought was correct. Indeed, that is the way mothers are instructed to serve the baby's food, particularly the bottle—at body temperature. We often test the temperature to see if it is just right by squirting a little of the formula on our wrist. That's a time-honored procedure. It just so happens, however, that some babies like their food best when it is cold and we are ready to discard it.

*"Is it possible to give the baby cold things? Doesn't everything have to be heated up to room temperature?"*

That's what was always taught in pediatric and nursing classes. However, some recent studies have reported that there were no ill effects from giving the baby the formula cold from the refrigerator. The food was warmed by the baby's body heat as it was consumed. So perhaps all our efforts to heat food are not entirely necessary for every baby. Perhaps heating food is only a cultural matter and not a natural need. Some babies are very slow in eating; by the time they get halfway through a meal the food is cold, but they seem to like it all the same.

*"My baby does that, and it makes me angry because I have taken such pains to get the food just right, and I try to hurry his eating so he'll get it while it is still warm. It makes me very tense."*

Being tense when feeding the baby and trying to hurry the eating process, which should be leisurely and pleasant for both of you, may make the baby a poor eater. As we have said before, it is important not to make the mealtime a battleground between parent and child.

*"I guess that's a carryover from my mother. That's the way she fed me. When she comes over, if I don't get the next spoonful into his mouth before he has quite swallowed the first one, she criticizes me. If he dawdles a little, she gets frantic."*

That can't be a very pleasant experience for any of us. Perhaps you could explain to your mother that the baby is really a good eater. Nothing serious will occur if he takes a little longer and the food cools a little. Tell her you discussed this with a doctor, and you were advised not to hurry the baby.

*"You don't know my mother!"*

We are not trying to prove grandparents wrong. They did what they were taught was best. In many instances, they are still correct. You must realize that child rearing wasn't so easy for them either. But some new things have been learned about child development since they brought up their children, and they probably would like to hear these ideas. Many ideas we teach here have been documented by careful observers and experimenters and should be shared with grandparents, other relatives, and neighbors.

*"My baby has a funny way of eating. I hesitate to mention it, but it has been bothering me. When I feed him, some of the food drops on the tray table on his high chair. That's just the food he is most anxious to eat. He doesn't seem to care for what's in the spoon. He'd much rather put his fingers in the food on the tray, mush it up, and then put it in his mouth. If I wipe it away, he gets irritable because that's what he wants. So he takes one spoonful that I feed him and some from the table with his hands, then another spoonful from me and then more with his own hands."*

## Readiness for Self-Feeding

Babies often do that. They are getting pleasure from the ability to feed themselves on their own. This is often the way self-feeding begins. Perhaps your baby is signaling that he is ready to try feeding himself. Some babies like to hold a spoon in their hands and feel that they are participating in the feeding. You can help the baby dip the spoon into thick food so it will adhere to the spoon long enough for him to get some of it into his mouth. This is a great achievement for the baby.

*"But it makes such a mess!"*

There are many things about a baby that are messy by adult standards, but babies are messy and clumsy while they are developing certain skills like eating or walking. They are not ready to be neat, and adults should not expect them to be. It is not the time for table manners yet.

*"What about entertaining and distracting a baby while you feed him, so he won't know he is being fed?"*

That is a way of getting food into the baby that many parents resort to. Your goal, however, is to teach the baby to eat food from a spoon, and the experience of eating should be pleasant for the baby. He develops a desire to eat from the spoon by the approval he gets. Mothers can show their approval by their smiles and expressions like "Good" and "That's nice." If the food is surreptitiously given to the baby or shoved in between distractions, the baby is not learning to eat from a spoon and gets no sense of achievement. In some cases, the baby may begin to clamp his mouth shut and refuse the food.

*"I tried playing with the baby to get him to eat, and pretty soon I ran out of ideas to entertain him. He didn't eat so well for a few days. Now we just sit quietly when it's mealtime, and he takes what he wants. It is probably enough because he is gaining weight. And I'm not a wreck at the end of the meal. My pediatrician approved of what I was doing, too."*

*"That doesn't bother my baby; she is a great eater. She can watch the company and eat too. I never force her."*

As we've said before, mealtime should be pleasant for both parent and baby. Babies eat well and learn to feed themselves best when parents are patient and recognize their achievements. The quantity of food consumed is less important than the atmosphere in which the feeding takes place. With the right atmosphere, the feeding process goes much more smoothly, and more food is ultimately consumed. Parents use a variety of techniques to achieve success in feeding, but, in general, the less forcing or deception, the better the results.

## Games and Social Activities

### "Pat-a-Cake"

Now that the babies are older, they are awake more of the time. This means there is more time to spend in play. Parents need to develop a repertoire of games that are appropriate for the babies' ages and that utilize the babies' competence and enhance their learning. One of these early games is "Pat-a-Cake." Interestingly, this game seems to be present in some form in the early play rituals of all societies.

At first the parents should demonstrate this game by clapping their hands together and reciting "Pat-a-Cake." Some parents simply say "Clap Hands," repeating the words in a rhythmic manner to arrest the babies interest. The baby, who can transfer objects from hand to hand, may now try to make his own hands approach each other in a clapping gesture. Sometimes the baby will watch the parents intently and raise his arms and drop them in response to the parents' activity. This response may be as far as the baby can go at this level of development, and it should be recognized by the parent with a smile and pleasant comment such as "Good," "That's nice."

Some parents take the baby's hands and put them together for the baby in a clapping position and recite "Pat-a-Cake" or "Clap Hands." Most babies chortle and enjoy this. It usually takes many weeks of watching the parent and having the parent manipulate the baby's hands before the baby begins to respond himself. For some babies, the clapping response may be to bang on something with one hand. After several weeks of this and further demonstration by the parents, they may begin to bang with two hands. Later, they learn to put their hands together, passing one hand with the other before they are actually able to clap them together. When they finally can clap their hands, they seem very pleased with themselves, particularly if the parent acknowledges their accomplishment by smiling, laughing, expressing approval verbally, or clapping in unison with them.

Have any of you begun to play "Pat-a-Cake" or "Clap Hands" with your baby?

*"We began several months ago, but we gave up because the baby would not let us hold his hands to guide them. That dampened our enthusiasm."*

That's too bad; it only means you may have begun the game too early. Perhaps the baby needed to watch you clap hands for a longer time before he was able to respond. It may be that he wanted to move his arms on his own in what he interpreted as imitating you. You can't expect the babies to have the coordination to copy your actions exactly. Clapping one hand against the other is actually quite a skill for a baby. He may be more ready now. Try again, and keep encouraging him. He will respond in his own good time.

*"I guess you are right. We expected too much too soon. Now that you mention it, he does sort of lift his arms and rock a little. I guess he is trying to use his whole body in rhythm because he isn't ready to put his hands together. We read that a baby his age should be ready for 'Pat-a-Cake,' and we just assumed he would do it as soon as we showed him. We were afraid there was something wrong with his development. Now we'll be more patient."*

*"We tried 'Pat-a-Cake' too, but all our baby would do was laugh at us. She wouldn't do it herself, even though she let us take her hands and do it. She enjoyed it, so that we got pleasure and didn't press her. We decided she just wasn't a genius, and we'd have to be satisfied. Now I feel better about her."*

*"We've been going through this too. Our baby lets us clap her hands. When we say, 'Clap Hands,' she puts her hands out for us to put together. She seems very pleased, but we can't get her to do it by herself. We wonder why."*

This is another example of how parental expectations may be too far ahead of an individual baby's level of development, causing the parents unnecessary disappointment and worry. It is fine to read about development and see if your child has reached the level indicated for her age. However, we have to remember that the book is written about babies in general and that each baby has his or her own maturational timetable, even in playing games. No general developmental chart can be right for every baby. Usually babies do things in the same sequence: They sit before they crawl, crawl before they walk, and so on. But few children begin walking at exactly the same age. It is the same with learning to play games.

## *"Bye-bye"*

There is another activity that is appropriate for babies of this age. It is part of socialization, and can also be a game. It is "Bye-bye." It is best to start this "game" when guests, relatives, or strangers are leaving after a visit and are waving "good-bye." The parent can then demonstrate the "game" by waving in response as she holds the baby. Later it can be done when Daddy leaves in the morning. After these preliminaries have been repeated several times, the mother, or whoever is holding the baby, should wave the baby's hand in a return gesture and say "Bye-bye." The words should be said in a musical, rhythmic manner, so the baby can get the rhythm of the intonation and learn to imitate it. After some repetition, the baby may be able to respond by waving her own arm. Some babies do not at first wave their arms but flex their fingers. Later they learn to use their arms to wave. This activity is an especially good one because the baby is not only learning to wave "Bye-bye" but is also learning about leaving and separation. She is adding to her vocabulary and beginning to verbalize a new concept.

When the baby has achieved a "Bye-bye" wave, parents will often try to show off the baby's achievement by saying "Bye-bye" when no one is departing. The baby may not respond because she has associated "Bye-bye" with someone's departure. If the phrase is then used when no one is leaving, the baby becomes confused. Saying "Bye-bye" should always be accompanied by the appropriate activity, even if someone goes out of the room for only a moment. As a matter of fact, leaving for only a moment is a very good activity because it gives the baby the experience of having the parent or other person return quickly. Then "Bye-bye" is not always associated with longer separation or loss.

Have any of you begun to teach your baby "Bye-bye"?

*"We have been saying 'Bye-bye' every time we go out of the room. The baby smiles at times and looks serious at others. He seems to know it's something special, but he hasn't moved his arm or his hand yet."*

*"Our baby just lifts his arm once and puts it down quickly. It's more of a bang than a wave, but he only does that particular gesture when we say 'Bye-bye' and leave. I'm sure it's his way of saying 'Bye-bye,' but my husband says I'm just imagining this because I want the baby to seem bright."*

You are describing the early steps in learning "Bye-bye." These very early gestures should be recognized as achievements and not dismissed as meaningless. As the babies get reinforcement from their parents, they go on to more accomplishments as soon as they are capable.

*"I'm afraid we were so excited because the baby does actually seem to respond to 'Bye-bye' that we've been showing off his ability to everyone, but not just when someone is leaving. So we are really using him like a trained puppy instead of realizing that he has to learn the meaning of 'bye-bye' too."*

That's a very good observation. Indeed, we are not training puppies. A baby is a person, a human being whom we are trying to help develop all of his potential. Sometimes when the babies are so young, it is hard to remember that.

## "Peekaboo"

There is another game for this age that is closely related to "Bye-bye," and that's "Peekaboo," or "Peek." Babies usually like this game very much. Begin to teach the baby this game by covering your eyes with your hands. Then uncover your eyes and say "Peek" or "I see you." Usually, the baby's expression becomes very serious when you cover your eyes or face, but she becomes all smiles when your eyes or face reappear. Later, the baby may begin to play the game by pulling part of her blanket or clothes over her face and then reappearing, or the parent may cover the baby's face and then expose it again, saying, "I see you."

The significance of the game, in addition to its fun for both parent and child, is that the baby begins to experience appearance and disappearance. The baby begins to deal with the concept that something that disappears from sight does return. It takes a long time for the baby to develop the understanding that there is existence beyond her field of vision. At first, she does not know that the person who is out of the room or out of sight exists. This is why the departure of the parent from the room is traumatic. It is also why you should not hide completely from the baby when playing "Peekaboo." That can become too threatening. "Peekaboo" is a game that helps the baby learn that someone or something exists even though not visible to the child at the moment.

When playing "Hide-and-Seek" with four- or five-year-old children, adults are often told to hide in a specific place. The children then joyously look for the adult because they are not made anxious by the adult's disappearance. When the children hide from the adult, they often call out to announce their hiding place in order to make certain they are found. They do this because they are still not sure the adult knows of their existence. This behavior seems strange to adults. They feel the child is not playing according to the rules. Actually, the children are playing according to their needs. This is what the adult always has to keep in mind in dealing with children. Their timetables and needs are not the same as the adult's. They need time and support to achieve concept formation on an adult level.

Have any of you begun to play "Peekaboo" with your baby? How are you going about introducing the game?

*"I began the game by hiding below the baby's changing table when he was on it on his stomach and could look over the edge. Then I'd rise up and stand, and he'd have to look up to find me too. He likes it, and his father does too. We began it as you showed us when the baby was four months old. As he began to respond to words, we began to say, 'I see you' when we got up, and he laughed and flung his arms out."*

Yes, that is the early form of "Peek," and it is a very good way to introduce the game—the action first and then the associated words. Have you extended the game now to covering your face with your hands or partially hiding behind something?

*"Yes, we have, and the baby likes that too."*

*"I began a few weeks ago just hiding my face and then saying, 'Peek, I see you' very loudly, I guess too enthusiastically. I think it scared the baby. So now we do it gently, and it is working all right."*

*"We've been playing 'Peekaboo, I see you' a long time with the baby just with our hands. The other day, her father came home and hid behind the open door before coming in. When the baby couldn't see him, she cried. We couldn't understand why."*

Perhaps it was because the baby expected to see Daddy when he came in, and was disappointed. The baby could not understand that he was behind the door. He may have been completely hidden from view.

*"Well, yes, he really was. My husband thought she was very silly to cry. He was a little bit upset too. Now that I understand, I can explain it to him."*

*"My husband is like that too, and so is my mother. They both think the baby should know they are there when they are completely hidden. But the baby usually cries, and they become annoyed. My husband sometimes says 'Dummy.' It makes me angry."*

Your husband doesn't really mean that. It is just that he is disappointed that what he intended as fun turned out badly. Now perhaps you can practice with the baby in the appropriate way and then show Daddy and your mother how he responds. When they can evoke smiles and laughter from the baby, they will be happy too.

*"Our baby enjoys it more when we cover his face with a diaper and then remove it, saying 'I see you.' Now he is beginning to pull the diaper off himself, and his grin when he sees us is just so nice. It's good to know that something that is just a game and such fun can also have real learning importance."*

That's the point of all these sessions: To help you enjoy bringing up the baby and to help you understand just how much what you are doing means to the baby.

## "So Big"

Another game you have been playing already is "So Big." By now the babies should be getting to the point of putting up their arms to show you how big they are.

Have you continued to play "So Big"?

*"Yes, and the baby can put both arms up now when we say, 'How big is baby?' She really gets a kick out of the game."*

*"I still have to pick the baby's arms up, but then he laughs and smiles. He likes me to do it over and over again."*

*"I am very glad that there are more games to play. We were getting very tired of 'So Big.' "*

*"Our baby gets mixed up between 'So Big,' 'Bye-bye,' and 'Pat-a-Cake.' When we say 'How big is the baby?' or say her name, she may clap or wave 'Bye-bye.' Why is that?"*

She knows she gets a positive response from you when she responds, but she hasn't quite sorted out which response is appropriate. Perhaps you introduced these games too close together, or ask her to do one after the other—for display rather than as meaningful play.

*"You know, that's it, because when she first learned a game, we'd have her do it to show off her tricks ('tricks' is good, isn't it?), and we may have mixed her up."*

That's the puppy-dog routine again, and we just have to remember that these babies are not puppies. The importance of "So Big" is that it teaches the babies some idea of the extent of themselves. Like the other games we have been talking about, it is a learning game, not just a "trick." As we have said before, playing is a baby's work because he or she learns through play.

We have discussed all these games for another reason as well: They provide a way for parents and baby to spend a happy time together. The parent-child relationship gains from this pleasant interaction.

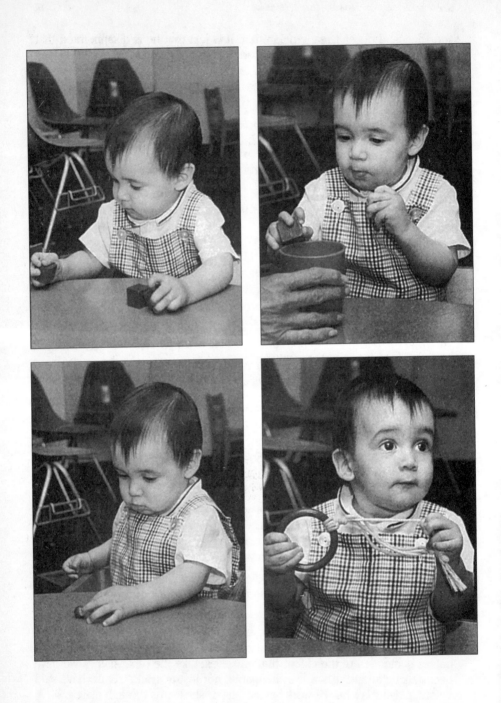

# *Age Forty-four to Forty-eight Weeks*

## *Highlights of Development— Forty-four Weeks*

The baby may now have the ability to stand and move along the rail of the crib. She may even be able to hold on to a couch or chair and move along it. Most babies will be quite adept at crawling, though some better at going backward than forward.

The baby may be able to take the bell by the top of the handle and may finger the clapper. She shows more manual dexterity and curiosity. However, she does not know yet that the clapper causes the sound of the bell. The baby notices the block in the cup and may reach in and get it out. She may be able to put the block back into the cup, but she may not release it. With this activity comes the beginning of the baby's understanding of the concepts of "in" and "out."

The baby may now be saying "Dada" and "Mama" more clearly. She may also have another word or two in her vocabulary. Acquisition of language is very uneven; some children may have no words and others five or six.

The baby is beginning to comprehend "Bye-bye" better, and while still concentrating on watching the adult make the gesture, she may lift her hand a little in imitation. She may respond to "Pat-a-Cake" by banging on the table with one hand, or she may begin to bring both hands together.

The baby can hold out a toy to the parent but will not yet release it. With a ball in hand, he reaches for his image in the mirror and may touch the ball to the mirror. He is beginning to accept the cup and drink better from it when the parent holds the cup for the baby.

## Holidays

### The Significance of Holidays for Babies

(The comments in this section are relevant for any time during the first year of life.)

Adults often feel that babies are not involved in big holidays like Thanksgiving, Christmas, Chanukah, Passover, and Easter because they are too young to understand what the holidays are all about. It is true that babies do not comprehend the significance that holidays have for adults and older children, but holidays do have a significance for them. It is important for parents to realize this because most parents have some holiday traditions they would like to continue or revive for their children.

*"I was wondering about that. At Christmas we always used to have a tree and hung up stockings when I was little. For me it always was such a happy time. But I was wondering about a baby that is under a year old. What is appropriate for the baby? Is it right to expose her to all that excitement?"*

Of course, the baby won't understand the meaning of the holiday, but she will sense the excitement. There will be a number of new and exciting happenings that will be fun for the baby. The baby will watch with great interest as the parents put up and decorate the tree, particularly if she can play with a harmless ornament. The baby will also enjoy seeing the tree lit up. Young babies love to look at the lighted tree and often engage in lots of cooing and babbling. Even though they will not understand the ceremony, babies will also enjoy the lighting of Chanukah candles. Babies may also enjoy playing with the colored wrappings of presents more than they enjoy the actual present. They will also like to watch presents being wrapped and later opened.

### Disruption of the Baby's Routine

At holiday time, there may be disruption of the babies' routines. For some babies, an occasional disruption is taken in stride and doesn't upset them provided the parents are there. Other babies get out of sorts just when the parents want to show them off to guests. The babies are irritable, won't take their feedings, have difficulty falling asleep, or don't stay asleep as long as usual. Although parents may think that they are doing things just as they normally do, they are usually under pressure to hurry a little, and babies sense this. This tension usually is felt when company is expected in the baby's home, and mother and father have extra chores to do to entertain their guests.

What plans are you making for entertaining at home during the holidays? How are you preparing for them physically and emotionally?

*"I'm worried. We are having a lot of visitors from out of town. The house will be full of people."*

■                                                                                   ■

Do you expect the baby to mind all the new faces?

*"Oh, no, he doesn't mind at all. He has a ball. I'm the one who doesn't like it. I think he gets overstimulated, and then when the company leaves, he becomes bored and wants the same attention from me just when I'm trying to clean up."*

That's one of the kinds of extra pressures, the hurry to clean up afterward. Since you have been through this experience before, why not have a quiet "winding-down" period with the baby and let some of the chores wait? If you can afford to have help, this is a good time for it. If not, just let things go until later. Perhaps some division of labor can be worked out with the rest of the family. Some of your relatives might be willing to stay and help with the cleaning up. If that arrangement is not to your taste, just do the cleaning up later. As they say, "cool it." Things work out better that way.

*"We have a different problem. As soon as company comes, the baby just clings to me and won't let me move. It takes him almost half the time the guests are there to get used to them and sit in their arms. He sometimes even won't go to his father or my mother either. That, of course, upsets them."*

Does your company usually swoop down on the baby and try to hold him?

*"Yes, that's it. Besides, they are very loud and exuberant people, and he just can't take the noise they make. They tell me I must be bringing him up wrong since he is so afraid of them. They say I should make him go to them, and that's how he will get used to them."*

That's the way some older adults feel babies should be treated. We do not happen to agree with that. From experience, we know that babies go through a period of stranger anxiety, and while they are in that stage, it is much better not to threaten them by placing them in a stranger's arms. Although most babies pass that stage by nine or ten months, stranger anxiety can linger on, especially if the babies are tired or have been ill. Then well-meaning but overly enthusiastic people can revive earlier response patterns. So you have to be your babies' advocates, and tell the guests gently but firmly and explicitly that the babies need time to adjust to them.

*"We've been through that, too. We used to think the baby was unfriendly, but now we can see that we just didn't understand how visitors come across to him. He isn't looking forward to the company as we are. He has no idea what it's all about. Now we just hold him or play with him ourselves and let the company settle down as best they can until the baby is ready for them."*

Trying to "cue in" to the baby's level of understanding pays off. Trying to make a baby, with his immature understanding, "cue in" to adult expectations is unreasonable and leads to trouble. Even older children can be difficult when you have guests because they feel that your attention is diverted. The baby can feel excluded from the adult activities.

■                                                                    ■

*"I guess we all have some problems entertaining when there is a small child in the family. Getting dinner ready used to be my worst headache, but I've worked out a simple menu that I can get ready with my eyes shut. I do most of the cooking at night when the baby is asleep. I fix a casserole that is all ready beforehand. My husband helps me clean up afterward. If we are too tired, we leave things as they are, and I get them done when I can. I've learned that I can't be overtired. So I spare myself, and that works out better for the baby too."*

That is a very good attitude and one that is helpful for the baby because it reduces the tension. The parent can function better, is not overworked, and can enjoy the holiday. The baby can too. It becomes a good experience for parents and baby. You don't have to feel that the baby has intruded into your social life. You can all enjoy the holiday together.

*"I suddenly realized that's just the way I've been feeling about the baby and the holidays. Instead of thinking of how to plan to enjoy it, I'm harping on the trouble the baby makes."*

It's good that you can see that. Many parents feel that way, and the holidays become unpleasant for all. You must be aware of the baby's level of development and not expect more from the baby than is appropriate for his age. The parents should not expect too much from themselves either.

*"I guess we are lucky because our families realize how hard it is going to be for me to get things together for dinner. Each guest is bringing something because everyone figured it would be less of a break in the baby's routine if they came to our house. We plan to have our dinner during the baby's nap. If he wakes early, it won't be too bad either. Everyone will see him when he is rested."*

## Holiday Visiting and Traveling

If you plan to visit relatives during the holidays, you will be relieved of preparing for company. But you will still have to prepare for traveling with the baby, as you have had to do on other occasions. You have to be sure to take all the things the baby will need on the trip.

The same problem with strange faces will occur, but, in addition, the baby will be in a strange place, so it is well to take some of her familiar toys.

Some babies enjoy the new surroundings and are stimulated and interested in all the new sights and sounds. Some respond by clinging and being a little apprehensive, so they need time to get adjusted. As nearly as possible, you should try to continue the baby's routine. If the baby is able to have a nap on the trip, she will arrive more rested. If the hosts have a high chair (and most grandparents and relatives do), the baby can be drawn up close to the parents while they are eating dinner.

*"We are going to my husband's family. The baby has been there before, so, aside from taking his food and diapers and a toy or two, I think we'll be okay."*

■                                                                          ■

*"We are going to friends who have no children and are quite fussy and formal. I warned them that the baby might be fussy if she wasn't having a good day, but they insisted. We're looking forward to it now, but at first we had some doubts."*

*"I suppose our plans are preposterous. We usually go to a club my husband belongs to for holiday meals, and we decided we'd do it this time with the baby. If he doesn't sleep in his carryall, we'll take turns minding him, but we will be with our friends; we won't feel left out just because we have a baby."*

It seems you have all thought out carefully how to manage with the baby and how to enjoy yourselves without looking upon the baby as a burden. If everyone is relaxed, the visits will be pleasant.

*"We are going to Florida. It will be the baby's first plane trip, and everything will be new to him when we get there. We are a little concerned. We'll take as many of his toys as we can. My parents are going with us, so we'll have some help on the plane."*

That certainly will be a big new experience. Babies usually take to plane trips very well. If the baby has a cold, however, you might run into a problem. The variations in air pressure may cause his ear canals to become blocked. If he is entirely well, there should be no problem with that. The baby can't chew gum as we do, but he can suck from a bottle during takeoff and landing. You should always have a bottle handy for this purpose, even for an older baby.

The first night in the new crib and new surroundings may change the baby's sleep pattern a little. She may not fall asleep as quickly, and you may need to stay with her until she does. She might also wake during the night.

The important ingredient in handling such changes in routine is your availability. That's what gives the baby reassurance and makes it possible for her to adapt to the change. If the parents are less available to the baby on vacation, the baby becomes upset, and no one can have a good time. It's also important to try to keep up the same sequence of daily events as at home. Sometimes the baby may sleep well in the new setting but not eat as well. All of these changes are temporary. The goal is to enjoy the trip and enjoy observing the effect of new experiences on the baby.

Whenever families go away for the holidays, they run the risk that the baby will not respond with pleasure. This happens because babies don't understand that such trips are for pleasure. They only know that something is different in their lives, and they can't quite cope with it. It may take a few days for them to settle down in the new environment and again when they return home. This does not happen in all cases, but parents should be prepared for their babies' responses and not feel that the babies are being "bad" just to spoil their holidays. Irritability, poor sleeping or eating responses, and the like are simply the baby's way of expressing her feelings about strange surroundings.

*"If babies sometimes respond so poorly to change, isn't it best to just stay home with them until they are old enough to understand what is going on? It's always such a hassle to get everything ready to go anywhere with the baby, and sometimes mine behaves so badly that it just doesn't seem worthwhile."*

Certainly babies are more comfortable in familiar surroundings, and it is easier not to try to take them on trips. However, parents must decide for themselves what sacrifices they want to make for their children. If parents understand, they can cope with their baby's behavior. The important thing is for the parents to be supportive of the baby and not become annoyed because the baby needs their support.

*"We've had different experiences with our baby. Sometimes everything turns out fine; other times it's just not her day and we go home early. We just play it by ear."*

Yes, that is frequently the story. Babies are not always predictable. Parents must get to know their baby and learn how to cope with the child's needs. It is not easy, but being aware of the baby's immaturity and need for help often makes the burden lighter.

Visiting and taking trips are part of the process of socialization, and some babies are able to socialize sooner than others. But being able to socialize is itself a process of maturation and learning, and here parental help and patience can really enhance development.

# Taking Trips Without the Baby

## The Babies' Reactions

We have talked about parental plans for spending the holiday season with their babies. There are some parents, however, who may be planning to spend the holidays or part of them away without their children. This may be the baby's first experience of prolonged separation from the parents, and it may be a very difficult situation for the baby to cope with. The babies are not yet old enough to understand that you are going away and will return. If the parents feel they must, need, or very much want to go away without the baby, they also need to make careful plans for the baby during the period of time they are absent.

*"We've been discussing going away for a four-day vacation over the holiday. We haven't been away together since the baby was born. My husband is very tired and needs a rest, which he can't get at home because the baby wakes us up so early. I could stand a rest myself. Do you think it would be so devastating for the baby if we were away just four days?"*

That depends on a number of things. Certainly your absence will have some impact on the baby. He will miss you, and when you return, he will show it in some way. If you are prepared to give the baby the extra attention he may need for a few days after you return, and if you can leave him with someone he is familiar with, then your absence won't be devastating. It's one of the decisions parents have to consider carefully. Sometimes, it is a very difficult decision to make. Occasionally, parents do need to get away for a short interval, but they must be prepared to deal with the baby's reactions after they return.

*"What would the baby do when we get back, or while we are away, that we should be prepared for?"*

When you come home, the baby will undoubtedly cling to one or both of you for several days. This is one of the most frequent reactions. Another thing the baby might do is wake at night. The baby will do this because he needs to be reassured that the parents are still there. Some babies get cranky and difficult to satisfy. Others change their eating habits for a few days.

Parents often think: "The baby will miss me and be so glad to see me that he will cuddle and be very loving." This is rarely the baby's response. Sometimes the baby may turn away from the parent and show his anger at being left behind. This is often the response that upsets parents the most. If parents are prepared for such behavior and understand that it is the baby's way of saying "I missed you very much," then they can respond without anger and disappointment.

The question was also asked about the baby's behavior while the parents were away. Besides the initial crying at the time of the parents' departure, the baby may show no other signs of missing them. Much depends on what arrangements are made for the baby, who takes care of the baby and where. The indications that the baby missed the parents may be evident only when they return.

In some cases, babies do give the caretaker some concern. It may be hard for the baby to get to sleep. The baby may keep looking for the parents, starting every time the outside door opens. The baby may be hard to console when he cries and may not eat as well. Some babies sleep longer than usual, as though to pass the time until the parents return. Some babies, if they have reached that level of speech, call for Mommy or Daddy when anyone comes in. These reactions may be minimal and hardly detectable, or they may be quite overt.

One more thing: We're not bringing this matter up to try to frighten you into not ever taking a vacation without your babies. Such an attitude would not be realistic. We are trying to help you understand the babies' needs so that you make the best possible arrangements for the child when you leave.

■                                                                              ■

*"What is the best way to arrange to go away? We were planning to have my parents, whom the baby knows well and who know the baby's routine, stay with the baby in our house."*

## Making Arrangements for the Baby

That sounds fine. The best arrangement is to have someone who is close to the baby and whom the baby knows and trusts come and stay with the baby in the baby's own house. Then the baby continues to have the security of his own familiar bed, room, toys, and equipment. The grandparents, other relatives, or close friends can carry out the familiar routines. That kind of arrangement is the least traumatic; the baby is less apt to miss the parents. It also gives grandparents or other relatives a great chance to get to know and enjoy the baby, as well as enlarging the baby's circle of trusted people.

It is a good idea if the substitute caretakers can come a day or two before the parents' departure so that the takeover of responsibility for care can be effected gradually. That way, the parents' departure is not so abrupt—at least, in the baby's eyes. The parents can leave for short intervals during this time, so that the baby has the experience of their leaving and returning; he may thus develop some sense that they will return again after the vacation. In this way, you will be giving the baby a few trial runs of short separations before the longer one.

*"In our case that won't work. If my parents come to us, it would mean a long trip for my father to his office. So we have to take the baby to my parents. We can go there a day or two before, settle him in, and see that all systems are 'go' before we leave. My parents' house is a place the baby is used to because we go there often for dinner and my parents have a high chair and a portacrib that the baby has used before. Besides, we'll bring his favorite toys and of course all his clothes, diapers, blankets, cups, and bottles. There will be many aunts and uncles with their children popping in, so the baby won't be lonesome."*

That sounds like a good alternative solution. Each family must work these things out to suit its own circumstances.

*"We've given a lot of thought to leaving this baby because we had a devastating experience with our first child. When she was a year old, we had an opportunity to go away for a month. We just took her to my parents' house and left her there without staying at all. She was upst all the time we were gone, so we know all about the clinging and crankiness you described. We didn't understand then what had happened, and we were very irritated at her when we got back. We thought my mother must have 'spoiled' her. Now we understand better about a child's reactions, and we don't expect the baby to understand. As a matter of fact, we are postponing a long vacation until the baby is old enough to understand. Our older one now needs more help to adjust to such a change than she would have needed had we not made the first mistake."*

■                                                                              ■

*"What do parents do if they must go away and have no one who will come to their house or in whose house the baby is comfortable?"*

This often happens in small families far from their relatives. In that case, it is a good idea to hire someone who does this kind of extended care for a living—a trained baby nurse, a practical nurse, or an experienced baby-sitter. It is not always easy to find such people at a moment's notice, but they are available. There are some agencies that specialize in this kind of assistance. Given sufficient time, appropriate arrangements can be made.

It is important to interview such a person first. Have the person come for a few hours to take care of the baby, and observe the baby's response. Then leave the baby for a short while in the person's care. If all goes well, you can feel comfortable leaving the baby for an extended time with the hired substitute.

*"Can you get hired caretakers to make such trial runs? Don't such things tend to make them feel from the start that you don't trust them?"*

The question here is not what the caretaker feels; the important issue is whether the particular caretaker in question is someone whom the baby can trust. Most people who care for babies professionally understand this concern on the part of the parents and will cooperate. If they do not, don't engage them. Many such caretakers are very glad to get acquainted with the baby and the baby's routine while the parents are still available because no one likes being left for several days with an unhappy, disoriented baby. Caretakers don't like to be left in such a setup any more than the baby does, so it is mutually beneficial to have the trial run.

*"We have some neighbors on our block who have a baby the same age as ours. We exchange baby-sitting services often. Their baby is used to being in our apartment, and our baby is used to being in theirs. Last week, these neighbors had to go out of town suddenly because of illness in the family, and they left their baby with us. He cried a little at bedtime the first night, but he settled down when I patted him off to sleep. The next day everything was fine. He was with us two nights. When his parents came back, he cried when he saw them and clung to them for a few hours. Then he was okay. My neighbor said she would like to return the favor and would be glad to take our baby for a weekend if we wanted to get away. Do you think we should do it?"*

*"That's a golden opportunity. Don't pass it up. It sounds like an ideal setup."*

It is a good setup if your baby can adapt as well to the neighbors as their baby adjusted to you, and if you feel your neighbors would take as good care of your baby as you did of theirs. The circumstances were a little different; you were helping out a neighbor in an emergency. The emotional framework is also a little different; your neighbors are returning what they consider a debt. You have to assess the quality and sincerity of the offer and how much you want to get away. When you have done that, then you can make a well-considered decision. It may turn out that this will be a nice arrangement that can occasionally be repeated. That's the next best thing to having one's own family close by.

*"What about going away to a hotel, taking the baby, and hiring someone there to care for him? There are many resorts that offer this service."*

What will happen in that situation is difficult to predict. The baby is with you part of the day and may take to the baby-sitter at once. All may go well. However, you must remember that the baby will be in a strange place and may have difficulty adjusting to new sleeping and eating arrangements with different people around. Some parents take care of the baby during the day. They put the baby to sleep and have a sitter there in case the baby wakes. The chances of the baby's waking in the new surroundings are good, and he will be confronted by a strange person. That may be traumatic. In that case, he may have difficulty getting back to sleep, and the next night the baby may not go off to sleep readily because he has fears of being left by his parents again. So even in the hotel setting—even if you are in the hotel dining room or elsewhere within reach—it is best to have the baby establish some sense of relationship with and trust for the baby-sitter before being left with her.

*"We had that experience. The advertisement seemed very enticing, so we went. We put the baby to sleep. Then the baby-sitter came. She was just a kid, and I was troubled by that, but since we were just downstairs in the dining room, we left the baby with her, The baby woke, took one look at her, and screamed. The sitter didn't know what to do, but she was very gentle and nice. The next day we took her with us to the beach, and the baby got to like her. That night she came before the baby went to sleep. He did wake up, but she gave him a bottle, and he went back to sleep. So it worked out all right. We just didn't use our heads the first night. We were too anxious to be free. It would have been better to hire the sitter for the first afternoon so the baby could get used to her. Even though we were together, it took several days for him to settle back into his routine when we got home. But now we understand that we should plan for the baby first and for ourselves second. It's not too awful, and it's certainly easier and more fun in the long run."*

That's a lesson well learned. It doesn't make so much difference who the caretaker is if the baby is given a chance to get used to her and the parents are confident that the caretaker can deal appropriately with the baby. Sometimes paid sitters are better at doing this than relatives are. Some grandparents and relatives get too anxious. You have to judge each situation for itself. But remember: Your vacation will be pleasanter for everyone—baby, parents, and caretakers alike—if you take the baby's needs and level of development into account when you make your arrangements.

■                                                                                              ■

*"Well, with so much attention being paid to the baby, what about the parents' needs?"*

You have hit on one of the big needs of our society: support and consideration for parents. This is one of the main purposes of our program, and that of many other parenting programs being established around the country.

Part of parenting is developing the ability to consider the baby's needs first. Yet, many parents are annoyed because the baby is inconsiderate of *their* needs, but we have also considered your needs as well. In this case, by planning well for the baby, you will ultimately profit by getting away for a rest, knowing that the minimum trauma will result. You will get a sense of achievement from having discharged your obligations with good sense.

## Parents' Vacations and Separation Anxiety

In our discussion of leaving babies for holidays or trips, nobody asked, "Why bother to go on a trip without the baby when it really isn't good for the child?"

*"Yes, that did occur to me. I thought we were making an awful issue about what to do for the baby in order to do something we knew was not the best thing for the baby."*

That is true. Leaving for a holiday or business trip means the baby is separated from his parents. This we know from experience is hard for babies. We have recently been discussing the manner in which to leave the baby, even for a short time, with a baby-sitter. We have said that repeated short absences teach the baby to understand that the parents will return. If left with a regular baby-sitter, the baby learns to manage, but even then the baby needs to cling to one or both of the parents when they return. How well the baby can tolerate even small separations depends on the child's level of development in this area.

We know that most children cannot separate well until they are about three years old. One of the reasons for this is that babies do not realize that their parents continue to exist when they cannot be seen. We have discussed how anxiety-provoking it can be for the baby when the parent merely disappears into the bathroom, as well as how annoying this anxiety is to the parent.

Going on vacations and leaving a baby is separation. If the baby has not learned to tolerate short separations and is very clinging when the mother returns, that baby is certainly not ready for the parents to leave for an extended period.

*"When would be the worst time to leave a baby for a vacation?"*

You know we believe that separation is very hard on children under three years of age. There are considerations that do make separation necessary, and it is not realistic to expect parents to give up all vacations or trips for the baby. That might be ideal in many cases, but to hope that it will happen is not realistic. Babies are probably most vulnerable from six months to a year. This is the period when stranger anxiety is most acute. Babies become less vulnerable as they approach three years. In the second half of the baby's first year of life the idea that a parent who leaves will return is just beginning to make an impact and needs many repetitions until the baby develops sufficient trust that the parents will return. So a vacation away from the baby at that age is not good planning and, if possible, should be avoided. However, if a separation is necessary, then you should follow the procedures we have discussed earlier.

*"If parents do go away, how long can they stay away without causing permanent or at least serious trauma?"*

I would begin with an overnight separation or, at most, two nights in the six-month-to-one-year period, if you have to go at all. In general, short vacations of not more than three or four days are better until the baby is three years old, or at least until the baby is verbal and can understand that you will return. It is also important for the baby to have a good relationship with the substitute caretaker while the parents are gone.

*"My! That seems like a lot of sacrifice over a very long time."*

*"Oh, it's not all that bad! You can get a lot of relief and pleasure out of an overnight away from home now and again. You can dine out, go to the theater, meet friends at a party, sleep late the next morning, go to a museum or movie in the afternoon, or shop."*

A mini-vacation goes a long way and does little or no harm to the development of the baby's sense of basic trust. A number of short vacations during this period are really better than one extended vacation.

*"Actually the time speeds by, and before you know it, suddenly the children are three, and you don't have a baby anymore! It's sad to think how fast the time passes and how quickly the fun you are having seeing them develop from one stage to the next is over."*

*"I didn't have that feeling with my first one. I just couldn't wait for him to grow up. I guess I know the reason why now. I didn't understand the stages of development, and I was in a constant battle with him because I expected more mature behavior. Then I left him for a month and didn't understand his behavior when I came back. I'm still trying to overcome some of the effects of that mistake. He is almost four, and he is still a clinging child who needs a great deal of attention and reassurance."*

It's obvious that we have a variety of opinions, feelings, and experiences. Each set of parents has to weigh the consequences of deciding upon early separation and make the choice that suits the family's needs best. However, we all have to remember that the best way to develop a whining, clinging child is to force the child into separation before the child is ready. A child who is fortunate enough to have parents who "cue in" and are sensitive to his needs and level of development repays his parents many times over by the way he develops and learns to cope independently.

*"What would be some of the consequences of experiencing separation too early?"*

One of the earliest consequences is the child who has difficulty going to school. Most children entering nursery school need to have their mother stay at first, sometimes for the first week or two. Others require their mothers longer. Some just can't separate; they are not ready for school and have to be kept home another semester or sometimes a whole year. Of course, in that case, the parents require some counseling.

Later, these children have difficulty going to another child's house to visit. They only want children to come to their house. They can't spend a night away from home visiting with Grandma or with friends. They often don't want to play outside with other children. Of course, all of these behavior patterns may have other causes, but when one gets the whole story of the child's development, early separation is often the culprit.

*"I've often heard of children who get so homesick at camp or college they have to come home. Is that the same problem in an older age group?"*

That's probably the core of the problem. Nothing can be wholly attributable to just one factor, but it is likely that early separation caused a very large part of the problem.

The effects of forcing separation too early also carry on into later life. There are individuals who, when they marry, have to live in the same apartment house or on the same block as their mothers. This can happen to a boy or a girl. In some cultures, this is looked upon as the norm, and we say such societies prize close family ties. Well, they do, but they may not be for the best reasons. However, developing such behavior may make for a more comfortable or a more secure life because it ensures the individual the support of the extended family. Thus, some advantages do sometimes accrue from that situation. The trouble comes when the adult child must move away from his relatives. Then the problem is fully exposed and needs careful handling. When the underlying cause is understood, it can be dealt with and, to some extent, overcome, but that is not so easy to do.

## *Fears: Strangers, Noises, Animals, the Dark, Doctors, and New Toys*

The separation anxiety we have been discussing is also related to the characteristic fears of early childhood. One is the fear of the unknown and the need to experience and re-experience things until they become familiar and the baby can cope with them. In separation, the unknown is the experience that the parent will return. The baby has to experience the return over and over again until he feels confident that the parent will indeed return.

Babies also fear strange people, particularly during the period from seven to ten months of age. But even later, they are usually wary of strangers, expecially if the stranger is very large or has a loud voice, or if the baby suspects the stranger will try to hold him or take him away from his mother.

*"My baby has developed a fear of fire engines. We live close to a firehouse, and one day just as we were leaving the house, the fire engine came clanging down the street with the siren going, and the baby began to cry. Now I try to anticipate this reaction by picking the baby up immediately and holding her. I also try to imitate the bell and reassure her. But there is just no way to avoid the problem. Even if we move, I guess there will be fire engines around sometimes."*

You are doing the very best you can with something you can't control. It is sometimes helpful to visit the firehouse when the engine is in place and not making noise, so the baby can study it a little. Sometimes a toy fire engine helps. That way, the baby gets to imitate the sound the real engine makes and gradually becomes able to deal with the fear. It is common for children to be afraid of loud noises.

*"What about dogs? Are children naturally fond or frightened of them? We don't have one, and I wondered if we should get a puppy that would grow up with the baby so she wouldn't be afraid of them. I'm especially concerned because I always had a fear of animals, dogs in particular."*

Most babies enjoy watching dogs and like to pet and play with them, provided the dog isn't so large that the baby is overwhelmed by its size. Dogs resemble the stuffed animals that the babies have been playing with, but they are more active and more interesting than stuffed animals. However, if the dog barks or sniffs and snorts too close to them, babies may become upset.

The usual approach to getting the baby to overcome his fears is to get him close to the dog and try to make him pet the animal. This usually only intensifies the baby's reaction. The best thing to do is to reassure the baby that everything is all right and move away from the dog to a distance that makes the baby feel comfortable again. The parent can say, "Nice doggie" and pet the animal, but they should not force the baby to do so until he feels comfortable enough with the situation to extend his hand to the dog. The baby may not reach this stage until several safe encounters have been experienced. Of course, you need to be certain beforehand that the dog is safe and will not bite or snarl at the baby. For that reason, stray dogs should be avoided. Only a dog whose owner is present and can vouch for the animal's gentleness should be allowed near the baby.

■       ■

It is not necessary to get puppies for babies of this age because the babies are really too young to enjoy them. Furthermore, puppies are babies too. They demand a lot of care, and providing that care may overburden the parents. Also, puppies are so high-spirited and undisciplined at first that they can easily frighten a baby. If the family already has a pet, of course, the animal becomes part of the baby's life experience. However, you must bear in mind that sometimes a pet can become jealous of a baby. If that happens, the baby may be in some danger from the animal.

Each family must decide whether or not to get a pet. We will be talking at a later time about the most appropriate age for children to have pets.

*"What about fear of the dark? When I was a child, I remember being afraid of going to bed in a dark room. Yet when I put the baby to bed, I turn out the light. She doesn't mind and goes right off to sleep."*

Usually babies do not start off being afraid of the dark. However, if they awake at night and the room is dark, they may become frightened when they can't make out any familiar landmarks. Also, if they are awakened by teething pains, they may associate the pain with the darkness and become afraid of the dark. Similarly, if they have been ill with a cold and wake in the dark with a choking sensation, they may associate this feeling with the dark. In any of these cases, the babies may not be able to fall asleep in a dark room.

*"That happened to our baby after a cold. I have tried to make her go back to sleep in the dark, but she won't. So I leave her door open and a small hall light on. Am I doing the right thing?"*

That's a reasonable thing to do. Some parents have a small night-light attached to the floor plug. This light gives off a very dim light, just adequate for the baby to make out familiar surroundings if he or she wakes, and also enough for the parent to be able to tend to the baby without turning on the overhead lights. There are also all sorts of table lamps with night-lights in them for babies' rooms.

*"We have covered a lot of fears I didn't realize babies could have, but there is one special fear I'd like to mention, and that is fear of doctors. Ever since she had her first injection at the doctor's office, my baby cries when we go into the doctor's office. She does this even before she sees the doctor in his white coat."*

It is unfortunate that inoculations have to be given as part of a regular checkup. Some doctors are very adept at it, however, and understand the baby's needs so well that they do the inoculation fast. Then the mother and child leave for a room with toys, so the baby can be distracted at once. That way, the doctor can also reappear in a pleasant, unthreatening setting and develop a friendlier relationship with the baby while he is giving the mother instructions. Unfortunately, such procedures take a little extra pediatric time, and some doctors are too busy to be able to provide them, but they do pay off because the baby is easier to examine when he is not afraid. Some doctors have an assistant give the inoculation so the baby doesn't become afraid of the doctor. Some have abandoned the white coat—that helps too.

Sometimes it's a good idea to bring a favorite toy to give to the baby to comfort him right after the inoculation; sometimes giving the baby a bottle will achieve this. The important thing is for the parent to be at ease, ready to console and comfort the baby, and not intensify the baby's feeling by her own anxiety.

*"My doctor gives the baby a lollipop right away. That keeps the baby busy, and he forgets his pain."*

*"My doctor does that too, but my dentist says lollipops are bad for the teeth. So I just bring a cookie or cracker, give it to the doctor ahead of time, and he hands it to the baby."*

It's good that many of you have worked out techniques to ease the way for your babies.

*"There is one more thing I wanted to mention and almost forgot. Are babies afraid of new toys?"*

That happens if the toy is very large or strange-looking. It also happens if the toy makes an odd noise or is a very dark color that doesn't appeal to the baby.

*"That's what happened to us. A friend gave the baby a large green, stuffed frog. The baby cried and wouldn't go near it. I tried to show him it was soft and nice, and he just cried more. I was so surprised and didn't know what to do."*

These things happen, but the mother should explain to the person who brought the present that perhaps the baby is just too young and will appreciate the gift later. Don't try to make the baby adjust to the toy to ease the visitor's feelings. It's the baby that needs the help. It's best to put that toy away, and try taking it out again when the baby is older, or after you have shown the baby pictures of the toy so he gets to deal with the strangeness in a less threatening situation. You can also make amusing animal noises for the baby and then associate these noises with the toy. The main job for the parent is to be the child's advocate and to be concerned about the child's reactions and needs, not about what an adult may feel. Sometimes this is hard to do because you may be dealing with the boss's wife, but it's the baby that needs help or consoling first. Then you can try to explain your child's behavior to the adult while showing your real appreciation for your visitor's efforts to please the baby.

■                                                                              ■

# Discipline Versus Punishment

## Setting Limits

Now that the babies are becoming more mobile, they can explore more distant areas and try out new activities. Adults recognize some of this exploration as dangerous, destructive, or painful to other children, and, therefore, they want to stop the baby from engaging in certain activities. Not to allow the baby to do anything that may be dangerous to the baby, destructive to property, or painful to another is part of the parents' job. How parents do this varies in different societies and households.

We have already talked about this topic several times from different points of view. Because discipline is teaching and because the baby's ability to comprehend what you are teaching develops over time, the parent-child interaction in this area changes and develops as well.

How are you dealing with situations calling for limitation? What activities do you limit? How do you go about setting these limits?

*"We live in a very old-fashioned apartment where the radiators are exposed. The baby likes to play with the radiator, especially when the steam comes up and begins to sizzle. When the heat's off, I'm not worried. But when the radiator is hot and he puts his hand out toward it, I say 'No,' but he still wants to be near it. At this point, I used to slap his hands. Since we've talked about the effect of slapping, however, I just shout 'No' and get very angry."*

It seems to me you are doing two things in this situation that confuse the baby. First, to let him play with the radiator when it is off and not when it is on is confusing. The baby cannot, at his age, understand why at one time it is all right to play with the radiator and at another it is not. You have to be consistent in your approach to this problem. The radiator should be off limits *all the time* until the baby is old enough to understand that something hot may be dangerous.

In the second place, to slap a baby is punishment, not discipline. He needs to be taught that he cannot touch the radiator and then be given a substitute that he can touch. He must be allowed to discharge the impulse to touch with another object. The parent can say "No" firmly and show disapproval by shaking her head and looking stern. Then the parent should be enthusiastic in her approval of the substitute activity. In this way, a parent teaches what is accepted and what is not.

*"Are you saying that we should not punish children, but we should discipline them? What is the difference?"*

Punishment means teaching by inflicting pain. That should not be the parent's purpose. The parent's purpose is to set limits—that is, to teach what is acceptable and what is not, what is considered right and what is considered wrong in the household. By doing this a parent disciplines, or teaches, the child. Parents are the primary teachers, the first and most important ones the child will ever have.

*"But doesn't a child learn by being hit? Isn't that a more certain way? That's what my parents did to me, and that's what my mother thinks I ought to do to my baby. She says a little slap never hurt anyone."*

That is the method of trying to teach by punishment, but a baby of this age doesn't even understand what the punishment is for because he does not know what is acceptable and not acceptable. There are many parents who pay attention to the child only when he is doing something wrong. Then he is punished physically. When the baby is doing something good, the parents just accept it as the routine. They may feel pleased by what the baby did but do not overtly convey that to the child. The child then only learns what is wrong because the parent only recognizes what is wrong. If there are many things of which the parent disapproves, then the child may get the feeling that he can't ever please the parent.

To this the child can respond in a number of ways: He can give up trying to please; he can keep trying by becoming overly compliant and ingratiating; or he can become overtly angry and hostile. None of these behavior patterns or character traits makes for a healthy adult personality. The child who gives up may have no incentive to learn in school because he has never experienced success and approval at home. The child who tries so hard to be liked may become insincere and harbor real hostility. The child who is overtly angry and aggressive cannot deal with authority appropriately.

We all know adults who have no "get up and go." We recognize the individuals who are ready to please everyone, the "yes men" who really aren't sincere. We also recognize the angry people, the individuals with chips on their shoulders. Are these really the character traits that we want our children to develop, or do we want them to develop a healthy sense of self-worth and self-esteem, as well as a solid understanding of the difference between right and wrong?

Children learn to accept limitations because their parents' method of teaching these limitations has been patient, firm, and consistent, but not punitive. Children develop self-esteem because approved behavior on their part has been recognized and encouraged by their parents. The same recognition and encouragement will lead children to internalize a healthy concept of right and wrong, without establishing an angry relationship with the parents. These children will develop healthy, active conscience mechanisms.

Disciplining rather than punishing children is one of the basic issues of child rearing, and we will be discussing it again at different age levels. For now, it is important to recognize the need for consistency and firmness when setting limits and for enthusiastic and positive recognition of approved behavior.

■                                                                      ■

The human being seems to have an inborn need for recognition and approval; this is the factor we should utilize in establishing limits or discipline. A person becomes self-disciplined when he can set his own limits and no longer needs parental or societal disapproval to discourage him from doing wrong. That is the kind of mature person we would like our children to grow up to be. We are setting a stage now for achieving that goal, and that's why we say "discipline—yes; punishment—no!"

## Permissiveness

*"Aren't you saying that parents should be permissive? Aren't we getting into the controversy between authoritarianism and permissiveness?"*

Both authoritarianism and permissiveness are extremes. Unfortunately, but rather commonly during our history, the changes that have taken place have tended to go from one extreme to the other. For example, we went from long, flowing skirts to the miniskirt and back again. Similarly, we went from enormous hats to no hats. In education, we moved from strictly prescribed courses to self-choice in the curriculum. Now we are moving back to requiring children and young people to take some basic courses again. In raising of children, we went from Victorian strictness to total permissiveness, and now we have begun to set limitations that are more appropriate to a child's level of development and understanding.

*"Why was permissiveness bad? What was wrong with it? We hear so much now about the aftermath of unhappiness in the generation that was brought up permissively."*

*"Well, those children who had everything their way never knew what they wanted and were brats. I saw some children raised like that, and they and their parents were not happy."*

Overpermissiveness seems to have led to quite a number of consequences that were not anticipated by the educators of the period. If everything is permitted and there are no limits, a child gets a sense of insecurity, a sense that no one cares what he does. It's a short step from this feeling to the feeling that no one cares for him. Children need help in identifying reality—what is harmless and harmful, good and bad, right and wrong. A parent can do that without being intrusive and taking away a child's initiative.

There is another aspect of permissiveness to be considered. If everything is permitted, there is little differentiation between right and wrong; there is also little special approval from parents when a child does do the right things. There is also probably less reinforcement of the sense of mastery and less recognition of achievement, and both factors are important in development of self-esteem and a good self-image.

From experience it has been found that children do not derive pleasure from doing just what they want to all the time. When there are

■                                                                         ■

certain restrictions, the child feels a heightened sense of pleasure from activities reinforced by parental approval and contact. Permissiveness took away this special pleasure from the child's experience and removed parents to a greater distance from their children. There was not as much interaction between parent and child, and some children interpreted this distance as parental indifference. Some responded to it with hostility and what some people consider being a "brat."

*"I think I was brought up something like that. I remember feeling as a child that my parents did not take as good care of me or love me as much as my friend's parents loved and took care of their child because my friend's parents told her when to come home and what to wear. This seemed so important to me."*

*"Well, my mother used to spank me a lot, and that was the way I thought children should be brought up. I soon realized I couldn't do that to my baby. Now I'm learning another way. But my problem isn't over because my mother sometimes baby-sits for me and I'm afraid she is going to treat my baby the same way she treated me."*

That punitive way of teaching children is still prevalent. The growing statistics on child abuse are further evidence of this because abuse often begins with what many people consider "legitimate punishment" to "teach the child a lesson." As we have said before, children are often punished as a means of getting them to behave in ways they cannot understand or perform. What we really need is an understanding of the infant's level of development and what an infant can comprehend at each level.

A great deal has been learned about the ways infants learn and the most appropriate methods for teaching them at different ages through the patient studies of many painstaking behavioral scientists. We are discussing these methods with you so that you can help your babies learn and grow in the best way possible. We also hope that the parent-child relationship will be made more enjoyable.

*"But the old methods are so ingrained and when we do anything different, someone—even a stranger in a supermarket—will come up and say: 'Don't you know how to raise a baby? He needs a good smack on the hand!' What do you do about that?"*

People who know little or nothing about raising children are often the ones who are most emphatic and certain in their opinions. They do make it hard for others. It is good to be prepared for them with a kind but firm reply.

*"I've got one I use. I say: 'That is the way you used to bring up children, but times have changed and so have methods. Your generation didn't do a perfect job. Now I'm going to try it my way.' I use that on my family, and they are getting the point. No one is going to hit my baby."*

If that works for you, that's fine. It is good that you have the courage to express yourself so frankly. Your family will respect you for it. However, for strangers in a store or elsewhere, it might be easier to say something like: "Oh, I see you think the baby should be slapped. Thank you for your advice; I'll think about it." Then move on. This way, you take yourself out of the stranger's control and leave him or her little opportunity to pursue the matter further.

*"I can hardly wait to try that because I have been bothered so much by strangers interfering in the way I bring up my baby."*

Probably the essence of all teaching is patience, kindness, firmness, and consistency. If that is what guides the relationship between parent and child, the results are bound to be effective, and no one will want or need to interfere with your child-rearing methods. Of course, babies have days when they are out of sorts and cranky, and outsiders often pick such times to comment or attempt to interfere. Parents must understand that such comments are made without knowledge of the whole picture of the baby's development and should be disregarded.

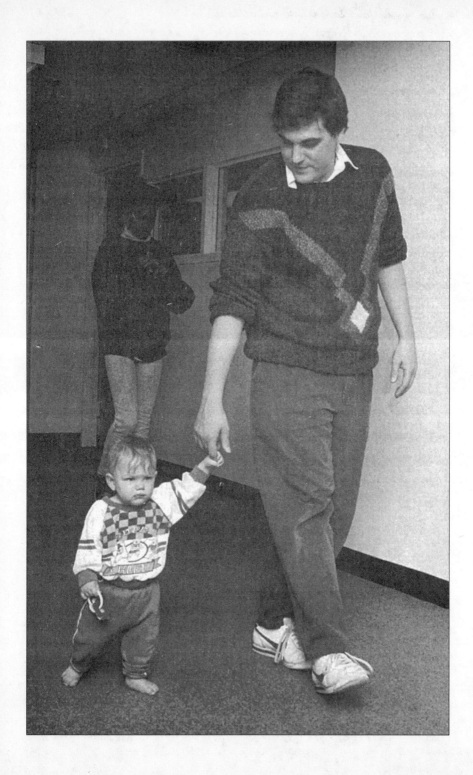

## Highlights of Development— Forty-eight Weeks

While sitting, the babies can now pivot and reach for things in all directions without losing their balance; previously they could only lean forward and straighten back to the sitting posture. Many of the babies can now stand  in their cribs and move around holding on to the rail. To walk outside of the crib, most babies still need support. (To provide this support, the parent may walk in front of the baby holding both of the baby's hands, or behind the child holding both of his hands over the child's head.) The babies may also be able to walk supporting themselves by pushing a chair ahead of them.

The babies are now able to pick up small objects (even small crumbs left on their high-chair trays) with a neat *pincers grasp,* an important fine motor achievement. When given several little blocks, the baby can play with them in several different ways—hitting them against each other, pushing them, and rearranging them.

Babies of this age are ready to be introduced to a simple formboard puzzle with round, square, and triangular pieces. When presented with such a puzzle with only the round form in place, the baby can remove it easily but will not be able to replace it. Practice with puzzles should, therefore, begin with the baby's *removal* of the pieces.

Most babies now have vocabularies including "Mama," "Dada," and one or two other words, such as "Hi" or "Bye." They should understand and be able to play "Pat-a-Cake" and "Bye-bye" more competently.

The babies can sit in their high chairs and play with toys for a longer period of time than previously. Usually the toys end up on the floor because the babies are now at the height of the period of exploring space by throwing things down—an activity that is important to their develop-ment, although annoying to some parents.

## New Developments in Exploration

We have talked about the babies' need to learn about space by pushing toys out of their cribs or off the high chair. For many babies this explora-tion is at its height. We hope that you are all taking advantage of this interest of your babies and teaching them the meanings of "up" and "down." This kind of teaching really assists the baby in understanding space and adds the verbal dimension to his exploratory efforts. Helping the baby achieve an understanding of these concepts can bring satisfaction to the parents as well as to the baby. There is nothing that enhances a baby's sense of achievement and mastery more than having the approving participation of the parents in his efforts to understand the world around him.

We forget how long it takes for babies to understand some concepts. They are true scientists. They have to experiment over and over again to verify their ideas. Each item that is dropped or pushed over the side of something makes a different sound or falls in a different way. The babies watch each one intently. Of course, we don't expect you to be as enchanted with this game as your babies are. For that reason, we have advised that you change the activity when you've had enough of it.

Some babies are probably already moving on to the next phase of this exploration—dropping toys and picking them up by themselves. Now that the babies are beginning to stand, they will hang on to a chair or rail with one hand and drop a toy with the other. Then they will lower themselves to pick the toy up, retrieve it, and then drop it again. They will do this over and over again because they are still not certain of cause and effect. In addition, being able to pick up a toy and throw it down by themselves without parental assistance gives babies a great sense of mastery. If your baby has not yet begun to do this, he will soon begin.

Remember: the babies will need to do the same experiment many times on their own because they were using the parent as an assistant when they could not do it by themselves.

Until now, we have been talking about throwing or dropping toys. What about food? Have any of the babies been dropping food off the table or high chair?

*"Oh, yes! Yesterday I was so angry. The baby pushed a plate off the high-chair tray. I scolded and yelled 'No' and slapped him hard. He looked very bewildered and cried and cried."*

It is very understandable that you do not find it at all amusing when the object used for exploration is a cup full of milk or the plate of delicious food you have prepared for the baby. From the baby's point of view, however, both kinds of things are fit objects for exploring space. It is hard for him to grasp the difference between a toy and a cup of milk, except that the latter falls in a more interesting way. At this age, it is better to place only a small amount of milk in a cup and sit close to the baby to intercept spills. In the coming year, the babies will be ready to understand the difference between toys and food.

*"I'm glad to know this because I'm sure I would have been ready to punish my baby. I so much want to be a good parent and not make the mistakes my parents made."*

Most mothers and fathers want to be good parents. The mistakes they make, however, do not occur because they are unkind, or unloving, but because they sometimes do not understand the meaning of their baby's actions in relation to his development. You cannot expect a one-year-old or a three-year-old to act like a five-year-old.

## Feelings About Parenthood: The Effect of Our Heritage

In this day and age, people do not have to become parents until they are ready to, until they want to have children. Even those who do not exercise this choice for religious reasons are helped by their beliefs to accept having a child.

However, in times past, many children were not wanted by their parents. As a result, child-rearing practices that reflected the parents' anger and feeling of being trapped by the child came into use. Indeed, such practices even became the accepted ways of dealing with a child.

Many of these questionable methods of child rearing were used on us when we were being brought up, and although most of us believe that we no longer endorse such outmoded methods, we still unconsciously replicate them because they are so deeply ingrained in our behavior. Indeed, it takes a great deal of effort to overcome our heritage, especially because we are not always aware of its place in our own behavior. But don't lose heart! With time, patience, and careful consideration of what you are doing and its effects on your children, you will be able to shed unwanted behavior patterns and assimilate new techniques.

Let me clarify what I mean by pointing out one such unfortunate remnant of the past—yelling at, scolding, or slapping a baby when he touches something or engages in some activity he shouldn't.

There was a time when parents had little or no understanding of early exploration and its importance in the child's development. In particular, they did not understand that a baby could not distinguish between what the parents considered healthy exploration—for example, playing quietly with a block or a doll—and what the parents looked on as dangerous, painful, or destructive—for example, reaching for mother's hair or pulling books out of a bookcase. To the parents, the child engaged in such unapproved behavior was just being "naughty" or "willfully disobedient." Thus, the parents felt justified in "teaching" the child how to behave by punishing him for wrong behavior. Usually this punishment involved yelling, scolding, or slapping the child's hands.

From the baby's point of view, however, such reactions are thoroughly unreasonable, and we feel such "teaching" techniques are inappropriate. The baby is exploring, trying to organize his world. He does not yet know that doing certain things is "good" and that doing certain other things is "bad." Such distinctions are way above his level of development. To the baby, everything he does is part of "exploring." It's neither "good" nor "bad"; it just is.

So, reacting to unapproved behavior with a yell or slap, especially a hard one, will only confuse or frighten the child. It may even discourage him from continuing to explore because he has been prevented painfully from completing the impulse he started to carry out. That could have serious consequences on the child's development of an ability or desire to explore and learn later on in school. Moreover, such a method of setting limits does not teach the child acceptable behavior. It merely punishes him for doing something the wrongness of which he cannot yet understand. Such a technique also inevitably puts the parent in the role of an inflicter of pain and fear, rather than in the role of a trusted guide and friend. This, of course, is hardly conducive to the development of a healthy parent-child relationship.

Instead of yelling at, scolding, or slapping a child, stop him from doing what he is doing with a firm "No," and immediately substitute some approved activity. This way, the child's impulse to complete the exploratory action he has begun will be diverted into acceptable channels. Thus, the child will not be discouraged from developing a healthy instinct to explore and learn, and he will begin to perceive what acceptable behavior entails. Finally, you will enhance, rather than impede, your relationship with the child by presenting yourself as a guide and friend.

Being limited in a harsh way is something we all experienced as children, and it is so deeply ingrained in our behavior patterns that we are all likely to react to our children that way. However, if you think through the consequences of such a "teaching" technique, you will see that it inevitably does more harm than good to the child's development.

*"I see now what you mean. That's just what I find myself doing. But when I use a more constructive approach such as you suggest, and it doesn't work the first time, I'm disappointed."*

Yes, of course, you are disappointed. The baby must still try his experiments until he learns, and you have to continue patiently teaching him until he does learn. The process takes time and patience, but it may make the difference between having a child with healthy intellectual curiosity and one who can't get involved in learning, or the difference between a child who learns to accept limitations and one who cannot accept them.

*"But not everything our parents did was wrong, was it?"*

There are many things that were right, and we have discussed some of them. Take, for example, picking up babies when they cry or rocking them to sleep. How do you suppose the lullaby began? We still sing babies to sleep or sing to soothe them. Similarly, we are going back to breast feeding and carrying babies on our backs or hips. Many practices from the past have value. Perhaps one of the most important of these is the establishment of regularity in the baby's day. We are returning to this time-honored practice—but with a difference—because now we recognize the baby's need for a routine that gives him a sense of security and order without the imposition of an exacting schedule unrelated to his own "biological clock."

All of the traditional practices or techniques that are appropriate and fit with the baby's level of development, we can and will hold on to. Those, however, that were not constructive, or that were harmful, we must unlearn by substituting better ways.

## The First Birthday

### The Party

Now that the babies are approaching their first birthdays, it may be helpful to discuss what would be appropriate for this big event. The most important thing to remember is that it is the child's birthday and should relate to his or her level of development. Grandparents naturally want to be there, and if they live nearby, that already makes a large group of guests. A very good "rule" for children's parties is to have one more child than the age of the child whose birthday it is. You will find that it is especially important to follow this "rule" when the children are two, three, and four years old. It is easy to overwhelm a child by inviting too many children and adults to the party.

*"Last week I saw that happen. I went to my nephew's party; he was two. His mother made it a great event with a beautifully decorated cake and table. There were ten children and ten mothers, plus grandparents. My nephew spent the whole afternoon crying in his room. I thought he must be getting sick. Now I understand that he was overwhelmed by the crowd invading his home."*

Exactly! There were simply too many children and adults at the party. We forget that each child comes with a parent or caretaker, and that doubles the number of guests. Following our suggested "rule," the appropriate number of children for the first birthday would be two: your child and one friend. If there is no other child available, your baby won't mind. (You must, of course, adapt all our suggestions to your own situation. If there are several siblings or other children that your baby is very used to, you may be able to have more children present at the party.) It is also important for the parent to stay close to the child to give the child a sense of security.

*"Another thing that surprised me was that none of the children ate the beautiful cake. It was a white cake with almond and bitter chocolate icing. I thought it was delicious."*

All the adults probably loved the cake, but it was too fancy for the children. You must remember what they eat every day and then prepare something that is not too different. Your one-year-olds may not eat any cake at all, but they will enjoy ice cream because they have had it before. Slightly older children may eat only a bite or two.

Another caution concerns the candles. Children, especially at this age, do not realize that they are hot. They are attracted by the brightness and may stick their fingers in the flame and burn themselves. It is a good idea, therefore, to keep a cake with lighted candles at some distance from the child—and then blow them out quickly after you have sung "Happy Birthday."

Remember also that one of the fears of this age is loud noise. It is a good idea to sing softly. A sudden rousing chorus of "Happy Birthday" can startle or frighten a child. The child may even burst into tears, which upsets everyone.

If you keep the party simple and at the child's level—not expecting her to understand it all—everyone will have a good time.

## Presents for the First Birthday

*"We've been talking a lot about our son's birthday, especially about presents. Just what presents are right for a baby this age, and how much is enough?"*

For the first birthday, there is a tendency to give a child too many presents that are too complicated. An appropriate present for a baby of this age is a small red ball that he can hold in his hand. It should be soft and chewable with nontoxic coloring because the baby will naturally try out its taste and texture with his mouth. Babies enjoy rolling balls along their high-chair trays or on the floor. They also like having the balls rolled back to them.

Other good toys include small rag dolls with the eyes, nose, and mouth embroidered on so they cannot be chewed off and brightly colored, nontoxic stuffed animals of a size the baby can hold—not enormous ones.

At this age, babies are also ready for small blocks about one inch square. They can hold them in their hands, put them in and out of cups, jars, or boxes, and perhaps begin to stack one on top of another.

The babies are also ready for the peg toy that holds a number of colored rings of graded sizes. At this time, the baby will be able to remove the rings from the peg and perhaps can learn to place one on the peg in the next few months. It is a good toy because it enhances development and, with maturation and practice, the baby will be able to place the rings on the peg in the appropriate order. This ability may not come until the child is two years old, so this is a useful toy for a long time.

Cloth books with one picture per page are also good presents and can be used for a long time. Musical rattles and music boxes are nice but not essential. The baby does not need too many new presents at once.

Clothes, small chairs and tables, electric trains, elaborate dolls with real hair and fine clothes, large stuffed animals, and the like are always things that doting friends and relatives feel moved to give babies on the first birthday (or first Christmas). At this age, such items are really presents for the parents. The complicated and elaborate toys can be put away until they are appropriate, or they can be used as room ornaments until the baby shows interest in them.

What feelings and ideas do you have about presents?

*"I have been wondering what to say if anyone asked what to get the baby. I can see to it that the baby's father and I get the few appropriate toys that have been suggested. We can decide afterward to do what seems right about whatever else the baby gets—use what is right for now and put the rest away."*

*"I know my husband is going to be very upset about the trains not being appropriate. He's been looking forward to giving the baby that for a present."*

Actually, you don't have to spoil the father's fun. We all know that getting the train set will give the father pleasure, and when he gets it set up and running, the baby will enjoy watching it for a few minutes at a time. However, you can hardly call the trains the baby's toy. A baby's toy is something the baby can manipulate by himself. Trains will not be appropriate for a few years yet.

*"If trains are really for fathers, how about the doll with change of clothes being for mothers?"*

If that gives mother pleasure, why not? Mother may have been looking forward to playing with dolls with her baby. There is nothing wrong in admitting that.

*"Well, I guess I don't need to play with dolls anymore. My baby is my big, live doll, and dressing her is the real thing. I guess I've worked out my needs in real life and don't need to do it symbolically anymore."*

Many women who like to sew get pleasure from making clothes for their children's dolls. Adults get pleasure in giving lovely toys. That's fine! The most important thing, however, is not to overwhelm the babies with too many presents and not to expect them to appreciate toys that are not yet developmentally appropriate.

## The Baby's First Shoes

The baby's first shoes are often given as a gift, especially by grandparents. There are differing opinions on when the baby needs shoes and what kind they should be. It is very important that shoes fit properly, and how to tell this is often a problem.

*"My pediatrician says babies don't need shoes until they are walking, and my mother is having a fit. She says the baby needs high shoes to support his ankles; otherwise he'll damage his ankles, and that is why he is not walking yet. We keep arguing about this."*

It's always a good idea to get your pediatrician's advice because he is the one who can best tell whether the baby is ready for shoes and what kind of shoes to get, particularly if a special type is required.

There are some facts about foot and muscle development that ought to be better known. For example, the belief that a baby needs high shoes for ankle support is a common misconception. A baby does not learn to walk because her feet are supported by bracelike high shoes but because her neuromusculature has matured to the point that she can support herself. Her ability to stand and move is helped by the freedom to flex and contract her muscles. The more freedom to exercise the muscles, the quicker the development of motor activity. A high, firm shoe can act as a deterent to this free exercise of the muscles and actually make movement more difficult and clumsy. We have often seen babies who clump along in heavy shoes and scamper freely when the shoes are removed.

*"Well, why put any shoes on the baby's feet in that case?"*

Actually, many doctors advise against shoes until the baby is walking well. However, in the winter when floors are cold and drafty, soft leather-soled moccasin-socks or slippers made out of corduroy, flexible leather, or felt are appropriate. Socks are also good if the baby doesn't slip or skid in them. These soft foot coverings serve two purposes: They keep the feet warm, and they protect them from pins or other sharp objects on the floor.

*"When babies are finally ready for shoes, what kind should they be? Should they be high or low shoes?"*

For normal feet, the high shoes are not necessary. Support for the child's weight comes from the bone and muscle, not the leather shoes. A low shoe is adequate. It is necessary only to protect the feet from the roughness of the pavement and such things as broken glass or sharp pebbles when the baby is walking outdoors. If the floor is carpeted, the baby certainly does not need shoes. If the floors are uncarpeted and cold, then some protective foot covering is in order. Parents have to use their judgment and find a shoe or slipper that allows freedom of movement but also provides protection for the feet.

*"What are some of the things to look for when getting shoes fitted? Stores make such a fuss about their brands, and some use X rays, although I hear that is dangerous."*

X rays are dangerous, and their use is now prohibited because there was too much X-ray emanation.

First of all, the thing to look for is a flexible sole on the shoes; you should be able to bend the toe toward the heel easily. Then you should be certain that the inner edge of the last—that is, the line from the big toe to the heel—is straight. When the baby's foot is placed in the shoes, the heel should not ride up. The back rim of the shoes should not curve and cut into the heel. Put your finger in and feel whether it does. When the shoe is buckled or laced and the baby stands up, there should be about half an inch from the end of his toe to the tip of the shoe. There should be ample toe room, and the top of the shoe should not overlap the sole. If a shoe does that, it is not wide enough to accommodate the foot when it is bearing the baby's weight. If the shoe has to be buckled or laced very tightly to keep the foot from riding up, then the shoe does not fit properly. A different size, width, or brand of shoe must be tried. Proper shoe fitting is difficult and very important.

*"Shoes are so expensive. The salespeople always try to sell you the most expensive ones. Can you tell by the price which to buy?"*

Certainly not. Look for the features just mentioned. They can sometimes be found in some of the least expensive shoes. The baby's foot grows very rapidly. When the shoes are very expensive, you try to get as much wear out of them as possible, and children often end up wearing shoes that are too small. It is not necessary to get the strongest, longest-lasting, and most expensive leather. The important factor is the fit, which should be checked every three months. Many babies need new shoes several times a year.

*"What about boots and overshoes?"*

Just now the babies are not spending enough time walking outdoors to need such footwear. In bad weather and in high snow, most babies are not outdoors very much at all. When they are older and do spend more time walking outdoors, these items will be needed. If some babies are out a lot in the rain and snow, they will, of course, need boots earlier. Parents have to decide depending on their own situations.

## *Weaning*

### *Breast Feeding*

Many mothers are breast feeding, and both baby and mother are thriving. Some of you have asked how long breast feeding should last. That is a very individual matter. If the milk supply is good and the mother is comfortable, it can be kept up until the baby is about a year old. Many babies have a natural inclination to stop when they are about eight or nine months old, and many mothers wish to encourage this.

Whenever the mother feels that she would like to offer a supplementary bottle instead of the breast, she can introduce it. It is best to offer this bottle at the same feeding each day so the baby gets used to it. Then, if an emergency arises when the mother has to be away, the baby will be more accustomed to drinking from a bottle. Your pediatrician will advise you about this and prescribe what formula is the best to use.

When weaning is decided on, it can be accomplished gradually as the baby becomes used to taking more from the bottle than from the breast. Nature has a way of taking care of the mother's milk supply. As the baby demands less and sucks less from the breast, the production of milk diminishes. Finally, the baby becomes entirely dependent on bottle feedings, and the breast supply of milk has ceased naturally, without trauma to either mother or baby.

Have you thought about weaning? What are your thoughts on the subject?

*"I'm perfectly content nursing, and I haven't used any supplementary bottles yet. Do you think it's a good idea to use supplementary bottles anyway?"*

Yes, it's a kind of an insurance, so that if an emergency arises, the baby won't be forced abruptly to use the unfamiliar bottle. But bear this consideration in mind: When using a bottle, you must be certain the milk flow is not too fast, so that the feeding isn't too quick. Breast-fed babies are accustomed to a lot of sucking.

*"If you keep up breast feeding as long as a year, isn't it harder on the baby to stop? Doesn't the baby become too attached to that method of feeding?"*

*"I had to stop suddenly when I was sick, and I hadn't started the baby on a bottle. The baby cried and cried and would not take the formula for two days. We were very concerned. Finally we sweetened the formula, and he took it. I wish I had given at least one bottle a day before that. Even now, he pulls at me as though he still wants the breast, but he is getting used to the bottle."*

Of course, the babies become attached to the method of feeding you've established. That is why the weaning should be very gradual. Perhaps one bottle a day for a week or two, then weaning to two and then three. The first morning and the last night feedings are usually the hardest to give up.

*"I heard that weaning should start when the baby begins to get teeth. Is that the usual guideline?"*

That used to be the guideline when breast feeding was the norm. When the baby bit the mother, she would then wean the baby. Often this was done quite abruptly, and the abruptness of the change caused the mother discomfort because she still had a large milk supply and had to have her breasts bound and use some form of dehydration. The baby was also miserable. Now we know better, and try to wean the baby more gradually on a time schedule that suits both infant and mother.

*"Do babies have to be weaned to a bottle? Can they be weaned to a cup?"*

This is often done, particularly when a baby has also been taught to take juice from a cup. When babies are used to taking juice, you can try giving them their milk or formula from a cup. This is a very nice way to wean a baby and eliminates the need for going through the bottle stage. Success, however, depends on the baby's level of development and ability to manage drinking from a cup. Cup feeding is an especially good way to begin weaning when breast feeding has continued for nearly a year. By this time, the baby has probably had sufficient sucking activity, and if the cup is accepted well, you needn't introduce the bottle.

*"What if the baby doesn't take as much milk from the cup as he would from a bottle?"*

The quantity that a baby needs has to be decided individually for each baby by the doctor. Usually if cup feeding is begun later, the baby is taking sufficient other food so that his nourishment isn't entirely dependent on milk. However, this is all very individual, and the timing has to be decided by the mother's assessment of her baby, her own needs, and her doctor's advice.

*"What about weaning from the bottle? Now that my baby is nearly a year old, I'm getting a lot of advice about weaning her to a cup."*

## *Bottle Feeding*

Bottle-fed babies need the same gradual weaning as breast-fed babies. Often such weaning is too abrupt because the mother does not have any personal physical need for gradualism.

Bottle-fed babies usually do not get as much sucking time as breast-fed babies because bottle nipples allow a more rapid milk flow. Bottle-fed babies therefore usually have a greater sucking need, and it is important to wean them slowly on their own timetables, not the adult's. Babies often find the last bottle of the day a comforting one to continue. If they still need to suck and are too abruptly weaned, they will find their own substitutes, usually their thumbs. Weaning from the bottle too early can lead to a habit of thumb-sucking.

*"Now that the babies have teeth, isn't it bad for them to go to sleep with a bottle in their mouths?"*

Doctors and dentists generally feel that allowing the baby to go to sleep with formula or milk in the mouth may result in damage to the baby's teeth. We, therefore, recommend that you do not leave the bottle in the crib with the baby. Instead, let the baby take her bottle; then give her a drink of water and put her to bed. If the baby will not relax and go off to sleep unless she is sucking on her bottle, use water in the bottle instead of milk.

Other babies who have stopped taking bottles may like to suck on a pacifier for a few minutes before they go to sleep. Such a child clearly needs the pacifier for additional sucking as well as for comfort.

*"What about the two-year-old who walks around with a bottle?"*

This child must still need some opportunity to suck. She may also need some extra comforting. It is a good idea to look at the child's life pattern and see whether there isn't something that is causing her anxiety. In any case, you often do more harm than good by trying to take away the bottle before the child is ready. No child goes to high school with a bottle, yet some at that age still surreptitiously suck their thumbs. Most children naturally give up the bottle when they are ready. Parents must "tune in" to the signs of readiness and be prepared to help the child take this step toward more mature behavior.

*"What is the latest that a child may need a bottle at bedtime or first thing in the morning?"*

About three years old is usually accepted as the average limit. The time factor varies, of course, with each child. Some manage cup feeding very well before they are three and are proud of their accomplishment. A few need one bottle a while longer. At no time should a child be shamed into giving up the bottle.

*"But you often see kids who are older than that walking around holding bottles. Why is that?"*

Such behavior is not usual or normal. The child in question is probably not using the bottle for nourishment but as a security measure or as a tie to the mother, from whom the child may have difficulty separating. The cause of such behavior varies in each case. You must look at each child's particular situation to determine the reasons for the behavior and the ways of correcting it.

## *Toilet Training: Some General Ideas*

*"What about toilet training? My mother keeps urging me to start training the baby. In fact, when he was four months old, she gave me a little potty!"*

That is the way older generations began toilet training: The mother put a small potty on her lap and held the baby on it. She, of course, did that about the time that the baby naturally had a bowel movement. For a baby with regular habits, this training could be quite successful. We maintain, however, that it was the mother who was well-trained, *not* the baby!

Other theorists held that one should start toilet training when the baby was about one year old. Once again the mother observed the natural time of bowel movements and trained herself to be ready for them.

More recently, we have come to understand that the child's ability to control the sphincter muscles of the bowels and bladder does not usually develop until the child is between two and three years old. In other words, children are physically incapable of controlling these body muscles until that time. As in every other aspect of child development, each child has his own maturational timetable. Some children may gain this control at a year and a half; others not until three years of age or later. Nonetheless, the ability develops, unless there is some physical problem, or unless the parents have tried to develop the ability too early or too punitively and the child has built up an emotional resistance to it. Such resistance comes from a battle for control between parent and child.

All of us must realize that this is the second major area over which the child has total control. The first, you will recall, is eating. No parent can force a child either to withhold or release his urine or bowel movement. The child must be physically capable of doing it, and—equally important—must want to. It is, therefore, a very complicated neurological, physiological, and psychological process. Inappropriate parental demands in this area can have deleterious effects on the parent-child relationship and turn it into an "angry alliance" that may affect the child's later development in the form of speech difficulties (speech delay and stuttering) and problems with self-control. How the child handles the demands of toilet training prepares him, more or less well, for the pressures of later life.

The appropriate timing for toilet training, the signs of a child's readiness, and ways in which parents can help the child learn this control with a minimum of stress to both parent and child will be topics for discussion in the coming year. We provide you with these general ideas on the topic now, however, to help you resist suggestions to begin premature toilet training and to enable you to relax and enjoy the developments that are appropriate to this age. They are greater motor activity, self-feeding, speech development, and concept formation; they do *not* include the ability to control the sphincter muscles of the bowels and the bladder.

It is also important that weaning and toilet training be kept quite separate. To place these two frustrations and limitations on the child's "baby ways" simultaneously is not a good idea. In the coming months, it is appropriate to begin gradual weaning. Toilet training should wait for the child's physical readiness and his greater understanding of the meaning of the physical feelings he has and how to act on them appropriately. It also helps tremendously if the child is more verbal and can understand and discuss the process with you.

*"I am very relieved to hear all this. My pediatrician has said very much the same thing. I'm glad you agree."*

Our suggestions to you on all these child-rearing topics are based not only on the thinking of child psychiatrists and psychologists but also on that of pediatricians. We always urge you to consult your pediatricians and certainly hope our ideas are not in conflict with theirs. All of us have the best interests of you and your children in mind.

*"My gosh, I thought we'd be getting rid of the diapers in a few months. But if the child's muscles aren't ready, I guess there's not much point in attempting to press toilet training."*

Pressing a child before he or she is ready only leads to frustration for both parent and child.

*"I am disappointed that it will take so long, but I am relieved that I don't have to start in yet because my friends are having such a struggle with the procedure."*

Your friends would not have a struggle if they were going about the training when the child was ready. You do not have to look ahead to toilet training as a struggle. It is a natural development that takes place without conflict or resistance if it is done on the child's timetable and not for the parents' convenience. We will be discussing this matter often in the coming year and will prepare you for action when the children are around two years old.

## Highlights of Development—Fifty-two Weeks

The child's first birthday has special significance for most parents. Development can still be quite varied, however, among children at the age. Some babies may be able to take a halting step or two alone, but most still need to hold on to a parent's hand for support. Some are more advanced and are walking quite well. It is fun for parents to recall the time when the baby's greatest accomplishments were lifting his head and waving his arms and legs about.

If the parent makes a tower of two blocks, the baby will try to build such a structure but often will not succeed. Even the attempt shows an advance over the last month when the baby could only bang blocks against each other. Practice helps the child to become more skillful at placing blocks on top of each other, and such play is a good game for parent and child.

The babies may be able to release a block into a cup after this activity has been demonstrated to them. They can now pick up a pellet more easily but have difficulty inserting it into the small jar, often missing the jar opening as they release the pellet. These activities can also be added to the child's playtime with the parents.

By now, the baby is able to dangle the red ring by the string, whereas several months ago she would only reach for the red ring, indicating an advance in manual dexterity.

When a simple puzzle board (for circles, squares, and triangles) is presented to the baby without the pieces in place and the round piece is handed to the baby, she will look selectively at the round hole, sometimes poking her finger into it. Most children do not put the piece in the correct place unless they have had some practice with the puzzle. This, too, is a good learning activity for parents to play with the child.

By now, most babies have a vocabulary of two or three words, perhaps "Bye" and "Hi" or "Ba" (for bottle), in addition to "Mama" and "Dada." The additional words in a child's vocabulary depend on what the child hears, what has been repeated most dramatically to him, and what interests him. for some it is "ca" (for cookie or car); for others, it is a syllable standing for the name of a favorite toy. In addition to expressive language, the children also show comprehension and may be able to hand toys to the parent on request, although they may not be able to release them yet.

The baby likes to gaze at herself in the mirror. If given a ball, she will place the ball against the mirror and look at it as well. While being dressed, the babies are beginning to cooperate by holding up their arms to be put through sleeves or holding up their feet for socks or shoes.

## *Review of the Accomplishments of the First Year*

The first birthday is really quite a milestone. It is a good time to review the accomplishments of this first year. What are the biggest changes you have noticed in your babies?

### *Communication*

*"For me the baby's first year went very fast. There were some bad days, and at times I wondered why I was so eager to be a mother, but on the whole it was a good experience. What we notice most is the increase in our ability to communicate and the increase in our ability to catch on to what the baby means. In the last week or two, she is really beginning to communicate with us."*

What do you mean by that?

*"Well, if she wants something, for instance, she gestures and grunts, and I can tell what she wants. When I get it right, she smiles and is very happy."*

*"As a father, I think communication is the most important thing, too. Now our baby can say 'Dada,' and I know what he means. He is calling to me; he wants me to come to him."*

*"Our baby only says, 'Mama,' 'Dada,' 'Bye,' waves, and calls out 'ca' (for 'car'), but we understand and that's a thrill. When we repeat words, we feel reassured that sooner or later the baby will catch on, and that language is on the way. I really have to admit that until he said a word that we could make out, we were really concerned about whether or not he would learn to talk."*

Parents feel that the baby is slow to speech, but three or four words at one year is normal. Sometimes parents do not "count" single syllables as words, even though they have meaning for the baby. Clear enunciation should not be expected at this age. The parents' sense of satisfaction will enhance the baby's sense of achievement if these words, no matter how rudimentary, are appropriately recognized as part of the baby's early vocabulary.

*"Even though our baby has only a small speaking vocabulary, I know she understands much more. If we want her to get something like a ball or a shoe or even go to the closet for Daddy's slipper, she can do it. Her ability to understand us is very satisfying."*

*"Even though we can't understand much of our baby's babbling, we can tell by her intonation that she thinks she is talking. We can only guess at the meaning of some of the clearer sounds, but there is much more of a sense of communication. We feel we are reaching a goal that we looked forward to very much."*

*"In our house we speak Spanish, so our baby is saying words in Spanish— 'Papy' for 'Daddy,' for instance. My husband is so happy. He says the baby is a real person now!"*

All of you seem to agree that communication is an important accomplishment. It is very interesting that this is the first acomplishment to be mentioned tonight. Naturally, communication is the most important accomplishment for a human baby. Language distinguishes us from the rest of the animal world, and good language development correlates highly with good achievement in school. All of you must have been doing a very good job in stimulating speech. That is clearly shown by your understanding of the importance of language and your interest in helping the baby develop the ability to communicate. Some parents place greater value on walking and often try to force a baby to walk before the baby is quite ready. As you all know by now, walking is a development that occurs spontaneously if the child is given sufficient freedom to move. However, language cannot be learned without stimulation and imitation. You are certainly doing a good job of providing this stimulation.

Is there anything else that you feel has been an important development during the baby's first year of life?

## Walking

*"Even though babies learn to walk naturally, it really is fun to see them take their first steps. They take a step or two ever so carefully at first. Then*

*they sit down. Then they get up and try again or reach for the nearest table or chair. We are delighted because our baby is so pleased with herself."*

*"I'm pleased the baby can walk, but I'm also a little worried. Now I have to watch him more closely so that he will not get hurt or get at something that he can break."*

*"I can't wait for the baby to walk by himself. To me that's very important—maybe because I enjoy sports and I want my son to be athletic too."*

Certainly, the increased ability to move around is an important advance for the babies. You'll remember the babies were unable to lift their heads from the mattress when they were first born. We understand your pleasure and the babies' pleasure in learning to walk. All parents look forward to this achievement.

## Exploration

*"The babies' greater mobility makes them more interesting as well, even if it makes us all work harder. We can see them explore things and try to reach out for, hold, and examine things. Sometimes they tear or break something, but I guess that's to be expected because they haven't learned yet just how to handle different objects."*

To permit exploration and provide the right playthings, such as small toys, plastic cups, measuring spoons, and small blocks, are all part of the parents' job. The baby's interest in exploration is one of the signs of progress and sets the groundwork for the desire to find out about things later in school.

*"There is one thing we haven't mentioned. I wouldn't call it an achievement, but it certainly is a condition or situation that you can't get away from, and that's the everlasting mess the baby creates in a house. My wife just can't seem to keep the place neat. I really love the baby, but the mess sometimes gets to me."*

Yes, there is apt to be disorder in the house where the baby is playing. At this age, babies are "messy" from the adult point of view. They are only exploring. They haven't yet learned what each object is. Soon you will be able to teach them where each thing belongs. They learn that by observation. So, a house should not be left in a mess all the time just because it's going to get messy again. There should be certain clean-up times—for example, before lunch or before bedtime—so the baby sees the house in order and begins to absorb that image of his home. When he is able to, the baby will begin to participate in the putting-away activities.

## Daily Routine

*"Another of our baby's accomplishments that means a great deal to me is that she is now on a good schedule and can sleep through the night. Also,*

*she takes a nap that I can count on during the day, and life is better organized for all of us."*

*"That accomplishment also means a lot to me. My baby isn't sleeping all through the night yet, but he wakes only once, at about eleven. Then he sleeps till six or seven in the morning. The day goes along pretty regularly. I'm not in a tizzy anymore trying to get him taken care of and do the housework too. Yes, I'd say it's quite a change for the better."*

*"I must confess that the first few times our baby slept through the night, I awakened, and so did my husband. We were used to getting up, and we had to go in and look at her to be sure she was all right."*

All of us like order in our lives; we also like to know more or less what's coming next. Babies like these things too, as you have found out. They give the baby a sense of security.

## Trust and Attachment

*"Yes, I'd have to say my baby is getting less restless and more confident. He seems to be simmering down, as though he was getting the idea that I'd be there to fix things for him. Could you say he seems to trust me more?"*

That's exactly the idea. Not only are the babies' nervous systems maturing and functioning better, but they themselves are developing a sense of security in their environment due to the consistency of your care. They are less anxious and more secure. This sense of security or basic trust is certainly one of the major achievements of this year. As you know, it is a very important element in personality development and helps the baby cope throughout life.

*"Of course, all the things we've talked about are accomplishments, but for me the most satisfying is the way the baby responds to us and acts like we are important to her. We see that she responds differently to her grandparents. She knows them and likes them, but her response is different from her response to her mother and me. You could say that the baby has a special attachment to each of us and that all these special attachments are different from one another."*

You are saying that the attachment you feel the baby has for you and the recognition you have of the baby's emerging personality are achievements to be recorded for this first year. That is a very good observation. It is very important to recognize the fact that you feel that each of you is becoming aware of the other as a person who counts, and, perhaps, is accountable to the other. Not so long ago, this feeling was not generally recognized as important, and babies were not thought to have such feelings and personalities until they were much older. Their wishes and preferences were never considered. But now we recognize that such is the case, and that constitutes a great advance in our understanding of young children.

# Changes and Developments to Expect in the Second Year

We seem to have covered all of the babies' major achievements during their first year of life. Now I wonder what you are looking forward to for the next year. What are some of the things that you are anticipating?

## Greater Mobility

*"I think one of the big advances will be in walking. The babies will be much more able to walk alone with less falling. It won't be such a tottering kind of walk."*

That's true. They will be able to walk faster and farther and even begin to run and climb stairs with help. Also, they will finally give up crawling.

*"That sounds great to me because our baby is getting too heavy to carry around, but he isn't making much effort to walk. He only stands. When should I expect him to walk?"*

Many babies walk by ten or eleven months. The average age for walking well alone is about fourteen months.

*"When should you begin to worry if they don't walk? Our baby seems so slow learning."*

If the babies are able to pull themselves to a standing position and shuffle from chair to chair, or along the crib edge, you know they will learn to walk. If you have any doubts, you should see your doctor about the matter. Some babies are very cautious; some are putting all their efforts into speech or the manipulation of toys, rather than walking. Parents must also remember that each child has a different maturational timetable.

## Increased Speech Development

*"What about speech? I know the babies will speak more this year, but how much more? What should we expect?"*

*"Maybe the babies will be able to name more things."*

*"I expect my baby to say sentences this year."*

*"I can't wait to have a real conversation wih my baby. When will that come?"*

There seems to be a variety of expectations. Some parents are quite modest in their expectations; others want a great deal. If a baby can say ten to twenty words by eighteen months, that is an appropriate vocabulary. By two years, the baby should be able to make a three-word sentence like "Daddy go bye" or "Baby want car," and their vocabularies will have increased to about 250 words. Of course, some babies will speak more fluently than others. Some will have a larger vocabulary but enunciate this vocabulary relatively poorly; others will enunciate clearly but possess a small vocabulary. There will be a great deal of gesturing and tugging to get parents to understand, and there may be tears and frustration when the parents don't. Parents who are patient and don't lose their "cool," however, will begin to understand their own child quite well, and that makes the second year more fun for both parents and child.

## Increased Socialization

*"What about play? Will the babies begin playing together?"*

The babies will become increasingly social and will enjoy being with other people and children. As we will see, babies of this age play *alongside* each other, rather than *with* each other, and will continue to need parental supervision.

## Self-Feeding

*"When can we expect the babies to feed themselves with a spoon?"*

Most babies begin trying to feed themselves between ten and fourteen months of age. Many of your babies are already doing well with finger foods. Gradually over this coming year, they will become more adept at using the spoon. It is important to let them begin doing this during this coming year, even though it is messy.

The babies will also become more adept at drinking from a cup in the coming year. Here again, you must expect some spilling and messiness.

## Increasing Autonomy

The desire to feed themselves is one of the examples of the babies' increasing desire for autonomy. Other signs of this desire include greater selectiveness about what they eat and the greater distance they run from the parent or caretaker. They will be able to play by themselves for longer periods as well and will be less willing to accept changes in activity. This will put greater demands on the parents' versatility, consistency, and firmness. The child's growing desire for autonomy can lead, therefore, to conflict with the parents. These conflicts can culminate toward the end of this year in the "terrible twos" if the child's need for autonomy is not properly understood by the parents. We will be talking more about this in the coming year to help make your relationship with your child happy and constructive.

## Increased Concept Formation

Most of the babies are now beginning to understand that people or objects they do not see still exist. When they drop their toys, they now look for them. They are also enjoying the game of "Peekaboo," and are no longer frightened or made uncomfortable when the parent's face disappears. Some of the babies are beginning to look up expectantly when they hear Daddy's key turn in the lock. The babies' understanding of the permanence of objects will be greatly strengthened during the second year.

In addition, children's concepts about the world will be related to their exploration and manipulation of objects. They will need to examine and physically handle a wide variety of objects. Needless to say, parents will often take a dim view of this activity, but it is essential to the child's development of concepts and language. Manipulating objects is the necessary precursor to naming them. Language, in turn, will strengthen conceptual thinking, so this will be another important area of discussion in the coming year.

## Closing Remarks

Now that we have had a "sneak preview" of the "coming attractions" for next year, let us say a few words about your part in your child's development this year.

You are learning the ropes of being parents. You have all acquired a greater understanding of your babies' developmental needs. You have helped the babies develop warm, trusting relationships with you, and you have come to enjoy them. When you were infants your parents imparted to you the best that they knew at that time. You have been learning the recent research information and incorporating that into your parenting practice. You are learning to become your children's advocates, instead of their critics, while at the same time helping them to accept your guidance in beginning to assimilate the socially accepted patterns of our society. You have helped them to learn about their world in a way that they could understand and to begin to recognize their own achievements and develop their own self-esteem. In all, you have contributed immeasurably to the great progress the babies have made. A mutually affectionate relationship has been established, and that is the best note on which to end the first year.

# The Second Year
## of Life

# 13

## Age One Year to Fifteen Months

## Highlights of Development—One Year

The child's first birthday has special significance for most parents. Development is still quite varied, however, among children at this age. Some children may be able to take a halting step or two alone, but most still need to hold on to a parent's hand for support. A few are walking alone quite well.

If the parent makes a tower of two blocks, the child will try to build such a structure but often will not succeed. Even the attempt shows an advance. Practice helps the child become more skillful at placing blocks on top of each other, and such play is a good game for parent and child. In a month or so, most children will be able to grasp two blocks in one hand and, therefore, will be able to hold three blocks. These achievements in small motor skills are often overshadowed by the gross motor developments of standing and walking.

The children may be able to put a block into a cup after this activity has been shown to them; soon, they will do it without demonstration. Parents can turn this new skill into the game of putting small objects into larger containers.

When a simple puzzle (of circles, squares, and triangles) is presented to the child without the pieces in place and the round piece is handed to the child, she will look selectively at the round hole, sometimes poking her finger into it. Most children do not put the piece in the correct place unless they have had some practice with the puzzle; they are able, however,

 to lift the piece out of the puzzle. In a month or so, most will begin placing the piece into the puzzle. This, too, is a good learning activity for parents to engage in with the child.

When given a crayon, children begin to imitate a scribble; some do it tentatively, and others more

vigorously. Parents are often worried about allowing drawing because they are concerned that the child will scribble on everything; but this activity is an important part of a child's development and should be encouraged with supervision.

At one year, most children have a vocabulary of two to four words, perhaps "Bye" and "Hi" or "Ba" (for bottle), in addition to "Mama" and "Dada." They are also beginning to carry on their own conversations using unintelligible words with the intonations of language. Children of this age comprehend considerably more language than they are given credit for or can express; they demonstrate this by pointing to and looking for things on parental request. A good game is "Find the ball" or "Get the doll," which encourages the child's language development and gives the parent a chance to show approval of the child's accomplishments.

The child also likes to gaze at himself in a mirror. If given a ball, he will place the ball against the mirror and look at it as well. In the coming weeks, the child will learn to release a ball toward the parent's open hands. As the child is encouraged to do this, another way of playing by rolling or throwing the ball to each other has begun. This game gives both parents and the child satisfaction and enjoyment.

While being dressed, the children are now beginning to cooperate by holding up their arms to be put through sleeves or holding up their feet for socks or shoes.

## Parents' Expectations of This Age Level

The children have made enormous progress in the last year, from complete helplessness and immobility to walking. They are taking on their own unique personalities, yet they are still very young and immature. We have noticed that parents' expectations of their children are often beyond the child's level of development. Are there some achievements you were expecting by now that haven't occurred? Are you surprised at things the baby doesn't do yet?

### Weaning

*"Yes, I was always under the impression that a baby would be fully weaned from a bottle by one year. My baby is so attached and dependent on his bottle that I don't think I can switch him to a cup for a long time."*

Weaning children by one year used to be the practice. We are now aware of the emotional significance of the bottle to the baby. It represents a time of closeness to mother. A baby cannot give up that closeness at a specific time determined by someone else. He should be allowed to give up the bottle gradually as he matures and can take more of his milk successfully from a cup. It must be done on the same maturational timetable as all the rest of his development.

■                                                                              ■

*"But my mother says she broke me and all of her children at one year. She just threw the bottles out and that was that. She thinks I should do the same. She said we cried for several days, maybe a week, and didn't eat; but she stuck it out and feels very proud of herself for it."*

At that time, it was the accepted procedure. Now that we think we understand a child's emotional needs better, we feel that this is not the best way to wean. We feel that weaning from breast or bottle to cup should be gradual and not traumatic. In our view, such abrupt weaning may set up the foundation of depression, interfere with basic trust, and give the child a sense of loss and separation too early for him to be able to cope with it. Because he is still essentially nonverbal at one year, the child really does not understand your expectations and cannot explain his feelings and needs.

*"I have been breast feeding my baby and I've been gradually introducing the cup. He takes it well when I hold him in my lap. I give him his milk from the cup twice a day. Is it possible to just wean him to cup feeding without going to the bottle stage and weaning him from that?"*

Since you have nursed him as long as this, it is perfectly possible to do it that way. As a breast-fed baby, he has probably had sufficient sucking. When one weans from the breast at an earlier age, before a baby has satisfied the sucking need and before he can take a sufficient amount from a cup, it's advisable to bottle-feed first and introduce the cup later.

*"When you say gradually, how gradually do you mean? My idea is to eliminate one bottle a day. Would that be too fast?"*

For some babies perhaps not; but in general at least a week should elapse before substituting the cup for another bottle feeding. The parent is the best judge of the interval, because she can tell how well the baby is adapting to the cup feeding. For some children, an even longer interval may be advisable.

## Ability to Separate; Parents' Time for Themselves

*"What bothers me is that my baby always wants to be near me. He can't seem to play alone. I can't get anything done around the house. I felt that I should be able to put him down for a while or be able to go on and do things in the house that I have to do."*

By this age, you expected the baby to entertain himself so that you would have a little more freedom. Then you would come back to him when *you* were ready?

*"Yes, and feel that he was all right; but I found out that it is not working at all."*

It is not working because at this age babies are not ready to play alone for a long enough time for mother to get the housework or cooking done.

There are reasons for it. One is that they still do not feel secure when they can't see you; another one is that they can't concentrate on any form of play for long enough on their own. They also cannot initiate activities without some help from the parent.

*"How long can they play on their own with something like a busy box?"*

Fifteen to twenty minutes is a very long time for them at this age. Then they have to be presented with something different. Some can be interested in a box with many little boxes, keys, small dolls, or blocks, which they can put in and take out. Others just like to roam about the room you are in and explore objects in it. Some can occupy themselves by turning the pages of a book.

*"I'm having the same problem. Even when my baby is in her room, she'll stay for about five minutes and then she comes to look for me. When she finds me, she takes me by the hand and leads me back to her room to play with her."*

That behavior is very typical for this age. There are ways, however, to do other things. If you have to be in the kitchen or the living room, you can take the same toy she has pulled you to play with and bring it back to the kitchen. Children need to keep in contact with you all the time. You would like some separation—time to do what you want to do. That's what every mother and father would like. You may be able to do this for a while with three-year-olds. At this age, children are still at the stage of beginning to separate from you.

It is important for working mothers to realize that their children will be acting the same way toward their housekeepers and baby-sitters. It is a good idea to talk with your caretakers and ask them how they feel about the baby's demands for closeness. Let them know that giving the baby appropriate attention is more important than doing all the housework. This is true for parents as well as other caretakers.

*"My baby is very demanding of my time on weekends; he won't let me out of his sight. I thought it was because I'd been gone all week. Do you mean he acts like that with his nurse? No wonder the house looks so messy sometimes!"*

A neat house and clean laundry are very visible things that housekeepers can show you at the end of the day. That you have kept the baby happy and interested and responded appropriately to his needs are not so easy to demonstrate. It is important to let your caretakers know where your priorities are and to help them to understand your baby's needs as you understand them.

*"I sometimes feel that I expect too much when I want my baby to under-stand what I am saying—especially if I take him somewhere and he is a bit frightened. I want him to understand that we are going back home soon,*

*that everything is all right, that I'm not going to leave him. Or if I am going to leave him, that I'm coming back soon."*

At this age, they are hardly able to be in a different room in your *own* house without seeing you. The *concept* of going to a new place and coming home soon is beyond the child's ability to understand. Each child will gain this understanding at a different time, depending on his or her temperament and level of maturation and experience.

*"Now that I have stopped working, what I am finding is that when she goes for her nap she will nap for a much longer time, knowing that I'm in the house. She'll also go into another room to play and come back to make sure that I'm still sitting there; and as long as I'm sitting there she'll play for a really long time."*

Her separation anxiety is diminishing because you're there.

*"Yes, and it's really noticeable in the way she plays with other people now. If I am there, she plays differently than when I am not. My husband says that he is amazed at the difference in the way she's trying to talk and to do things because I am there with her."*

She isn't so torn by that anxiety of separation that we talk about and that parents find so hard to accept. It is not that the children are not well cared for or happy while you are away. It is just that their primary attachments are to you and they cling to you. It is still a good sign, for it shows how strong their attachments are. It will probably be a while before they understand and feel secure that you will return when you leave.

What you all seem to be saying is that you were expecting the children to give you a little more time to yourselves. A lot of you are saying that you don't get a lot of free time because the babies want you by their side all the time. But they do have naptime. How do you use that time? Do you use it for reading or rest, or do you use that time for housework? When do you get any rest?

*"At night mostly. I go to bed at nine. I'm dead tired and can't get anything done the next day if I don't go to bed early."*

*"I work while she is napping rather than rest when she does."*

*"I feel I should get a break then, too, when she is napping."*

Mothers should take a break. Anyone working at any other job gets a ten- or fifteen-minute break for coffee. You will find that you are much more patient and enjoy your child more if you take a little time for yourself. The last thing you should forgo is that little bit of rest and relaxation.

*"I find that I rest a lot when she plays alone. She does that more now."*

*"I don't need the rest so much, but I can't even talk to my friends on the phone to relax. She always wants me with her just then."*

Yes, the telephone is a problem. Most children resent very much when you talk on the phone, because you are physically present but your attention is elsewhere. One of the best solutions is to take the child on your lap and include her in your conversations or give her something to play with on your lap so she doesn't feel left out.

Are there other areas in which you feel your expectations have not been fulfilled?

## Communication

*"Yes, I always thought that a one-year-old baby communicated more. What I really mean is that sometimes I talk to her and she seems to understand me and sometimes she just doesn't seem to know what I am talking about, even if I've said it before."*

Babies need to hear the same word or phrase repeated slowly and rhythmically many times in order to associate it with a specific item or situation. For example, if we say "Bye-bye" to children and wave but do not leave, we don't convey the meaning of leaving to them. We communicate to them by our expression and gesture and by repeating the words. They "catch on" when we have done it in the same way sufficiently often. The baby's readiness for language varies with each baby. Sometimes babies are in a more receptive state and seem to catch on better. The next time you say the same thing, the baby may be working on motor activity and may not respond as well to speech.

At this age, if they say about three or four words besides "Dada" and "Mama" and seem to understand a few others, that is all that is expected. Some children may take longer than others.

Has anyone else been feeling that the children should be further along in speech?

*"In our family we speak two languages. We speak Spanish among ourselves at home, but outside the home we speak mostly English. Does that confuse the baby?"*

It may. There are some babies who can grasp two languages at once, but most children do better if they learn one language at a time. This is especially true of those who have a slower maturation rate for language. There are some who are just not talkers and do better at other activities like walking or putting things together, such as puzzles.

*"I guess I never expected much of my baby. I thought babies didn't begin to talk or understand until they were three or more. So to me, it is a great surprise each time he seems to catch on to a new word. Maybe I'm not stimulating him enough. Do you think I ought to talk to him more?"*

It is important for parents to talk to their babies. At this stage, they may not grasp a long, unmodulated sentence all in a single tone, as adults talk to each other. They can understand when you hand them a bottle and say,

"Bo-ttle," or "Here is your do-llie" when you give them a doll. They are at the stage of learning names, identifying objects. They are not yet ready for sentences.

*"Would you consider it a word if a baby says 'Bo' for boat and 'Ca' for car?"*

This is the beginning. They may not be able to pronounce the whole word. It is important for you to recognize the sound as the word and show recognition and approval by saying enthusiastically, "Yes, boat (or car)." In this way the baby hears the complete word and knows that he has communicated with you and feels pleased about it. Perhaps there are many times that babies do this and parents do not listen closely enough to what the baby is really saying. The baby is looking for recognition and reinforcement. If you don't notice, he may try less. Babies need encouragement and recognition. This recognition adds to the baby's sense of achievement. We will talk more about this on many levels.

## Toys—Sharing and Possessiveness

Now that the children are more active, they are playing more with other children. At first, they just play alongside the other child. If the other child is playing with an attractive toy, there is often a tendency to take it. This can prove to be quite a problem. Has this been happening? How do you handle it?

*"I'm always having that experience, and I don't know quite what to do. If the other child doesn't protest, then I let my child have it. If there's a protest, then I give it back and give mine something else. He usually still wants the other child's toy."*

That is a difficult and important issue. The child who doesn't protest may be getting the message that his things are always going to be taken away from him. He may move away from other children in order to protect his property. We have all seen children who clutch their possessions and isolate themselves from other children. Or the child may feel he has no right to his toys and he becomes submissive and gives everything up. Neither response is healthy.

A good practice is to return the toy to the first child. Then give the other one who took it a substitute, telling him he can have the toy later. At first, there will be a great protest; but if you are consistent and allow the child to play with the toy later, the child gradually learns to wait and trust.

*"Shouldn't children be taught to share their toys? Last week, my son was playing at a friend's house. Every toy he picked up, the child would come over and take it, saying 'Mine.' Wasn't that child selfish?"*

"Selfish" is a label we apply too easily to young children. A child of that age is establishing his autonomy and identity. He is beginning to know "I," "my," and "mine." The mother could have said, "Yes, it is yours. He is not taking it away. You can let him have a turn playing with it while you play with your other red car."

Another way of negotiating this toy problem when visiting is to bring one or two of your child's toys, so that if the problem comes up, you can give your child his toy and say, "This is yours; that is his." Later, they will each pick up the other's toy and play for a while without difficulty. However, all play at this time has to be monitored by the adults present.

*"When I do this, my friends say I'm bringing up a selfish child. I have to teach him to share."*

Certainly you will teach sharing, but when he can understand it. Most parents try to teach sharing much too early, before a child has really gotten his sense of self. Acquiring a sense of self is important now. Sharing comes later. You have to supervise; there is no such thing as visiting with children under three and expecting that they are going to be able to manage the business of sharing. If they do, it's really quite remarkable; but you can't expect it.

## General Physical Care

### Need for Medical Attention—The Ideal Doctor

We know that in the baby's first year, you were all having regular contact with your family doctor or pediatrician or clinic. We feel that continued medical care is very important to your child's healthy development. How often are you visiting your doctors?

*"Well, I do take the baby if he is sick. Otherwise I don't, because there is always such a long wait. Even when we have an appointment weeks in advance, we have to wait forty-five minutes or more. It is very hard with an active baby—bad enough when he is well and, of course, more agonizing when he is sick. But my doctor is good, and I trust him. I know he will pay a lot of attention if there is something seriously wrong."*

Our reason for talking about medical services is to help you use your doctor's expertise to the best advantage. Your doctor should continue to monitor physical development and give appropriate inoculations and advice about diet, visual and auditory development, neuromuscular development, allergies, injuries, and hosts of other things. A good doctor who knows your family and your child detects such problems in physical examinations because he knows what familial diseases and characteristics to look for.

*"I can't afford to go to a private doctor. I have to go to the clinic. Each time I go, I see a different doctor. I know that they try to read my baby's history, but I keep wondering how much they know about her after a brief glance."*

■                                                                      ■

It is much harder to feel you are getting good medical care when you see different doctors each time. Some clinics have a team approach in which you and your family always see someone from the same team of doctors and nurse practitioners.

*"You said babies should be having regular contact with the doctor. What does that mean? How many times a year?"*

Every three months in the second year, in order to be sure developmental defects undetected in the first year, such as cardiac murmurs and difficulties with hearing or visual development, will be picked up. Also, during the second year appetites are often poor; nutrition and total growth need to be evaluated.

## Poor Appetites During the Second Year

The babies have all grown a great deal in the past year. Their growth rate and weight gain in the second year, while marked, are not as rapid proportionately as in the first year. With the change to table food and a normal decrease in appetite, they may not seem to be eating as much. Have any of you been noticing this in your babies?

*"This is a problem I have been having a long time. It didn't just begin this year. My baby has always been a very poor eater. She takes her milk, but only enough solids for a bird. This is one of the things I want to talk over with my pediatrician. I wonder if there is something I can do or should do to stimulate her appetite."*

If your doctor were worried about her, he would probably have suggested something himself. If it worries you, however, you should talk it over with him. In general, a child's progress is not measured by weight alone. It's not like putting weight on a turkey to get a good price for the holidays! Although most parents do have the feeling that weight is an important indicator of good development, it is only a small part of the picture. The baby's general health is revealed in her social and emotional responses, her activity level and motor development, her speech—spoken and understood. All these are very important characteristics of development. These are more important than weight and size unless there is something extremely abnormal.

*"My baby doesn't seem to care much for the food I give him; but when he sees us sit down to eat, he almost jumps out of his high chair to get it. So I give him some of what we are having: pot roast or chicken or chops, rice, such things. Is that all right?"*

There is no reason why your baby has to eat "baby food" if he likes to eat your food. It should not be too highly salted and seasoned and shouldn't contain preservatives that are inappropriate for babies. The only other concern is that you give him small pieces so that there will be no danger of choking.

■                                                                              ■

The important thing is not to make feeding time a battle. Sometimes babies eat much better in the company of their parents when they see adults eating. Often you can interest a baby in new foods this way. If she reaches for some of your food, you may give her very tiny pieces, one at a time. As she finishes each bit, without any eagerness or urging just acknowledge it with, "Umm, so good." In that way, a baby may consume a considerable amount happily, without a fuss being made.

## Changing Nap Patterns

At the same time as babies seem to be developing poor eating patterns, their sleeping patterns may be changing as well. Gradually during the first year, your babies have been sleeping less and less but generally for a longer stretch at night. Most of the babies during the past months have been taking a morning and an afternoon nap. Are they still doing this?

*"It's funny you should bring this up now. For the last three days my baby has refused to sleep in the morning, so we've gone outside earlier. By the time we get home, he is tired and falls asleep over his lunch. His schedule is all off."*

In that case it may be better to come back earlier so he can eat his lunch and then nap.

*"My baby is doing the opposite. She still naps in the morning but won't sleep in the afternoon. By the time my husband gets home, we've played all our games twice and we are both 'basket cases.' I don't know what to do with her."*

Your babies have given up one nap, but they seem to get tired without it. This is a developmental change that the children are unaccustomed to— and so are you. When they begin to nap less, it is important to see whether the one remaining nap can be lengthened. If not, then it is often necessary to try to do something quiet with the baby at the time of the former nap: listening to a soothing record or looking at picture books. Sometimes the babies will fall asleep in their carriages or strollers if you take them out at the former naptime. Usually, after a week or so, both you and the baby will settle into a new routine that has only one nap but less strain than at first. In general, the babies seem to need less sleep now. You may also find that, as they walk more and get more exercise, they sleep better at night.

*"I look forward to that! Now that the baby walks around he gets into everything. When we're outside, he's constantly on the go. He comes in tired, but I'm exhausted. Yesterday, we both slept for two hours!"*

Sometimes when the children first give up the second nap, they may still miss it. They are not quite ready to be active that much more of the day. Sometimes parents plan too many activities with the new time and overtire the children, who become irritable and need a quiet time. Each of you will

■                                                                          ■

have to experiment a little as you rearrange routines to accommodate this new development. It is also a good idea for those of you who are not home with your children all the time to discuss these changes in napping and eating patterns with your caretakers.

# Attachment and Separation: The Child's Needs

## How Attachment Develops

The babies are now at the beginning of their second year. Let us review for a moment how their attachments have developed. Gradually, as they are cared for by mother, father, or other caretakers, they become familiar with these persons. This familiarity establishes the baby's sense of security and attachment. Generally, one person takes primary care of the child and the child becomes attached to that person.

Many of you decided that you wanted to be the one to provide the primary caretaking and that you enjoyed child rearing. You have decided to stay home with your children and provide the quality of care that is very hard to replicate: the full-time care of the mother. The babies have become primarily attached to you, but they have also formed attachments to the father and other relatives as well. This was a good decision for you and your children, and this job you have undertaken should not be considered "nonwork" or any less professional than a paid job outside the home.

Others of you felt the need (for economic or professional reasons) to continue working outside the home. We advised you that it was best to return to work before the baby had formed such a strong attachment to you that leaving him or her would create great separation anxiety. We advised that you go back to work when your child was three or four months old, so that he or she could form a strong attachment to the substitute caretaker as well as to you and the father. Some of you have done this. You have found that the baby was able to become attached to each adult in a special way because of the particular routines that each has with the baby. Your babies have come to depend on you because of this special relationship, and yet they feel secure when you leave. In this way, they have not had to experience the trauma of premature separation. The baby has learned which adult fills which part of the daily caretaking and feels secure.

*"You know, I do think it has worked. I was afraid my baby would be attached to the sitter and not to me. I know now that she is attached to all of us."*

She *should* be attached to the caretaker. It is important for her to form an attachment to the person who gives her consistent care. Most children will form a different and very special attachment to their parents if they give the child regular and consistent care in their own special ways and times.

■                                                                                              ■

By now, whether the parents are both working outside the home full time or not, one would hope that the babies have established feelings of attachment to both parents and caretakers. Those of you who have been home all the time may be thinking that this is about the right time to go back to work or get out of the house more with your husband and friends. You are feeling ready to separate yourself from your children, and you are thinking the children should be ready as well. In fact, many of the children have recently learned to walk and seem only too eager to toddle away from you. Often their exhilaration in being able to move away confirms your feelings that they are ready to be away from you. Actually, the children are not as independent as they seem; they move away from you, but they prefer that you be stationary—a secure "home base." If it can be arranged, part-time work would probably be better.

*"I am not thinking of going back to work. Eventually I may feel that way. What is the ideal time to consider going back to work?"*

## Ideal Time for Separation

When you ask about the *ideal* time, we think that *from the child's point of view* the child should be about three years old. Children need a consistent mothering person around them until they are about three, the age at which most are able to function independently. By that time, they are able to talk and communicate their needs and to feed themselves. Most are also toilet trained and able to spend time playing alone or with friends. They are ready at that age to start nursery school or a day-care program and are able to separate more easily from the parents.

We are talking now about the ideal situations from the child's point of view. There are two of them: either to have a nearly full-time parent for about three years (we say "nearly" because everyone needs time off, and it is good for the child to get used to other caretakers for short periods of time) or to have the consistent care of another relative or baby-sitter or housekeeper who shares the caring role with the working parent(s) during the first three years. We recognize that it is often very difficult to achieve these ideals. The most important thing to remember is that children will experience feelings of separation anxiety and abandonment if the parent or other caretaker leaves them too abruptly before they have become accustomed to the new caretaking situation.

*"My husband is not working. Very soon I may have to go back to work. Is there something special in the baby's behavior that I should be prepared for?"*

You have all noticed that often, when a mother leaves her child, the child clings to her on her return and needs undivided attention. A baby who has become accustomed to his mother's care will protest at her leaving. After being without her all day, no matter how good the substitute care, this child will at first cling to her. She needs to expect this and plan to spend time with him.

## Helping Child Adjust to Substitute Care

*"Is there some way to ease the baby's anxiety and make it easier for him?"*

The best way is for the change of caretaker to be gradual. Sometimes the mother can find work and the father cannot; so he can care for the baby. In our experience, fathers are very good caretakers. Sometimes, when both parents work, their schedules can be arranged so that one of them can care for the child while the other is out—at least, most of the time. Grandmothers, sisters, and other relatives make good caretakers because they have a sense of affection and responsibility toward the child.

If no member of the family is available, then you have to hire a caretaker either to come into your home or to care for the child in her own home. It is best if she can be at home with you for a few days, watching your way of caring for your baby and gradually taking over some of your functions. In this way, the baby gets to know her and becomes accustomed to her way of doing things with him. During this time, you can go out for short periods, so the baby begins to learn that you will return.

As mentioned earlier, many parents may not be able to find an appropriate person to come to their homes to care for their children. They may opt for another solution: family day care. This means care given by a qualified person in her own home. Regulations vary in different states, but generally, licensed family day care strictly limits the number of children who may be cared for by one person and assures a certain level of competence. Care in a day-care center is also a possibility, but we feel it is a less desirable alternative *for children of this age* (actually, center care is rarely an alternative, since few centers take children under two years of age).

Whether you leave your children with another mother, in family day care, or in a day-care center, the process of separation should be gradual. The child then becomes familiar with the new caregiver, the new routines, and the new environment while the parent is still available for support. To make the transition, it is necessary to bring a few of the child's own toys from home, especially a special one such as his blanket or other favorite object. In the long run, extra time spent at the beginning of different care is time well spent in maintaining a child's sense of security and well-being.

## Child's Reactions to Parents' Absence

*"But what if you have to make a change in a hurry? You have no choice."*

We know that happens sometimes. You must then be prepared for the baby to cling to you, cry a good deal, and not let you out of sight when you come home. You just recognize that this is his way of saying, "I missed you; I was afraid you would never come back," and give the child your undivided attention for a while when you come home. Don't feel that the child is too demanding and being naughty and nagging just to upset you. If you react that way, the child will pick up your negative feelings and his anxiety will increase.

*"What about the mother who comes home after a hard day's work? Isn't she entitled to some peace and quiet?"*

You mean that after working she feels entitled to some relaxation; she feels the baby should realize how hard she has worked and that she is working for him? The child simply cannot understand that concept. All he or she understands is "Mommy has been away and I want her back."

*"Usually I work part-time; but yesterday I worked all day and I came home exhausted. I did play with him, but I had the feeling that he was angry at me, and that made me angry."*

That is another way children show how much they have missed you—by being angry. That is because they are not yet verbal and cannot say, "I missed you; I'm glad you are home; please play with me." Parents should be prepared for this kind of response and not get so upset by it. If the parent can understand the child's needs, he or she can deal with them upon arriving home. The child needs special attention and time after a day's separation from the mother (and father).

*"What if I have to do the cooking, or the laundry, or some marketing when I get home?"*

You can do all those things *after* you have given the baby some undivided attention *first*. Have a snack together or play for a while. Then involve the child in whatever you have to do so that he or she does not again have the feeling of being left out. It is also important to realize that you don't have to be a "superwoman." Perhaps the marketing and laundry should wait until the weekend; or the baby's father can help. You know we believe that parenting is a shared enterprise. Planning your time so that you get some relaxation is important. Sitting down and looking at a book with the baby may be a good change of pace for you. The baby will be so pleased with your attention that she may be willing to play with some toys near you. You will be surprised at how cooperative the baby can be if she feels close to you.

*"You were saying that until they are two and a half or three most children are not ready to separate from the parents once they are attached. That seems like a long time. I'd like to be doing something else part-time earlier. Parenting sounds like a job I am going to have forever!"*

Yes, that's right. Once a parent, always a parent! But getting your child off to a good start in the early years should make the job easier later on. You see, the generation gap can start here if early separations upset the child's development of basic trust and self-confidence. You need to understand that your going away upsets him. You will then expect clinging and you won't think he is naughty and react with anger, thereby adding negative feelings to his feelings of distress at your absence.

*"It sounds like parenting should be a twenty-four-hour job. Can't the mother and father have some time off?"*

No mother and father—no matter what the age of the child—can be with the child all the time. Most fathers and many mothers work outside the home. Parents also need time to pursue activities that they've always liked to do as adults. No one can do the same job well twenty-four hours a day, seven days a week. No profession requires that. No lawyer, businessman, nurse, mechanic, or doctor keeps those hours. Each needs relief and change; this enhances one's ability to do the job well. It is so with parents, too. Each family has to work this out in a way that suits its needs best. That is not the issue here. What we are trying to emphasize is the way the baby may respond to separation and how best to deal with his attachment and separation in order to cause the least difficulty and the most positive personality development. We want our children to be self-reliant, self-confident, trusting, and compassionate individuals. The foundations for these character traits begin in the early years.

## *Parents' Feelings About Parenting Roles; Mothering as a Profession*

### *"No-win" Situation for Mothers*

Some of you have decided to take off from your jobs to be full-time mothers; others have made the decision to continue in your professions. As you know, we hope to help all of you to raise your children with the minimum of stress and the maximum of pleasure, no matter what your decision about your jobs. We wish to be supportive of all of you. We do find it startling that the women who work outside the homes are labeled "working mothers," while those who stay home and care for their children, husband, and home are considered nonworking! We believe that full-time mothering requires as much, if not more, stamina, ingenuity, knowledge, understanding, diplomacy, and common sense as other professional positions. We stress the importance we place on full-time mothering because the value of mothers and homemaking is often downgraded. At the same time, society in general has made mothers who work outside the home feel guilty. It's kind of a "no-win" situation for young mothers right now.

*"I enjoy this age more, but it is much harder in some ways. What annoys me is that people at a party ask me what I do. When I say I take care of my child, they look at me and say, 'And what else?' That gets to me."*

That is something to overcome. This is an area in which we have to enlighten society: that being a mother is just as important a profession as any other. As we have said before, and we will have to repeat often, mothering (parenting) is the most important profession because it is the profession on which the success or failure of our society depends. This recognition of the value of parenting has to be fought for.

*"I've noticed that when a woman goes to register to vote, if she says she is a teacher, doctor, etc., that is well regarded. If the woman has no paying job, then* housewife *is entered in the book with a little disdain."*

## Motherhood Requires Versatility and Skill

It is not recognized in our complex society that being a wife and a mother requires a great deal of versatility and skill. When you are in the kitchen preparing dinner, you also have to have your mind on whether the child is safe. Or maybe you have your mind on whether what you are doing is a way to teach your child a new experience. You also have to think of things to do to divert the child if he is getting in your way. This really takes a lot of ingenuity, much more than you have to use in the average paying job. Mothering is a far more responsible and demanding job than is generally recognized.

*"When it's put that way, it raises my self-esteem no end. It's such an important job; what if we make mistakes?"*

Everyone makes mistakes in all areas of life; that is how we learn. Recognizing the importance of your role should make you want to know how to do it better. For instance, if you were a pianist, it wouldn't scare you because you couldn't play a sonata the first time you tried it. It's the same with mothering (parenting). It's not fatal if you make a mistake once or twice; the danger comes when we keep repeating the same mistake.

*"I agree that being a parent is a complex job. I was a schoolteacher and I prided myself on my ability to understand preschoolers and conduct a class with pleasure and satisfaction. But let me tell you that nothing requires as much patience, understanding, and savvy as bringing up your own child. This sounds 'corny' to my friends who are still at work and have no children. I understand them, because that's the way I used to feel."*

*"I never wanted to be a mother, and I frankly don't think I'm a model one. I don't enjoy it all that much, but I could never let anyone else take care of my child. No one would do it the way I would like it done. Besides, I've had a career in advertising. I was succesful, but I would not go back to it. When my son is older, perhaps I'll find another career. At the moment, my child is my job. Certainly, I like my time off a couple of afternoons a week. I shop or visit with friends, but my son is so glad to see me when I get home that I know my being there makes a difference to him."*

That is an important discovery. Many more mothers need to be able to understand that so they will take pride in their efforts and feel worthwhile.

■                                                                          ■

We believe women should be able to choose how to lead their lives. That includes seeing motherhood as an occupation of value.

*"There is another aspect that I'd like to emphasize because I am a 'working mother.' When you are single and you work, there is only one job to do. When you marry and work, there are two jobs: keeping house and working. But when you have a child, too, then it's* quadrupled *because you have just as much work at home—a husband rarely pitches in sufficiently. Even if he doesn't mind a little housework, there is the job, the child, and the responsibility of getting across to your caretaker what you want done for your child."*

*"I think too much is expected of women without at the same time giving them the credit they deserve for raising a family. In the law office where I worked, women were often passed over in promotions because they were not considered as continuously employed if they took maternity leaves. So, I just left. When I go back to work, I'll begin with another firm."*

*"It's quite unfair. Women are passed over for promotion in industry for the same reason. No provisions are made for a 'buddy' system, so that two people can do the same job. The excuse is that the fringe benefits would be too expensive."*

We are living in a period when more and more women, including an increasing number with children under six years of age, are entering the work force. Insufficient provisions are made by society for the care of these children. They may be given the least effective care at the time when intelligent care is most important. The first three years are considered by most experts the most crucial; that is why we concentrate on that period. The extended family with a grandparent or aunt available to take the mother's place when she goes to work is a rarity. In many cases, the grandmother is working, too! In some areas, one can find a good day-care center small enough and intimate enough to give children of this age adequate individual attention and appropriate physical surroundings and equipment—at a fee that parents can afford. But that is quite rare, especially for children under three.

*"Well, I have decided not to work, even though we could use the money. My husband has had to take two jobs; but he is willing to do it, and I am willing to spend a lot of evenings alone because of it. We think it is worthwhile because we have been observing the children of our neighbors who work and leave their children in day-care centers or in a relative's house. They don't speak as well as our son; they don't socialize well; they cry a lot. They just don't seem to be happy. Those who do seem to be doing well relate to their caretakers as though they were the parents. I wouldn't want my child to do that; I want to have his affection for me, not for the caretaker."*

*"Suppose a mother does have to work for whatever reason. Does she necessarily lose her child's affection? Isn't she still the mother?"*

She is still the mother; but if she is away most of the time and the baby's needs are met by another caretaker, that person may become the "psychological" parent. It is important, however, that the child establish an affectionate relationship with the caregiver. The relationship indicates that he is well cared for and that he feels secure and is developing basic trust. That does not mean that the biological mother has lost her role or the child's love. She may fill her role in another way when she returns from work. She has to establish her own way of spending quality time with her child. As we have discussed before, the mother should, upon first returning, spend time with the child, playing with him, talking to him, having a snack with him and later involving him in any household chores. She can also spend time bathing and putting him to bed, either by herself or with the father when he returns. Parents can establish special pleasant play and bedtime routines in the evening. Working parents will then be establishing different roles for themselves with their child, but ones that are *just as important* as the one with the caretaker. Weekends are another period that can be used in expanding one's parenting role with the child.

*"But isn't a mother who works all day at some job or profession—no matter how interesting—too tired to be patient and involved with her child? Isn't that asking too much of her?"*

It is true that the parent may be tired, but she is tired of doing her outside job. There is plenty of energy left to do a different job at home, especially if one regards it as a pleasure to be with one's child. We all know that after work tired businesspeople have enough energy to go swimming, play tennis or squash, ride bicycles, or jog. The tiredness is from doing the office job. There is plenty of energy left for other activities, and caring for one's child can be one of them.

*"It is true that the 'working parent' can establish a good relationship with her child. But doesn't she miss a lot of the firsts: the first step, the first word—all the new things a baby learns? I have had that thrill. I wouldn't have missed it for the world. It only made me sad that my husband wasn't home to share most of these 'firsts,' too."*

These are all important considerations. But each family has to make its choices according to its needs and compensate in other ways.

## Working Mothers Need Help with Housework

*"It seems that mothers have to take the major burden in any case—and if you work you feel guilty."*

Our society seems to place the major burden on mothers. Research shows that the increase of women in the work force has not been paralleled by an increase in male participation in housework. But it need not be so. We believe parenting is a shared responsibility. Household chores and baby care are not something that only a woman can and should do. Societal attitudes have to be changed. Fathers are equally capable of caring for children—given the time and the inclination. Fortunately, some fathers are getting more involved with child rearing. If parents understand child development, child care can be an exciting challenge, not a chore.

A rather radical idea, but one that would relieve many of our present tensions, would be to pay mothers to stay home if they wished to take care of their *own* children, while at the same time learning how to do this better. This would be an enormous step forward in our society. It would be more economical than day care for very young children. Courses on child rearing would help as sources of information, as support groups, and as an economical way for early detection of children's difficulties. This approach would begin to educate society to advocate the appropriate care of children in the preschool years and beyond.

At the same time, greatly improved and expanded day-care services should be made available, especially for preschoolers aged three to five. Parenting education classes should also become a part of the day-care system, to help these parents meet their children's needs.

Such a dual system would give all women the *real* choice of remaining at home to rear their own children, especially in the early years, or joining the work force with the feeling that their children are being adequately cared for. In the meantime, it is our concern to look at this dilemma as objectively as possible. Our purpose is to enhance parental understanding of child development so that good parent-child relations can be established. In that way, parenting can become a happier, more satisfying role and the child can be helped to reach his or her maximum potential, whatever the family's particular circumstances.

## Discipline: A Teaching Process

Your children are now more mobile and are exploring and trying to manipulate more of the objects in your houses. Many of these objects are dangerous for a child of this age. What do you do about it?

### Toddlers Don't Understand Consequences

*"We are having quite a time with that. Our baby can feed herself with a spoon. We are proud of that. But she starts walking with the spoon in her mouth and I take it away from her and give her something else. She throws herself on the floor and looks as if she's about to have a tantrum, and she is not satisfied with the substitute. She isn't even certain what it is; but whatever it is, she doesn't want it. She wants what she had before."*

Children are very insistent on continuing their activity, and they do protest. That is normal. We want them to understand that walking with a spoon, pencil, or other object can be dangerous if they should fall and jam it into their eyes or throats. We want them to understand this and be reasonable. That would make life easier for us. However, we cannot expect it of children this age. They cannot foresee such consequences, and therefore they do not comprehend our concerns.

One way to make such an incident easier to handle is by offering the child something more attractive to hold: perhaps a small soft toy, ball, or a small jar with a block in it. Then, as the baby reaches for the toy, remove the spoon instead of pulling it away and give the substitute before the baby has begun protesting.

*"But that way you are not teaching the child that it is dangerous to walk with spoons and such things."*

The children are too young to comprehend this danger, but you may begin trying to get the idea across to them if you don't expect too much. After the spoon has been taken away and when the child is not protesting and can hear you, you may say, "Spoons are for eating. We don't walk with spoons. We walk with dollies or teddies."

## Importance of Safety and Exploration

If a parent is consistent and persistent, the child learns in time that some objects are not allowed in certain situations. It takes patience. It is not easy. Once this understanding comes, it is a very important milestone. Homes should be arranged so that you do not have to limit the child all day long. When the children were younger, we talked about the dangers and mess associated with their increasing motor ability. Now the children are even more mobile; most are walking and some are beginning to climb a little. The danger increases for pulling things over and getting into cupboards with medicines or poisonous cleaning materials.

We do have to try to confine the restrictions we place on children's exploration to matters of safety rather than whims of ours to keep our houses neat. Precious objects should be put out of the way for their preservation. If they are too large to be moved, then the baby has to learn to avoid them and be given interesting substitutes to play with. In the kitchen, for example, the stove and certain closets are off limits, but one cupboard can be made safe for exploration with a set of cups, pans, measuring spoons, and jars. Most children are fascinated with these domestic utensils, often preferring them to elaborate toys.

The important thing to remember as children reach this stage is that they need to explore. Their curiosity about the world around them and their understanding of the properties of objects—what makes things work—comes from their manipulation of the objects around them. This understanding and the desire and drive to understand are not enhanced if everything the child tries to do or touch evokes a stern parental "No." The parent can become a real guide during this phase. The child begins to learn what is dangerous and what is safe, what is appropriate and what is not; he learns what his parents approve and what they don't approve.

■                                                                    ■

## Child's Need for Approval

Parents often emphasize limitations and disapproval with a firm "No" or, in frustration, angry words. Approval is often not overtly expressed to the child.

How do you show approval when your children are doing the right things? Do they get the message that these actions are approved?

*"I say, 'Yes, very good, nice!' "*

Do you say it dramatically enough so that it is more important than the "No"? That's the key, to make your approval much more important than the "No." When the child is doing something that we like, many of us just smile. The child may not see it and may not get the message. The child must really hear the "That's good," so that she will know that you approve of what she is doing. That approval gives children a sense of self-esteem or well-being about themselves. Not only is this sense of self-esteem important, but parental attention for *approved* behavior is an important pattern of parent-child interaction. If we pay attention only when our children are "naughty," then our attention is counterproductive—and the relationship becomes one of an "angry alliance." If we pay more attention when children behave appropriately, or as we approve of them, then our relationship can be positive. Children look for attention and approval and will work for it. They will try to avoid disapproval; they will see that they don't have to be "naughty" to get attention.

Often you see your child about to touch something, then he looks at you because he wants to know if you are going to say "No" or "Yes." Have you seen this yet?

*"I have seen my child do that. But I thought he knew he was not supposed to touch the light cord and that he was just teasing me. So I became angry and slapped him."*

It is very common for parents to mistake the child's testing of limitations as teasing. Children need to be shown over and over again what is approved and what is disapproved. Children will work for the approval. The trouble with us is that we're often much more emphatic about the "No"; we sometimes shriek and yell! We feel the child is bad and we give the child the feeling that he is bad.

*"Well, isn't the child being bad when he does what he isn't supposed to?"*

He is not bad. He is just trying to find out what is right or wrong. We, the adults, are the teachers. We have to repeat the response until the baby learns. Some children learn after twenty times; some may take what seems to the parent like two hundred times! It depends on the child's neurological maturity. At this age he doesn't have control of his impulses. He still needs the parent's *help* in *not* doing what he is beginning to sense is wrong. That is why he looks back at the parent. He is not teasing. He is looking for his parent to help him control his impulses.

*"I have tried to be firm, but sometimes I'm gentle and say 'Please.' "*

You cannot vacillate; you have to be *very* firm right from the start. It has to be a firm "No" instead of a gentle "Please don't, dear."

*"He often cries and cowers away from me. Then I feel guilty and give him a hug. A few minutes later he goes back."*

You are giving your child a double message. You are being very stern and scaring him; then you are cuddling him. He feels your ambivalence. So you really haven't accomplished anything. It is important to say a very firm "No." The impulse to do something is there; you have to give another outlet for that impulse and show your approval for the substitute. When you understand that you are teaching your child an important lesson for her future life, then you will realize that you don't need to feel guilty about imposing limits.

## Importance of Substitute Activities

*"I used to be able to substitute a toy when my baby was doing something wrong or harmful, but now that won't work. He always likes to be in motion since he learned to walk. He used to be able to play with a toy, sometimes for forty-five minutes."*

In that case, a motor activity has to be the substitute for him. For example, take him to find something in another area of the room. Your child has achieved a new level of development. He is concentrating on motor activities now, and you must utilize this level to absorb his interest. Parents have to move with the child's level of interest. Different responses are needed at different stages—this is called "cuing in" to your child.

*"Are they too young to understand that if they do something bad, they won't get a cookie; and when they are good, they will?"*

That is a very difficult way to set limits, even with an older child who is verbal. When a child is removed from some unacceptable activity and is happily engaged in another, a cookie may be offered to reinforce the pleasant atmosphere. Cookies should not, however, be offered as rewards. If this has been the usual procedure, the child may begin to associate approved behavior with oral gratification. This is a habit best not initiated.

*"I just think a lot of the time is spent diverting. I find, too, that my son likes to be in the same room with me. If I'm in the bedroom, then he must be there, and I'll give him a brush or some knickknack to play with."*

Yes, for effective diversion an adult has to be there in person.

*"I like everything to be very neat when I get home from work. I get annoyed at the baby-sitter when the house is a mess. I wonder if that attitude is making her say 'No' too much to my daughter."*

■                                                                          ■

That is possible. It is very important to try to limit saying "No." We have to accept the fact that a house with a baby cannot be as neat as it was before the baby arrived. But it doesn't last forever. If regarded as part of the child's growing and learning, it may be seen in a better perspective.

*"I guess I'd better discuss this whole business with my sitter. I need to be more understanding of her. And we both need to agree on how we discipline my baby."*

That is a very good idea. It is very important for everyone involved with the child's care, especially mothers, fathers, and sitters, to be consistent in their teaching of discipline. Inconsistent discipline—like the ambivalent messages we discussed earlier—can be very confusing to a child and will slow down the learning process. Different adults have different personalities and styles; each will interact with the child in his or her own special way. But in some areas like discipline, there should be as consistent a message as possible. Inconsistency in our responses to children is, in our view, what "spoils" them.

## Different Cultural and Ethnic Attitudes Toward Child Rearing

Do you find that some of the attitudes we discuss here are quite different from the way your parents and neighbors view child rearing? Is this upsetting to you?

*"I find that when I tell people I attend parenting classes with my baby, they say, 'What's wrong with you?' "*

*"Yes, I get the same thing. 'Why do you have to learn how to be a parent? That just comes naturally.' "*

### Why Teach Parenting Skills?

Parenting in our complex society does not come as naturally as it does for the lower animals. Parenting has always been taught. From the beginning of time, the care of children and the teaching of the culture and mores of tribes, peoples, and nations have been passed down in families from generation to generation. The phenomenon that has seemed so new in the last decades is the teaching of parenting skills by people *outside* of the family, a trend made necessary by the many changes and far greater mobility of our society.

In the past, when several generations lived in the same house, or at least nearby, there were family members around to help the new parents. Most young mothers had also had experience caring for younger brothers and sisters and cousins. Now families are more scattered. Most of you have had little experience with children until you had your own, and families are not usually around to help except at the very beginning, and then only if you are lucky.

## *Appropriate Attention Is Not "Spoiling"*

*"My father-in-law used to tell me that my child was going to be a spoiled brat if I kept picking him up when he cried. He is a strict, European disciplinarian. My husband tries to support me, but he wonders sometimes."*

As we have said before, *appropriately* attending to children's needs does not spoil them. Crying is the infant's only language. He cries for a reason: because he is hungry or wet or lonely. When the parent or caretaker satisfies or gratifies this need, a child learns to trust the people around him or her and gains a sense of confidence and security. She learns how to "communicate" and interact with the world around her. Actually, the children who do not get picked up when they cry as infants, and do not have appropriate attention paid to them, often become the demanding adults who fume in restaurants and stores if the service is not quick enough. They are still afraid their needs will not be satisfied.

Your father-in-law's attitude is not too different from the attitude promoted by American pediatricians some years ago, or that advocated by behavioral psychologists. They believed that children only cried more if parents "rewarded" crying by responding. Other psychologists have demonstrated the opposite: that children whose cries are attended to become more trusting and cry less, and those who are ignored tend to become the clingers and "cry babies."

## *Development of Trust and Self-esteem*

*"My family also objected when I picked up the baby when he cried. They said that does not relate to a black child. They said, 'They have to learn to wait out in the world and you have to let them know it right away.'"*

What they are saying is that the world is much harder for a black child than it is for a white child and that he's got to learn this early. Unfortunately, they are probably right about the first part. But what will help a black child—or any child—succeed or overcome difficult situations in life is a sense of trust in his parents, self-confidence, and self-esteem. A child who does not develop a sense of attachment and trust because his needs are not met has a harder time. A child whose parents value him and respond to his needs learns that he is recognized and develops self-esteem. This child is willing and able to strive for further achievements with confidence. If parents do not respond and build trust, the child can become "turned off" from other people as being of no help or can become angry and disappointed or unnaturally submissive and ingratiating in order to get attention and care. We believe that this is what all parents, including black parents, want to avoid.

You have a real job helping your friends and neighbors understand that all children have similar needs, whatever their race or ethnic group. There is no biological difference in infancy other than that ordinarily found among all children, because each child is unique. It may interest black parents that some of the early studies of infant attachment and the infant's need to be picked up by the mother were done in Uganda. These studies were repeated here in the United States and form the basis for what we have been saying about attending to a baby's needs as soon as you can, no matter what his or her color or national origin. There are few differences between one infant's needs and another's. It is *our response* to those needs that can change his or her personality development. We can enhance it or hinder it. It is up to us in our own immediate families and in our religious institutions and in our community organizations to help people understand children's basic needs.

*"Well, this helps me. Now I also understand a little better why my child cries when some of my neighbors try to touch him or play with him. Their whole approach is rough and tough; he is afraid of them."*

*"I have the same problem with my in-laws, who come from Europe."*

Many people have the same problems, because the ideas of past generations and different cultures have been that you have to toughen kids to face a tough world. Well, you don't toughen a child at four weeks or at four months or at two years. First, children have to develop a sense of security, a relationship to their families, and a sense of their own worth. If children don't begin to develop these within the first three years, they are beginning with deficits that make it harder, if not impossible, for them to develop to their fullest potential.

*"Doesn't this idea of being tough apply more to boys than to girls?"*

That is another one of the "sacred cows" that we have to overcome. Many people still believe that boys will be sissies if they are not toughened up early. Actually, boys of this age need the same attention and protection as girls.

*"You say boys need the same protection as girls. I would say girls need to be toughened as much as, or more than, boys. It's a man's world; our daughters need to be tough to get ahead."*

*"I come from a Spanish culture, and there, too, the idea that a boy has to be tough and continue to be so as a man is the accepted attitude."*

First, we must consider the child's developmental needs. Response to children must be adapted to their age. At this age, all children need attention and protection, not toughening. Instead of making girls and women fit into the old male stereotype of being "tough," however, perhaps we should be thinking of how we can help boys *and* girls to become competent and self-confident and sensitive to the needs of others—as well as the other qualities we admire in men *and* women.

## Spacing of Children

Some of you are beginning to think of having another child. What are your thoughts?

*"The only reason I would think of having another child is to give my son company and keep him from being an only child."*

You think you are going to provide a playmate for your child. You may find, however, that the children are rivals and are not such good friends after all. The spacing can make a lot of difference. If the first child is too young to share his parent's attention and parents are insensitive to his needs, his initial resentment to the new baby may linger on.

### Ideal Spacing: The Child's Viewpoint

*"What is the best interval to have between children if you plan to space them for the best interests of the child?"*

Each family has its own way and reason for the spacing of their children. However, thinking of what is best for the child, the ideal spacing is about three years. The reason for this is that a baby needs a great deal of attention for the first three years. A child of three usually has developed many competencies. She is verbal and can communicate, saying how she feels and what she wants. By this age most children are independent and can feed and almost dress themselves. They are probably toilet trained and, most of all, can separate from their parents and socialize with their peers. A child is in a better position to cope with and enjoy a new baby when he has a sense of self and is more ready to share his parents with another child.

*"Logically and developmentally, I can understand and appreciate what you are saying; but my doctor has warned me that I must have another child right away because of my age—I'm thirty-five."*

After thirty-five there is increasing risk of difficulties in pregnancy and fetal abnormality. That is a medical issue for serious consideration. However, we are discussing what is best for the child. One must realize that a child of eighteen months usually does not have the capacity to understand the situation as well as an older child. She will not be able to tell you how she feels or to express her resentment or hostility toward what in her eyes is an "intruder." There will be times when she needs your attention, but the new baby's needs will have to come first. It is more difficult for the mother to take care of an infant and a toddler who is not yet ready to separate.

With appropriate expectations of each child's needs, you will have a much better chance of coping.

*"I am interested in what you say because my husband and I want to have all our children close together so that I can go back to work before my training is useless. It sounds like it will be harder—but possible."*

It is possible, but harder, as you say. You may need more help from your husband and other members of your family. It may even be necessary to employ help in caring for the home and children.

## Why Have Another Child?

*"This just makes me feel more than ever that I am not sure I want another child. I enjoy our baby, but he takes so much time and effort. Why should I have another child?"*

The best reason for having another child is that the parents want to have one. You should not have a child because somebody else thinks you should or because you would like company for the first child. Each child should be wanted for himself. The best reason for having a child is that you love children and look forward to bringing up more than one child—you think you will enjoy the challenge of having two (or more) children, each with a different personality. For those who feel this way, it is exciting.

*"I love my son so much. I don't think I could love another. I still feel that I couldn't put the time and energy into another child that I have into him."*

This is a very common feeling; one can't imagine loving another child or going through all those sleepless nights again. But remember you are now an experienced parent, and probably the things that you found very hard the first time will not be so hard the second time. You know a good deal of the mechanics now that you didn't know the first time. So you will probably be more relaxed.

*"We can't afford another one now, although we would like to have another baby someday. If we do, we will have to move, because there just isn't room in our present apartment—and that will add to the expense, too."*

*"I really feel now that I would like to get back to school and do the things I couldn't do before. That's my reason for not having another child."*

Each family has to make its own decision. Now that our whole society is working toward population stability, there isn't that pressure for everybody to have large families.

## Only Children

*"Isn't it bad to have an only child? Aren't only children usually spoiled children?"*

Only children are not necessarily spoiled children. It depends on what you mean by spoiled. We feel that children are spoiled when their needs are not consistently attended to—sometimes getting attention and sometimes not. This can happen more easily in a family where there are many children close together, with no one getting sufficient or consistent attention.

*"I read some research on only children in which they seem to think only children might be better off than other children. Is that true?"*

There are reports that indicate that the first child in the family is the better achiever. In effect, he has had the advantage of being the only child until his siblings arrive.

*"One of the things you associate with only children is that they always seem to want to be the center of attention. I call that spoiled."*

Only children spend a good deal of time with adults. When adults are around they expect to be involved because they are used to being with adults.

*"Don't parents of only children have to make more of an effort to see that their children have companions?"*

That is, of course, one of the extra responsibilities of having an only child. However, there is no reason why an only child's day should be so different from other children's. Many people have no choice about having another child—or not having one. All of us can learn to adjust. Only children can have happy, cheerful childhoods; sometimes a child with brothers and sisters can be lonely. There is no *one* best number of children. It depends on how parents respond to children's needs and on each family's circumstances.

*"Well, I can tell you that I wish I had heard this discussion long ago. This is my second baby, and there are only two years between the two. It is very hard. One year more would have made quite a difference. My reasons were wanting to get back to my profession and have child rearing over faster. I'm learning to manage, but it's hard. I would tell someone else to think it over carefully."*

As we have said before, each family must make its own decisions. Some are based on emotions or economics or age factors; some are cultural or religious. Each family, if well informed, can be prepared to cope effectively for the good of the entire family.

## *Emergency Measures for Accidents: Poisoning, Cuts, Splinters, Head Injuries, Burns, Choking*

During the second year, children often have more accidents because of their increased mobility and exploration. Knowing simple first-aid procedures will help you to keep calm and enable you to reassure the children while coping with the emergency.

## Poisoning

The best way to deal with accidents is to try to prevent them. All poisonous cleaners, detergents, or paints should be put on high shelves or in cupboards with safety catches or locks (with the keys kept well out of reach). This same precaution should be taken with all medications. As you probably know, even drugs commonly used for children, such as children's aspirin or vitamins, can be toxic if taken in amounts over the normal dose for age and weight. Care should be taken not to leave medications in purses. Children of this age enjoy exploring mother's purse when it is left in an accessible place and sampling its contents. (Lipstick can make a mess, but a parent's medication could be lethal.) These precautions seem self-evident, but too many of these avoidable accidents still occur. Parents may feel that the medicine cabinet is "safe" because the child is not a climber. But there is always a first climb or another new development that enables the child to get into trouble. Therefore, parents must get into the habit of observing these precautions. In this year, the need to watch the children carefully is more demanding on parents because of the children's natural curiosity. We don't want to inhibit this exploratory drive, but at the same time we want to keep the children safe.

*"What if the child, no matter how careful you are, does get into a poisonous substance. Then what should you do?"*

There are certain precautions you should take to be ready for such an accident. One is to have the number of the Poison Control Center in your area posted near the telephone. If there isn't one, then you should have the number of the nearest hospital emergency room and your doctor's number posted. (It is a good idea to have these numbers in your wallet as well, so they are available when you are out visiting or shopping.) The second precaution is to have on hand syrup of ipecac, a medicine to induce vomiting, in case you are directed to give it by the doctor. It is also useful to keep sufficient cash for taxi fare posted near your phone so that you or the sitter can get to an emergency room or doctor. When the child ingests something that you suspect is poisonous, have the container in hand as you phone so you can read off the ingredients. If Poison Control or the doctor advises giving ipecac, give one tablespoon to a child of one year or over with a glass of water. If no vomiting occurs in twenty minutes, the dose may be repeated *once* only. If there is still no result, then take the child to the nearest emergency room or doctor, taking the container or label with you. Keep the child upright, so that if he or she vomits there will be less chance of choking. *Ipecac should not always be given,* so it is best to consult Poison Control or the doctor first. If the ingested material is caustic, such as lye, for example, ipecac should not be given. Instead you should give milk or water, anything to dilute the poison, and go to the emergency room as soon as possible. You can call your doctor from there.

The same procedure of calling Poison Control or your pediatrician should be followed if the child ingests too many baby aspirins or vitamins or any adult medication.

## Cuts and Splinters

*"Could you talk about scrapes and cuts? Because that's my son's problem. I know I should wash off a scrape, that soap and water is the best treatment, and if there is dirt in it that I can't get out, to see a doctor. But he raises so much more fuss now than before and kicks and screams. I was wondering if it wouldn't be just as good to simply put some antiseptic on and a Band-Aid and let it go at that."*

It is very unpleasant and unnerving when the child puts up a fight against first-aid measures, but the parent still has to do the right thing. The compromise may lead to unnecessary smarting of the wound by an "antiseptic" that may not avoid subsequent infection because of the contamination of the wound by the remaining dirt and germs. Washing the area involved with soap and water is the best procedure. Then the wound should be covered with a light sterile dressing or Band-Aid. If the accident occurred outdoors or in the street and there is soil embedded in the wound, your pediatrician should be consulted to make sure the child's immunization for tetanus is up-to-date. While attending the child, the parent must bear in mind that the child is frightened and needs to be assured that the parent understands and is going to help, not scold.

Another way to ease the situation is to get the child involved in the process. As many of you have probably discovered, the children are entering a period when Band-Aids are a kind of magic "cure-all." There are some kinds that have decorations on them—stripes and stars. After getting the child calmed down, hand her the box of Band-Aids and ask her to pick one. Explain that before the Band-Aid is put on, the cut must be washed. Then you can partly open the Band-Aid and let her get it out. Talk about the colors or stars and then make a little ceremony out of the Band-Aid.

*"Now that you mention it, I did see a child in the park with about five Band-Aids on his leg. He kept looking at them and touching them. I think they made him feel more comfortable. I will try that."*

*"I will, too. But you know it is so hard not to scold the child, especially when she hurts herself doing something that I told her not to do."*

That is very understandable. But parents must remember that children of this age, while they may be aware that they are doing something forbidden, still do not have the self-control to resist. So parents must control their first impulse to scold, and comfort the child while they are administering the appropriate help.

■                                                                    ■

*"My trouble is when there is a cut and a lot of bleeding. I get excited. My baby fell and hit his mouth, and his teeth cut his lip. I remembered to soothe him but I couldn't remember whether to wash his lip or press on it or what."*

Bleeding usually washes away the dirt unless it's a very jagged, dirty cut that needs professional attention. Usually, just applying pressure for a few minutes with a clean cloth or dressing is sufficient to stop the bleeding. Constantly washing the cut after the first cleansing only washes away the clot and the natural clotting substance that stops the bleeding. If the cut is large, open, or continues to ooze or bleed for more than five minutes, it is best to see a doctor, since stitches may be needed. If the blood is not oozing out but spurting out, apply pressure above the bleeding point and go to a doctor or a hospital emergency room at once. An artery may be cut, and this requires immediate medical attention.

*"My baby stuck a tack into his finger. There was a hole and it didn't bleed at all. My doctor took that very seriously."*

Puncture wounds that don't bleed are often overlooked. They can be the most serious, however, because the puncturing objects may have been carrying infectious germs, pushing them deep into the wound. To avoid infection, the child may even need an antibiotic or a tetanus injection, depending on the last immunization date. A doctor should be consulted to determine the treatment.

*"We have a wooden floor on the porch of our house. Sometimes, when our child plays on it, he slips and falls and gets a splinter in his hand or leg. We try to keep him on the rug, but it doesn't always work. We remove the splinter with a tweezer if we can and then wash the area clean. It is a trauma all around, however, because our child cries and screams. Some friends have told me that small slivers work their way out and that I am causing more trauma than necessary. Is that so?"*

It is best to remove a splinter. Wash the area first with soap and water, then wash again after the splinter is removed. If the splinter isn't easily removed with tweezers, or leaves a deep hole, consult the doctor.

## Head Injuries

*"My big worry is that my child will fall or hurt his head seriously because he insists on climbing. I try to keep hold of him when we are in areas where he could fall down stone steps and really hurt himself. But just in case—what about head injuries? If a child bumps his head really hard, should you try to keep him awake or let him fall asleep?"*

In case of head injuries, rest is the most important thing. If the fall causes unconsciousness immediately or later, consult the doctor at once. The child should not be shaken to keep him awake because further damage may be done. It is best to keep him quiet and take him at once to the

■                                                                              ■

nearest doctor or hospital. If there is vomiting, bleeding from the ear or nose, pallor, or unequal size of the pupils of the eyes, immediate medical attention is necessary. None of the child's symptoms can be assessed well if the parents are too excited themselves. The most important thing in an emergency such as this is to reassure the child that you are there and that you will take care of him. Then assess the situation and get proper help. Keep the child as calm and quiet as possible as you go to the doctor or the emergency room of the nearest hospital.

## Nosebleeds

*"My little girl fell while we were visiting yesterday and came running to me with her nose bleeding. I don't know how it happened. My friend got very excited, laid her down, and put a cold compress on her nose and one at the back of her neck. But it didn't help much and the baby kept screaming. I tried to soothe her. Then I remembered that it is best for the child to sit up while you squeeze her nose closed."*

That is the correct procedure. In case of a nosebleed, the child should sit up while you squeeze the nose closed by pressing the nostrils together, where the soft part meets the bone. This stops the bleeding. It is better for the child not to lie down, because then blood may run into the back of the throat. Most children hate cold compresses on their faces or necks, so their use is often counterproductive for nosebleeds. If nosebleeds are prolonged or frequent, the doctor should be consulted.

## Burns

*"I was able to keep my baby from going near the stove by saying 'No, hot.' But now he's so active I'm afraid he'll run into me when I am cooking and tip over something hot that I'm lifting before I can warn him away. In fact, he did tip over a cup of hot soup, but only a little splashed on his hand, leaving a small red spot. I just put a cold cloth on it. But if it had been more severe, should I have used butter or some salve? That's what my mother always did."*

For just redness, which is a first-degree or superficial burn, use cold water or an ice cube or cold compress until the stinging pain subsides. Then a nonadhesive dressing, such as Saran Wrap, can be put on to protect the area. If blisters form, the burn is more serious. The blisters should not be broken or opened. The child should be taken to the doctor or emergency room. If burns are more extensive or severe, remove the clothing around the burn, apply cold compresses, and get to the hospital as quickly as possible. If the trip is long, give fluids in sips frequently on the way. At no time should butter or oils or powders be applied. Oil applied to the hot flesh will continue the burning action; ice, or even cold water, will stop the actual burning process. In addition, oils complicate the proper cleaning of the area and may serve as a culture medium for the growth of

■                                                                                    ■

bacteria, thus causing infection. The first impulse may be to put on a salve, but it is better to wait for your doctor's instructions.

One can't reiterate often enough that matches must be kept away from children and that children should never be left at home alone, because they can start fires by playing with matches or tipping over electric lamps and heaters. If you have to leave the house, even for a few minutes while you think the baby is asleep, it is better to wake the child and take him with you. In addition to having an accident, the child could awaken and become frightened at finding himself alone.

## Convulsions

*"My baby had a cold, sore throat, and very high fever and suddenly he had a convulsion. I took him to the emergency room. They gave him a cool sponge bath and some aspirin and, I think, a sedative. He was better the next day, but it was frightening. Is there any way to be prepared? Does that happen often with small children?"*

Some small children do not tolerate high fevers well and have convulsions whenever their fever gets high. Your doctor can best advise you what to do for your child. In general, it is well to give something to control fever, such as Children's Tylenol (whatever your doctor recommends), at the first sign of fever. Be prepared to give cool baths or sponge baths if the fever gets high. Any child who has a convulsion should be seen by a doctor to determine the cause. During a convulsion, parents should keep the child's head inclined and the tongue extended, to avoid choking or aspiration.

## Choking

*"My child is at the stage of putting everything in his mouth. I'm afraid he'll choke on something or swallow something harmful. What is the best thing to do?"*

It's best to keep an eye on him. But even so, we can't always prevent swift action on the part of the child. If the baby actually swallows a small, smooth object, the most important thing to do is keep calm and not frighten the baby. Then, it is a good idea to give her something soft to eat, such as bread or thick cereal, so that the object will be coated. If the object is sharp or jagged and could cause a perforation, you should also give the child something soft to eat and then get in touch with the doctor immediately.

If the child is choking on an object or piece of food, again it is most important to keep calm and not frighten the baby. The first emergency procedure is to quickly inspect the baby's mouth to locate the object. If it can be reached, it should be pulled from the mouth immediately. If it is in the baby's throat, do not try to dislodge it with your fingers, because you may push it farther down and cause more difficulty. The best procedure is to make use of gravity by inverting the baby and slapping his back firmly.

■

A good way to do this is on your lap or along your extended legs. If the object is not dislodged, place the baby facedown along your forearm (or, for a larger child, you may use your knee) so that his abdomen rests against your arm (or knee). Then, quickly and firmly press down three or four times with the heel of your hand between the child's shoulder blades. This usually causes the baby to cough up the object so that you can remove it from his mouth.

If these emergency measures fail, take the baby immediately to the nearest hospital emergency room. Even though an object is obstructing the baby's throat, enough air may be getting through to allow him to breathe. Soothing and calming the baby is important at this point, so that the spasms or crying are not intensified. Crying itself constricts the throat muscles, creating less air space.

We have talked about these emergency procedures to help you feel prepared. It is always important to remember that the child is even more frightened than the parent. Therefore, the first step is to soothe and comfort the child. Then assess the situation as calmly as possible so that you can take the appropriate measures.

## Socialization

As the children are getting older, your social life may be increasing and the children will be introduced to new situations. At this age, the children can begin to enlarge their social horizons. They need to emerge from the confines of the immediate family into the world of friends and neighbors. Have you been venturing into new situations with them? How is it going?

*"We've been trying to get out on weekends with the baby. Sometimes we just go for a ride in the car, and he likes that. It gives us a change of scene, and we can show him things. It works all right."*

*"We've had some trouble visiting friends. Whenever we go to a different place, a place the baby has not been before, he stiffens up, cries, and seems frightened. We've almost decided not to go out at all with him. What should we do? We want to get out, but we can't have baby-sitters all the time."*

### Children's Responses to New Situations

Many babies don't feel secure in new surroundings. This is normal because the new or unknown is strange and can be frightening. Your baby responds vigorously to change; other children become very quiet and clinging. Some babies are wary of strangers and strange places because they have been frightened by well-meaning but overenthusiastic friends or relatives who rush up without giving the baby time to get used to them. Even some babies who have not had that experience are very cautious of strangers;

some sense that the parent may allow the stranger to pick them up and hold them.

If your baby responds fearfully to new places and people, you can help him feel more secure by holding him close to you. Instead of not taking him out and increasing his isolation, you need to help him learn about new situations. Talk to him. Show him interesting things about the new place. If the baby doesn't relax, then stay a short time and repeat the visit another time.

*"I think our problem is just the opposite. We took our baby to visit friends. She made herself right at home. She was into everything. The house was so 'unbaby-proofed' that when we weren't holding her she had to be in a playpen, which she hates. So either she was in the playpen or we were following her like policemen. We had no time with our friends."*

When babies of this age (twelve to fifteen months) are taken to visit friends, the parents must not expect the same kind of relaxed visit, with uninterrupted adult conversation, that was possible before the baby was born. It is inappropriate to expect the baby to be quiet and not explore interesting new surroundings. Actually, this exploratory behavior indicates healthy curiosity and appropriate cognitive development. Visits at this age have to be more baby-centered than adult-centered.

*"I think we could manage visiting when we have the baby if my husband and I could take turns watching and playing with him; but it doesn't work that way. Before I know it, my husband is deep in a political or business conversation, and he just doesn't seem to know the baby is there. I get so angry. I've just given up, and don't think it's worth the trouble getting all the gear together and then minding the baby just as I do at home all week."*

Child rearing is a shared parental activity. Some fathers do need to get more involved. Before going out, it would be a good idea to talk about your expectations. Explain that you would like to participate in the visit, too. One of the ways to encourage the father to be more involved is to indicate how he can show your friends the baby's achievements and the games that he and the baby play together. It also sounds as if you need to get out a little by yourself. Some mothers, without realizing it, actually prevent the fathers from being involved with the baby because she never leaves the two of them alone together. Why don't you try going out for an hour or so on the weekend and let the father take full charge of the baby?

*"That's what I've been doing. I go out each Saturday afternoon for a while. Now my husband has a much better appreciation of how tiring the baby can be. But they have also developed some special games on their own. When we go visiting now, my husband really does share."*

*"We are having trouble with older children. When we go to the park, there is no place just for little children. Sometimes older children of five or six play roughly and knock the little ones over or take their toys. I've made it*

*a practice to sit at the edge of the sandbox. I'm the only mother who does that. I know the others think I am overprotective. Is that overprotective?"*

"Overprotective" is a very commonly used expression of disapproval of mothers who are concerned about their children's welfare. There is a great difference between appropriate protection or anticipation of trouble and overprotection. In this case, you know that the sandbox has a mix of children both older and younger. Some older ones, either inadvertently or purposely, are dangerous to children of this age. You can't expect a baby to protect himself from an older child, or even from one of his peers who may poke at him innocently. It is the parent's job to be available to intervene before an unpleasant encounter has occurred.

*"My husband says that if I always stand up for our son, he won't learn to stand up for himself and I'll make a 'sissy' of him."*

From our experience it seems that quite the contrary is true. If young children are exposed to situations that are frightening and perhaps even dangerous before they are old enough to have developed coping mechanisms, they may always be afraid of situations that involve encounters with others. Such children will hang back and will develop the characteristics that have been labeled "sissy" or "crybaby." Other children may respond by becoming overly aggressive and punching other children without provocation. In this situation, as in so many others, parents must respond appropriately for the child's age. At this age, your children need protection. If you help them now, they will gain the ability and confidence to cope on their own later in life.

## Child's Need for Reassurance

Some fathers feel that little boys, particularly, should not be treated in this way. They are more willing to be protective of their daughters. Both boys and girls need protection and help while they learn to socialize. A boy who cringes and cries when threatened by another child should not be considered a sissy any more than a girl would be. Many tend to think it's okay to be protective of little girls and comfort them when they cry; little boys of the same age are often scolded for crying. Parental attention and protection must be age-appropriate and not determined by the sex of the child. At this age, your children need your help as they learn to cope in social situations.

What are some of your experiences? What are your ideas about intervening when children play?

*"I guess I expected too much and didn't intervene soon enough, because my child begins to whimper and cling to me as soon as she sees other children approach her. They may not be stopping, just passing by, and she seems to cringe and cling to me. I pick her up and hold her till they pass. How can I help her overcome this?"*

When a child has had an unhappy experience, one has to be very supportive and stay close to her until she begins to feel secure again. As she has good experiences with other children and matures, she will feel more secure.

*"What should we do when our children are playing and start to pull toys away from each other? Some people say to let them settle it themselves so they will learn what to do."*

The adults have to intervene. Children of this age cannot settle things themselves. They are not verbal. They do not yet know how to play with other children.

*"You know, I think that may explain something that has puzzled me. I do take my child to the park on weekends, and she cries when I take her to the sandbox. Perhaps my sitter did not intervene soon enough."*

For those of you who work, it is a good idea to discuss these ideas about beginning socialization with your relatives or sitters. It is important for the child to receive this kind of help and support from caretakers as well as parents.

*"My policy has been to ignore it unless the child protests when the toy is taken. You are saying that is not a good idea?"*

What you have been practicing is "peace at any price." Actually, you may be giving the nonprotesting child a feeling that his rights are not recognized and are not important to you. He is simply *not* protesting. If this happens too often, the child may become apprehensive at the approach of other children. He may draw back from other children because they have come to mean that he has to give up his toys. The nonassertive child becomes the victim and the assertive one is rewarded. Projecting that to older children, we can see that this is rewarding the "bully." That is not the attitude we want to foster. We have to be sure that the nonprotesting child is protected as well as the one who loudly protests. This is all part of the gradual process of developing social skills, in which the parent or other caretaker plays a very important guiding role.

## Outdoor Activities

Now that the children are older, the way they behave outdoors changes, too. Some are very content to be wheeled in their carriages or strollers. Others, now that they can walk, are no longer so willing to sit still—causing parents some concern. How are you managing now when you take the children out?

*"I have a great deal of difficulty keeping her sitting down. She wants to stand up in her carriage. I have to keep her harnessed. I'm afraid she'll fall out."*

■                                                                                          ■

*"My son doesn't like walking. My husband is always telling me, 'Make him walk, make him walk.' When we're out in the street, he likes to be held. Sometimes he'll get down and walk for a couple of feet. Then he'll lift up his arms, and I usually pick him up. Is that okay?"*

Children do like to be picked up and carried. It takes a while before they can do as much walking as we expect. In the house they run around, and you think they'll be able to take a good walk. But when you take them out for a walk in the street, they get tired. They're not ready for much walking in the street yet.

## Need for Autonomy and Protection

*"I have a different problem. When my child gets out of the stroller, she refuses to hold my hand and starts to run. Fortunately, she's not too fast yet."*

Now that the children can walk, they are feeling more independent. Their unwillingness to have their hands held does present concerns about their safety. Parents must be very firm in order to protect the child. Sometimes at this age you can use a special harness that allows the child to walk without having his hand held. In this way, the child feels independent, but you are still able to maintain some control over how far away from you the child can get. Another technique is to hold the child's hand until you are nearly at the playground and then say, "Okay, you may walk by yourself now." You can do the same thing as you are returning to your apartment or home entrance.

## Tantrums Caused by Frustration and Fatigue

*"My son hates to have me hold his hand. When I insist, he lies down on the sidewalk and has a tantrum. People stop and look at me; it's embarrassing. I don't know what to do."*

*"My child did the same thing the other day. I got so mad I shouted at him and smacked his bottom. Then he really started to cry."*

This is very typical behavior at this age. Children feel more independent and they don't like to be restricted. Or they may have been walking quite a distance and they get tired. Lying down and refusing to get up are common responses. If you are in the middle of the street, you simply have to pick the child up and carry him or her. If you are on the sidewalk, sometimes you can just let the child lie there for a few moments. Then you can say that it's time to ride in the stroller, or time to go for lunch, or time to look in the store window. One must handle these outbursts in the same way that one does a tantrum in any other place. It is also important to try to keep your cool and remember that everyone on the street who is a parent has probably been through a similar episode. It doesn't help to get angry yourself and to shout or hit. Children having tantrums are often

■                                                                                    ■

frightened by their inability to control themselves; they need your help in regaining control. You will be most effective if you keep yourself under control.

From this age on, it is important to find a good playground where the children can run around safely. A playground should have a fence around it and only one entrance. Then you can watch your child from a distance, giving her the feeling of freedom and independence. At first, the child may wander outside the entrance. This provides another teaching opportunity. You say firmly, "No, we play in here," and lead the child back into the playground. Gradually, children will learn to stay there.

## Mobility of Child Demands Vigilance

In the next few months, the children's motor abilities will be improving. At the same time, some will begin to separate more from the parents. These combined developments will mean that the children move farther away from you and that they have the ability to move faster. It is therefore very important to be vigilant in the playground. If they are near the entrance, they can dart out quickly. Or if they are near the slide, they can suddenly be at the top. If one sits down to chat with friends, one must always be watching and ready to dash to protect one's child.

*"You are right. My son loves the playground, but I see it as a million hazards. Sometimes I'm sorry that he's become so mobile. It used to be so peaceful to be able to sit on the park bench in the sun and know the baby was safe in the carriage. Those days are gone for good."*

Those days are gone for good. Just as one gets used to the child's level of development, she reaches a new level that requires adjustments on the part of the parents. The stage that the children are coming into now is quite trying: they have lots of energy and no idea of the consequences of their actions. Most of the learning at this stage comes from doing and action. Gradually, as the children approach two years of age, more of their learning will come from observation and thinking.

# Cuing In to the Child's Needs

Are you finding it difficult to understand your child's new level of development? Are the changes frustrating to you?

## Accommodation to Child's Needs

*"I think I had the notion before the baby came that I would have the baby fit into our way of life. I learned that it led to an irritating situation between us, and I've gotten used to doing what he needs and not feeling upset."*

I think you are right. The baby cannot totally accommodate to the adult world. The adult cues in to what the child can tolerate and needs on the level at which he or she is—that's the whole idea. You know, grown-ups think that they are going to train children to fit into their lives at once; but you can't do that. You have to recognize the various levels of development and adjust your behavior accordingly. This doesn't mean that there will be no adjustments by the baby. Each family has a somewhat different life-style, and by trial and error you are all finding out how much you *have* to adjust and how much the baby *can* adjust. Some of you work part-time or have regular times you go out, so your children have gotten used to being cared for by a grandmother or a baby-sitter. In other families the fathers work late; so you have helped the children to develop a schedule in which they take long afternoon naps and may stay up late to be able to play with Daddy. In some families both parents work outside the home, and a similar schedule is usually worked out: the evening becomes the child's playtime with the parents. These adjustments are made gradually by both parents and child—with the parents taking into consideration the needs of the child for adequate sleep and time with the parents. This kind of scheduling does put an extra burden on parents who have a busy, tiring day. Spending quality time with your child, even when you are tired, is the adjustment you make to the child's needs.

Although you can't train a child to fit completely into the pattern of your life as it was before the child was born, you can, with some adjustments, find a new pattern for your life as a growing family.

Making adjustments for the child's needs does not mean that the child "rules the roost." There are many areas in which you are teaching the child to accommodate to the values of your family in particular and of society in general.

The main thing that children must conform to at this age—and they learn to conform only by consistent training—is that there are certain things they cannot do because they are dangerous to themselves or to others.

## Accommodations to New Levels of Development

In all other areas, you should be cuing in to them at their level. You cue in to their level of development regarding what they can eat, how many hours they can sleep, how long they can play with a toy, what toys interest them, and how much they can socialize and separate from you. At the same time, you are also trying to stimulate them to go to the next level of development. As their central nervous systems mature, they will move to a new level. They need the opportunity to advance step by step at their own rates, not at the rate the parent might find more convenient or pleasurable.

*"I have had to say 'No' when something was dangerous, but I felt like a heel. I avoid the negative as much as possible. I guess that makes me pretty inconsistent; but I so want to avoid being like my parents, who were so strict."*

■                                                                                     ■

We are not suggesting that you be strict in the sense that left an unpleasant memory for you, but that you be firm and consistent about a few necessary limitations, such as touching a hot stove or pulling over a large lamp or plant or hitting another child. The important part is to limit and offer a substitute activity appropriate to the child's level.

*"But won't the baby be angry with me? I want my baby to love me."*

Your child will not be angry with you because you are firm. One can be firm without being harsh, mean, or angry with the baby. Consistent limitations give the child a sense of security as he or she begins to learn what is forbidden and what is allowed. It is the parent's duty to set limits.

*"Can the baby understand why you are setting limits? If my baby climbs on the couch and falls off, will she understand the next time I stop her that it is for her safety?"*

At this age children do not understand the why, the reason. That understanding comes much later, when they begin to learn the concepts of cause and effect. They are just at the stage when they are beginning to discover that a toy falls down if it is pushed over the side of the high chair.

*"Is it wrong, for instance, if while she's playing with something and I can sort of tell that she is about finished, to get her interested in something else before she's fretful?"*

To be able to anticipate like that is very good. It is something that parents—and nursery school teachers—learn to do. When parents have difficulty in doing this, the child can become cross and fretful or frustrated. It is very appropriate to change the activity when you see it is reaching an unproductive stage. Often it is possible to show the child a new way to play with a toy. For example, when a child looks as if she is tired of rolling a small ball back and forth, you may pick up a box and let the child drop the ball into the box. A little later, you can show her how to roll the ball toward the box.

## Gratifying Needs Is Not Spoiling

*"How can you anticipate the baby's every want and need? If I could, wouldn't that spoil her? Does she have to have every need gratified?"*

We are not talking about gratifying every wish. That's not possible. If we can anticipate some of them, it makes life run more smoothly for the parent and gives the child a sense that the parent is there to help. It fortifies basic trust. We are talking about children who are nonverbal and can't always express their wishes or needs clearly. It is indeed the parents' job to anticipate as much as they can. If the parents get it right even half the time, that gives the child a feeling of trust and security.

I think you are touching on another aspect of this question when you mention spoiling. Gratifying a child's need is not spoiling. Often, when parents are trying to anticipate or meet their children's needs, they are concerned that other people will think they are spoiling the children—in fact, some people may even tell the parent exactly that.

Very often in crowded places such as shopping centers, buses, or trains, children will be restless. Sometimes they cry and the parents have difficulty discovering what is needed to quiet them. They often want to run around and explore; or they may be frightened by strange places or people. Parents often feel embarrassed and often appear to be placating the other adults rather than satisfying the child's needs. The child is scolded, told to be quiet, sit still, and stop bothering. Does this sound familiar to any of you?

*"That has often happened to me. Especially on a bus. My baby will cry and want to get down or tug at the newspaper of the person next to us. I feel embarrassed and try to quiet him down to avoid disturbing others, but he only makes more of a fuss. It's a hassle. It's not every time; some days he is fine."*

It's a natural thing for us to say, "Now, sit down and be quiet. There are other people around and you must be quiet," trying to show the other adults you know how to bring up a child. At the same time, you imply that your child is at fault. Your child senses this and protests more vigorously.

*"What should one do? What would be the proper procedure, given that situation?"*

To respond to each situation, one has to know the child's state. Is she overtired? Is she hungry? Has she been confined for too long? Is she frightened? One must assess the situation. If the child is overtired, she needs soothing—a little patting, soft talk, some rocking. If she is hungry, a snack or a bottle is in order. It is always important to have a few diverting things in one's purse or bag—a toy or book and a snack.

*"I have trouble in the supermarket. My baby tries to reach for everything she sees as we pass the shelves. She cries if she wants to touch something and I won't let her. Once, a woman came up to me and said, 'What your baby needs is a good sound smack on the hand.' She made me very angry. But she said it so emphatically, as if she knew so much about raising children, that I began to wonder if she was right and if I am spoiling the baby by not slapping her."*

## Alternatives to Slapping

Slapping or hitting is never a satisfactory form of teaching. The baby is attracted by all the brightly colored packaged items on the shelves and wants to explore. The trip to the market can be a very important part of the baby's day. As you take down an item and put it into the cart you can name it. Try to give one or two small things to the baby to hold. Talk to the baby and describe what you are going to get next. In this way, the

■                                                                    ■

baby becomes involved in what is happening. She absorbs what you are saying, and the entire activity can be productive instead of aggravating.

*"When I do that I feel self-conscious. I think people are looking at me as though I were crazy."*

You seem to be worrying more about what other adults think than what your baby is learning from this experience. Think, instead, of enhancing your baby's understanding of the world around her and of your increased communication with her. What the other adults think doesn't matter. How your child feels does matter to you.

*"I can do that and enjoy it when I have a few things to buy; but I can't do it when I have to do the shopping for the week. It takes too much time, and the baby gets tired or fussy."*

That's true. If at all possible, the baby should not be with you for a long shopping trip. If someone can't watch the baby while you shop, it might be better to rearrange your shopping. Do a little each day so that the baby gets used to the routine without getting overtired and irritable.

This is what we were talking about earlier. You can't expect the baby to accommodate completely to your needs. You need to cue in to how much the baby can tolerate. Several shorter shopping trips a week may, in the long run, be better for both you and the baby.

*"I guess I fall into the trap of being more tuned in to the adult than my baby when we have company. Somehow, at that time, she seems to want the most attention. I feel that the guest's needs are more important than hers, that the baby should wait."*

Waiting is something we learn as we mature. The younger the child, the less she can wait. It is a sign of maturity to be able to wait. Our babies are now at the stage when they can delay gratification of their needs only briefly. It is the adult who should be patient. Parents have to be on the child's side—and not expect more of the child than she can deliver. Children who feel that their parents are on their side—helping them get what they need—develop trust and self-confidence. Children who feel that their parents are always disappointed in them or not satisfied with them take on these feelings about themselves. The way one responds to one's child, therefore, goes beyond the resolution of the immediate situation. It has a lot to do with the development of the child's personality—his feelings about himself and about others.

## *Dealing with the Child's Fears*

### *New Places and Situations*

Are your children beginning to show fear in certain situations?

*"Yes, I was going to ask about that. I find now that when we go to a new place my baby shows much more anxiety than he used to. He cries and pulls me away from a house where we have not been before, or where we have not been for a long time."*

The important thing is to reassure the child. Pick him up and hold him so he feels secure. Point out things he might be interested in. Tell him you are going to stay a little while and that you will be going home soon. Make your visit very short if he doesn't overcome his anxiety. Try not to give him the feeling that he has done something wrong. This anxiety is age-appropriate behavior. It indicates that the child recognizes the difference in his surroundings and that the "known" is different from the "unknown." It indicates an advance in cognitive development. Some children are more anxious or shy than others in accepting newness. Many parents give children the feeling that they are naughty and that they are displeased with them. If you return to the same place again and the child has not been forced to accept it the first time, it will be easier the second time. As he matures, he will be more ready to explore and socialize. Some children are not yet as ready as some parents would like them to be. We can make them more apprehensive by forcing too much exposure too early. That does not mean we should not try new situations. We should, however, respect the child's apprehension and reassure him.

## Loud Noises

*"My child is afraid of loud noises. Whenever we are in the street and a car backfires or a loud truck comes along, he starts running to me and cries. So I pick him up till it passes, and then he is all right until the next time. I always say, 'Mama's here; everything is okay. The truck will soon be gone.' As it disappears, I say, 'Bye, truck.' That seems to make him feel better."*

Many children are afraid of loud noises. In fact, some people seem to be more sensitive to noise and even as adults will be startled when they hear sudden loud noises. The important thing is to comfort and reassure children that everything is all right. Gradually, they learn that loud noises per se do not hurt them. Again, one must not belittle children for this kind of fear.

## Elevators

*"My child has fears, too. Especially of the elevator. The door makes a noise as it closes. Right away, the clutching begins."*

Elevator phobia is not uncommon in large cities and can start early. Once you know that some elevators bother your child, you must be prepared to distract the child with something interesting to do. One could say, "Let's look for Mommy's keys so that we can open the door" or "Let's look in our bag for your car so that you can play as soon as we get up (or down)" or

■          ■

"Let's watch the numbers light up." Counting the numbers up and down is a particularly good game when the children are a little older. Another good diversion is to show children how to push the button (in a self-service elevator) and let them do it. Say, "We push the button and the door will close. Here we go up to see Granny." When there is an operator, one can say, "Let's watch the man drive the elevator. First he shuts the door; here we go up, up, up."

Of course, for small children there may be too many strange things at once. They may be afraid of the elevator operator as well as the elevator itself. We are often beset by people who are trying to be kind but sometimes interfere.

*"You're right. My daughter was frightened by an elevator man who suddenly poked her in the stomach and gave a big laugh. I guess he was trying to be friendly, but my daughter was terrified."*

Some people come upon children too quickly. We need to hold the children and reassure them that we will protect them. What is fun or funny to an adult is not always funny to a child. Children do not understand jokes, or sarcasm for that matter, until they are much older.

## Animals

*"My little girl just became afraid of dogs. One day when I was taking her home, this very big collie started barking excitedly. She was very frightened of him. Now she is afraid of all dogs."*

Fear of all animals—dogs, cats, and horses—is a very frequent fear. One of the most common errors adults make is to try to make the child pet the animal. This often intensifies the fear. The best thing is to hold the child and move away from the animal. Let the child observe from a distance until he is older and has seen you or others pet the animal. It's a good idea to give the child a small toy replica of the animal and show him pictures of the animal. Gradually he may show some desire to get close to the animal and you will allow him to do it. Often, a lifelong fear of animals is started innocently by forcing a child to make contact with them before he is ready.

*"I think my child is afraid of dogs because she senses that I am. Is it possible that she knows? I try to hide it."*

We know that children are much more sensitive to our moods and feelings than it might appear. Even though you try to hide your fear of dogs, you may be startled or become tense. If you are holding your child, she will literally feel these physical responses on your part. In this case, it is a good idea for both of you to remain at a distance looking at the dog and talking about his actions. Discussing the fear is hard at this age because children do not understand exactly what you are saying and they are not able to express their own feelings, except by crying. By the third or fourth year, you will be able to talk together about the child's feelings—and your own as well.

When one encounters a dog in the park or on the sidewalk, one should not let one's child rush up to it, no matter how small and friendly looking it is. Sometimes the dog's owner will actually say that the dog is frightened of children and may bite. Others will say the dog likes children and encourage you to introduce your child. Again, the most important thing is not to force the child and to let him or her observe from a distance.

### Strangers

*"My son is frightened of people, strangers who come up and talk to him. They say 'Hello' and he hides behind me. It's embarrassing."*

The best thing to do is for you to say "Hello" in a friendly way and move on. Some parents stop and insist that the child reply. These children are really too young for that. When the child is older, having watched you model the greeting procedure sufficiently, he will be able to do it on his own without coaxing. Parental insistence lowers the child's self-esteem and intensifies his reluctance to meet new people because he senses your disapproval of his behavior.

*"When my little girl sits on my lap, she is very friendly; but she won't go to anyone. If anyone comes too close, she cries and pulls back."*

Adults have to be warned that they must let the child get used to them first, that children need to "size them up" as it were. The child makes the approach to the adult when she is ready and feels comfortable. A little patience on the part of the adult will be well rewarded.

*"My child is afraid of her grandfather, who has a muscular condition and walks with a limp. He uses a cane—he is not steady on his legs and he sort of falls into the chair. When he wants to pick her up, she shrieks. I think she senses his weakness."*

She notices his disability. The cane and his unsteadiness may scare her; she may sense your concern. This is very hard to explain. Instead, you can explain that children are very often afraid of grown-ups if they are not used to them. Make it general, so Grandfather isn't hurt; but still make it comfortable for the child. After a while, instead of picking the child up, Grandfather should be encouraged to hand her a toy or roll her a ball.

*"That reminds me of my childhood. I can still hear my mother say, 'Shame on you; say hello to so-and-so.' I still have a funny feeling when I'm introduced to strangers, but the grown-up part of me goes through the formalities. Are we helping our children to avoid this? Are we sowing the seeds of easy social poise by being supportive of the children at this age?"*

Yes, that is exactly it. We are trying to help them deal with their age-appropriate anxiety by recognizing their need for support.

■                                                                    ■

*"This seems to be an age of lots of fears. When will it end?"*

As you reassure the children about one set of fears, they will gradually overcome them. Then suddenly you will discover that there is something new they are afraid of. This is part of growing up and learning about the world.

### The Water

For example, you take your child to the beach this year and he loves it, running into the water without fear. Next year, you may take him back to the very same beach. He will be a year older and will be frightened. You just can't understand what it is. This is the year he realizes how large the ocean is and how big the waves are. You have to get him used to the water in gradual stages.

### Masks

Halloween masks are something else we might mention at this point. From this age until children are about three or four, they will be very fearful even of other children wearing masks. If children wearing masks come to your door, you should ask them to take off their masks so the baby can see their faces. Even if they see the other child's face, that child is "gone" and the "pussycat" or "witch" is back as soon as the mask is replaced. Even when as familiar a person as daddy puts on a mask or a Santa Claus beard or even sunglasses, he is no longer daddy to a child of this age— even though all the rest of daddy is showing. Daddy should not be hurt. Everyone must realize that this is a phase of development that all children go through.

### The Dark

*"One fear we haven't mentioned yet is the dark. Our baby screams now if her room is dark."*

Yes, and that is a fear that may last several years. Some of you may already have started using dim night-lights. You can get either a small lamp or a little bulb that fits into a plug—the kind that many people keep lit all night in a bathroom or hallway. A little bit of light helps the child to see the familiar objects in the room and feel reassured. Fear of the dark is probably the most common childhood fear of all. As with all other fears, one must reassure the child.

Some children are quite independent and can always do many things on their own and not get into trouble. Others are more sensitive and need more emotional support. Parents have to tune in to each child's needs in these situations. With parental reassurance, fears are gradually overcome.

## The Child's Daily Routines and Activities

Now that the children are older, do you find you are able to spend time together in more satisfying ways? Is there any difference from when the children were younger?

■                                                                      ■

"There is a world of difference. At first, I was so busy just making sure he ate, slept, was bathed, changed, and kept reasonably entertained. Then when he began to walk, it seemed all I did was run after him to keep him out of trouble. Now he is beginning to talk. There is communication, and I feel I'm spending time with a real person; I am having a great time. This is what I thought having a child would be like. We can do so many things together."

"My son seems to want to be on the go all the time. From the minute he wakes in the morning he is ready to go out in his stroller. Of course, I dress him and give him his breakfast first. That he seems to be able to wait for, but then he wants to go. I feel frustrated because I would like to straighten up the house first and get some cleaning done. That was my old pattern when he was a baby. Now I know that if we go out first, he is happier. I get a little marketing done before the stores are crowded. If it's nice, we go to the park for a while. Then he seems tired and ready to come home for lunch. Then he naps and I do the laundry and some cleaning . . . and then we go out again. By the time his father gets home, we're both pooped! The only good part is that after some quiet play with his daddy, he goes right to sleep."

"I also go to work. My son eats breakfast with his daddy and me. Then we dress him. Both of us get up early so as to avoid too much rush before we leave. Then his sitter comes; her main job is the baby—not the house. She plays indoors with him, if the weather is bad, or goes out to the park. In the afternoons it's a walk outdoors again, or maybe she gets together with another sitter and baby and they play indoors. Then I get home and take over: bathing, supper, and bedtime about nine. Sometimes my husband is home in time to join us. Then it's easier and more fun. I'm trying to take it easy and have more fun; a lot of housework just doesn't get done."

"I used to work full time, too. But it was too much of a hassle for me, so I decided to work part-time, just in the morning. Now I can take my child to the park, or we visit a friend or play games at home. Sometimes we go to the children's room at the library. Now I feel I'm giving my child the stimulation he needs, which I wasn't sure the baby-sitter was doing. The best part is that I have been around to see most of the 'firsts.' We talked before about how a working mother may miss these."

## Importance of Play Versus Housework

It seems that those of you who leave your children in the care of others worry that the child may not be getting appropriate stimulation, while the "at-home mother" is there all the time and can make sure. However, some of the mothers who are at home seem to have difficulty tearing themselves away from household chores and seem overburdened. Others seem more willing and able to accommodate to the child's needs and put housework aside. Each one has a choice to make. We believe that the child is more important than the house.

■                                                                    ■

*"I'm glad to hear you say that the child is more important. It's what I feel, but my husband says his mother always kept a neat, clean house and she had four kids."*

We don't know exactly what her circumstances were or what other help she had. Often it is easier for adults to get things done in the house when there are several children in the family who can play with each other. But your child can't be expected to entertain himself for very long. He won't be able to for some time, in fact.

We believe that child care should have priority over housework both for the parents and for caretakers. Most mothers will make that choice— or wear themselves out trying to do both. Housekeepers may get the idea, however, that the house is their priority. After all, it is easy to see when the laundry isn't done or the kitchen floor is not washed. It is not necessarily so easy to show the results of a walk in the park or time spent looking at a book or playing games with a child. To show that the child— and appropriate stimulation of the child—is more important, parents should make a point of asking about the child's day and what activities the caretaker and child have engaged in. It also doesn't hurt if every once in a while you come home when you are not expected, to see what is actually going on. This occasional checking up on the child's daily routines and welfare is also a good idea if the child is left regularly with a neighbor, in family day care, or in a day-care center. Remember, your children are too young to tell you what is actually happening to them.

Children who do not see their parents all day do need time with them in the evening but, after working all day, parents need some time to themselves as well. Though a caretaker may not be as exciting as the parent, she can provide some stimulation and outdoor activities.

*"I'm afraid my baby-sitter doesn't have much imagination. I know they go out when the weather is good, but I guess I will have to make some suggestions about games for rainy days."*

*"Of course, the rainy days or sick days are hard, and the child gets restless and cranky. I have a bag of some new toys he hasn't seen before that I save for those days. I have also put away some old ones. He has a ball trying to play with the discarded ones in a new way. It gives him quite a lift and me a breathing spell."*

*"A cranky child is no worse than a cranky, demanding boss. Some days at work are just as trying. It seems that every minute of life can't be a thrill, either at home or in the office. You just 'roll with the punches'—it's a challenge."*

There is no doubt whether one is an "at-home working mother" or an "outside working mother," it is a challenging job. It takes patience, ingenuity, creativity, and knowledge and understanding of the level of your child's development, his personality, special needs, and how to accommodate the child's and parents' needs. No one ever said it was easy to be a parent, but it can be interesting and fulfilling. No profession—and parenting is an important profession—is without its hard and dull days, its frustrations and annoyances. The difficulties need to be examined thoughtfully so that they can be minimized. Often, that can be profitable.

## Daily Routines Should Be Pleasant for Parent and Child

Emphasizing the negative, however, and not focusing on the positive aspects of any job can be destructive. That's why it is important for parents to work out their priorities and establish a consistent framework of daily activities that is pleasant for parent and child. Pleasant daily experiences enhance the relationship between parent and child or housekeeper and child. The child needs the security of familiar activities and the stimulation of new ones. For example, children enjoy becoming more proficient in rolling a ball; at the same time, the game becomes more interesting if they roll the ball into a box, or even try to throw it.

*"I just couldn't take the routine at home. I am much better off working all day. When I come home, I am glad to see my son, and he is glad to see me and his father and plays with us. Before bed, we take time to get him simmered down. On the weekend we take turns taking him to the playground. One day each; we can take it. His father is better at it than I am. We both relax when he naps. He seems to be thriving, except that we notice he doesn't talk as much as some other children his age. Can it be his rate of development, or isn't he getting enough speech stimulation?"*

## Language Stimulation

Some children develop one area more quickly than another. Your child sounds as though all his energy was devoted to motor activity. There probably is no cause for worry. However, one needs to know whether he is getting sufficient speech stimulation so that when he is ready, he will achieve appropriate language development. Some caretakers may not stimulate speech sufficiently. If that is a concern, then the parents can try to make up for it when they are with the child at night and over the weekend.

*"I'm afraid we have the same problem. Our housekeeper is Spanish-speaking and she apparently doesn't talk much to our little girl—although she is fine in every other way, gentle and efficient, reliable in everything one would want."*

Your housekeeper may feel that you don't want her to speak Spanish to your child. Actually, it may be a good opportunity for your child to learn two languages. Usually children who learn two languages at the same time learn both more slowly, but they can learn both well. The important thing is for your child to be spoken to, to hear language, and begin to say words and communicate. It is much better for her to learn Spanish from your sitter than not to have any verbal communication while you are gone. Reading books that have pictures with names or simple captions underneath may be a good way for your housekeeper to learn some English, too. With encouragement from you—and some help in pronunciation—your housekeeper may find she enjoys this activity.

*"I like that idea. I'll try it. Also, I think we need to talk more to our baby ourselves. I did not realize it would make so much difference."*

We've been hearing about the many different ways that parents plan for their child's day. Each family has to make the appropriate adjustments to suit the child's and their own needs. Routines will vary, depending on the time parents can spend with their child, their own emotional needs, the child's endowment, and the kind of substitute care that is available. All of this takes a great deal of thought. The important issue to bear in mind is that the child is dependent upon the parent. Each child has his own endowment, but the parent supplies the environment in which the child develops and flourishes. Not every day will be great; but as the children mature and, as some of you have said, "get to be real persons," more days can be happy and productive for both parent and child.

## *Marital Relations: How to Revive the Romance*

How do you feel the care of a child has affected your lives? Has it been what you expected?

*"Well, I'll say it's changed our lives enormously in a way we didn't expect. We knew the baby would be an added expense, but we figured that we could manage; and that part is okay. But we didn't figure how much time he would take away from our doing things together, such as going out to dinner, or entertaining, or just talking alone together. The baby himself is a joy, and we are getting to understand his needs better. The older he gets, the better it is getting. But we rarely are alone together—and when we are, we're too exhausted for romance and sex."*

*"We find this, too. We can't be spontaneous anymore. We have to plan on the baby's needs and then ours. It's a growing experience, I suppose, to look out for another before yourself. Sometimes I wish I could just think about myself."*

Certainly, raising a child is very time-consuming and demanding. Many of you are experiencing some satisfaction, even though there are times of frustration. Occasionally, the frustration comes from unrealistic expectations of what child rearing will be like. Other times, frustration comes from unrealistic expectations about what marriage will be like and what each partner can realistically offer the other. Sometimes, a husband may expect his wife to be just like his mother, and the wife's care of the child interferes with the care he desires. The same may be true for a wife.

Much more common, however, are the cases in which parents become fatigued by the many responsibilities of child care, housework, and jobs. "Romantic love" then becomes lost in the other pressures of the marriage. Sometimes, parents don't know what to do about this—or don't recognize the lack for what it is—and develop feelings of anger and frustration toward each other and the baby. Toddlers are very active, and often their sleep is still disturbed by dreams or teething. Parents therefore are often tired and have no energy left for lovemaking, or even for affectionate gestures toward each other. As soon as couples notice such feelings, they should discuss them with each other.

*"We had that situation after the baby was born. It took a long time before we were able to talk it out."*

Each one has feelings of concern and regret or resentment. If one doesn't discuss one's feelings, it is easy to think that the other doesn't notice or care. Often, it's hard to find the appropriate time for such a discussion because you are so busy getting the child to bed, doing the laundry, and other chores.

## Parents Need to Discuss Their Feelings

*"We have found we spend most of the time discussing what the children have done or what my day was at the office—and not addressing our feelings. The whole business of being affectionate to each other got lost somewhere. My wife was so busy being cross because I wasn't helping enough; she didn't seem to be making me the center of attention. I thought she ought to, because I'd been imposed upon in the office. I wanted to come home to a haven, and it's not a haven at all—so I was terribly disappointed. I didn't realize that was the trouble until we talked about it."*

In all our relationships—whether professional, social, marital, parental—we have to think of the other person's feelings, just as we have to think about how the child is feeling. Each person has to consider how the other one is thinking and feeling about the marriage as well. When the husband comes home and says, "Dinner ready?" and the wife says, "No, it isn't," and he says, "Why not?" then she starts telling him that she hasn't been wasting her time, that she has been busy all day. He can't understand the outburst because he doesn't fully understand what she has been doing and that she feels overworked and unappreciated. At the same time, she may not know what has been happening to him.

*"That is exactly the scene in our house. My husband expects dinner to be ready and our son put to bed all between the hours of 7:00 and 7:30. Our baby doesn't finish eating until 6:30. Then I have to bathe him and get him to bed by 7:00 so I can clean up and get dinner ready in thirty minutes. It's a mad rush; so when my husband comes in I'm feeling harassed—and certainly not loving."*

## Parents Need to Help Each Other

This kind of situation does not need to go on. Parents can try to work out their time schedules and help each other a bit. If it's the mess that bothers the

■                                                                    ■

father, it would not be a big deal for him to toss the toys strewn about into the toy box. Sometimes the mother and toddler of this age can do it together as a "cleaning-up time" before bed. Simple dinners can be planned that can be cooked while the mother is tending the baby. It takes a little forethought and planning, but it can be done. Such planning will help to avoid an angry welcome home that is unpleasant for parents and baby alike.

*"We overcame that situation by sharing the bedtime routines. I cook while my husband takes over and plays with the baby. Then we put him in his bath together while dinner is cooking. Then one of us reads or sings to him, whichever he seems to want that day. Usually a little holding or quiet play works best; and he is off to sleep. Then we have a quiet dinner alone and talk over the day. Sometimes we make plans for going out and getting a baby-sitter. I think we are really getting to feel good about being parents, and good about being with each other as people and parents. Somehow we expected that from the start, but it took work to make it come out that way."*

*"My husband and I seem to be on different wavelengths. He was always loving, but in a way that made me feel like a child. Now, as a mother, I feel more grown up and want to be treated that way—not criticized all the time, no matter how tactfully, and I'd like a little praise."*

It may be that your husband was brought up in the way that many of us were brought up—if you don't like something, you say so; but if you like it, you make no particular comment. There are many people who will tell you when something is wrong. If it's right, well, that's the way they seem to expect it. If you are really looking for a compliment from that kind of person, then you are doomed to disappointment. It's not that such a person doesn't recognize what you have done and doesn't approve of it; he simply doesn't think to express approval. He may never have had the experience of being overtly approved of in his own bringing up. Therefore, he can't express what he has never experienced.

*"I guess that is our situation. I recognize it; so now I will understand better if there is never a compliment. I'll try to consider the lack of criticism as a compliment."*

That is a way to deal with the situation. However, it may also help if you express your appreciation for whatever your husband does; it may make it easier for him to respond the same way. All of us like to be recognized and praised a little. If we can do it with our children appropriately, then perhaps we will raise a generation with fewer people who can make only a critical response. In addition, we have to realize that as parents we are growing, too. We must be able to recognize when we have done something right ourselves. Then we will not be dependent on others' recognition, although it is always nice to have it. Truly mature individuals recognize their own achievements without being smug.

■                                                                    ■

## Parents Need Time Off Together

*"Isn't it possible that sometimes parents can't get time with each other because of the demands of the household and that they need time away from home?"*

That certainly is often true. That is why we have always advocated that parents should spend time alone together regularly one afternoon or evening a week. Occasionally, parents should plan a "mini-vacation," such as a short weekend alone in a hotel in the city or at a resort with friends or relatives in the country. The best way to do it is to have someone the baby likes stay with her in the familiar surroundings of your own house so her routines and sense of security are not disturbed. Then separation will be as painless as possible for the baby.

*"What about longer vacations? Would the baby be too upset at this stage?"*

It all depends on the individual child and the arrangements the parents can make for baby-sitters. Having the baby at home with a capable baby-sitter whom the child knows well or a family member is best. Leaving the baby with friends or relations whose home he is used to and who knows how to carry out his routines is next best. Sometimes close friends and neighbors carry out these services for each other on an exchange basis. If the child is experiencing separation anxiety in general and is very clinging already, that would not be the best time. If parents have no alternative, then they will have to understand the repercussions of the baby's separation anxiety and deal with them on their return. When the parents understand that often the baby feels abandoned when they leave for an extended period, they can respond patiently and appropriately when they return. They can help the baby deal with the separation by allowing clinging and giving extra attention and reassurance.

It is when we get angry and impatient with the baby for expressing his normal feelings that we get into trouble. A vacation should make a parent feel more relaxed and willing to spend more quality time with the baby. Many parents, in fact, find it nicer to be home with the baby than away from him.

*"We went away for a week and left the baby with his regular sitter. When we came home, the baby turned away from us at first. After about twenty minutes, he seemed to recognize us and was all smiles. Didn't he know us?"*

My interpretation would be that he was letting you know that he missed you and was possibly a little angry. As he is still not very verbal, he could express himself only in that way.

*"Now I understand why our baby is so cross when I first come home after a business trip. It makes me feel better to know that that is his way of expressing that he missed me. I always expect him to get excited and smile; and I'm so disappointed when he doesn't. When my husband is away on a trip, he does the same thing to him."*

With children of this age, it is best to take frequent "mini-vacations" rather than an extended vacation. When the child is older, you will be able to be away longer.

Even if you are not able to get away, you should make a point of getting out occasionally in the evening. Also, it is important to stop your work while you are home—at least a couple of evenings a week—and talk to each other. Sit down and relax with each other. If, after supper and the baby's bedtime, both parents continue to do work—whether office work or housework—until bedtime, they will be too tired to think about enjoying any intimacy with each other. The decrease in sexual relations between married couples because of other life pressures and fatigue is very common, but it can be overcome with a little effort and mutual consideration. Ultimately, the best thing for the child is to grow up with parents who are happy with each other as well as with him.

## Recognition of the Child's Personality as Unique

Now that the children are well into their second year—walking and perhaps saying a few words as well as understanding much more about the world around them, they are beginning to have more distinctive personalities. They are also able to express their likes and dislikes more clearly. Many are already showing early expressions of a desire for autonomy. This is a normal progression in child development that catches many parents by surprise.

Some of you have commented that they are beginning to be "real people." By that you mean that their character traits and personalities are becoming increasingly distinct and individual. Many of you have expressed enjoyment and interest in this development—often when the child begins to express himself or herself in ways that match aspects of your personalities. For example, active, athletic parents enjoy active children; and more verbal parents are especially thrilled when their child begins to say words and communicate. Often, however, children's personalities are quite different from one or both of their parents', and this mismatch can cause difficulties. The active, energetic child can be exceedingly tiring and may appear abnormal to the quiet, reflective parent; similarly, a cautious child can be a total puzzle (and embarrassment) to the active parent.

Have any of you found this to be true in your family? How would you describe the match between yourselves and your children?

*"My husband is quiet and likes it that way. I'm more exuberant, and so is our little girl. So I find I have to try to counteract his attempts to keep her quiet; I try to strike a happy medium for her."*

*"We have just the opposite situation. Our boy is quiet, sensitive, and emotional. I can accept that, but my husband can't understand it. He thinks a boy should be all 'go.' Gradually, he is becoming reconciled and can see the baby's progress in other than muscular development now that he is beginning to talk. I think he is still disappointed."*

### Temperamental Differences

It does make it difficult if a parent's temperamental makeup is different from the baby's. It is important to remember that the baby is a unique individual, not a duplicate of the mother or father—or even an equal mixture of both. If one recognizes his uniqueness and respects it as the child's normal endowment, then some thoughtful adaptive arrangements can be made to ease the frustrations that differences can cause. For example, if a very active baby is really troublesome to a quiet mother but enjoyed by the father, the father can assume major responsibility for the outdoor activities that cause the mother anxiety. The mother can concentrate more on the quiet activities such as looking at books and playing games, which are also important to the child's development, while understanding that her son's attention span for such activities will be quite limited.

Mothers and fathers who like quiet may be lucky to have quiet, reflective children. Those households will appear quite subdued to others. Other children may be rather noisy at times. Before they learn to talk, there is a period of screaming. That is the way children express themselves. Also, they simply do not know how to modulate their voices or talk in a whisper. It helps for quiet parents to realize that this behavior is a normal part of development, and not a malicious attempt on the child's part to disturb their peace; and it should be allowed at certain times, such as in the park. Sometimes a child becomes very noisy and disruptive to gain attention; so parents should be sure they give enough attention to the quiet behavior they claim to appreciate, and not use the child's quiet periods as times to ignore him.

*"You are right. My daughter is sometimes most exuberant when my husband is reading and paying no attention to her. When he stops his book and reads to her, she quiets right down."*

While it is important to recognize and respect the uniqueness of each child's personality, this does not mean that one cannot also encourage a child to develop in areas where natural inclination is not evident. For example, the active child may learn to enjoy quiet activities once in a while. With appropriate encouragement, the quiet, sensitive child can learn to take more interest in more active games. The way to do this is not for the parent to force motor activities on the child and berate him or her for being reticent, but to encourage more activity gradually and gently. Children should be exposed at the appropriate ages to all kinds of activities, such as sports, music, dance, and art. Parents cannot assume that children will have the same interests as they have; but often children develop similar interests if the activities are presented without pressure.

## Child's Need for Appreciation as an Individual

*"Our son is adopted, so we have no idea about his natural endowment, whether he is artistic, mechanical, musical, or what. He seems to us to be bright, but we really don't know what his potential is. We plan to introduce him to lots of things to see where his talents lie, though I guess we will probably concentrate more on the things we enjoy and understand ourselves. But we love him for himself."*

■                                                                        ■

That is an attitude that would be healthy for all parents to have regarding their children. A child can have a wonderful personality or talent that, if unappreciated or misunderstood by the parents, can be inhibited or prevented from developing to its fullest potential. There is nothing sadder than to see a perfectly competent child who doesn't "measure up" in his parents' eyes because he can't do what they want him to do.

Growth is a two-way proposition. Children with different character traits and talents cause parents to grow and develop with them. These differences make child rearing a dynamic, interesting interaction between parents and child. Very often parents become interested in new things through their children's interests. If our children were just like us and did just what we always expected, life would be nice and stable and probably a bit dull.

*"I'm glad you said that. I was getting the feeling that differences only cause trouble. My husband and I are quite different, and I think our daughter is an unusual combination of two grandparents. It is quite fascinating and fun to watch her develop. We love it."*

*"You seem to be happy that your child resembles the grandparents. In our case it is just the opposite. I worry that my daughter will be just like my mother-in-law—dictatorial and opinionated! I think I may be mistaking our child's natural development for imitation of her grandmother, and I may be squelching the natural development of her personality."*

Often parents may see in their children characteristics of relatives, or even of themselves, that they do not like. It is important to recognize that in most cases these are just associations you have made. They may cause you to relate to your child in such a way that you are always emphasizing the characteristics that you do not like rather than recognizing all the other likable characteristics of your child. In some cases, the very thing you don't like because you associate it with someone you don't like may, with proper guidance, become an asset to the child.

There is much to appreciate about each individual child's personality and achievements. Parental approval stimulates further growth and development in a winning cycle of parent-child interaction. Disapproval and inappropriate parental expectations produce just the opposite: the vicious cycle of the "angry alliance" between parent and child or the child who lacks self-esteem. None of us wants to do that, but sometimes we need help in fully appreciating our children when they are very different from our expectations or from us.

The child whose individual traits and personality delight his or her parents will gain a sense of acceptance and self-worth and self-confidence. Each child develops somewhat differently and needs to be accepted at the level that he or she has achieved. Children thrive when their accomplishments are noted by the parents and when they receive the appropriate mixture of challenge and support.

# 14

# Age Fifteen to Eighteen Months

## Highlights of Development—Fifteen Months

Most children have now advanced from standing and holding on to furniture and taking a few steps to walking alone. Some may have abandoned creeping except for climbing up stairs; most will begin climbing down stairs backward. Greater small motor dexterity is evident in the child's ability to put a marble into a small jar without prior demonstration and to help turn the pages of a book.

When given several small blocks, the child can make a tower of two and can put six blocks in and out of a cup. Putting small objects into larger containers is a favorite activity of this period and is therefore a good game for parents and child.

The child can now grasp a crayon more firmly and may begin to imitate a line as well as a scribble drawn by the parent. She can also place the round piece in the puzzle without demonstration.

The child's vocabulary may have increased to four or five words; some children will have many more words. Most will still be using jargon, unintelligible words with the intonation of speech, much of the time.

While a child's language is related to his or her own maturational timetable, it can also be enhanced by parental stimulation and language modeling. There is still more understanding than production of language. When looking at a book, the child now pats the picture, indicating recognition or interest; parents should name the object to which the child points.

The child may grasp his dish when his food is served and need to be inhibited from spilling it. He may respond with some version of "thank you" occasionally if it has been modeled for him. He now points at things that he wants. He likes to show or offer a toy but then may not actually give it up. He may throw a ball or refuse to throw it. These options are more complicated than parents often realize. Knowing he has the ability gives the child the choice of doing it or not. Learning to throw is very exhilarating; but the child still has no appreciation of what is appropriate—he will need to be intercepted if he decides to throw his dish or food.

# *Language Development*

Language at this age consists mostly of naming objects. A child's vocabulary is normal if he says about five words, including names, at fifteen months. By eighteen months most children have a vocabulary of about ten words. Most parents expect more, and indeed it would make life simpler if children were more verbal earlier. However, although children are not able to say much, they do understand a great deal more than some parents realize.

*"I must admit I expected more speech by this time. My son knows 'hi,' 'bye,' 'Daddy,' 'Mommy,' 'car,' 'hot'—and that's about it."*

*"I am just realizing that my son knows a lot more than I think he does."*

## *Toddlers Understand More Than They Can Express*

Children do know a good deal more than they are able to express right now. They take in a good deal more than we recognize. They have a large store of receptive speech and many concepts that they cannot express.

*"Yes, I had a good example of that when we were eating out last week. I have never given my daughter a spoon, mostly because I do not have the time. But we were in a restaurant, and she picked up a spoon and put it straight into my mouth."*

She really knows what a spoon is for; and if you are eating, then she is going to help you eat. The concepts are getting there. They aren't always as fully developed as we expect them to be; but if the children are given the time and opportunity to experiment, the concepts will come.

*"I think I'm doing the same thing with my daughter. I will say to myself, particularly when I'm reading a book, 'She won't know that is an elephant.' So I'll say something simpler. Maybe I'm not really being fair to her."*

She may not be able to repeat the word, but you should say "elephant." Finally, one day when you point to an elephant, she will name it—and you will be surprised and pleased.

*"My inclination is to say 'No, say cat' if it is a cat, because I feel the child won't learn if she is not corrected."*

Correction like that sets a tone of disapproval when what is needed is approval and good speech modeling. You say the correct name when you point out the animal. The child will do the best she can, and one day you

■                                                                            ■

will realize that she is saying the word correctly. Then you should recognize her achievement with approval. There should be no attitude of disapproval if the sounds do not seem quite correct to you.

## Appropriate Speech Stimulation

*"So you are saying that I shouldn't correct her?"*

At this stage children need encouragement, not disapproval. Their vocabulary is very limited, and "dog" means all animals. If he says "dog" now for all animals, you don't say "no." Later, they will be able to differentiate.

*"What should you say in that case?"*

Just say "Um" in a sound of acknowledgment and go on to the next picture. You don't correct him; but the next time, you say, "There is a dog, and there is a cat, and there is an elephant." He looks at the book and may still say, "Bow-wow, bow-wow" or "Doggie." For him, bow-wow represents all animals. Later on, as you point out things, he will learn to say the correct name. In another picture you point out that this is a moon, or this is a star. He may say "moon" for everything. Don't say "no," because that makes him feel that he is doing something wrong. Then the next time you show the picture, you say "moon" and "stars" again. You may have to do that for several months, until one day he is saying "moon" and "stars" for the appropriate items. When he does this, it has really registered and he has been able to put together the physical ability to verbalize the visual image. The brain center has matured, and he has reached the stage of being able both to differentiate and to express it. In the beginning, it is enough if he says "bow-wow" for every animal. It is also enough if he says "dada" for every man.

*"I guess we are all too impatient. You keep telling us that each child matures at his or her own rate and we have to allow for it."*

That's the message. The difference in rates of development is especially evident in speech. The baby will develop speech as soon as his central nervous system matures sufficiently in that area. His speech will follow the parents' model but will also contain a lot that is original to the child. Children learn to name objects from hearing them named—there is no other way to do it. They learn how to put sentences together from listening to others talking. They also have the innate capacity to put words together in a way that goes beyond imitation and is original, as we will see in their speech toward the end of this second year.

## Language Development in a Bilingual Family

*"We speak two languages at home, Spanish and English. My husband and I generally speak English to each other, since we were born here and went to school here; but my mother, who speaks only Spanish, came to live with*

us last year to help with the baby. We noticed that our baby seems to be slower in saying words than some of the babies here. That worries us a little. Do you think that it is because he is confused by two languages?"

Some children in bilingual families do begin to speak later. They understand words in each language, but are slower in expressive speech.

*"Is it bad? Should we speak only one language to the baby?"*

There are speech specialists who believe that it is best to concentrate on one language at a time. That is especially important if the child is having difficulty with speech. However, there are many children who are able to learn two languages at the same time and can distinguish between them from a very early age.

Parents have to observe their child. If they observe that the child's speech development is quite late, even though they speak slowly and clearly to the child in each language, they may want to consult a speech specialist. In that way, they will be properly advised whether the problem is due to the use of more than one language. If it is, they can then concentrate on speaking only one language to the child.

*"My native tongue is Swedish. I always speak to my son in Swedish, and he is learning very well. My husband speaks only English; so our child says words in English, too. I do not see how it can be bad to learn two languages at once—in Europe, it is common to do that."*

It is not bad to learn two languages at once. In fact, it is very nice if the child can do that. It is also important for parents to communicate with the child in a language the parents are comfortable with. However, there are some children who cannot do this. For them, it is better to concentrate on one language until they have acquired it and can use that language for communication.

*"Which language should the parents choose? I want my child to know French because that is the language we use in our home. But when we go to the park to play, she does not seem to understand the children very well. Will that be a handicap for her?"*

At this age, there is not a great deal of verbal communication among children. It is mostly gesture and crying. If you speak your native tongue at home, she will learn that first. As she gets older and associates more with children, especially at nursery school, she will learn English and will achieve a knowledge of two languages. She will have the advantage of the background of your language and culture and will learn ours, too.

*"How can you tell if the baby understands what you say? She says so little that it worries me, especially since we speak two languages at home. I am worried that it confuses the baby."*

One way to tell is to ask the child to look for something that you mention every day and that you think the child should know. For example, "Where is the shoe?" or "Where is the light?" The child will turn toward that object or walk toward it. Then you know the child understands, even if he cannot repeat the word yet in whichever language is used.

*"Well, my child can do that whether I say it in English or Spanish. I guess it will just take time, and I can stop worrying."*

That is right. We always have to remember that each child has his or her own maturational timetable. Some children are so endowed that they develop speech later. These very children may be walking early; others may both walk and talk later. Each child is different. So, while we have to bear in mind the effect that being exposed to two languages may have on the child's speech, we must not forget that each child's natural endowment and timetable for development is unique.

However, no matter what the child's endowment, and no matter which language we use, we should talk to our babies. We should name things for them slowly and with a rhythm and intonation that they can pick up and imitate as soon as they are ready.

## Organic Causes of Speech Impairment

*"Aren't there some physical things that are sometimes the reason why a baby doesn't talk?"*

An important function for speech is good hearing. Deafness retards speech development. Normal hearing can be interfered with by ear infections. So ears should be checked during bad colds, and hearing should be checked after each infection. Then, if hearing seems impaired, proper measures can be taken.

*"Is there anything else?"*

The issue to be most concerned about is understimulation. The child who is not spoken to early or clearly has no speech models and little opportunity to practice language. All children make sounds, but those sounds do not become a specific language unless the child has a speech model. Earlier we spoke about what may be overstimulation, the introduction of two languages; but we must not overlook the fact that some children are not sufficiently stimulated to speak even one language. For each child the parents are the first models and teachers. Stimulating speech does more than teach the child the cognitive skill of language concepts; it also develops the social and emotional skills of communication.

## Appropriate Play Activities and Toys

Some parents enjoy playing with their children; others set up the toys and hope the children will play alone so that they might have some time for themselves. Some parents find playing games with children of this age boring and some enjoy it.

How much are you playing with your babies now? What kind of games do you play?"

*"I put a bunch of his toys in his playpen or crib and let him do what he wants. Or when he is on the floor, I put them down near him and let him crawl or walk over and get them. But that doesn't keep him quiet very long—he soon tires of the toys. Is there some way of getting him to spend more time playing on his own?"*

Very often parents give children too many toys at once. Children often can't deal with that. They don't know what to select and just give up and cry. They need the parents to show them the way to play with one or two things. For example, at this age putting some small blocks or small animals into a box or other container and then taking them out is very entertaining. The child then does it on his own—often many, many times. This is also an instructive activity because it is giving the concept of "in" and "out," especially if the parent participates and verbalizes "in" and "out."

*"I just don't seem to know what to do, either. What are some of the other things to play with them now?"*

At each age, one has to utilize the level of the child's interest and development. At this age, children also enjoy handing things to you and getting them back. Sometimes they want to give the parent several items and then have them given back. This giving and receiving is the beginning of sharing and getting a sense that giving is not a loss, because the toy will be returned.

## Games for Toddlers

*"My daughter started that. We do that all the time and I thought it was silly. I couldn't understand why she got such a kick out of it. Now I feel differently about it."*

Rolling a ball back and forth serves the same purpose. It is a game that can be shared with the parent and gives pleasure to both parent and child. When the ball rolls out of reach, the child can go after it. If this, as well as catching the ball on the roll, is recognized as an achievement, the child's sense of mastery and the parent's sense of pride in the child's accomplishment are enhanced. In addition, the "rolling ball" game is a precursor of later "catch" games and gives the child experience of what rolls and what does not. This game also leads to the game of hiding and finding things when the ball rolls out of sight. It also helps children to learn the concepts of "in front of," "behind," "on top of," and "under."

The child's limited level of understanding about looking for objects may surprise the parents. At first, parents will see that they need to hide the object while the child can see where it is being hidden, even leaving part of it exposed. Then say, "Let's find it," and the child will excitedly and confidently find it. If you hide the object without the child's knowing about it, the child may have no interest, for the hidden object seems to be "gone." After some experience, the children get to the point where you can hide the object and they can look for it without seeing where you put it. But when you first begin hiding things, you have to let them see where you hide them. Children also need the experience of hiding things from you. At first, they will put the object right in front of you, and you have to pretend that you have looked and found it. This game increases in complexity when you put the object "in front of" or "under" something and say, "The ball is under the cushion. Let's look there." Or, "The ball is in front of the table." This variation helps teach the concepts of different spatial positions.

Even if you play with the children for just a few minutes, you as parents can make their games more stimulating. Then their play becomes interesting to you because you see that they have learned something new. By participating in this way, you make their play more challenging and more interesting for both of you; such play is no longer a boring routine.

It is the same with books. Children love to read the same book and point to that same moon or house over and over again. But they need to find out about other pictures they haven't noticed before. You can point out something new to them each time you look at the book. Then the next time you read the book, the child has something new to name. The child will gradually develop a repertoire of things of special interest, and you will be interested to see if she can find these in the book. Then she will find her favorite items in other books. In this way, children enlarge their experience and vocabularies, making the reading of the same book over and over more interesting to you as well.

Children will still enjoy tactile games such as "This Little Piggy" and "Pat-a-Cake," which they can now do more competently than before.

## *Songs and Nursery Rhymes*

At this age children may also like to listen to nursery tunes, and may even sway to a tune. Some parents have been singing the baby to sleep for some time, so singing may be a more familiar form of play in some families. Some children are now beginning to recognize favorite songs and rhythms and like to sing some of the words and clap hands or dance.

*"My baby is learning to do that. If I sing and stop before the end, sometimes he will put in the word. It is such a thrill."*

That's very good; that is one of the ways to learn to talk. Sometimes, when they are in the kitchen and they're bothering you, you can starting singing a song and they will become interested in putting in the words you leave out. In this way, you get them occupied and diverted from doing the things that you don't want them to do. Some children are ready to play in this way now; others will do it at a later date. Most also enjoy listening to children's songs on records. They all want to touch the phonograph, but they are not yet ready to handle it safely. The phonograph, therefore, should not be put in a place that is accessible to them.

They are getting to the stage of beginning to play "Ring-Around-a-Rosy—All Fall Down." While they can't say all the words, they may enjoy the movement to the song. Some children can respond to this now; others are not quite ready. Parents should not be disappointed if their child is not ready now; they can try again in a week or two. The change in responsiveness may be quite remarkable, and parents will find that their children are suddenly understanding and remembering much more than they expected.

*"I know all these things and I always thought I would be playing a great deal with my baby. But somehow one gets caught up in household chores and neglects to play."*

That's a rut one sometimes gets into. That's why we like to remind you that household work can wait. The child's developmental stages will not wait, nor can they be hurried. So parents need to be tuning in to their own child's readiness for play activities, and not letting important learning opportunities pass by.

## Toys and Play

Have you noticed that your children seem to be less interested in their old toys and are less easily distracted by them? What are you doing about that?

*"I was out shopping to pick up a few things for the baby. There aren't too many things available for this age."*

*"There are many things that one can make, however."*

*"Yes, but I just don't have the time."*

It's often hard to find time to make toys for your children, but some things that you have around the house make wonderful toys. For instance, your measuring cups, the ones that fit into each other, make interesting things for children's play. At first they will only separate them. Gradually, they will learn to fit them back together.

All kinds of household objects can be used for the "in and out" game described earlier. Spoons, clothespins, little empty boxes, small cookie cutters, and jar covers—as well as small blocks, toy animals, and cars that most children may already have—can be put into (and then taken out of) pots, plastic containers, and jars.

They also like to play with a comb and brush. They try to comb their own hair and that of their dolls. They like to play with toys that simulate the things parents are using.

*"My baby only wants to use the phone. So we got her a plastic one that is a pretty good imitation and that keeps her busy for a few minutes when I want to use the phone."*

That is a good toy. Another one that simulates something of yours is a pocketbook. An old purse with a few keys, a small change purse, a little box that can be opened and shut are all things that one can find in the house. They keep children entertained and stimulate their manual dexterity, parental imitation, and concept formation.

## Books

*"My baby likes books, but I find it difficult to get the right ones. Most are too complicated for him right now."*

Although there are many good books for children, most are too complicated for this age. *(Suggested reading for children twelve to thirty-six months can be found on pages 687–89.)* When you or your child notice something in a magazine, such as an apple, a baby, keys, a cup, or a shoe, cut it out and paste it on a piece of cardboard. Shirt cardboards can be saved for this purpose. Sometimes you can make up a story, using these pictures of familiar objects. The stories that children like best are the ones you make up about their own experiences. For example, you say, "This morning *(child's name)* went for a walk with his daddy. They went to the store and they bought an apple." Point to the apple. "Then they went to another store and bought shoes. When they came home, Daddy put a key in the lock, and here is the key they used. They opened the door, and there was Mommy at home waiting for them." Children love this sort of story. At this age, it is best to have a single picture on each page of the book. You turn to that picture as the story is told. Soon, the children will be turning pages, mumbling their own version of the stories, and naming the objects.

## Other Toys

*"How about blocks? Are they good toys for this age?"*

Blocks are always good toys because they help in organizing spatial relations and assist in manual dexterity. Small blocks about one inch square are good for small motor coordination and for putting inside other objects. If the child is at a stage of throwing things, it is a good idea to make blocks by cutting up a sponge. These can be covered with cloth or left as is. Such blocks can be cut into various sizes and shapes and the child will enjoy arranging them in various ways.

Toys that can be pulled are also very good for this age. Some, of course, can be purchased; you will see all kinds of pull toys in the stores. But most children are very happy pulling a shoe box with a string attached. It is very exciting for them to have it filled with small items such as a doll, a small car, or a few small boxes. They like to make stops, taking things out and putting other things in as they move around the house.

Other toys that interest children of this age are the large snap-lock or pop-it beads (they will be able to pull them apart but not snap them together); bath toys such as bath boats and fish; and stacking rings (again, don't expect stacking in correct order yet). Some children of this age may also be ready to play with a small doll's house, with a few people to go in it. As they get older, more people and furniture can be added. Some parents may be able to construct this kind of house themselves.

Toys that provide stimulation to the larger motor skills, and ones that parents can begin to introduce with supervision, are small riding toys. Parents should make sure that the child's first riding toys are well balanced. Some are too high and narrow and tip over, causing the child to fall. For maximum safety, the toy should be low and not too narrow. Among the best designs are several types of toy cars, because they are broad and low to the ground—the design of some riding horses is too narrow and unstable. These toys should not have pedals but should be the kind that the child propels by his or her feet on the ground or floor.

We have been talking about a number of new toys that will interest and stimulate your children, but it is important to remember that children like to keep their old toys around as well. Sometimes a parent will throw out some scruffy old toy that the child seems to have discarded, only to find that it is very much desired again. When children seem to be bored with their toys, it is a good idea to remove them. A month or so later, going through such a box of old toys can provide a wonderful rainy-day activity of rediscovering "old friends." As children mature, they often find new ways to play with old toys.

When we speak of toys, we must remember that the greatest "toy" and stimulant for the child is the interaction with another human being, particularly his parents (or their substitute). Playing with parents, and then gradually learning to play with other children, is the most important kind of play. Interesting toys and objects that the child learns to manipulate and understand are valuable for the child's learning experience; but children need the physical and verbal interaction with people in order to develop emotionally, socially, and intellectually.

## Independence: Autonomy Versus Limitation

The children are getting more competent now that they are between fifteen and eighteen months old. They are walking quite well on their own and exploring more and more of their surroundings. To some parents this means that the children are "getting into everything," and this is not too welcome a development. Some children insist on feeding themselves and refuse to be fed; others are refusing to get into their strollers and instead want to push them; some want to walk only in a certain area or toward a certain part of the park. They are beginning to show a desire for independence—for autonomy. This is a normal stage of their development. At times, their wishes are in harmony with the parents', and all is well. However, when the desires and expectations are contrary, there may be a confrontation—with a resulting angry parent and tearful, screaming child. Have you had any incidents like this yet?

*"One of the problems I am having with my son is that he wants to climb up every step he sees. When we are going outside, I hold his hand; but in the house he wants to climb upstairs alone. I can't be with him all the time to watch that he doesn't fall. I'm always in a frenzy at home when I can't see him."*

That is a problem. The steps are very tempting. However, one cannot expect that an admonition will work when the parent is not present. One has to anticipate that the child will want to climb the steps. To avoid accidents and constant conflict, gates have to be installed at both the bottom and top of the stairs.

*"We have gates in our house. But when I go to someone else's house where there is no gate, then what?"*

In that case, you have to keep your child close to you and occupied with a toy. If it is possible, close the door to the stair hall or put up some makeshift barrier to the steps, such as a chair on its side.

## Saying "No" Too Often

*"I think I've reached that stage with my baby, too. I find I'm beginning to say 'No, no' most of the day."*

When you are always saying "No, no," the children may begin to think that the parent is a person who always says "No." They may just tune you out. The good relationship that you've had seems to disappear. They need to know that a parent says "No" but she also says "Yes"—that she does recognize the good things. These have to be recognized with a more emphatic voice, with much more enthusiasm than the "no" things. You must also remember that many of the "bad" things are quite interesting to the child, and learning to stop doing them takes time. If you are aware of this, you may have more patience; you will also learn to avoid certain situations that lead to confrontation.

*"I'm having a tough time with my son. When he can't have his own way, he gets mad. Sometimes he will grab a glass and try to throw it on the floor!"*

In such an instance, the child certainly has to be stopped. You can't let him do that; you have to say "No" firmly and give him something he can do. He will fuss, and he may scream and kick and try to get what he wants. If you get mad at that point and raise your voice, this only intensifies the situation and it becomes a battle between the two of you. The only thing to do at this point is to say "No," and give him something that he can do.

Let him cry and fuss; let him bang something safe. This is a stage that children have to go through: learning what they can do and what they can't do. If you continue to be firm about a *few* important issues, the child gradually learns. If, on the other hand, confrontation becomes a pattern between you and the child, the relationship with you is always going to be one of conflict. Conflict will become a part of the child's way of relating; he or she will act in this combative way with friends, with siblings, with teachers. This sets the stage for the development of the angry character structure.

*"Is this what happens if the parent always makes too much of a fuss?"*

It may, if a parent emphasizes only what is not approved and does not recognize just as emphatically the good things the child does.

*"Should you say 'No' just firmly, or loudly?"*

It has to be loud enough so that the child can hear it. Very often parents say "No" and smile. That confuses the child. You must say "No" very firmly and look firm. Then offer a substitute, saying, "You can have this (or do this)," and you make "this" very appealing—and smile. Or pick him up and take him into another room where there is a new interest for him, "something special." Change his entire focus. Finding an appealing substitute takes a lot of effort and patience; and no one says it is easy. This is one of the hardest things to do, but it's one of the things that pays off in the long run.

*"Suppose you go visiting in someone else's house. They allow the child to take things off the table, and you don't. What do you do then?"*

When you are visiting and you see objects that are dangerous for your child to have and that you don't allow to be touched in your house, you have to make the same restrictions. You have to be consistent, even if the host doesn't mind whether the baby does some things he is not allowed to do at home. You explain your standards and see that the baby carries them out in another home. Then you have to help your child in a strange house. The easiest way is to remove the objects that are fragile or dangerous.

*"What if a mother and father do not have the same standards? That's what happens in our house."*

## Need for Consistent "No's"

You can't say "No" and have father saying "Oh, let him do it." Or father saying "No" and mother saying "Oh, he's only little and you're too strict with him." You have to establish uniform standards that you both are going to accept; both father and mother have to establish these together. You may find that one day while father is with the baby and mother is in the kitchen, father says, "No, you can't do that." You can't rush from the kitchen and say, "I always let him do that." You can talk to father afterward; but in front of the child there should not be any kind of disagreement.

If limits are not the same, the child may become manipulative later, playing one against the other. Setting consistent limits is very important for the child's personality development.

*"We seem to be able to do that. It seems to me it only takes a word on my husband's part and the baby responds, but I have to scream."*

It may be easier for father to be consistent and firm and get a response, because father's manner is often firmer than mother's. However, if mother uses the same tone and is firm and doesn't scream, the child learns she means business, too, and responds just as well. Sometimes, because he sees less of the child and wants to be loved, the father tries to ensure the child's affection by being less firm than mother.

*"We are having a different kind of irritating time with our baby. She is just learning to pile up her blocks. She gets up to three, but when she tries the next one they topple over and she gets very upset and screams. I try to soothe her by putting the blocks up again, but she will have none of it."*

They are at the stage now when they want to do things by themselves but they are not competent enough. They aren't helpless babies, but at the same time they can't do all the things they want to do on their own. It is a very difficult time for them and for the parents. If a parent knows, for example, that the baby cannot pile more than three blocks, give her that number and let her feel success. Then, in a week or two, give her a fourth. Having had success, she may then be able to handle the frustration of its falling off. With the passage of time and practice, she will reach the point where she can manage four, or will let you show her how to manage. A difficulty at this stage is that children are often not competent enough, but they won't accept help, either. Another situation that arises frequently at this age, and later, is that children are given toys that are too complicated for them to play with. A parent needs to be aware of this and be ready to put away those toys and reintroduce them when the child is ready.

*"Does that mean that children should never be given anything that is difficult to do—that they must never be frustrated?"*

No, that is not what is being advocated. Children should not be given things that frustrate them beyond their tolerance. Parents have to observe their children, understand their level of frustration tolerance, and help them overcome it by tuning in to the child's level of development. This will vary with each child. Some children can tolerate their blocks falling down and will try over and over again to set them up. Their frustration tolerance level is high; that is their endowment. Other children become upset quickly; their frustration tolerance has to be patiently increased by slowly introducing more difficult tasks. This is what good teaching is all about; and parents are the most important teachers the child will ever have.

*"Is what we have been talking about the beginning of what some people call the 'terrible twos'? Are we approaching that time?"*

It seems that you are. What we are trying to explain is that the twos need not be "terrible." Parents need to understand how to permit and encourage the independence that is necessary for development; they need to find appropriate areas in which the child can express his or her independence and sense of autonomy and achievement. At the same time, they need to set consistent limits when the child's desires can harm him, others, or valuable property. This principle remains the same throughout life, though the items may change with growth. This is a time when the child's desire to do things is not equal to his ability to do them for and by himself. The parents need to understand the child's level of development, his or her level of competence. If they also tune in to or anticipate some of the child's desired activities, parents can tactfully help the child handle the situation—or prevent him from getting into a situation that will be too frustrating or dangerous.

## *More on Autonomy: Eating and Dressing*

One of the areas in which parents can sometimes come into conflict with their children as they assert their growing autonomy is eating. Are any of you beginning to see signs of this?

*"I am having that problem, I think, especially when he spills his milk. I leave a cup of milk on his high-chair tray so he can have some whenever he wants it. When my back is turned, he just picks it up and pours it on the floor. Of course, I scream at him, but he does it all the time. He seems to enjoy the battle."*

### *Avoiding Conflicts About Eating*

It seems you are setting up a situation for an angry confrontation. For him it is a new experience; it gives him a sense of achievement to pour something. If you want to teach him to drink his milk from a cup, give him a small amount. Sit with him until he finishes it and recognize the achievement by some comment such as "Good, you drank it all up." Give him more if he seems to want it and repeat the recognition when he finishes. Let him learn that milk in a cup is for drinking. Then, when he is in his bath, let him have a few small containers that he can fill with water and pour out. He may pour some on the bathroom floor, but that can be absorbed by the bath mat. In the bathroom you teach him to limit his pouring to the tub. The point is that he needs to be given an appropriate outlet to get a sense of achievement in pouring. He needs to have a chance for exploration, without angry confrontation all the time.

*"My problem with independence also concerns the way the baby eats. It drives me wild. She won't let me feed her anymore. Most of the time, if I*

make her cereal thick enough, she gets it into her mouth by using the spoon, which is usually upside down! Sometimes cereal drops on her table. Sometimes she mushes it up all over the table; after she has done that, she'll eat it with her hands. Other times, she just loses a lot and won't eat it from the table. Can I just let her go on like that?"

All babies are messy eaters. In most cases, if they are hungry and they like the food offered, they will eat enough. We expect them to like the food warm and eat it neatly from the spoon. But warm food and neatness are not important to them now. It really doesn't matter from a nutritional point of view if they eat with the spoon or with their hands, or if the food is cold or has been smeared over the tabletop first.

*"Is there any way to teach them to eat from the spoon?"*

The mother can fill the spoon and help the child guide it to her mouth. She should then make some favorable comment such as "Good" when the child is successful. That may reinforce interest in eating with a spoon.

If one is too fussy about neatness, it sometimes diminishes the child's interest in eating. Teaching manners will come later. Now the child needs to develop the skill of eating by herself and to have the satisfaction of that competence.

*"But what if she just takes a few mouthfuls and then begins to smear the food over the table and doesn't eat it?"*

A parent can usually tell when the child is hungry and interested in food. If she begins to smear it about, just remove it. The less fuss made the better. When she eats, make a favorable comment.

*"Shouldn't a child be made to eat his food? It is such a waste to make good food, which is now also expensive, and have him waste it all. My mother says she always made her children eat what was set before them. If they didn't finish it, she just gave them the rest at the next meal. Sometimes I am tempted to do that."*

That is not really an appropriate way of handling a poor eater. There are several things to consider. In the first place, one has to remember that at this age, in the second year, appetites usually diminish. A baby who was an avid eater before may become much less interested in eating. That is a natural physiological process that occurs in most children. So, of course, they should not be forced to eat. If they are forced to eat when their appetites are poor, they may become resistant to eating. Then when their appetites normally improve, they will not resume eating as they ordinarily would have if they had not been forced to eat.

*"That is the mistake I made with my first child. We had a battle royal every mealtime. In the end, I lost. She is still a finicky eater. I am not going to make the same mistake with this baby. His appetite has slowed down, and I am just letting him eat what he wants the way he wants to."*

That is a good way to respond to his changing appetite. Parents also have to remember that a child who normally has a good appetite may have a meal or two (or even a day or two) when he is not hungry, just as there are certain meals when adults are not as hungry as at others.

*"I know that and I try to remember it; but it always seems to happen just the day I think I've made something that he should eat and enjoy, such as scrambled eggs or chopped steak. Then I find I urge a little too much. He refuses, and before I know it, we've started a small war."*

We have to remember that children's appetites can be very variable, especially in the second year. We also need to recognize that our children may not now care for the foods we like or think are best for them. Later, they may develop a taste for the very thing they turn down now.

## Children Do Not Need Varied Menus

*"But what does one do about a child who eats no variety at all? He'll only eat one cereal—Rice Krispies, which he picks up with his fingers—hamburgers, carrots, and apple sauce. Very rarely will he eat chicken or anything else, except his milk."*

Children do not need the large variety of foods we offer. Your child's tastes will change in time. Some children have an innate feeling for the foods that agree with them and may be upset by the other foods a parent thinks they must have. This is often true of children with allergies. They seem to have a sense of what agrees with them. The child's preferences should be respected. Food should not be forced on a child.

## Eating Patterns

*"One of the things that upsets us is that the baby won't sit and finish a meal. He'll have one part of it, then get up and play a little. Then he is ready for his fruit and he'll sit for that. Then he wants more play. It seems to us he is eating at short intervals all day instead of having full meals. That bothers us, and we try to make him sit still and finish the whole meal. But it's a battle, and then he usually won't eat as well."*

Part of the problem is that your child—and this is true of many children— can't eat what we consider a full meal because he does not have the capacity to consume that much food at one time. The parent should not take it personally and feel that her culinary efforts are being spurned. The child simply cannot eat so much and cannot sit still for a whole meal, either.

We are accustomed to the idea that one has to have three square meals a day. That's really for adults. This eating schedule was convenient for work. It is better for your digestive system, however, to have a small amount of food more frequently than to have three big meals. More recently, industry has discovered that productivity of the work force increases if there are additional breaks for nourishment. That is how coffee breaks came about. Our children also need several "coffee breaks" a day as well as regular small meals. Gradually, as they get older and become more socialized, the children will want to participate in the family meal-times. You need not feel upset now if children do not eat a meal from start to finish with the family. If there is recognition and approval when they do sit down at the table, rather than a scolding when they don't, they may learn to eat with you sooner.

So for now, it is better to put very little on the child's plate in order that the child will be able to finish it and ask for more. When he finishes, even if it is very little, he should receive positive recognition so he will have a sense of accomplishment and a good feeling about mealtimes. The parent, too, will not feel so frustrated.

*"I have no problem with my baby's eating. It's just that when he finishes his food and I'm not close by, he throws his empty plate on the floor."*

These actions can be anticipated. When the child seems to have had enough, ask him to hand the cup or the plate to you and say "All gone." He can be rewarded by your approval when he hands you the cup or plate. Such anticipation can turn a frustrating and messy situation into a happy learning situation.

Of course, we must also remember that children have to do some experimenting. They are really scientists in their way of trying to find out about the world they live in. They have to learn that tipping a cup over spills the contents; they have to have a chance to find that out. Some parents prefer this experimentation in the bathtub. However, if a small amount of liquid is placed in the cup in the first place, not too much will be left to spill. When the baby finishes her milk and does not spill it, the mother can smile and say, "Good, you finished your milk." If she says it with some enthusiasm, the baby will feel that she did something well and is approved of.

## *Avoiding Conflicts About Getting Dressed*

Another area in which the child's need for autonomy often manifests itself at an early age is dressing. For many months children may have been "helping" in their own dressing by bending an arm when they see the sweater sleeve approaching or by lifting a leg to step into pants. Some will continue to do that for some time to come; others will suddenly refuse. Often this behavior develops because the child does not want to stop the play activity in which he or she is engaged. Getting dressed is a signal that another event is going to take place, perhaps even as welcome as going out to the park or as unwelcome as mother's leaving for work. In any case, the child does not want to be dressed, and a battle for control of the situation can easily develop between parent and child. It is often helpful if children are given some warning that "in a few minutes" it will be time to get dressed. Or you can indicate that when the child gets dressed, there will be play. Because the process is slow, the parent can become very impatient. Parents need to use a lot of tact in such situations, saying, "Let me give you a little help with that shirt, and then you can put on your pants." Approval of whatever part of the dressing process the child can accomplish will give the child a sense of achievement and pride. Again, it is important to allow enough time so that the child does not become rushed. Perhaps you are interrupting play or an activity the child wants to continue, just as an adult absorbed in an activity may wish not to be disturbed.

*"You are talking about my biggest problem. My daughter refuses to let me put a sweater on her. It's too cold outside to let her go without one. I get furious and she screams."*

In cases where the child is striving for autonomy but is not really ready, it helps sometimes to give the child a less frustrating way of exercising her independence. Perhaps the next time you can show her two sweaters and ask her which one she would like to put on. She then has the choice of the red one or the blue one, but she does not have the choice of whether she will wear a sweater.

Confrontations over dressing do not have consequences as serious as confrontations over eating; but if they become part of a daily pattern between parent and child, they are not healthy. Understanding what is going on in the child's mind may help you to be more patient and think of better ways of handling difficult situations.

## Sleep Patterns and Bedtime Routines

How are you managing in getting your babies to sleep now? Have you been able to establish a good bedtime routine and pattern, or is it still unstable?

*"Now we do very well getting the baby to sleep, but we have trouble with him waking once or twice a night. Sometimes it's just for one night, or maybe for a few nights in a row—and then he is back to sleeping through the night. It always worries us, because we think: here we go again, back to the old days of being up half the night. Will this continue?"*

### Sleep Patterns

You know, we all sleep in cycles. We have periods of deeper sleep alternating with lighter sleep. If during one of the periods of light sleep, the baby should be aware of some sensation in her stomach caused by gas, or if she bites down on a sore gum when she is teething, or if she hears a loud noise in the street, she may wake up. Some babies cry out momentarily and then go off to sleep by themselves. Occasionally, they may need comforting for a few minutes before they go back to sleep. This does occur from time to time and should not be a cause for alarm. As adults, we are often awakened by something, turn over, and go back to sleep. Few people sleep all night without waking at all.

*"Our baby sleeps well, except when she is teething. Then she may be up for a while several times during the night until we find a way of soothing her gums by rubbing them with our fingers or bits of ice, or by giving her something to bite on. Sometimes she needs a bottle. It's miserable on the nights when it happens; but as soon as the tooth comes in, she is fine again."*

*"We have a different situation. Whenever we expect company at night, our baby seems to sense it; and then it takes forever to get him to go to sleep. How do they know? I try to do everything the same way, and he just knows."*

Perhaps you think you are doing everything the same way. But you may be communicating some tension, hurrying things a bit, just enough to alert the baby to a feeling that something is different.

*"What is so awful if your baby isn't asleep when the company comes and stays up a little while and sees them? Then you can put the baby to bed."*

There is nothing wrong if you are comfortable with that and can put the baby to bed more easily later. It depends on what is the most comfortable way for you and for your baby. Some babies get overstimulated by visitors before bedtime and then have difficulty going to sleep. If that is your experience, perhaps it is best to invite the company for a later time when you know the baby will be asleep.

*"If I am having company, my system is to start preparing several days ahead after the baby is in bed. On the day, I try to keep the same order of things, just doing everything a little earlier, so I'll be sure he is in bed and asleep. It usually works out all right."*

That is a fine arrangement if your child can respond to that system. Some children's biological clocks can't be manipulated that easily. Many of us see that when we have time changes and the clocks are put ahead or back one hour. The children do not change their rhythm all at once; and so, in order to make the changes in time coincide with daily routines, parents have to alter the schedule by ten to fifteen minutes every few days until they have overcome the hour change.

*"You know, I never realized that until we went back to standard time. My baby used to get up at seven in the morning and when the time changed he was getting up at six. That upset me, but he was really getting up at the time he was accustomed to."*

That's true; but by shifting ten to fifteen minutes a day, most babies gradually get into the new time sequence. Have any of you observed that?

■                                                                                                    ■

*"That's what I tried, but it took about two weeks to really get him settled into the new time."*

*"Our baby is a good sleeper except when he is sick. If he gets a cold he may fall asleep, but he wakes many times during the night. When he is well, it takes a few days to get him back to sleeping all through the night. I may have to go in to soothe him once or twice a night for a few nights. My mother says I should not do that, that I may get him into the habit of waking."*

## Disruptions to Sleep Patterns

If your baby wakes a few times after an illness, it may mean that he isn't quite over it, or that maybe he is experiencing some of the unpleasant sensations of his illness in his dreams. In any case, he should be comforted. He will not make a "habit" of it if he has no need to wake. If he was a good sleeper before the illness, he will return to his usual routine. It is important, however, not to let the moments of comforting in the night become playtime. Responding to the child's cry should be brief and low-key, with as little extra light and stimulation as possible.

*"Our baby also is usually a good sleeper. But to go to bed, he has to have everything done in the same way each night: the same song on the music box, the same teddy bear in the corner of his crib. Last weekend we visited friends for the weekend. We took the Portacrib, blanket, and teddy but forgot the music box. We had a terrible time. He finally went to sleep when I patted him and sang the same song for him. That made us wonder if we had done the right thing by getting him so used to the same routine. Wouldn't it have been better if he had gotten to bed with a different pattern every night? You see some children who can go to sleep anytime."*

There are some children who are very relaxed and easygoing, who sleep whenever they are sleepy, anywhere they happen to be. However, that is not the case with most children. Most feel insecure in strange surroundings and need the support of a familiar routine and familiar things in order to fall asleep. It sounds as though you responded appropriately to your child's needs for security. When he becomes more accustomed to traveling, he will be more able to fall asleep in strange places. It is a matter of maturity and endowment. Parents have to respond according to each child's individual needs.

## Importance of Relaxed Bedtime Routines

*"We used to have a good bedtime routine with our baby. My husband would play with her and look at a favorite book with her, and then we would put her to bed with her ba-ba (blanket). Now my husband's schedule is changed and he gets home later. He is hungry and wants to eat; she's tired but won't go to sleep. Suddenly we find she's up until ten o'clock and very cranky."*

■                                                                              ■

Changes like that in a parent's schedule can be upsetting to the whole family. Some thinking needs to be done on the best way to reintroduce a playtime with daddy and a bedtime that is comfortable all around. Perhaps, since it's important for the baby to see her father, she could nap a little longer in the afternoon. Then she would not become overtired so early. Perhaps father could have a small snack when he first gets home and then play with the baby. Then you and your husband can have a later, more relaxed dinner. Another solution is for you to serve dinner right away, letting the baby sit with you or play near you. In this case, you will have to expect that she will demand attention and be very unsatisfied if you talk to each other and ignore her. After dinner, your husband can play with her for a while. The important thing is for the child to feel that the evening playtime and bedtime routine are pleasant and unhurried. Children are very sensitive to particular tensions and the parents' desire to rush. It is our experience that an hour of undivided, loving attention works better in the long run than the begrudged twenty minutes that don't satisfy the child's need and that can therefore stretch into *hours* of crankiness and crying.

*"That sounds great for the baby. But what about me? I've been home all day and I'd like to talk to an adult. My husband and I rarely get to talk alone."*

It is hard when the needs of family members seem to be in conflict. The child needs to be with her father, and you and your husband need time together. You have to satisfy everyone as best you can and recognize that this stage won't last forever. Soon your child will be able to play a little more by herself and you and your husband will be able to talk more. It is important for parents to plan times alone, without the baby, on a regular basis to satisfy their own needs.

*"My problem is similar. My husband and I both get home from work late. We want to play with the baby, but we are both tired. She is a bundle of energy."*

Again, each family must make its own plans on how to handle these situations. The child doesn't have to play with both of you at once. One parent can play while the other relaxes or prepares dinner. One parent can go through the bedtime routines while the other washes up. The important thing—to get back to good sleep patterns—is to establish a bedtime routine that is as unvaried every night as possible. This helps the child feel secure and relaxed: a state of being that is important for relaxed sleep. It is also a good idea not to let play activities in the evening become too stimulating, because the child then takes longer to wind down.

*"Are there babies who are naturally poor sleepers and never overcome this?"*

We know that there are adults who for some reason require little sleep and manage very well this way. In the same way, there is a great variation in how much sleep children need. Some need to sleep a great deal; others need much less. There are some children who wake at night to play in their cribs, and then go back to sleep. That is their pattern. Others wake and cry and need to be comforted and helped to relax and fall asleep again. The majority finally develop a pattern of sleeping through the night. Sometimes this may not become fully settled until they are two or three; but it does finally come.

# Crankiness and Its Causes

Do you think you are getting to understand your child's personality? Do you seem to be able to get along with each other comfortably, or are there times of frustration?

*"I think I understand my baby most of the time, but there are times when she is very cranky and I don't seem to know what to do. What is the explanation for it? And what should I do?"*

## Fatigue

There are many things that can make a child cranky; and most children are cranky at one time or another. One of the most frequent reasons a child is cranky is that he or she is overtired. Some children tire very quickly from stimulating play, a shopping trip, or visiting. Others seem to have a greater tolerance for these activities.

*"My baby fits into the first category. If we stay at home and keep to a routine, she is fine. A short shopping trip or just stopping in a small shop for a minute or two is okay, but shopping for a week's supply in the supermarket—forget it! She ends up having a tantrum and screaming. So now my husband or I do it alone. That way we aren't upset and angry with the baby, and actually we get it done faster, too."*

That shows you have tuned in to the baby's capabilities and are dealing with them comfortably.

## Illness and Teething

Sometimes, children are cranky at the onset of an illness, often before there are any overt signs such as fever, cough, vomiting, diarrhea, rash, or runny nose. Crankiness is a warning signal in a child who is usually quite contented.

Another common cause of crankiness at this age is teething. The gums are sore and make the child very irritable. Most of you recognize this. You see the drooling and the chewing of the fingers and toys, often accompanied by a decrease in appetite and waking at night.

■                                                                                                              ■

*"Of course, we know about those things. Even so, they seem to come unexpectedly and always jolt me. The other day, the baby was so fussy when we were in the park that I came home a little annoyed. As I was undressing her I noticed she was quite warm, so I took her temperature. It was 102 degrees. I felt so guilty for being cross with her."*

To be annoyed when you don't realize that there is a problem is a very usual response. Perhaps one of the reasons you are annoyed with the children at this stage is that you expected easier sailing after the difficulties of infancy. This crankiness frightens you a little unconsciously and you are feeling, "No, not that again." But it's only for a short time, until you've found the cause and can cope with it.

*"Teething is the one that is bothering me. Does every tooth that comes in cause so much pain and crying?"*

It varies with each child. Some have thick gums and do have a hard time with each tooth; other children have pain only with certain teeth. Some have no problem at all: the parent simply discovers that a tooth is there by the click of the spoon on a new tooth.

There are some remedies that work for some children, such as rubbing the gum, applying something cold like a chip of ice, or using a refrigerated teething ring. There are also medications to rub on the gums, which your physician may prescribe if he or she thinks it is advisable.

## Inconsistent Routines

There are other causes of crankiness. Sometimes, now that the children are older, we may not be as consistent in our dealing with them. Baths, play, and feeding routines may not be followed in their usual order, and this may bother them. You've begun to do things one way one day and another the next, and the children don't know quite what to expect. This, too, can be upsetting and make them cranky. They are not yet verbal, so they can't say, "Isn't it time to go for a ride in the stroller?" or, "I'm ready for my nap now," or, "I'm hungry. Isn't it lunchtime?" We have to recognize that they are not as flexible as we think they should be at this age.

## Growth Spurts

There is another situation that seems to make children irritable, which we've mentioned before. Children often display irritability just preceding a growth spurt or change in level of development. When they are reaching to a new level of achievement, they have a feeling of disequilibrium that expresses itself in irritability. No amount of comforting seems to resolve it until a day or two has passed and they suddenly seem to have arrived at the new level of achievement. These changing levels may range from crawling to walking or from babbling to saying some words. Then all is serene again. It may help parents tolerate the irritability to look for signs of new development.

Whining and crankiness are especially irritating to parents, because this behavior often occurs when the parents are overtired or preoccupied with other things themselves. Many parents are fatigued by long trips to the supermarket or by visiting; so just when the most patience is needed, the parent is least able to give it. As we've noted many times before, children are very sensitive to their parents' moods and tensions.

The worst time for parents comes when they plan some excursion or activity especially for the child and the child becomes irritable and cranky. What you have planned as a nice treat becomes a nightmare all around. Your feelings of disappointment and frustration are understandable. It is important, however, not to blame the child—he or she is *not* purposely trying to irritate you. The child may be tired or sick or in a state of developmental disequilibrium—and unable to enjoy the treat you planned. Or perhaps the activity—a puppet show or a library story-telling—is too advanced for the child's level of development. At this age the child cannot say in words, "I don't understand this." All he or she can do is become restless and irritable. Better understanding of the child's level of development and what activities are appropriate helps parents to avoid situations like these.

## *More on Socialization: How to Handle Biting and Screaming*

### *Biting*

Many parents are bothered because their children are biting them or other children. Nursing mothers are somethings bitten, and this has often been a signal to begin weaning. Some babies never bite the breast, even when they have teeth. Sometimes biting is a way of showing anger. Often it is a sign of frustration in the nonverbal child who cannot express what he wants. Sometimes biting is the child's way of showing affection.

From a purely physical point of view, biting may signify the discomfort caused by emerging teeth. The baby bites for relief of discomfort and may bite anything! If the biting is due to teething, the proper response is to soothe the gum by giving a teething ring or teething biscuit, or by rubbing the gums with a chip of ice—or even with an analgesic medication prescribed by your doctor.

The parent's first response should be to try to discover the cause of the biting. This is not always easy, since the child cannot express himself or herself verbally. The answer may be reached only by trial and error. In the past, one could soothe the baby by diverting him, even if one didn't discover the cause. A toy or food or some attention was all that was needed to stop the biting. But now that the children are older and are beginning to be verbal, the parent should show displeasure, firmly saying,

■      ■

"We don't bite Mommy (or Susie or Johnny); we bite on this." Then, give the child something appropriate to bite on. You may also say, "Biting hurts Mommy."

Showing your displeasure by hitting the child is only more anger-producing and may intensify and perpetuate the behavior, so that it becomes the usual way of showing anger. When parents hit a child, the child's response is often to hit back or to hit a younger sibling or pet. This can be avoided by dealing with the situation calmly and appropriately from the start.

Biting is not always an expression of anger. It can also be an attempt to express affection. This may be the baby's attempt to kiss the parent or other child, and it is mishandled due to the child's lack of experience. In that case, the baby has to be shown how to pat or kiss. Showing affection by biting does, however, have a certain place in our culture as evidenced by the expression "I love you so much I could just eat you up."

*"When my baby bites me, I get very upset because it hurts. Someone told me to bite him back so he would see how it feels and that would stop him."*

That is a very common suggestion. Biting may frighten him and make him stop. It may also make him more angry and give him the sanction to repeat the biting: if a parent does it he can do it, too. The same applies to hitting. It has been noted that children who are hit or spanked tend to hit others. To teach by frightening the child is not a solution we advocate. To teach by good example is more productive and doesn't undermine the child-parent relationship.

*"When my baby hit another child who was visiting us, I think he did it as a way of making contact. But I was so embarrassed I slapped his mouth. I wanted to show the other mother that I really didn't approve of it. He cried and didn't seem to know what to make of it."*

When toddlers are playing together, parents have to anticipate their activities and separate them before they bite, if possible. If the parent is too late, she should show her disapproval by saying firmly, "We don't bite," and show the child how to stroke the other child and say, "Nice." In that way, you can teach your child what to do while showing the other parent that you do not approve of the behavior. Then get the children started on some other activity.

*"How long does this biting last?"*

It disappears more rapidly when appropriate alternative activities are substituted and when verbal communication is stimulated. It is quite common in the preverbal stage, but it passes when the child can express himself or herself in other ways. Teaching by parents and maturation both help in this process. The important thing to remember is that this is a phase; it will pass. The parent needs to be a teacher, and not a lion tamer with a whip!

## Screaming

We have been noticing that in the children's play here some of them are beginning to run back and forth screaming. Are they doing this at home? How does it affect you.

*"Have I noticed it! My little girl runs around screaming like a wild Indian, especially when we open the door of the apartment and let her run down the hall. She scares all the neighbors with her screaming."*

*"I don't allow it. When my child screams, I just put my hand over her mouth and say 'Stop it' or 'Shshsh,' and she stops for the time being, anyway."*

They all go through a stage of screaming when they are learning how to use their voices and how to modulate them. They are making discoveries. This is perfectly normal and should not be limited all the time. There are times, of course, when one must limit screaming. If someone in the house is asleep or ill, the child should not scream. The best way to stop it is to get the child interested in another, quieter activity.

*"I'm very upset when my little girl screams. She used to scream so loud when she was an infant and was hungry and wet. Now that she is beginning to understand more, I thought we were over the screaming."*

You thought it was just a continuation of the same pattern. Certainly, children may still scream if they are frightened, hurt, or frustrated. But the screaming we are talking about now is more like the vocalizing they used when they first discovered their own voices. Now they are screaming with a sense of achievement, and also as a way of letting off excess energy. It is a form of play and exploration. When it gets to be too much for you, start another activity. Look at a book, play some music, or take a walk in the park. You can begin to say, "Not in the apartment (house). Let's go out." Children need to let off steam.

*"I have a different worry. I am haunted by a friend's three-year-old. When he does not get his way, he stands there and just screams. And of course, the more his mother says, 'Stop that,' the more he screams. He is obnoxious. I don't want my child to become like that."*

It is very risky to make a judgment about a child's behavior when one does not know the whole situation. From past experience, I would hazard a guess that the boy you describe may not have had his needs met in the appropriate manner. It seems to me that you should not worry that your child will behave in the same way as your friend's child, because your approach has been different.

*"Well, I guess there are different screaming situations and no two are alike. We have to distinguish between them, just as we had to learn to understand the different cries when they were infants."*

Children do have different screams, as you say. We have to remember that children aren't the only ones who scream. Sometimes mothers scream. If a child is about to pull something down over himself that is hot, or runs away toward the street, a parent screams out in fright. That occasionally happens and can't be helped; it's a spontaneous response. However, when parents use screaming consciously as a means of setting limits, then it is not appropriate or useful. In fact, it may be counterproductive. It may serve as a model for the child on how to relate to others, who will then find the child "obnoxious." Finally, the child may begin to ignore parental screaming and just tune out the parent. Children do not like to be screamed at any more than adults like to hear children screaming.

*"I can remember to this day how my mother always screamed, and I hated it. But I find that I do it sometimes, too. I guess it's ingrained. I hate myself when I catch myself doing it, because I had resolved not to do it to my children if I ever had any."*

Perhaps you are unconsciously modeling yourself after your mother. When you are aware of it, you can control it. That happens to all of us. Some parental models were very good, and we want to emulate those; some others, it is better not to follow. It is good that you are beginning to understand which models are beneficial to good growth and good parent-child relations and which are not.

# Recognizing the Challenge and Responsibility of Parenting: Baby's Needs Versus Parents' Needs

## Parents' Feelings About Responsibility of Child Rearing

How are you feeling now in your role as parents? Do you have more time for yourselves? Do you still feel that you are a "hostage" to the child?

*"At first, I had that feeling a good deal of the time. I felt, here I am so young sitting at home all day with the baby. I don't know yet exactly who I am, and I'm responsible for a baby. What should I do? I can't complain; he is a good baby. Sometimes it is fun. But it's not like playing with a doll. There is so much responsibility."*

You sound a little overwhelmed by the responsibility and perhaps feel that you should not have to be responsible. You miss your freedom to come and go, those carefree days when you could read a book or go to the movies on a last-minute whim. That is natural and understandable. Everyone goes through those things. Accepting responsibility is part of growing up—and sometimes we would rather not grow up. But there is satisfaction in discharging a responsibility well. That's what maturing is all about: learning to manage life's experiences to the best of one's ability. Raising your child is part of growing up and a part of maturing that has to take place. Some parents naturally take on the responsibility of child rearing and become more mature and parental. They had good parenting models themselves and they carry them on. There are other parents who did not have this kind of model and feel frustrated all the time and angry at their children.

*"What if a mother feels this way and is cross and angry a lot? Don't the children get used to it?"*

The result of a continuing battle between parent and child may often be seen in the personality the child develops—one that is angry and irritable, too. This is not a personality structure that makes for success or happiness for the child or the parent. That is why it is important to recognize how one feels and acts and the consequences of persistent anger or frustration.

Learning to assume responsibility and to enjoy discharging it successfully is important in any endeavor—whether one is a dress designer, a mechanic, an office worker, or a doctor. Each situation requires the assumption of responsibility, and we mature as we work at it. It is true of parenting, too.

*"But when a mother devotes herself to child rearing, she must give up so much if she has had a career."*

*"I used to think that, too, but I see now what it means to be a mother. I am learning so much about personality development and how a child grows to be a person that I really feel that when I go back to work I'll be more valuable. It's worth it to me to take time off from my career to see my child develop well."*

*"As you know, I decided not to give up my job. I really could not afford to, financially or professionally. My child seems to be adjusted to being cared for by us and by my mother, who helps us. I agree that I may have to advance more slowly, because I do not accept overtime assignments. I want to have time with the baby, but it is tiring. I am often cross."*

*"I refuse to settle for advancing slower. I take on all assignments. In my firm, it is 'up or out.' Fortunately, my husband is settled in a more nine-to-five job. He is more the 'mommy' in our family—and truthfully, we both resent that sometimes."*

These issues are of prime concern these days, and parents, especially mothers, are under tremendous pressure, whether they are staying home with their children or working outside the home. Right now, we are discussing how you feel about your responsibilities. Certainly, holding down a job in addition to caring for a child (or children) increases the responsibilities and, often, the feelings of being overburdened. Whether you are at home or at an office, there are times when you "want out." We understand that, and we want to help you slow up and take stock. You don't have to be superwoman or superman.

*"The problem with mothering is the long hours: it's never over. I have so little time for myself."*

■                                                                        ■

If you think back to what it was like when the children were infants, you will realize that you have come a long way. You have developed successful patterns for yourselves and for your children's days. Learning how to do it is all part of the maturing experience. Now that the children are older, you are expecting more time and you are frustrated that at this toddler stage the children are putting demands on you in a new way. But you are becoming more experienced, and soon your lives will begin to assume more of the characteristics they had before the children came.

*"When we first talked about this, I could not believe I would adjust. I just 'wanted out,' as they say. As my baby learned to sleep, I began to enjoy the situation more and more, and now it's a real satisfaction for me. Of course, I'll go back to my firm when my children are older. My profession will still be there. I may need to brush up and make new contacts, but this is for the future. Now it's my children's time."*

*"My mother always went to business. I resented her being away so much and I hated the people who took care of me. I vowed I'd stay home if I had a child. Well, I am staying home, but I find I'm angry about it. It surprises and worries me. I realize now I did not have a good model for being a mother. I will have to try to work at it, because I really do want to be a good mother."*

Parents want to be good parents. They come to parenting with different past experiences, so for some it is harder than for others.

Part of the reason you feel burdened by child care *now* is that you expected the children to play on their own without as much parental involvement.

## Child's Need for Parents' Company and Attention

*"I find my child wants me with him as much as ever. He pulls me to his toys, says 'Sit,' and then he can concentrate and play for quite a while. But I must be there in the room."*

This is still part of the separation struggle. It is important to be available to them when you are there—not to just sit in the house, but to be there and to be involved with them. That is what you are complaining about. Right now, in order to keep you there they try to keep you involved. It is a way of reassuring themselves that you are really there. If you are involved with them, you can't possibly go away. That's one of the reasons why they want you to play with them all the time. When they feel secure, they will gradually do a little more on their own. Of course, playing with you is also more fun and stimulating.

*"That's all well and good, if you have time to do that. What if you have to make the bed, or fix a meal? Then what do you do?"*

In that case, you take the toys the child is playing with and say, "Let's play in the bedroom or kitchen," and arrange a place for the child to play beside you while you work. He is with you and you can talk to each other. The child will feel included in your activities. You can get involved momentarily in the play and then continue your work. Both can be satisfied; no conflict need arise.

*"That works for me most of the time, and I feel I have a good relationship with my child. Once in a while she is resistant and we have a little crying."*

Sometimes that happens when the child is very absorbed and doesn't want to be disturbed. Then one has to give a little time and say, "As soon as you finish this, we'll play some more in the kitchen (or whatever room you need to be in)." Children can't always switch their interest to another area quickly and need a little time to adjust. Remember, they do not yet have a smoothly working nervous system. It's still immature and does not respond instantaneously, as adults would like it to do.

*"Whenever I try to visit with other people she wants me to be with her. Even if we are home and she has been playing with her toys all on her own, the minute someone walks in she is right there and wants me to play and pulls me. Should I allow it? It makes me angry, and I know my friends think there is something wrong with the way I am trying to bring her up."*

She doesn't want you to be monopolized by someone else. To her, that means that she is excluded and that you are, in fact, "taken away" from her. If you recognize this, you can pick her up, put her in your lap, and include her in the conversation. Let her get acquainted with the visitor. When she feels secure and included, she will interest herself in her toys. She may make frequent trips back to you to assure herself of your attention to be sure you are still there.

## Child's Need to Feel Included

*"It is not so bad when we are at home. It's just when we go visiting that it is a problem."*

Children need to feel included when they go visiting; they often feel excluded. They can't tolerate exclusion. If you put them on your lap while you talk, and talk and play with them too, you help them feel included. In this way, they are also helped to socialize.

*"My biggest problem is when I'm doing something in the house and he just wants to be with me."*

Getting housework done is a problem. It has to be patterned into the daily routine just the way you patterned the bath, the feeding, playing, and other activities. You say, "I've got to do the dishes. Now, it's Mommy's dishes time," and you do the dishes. Say it firmly, not as though you were asking, "Will you let Mommy do it?" but as a fact: "This is what we are going to do." Then make a habit of saying it that way, so that he knows this is "dishes time," "cleaning time," or "cooking time." Children learn that when you are cleaning or cooking, you are still around. They will come in and out of the room. This gets to be a habit; it gets to be something that's expected, a part of their life experience. If you are cooking, talk about it and show what you are doing. Give the baby a spoon to play with or a taste of something you are stirring once in a while.

*"Suppose the child doesn't respond by getting interested in what you are doing?"*

Then you have to find some other activity the child can engage in near you while you work. It certainly may not work the first time. It has to be repeated until it becomes an accepted part of the baby's life, too. You have to say, "Mommy has to do this; this is Mommy's job." When you are finished say, "Mommy is finished. We can play now."

*"I have two old pails with pieces of cloth in them. When I am doing dishes, I give her some plastic shapes—it doesn't matter what it is—and she does dishes too."*

That's fine. If you set it up like that you can get your work done. However, there are some mothers who prefer not to involve the baby in their work and wait until the baby is having a nap. That is when they do their work. Are some of you managing that way?

*"I prefer to do my cooking when she naps in the morning or afternoon. I really enjoy cooking, and it is relaxing not to be interrupted all the time."*

*"Well, I don't do any housework during my child's naptime. That's my time for myself, to relax and read or wash my hair. That refreshes me and I feel better."*

Mothers do need that little bit of relaxation and time for themselves. There is no one, not a doctor or a secretary or a businessman, who does not need a few minutes for a rest break at some time during the day. A mother should program some relaxation into her job, too. Some mothers may even find they need to nap for a little while themselves.

As in every other profession, parents must try to have some balance between work on the job and relaxation. As they learn more about child development and the child's changing needs, parents learn to make adjustments so that the child's needs—and theirs—can be satisfied. Bringing up children *is* a big responsibility, but it can also be a lot of fun.

## Integrating Child into Family's Social Life; Parents' Need for Time as a Couple

Most children are ready for more socialization. Are you able to participate in more social activities now with your children than you were before?

## Taking Children Visiting

*"I take my baby almost everywhere with me now. What bothers me is that some older women make remarks about it. I take my baby in her carriage when I shop in a department store. I've had some older women be very rude about the fact that her carriage takes up a lot of elevator space, which is true, but I just don't say anything."*

Older generations were used to keeping babies at home. That was the time when there were extended families or hired help with whom to leave the babies at home. In this day and age, a mother would be totally isolated if she could not take her baby with her. You are quite right not to become involved in arguing with people who are simply not in tune with the times.

*"I feel very uptight about taking the baby to somebody else's house where there are no children. We've been married about six years, and most of our friends either have children in their teens or none at all. Our baby is over his shyness of new places and he is into everything. He wants to look at and touch absolutely everything. Also, sometimes he screams with delight. It can be nerve-racking if you are not used to it."*

Some adults do believe that children should be seen and not heard and that a quiet baby is a good baby. They do not know that screaming is one form of expression before children learn to talk. As for the exploratory behavior that you describe, that is perfectly natural at this age and it does make visiting difficult if your friends are not used to this stage of children's development.

*"We have the best time now, visiting relatives or friends with somewhat older children. They love playing with the baby and he loves it, too. I feel comfortable because he can walk by himself and I don't have to worry about their dropping him anymore. It's really great; I recommend it to everyone."*

That does sound like a very good arrangement for all concerned, including your friends' children, who enjoy the responsibility of looking after the baby.

*"We are trying to begin to entertain a little, but we have a problem getting the baby to go to sleep. She just seems to want to stay up with the company. Is it wrong to let her stay up past her regular bedtime?"*

You have to experiment and see how disturbing it is to her sleep pattern and whether it's better to get her off to sleep before the company comes. Children really have social aspirations; they want to be part of the family's activities. Formerly, in large families, the baby was wherever the rest of the family was; the attitude that "it's six o'clock and the baby has to be in bed" is a modern concept. Different cultures have different patterns. Each family has to establish the pattern that suits its style of life. What is important is to keep that pattern consistent. However, occasional deviations can usually be tolerated, provided the parents recognize that they need to make patient effort to get the baby's schedule back to its usual form in the next day or two. Maybe the next night the baby will take a little longer to go to sleep. Or she may be a little cranky the next day because of lack of sleep. None of this is serious. If the parents understand what is happening, they can be patient with the baby when necessary but continue the social life they enjoy. It usually works best when parents integrate the baby gradually into the kind of social life they want to have.

*"We take our baby everywhere we go—shopping, visiting relatives, or to the museum. It works well, but we have to accommodate, as you say, to her tolerance level. Sometimes I wish we could just go by ourselves. I'm tired of short visits and seeing half an exhibition."*

*"I agree with you. We tried to go to an adult restaurant and it was a disaster. Now we eat at McDonald's and other places that are good for kids."*

That is a compromise that is appropriate now. When you go out for dinner without the baby, you can go to a restaurant of *your* choice.

## *Parents Need Time as a Couple*

You are also raising another important issue. Now that it is becoming a little easier to include the children in your social activities, at least at a certain level, you find that they are always with you. Not only do you need to see the whole exhibition or finish a whole conversation, you also need time by yourselves as a couple. You need time to find out how you are thinking about yourselves as the individuals you were before you had the child—and as the couple you were. Sometimes a father feels neglected and thinks the mother cares more about the child than about him. Some mothers feel quite isolated from the adult world; they haven't had time to hear much about the father's work outside the home or to keep up with their usual interest. If both parents work, they have spent most of their nonworking hours caring for the baby. They haven't had much time to talk to each other; except for the baby, their lives seem quite separate. This is not very good for the marriage.

*"My husband was just saying that. We both work, and he said, 'You know, I think I come last in your life, after the baby and your job.' It gave me quite a shock. I'm still thinking about it; he may be right."*

*"My husband is complaining that we never go out without the baby. Personally, I like it that way. I don't want to leave her with a sitter. I have no relatives nearby."*

*"In our family, I'm the one who is complaining. My husband loves to play with the baby. He hardly talks to me anymore. I feel like the third wheel."*

It is important for all of you to make an effort every once in a while to go out together by yourselves—and do something that you enjoyed doing together before the baby arrived. While we have always stressed being considerate of the child's needs for security, we do not think that you should never leave your child. It is healthy for you to pursue your own interests, and it is important for the child to learn to separate from you and to feel comfortable with at least one other caretaker. If a child has no sense of your leaving and returning, an emergency situation in which you have to leave would be all the harder for the child to tolerate.

*"My mother left me with baby-sitters I hated. I was terrified of them. I decided never to leave my child."*

Often, the way we were raised carries over into our own child-rearing patterns, either as similarities or as opposites. Sometimes we go to extremes to spare our children the discomforts we felt. This is understandable. However, we need to be aware of our own maturation and assess whether our response is appropriate. While it is a good idea to be with the baby as much as possible, the baby does need to be able to trust and relate to other people, at least one other adult besides the parents.

## Separation Anxiety: A Resurgence of Clinging

Have you noticed that the children are going through a period in which they find it more difficult to separate from you and stay closer to you physically—actually clinging to you sometimes?

*"My child is doing that just when I thought she was getting to be more self-sufficient."*

*"My son was so independent when he started to walk. Now his constant clinging makes me want to get away from him."*

### Resurgence of Dependence

Parents are disappointed when their children seem to become more, rather than less, dependent. When they first learned to walk, the children were so exhilarated and pleased with their new mobility that they didn't notice when they strayed far. They didn't even notice the bumps and bruises when they fell. Often, you were anxious and ran after them. Now they are bigger and older, and you think they should be more independent. But when they move away from you now, they discover that the world is pretty big and they have much more comprehension of how far away from you they are. They come running back and cling to you for support. It is a stage when they need reassurance that you are *there* for them; that you are not trying to run *away from them*. When you try to get away from them, they cling even more. If you try to hurry independence, you defeat what you really want to accomplish: the child's development into a self-sufficient, independent individual.

*"Does that mean that during this stage mothers should never go away and leave them? That I must give up my afternoon off? That throws me into a panic, because I look forward all week to that time away."*

No one is saying that mothers should not have some time off. Mothers need time for themselves in order to be able to cope with their job of child rearing. Child rearing is a very hard job, and parents have to have relief. Nobody works twenty-four hours a day, every day of the week.

*"My son used to like our baby-sitter and was glad to see her; but now the minute I put on my things to leave, he begins to cling to me and cry a little. Should I stay with him longer, or not go? The minute I'm out of sight, he stops and begins to play as if nothing has happened."*

He has to protest; he has to show that he is attached to you. It wouldn't be good or healthy if he didn't notice that you were leaving. He has a sense of attachment to you and he makes that attachment known. A child of this age should notice your leaving. If he did not protest, it might mean that he was not sufficiently attached. Of course, it would be more understandable if he could say, "Please don't go. I'll miss you." You have to understand that is what he is saying when he cries when you leave. It is important to say "good-bye" and that you will be back soon. Talk about the things he will be doing and tell him when you will be home—for example, after his nap or before his bath. He can understand that. Then when you return, make the greeting happy and let the child rejoice that you are back.

*"Should I promise to bring him something if he is a good boy and lets me go?"*

That is a bribe. A child will get into the habit of expecting something material in exchange for your going. The present that a parent brings back each time is herself or himself. A toy can be given to the child occasionally when you find something appropriate and want him to have it—but not as a bribe.

*"Since I have begun to go out more often now that I have a good caretaker, the baby does not go to sleep as easily. He needs me to be with him until he falls asleep. He seems afraid to let me go. Should I sit with him?"*

It often works out better, if children are very anxious, for you to sit with them until they are asleep. When they know that you are going to be there, that you are not going away, the time that you have to sit with them gets less and less. This new clinging is a transitory stage, and they will get over it. They are working out their separation from you; it is not an easy task for them, and they need help. They need to establish the habit of preparing for bed and sleep with a special story, record, or song the parent sings.

During this period, children need more parental support. If you go to the door or phone, they are right after you. As they cling more, you in turn get angry and feel more confined. You feel you can't do anything that *you* want to do. But you must remember that it is only a transitory phase. If you can reassure them during changes that cause anxiety—when a new caretaker comes to your house or one of the parents is ill—they will gradually stop clinging. Most parents don't expect this resurgence of clinging; that is why you are asking about it. This is something that has been well understood only recently. In the past, parents often dealt with it by slapping the children, putting them to bed, and letting them cry. And it seemed to work. The children did become quiet, but some needed psychotherapy later to overcome their insecurities.

If you go through the inconvenience now—and it is inconvenient and does make your life miserable for a while—your patience and attention will be rewarded by a child with greater self-confidence.

*"I have no problem putting my son to bed for his nap, but at night I have to give him his bottle and hold him till he's sound asleep; otherwise he just clings to me and doesn't want to let me leave. I was wondering why only at night. Is it because his father comes home for dinner and then leaves for another job? Is he afraid that at night I will leave him, too?"*

That sounds like a very good interpretation of his behavior. He is clinging because he doesn't understand that his daddy has to go to work but that you will be there. When he is older and understands more, the clinging will end.

### Separation Problems at Bedtime

Difficulty in separating at bedtime is a very common situation. All children need special attention at bedtime: stories, a special song, and sometimes a drink of water. Children do not like going to bed because it separates them from the family. Some children play very hard and get very tired; they fall asleep the minute their heads touch the pillow. There are others who do not. That doesn't mean they are "bad" children; each has a different pattern. Some may not separate easily at bedtime until they are three; others may do it at one and a half or two. Everybody envies the parent whose child goes off to sleep easily. With understanding and patience, all children do it eventually. One hastens the process not by force, but by allowing the child to deal with it on his or her own maturational timetable.

*"My problem was different. I went back to work for five days and left my son with his grandmother, who often stays with us. I worked from 8:30 A.M. to noon; I never had trouble when I left. But Saturday morning he would not let go of me; Sunday, the same thing. Then, on Monday when he saw his father getting dressed, he would not take his eyes off of me. When he saw that I wasn't getting dressed, he was satisfied that I wasn't going out, too. The minute he was satisfied, he went to his room to play. But for three days he followed me everywhere like a little puppy. I thought he was beyond that stage; his behavior made me kind of angry. Now I'll know what to expect."*

When you know what to expect and understand what the behavior means, then it is easier to deal with.

■         ■

The children are now getting to the age when they can relate to more people than Mommy and Daddy. They can relate to others now because they have learned to trust their parents. That is why it's very important in the beginning to establish a good relationship with the parents. When children feel secure with their parents, they are able to feel secure with other people. But they still do not like to separate from you, and they show you they don't like it. You have to continue to reassure them.

*"When I go away, she cries a lot because I once left her with a person she didn't know. She cried from the moment I went out until I got back. I will never do that again. She never behaved that way when I left her with someone she knew. Now it is hard to leave her."*

It sounds as though you have to reestablish her sense of trust. She must relearn that you will come back and that you will not leave her unless she is comfortable with the person who is taking care of her. Just one unfortunate episode can undo so much effort in helping them separate. Parents often find this hard to understand.

## Sneaking Out Causes Problems

Do some of you find it so upsetting to your baby when you leave that you sneak out?

*"Well, I used to do that. But as we learned here, it just upsets the baby more. When I came home he cried and stayed glued to me. I realized that he thought I might disappear again. It's hard to make them understand that you won't go away again—that day, anyway."*

That is indeed the problem. Once you have sneaked out, then the child no longer trusts you. He or she does not know that you won't disappear from the bathroom or from the kitchen, even if you are in the middle of cooking. It is exceedingly important to say—and mean it, "Mommy is home." When you really practice this, the child will gradually regain trust and feel secure that you will stay, that you are still home—even if you are in the next room. Gradually, he will not be so anxious when you leave the room or go to the door to answer the bell. Then, when you do have to go out again, you tell the child before you go and reassure him that you will return. When this pattern is established between parent and child, there is a mutual sense of trust. The child will feel secure that he knows what is going to happen to him.

Children do not like surprises; they like to be able to prepare for what is going to happen to them. They feel very vulnerable and they constantly need reassurance that someone, preferably the parent, will be with them, that they will not be abandoned. Just because you tell them that you are going out and will be back does not mean that they will not fuss when you leave. They may, indeed, fuss or cry; the important thing to remember, however, is that these tears do not mean broken trust. They simply mean that the child is sad to be left behind; they mean the child would rather be with you than with the substitute caretaker. This behavior shows appropriate attachment.

*"I have noticed that sometimes when I come home the baby turns away from me. Does that mean he did not miss me or recognize me?"*

## How Children Show They Have Missed Their Parents

Sometimes when they have really missed you a lot, they won't come to you when you return. That is one of their ways of saying, "Look, you left me and I'm angry." You will not be as disappointed when this happens if you understand what it means. They have felt abandoned. It is hard for them to suddenly change their mood when you return.

*"It's hard to take. I come home ready to hug and kiss the baby, and he turns away. I have noticed that in a few minutes he comes over and won't stir from my side. Now it's clear to me what it all means."*

*"I have a dilemma just now. I had a separation problem when I had to spend time in the hospital with my father. My daughter had to stay at my parents' house with a sitter and was upset for months. Afterward we finally reestablished her sense of trust in us, and I would hate to undermine it now. However, my husband is getting a two-week vacation; he hasn't had one in two years, and we would like to go away together. I've made plans for my parents to come and stay for a week before we leave so she can get used to them. It's making me very uncomfortable and I don't know what to do. It seems to me she knows my neighbor better than she knows my parents and would be happier with her, but I can't ask for such a favor."*

It sounds as though your parents were quite willing to try to get to know their granddaughter better. In the week while you are at home, you can leave her with them for short periods of time and see how they get along. Remember, she is older now. She will be in her own home, not in a strange place. She will have her own bed and toys and the playmate next door. Her grandparents can carry out her daily routine in the same way you do. Everything will probably go very well, and she will learn to trust her grandparents, too.

*"But what if she doesn't take to them?"*

You will be able to determine this before you leave. Then you can decide what is best to do. No matter how well they get along, you have to be prepared for signs that she missed you. She may cling for several days or she may be a little bit cranky when you return. As long as you understand, you can try to meet her needs without feeling guilty or angry.

*"Don't you think making this effort and possibly changing your vacation plans is catering to the baby too much?"*

It is not a matter of "catering." It is a matter of understanding the baby's needs. In this case, there has already been an initial unintentional trauma. It shows a great deal of understanding and sensitivity on the parents' part to understand this and to want to avoid a repetition. Most parents will not really enjoy their vacation too much if they feel that the child is suffering. Everyone needs time off; parents of young children certainly need time off as much as—or more

■                                                                          ■

than—most. This is a case, however, in which a little extra thought and planning by the parents can avoid problems later. Understanding and consideration for the child's needs sometimes takes more time initially but can make life easier and more pleasant in the long run.

## Comforting: What Is Appropriate Now?

How are you comforting your children now when they cry and need soothing?

### Oral Comforting

*"I find a bottle or a cookie works surely and quickly. I guess that is why I offer those first."*

*"When my baby stumbles and falls, I go and pick him up and hold him; but that is not enough now. I have to talk to him and say, 'It's okay. Mama's here.' Sometimes he will run and get his bottle himself if it is nearby."*

That certainly indicates that he still finds the bottle the best form of comfort. That is what we are concerned about: that there may be too much dependence on bottles or food for comfort. Gradually the parent has to begin to substitute other forms of comfort so that later in life drinking or eating are not the main sources of comfort. There may be some connection between too much dependence on oral comforting in early childhood and overeating, alcoholism, and smoking as ways of overcoming trouble later in life. These oral satisfactions may become the way of allaying anxiety or distress in adult life.

*"What about a pacifier instead of a bottle?"*

A pacifier may give immediate comfort; one sees many older children still sucking on pacifiers. As we discussed when the children were babies (*see pages 36–37*), pacifiers should be used only to provide additional sucking for a baby who takes bottle feedings too quickly and has insufficient sucking. The problem with both the pacifier and feeding as automatic comforting devices is that they tend literally to plug up the child's feelings. When the child is sucking on a bottle or pacifier or chewing on a cookie, he cannot express himself verbally. Children often cry now because they cannot express themselves in any other way. But if we hold them and calm them down, we can try to ask them what the problem is. At this age, they may be able only to point or say one word, but the parent may be able to understand what the problem is. If another child has taken a toy and we have not seen it happen, the child may point to it if we take the time to ask. Getting the toy back is, in this case, more appropriate comforting than being handed a cookie. In another case, the child may cry because he cannot do something he wants to do. Help in mastering the activity is more beneficial to the child than any oral comforting. In a few months, the children will be more verbal and it will be even more important to try to communicate with them about what is upsetting them. Always

■                                                                                                    ■

handing a child a pacifier or cookie—"peace at any price"—turns off the child's natural inclination to communicate his feelings and concerns.

Just as we learned to listen to different cries and tried to understand them, we must now learn to *listen* to words. Such a pattern will lead to good parent-child relations and open communication, without which both parent and child may feel misunderstood.

*"It takes a lot of ingenuity sometimes to find what is making the baby unhappy and just what will comfort him."*

Yes, to be a parent requires a lot of ingenuity and versatility. That's why we keep repeating that being a parent is an important job that requires knowledge, understanding, patience, and a dedication that puts it into a category of profession—not just a job to be done somehow or other.

## Other Forms of Comforting

*"My husband is more adept at diverting the baby than I am. I catch on when she is wet or hungry, but he seems to know just when to tickle her, or jog her on his knee, or show her pictures in a book."*

*"My best bet is to turn on some music; sometimes just my singing does it! Of course, it's nice for me, too, because we all like music."*

*"Are you saying that we should never console them with a cookie?"*

No, that is not our intention. We are saying that comforting by putting something into the mouth is no longer the appropriate form of comforting. Furthermore, used as the sole form of comforting, it may lead later in life to unpleasant consequences. At present, the child should experience a whole variety of comforting mechanisms and interchanges with the parent that can enrich the relationship between parent and child. The emphasis at this age should be on establishing an open communication pattern.

One must always make the distinction as well between oral comforting and satisfying a child's hunger. Often children will cry and become fussy when they are tired and hungry. Sometimes a child will tell the parent he is hungry, but many children still cannot tell you at this age. The parent must then guess, by knowing the child's schedule and recent food intake, whether the child needs food or another form of comforting. If the child is really hungry, then the bottle is more appropriate than a cookie from a nutritional point of view.

The main point is that parents' styles of comforting need to progress in keeping with the child's new development capabilities. Only oral comforting is no longer age-appropriate.

# Rivalry with Siblings and Other Children; Children's Need for Attention and Inability to Share

## Sibling Rivalry

Most parents are generally aware of the potential for sibling rivalry, and most parents try to plan for the older child when a new baby comes into the family.

They recognize that the older child should not feel left out. They may also not realize that their child feels left out if another child, outside the family, gets too much of their attention, even briefly. Have any of you been noticing your child's need for attention?

*"Yes, our child seems in constant rivalry with her baby brother. Although I take primary care of her and our maid does almost everything for him, I still have to give him some attention. He is my baby, too. It is very disturbing."*

It's very hard for a mother to apportion her time and attention to satisfy more than one child at a time. The closer the children are in age, the more difficult it is, especially if the parents do not understand that it is natural and normal for the older child to want as much attention as the younger one receives. Parents often feel that the older one should understand that it's the younger one's turn. They think the older one is selfish and that he should relinquish his mother's attention for the baby's good. This is an expectation that is in no way realistic. The older one may not yet be mature enough to understand sharing his parents' attention. He still requires a great deal of recognition of his needs, and his emotional needs are much greater than parents anticipate. No matter how bright the child may be, his emotional development and experience are only at the level of his chronological age.

*"I know what you say is true, but it is so hard to live through the situation. My son is even upset if I pay some attention to the dog. He comes running over to get into the act!"*

Yes, that's just it. Children need to feel "in the act," as you say. There seems to be an inborn quality in the child that makes exclusion of any kind impossible to tolerate.

We have been talking about sibling rivalry, but children can also be jealous of parents' attention to each other. When parents embrace, the child comes right over and wants to be part of it, too.

*"Does that mean parents should not embrace in front of the child?"*

Not at all. It is good for the child to be aware of the loving relationship between her parents. It is a good example for the child; but the child should be included in the demonstration of affection if she seems to desire it. She should be included in all greetings to family and friends. She is part of the family, and this needs to be recognized. Some children are more insistent about this than others. Parents should not become angry and feel this is an intrusion, considering the child's actions out of place. The child is behaving as a child. The problem is with us adults. We want children to grow up faster than they can.

## Rivalry with Other Children

Have you also noticed how your children behave if you hold another child on your lap or pay attention to another child?

*"As a matter of fact, I have found it quite embarrassing when my child raises a rumpus if I pick up another child, especially if he falls and I am nearer than his own mother."*

It is considerate to pick up the other child if you are nearer, but do not expect your child to like it. For her, you have become unavailable when you tend to another child. The hurt child needs his *own* mother's comforting. Mothers really have to console their own children. If for any reason you have to care momentarily for another child, it is best to step aside as soon as the mother arrives. Then pick up your own child, assuring her that you are there for her, and get her interested in some activity with you.

*"I have noticed that even at home. My baby can be playing and concentrating on his play, but if he sees out of the corner of his eye that I am going toward another child, or even to our pet dog, he comes running right over. In a way I find it funny, but also embarrassing, because it seems to me that he is developing into a selfish person."*

At this age, it is not selfishness but an age-appropriate and primitive need to be assured that he is not going to be separated from you by anyone else. The parent needs to give the child that assurance.

*"If we do what you suggest, aren't we catering to this behavior? Won't it encourage the children to demand attention and condone jealousy?"*

We want to help you avoid reinforcing this behavior. Parents invite this kind of behavior by ignoring the child's needs and causing him or her to be more demanding. Children whose needs are not met become very demanding. This may continue into adult life. Some adults are still trying to get their primitive needs satisifed. We are trying to help you meet your child's needs for attention and to understand how upsetting attention to another child can be at this age. When your children are older and more verbal, they will be able to tolerate your attention to others better.

*"You are right. My older son is quite tolerant of the baby now. But he got quite clinging recently while he was sick. This baby is much more dependent on me, and she was terribly jealous. Every time I went to my son, she wanted to be right with me, too. The hardest time was when his fever was really high, and he wanted me to stay with him."*

Couldn't you get someone to help you with her, to give her the attention that she needed?

*"No, she wanted only me. There was one day that was really rough. That was the next day, when he felt better but was still very demanding and cranky from being sick. It was really impossible."*

That's a good day for grandma to come and help. Sometimes you really do need help, because you have only two hands. When one of the children is sick, you can't be close to both of them together.

■          ■

*"I would try to explain to her and kind of pat her head and say I knew she wanted me to hold her, too, and things like that. But it didn't really work."*

One way to try to ease the situation is to give her attention before she has to ask for it. If you give her attention *only* when she asks for it, then she has to keep asking for it. For instance, perhaps when your son was sleeping, you could have given her some attention, even though she did not ask. It is very hard. But if you understand what is going on, then you don't get so angry at your child.

## Understanding Child's Need for Attention

*"But don't they become spoiled 'nags' if you always try to do what they want? That is what my husband and his parents seem to think."*

That attitude is a misunderstanding of a child's needs. If you understand what is going on, and you try to give the child a little bit of attention when she is not asking for it, that keeps her from thinking that she gets attention only when she demands it. A "nag" is a child who continues to ask until he or she is satisfied. If the child is responded to promptly most of the time, and even has some needs anticipated, he or she develops a sense of security and trust and does not become a "nag."

*"I have a problem when we have visitors. When my son is on somebody else's territory, he is a perfect gentleman. But if somebody is here, he even takes toys away from small babies. He pushes other children around. He is bratty on his territory."*

It is his turf, and he has a feeling that the other children will take his things away from him. He may have already experienced that. In order to be polite to a visiting child, you may have inadvertently offered her one of your child's favorite toys. So he is now expecting the worst when someone comes.

Children of this age are now just coming into the "I, my, mine" stage *(see pages 396–98 for more discussion on this)*. They are just discovering who they are and what is theirs. You must assure your child that the toys are his. Ask him which one the visitor can play with for a few minutes and explain that his toys will not be taken away.

It's a good idea also for children to take one or two of their own toys with them when they go visiting, so that there will be less conflict with the host child. In addition, their play will have to be supervised by the parents.

*"I find the most rivalry is over toys in the park. My child seems to want whatever the other child has. If he picks up another child's toy and the other child wants it, what should I do?"*

First, it is important to bring some of your child's toys to the park. When this situation occurs, give back the other child's toy. Then give your child his own toy and say, "This is yours," and begin to play with him. You may have to move away from the other child to another part of the playground.

*"But what should I do if the situation is the opposite—the other child takes my child's toy? If I take it back from him, the other child's mother thinks I'm mean."*

That is not your primary concern. You help your child retrieve his toy, if he wants it, and say, "I'm sorry." Try to find something to give to the other child and explain that he or she may have a turn with the toy later.

*"You don't think they should be left to fight it out themselves?"*

They are too young for that kind of negotiation. They are still nonverbal. They know what they want, but they can't express their feelings verbally. All they can do is cry, kick, bite, and scream. If this physical way of handling a situation is allowed to continue, it becomes the pattern for social contact. It encourages physical violence rather than verbal resolution of arguments. That is the making of a "brat" and a "bully." What we are doing is setting an example of appropriate negotiation. This procedure takes patience, but it works and avoids fights and bad feelings between both adults and children.

*"How long does it take for them to get over this need to be included all the time? I can't even talk on the phone without having her cry, crawl to my lap, and pull on the phone."*

That depends on the kind of relationship you have established with your child and his emotional development: how far along the child is in his ability to separate from you; how verbal he is; how long he can concentrate on an activity of his own; how secure he feels.

## *More on Discipline: A Positive Approach*

Now that the children are more active, do you find it more difficult to set limits? What are your concerns now?

*"My big problem is at the park: my son runs out the gate of the playground. The minute the gate is open, he runs for it and gets out. I have to be on the watch all the time and stop him before he gets out. Sometimes I'm too late. I have to chase him, and he just loves it. For him, it's a game!"*

*"I have the same problem. My daughter knows she is not supposed to go out the gate. She goes to the gate and looks back to see if I am looking at her. I look at her and say 'No,' and then usually she just runs back. Sometimes she does run out and I run after her. But she knows she is not to do it."*

She is looking at you to say "No." She still does not have the ability to limit herself. You remember what we have discussed *(see "The First Year of Life")* about learning limitations: that the baby would go up to an ashtray, and you would say "No" to her and give her something else to do. After several weeks or months, she would go up to it and say "No" to herself but still pick it up. Then finally she would say "No" and would not pick it up. It may take a little more time before she goes over to the gate, hears you say "No, don't go out,"

■                                                                            ■

and comes back herself. Learning self-control follows much the same process in each case, but running away is even more tempting than touching an ashtray. There is such a sense of mastery in being able to run. We must recognize that. Our problem is to teach the limits of where children can safely run. That's the hard part. If we are consistent in our limits and don't permit them to become a game, the lesson is finally learned.

## Children Don't Yet Understand the Consequences of Their Actions

*"In the park, I have a different problem. My baby likes to play in the sandbox. He picks up the sand in his fingers and lets it drop; sometimes it blows in his or another child's face. Other mothers accuse him of throwing sand. Usually, it isn't really on purpose, but other mothers don't understand that. So I've stopped going to that part of the park, although he enjoys it, because I don't know how to handle him there."*

You are right; he doesn't understand the consequences of throwing sand. He needs to learn how to play appropriately in the sand. *You* should be with him and show him how to shovel and build in the sand. Children of this age should be watched in a sandbox.

*"Last summer they were all eating sand, but that has passed. Now they are in the running stage. How does one take a child this age to the beach?"*

You can take her for a walk on the beach holding her hand. You can help her make sand castles and dig holes into which the water can come. You can keep her busy doing things such as playing with a beach ball or other sand toys. When she loses interest, you can go for a walk with her again or collect shells. Often, she will be interested in playing beside another child. Then you can enjoy talking with the other mother as long as the children are near you. Children of this age should never be out of your sight at the beach.

One of the things you have to stress is that the child cannot go into the water without you. You approve all the safe things that the child can do at the beach: how much fun it is when the sand dumps out and makes a pie; how nice it is to make a little trough for the water to run into. What fun it is to run *with mommy* down the beach. If the child runs away, you have to say "No" firmly and bring him back, just as you would in the park. The danger in the park is running into the street. At the beach the danger is running into the water alone. No child should be permitted near the water without a life jacket. That should be standard equipment at all times, but parents must still watch closely.

*"I do all of these things and I actually enjoy being there. Sometimes some of my friends are there with their children, and that makes it very nice, too. But the other adults seem to think I spend too much time with my child and should let him occupy himself."*

Again, we find that the adults without children are making parents who are giving their children appropriate attention feel uncomfortable. It is true that children should be allowed to occupy themselves, but that comes at a later stage. At the beach, children of this age need close attention and supervision.

We have been talking about the kinds of activities that require new limitations. We have not yet spoken about whether you feel you are saying "No" about more things, or whether you are saying "No" too much.

*"I find I am doing that. Whether we are in the house or outside, my child seems to be doing something she shouldn't: putting dirty paper in her mouth or jumping on the sofa or running out of the playground."*

## Positive Approach to Teaching Discipline

Instead of saying "No" all the time, it is good to use a positive approach whenever you can. When the child is about to put paper from the floor in her mouth, say, "Paper goes in the basket," and get her to throw it there. Then you give her a cracker and say, "The cracker is to eat; paper goes in the basket." She has an impulse to put the paper in her mouth, but it can be diverted to the appropriate action of putting it in the basket. This approach enables you to be more positive. Do you ever try that?

*"I try to. I try to be positive, but he goes right back to whatever I tell him not to. So I end up saying 'No' more times than I'd like."*

One of the reasons we have trouble is that we were brought up with "No." Unconsciously, our first impulse is to say "No" because it was said to us. We treat our children that way because that is how we were treated. It may take a while to change that pattern, so you mustn't be disappointed with yourselves if you don't always respond more positively. The important thing is that you understand the concept and try as often as you can to say something other than "No," which should be saved for the hot stove, crossing the streets, pulling down the lamp—things that are dangerous. Try saying, "The cup is for drinking; the ball is for throwing." When the children accept the appropriate action, then give them recognition for their achievement.

*"I know. I find that when he does things I approve of, he will come back and do the same thing again, even the next day. When we go out on the terrace to play with his toys, he puts any papers that are lying around into the basket. That has become part of his routine each day. He knows I approve."*

Now you see that it works. You can continue that kind of experience. It gives the children a great feeling when they are doing many things that you can approve of. It is very important for them to get the message that what they are doing is good. Then, they can approve of themselves; the approval doesn't always have to come from somebody else. Many people never experience this educational process of learning to recognize when their efforts are good. These are the people in therapy who are afraid of others finding fault with them and who are never sure that what they do is right. These feelings come from very early lack of positive recognition. We want each child to feel, "Yes, I am okay. I am doing right. I can do things and I am an achiever."

■                                                                                              ■

## Development of Self-confidence

*"Won't it make a child 'stuck up' to feel that he is approved of and to think well of himself? Doesn't that make a conceited grown-up?"*

To be aware of one's ability and to have a sense of self-confidence are characteristics of a healthy, mature adult. A person whom we refer to as "stuck up" is usually a person whose sense of security is fragile, who did not develop a realistic sense of his own ability and needs to reassure himself by bragging about his actions to others. We are aiming for the early healthy development of a sense of achievement in our children, to enhance their motivation to achieve in school. Motivation for school achievement continues in children who feel confident about achieving by their own efforts. Early recognition of children's achievement enhances these feelings.

*"I wish my parents had known this. I was always trying to please and I never got any response from my parents except disapproval. It's funny; they continue it even now. I think I could have gone to college if I had had the least encouragement."*

*"I think my husband's family must have been like that, too. He feels he made it in spite of his parents. He often thinks I'm coddling our child."*

It is a good idea to talk these ideas over with the other parent (and the caretaker). As we've said before, it is important for the child to receive similar approval and limitation from all of his or her caretakers. It is confusing to the child to receive different limitations from each parent. Perhaps you can help your spouses (and caretakers) to use this more positive approach to discipline.

We believe parents sincerely want to see their children achieve. They have the mistaken idea that pointing out all the negative aspects of behavior will help their children overcome them. They do not realize that this approach is counterproductive and discourages the children from trying because they become afraid to fail. Instead, parents need to emphasize their approval and recognition so that the children develop self-confidence and a sense of self-worth.

# The Child's Ability to Delay Gratification and Respond to Parental Requests

## Children's Inability to Wait

Are you finding that these toddlers still need to have instant satisfaction of their needs? Or have you noticed the beginning of some tolerance for delay?

*"This is a subject I discuss with my husband all the time. He thinks that at this age our son should be able to wait for anything. It bothers him most when we have to stop the car for a red light and the baby begins to fidget and cry, saying 'Ca, go.' My husband thinks there is something wrong with the baby."*

■      ■

That is a very common situation. It is a good opportunity to say to your son, "Soon the light will be green. Red is stop. Green is go." Tell him that now is *their* turn to go; soon it will be *ours*. You may have to do this for weeks until the idea of stopping, waiting, and going becomes familiar to him. It can be a game as well as a chance to understand the new associations of red for stop, green for go. It will help him cope with a situation in which delay cannot be avoided. It may also help him begin to accept delay in other situations as well.

*"We have tried to play the 'stop and go game' in traffic because our daughter hates to wait. My husband added to the game by counting the passing cars and, although she can't count, it seems to help her wait."*

*"Trying to get my son to wait affects me a little differently. He wants me to come and play with him 'right now!' I can't stop instantly whatever I'm doing; yet I want to, because I'm worried that he will feel I'm rejecting him."*

If you didn't ever stop to play with your child when he asked, he might get the feeling of rejection. At this age, most children can wait a little while without feeling rejected. When babies are very young, they cannot wait. You have all been through that. When they were hungry, they needed feeding pretty quickly. When they got a little older and began to know that the sounds you were making in the kitchen meant you were preparing the bottle, their cries were less insistent. They were able to wait a little while. Now that they are beginning to be verbal, it is possible to say, "I'm coming in a minute (soon)," or, "Just a second," and then go to them. Now they are able to tolerate a little more delay. As they get older, the delay can gradually be increased. That is one of the ways to help your children develop the ability to delay. The ability to postpone gratification of one's needs or wishes for an appropriate time is a measure of maturity. Children who are not verbal cannot be expected to respond to "Just a minute." They have to learn by patient repetition of the situation what "Just a minute," "I am coming soon," or "Wait for Mommy," means.

## Helping Children Learn to Wait

We have talked about the importance of daily routines—of sequencing the events in a child's day so that he or she knows what is coming next. In addition to establishing a sense of security and trust, knowing what to expect also helps the child to wait. If the child begins to understand that a certain activity usually happens next, she can tolerate a little delay more calmly. She learns that this is the time for eating, sees the preparation of food, and *knows* that food is coming. This growing ability to delay develops more quickly and with less fussing from the child if we are patient and don't exploit the child's acceptance of some delay. For instance, if the phone rings as you are preparing dinner and, because the child is quiet, you think you can talk for a while, the child's tolerance limit may be surpassed. Often we expect too much of children too soon. Sometimes we even expect them to understand *our* needs and to delay gratification until we are ready to serve them. Then we get impatient when they fuss.

*"Something that I find takes patience is giving my son medicine. He won't take any kind of pill or medicine without a fight."*

Never rush him. And never urge him to take the medicine "for Mommy."

*"I used to have that problem. But now I say, 'Tell me when you are ready,' and she turns right around and takes it."*

That is something we can all learn. Saying "When you are ready" or "Tell me when" often works with children. If you want them to come to the table to eat and they resist, you may say, "Your dinner is here. When you are ready, you can come." Often, in just a few seconds, they turn around and sit down. But if you say, "Sit down right now and eat your supper," you are not allowing the child any autonomy. Remember, this is the age of beginning independence, and children balk when they feel too dominated. Many of us were brought up with "Sit down right now" and feel that our children should be, too. Often one parent holds this view and the other doesn't. Do you find that you are having disagreements about what to expect from your children?

*"Not from my husband, because we discuss these topics when I get home. Some of our relatives are critical; they think we cater to the baby."*

## Appropriate Responses

As we have said before, meeting the child's needs at his or her level is not catering. In the same way that we expect children to wait longer than they can, we often expect them to respond more quickly than they can to our requests or demands. At this age, the children's central nervous systems are not sufficiently developed for immediate responses to our requests. It is unrealistic to ask them to "come right away" or "sit right down." The message has to travel to the brain, register, and travel out again to generate the appropriate activity. Children cannot make quick transitions from one activity to another. If they are playing, they also may not want to stop suddenly to get dressed or to eat. If we look honestly at our own behavior as adults, we will recognize a similar attitude in ourselves. How many times has a child—or another adult—asked us to do something and our reaction is, "Just a minute. Let me finish this chapter (or this phone call)?" Children of this age are not verbal enough or socialized enough to say to you, "Just a minute," but they have similar feelings. Demanding immediate response from a child leads most of the time to a confrontation between parent and child. We, as adults, must be patient. We must understand that children are *unable* to respond quickly. Often they are also *unwilling;* but with a little forewarning and patience, they can be encouraged to do what needs to be done.

Understanding the child's inability in these areas as *immaturity* and *lack of experience* will help us to be more realistic in our expectations and more patient. This understanding will help us avoid unnecessary frustrations.

# Family Differences in Child-Rearing Attitudes

Do you find that your ways of being parents are very different from your own parents' and friends' ways of parenting? If so, how are you managing?

## Responding Is Not Spoiling

*"I have a lot of trouble not only with my relatives but sometimes with my husband, because he is so influenced by them. They all think I'm spoiling the baby when I respond to his cries."*

We have talked before about how different cultures and different generations view the question of spoiling. Introducing new ways of child rearing is often threatening and upsetting to people who have reared children themselves. It is really very difficult. It takes persistence and patience—you do have to be patient teachers. If you get angry at the advice and just seethe inwardly when your relatives don't view things your way, you don't accomplish much and may hurt your relationships. It may help to say something like "I respect your point of view; I know you've had a lot of experience. Let me try to explain why I am doing it a little differently. I think this way is working out; if it is not successful, then I may try your way."

## Intimidation by Family

*"My family says, 'You and your special methods! You think your child is something special.' And I have to admit I do. I tell them he is something special and remind them that they must have felt the same way about their children."*

*"It's very hard for me to speak out like that. I have an aunt who has three grown children, and all are in psychotherapy. All have had a real bad life, so to speak, right? And she was scolding me unmercifully for letting my little girl hug me. I felt like saying to her, 'Well, if you did more of that with your children, they wouldn't be where they are today.' I had to use my self-control to keep quiet."*

It is easier to keep quiet. You might be able to handle her by saying, "You know, Auntie, everybody has her own way of bringing up her children. You brought up your children your way, the best way you knew; and I am trying to bring up my child the best way I know."

*"It is very easy when we are talking about it here; but when I am there and she is literally screaming at me, and that is exactly her method—screaming—I just go to pieces. My husband just laughs. He says that as soon as I know she is coming, I get nervous. I open the door and I am a different person. I can't control the feeling. She made me feel that way when I used to visit her when I was little, too."*

Her behavior to you revives your whole childhood experience. She's still doing just what she did to her own children and to you. You are responding

■                                                                          ■

automatically to your emotions and not using your head or your professional expertise as a psychiatric nurse. It is very hard to escape from your childhood role when it is forced on you. That is one of the reasons that we talk so much about helping our children to establish self-confidence. Now you see why it is so important. If they develop self-confidence early, it will be easier for them to cope in such situations.

*"My father has the same ability to put me in a state of total panic."*

Yes, and then it's hard for you to remember that you are a grown-up. You are an adult and you are really on a par with him now. You are a parent. He has a great deal of interest in you. He has a right to have an opinion and to express it, but he really has no right to direct you. It is perfectly all right to listen to him and then say, "Yes, I see you would have liked that better."

*"It is so easy to say it here but so difficult at home."*

That is why we repeatedly talk about these issues here—so that after a while, you will learn how to make use of what seems helpful. It is very, very hard. It is like a music lesson. It seems so easy when your teacher explains it. The hard part is to go home and use what you learned. It is much the same for you. Practice makes it easier each time.

*"I have trouble with my older brothers. My son often wants to be carried after we've walked a short distance outside. Sometimes he is tired; and sometimes I think the traffic frightens him, so I pick him up. They say, 'Put him down. Do you want him to be a mama's boy?' I get upset. What makes me so insecure that I listen to them?"*

It is not a sign of your feeling insecure as a mother. You know what to do as a mother. But your behavior suggests that your original relationship to your brothers is continuing. Did they always make you feel they knew better in regard to your schoolwork, clothes, or boyfriends as you were growing up?

*"They were always telling me what to do, and I was always intimidated by them."*

They are still doing that to you. You know very well what you expect of your child and how you want to bring him up. You are not reacting to them as your child's mother. You are reacting to them as the little sister. They are putting you back in the mold of little sister, and not allowing you to emerge into your role as mother.

It is not a conflict that is being induced so much by differences in the ways of child rearing as it is the difficulty in recognizing that you have grown up to be a parent. If you deal with the situation maturely, your relatives may soon respond with less of an authoritarian attitude. In any case, you can hold your ground with more sense of security. There are conflicts, however, that do arise over different attitudes toward child rearing. We spoke earlier of spoiling. Are there other areas that cause disagreement?

## Permitting Exploration

*"Yes, I'm in trouble with my mother most of the time, now that the baby is getting around on her own, especially if she tries to climb up into a chair or even run down the hall. She is always saying, 'Be careful.' "*

This anxiety may carry over to the child. If the anxious adult is present often enough, it can influence the child's development. This is another instance in which the parent has to stand up firmly for the child's freedom to explore. It is not easy, but one has to assure the anxious relative patiently that the child is capable of climbing or walking. Stand by and show the grandmother how well the child does and overtly recognize the child's achievement. Say that you know children do fall and that you watch to see that the child does not injure himself.

*"You know, I try to do that with an aunt who just dotes on the baby, but I find myself getting angry at her. She acts as though I'm not aware or don't care— that only she has the baby's interest at heart."*

That is a tough situation to handle. Try to stay calm and collected and don't compete with her to demonstrate who cares more for the child. Show her calmly what the baby can do now. She may then be able to appreciate the baby's achievement, too, instead of worrying everyone about it. This will diminish some of your tenseness.

## Allowing Normal Activity and Noise

*"My father-in-law thinks children should be seen and not heard. He expects them to sit still and be quiet, even at this age. He keeps saying, 'Shhh, shhh,' with his finger to his lips whenever the baby begins to make a sound. Now, whenever he comes, the baby just clings to me and won't go to him at all."*

It is very inhibiting for a child to be told to be quiet all the time. Children need to be free to express themselves. Older people often think the quiet child is the good child. Such constant disapproval is not a good way to build the child's self-esteem. Perhaps you can explain some of this to your father-in-law. Someday he might go out with you to the park, so that your baby can run around and make noise without disturbing his grandfather. Then, when you come back inside, perhaps the baby will be ready to look at a book quietly with his grandfather.

*"When my parents come to look after the baby, they skip her bath and let her stay up an hour later. Then she seems cranky the next day. When I suggest that they follow my routine, they say, 'Oh, it won't hurt her every once in a while.' It makes me not want to have them again."*

Life is much easier when parents, grandparents, and baby-sitters all follow about the same routines with a child. It can be upsetting all around when things are changed. On the other hand, if it is only occasionally and the child really enjoys her grandparents, it may not be so bad. Having a good time with the grandparents is very important in building a relationship with them. Parents should try not to be disapproving of the grandparents' care. Within reasonable limits, children can accommodate to some variations in their routines. If the baby gets back to her schedule after a day or two, it's probably all right. If it takes longer, then you must explain that to your parents. They may be skipping the bath because they do not feel secure in handling that. We stress the security that children get from following a routine, but we do not want you to become inflexible about it.

## *Favorite Toys and Security Blankets*

Have some of you noticed that your children are becoming attached to certain toys or other objects that they need to take with them wherever they go?

*"She mothers her bear all the time; she puts it to bed, gives it a bottle, and sleeps with it. I look on it as a little playmate for her. My mother says, 'Oh, what a dirty bear. Does she have to take it everywhere?' I say, 'She really likes that bear. So why shouldn't she take it?' Then I think to myself: have I really failed her somewhere?"*

At this age, most children are attached to such objects. So you shouldn't be affected by the comments that other people make. If she really wants to take her bear, and it makes her feel secure, then she should have it. When a child has this need, it indicates that his or her sense of security and ability to separate from home are not yet well established, and that is perfectly normal at this age. Removing the toy only intensifies the feeling of insecurity; it does not help to deprive the child of this object. Doing so may satisfy the adult's sense of control, but that is not the goal in this situation.

*"My baby has a favorite blanket, which he clutches and rubs against his face when he goes to sleep. He likes it best, it seems to me, when it gets smelly and dirty. When I wash it, I have to return it at once to his bed. He won't accept a substitute that looks just like it. Is that normal?"*

This is a very common situation. The blanket represents a comfort that the child has found for himself. Some children relinquish these early comfort mechanisms and move on to others as they get older; others cling to them for a very long time. In some cases, it becomes a symptom that requires special intervention, but in most cases this attachment to an object disappears as the child matures. It is interesting that you mention your baby likes the blanket best when it is smelly. Certainly the sense of smell is important to children in the early months. The smell of mother distinguishes her from others. The freshly washed blanket smells of detergent, not the familiar body smells permeating the unwashed blanket.

*"My sister's child is five years old. He had a favorite blanket that is now in shreds. He still carries one of those shreds around with him when he seems a*

■                                                                                                    ■

*little unsure of what's in store for him. My sister and her husband are very upset. They scold him and hide the piece of blanket, but he always finds it."*

Fortunately, they have been sensitive enough not to throw it out. This need to carry around a blanket is so common that a cartoonist has used it for a popular cartoon character, Linus. You may have seen it. Linus always carries around his blanket. In fact, many people refer to the child's blanket or toy as his "Linus blanket." In any case, such objects should not be taken away before children are ready to relinquish them or find their own substitutes.

*"One little girl I know had a knitted afghan that she gradually unraveled. For years she carried this ball of yarn around in her pocket. It became dirty and raveled, but she had to have it. Finally she outgrew it. Her parents understood she needed it and never embarrassed her with unkind comments."*

There are many instances of that sort. However, there are more in which the parents interfere and take away the blanket. Then the child may become irritable and even depressed. A pattern for depressive responses to separation or change can sometimes be traced, in later years, to what seemed like such innocent episodes in the child's early life.

Think about the college student who takes pictures, blankets, books, and other items from home to decorate a college room. It's considered appropriate to give the room a "homelike look." Yet this may be a later stage of the same need that was not sufficiently gratified by the blanket in very early childhood. There are adults who never leave home without special items from their dressing table or desk, even for a short visit. We call this sentimental, but it, too, may be a vestige of the "Linus blanket" or transitional object syndrome.

We tolerate many things that adults do, but we often give small children a hard time when they are only behaving appropriately for their age.

*"Well, that gives me a new perspective. I was getting a little ashamed of having my baby drag around his battered, dirty, stuffed dog Spot and I was on the verge of throwing it out. Now I know better and I'll be prepared to protect him from others who are critical."*

There are a lot of pressures on parents these days. Our society has become very complex. We are often surrounded by conflicting demands and tensions. These tensions are very quickly felt by our children, no matter how hard we try to protect them. Perhaps this is one reason that "Linus blankets" have become so prevalent. We must recognize our children's needs for comforting, especially when we are not able to be with them all the time.

This tangible bit of security is the child's way of coping with feelings of anxiety. By taking the object away, we only increase the anxiety, which may then be manifested in other ways that the parents may find even more annoying.

In the normal course of development, such objects are used by children in making the transition from complete dependence on others (parents) for security to more independence and self-reliance. Children should therefore be allowed to keep the object while they are making this transition and not be forced to relinquish it before they are ready. Once again, this is a passing stage. It helps the parents to be more tolerant and patient when they understand the meaning of this behavior.

# *The Child's Sexual Identity*

What are your feelings about this issue? Do you think that boys and girls should be brought up differently? Do you see differences in the way boys and girls behave?

*"You know, I've been wondering about that. We went to visit some friends who have a little girl about my little boy's age. She has a baby doll. My son has no doll, and he seemed so intrigued with hers. When we were going home and he had to put the doll down, he began to cry. My husband seemed upset at the time and when I suggested that we ought to give our son a doll to play with, he had a fit. He said, 'Do you want to make a sissy of our boy?' Was he right? Would playing with a doll at this age make him less masculine?"*

The question boils down to this: how much is an individual's identity as a boy or girl determined by biology or endowment at birth, and how much does the way society treats each sex determine sexual identity?

## *Are Girls and Boys Born Different?*

*"That's just what I want to know. Are boys naturally more athletic and aggressive than girls, and are girls naturally more gentle and 'motherly' than boys?"*

A recent review of the literature on sex differences seems to point to only four real differences. Boys seem to be more aggressive both physically and emotionally, excel at visual spatial tasks, and are better in math. Girls are superior in verbal ability. There seems to be no difference in how boys and girls are endowed in other areas such as ability to learn, to achieve and analyze situations, or in self-awareness or response to social pressure. The question remains whether these differences are psychobiologically or environmentally produced. We know from the research that small differences in infant behavior can subtly influence the parent's response. For example, infant boys are more muscular than infant girls; they are neurologically less mature at birth and startle more. Mothers (statistically) comfort infant boys more by holding them close, while they comfort infant girls more by smiling and talking. One may well ask, therefore, whether the verbal superiority of girls is *caused* by this differential parental treatment or whether innate, subtle sex differences *cause* different parental responses. Many child development specialists are working to find the answers to this question, for there is much about the relationship between biological endowment and environmental influence (nature versus nurture) that is still not known.

■                                                                                             ■

*"You were saying that aside from those four areas, a girl and a boy aren't very different. So how come we see so much difference in the way they behave?"*

Your children are about eighteen months old. By this time, we have consciously or unconsciously given them cues on how we expect them to behave. Even though we usually dress boys and girls in overalls, we do at times dress a little girl in a dainty dress and let her know we admire her femininity. Many people are consciously or unconsciously more gentle in their approach to a baby girl. With a boy, we show approval of evidences of his masculinity. We say, "What a big boy you are!" or "My little man!"

*"We do that all the time with our little boy. He just beams and, of course, so does his father. I guess I would say different things if I had a girl."*

*"Well, I have a girl and a boy. There certainly is a difference in the way I treat them. I guess a great deal of it is caused by the difference in sex. I always wanted her to look pretty and be neat as a pin. I never gave her cars or trucks to play with. With my boy, I'm just not so fussy about his clothes. Now he has cars and trucks and my daughter plays with them, too. It surprised me that she was so interested. Sometimes she acts as tough as he does, and sometimes he is very gentle with a doll. I find I like that."*

## Should Boys and Girls Be Treated Differently?

The issue you are raising now is really more important than what toys are appropriate per se. Do we expect only girls to be gentle? Is it wrong for boys to be gentle, tender, and considerate? Should these characteristics be feminine only? To be rough and tough has been considered appropriate for a boy; but if a girl is like that, some think she is not fulfilling her role. Many people believe that boys should not cry, that only girls may cry.

*"My husband made a strange remark yesterday when he came in. He said, 'Is he still all boy?' I wonder what he means by 'all boy.' Does he mean rough and ready? I think that he has the feeling that he must be ready to meet the world outside—the hard man's world."*

That's a very common attitude. But treating a little boy in a tough manner before it is appropriate may have the opposite effect. It may undermine his trust in adults as advocates for his welfare and make him timid and distrustful or extremely aggressive. At the same time, following the opposite attitude for girls by sheltering them all the time may have the ultimate result of making them helpless. These are the stereotypes of masculine and feminine roles that have been traditional in our society. We know from our own observations, as well as from the research, that many differences in girls' and boys' behavior and aptitude develop because of differential parental treatment. We see that boys' aggressive behavior is often overlooked, or even encouraged with a paternal smile and a shrugging "Boys will be boys," or, "That's my tough guy." Boys are more often encouraged, "Hit back; don't be a sissy." Girls are encouraged to settle their differences verbally. Similarly, girls have traditionally been rewarded for quiet, compliant behavior, while quiet boys cause concern, particularly to their fathers. Such sex-role expectations and taboos have led to many differences in how children have been treated and in how they come to view themselves. The question is: Do we as parents want this to persist? If we can influence our children's development, what is best?

*"I agree with the earlier comment that it's a man's world—and therefore I want my daughter to be as tough as possible."*

*"I want my daughter to grow up able to cope on a par with men, but I don't want her to be masculine and lose her identity as a female. Women need to be considered equal to men, but they don't have to copy men."*

*"I would want my son to be able to compete in the world. But I would still like him to be kind and loving to his family, and not be so 'macho' that he couldn't help in the house or take care of his children."*

I think you are expressing new expectations for male and female roles. You want children who become assertive *and* kind, self-reliant *and* sensitive, competent *and* compassionate.

*"But how can we, as parents, achieve that? Do you think the way we act to them now makes a difference?"*

*"My husband tends to comfort our son less when he hurts himself than he does our daughter, although she is older. Is that one of the ways we encourage an inappropriate difference?"*

Yes, I believe so. When a small child is hurt, that child needs attention appropriate to the extent of the injury and age of the child. The child's sex is not the issue. The issue is the child's need to be comforted. We comfort babies with holding, rocking, feeding, and singing. We comfort older children by helping them up, rubbing the sore spot, talking to them in a reassuring way, and then getting them interested in some other activity. It's the question of level of development, not the sex of the child.

## Parents Are Sex-Role Models

Another way we influence children is by the model we set as parents. Each of us has been influenced by the models in our own families, some of which were more traditional than others. If the father, in addition to his work outside the home, also helps in child care, cooking, and housework, he sets that kind of model of masculinity for his children, both sons and daughters. If the mother engages in some athletic activity, has a job, or engages in volunteer work as well as cooking and housework, she sets that feminine model for her sons and daughters. These children will see a father who does things that were once considered only suitable for a woman and a mother who does things that were considered appropriate for a man.

That brings us back to the question with which we began this discussion. Should a little boy play with dolls? If we want him to become a father who can take care of babies, the answer is "Yes." Playing with dolls is practice for child care; he is not learning to be a girl. Later, still without learning to be a girl, he may be a baby-sitter. By the same token, a girl can play with cars and trucks or throw a ball because she is learning to be a more versatile woman. She isn't learning to be a boy. In addition, we must remember that children of this age are learning by doing—by acting on the objects around them. The greater the range of objects they have to interact with, the greater their range of experiential learning. When children play with dolls, they have an opportunity for imaginative, creative role-playing as well as for imitating real life. As in their play with many other kinds of objects, they are learning about classification, size, and relationships. The exercise of putting on and taking off a doll's clothes is as valuable for increasing manual dexterity in boys as in girls. In other words, some of what children learn from objects has nothing to do with sex roles assigned to those objects by adults.

*"That makes me feel much better and gives me a good, sensible explanation for my father-in-law."*

*"But what about the girl who is a complete tomboy or a boy who just wants to play house and dolls?"*

Such situations arise for girls when they have only brothers or boy neighbors to play with. The same is true for boys who live in a household of females and have only girls to play with. If children play with others of both sexes, then such a concentration on one type of play is usually transitory. To return to what we were saying earlier, it is best for children to have a wide variety of experiences. We should try to encourage our children to develop many interests. To do this, boys and girls need to play with dolls *and* trucks, blocks *and* crayons, books *and* baseballs.

We must be aware that in speaking of the differences found between boys and girls in the literature, we mean the statistical differences between large numbers of boys and girls. That a greater percentage of boys are superior in mathematics does not mean that there aren't large numbers of girls with superior mathematical ability. Each child is an individual with his or her own endowments. Parents themselves vary in their interests and endowments. In some families, it may be the mother who tends to the athletic development of the children while the father encourages the arts and music, even though the opposite may be considered more common. Parents provide role models for their children. As people play different roles in our changing society, these models are changing. What children of both sexes need is to have the opportunity to have both male and female role models.

*"What about single parents? They can't supply both models?"*

That is true, and it is one of the difficulties of being a single parent. I would hope that friends, relatives, or teachers could provide the child with the other model. Such models may be hard to find, with the high incidence of divorce in our country; but single parents have a great need for help so that their children can have this experience. We are now in a transitional period, and our society must explore ways to meet this need.

*"This is a very complicated problem. I think I've taken too many myths about sex characteristics for granted. At the same time, I want my son to be clear that he's a boy."*

You are raising a concern of many parents. Even though they may not like sexual stereotypes, they are also very interested in having their children develop healthy heterosexual orientations. A woman who is satisfied with being a woman—even if she yearns for greater fulfillment—communicates this satisfaction to her daughters and sons. A little girl then finds satisfaction in being a girl "like Mommy." If the father values the mother and the daughters as individuals and women, this satisfaction is enhanced. The daughter must be loved *as a girl,* not only as an individual, by the father. If he is disappointed that he didn't have a boy and this is communicated to the daughter, she may deprecate all that is feminine. In our opinion, that is not healthy. Similarly, a boy finds satisfaction in being a boy "like Daddy" when his father is confident of his own masculinity and his masculinity is valued by the mother. The mother who constantly denigrates the father does much to place her son's heterosexuality at risk. Once again, therefore, parents' feelings about themselves serve as conscious or unconscious models for the child's developing sexual identity.

As all of you are well aware, we are now in the midst of a sex-role—and sexual—revolution. The answers are not easy or simple, and we will be talking about the implications for child rearing again.

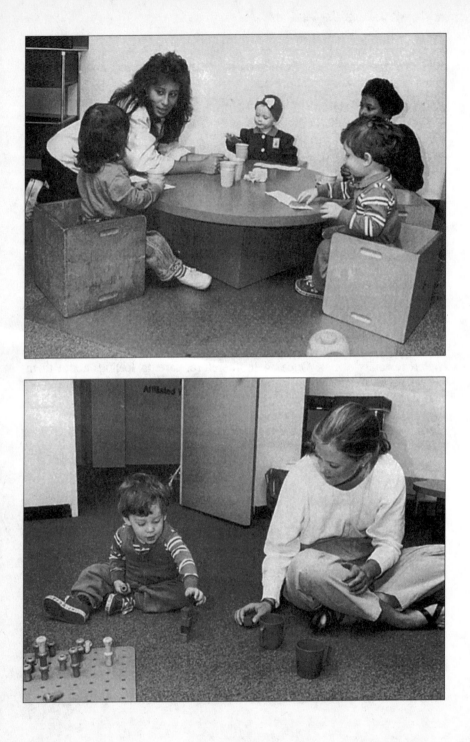

## *Highlights of Development—Eighteen Months*

Most children are walking well now and seldom falling. Many may also have begun to run, although a little stiffly. Most children can climb stairs with one hand held. They can seat themselves in a child's chair and climb into an adult chair. They can throw a small ball and walk over to a large ball placed on the floor, preliminary to the skill of kicking.

Children of this age can make a tower of three or four blocks and can put ten blocks in a cup. They can get a marble out of a small jar by dumping it out (instead of trying to reach in) and can put it back in. When given paper and a crayon, most children take the crayon at once and scribble spontaneously; they can also imitate a single line drawn by the parent.

Most children enjoy puzzles and can place the round piece and often several others in the puzzle board. They can turn the pages of a book, usually two or three at a time rather than singly.

While looking at a book, the children may point to the pictures and name one; some may only point or look selectively at familiar objects.  Most children now have a vocabulary of about ten words and should be able to name at least one object on request.

When feeding themselves, the children may hand the empty dish to the parents. If the parents' responses are not quick enough, however, some children push the dish off the high-chair tray or table. Children can now feed themselves with some spilling. When playing, children are able to pull a toy along the floor after them. They like to carry and hug a doll or stuffed animal.

# *Changes in Sleeping and Eating Patterns*

## *Sleeping Patterns*

Are you finding that just when you felt you had the child's routines stabilized, the children are changing waking times and eating habits—that many changes are taking place?

*"There has been a great change in my son's waking routine. He used to wake, take the bottle, and go back to sleep until 7:00 or 8:00 A.M. Now he wakes at 6:00, drinks an ounce of milk, and then wants to get up. He keeps coming into our bedroom and wants us to get up, too. We keep saying: 'No, we are not going to get up now. Go in your room and play.' Should we get a gate for his room and make him stay in there?"*

Can you go back to sleep, knowing that he is up and moving around? Would he stay happily in his room behind the gate?

*"Well, it is not so much sleeping; it's just that I want to stay in bed. Now that you mention it, he probably would scream if he couldn't come out."*

Could he play in your room, then, while you were in bed? Sometimes children will bring some toys and play in the parents' room or on their bed.

*"He brings his ball and giraffe in and says, 'Daddy go,' and 'Mommy come here.' He doesn't leave us alone."*

He has had a good night's sleep; he's all rested and ready for action. It might be better if you took turns getting up while one stays in bed, instead of both of you getting agitated about it.

*"Sometimes my husband does get up and goes into his room and lies down on the daybed. This seems to satisfy our son—he doesn't want to be in his room by himself."*

I think he wants to be sure that you are available; he has that need. It is a stage of the separation issue. When he wakes up, he needs to know one of you is available.

*"We have been having the same trouble. All of a sudden, our little girl is waking at 6:00 A.M. I don't want to get up, so I take her into our bed. We talk or sing songs. I can't go back to sleep, but I rest."*

A lot of parents seem to resolve the problem of children's waking early in this way. It keeps the child quiet and in view and enables the parents and child to get a little more rest.

*"I thought that it was bad to take the child into bed with you—that it was a bad pattern to establish."*

Letting the child spend a little time in bed with you in the morning to have a short period of quiet conversation or play is quite different from letting the child sleep with you all night. This period is not a sleep time; it's a quiet playtime. It is probably good to say to the child, "Come in and talk with Mommy." Emphasize that it's quiet playtime before the day begins. It is only a good idea to do this if you will be getting up soon. If it is the middle of the night, say, "It is still nighttime; we sleep in our own beds at night. In the morning, you can come in for a few minutes."

*"Does it help to put the child to bed later so he will wake up later?"*

Sometimes putting children to bed later works if it happens to meet their biological needs. Some children get a second wind; others get overtired and do not go to bed as easily. Many continue to wake early. Most of your children will begin to sleep later in the morning. One day, you'll find you are complaining that you can't wake them up in time for school. You are all laughing now, but the time really will come!

*"I think my daughter is in a transition state. Sometimes she'll wake up at 6:00, and the past two weeks she has been getting up at 7:30. She seems to switch back and forth."*

This is an example of what we were saying. These changes occur for most children but at different times, in keeping with each child's rate of development.

*"What are the causes of these changes?"*

One of the reasons is that their growth and metabolic rates are changing. Some are teething. Some are experiencing changes in eating habits as well. They may not have been hungry at suppertime and didn't eat well; then they get hungry earlier and wake earlier in the morning. Some need less sleep than they used to. If they are continuing with long naps, they may wake earlier. Sometimes this change suits the family. Sometimes there is a misfit between an early-rising child and a late-sleeping parent. The parents are night people; they stay up late and want to sleep late. The child's schedule is different. He goes to bed early and wakes up early—at the right time for him, but too early for his parents, especially on weekends. But even now, there are some children who have become accustomed to being quieter on weekend mornings.

*"I think our baby is beginning to notice that we sleep later on weekends. Either we don't hear her, or she is really sleeping later."*

Some children adjust early to differing family tempos. You are lucky if that is happening.

*"Our child was doing fine until the time changed. Now she wakes at 5:00 A.M."*

■                                                                              ■

Of course, there are always external reasons such as time changes, family trips, or vacations that cause disruptions in children's routines.

*"I'm glad you mentioned vacations. We are going on a vacation and are a little concerned because even at home she has sleep problems. I know I should take her blanket and her teddy bear, but is there anything else? There is going to be a crib there."*

Are there any other things that she especially likes?

*"A musical pillow that I always play when she goes to sleep."*

It is always a good idea to take along all the baby's favorite sleep toys as well as other toys, blankets, and pillows, so that the child has familiar things to help her make the transition to the new setting. Then the new place will not seem so strange or threatening. In addition, I would follow the same bedtime routines as at home.

*"We've noticed a different kind of change. Our daughter has been waking early lately because she seems to be getting much wetter. The last few nights she has awakened at 5:00 A.M. with her whole bed so wet that even her face and hands are wet. Is there any way to prevent this? I know it is hot and she is drinking a lot."*

If you are having problems with very wet beds, it is a good idea to place a second soak-proof pad and sheet on the bed. Then, when the bed gets wet, you will need only to strip off the top sheet and pad, leaving another dry sheet underneath. This takes less time than making up a fresh bed in the middle of the night and is less disturbing to the child.

*"We have had the experience of our baby waking wet, too. After he's changed we go through his whole bedtime routine again and it works well. The last thing before he goes to bed he switches off the light. He loves to do that. So when he wakes, we turn on the lights and change him. Then we tell him to turn off the light. He does it happily and goes right off to sleep without any hassle."*

You have apparently set up a good routine for him. That's a nice example of how it can work. For some children, just putting them back in their favorite sleeping positions with their bedtime toys is sufficient. Each family needs to tune in to their own child and follow the appropriate routine consistently and patiently. It's hard in the middle of the night, but it's the most productive way to do it. Once the child senses irritation and impatience on the part of the parent, he becomes tense and irritable and harder to get to sleep.

## Eating Patterns

*"I find changing him isn't enough. He needs a bottle. He takes all of it most of the time. So I think hunger is what wakes him. Is it normal to be waking for a feeding at this age?"*

It depends on the child's metabolism and biological clock. Perhaps he is having his last feeding too early and is getting hungry during the night.

*"He eats at about 6:30 but he doesn't finish his milk then. Is there some way to get him over that?"*

It may be that your child is a little overtired at the time you feed him. It might improve the situation if you were to give him his supper a little earlier. Then he might not be overtired and might be able to take more. Or just before bed he may need a small bottle or cup of milk so he won't get hungry during the night.

Many children seem to wake because they are thirsty. They don't need a feeding, just some water. Have any of you had that experience?

*"Yes, my son was eating a good supper and was still waking up at night. At first, I gave him a bottle and he took most of it; but I didn't want him to be too fat. I spoke to my pediatrician, and he advised water instead of a bottle. That's what I give him now and it works fine. He takes it and goes right back to sleep."*

*"We are having a different problem. It's a change in eating. Our daughter used to gobble down her breakfast, but now she is not a good eater in the morning. I go through all the trouble of making a really good breakfast, such as cinnamon toast or pancakes, and she won't eat."*

I wouldn't go to all that trouble. I'd sit down and eat my breakfast in front of her and say, "Mmmm, this is good." She'll see that mother is enjoying her breakfast and she'll want some. If you make something especially for her, she may not want it. There are some children who don't want to have their breakfast when they first get up; they don't get up feeling hungry. If you have that kind of child, there is no point in struggling with her or forcing her to eat. We have talked about the importance of not making eating a battleground. It is very common in the second year for the child's appetite to slacken off, even in the best eaters. It is a natural stage of development, and knowing this should help you resist getting into battles over eating. For some mothers this is very hard to resist, because they worry that there will be malnutrition and a decline in health. Many of these changes in eating patterns will be transitory if the parents don't make too much of an issue over them.

# The Beginnings of Self-control

## Temper Tantrums and Crying Fits

Are you finding that you are having more difficulty with enforcing limits, with your child crying and having temper tantrums just when you thought the children were understanding more and should be able to do what you ask? Do you find they are suddenly bursting into tears?

*"Exactly. Often, when I look up at my daughter, she runs away and lies down on the bedroom floor and cries."*

*"My son did that yesterday. He was perfectly fine, sitting in his high chair having dinner, and then all of a sudden he started to cry and struggle to get down. When I took him down, he ran away."*

Sometimes there are physical reasons for such outbursts. If it happens while the child is eating, he may have bitten down on a sore gum or on his tongue or cheek. This happens frequently and causes the child a sudden, sometimes sharp pain. There are also emotional reasons. The child may have spilled his milk and be concerned that he will receive a scolding. Or he may want to pour out his milk—something he knows will earn him parental disapproval.

*"But why do they try to run away from you when they start to cry?"*

Children may run away because they think they will be scolded. Sometimes they run away and cry because they know they've done something they shouldn't have.

*"But how do you know what the real problem is when they suddenly cry?"*

Sometimes it is very hard to tell. Often, if the child bites his tongue or cheek, he will cry very hard and put his hand to his cheek or mouth. He will appear to be in pain. If the cup is nearby and there have been problems about cup throwing, the parent may guess that this is the problem. Again, it is a question of each parent's tuning in to his or her child's particular behavior and needs.

*"If they are afraid of being scolded and run away, why do they do it?"*

The temptation to carry out their impulses will win out most of the time for quite a while. First, control has to come from the parents, control from without. Later, after patient teaching, control from within—self-control— is established. At this age children still need to be prevented from touching a hot stove, or putting their fingers in light sockets, or running across the street. The parent must exercise these controls for a long time before the child can control himself or herself. At first, you say "No" and find an alternative for the child. Later, the child stops momentarily and looks back at the parent. Finally, he will say "No" and have enough self-control not to do it. That is the story of how self-control develops. Children don't learn self-control until we have consistently helped them with control from the outside. Most parents expect children to achieve self-control sooner than it can possibly come.

## Helping Children Learn Self-control

Helping children to learn self-control is one of the big jobs that parents have. Teaching this begins at home and is continued in nursery and

■                                                                                      ■

elementary school. Children learn self-control bit by bit. For instance, you tell your son not to touch a plant; after a while, he doesn't touch it anymore. He has developed that bit of self-control—and you don't have to say "No" for that anymore. Gradually, he will add other areas that he can control, but not everything. The parents will think, "Well, he stopped doing that; why can't he stop doing this?" For each child, this process takes a different length of time. It depends on the individual child's maturational timetable, combined with the parents' consistent and patient help.

*"Are there some children who are not able to develop this inner control?"*

There are some children for whom it is much more difficult. They have trouble accepting "outer" control as well as developing "inner" control. Children of this type either don't have intact central nervous systems or they have never had anybody patiently help them achieve self-control. The latter cases are in the majority. Children born with injured central nervous systems, or those who do not develop properly, are relatively rare.

*"Is there anything that can be done for these children?"*

When such cases are detected early, procedures can be instituted that will be helpful. What concerns us most here is much more commonplace. More often, parents haven't been consistent and expect too much, too soon. By being too demanding and impatient, the parents can create discipline problems. Learning self-control takes time and is very variable. Children may get the concept of what is appropriate in one area, and in another area they may not get the idea at all. Parents have to be very consistent, and this is hard. Have you been experiencing that.

*"My daughter pushes her baby brother roughly and grabs his rattle or teddy bear. I keep saying, 'No, no, you love the baby.' But she does it again."*

And are you very angry about it?

*"No, I don't get angry. I understand that having a baby brother is very hard for her. I don't think she would really hurt him, but I let her know I don't want her to hurt him."*

She really doesn't care if the baby gets hurt; and she certainly doesn't love the baby right now. You can accept that and be understanding of her feelings, but you *cannot* accept the possibility of her hurting the baby. She doesn't understand what she could do, the possible harm she could cause the baby. But she can understand that you are very displeased—and even angry at her. She needs to learn that what she has done does not meet with your approval.

*"You mean I should say, 'Mommy does not like that; that makes Mommy angry'?"*

■                                                                    ■

Yes, and you should be pretty emphatic and dramatic about it, and say sternly, "No, we don't do that." Then give her something to do that you can approve of. You apparently are not emphatic enough; you are too objective and not emotional enough. You recognize that she is experiencing jealousy toward the baby and you feel a little guilty about causing her this pain. But she could very easily harm the baby, and he deserves your protection. He cannot protect himself. Children need to understand that you have strong feelings about certain things that they do.

*"When she goes near the stove, I just say 'No' once, and she runs off."*

Her getting near the stove really frightens you, so you are very emphatic about that. When you say "No," you mean it and she knows it. You must do the same thing about the baby. Then, immediately give her something else that she can do. Or say, "Let's play with the baby; look at him smile at you when you give him his rattle." Then be very approving. She will need help in having a pleasant encounter with the baby. Give her approval when she is nice to the baby, not just attention when she is not so nice.

*"I had that problem with my son. It's better now that he's three. It usually happens when I'm not in the room. He usually knows enough to be nice to his sister when I'm around."*

Your son is making progress. He has learned what you expect and what you approve of, but he cannot control himself all of the time. Children under three or so should not be left to play unsupervised. If you need to leave the room, take one of them with you. This is a stage that will pass. If parents are constantly in conflict with one child because of the other, sibling relations will be difficult. If you can separate them sometimes, the problem situations are fewer and the relations between parents and children will be easier and more pleasant.

### External Control Before Inner Control

*"I have a good friend with a child the same age. Sometimes they play well together and sometimes there's a lot of pushing and grabbing toys. Once my daughter was bitten."*

A good deal of the difficulty between children of this age is that they are not yet verbal enough to say, "Give me back my ball," or, "Mommy, Lori took my doll." They can't explain the problem. The only thing they know how to do is to bite, pull the toy away, or hit—these are the only weapons that they have to defend themselves. And they have not learned to control these impulses yet. They will need parental control in most areas, including play with other children. The areas where they can exert their own inner control are still few. Parents have to be patient and consistent in helping children to develop these inner controls.

The children are torn between carrying out their impulses and seeking parental approval. This conflict causes frustration, which is then released by screaming and kicking, because they cannot express themselves adequately in words. Parents often escalate the number of tantrums by concentrating too much on limitations and behavior of which they disapprove. It is important for children to receive attention and approval for the things they are doing right. If children get attention only when they are doing something the parents don't like, they tend to do those things more often.

It does help us to feel better about our role as parents if we "take stock" every once in a while and recognize how much the children have learned from our patient teaching—and from their own increased understanding of the world around them. Self-control develops little by little with parental assistance, and we are seeing the beginnings now.

## Obedience: Parents' Desire for Instant Response

As the children grow older, parents are expecting more mature behavior, particularly in the area of obedience. Are you beginning to feel that these toddlers should be responding more quickly to your requests? Do you think they should be able to "obey" more quickly now?

*"It seems to me my son never does what I want him to when I want him to. I have to tell him over and over. It makes me angry. When do they begin to respond? I don't want him to be a brat. I want him to behave."*

### Children's Inability to Respond Immediately

We understand that you do not want your child to be a brat, but no child of this age is neurologically able to respond instantaneously. Most parents do not understand the very complicated process involved in an individual's response to another's request. First, one hears the message, which goes to the brain for registration and decoding (*understanding*). Then the reply (*words* or *actions*) must be formulated and the responding message must be sent to the body. Finally, the body responds to the message. The pathways on which these messages travel—the pathways of nerves—are not fully established at birth. Gradually, the nerve pathways develop and messages travel along them. At this age, the messages are moving slowly along the pathways of the central nervous system.

If a child is about to bang on the coffee table with a block, he is following the impulse to do that. This activity cannot be stopped instantaneously. The parent needs, instead, to give the child another outlet for the impulse. Point to the floor and say, "Bang the block on the floor." Children of this age cannot respond instantaneously; neither can children who are considerably older. You hear the parent of a three- or four-year-old say, "You stop, and you stop this minute." But the child can't stop; he goes right on doing what he started because a message has gone up to the brain and needs an outlet. If you haven't given him another way to finish that message by giving him a substitute activity, he will go on with the act. Even when an alternate response is offered, the child may not be able to act on it at once (no matter how much he may want to), because his nervous system is slow in responding. The system simply does not have the facility for quick changes until its pathways have had a great deal of practice.

*"Is that why my child can't stop and I can't make her hurry? When I try to make her hurry, she gets all upset and can't do the simplest thing, such as putting down a toy to get her hand into a sleeve."*

It's the same reason. Her nervous system can't stop or speed up on short notice. As a matter of fact, the circuits seem to get jammed, and it seems as though the child becomes paralyzed and can't act at all. When we understand the level of maturity of their nervous systems, we can be more patient. We can give them some warning about the need to do something. We can say, "In a little while we are going to get dressed . . . take a bath." We can give them a little time to respond.

*"That procedure drives my husband crazy. He says our child has got to learn to obey—immediately."*

Your husband may be reenacting his own childhood. This may be the only model of parenting that he has. He needs to understand the level of development of the child's central nervous system and that the child cannot respond instantaneously.

*"But what about safety? What about when they may run in front of a car?"*

That is a very good question to ask right now. You cannot depend at all on a child's stopping in time to avoid being hit because you yell "Stop!" You must keep the child close enough to you to stop the child yourself. There are many things that we expect from children that they cannot do yet.

*"But when can we expect instant response—for safety's safe?"*

We really cannot expect an instantaneous response until children are between eight and ten years old, depending on each child's development.

*"Is it too much to expect my little girl to stop pulling my hair when I tell her to? Sometimes she also pulls the hair of a child while playing. She seems to enjoy touching hair, but it soon becomes pulling. The last time, I slapped her, and she hit me. It made me more angry."*

You have a twofold problem now. First, you need to understand why she is pulling hair. From your comment, it sounds as though she enjoys the sensation of touching and exploring the texture of hair. Pulling, then, is another related activity. She is not doing it to inflict pain; she doesn't know how hard she is pulling. You have to indicate that she can pat your hair, but that you don't like her to pull it—that it hurts. You can take her hand and show her how you like to have it done. You may need to do this many times until she gets the message and derives satisfaction from the approval you give her when she does it correctly—that is, without causing pain. This impulse to touch your hair might also be diverted into brushing your hair or her own hair. The second part of the situation you described is the hitting. You have set the example by hitting her.

## *Hitting and Slapping*

*"You mean she hit me because I hit her in punishment?"*

Yes, you gave her the example. She doesn't know that in your view only grown-ups are supposed to hit. A child doesn't understand that. Whom would she learn that from? Children imitate everything we do. That is how they learn. When we realize this, we may want to consider carefully what we are, in fact, teaching. Do we want them to learn that there are things, such as slapping and spanking, that adults can do but children cannot do? Children may, indeed, learn this lesson but reshape it to the concept that if you are bigger you can hit smaller people. One finds children who then hit younger and smaller children. We believe it is better to teach what is accepted and what is not—what is right and wrong—*without hitting*. With understanding of their levels of development and provision of substitute activities, we can teach them to behave in appropriate ways. If we understand that instant obedience is not possible, we will be more patient and think of more constructive ways to get our children to do what needs to be done. In this way, we will avoid angry confrontations and punishment.

Patience and understanding on our part are also better ways of eliciting the *desire* to do what we ask. Angry confrontations usually dispel any desire the child might have had to willingly do what we ask. If we adults are given ultimatums, we usually respond negatively. If someone tells us to "type this report" or "cook dinner right now" while we are doing something else, we become annoyed. Our need to manage our own lives is threatened by such demands. Our children feel much the same. They are just now starting on the path toward autonomy. They don't like being told what to do. If they are given the opportunity to respond at their own speed to our *requests,* and are given approval when they do, children willingly begin to behave the way we wish. They do not become brats from being treated with consideration for their level of development. Children become brats, or "spoiled," when they are treated inconsistently and when inappropriate demands are made on them. Because parents often do not understand this aspect of child development, conflict between parent and child develops, causing poor parent-child relationships and the kind of behavior that has been labeled the "terrible twos."

# How to Handle Temper Tantrums

Are you beginning to think that your children are hard to control, that they cry and kick and scream when you want them to stop doing something or do something they don't want to do? How do you handle these situations?

*"I've been troubled with that lately. My little girl was so easy to handle. I only had to call to her and she would come. I could stop her from doing something that I didn't want her to do and give her a substitute, and she would accept it. But now, she has a mind of her own. If I take something away from her, she has a fit. She cries and gets so red and stamps her feet, I stand there shocked at times; sometimes I get just as mad and want to hit her."*

*"When I have to take something away from my son that is dangerous or breakable or when I have to stop him from banging on a table, he lies on the floor and kicks and screams."*

## Temper Tantrums Are a Signal

Temper tantrums are one of the ways children have of telling you something is wrong in their world. They are still unable to modulate their reactions—to make a small protest for a small thing and a proportionately larger protest for a more important thing. Children always give such protests all of their energy. The uproar is upsetting to parents. They are frightened and annoyed, too, because no one likes to have a screaming child. Most of us have said, "I'll never let my child kick and scream and become a brat." Then you see this behavior and you are afraid it is happening to you. You wonder what you have done wrong.

When a child acts like this, the most important thing that a parent can do is to keep calm. The next step is to recognize that the outburst is a *communication* that would probably not be as upsetting if it could be converted to language. It would be different if the child could say, "Mother, I want to play longer. I don't want to go home yet"; or, "I am upset with myself because I can't make this toy work"; or, "I want to push my *own* stroller."

So the next step is to try calmly to understand what the communication means. You must ask yourself whether the child is overtired or overstimulated, frustrated, unable to understand your request, not ready to make the transition from one place to another, or trying to get your attention. Depending on your assessment of the situation, you will respond in different ways. The overtired child may need soothing and gentle reassurance and then a bottle quietly on your lap. The frustrated child may need your quiet assistance in making the offending toy work. Once the parent has handled the current outburst, it is important to keep in mind the situation that brought it about and try to avoid the repetition of

■                                                                    ■

that situation in the future. For example, some parents leave the children in their pajamas playing after breakfast. Then, when it is time to dress to go out, the children make a fuss because they don't want to stop playing. This rebellion might be avoided if the children were dressed as soon as they got up. That kind of rescheduling to avoid conflict situations is one way to cut down on the number of tantrums. If you think about your own situation, you may be able to apply it to your way of doing things.

*"Well, I know most of our tantrums come when he is overtired. Sometimes it takes us too long to get home from a visit. We're having too good a time and we don't leave early enough. I guess it's up to us to adapt to his needs if we want to avoid problems. Just recognizing the situation and knowing how to avoid it will really help me. I won't feel that I have a rotten, spoiled child—just a tired one—and I won't get so angry."*

*"Suppose you haven't been able to avoid the situation, or you just don't understand how the tantrum came about. Then what do you do?"*

If the tantrum develops in spite of your efforts to avoid it or you do not understand the cause, the first thing, as we said before, is to remain calm and not to scream louder than the child. This is often the way parents respond, and it's easy to understand their anger. However, it's the least productive and most harmful way to respond, because it only makes a bad situation worse.

## Different Approach for Each Child

*"I agree that's a bad way, but I can't seem to do anything else. That's what my mother did to me. What can I do?"*

Each child may need a different approach. You have to experiment and see which way is most helpful to the child. Some children should not be given too much attention. Others respond best if you sit quietly near them— available to them but not intruding on "their space." Some children respond best if they are held and soothed and told that the parent understands they are upset and will try to help them.

*"Well, isn't that catering to a child? Won't it encourage them to always respond that way?"*

Most children will not continue to have tantrums if the parent's response is appropriate; responding to a child's needs is not catering.

*"What about the child who always makes a fuss to get his way?"*

The child who *always* makes a fuss is usually the one who hasn't been able to get an appropriate response, the child whose communication is not understood or who hasn't been heard unless he makes a fuss. Getting attention in this way becomes the pattern for the way he and his parents relate to each other. We call it the "angry alliance." This child is often referred to as a brat. It is important to understand that he was not born a brat—he became a brat.

## The Problems with Spanking

*"Don't some children need to be spanked to make them behave? My parents spanked all of us?"*

We do not believe that children need to be spanked to be taught what is acceptable behavior and what is not. If the relationship between parent and child has been one of trust, with consistent limitation and approval from the parent, the child learns what is acceptable and what is not acceptable. Spanking is a dangerous form of discipline, because it sets a bad example and can lead to child abuse when carried to an extreme. We do not believe that teaching discipline needs to depend on causing pain. If spanking is the usual form of discipline, it may cause loss of trust in the parents and make children hostile and irritable, fearful and inhibited, or compliant and ingratiating. Discipline should come from the parents' desire to *teach* rather than to *punish*. Punishment is unfortunately in-grained in the upbringing of many of us. We are struggling here to overcome that legacy.

*"Well, in between spanking and comforting the child, are there other ways of overcoming a tantrum?"*

Yes, there are. They all take thought and ingenuity and an understanding of your child's behavior. Sometimes, when a child is having a tantrum and is lying on the floor kicking and screaming, a parent can sit beside him and quietly begin playing with a toy. The parent does not pay attention to the child, but just makes remarks about the toy, such as, "My, this car goes fast," or, "I am building a very high tower." In a short time, the child's attention is attracted and he joins in the play without "losing face."

A recent research study has shown that praising the child's acceptable behavior rather than concentrating on bad behavior dramatically reduces the frequency and length of violent temper outbursts.

*"Sometimes I have done something like that or just left him alone, and the tantrum passed. Now I do it regularly, and it seems to me the tantrums are fewer and shorter."*

*"I used that method and I felt it was working. But one day my mother was over. She said I was doing it wrong—that I should put my child in his room and close the door until he stopped. Is that a better method?"*

At this stage of development, isolation may cause fear and an even greater sense that the child can't communicate. When he is verbal, the child may understand and appreciate the request to go to his room until he feels calmer and like talking about his problem. But that is not an appropriate response for this age.

## *Take Time to Assess Child's Request*

One last piece of advice on how to avoid tantrums: avoid unnecessary confrontation by carefully assessing the child's requests before saying "No." We often find ourselves in conflict with our children because we have said "No" too quickly to a request that, upon reflection, is fairly reasonable, or at least not worth fighting over. Then we are in the uncomfortable position of "rewarding" the child's outburst by backing down, or of sticking to a position that we wish we were not in. When a child asks for something, there is no harm in saying, "Let me think about that a minute." Then use the time to decide whether you will stick to your position if the child fusses. If you are ultimately going to back down, it is better all around to say "Yes" in the first place. You avoid a confrontation and your child learns that a less frequent "No" really means "No."

We believe that if you respond now in a manner that suits the child's temperament and level of development, he or she will be better able to cope in the future with limitation, frustration, or changes in developmental equilibrium. The stage of temper tantrums does come to an end with appropriate handling by the parents and maturation by the child.

## *Appropriate Response to the Child: Meeting Needs or Spoiling?*

The underlying theme of most of the discussion topics in this book is the importance of parents' knowing the level of their own child's development and the responses appropriate at each given age. Many of the topics have touched tangentially on the issue of "coddling" or "spoiling." Parents sometimes feel that what we recommend as appropriate at a given age looks like coddling to others, if not to themselves. Is that still an issue, and if so, how do you cope with it?

*"I get that all the time from my family—not from my husband, but from my father and mother and aunts. They are European and think children should be seen and not heard. If my little girl wants something while I'm talking to one of them, they think she should wait till they are finished. I'm told I'm catering too much to her if I pick her up and attend to her. When they leave, I'm a wreck, because they have been telling me in no uncertain terms that I don't know how to bring up my child and that's not the way they brought me up. I can't tell them it's just because I remember that upbringing that I want to treat my child differently."*

There is certainly a cultural clash in your family. What you are doing is appropriate. Your daughter comes to you because she needs something or because she does not want to be excluded from the family conversation.

You have a right to bring her up in a way that you feel is correct. It is hard to stand up for your viewpoint against a continual barrage from your family. If you and your husband agree on your method of rearing your child, that is all that is necessary. You may still be trying to get the approval of your family that you did not get as a child and you would like them to recognize now how well you are dealing with your child. It is difficult for them to recognize now how well you are dealing with your child. It is difficult for them to show approval because it is not their way. In time, they will begin to notice what a secure and friendly child she is. You can listen to them and then do as you see fit. Only you and your husband need to agree on what is right. Part of the tension for you is brought on by your need for your family's approval. You need to approve of yourself and your way of doing things.

*"My husband and his family think I am making a mommy's boy of our son because I pick him up when he wants to be carried, or because I stop doing something and play with him for a few minutes if he wants me to. They say he won't get this attention all his life, and since he won't get it, he may as well get used to it now. It's a hard world, especially for a black child, so he might as well learn it now."*

## Gradual Delay of Gratification

There certainly is a time for learning that one cannot have instant gratification. We begin teaching this by delaying gratification in small doses as the children get older, according to their developmental level. Now we also deny them the things they cannot have, either because they are dangerous to the child or too fragile for the child to handle. We introduce an alternate activity. There is a time and way to teach a child limits and delay according to each child's developmental level without destroying a child's basic trust, security, and self-image. That is what we are trying to do without introducing harshness into the child's life when he or she can't cope with it. By making children secure now, they will have the self-reliance to cope later when they are ready. And if the black child's world is more difficult, all the more reason for the parents to help their children establish basic trust and a good self-image early, so that they can succeed in the world.

*"My husband has the same attitude. He thinks I coddle our son and that he's going to be a sissy."*

We have recently talked about expectations that parents often have for their children, based on the child's sex rather than on the child's level of development and needs. Your husband's attitude stems partly from wanting to make sure that his son becomes manly and partly from not wanting him to be a "spoiled brat." What he needs to understand is that the child must have his *needs* met in order to feel a sense of security and trust in people. How can a child trust those closest to him if he feels that something that he needs is denied? Children need to feel capable of evoking appropriate responses from people. By learning that they have this capability, they develop self-confidence and a good self-image and better coping mechanisms for the hazards of later life. Think of your own lives. If one rarely succeeds in getting what one needs, one develops a sense of powerlessness. We don't want that for ourselves or for our children. We want to see our children become competent, self-reliant individuals with a drive to achieve without hurting others.

*"Do you mean we should give our children everything they want—to develop self-confidence? We can't deny them anything?"*

## Emotional Needs Versus Material Wants

We believe children should always be given what they *need*. In other words, when they express hunger, they should be fed; when they feel insecure or express fear, they should be reassured; when they hurt themselves and cry, they should be comforted; when they feel excluded, they should be given attention. These are some of the needs that parents should satisfy. At the same time, we have to distinguish between emotional *needs* and material *wants*. We should not—often we cannot—give children everything they *want*. We believe that children who express excessive wants are really in *need* of something else. For example, a child who wants every toy he sees and has a tantrum when he doesn't get it probably desperately needs more consistent, loving human attention. A child who wants her parents to watch everything she does and looks for approval all the time probably needs more attention and time with her parents—and more approval *before* she asks for it. One often sees behavior like this in children after the arrival of a baby brother or sister. Children cannot say, "I need your attention." Instead, they are clinging and demanding and perhaps say, "Mommy play," or, "I want that and this" in a very command-ing way. This often irritates parents who feel that they are catering to a lot of demands. One must step back from such situations and try to analyze what the reasons might be for such behavior. More often than not, one will find that some basic need is not being met. Now is the appropriate time to meet such needs.

*"But won't that make a child expect it for the rest of his life?"*

On the contrary, meeting a child's needs at this age builds self-confidence and the child's feeling that he or she can obtain what he or she needs. The person whose needs are not met *now* will continue to try to find such satisfaction throughout life. Often such people are never satisfied—no matter how outwardly successful. You can probably recognize this person-ality structure in some of the people you know.

*"But some kids really are spoiled brats. How do they get that way?"*

We believe such children have been "spoiled" by their parents' inconsistent handling of them. These children have low self-esteem and low self-confidence. To make up for these bad feelings about themselves, they often become aggressive and unruly or whining. They have found that bad behavior earns them more attention than good behavior. They do become brats; they are not pleasant to be with—and yet, one must feel very sorry for them. Their legitimate needs for approval and attention and satisfaction have not been met consistently and appropriately. They are not learning how to cope appropriately in the family and will probably have trouble entering the larger world of school and community.

## *Sharing: The "I, My, Mine" Stage*

Are you worried because your children are having difficulty in sharing toys when they have visitors or are playing in the sandbox at the park?

*"Oh, yes. It's a battle every day when we go to the park. I almost hate to go, but I can't keep him inside in such nice weather. No sooner is my son in the sandbox than some child comes up and wants his shovel and may take it. If my son cries, I go and get him something else to play with, but I'm upset by what the other mothers think because my child won't share his shovel or any other toy."*

You seem to be more concerned about what the other mothers may be thinking than about how your child is feeling. When a parent allows other children to take her child's things and intervenes only if he protests—and then does not retrieve his toy but gives him a substitute, the child may get the feeling that he has no right to his toys. He comes to see the other children as a menace to his toys. He feels helpless when his toys are taken. If his parent doesn't help him retrieve the toy, his self-confidence and sense of self are undermined. This can create difficulty in his social relations; he may withdraw and not want to play with other children. If he is more assertive, he will hang on to his toys and not let the other child have them. In that case, he is considered selfish.

*"Well, isn't that selfish?"*

### *Beginning of Sense of Self*

This behavior needs to be regarded from another point of view: the maturational level of the child and what he is ready for in the way of social relations. At this age, he is just beginning to establish who he is, where he belongs, what belongs to him—the "I, my, mine" stage. He has to learn that certain toys are his and that he has a right to keep them. He has to learn that other toys belong to other children and that they have a right to keep them.

Children do not know this automatically. They have to learn it. Parents' intervention and patient teaching are essential in this learning process. They must reassure their child by retrieving toys that are taken from him and by giving a substitute to the other child, saying, "Johnny wants to play with *his* truck now; you may play with this car." In the same way, when your child takes another's toy, you should return it and give your own child a substitute.

Gradually, the child learns that what belongs to her *is* hers and that she has a right to it. She also learns that other children and Daddy and Mommy have a right to their things. She gains confidence that she may keep her toys because her parents have helped her achieve this sense of possession by helping her retrieve her things. She may then have the confidence to let other children play with something that belongs to her when she is not playing with it. She learns she can play with another's toy when he doesn't want it. This is the beginning of learning to take turns— and the beginning of sharing.

*"I have a girlfriend who has two kids, one three and one a year and a half, and they both share. She says, 'Oh, when my son was alone, he was spoiled like that, too.' "*

Being possessive of one's things at this age is not being spoiled. That is simply a stage the children are going through—not being ready to share yet. Your friend may be making her one-and-a-half-year-old child share earlier than she is ready to. Actually, the child may be giving up—she may not understand that anything is hers. She may think everything belongs to her brother.

## Parental Help in Social Situations

*"I have another question about this. When I see my son fighting over a toy and it belongs to somebody else, I get my son's toy and say, 'This is yours, and that is the other little boy's.' Is that helping him? My husband thinks the kids should settle it themselves."*

At this age, the parents must intervene. The children are not ready to settle it themselves in a way that is beneficial to both. The stronger child will keep the toy and learn that "might makes right." The less assertive child will be the "loser" and may then tend to want to withdraw from contact with other children. Children need help in learning to socialize and interact with others. They are too young to "settle" such situations by themselves.

*"It's not so much the other children as the other mothers who concern me by saying I'm teaching my son to be selfish."*

Then you have to explain to them that he is in the "I, my, mine" stage and that you are teaching him to take turns. Explain that you are teaching this by allowing the child who has the toy first, or who owns it, to keep it and by giving the one who grabbed the toy an alternate. One of the mothers who comes to the Center was able to teach the mothers in her playground this technique. They found it works, and now they all have a similar attitude. If you think this is a good idea, share it. It may make it easier for everyone.

## Genital Play: Self-discovery

Have you noticed that your babies are beginning to touch their genitals? How do you deal with it?

*"I am so glad you brought this up, because it has been bothering me. Lately, every time I change my son's diaper, he puts his hand on his penis and pulls on it before I can get him changed. I try to change him as quickly as possible so he won't get a chance to do it, but he is faster than I am!"*

Why do you think this worries you so much?

*"Well, I think he may harm himself because he doesn't know what he is doing. That's my reason; that's why I get him diapered as fast as I possibly can."*

*"When my son does it, I just take his hand away and then I hurry and dress him. Why do such young children touch themselves?"*

### Normal Exploration

Children touch themselves because they are exploring their bodies. The genital area is another part of themselves with which to get acquainted. They put their fingers on their eyes; sometimes they even poke them in. When they find it uncomfortable, they remove their fingers, or we stop them. They explore their noses by putting their fingers in their nostrils; they explore their ears in the same way. When sitting on our laps, they may explore our eyes and noses as well as our mouths, hair, and ears. We seem to understand and tolerate this exploration, except when they become too vigorous and hurt us. Then we inhibit them. As a matter of fact, as they touch these body parts we name them. Then we are pleased when the baby learns the names and can point to them. However, the genital area is different. We are disturbed by that; it is taboo, somehow.

*"Well, isn't touching the genitals the beginning of masturbation? My mother says it is. She told me to pull his hand away as soon as he reaches for that area, or else he will become a masturbator. She says this is very unhealthy."*

*"My mother isn't nearby, but she doesn't need to be. I remember what she used to do to me. She made me feel so bad if I even put my hand to my panties to scratch! I'm determined not to make my child feel like that, but the whole thing makes me uncomfortable. I'm surprised at myself."*

You have raised an interesting issue. Many of us were made to feel anxious and guilty about our developing sexuality. Intellectually, we understand that it was not a healthy way to deal with sex, and yet we find those old feelings and fears coming back to us as we raise our children. It may help all of you to express those feelings and to understand that your anxieties are natural, given your own upbringing. Some of you will be able to cope more naturally with your children about this issue than others.

*"It isn't only little boys who do it. My little girl reaches for her labia when her diapers are off. What should I do?"*

The simplest thing to do if that bothers you is to finish dressing the baby as quickly as possible. Pulling the child's hand away repeatedly seems only to intensify the need to touch. If you want to limit this activity, give the baby something else to occupy her hands while the diaper is being changed, without frustrating the child by pulling the exploring hand away.

## Good Feelings About One's Body

Although this diversionary tactic may be a more comfortable procedure for parents at this stage, one needs to remember that masturbation is a normal phase of sexual development and should not be regarded as a disease or crime. Touching the genitals creates a pleasurable sensation for children, as it does for adults. Having good feelings about one's body is an important aspect of the child's developing sense of self-worth. Therefore, we must try not to interfere with the child's discovery of, and pleasure in, his or her body. Parents do need to teach their children, as part of their growing social sense, that masturbation is a private act. Most children will only need a few kindly parental reminders to that effect; but it will be important not to convey disapproval of the act itself.

*"Rationally I agree with you, but I find I get emotional about it. Isn't there a danger that children will spend too much time giving themselves plea-sure?"*

If children do not receive any other kind of pleasure, they can become overly engrossed in this kind of self-initiated pleasure. But this will not happen if children are properly attended to and their needs for stimulation and love are met.

*"You say it is important to teach them without conveying disapproval. I don't quite see how we will do that."*

Now, while the children are still in diapers and are still not verbal, it is premature to think of doing that. For now, as they show interest in touching and exploring their bodies, it is important to be as matter-of-fact as you can while you are changing diapers or bathing the children.

*"Then would you suggest that when the baby touches the genital area you name it and say, 'That's your penis' or 'That is your vagina,' just as we say eye or nose or mouth?"*

Yes, that is the correct terminology and should be used as we would for any other part of the anatomy. One does not have to either emphasize the genital area or avoid mentioning it.

■     ■

*"Is it important to use the correct anatomical name? I've always referred to that part as the 'wee wee.' Is that wrong?"*

It's a matter of family feeling and custom. Some families use "penis" and "vagina"; others use "wee wee" or "tinkle" or some other term with which they are more comfortable. It's really not the word that matters; it is the attitude of the parents—and whether it conveys information or prohibition. "Wee wee" and "tinkle" are nursery language and easier for children to imitate. That may be why these words are so commonly used, especially at this age. Often parents begin with these words and then switch to the correct anatomical names when the children are more verbal. Some families may find the nursery words less threatening and may continue using them.

## Honesty About Sex Is Important

The most important thing is to try to deal naturally and honestly with this issue. As we said earlier, interest in the genitals at this age is largely a part of children's natural exploration of their bodies and the world around them. The more matter-of-factly parents handle this exploration, the easier it will be for children to gain a healthy attitude toward sex as a normal part of life that has its proper place and time, just as other aspects of life have. Of course, sexual satisfaction in adult life depends on more than this, but honesty about sex is an important beginning.

# Fathers' Expectations of Their Children and Wives

## Differing Feelings of Parents

Mothers and fathers may, however, have different expectations and feelings about their child's development and their parenting roles; and it is healthy to discuss them.

The children have changed a good deal in the last few months. What have the fathers been observing? What strikes you as the most important developments?

*"To me it's the development of the personality that is beginning to emerge. At first, the baby seemed like an undifferentiated blob to me, really. I mean that. But as she begins to develop she is becoming somebody."*

*"I keep wondering how much of the change is due to our influence and how much they would be as they are, anyway?"*

The child's genetic endowment comes first; then comes the influence of society. You are the child's first contact with society. The child is born with a certain potential—sometimes greater, sometimes lesser. Some have potential in certain areas and not in others. The job of the parents and grandparents and society is to help them develop that potential to its maximum.

*"That's certainly true, and I agree with that. But there are times when what children do is so hard to figure out: what things upset them, how much they understand, and that sort of thing."*

It is a puzzle at times, and at times we don't get it right, but by spending time with the child we get more experience and understand his frame of reference. It then becomes easier and more fun.

*"I'm afraid I have certain fixed ideas. At least, my wife says I have and that I expect my child to behave in a certain way—that I'm expecting immediate responses from him that he is not able to give. We argue about that because I think I was that way—or brought up that way—and I'd like him to be that way, too."*

Do you think that you are trying to make him respond as you think you did at nineteen or twenty months? Is it possible that you are remembering yourself at a later age? Most studies show that few of us remember much before we are three or four. But even if your memory is correct, or refreshed by what you have heard about yourself, would it be fair to expect an exact replica of yourself?

*"You may be right. Perhaps I am trying to push him into a preconceived notion that I had."*

Perhaps you are. That is not unusual, but it is not a good idea to try to mold a child into something he wasn't meant to be. All of us can probably think of examples of this kind of parental pressure. There is the parent who wants the child to be a musician, and the child wants to be a baseball player. The child's natural capacity doesn't suit him for a musical career. Another example is that of a child who is a bookworm and the athletic father who wants him to be a football player. That doesn't work, either. So you have to go along with what the child's potential is, allowing and encouraging the child to reach that potential. Parents really need to understand the messages children give them. They need to let children tell them what their special needs are and what their special talents are. Parents have to listen to their children and watch their development and behavior. Children give off cues all the time about their interests and preferences.

*"I remember as a child always being lectured by my parents and being told what to do. I know I hated it, but I've since figured it was for my good. Is that out of fashion?"*

It's not that it is out of fashion, but that we understand more about personality development. We understand now that the parent is a model, and the child will often follow what the parent does much more readily than what the parent tells the child to do. It's the unspoken word, the model that the parent sets, that is more effective than a lecture. If the parent is the kind who is very angry and short-tempered, the child models that. If the parent always speaks in a very gentle voice, the child will then have that model in mind. If the child grows up in a family where the means of communication is always shouting, that will be natural to her—unless her own endowment is such that it intimidates her, and then she may be inhibited. You see, it's the interplay of endowment and environment that determines the person's development. We are trying to help you combine these factors in the most effective way for each child.

Thus far, we have been talking about the need to understand our children and their changes in development. Since the child has come into the home, there may have been a change in the relations between spouses. Fathers have certain expectations of their wives, and vice versa. Sometimes it is hard to adjust to a wife when she has taken on the new role of mother. Most of the mothers have worked up to the time of the child's birth. They were fairly independent and enjoyed their contacts with the other people involved in their work, as well as the socializing they did with their husbands and friends. Some of the mothers decided to go back to their jobs, and a caretaker stays with the child. Others have temporarily given up their jobs to be at home with the child. In either situation, they have a number of adjustments to make. Though many fathers do help with child rearing, many may have little idea of how time-consuming child care can be. They may expect that the household will continue to function as it did before the child's arrival, or that it should be returning to normal now that the children are getting older. Perhaps we can talk a little about the fathers' expectations. It is very important that these expectations be appropriate and realistic for the well-being of the entire family.

## Need to Share Feelings

*"I must say I was completely unprepared for the change in our life. Before the baby came my wife was everything to me, and I thought I was to her. It never occurred to me how much of her time and attention would be given to the baby. We wanted the baby and had him when we were ready—or so we thought. When I come home now, she barely greets me. She says, 'Why don't you play this or that with Sammy?' Then she dashes off to get our dinner ready. I thought we would share more, having the baby, but instead he seems a wedge between us. That's not true all the time, but just at times."*

This happens often, but it is not a situation that cannot be changed. A husband can communicate to his wife how he feels. She may actually be having similar feelings. She may feel that all he wants is his dinner ready and the child in bed. He may want to share playing with the baby, and she may want that, too. It has to be verbalized and worked out. It doesn't happen automatically.

■                                                                    ■

*"I'm not disturbed by the attention our child requires. What bothers me is that my wife doesn't seem to have any control over him. For instance, if he wants to drink his milk rather than eat his food, she lets him. When I feed him, I won't let him do that. I just look sternly at him, and he doesn't ask for his milk."*

You are saying that your wife should be more insistent. Does the baby eat as well when you are feeding him?

*"I don't know about that. I just know he doesn't ask for his milk first. His mother lets him have a drink first, and then he gets the food in between sips. I think that's wrong."*

It sounds as though eating might become a battle for all of you. That is not an issue that should be a battleground. It may eventually make eating a problem.

Parents should agree on a consistent attitude toward, and routine for, their child. The pattern of the day—the order in which things will be done; what things a child may play with, which are forbidden; bedtimes and playtimes—are all things parents should agree on. We have talked before about the importance of consistent limitations and how inconsistency creates the spoiled child. The child also needs consistency in order to feel secure about her environment and her place in that world.

*"Is it too much for a man to expect his wife to have a little time for him after she takes care of the kids? Some days she is so pooped that she goes to bed at seven when the kids go to bed. Her going to bed at that hour is a bone of contention between us."*

Maybe you think that she could get some rest during the day so that she would have more time to spend with you?

*"Yes, that's just it; I do think so."*

That's a very common feeling with fathers: that their wives should save some energy for them. Many husbands do not realize how tiring a day with young children can be. But if it is a constant pattern, then one can understand that a husband would be a little upset.

*"It isn't a constant pattern; I don't mean to say that. Sometimes, of course, I come from work tired, too."*

Having two children so close in age is very demanding. Maybe what your wife really needs is someone to come in for an hour or two and relieve her during the day. Then she would not be so tired in the evening. Sometimes husbands are not aware of how their wives feel, and wives are not aware of how their husbands feel, about certain situations. While you are complaining about not seeing your wife enough in the evening, she may be thinking, "Do I have to drop dead before he realizes how much I need help?" Husbands and wives need to talk honestly about how they feel. It

■                                                                                              ■

helps to try to approach the problem from the other's point of view. What do you suppose would happen if the husband, instead of complaining about being neglected, said, "I am sorry you are so tired. What can I do to help you out? I miss talking with you in the evening." When husbands and wives face these situations together, solutions can usually be found.

Sometimes a very small reorganization, such as having a high school girl in to play with the children for an hour or two or take them out for a walk so the mother can do something else or take a nap, makes a lot of difference.

*"We have had our moments, but I think my wife is doing a nice job. I realize it's hard for her; she's given up her career temporarily for the baby's sake. I really appreciate that. I try to help her and give her some time off. I try to let her know what a great job she's doing."*

It is important to let each other know our good feelings, not only the bad ones. Many husbands feel that they lost their wives after the babies were born, that the wives are spending all their time and their whole effort on the baby. These husbands don't look at the situation from the wives' point of view. They don't realize how much the wives miss their freedom and how much they might like a little help.

*"I guess I felt that I'd lost my wife at first, but not anymore. I try to help now. I don't think I'm overtired in the evening, and my wife tries to rest during the day. So we both arrange to have some energy left for each other when the children are asleep."*

*"I take care of the kids one day on the weekend, and I do other things: washing and cleaning, occasionally."*

Do some fathers feel that they work for a living and then work more at home? Do they feel they do so much and get nothing in return?

*"No, I don't think that now, but at first I sometimes had that feeling. We talked it over and divided up the responsibilities as we thought we needed to."*

*"In our case, I work late, so I can't help at home; but I do all the food shopping and other errands. It's easier for me to do it. She, in turn, does all the housekeeping and baby care."*

*"Our situation is different, because my wife has returned to her full-time job. We have a good housekeeper, so things are pretty well organized in the evenings as far as housework goes. But the baby is exceedingly demanding now. We have very little time—and no energy—left for each other. Sometimes I feel as though I've lost my wife; her responsibilities as a mother always seem to come first. Our romance is over."*

*"We have a problem, since we both work. We were getting so far apart we decided that we had to do something about it. Now we try to have lunch together once a week."*

■                                                                         ■

That is a good idea that we would certainly recommend to all working couples whose locations of work make it feasible. Your baby will thrive best in a home where the parents are close and happy. It would therefore be good for you as a couple and for your child if you could regain your former closeness. Your child will ultimately benefit from the opportunity to live in a family with two parents committed to each other (as well as to the baby).

It sounds as if there have been times when all of you—whether the mother has gone back to her job or not—have experienced the children as an interference in your lives. Because of the various accommodations that you are learning to make, this feeling of the children's being an interference is beginning to pass and your marriages are beginning to come together again. Children should be part of the family, and not blocks between mother and father. Most of you sound as though you are working on ways for this to happen, and this is a positive approach; but it requires effort, patience, and understanding.

## *Mothers' Expectations of Fathers*

How do mothers feel that a child affects your relationship and social life? Do you think it has affected you and your husbands differently?

*"I guess after the first few months I expected that there would be more time and that I would have more energy to entertain and go places with my husband. I thought it would be easier to leave the baby with a sitter as he grew older. Instead, I find that as he grows older he needs more experienced sitters and I am more anxious about whom I leave him with and how he relates to my substitute—because that is what a sitter really is. My husband thinks I'm too fussy."*

### *Who Has Primary Responsibility for Child Care?*

Usually mothers make the decisions about sitters, but it is important for the fathers to know that these are sometimes difficult decisions. They relate to the management of your life and to the healthy development of your child. To fathers these decisions may not seem like difficult or large problems, because they are not home with the child all the time. Child care is not their total responsibility; they have largely delegated this responsibility to the mothers. Concerns about getting sitters or the need for relief from child care have not been part of their experience, so they have difficulty understanding the problems. Mothers should explain how they feel about this issue.

*"It is always a surprise to me how little notion my husband has of how hard it is for me to get the housework done and tend to the baby. He thinks the baby plays a lot while I take care of things or read the paper. When did I last do that?"*

Many men have no notion of what really goes on at home. Fathers need to learn what it is like to care for a child all the time and why and when the mother needs help and relief.

*"My husband is helpful with our son. He used to help me more with the cleaning, but he really doesn't have the time for that now. I'd rather he spend the time with the baby. I do the cleaning when I can! I just don't clean that much anymore."*

All that is really needed is to have things in their place and relatively clean. The fixation on having a spotless house seems to be the wrong emphasis. Spending time with the children and sparing yourself so that you, as a person, can relate to your husband and your children is much more important.

*"My husband minds when he comes home and finds toys strewn around in every room, wherever the baby happened to leave them. He says, 'What have you been doing all day? The place is a mess.' I couldn't care less at that point. What I'm concerned with is getting our dinner and getting the baby ready for bed."*

If you know that this kind of thing bothers your husband, it is a perfectly good technique to let the child know that cleanup time just precedes Daddy's coming home. The child learns to participate in "putting away" time. Of course, the mother may do most of it at first, but as children get older they will do more and more if their effort is recognized. Then, when your husband comes home, you can say, "Johnny is learning to put his toys away." Sometimes, if you are behind schedule, your husband might help. In some families, the father doesn't mind the job of putting all the toys into a box himself. Each family has its own way of settling this kind of thing.

## Mother's Viewpoint

We have been discussing how you feel about the father's expectations of the mother's role and how his home life is managed. Now, perhaps, we can talk about what mothers expect of fathers.

*"I'm glad we are going to talk about that. I think we are drifting further and further apart because my husband doesn't concern himself at all with what is going on in the house, what the baby is doing, what I'm doing, or how I feel. What makes me so mad is that he comes home in such a pleasant mood and says 'How are you, dear?' then kisses us. Asks, 'Need any help?' And before I can answer, he is off to the bedroom, showers, changes, turns on the TV, and waits for dinner while I get it ready and put the baby to bed. When I ask him why he never helps, he says he would be glad to but there doesn't seem to be anything for him to do—that I have it all in hand."*

Are you that efficient? Perhaps you are so efficient that you appear critical of what he does to help you, so he may have given up.

*"You may have something there, because I do want things done in a certain way. The baby is used to a certain routine, and my husband does things differently."*

The baby can get used to daddy's way of doing things. In fact, children should have the opportunity to experience the father's care. They can get used to each parent's style of caretaking.

*"Well, my husband isn't much for helping in the house, and I don't expect much: just taking the garbage out and once in a while shopping on his way home. If I ask too often, he acts imposed upon. You see, he thinks that is not his job; marketing is my job."*

*"In my family, it is just the opposite. My husband does all the marketing on his way home. He prefers it that way. He can see where the money is spent, and he sometimes gets just what he likes, too. It suits me fine and relieves me of having to shop in the supermarket with the baby. It is really a big help."*

Husbands do have different views of what is their job and what is the wife's. Some of it depends on the home they came from and what examples their parents have set. If they were accustomed to having the mother assume all the responsibility for the house and care of the children, as well as catering to dad's needs, then they expect this from their wives. If it was a household in which the parents shared chores and child care, then it is easy for them to do the same. If it was one in which the mother played the helpless role and the father assumed major responsibility, that is what a husband will expect and he may be a little uneasy if his wife is too efficient. All of you have different family patterns to cope with as you build your own families.

*"But don't you think wives sometimes need help, even if they are efficient?"*

Everyone needs help sometimes. When two people plan to marry, they should talk about how they see each other's roles in the marriage and later when they have children. If they haven't discussed this beforehand, then they haven't talked about some of the important issues that they are going to have to face in their life together. In any job, you sit down and deal with a problem; you discuss what is the best way to solve it. In marriage we should do the same. Problems should not be dealt with emotionally, with recriminations. If you act emotionally in your business and not objectively, then you are not going to make it. Marriage and running a household and raising children are among the most important projects you will ever be involved in; they are not accomplished without thought and effort. You always have to work at it; it isn't something for which you can say, "Now it's done." There are changes taking place all the time, requiring constant effort and adjustment.

## Need for Parental Adjustments

As with all aspects of life, you have to adjust yourself to the many changes taking place in your marriage and in your children's interests. There are opportunities to make friends and keep friends, there is your individual social life and there is your social life as a couple. There are also all the changing stages that your children go through as they develop. You will get to know the parents of the other children in school; you may prefer these to some of the friends you used to have. Many changes take place, and you have to grow with them. You may move to a new neighborhood. Your husband's job situation may change. You may not have the money to buy a home, or you may have to live in a smaller one. Some changes may be pleasant or challenging; others may be difficult and unpleasant, but all are part of life and growth. Parents grow and change, too, just as the children do.

*"We have found that having children has changed our marriage in ways we couldn't have predicted. We did discuss the issue of sharing responsibility financially, socially, and as parents. It has enriched our lives at the same time that it has created problems."*

What kind of problems?

*"My husband would like to spend more time with me alone. Our child is always with us except when we go out, and we don't go out very often."*

This is part of the management of your life that you really have to work at. It is very important to arrange time together.

*"Sometimes I get the feeling that my husband and I have drifted apart since we got married."*

Do you feel that you had a relationship that you have lost.

*"We haven't really lost it; it's still there, but it's more diminished now than it used to be. We used to be such 'lovebirds.' Now we are sometimes so matter-of-fact and cold. At other times we are considerate and loving to each other. It seems to depend on how tired we are and what kind of day we have had and how much time we've had together. When the baby does something cute that I can show my husband, it brings back a lot of the feeling, too, because we can both share that."*

## Do Fathers Consider Child Care Unmanly?

*"The thing that bothers me is going visiting with our child. My husband will sit and visit and expect me to take care of the baby when I would like to participate in some adult conversation, too. It's the same on vacation. I would like to have a division of labor. If he wants to go fishing in the morning, I'll take care of the baby then; but then I want time for my fun in the afternoon. I think that's only fair, but I can't get him to agree to such an arrangement beforehand. He is very old-fashioned in his ideas of what a*

*father should do. If he takes him for a walk, he will come back and say, 'I sure did a lot for the baby today.' I am of the opinion that the father should take some responsibility for the child and not leave it all to the mother. He thinks the father's role is one of providing security. He is a good father in that respect, and I do appreciate that. I guess I can't have everything. It's hard, though, because my own father helped my mother a lot."*

It is especially difficult for you because you were brought up with a different model. You will have to be patient, and perhaps your husband will become more helpful as he sees how the other fathers in the group act. Many men are afraid they will appear unmanly if they help too much. What about some of the other fathers? What kind of models did they have for their roles?

*"Well, actually, when my husband was growing up, my father-in-law spent a tremendous amount of time at work. He really didn't have time to help. He's now enjoying our baby, which he didn't have time to do with his own son, and he even helps me. My husband is now sharing more and more chores around the home. Come to think of it, he and his father are kind of modeling a new way for each other."*

*"I am very lucky, I guess. My husband gets involved in everything our daughter does. His father was like that, too."*

*"My husband is struggling with two jobs, and I don't expect much help. When he does have time, he's very good."*

*"I have gone along with most of the things my husband doesn't do because he has very demanding work. The baby is work, too, but if I'm awakened during the night, it's not too bad for me because I can get a nap during the day. So I do not bitch about that; I do agree that he has to concentrate on his job. It may be Victorian, but I agree."*

That is a wise attitude. Some young men's work *is* very, very demanding. Men are often not able to take as much strain as women. If we look around us, we see that; the life span of the male is shorter than for the female. It appears to be a physiological given; perhaps it is related to the endurance needed for childbearing. Research has actually shown that the life span of the male in this country is shorter than that of the female by about eight years. Perhaps we must recognize that for physiological reasons men need to play golf, or tennis, or swim, or do something relaxing. American men are exposed to quite severe tension, and they do need to have some relaxation. Wives should accept this need and not feel that they are being neglected.

Of course, what many men may not realize is that interacting with a child can be relaxing, because it is such a different activity than what they have been doing in the office. They are tired of their office work, but they are not too tired to do something different. We have found that some fathers love to come home and lie on the floor and play games with their children. This kind of activity takes their minds off their office problems and relaxes them. If the father looks on such activity as a pleasure, it can be. All fathers should be encouraged to try this. Of course, it may not be relaxing for other men; they may need some time by themselves to unwind at the end of the day. You may find that the husband who falls asleep in front of the TV is protecting himself because he has an unconscious physiological need for rest. We can't expect fathers to be supermen, doing everything all the time, any more than we should expect mothers to be superwomen. Just as mothers may have to do some reorganizing so that they can get more rest and relief, fathers may have to do the same.

*"You know, a lot depends on attitude. If my husband comes home and compliments me on the job I'm doing, then I don't feel put upon. I can willingly let him have a recuperation period. If he comes home and gripes, then I gripe, too."*

*"You talked earlier about men's shorter life span and greater vulnerability, and I guess that's true. But with more women working in executive jobs, it seems that they are developing many of the same problems, such as ulcers and heart attacks. Since my husband and I both work, I don't think it's fair for me to shoulder the whole burden at home after working myself."*

## Parenting Is a Shared Responsibility

As we said, mothers should not try to be superwomen. Ideally, mothers and fathers should share the care and responsibility of child rearing—and many young couples are doing that. Other parents may divide up the responsibilities differently; each family must suit its own needs and situation. The important thing is to talk about each person's needs and to work out the best arrangement you can—for yourselves and for your children.

Many people think that when they get married, it just works by itself. But it doesn't. After you have children, the relationship is different, and it has to be worked at also. You have to work at creating a marriage just as you would if you were creating a painting or a sculpture or solving a mathematical problem. It's a relationship that has to be worked at; it's not static. It can't be static because the outside world is changing, and so is your inside world and the children. The emotional climate that exists between the parents affects the children. That is why we talk about your feelings toward your spouses. Your children are going to be getting more and more aware of your feelings. You are presenting the model for how they will handle relationships when they grow up, so your marital relationship is important not only for yourself but for your children. This is something many people aren't really aware of and should talk about, because the children are taking it in unconsciously all the time. Your smiles and affectionate touches are unconsciously absorbed by the children and become part of the way they are going to be. If you are quarreling and angry, this becomes the child's model for later life. Therefore, to make your own lives and your child's life happier now and in the future, it is important to work out and resolve the problems that cause conflict in the relationship.

## Family Excursions and Travel

Now that the children are older, do you go on family outings, or vacations, or to visit distant relatives? How do things go?

*"When we go on family outings, everything just seems to go wrong and we end up fighting."*

### Need for Flexibility in Planning

When adults go out socially, they often expect the children to be interested in the same kind of things they are interested in. They expect children to participate in the same way as they do. At this age, the children get tired, or they sometimes get bored by the things we think will interest them. When this happens, the thing to do is to modify the plans right away. Such changes take a great deal of flexibility and maturity on the part of the parents. No one likes to give up nice activities that have been planned for the family's entertainment. Parents may plan a drive up to the mountains. The child gets tired after the first five miles, wants to stop at a hamburger stand, and then go home. Some parents will be perfectly willing to go home and do not insist on going all the way. Other parents won't see any reason to change their plans. Sometimes it will work out all right, because the child will fall asleep and wake refreshed. At other times, the child will become increasingly cranky and the trip will be spoiled for everyone. Children of this age cannot necessarily tolerate the excursions that we plan. It is best not to make plans that are too elaborate and to be able to make changes if the plans aren't working.

### Car Sickness

*"My child usually gets carsick. Is there any way to stop that?"*

Car sickness is caused by different things. In many cases, it's a disturbance affecting the semicircular canals in the ears. In some, it happens only on long trips if the speed of the car is above a certain level. If children are better on shorter trips, one can take that into account and break up the trip. In other cases, it is best not to give the child liquids such as milk before the trip and only dry foods such as plain crackers during the trip. Some pediatricians may think that an antiemetic medication is needed and will prescribe the appropriate one in the correct dosage for your child. Some children may be sick because of anxiety about travel. In most cases, children outgrow car sickness in time.

*"I find that train trips are easier because the baby isn't so confined. Maybe the other passengers are not happy when we walk up and down the aisles,*

*but it takes up some of the time. Once in a while, we meet a friendly person. If they are unfriendly, we just move on."*

*"For me, a bottle still soothes my son and keeps him from being too restless when the books and toys get boring. Traveling alone is a lot harder than traveling with my husband or a friend, but it's manageable."*

## Air Travel

*"We're taking a plane trip, and I dread it because it will be for several hours. We hope the baby will sleep part of the time; but if not, how do we amuse her? It's not like car or train travel; there usually isn't anything to point to outside the window except clouds."*

Certainly traveling in a plane is difficult for that reason. Also, there are certain times when the child must be confined by a seat belt: at takeoff and landing, and during rough weather. One cannot stop the plane to give the child a chance to run or play. But there are occasional times on a plane when you can walk in the aisles with a child; and children are usually entertained by the serving of food. Sometimes the flight attendant has a children's play kit; and the airlines often give special treatment to families with small children by serving their food first or letting them embark and disembark first.

Another aspect of plane trips that is very different from other kinds of travel is the difficulty caused by altitude. The altitude often causes children's (and adult's) ears to hurt, especially on takeoff or landing, if they have a cold or respiratory infection. Adults often chew gum for relief of this condition, but these toddlers are really too young for gum. Swallowing is the natural method of physiologically relieving the pressure on one's ears. Therefore, it is very important to have a bottle or pacifier handy for children of this age. Children should be offered a bottle or pacifier if they begin to cry suddenly on a plane, because they may feel a change of pressure. The swallowing that results from drinking from a bottle or sucking on a pacifier will relieve the pressure or pain in their ears. Parents must know about this, because these toddlers are usually unable to say that their ears hurt. Much of the unpleasantness of traveling by plane can be avoided if parents are prepared for this occurrence. In fact, if the child—or the adult—has had a cold immediately prior to taking a plane trip, it is a good idea to consult a physician to see whether some medication can be prescribed as well.

Parents must be *prepared* for all eventualities when they are traveling long distances with young children. You never know when there may be a delay. You should always have extra diapers. Some airlines are prepared to help out with extra baby supplies, but you should not count on it.

In general, traveling with children of this age is difficult because they want to be active and can't be absorbed in any one thing for a long time. Every activity works for a while. A cookie works for a while, and a little car or a doll works for a while; nothing distracts them for very long. You have to work out a whole repertoire of activities that you know will engage your child. It is also a good idea to have a toy or two that are new, as well as some old favorites.

## Entertaining

Are any of you beginning to entertain at home? How are you managing? When you have company coming to your house, do you arrange it so that your child is asleep and the guests come later? Or do they come during the time that your child is awake?

*"There are some people who really don't care to be around children, so we ask them for later; and there are others who come just to see the children—they just love to see them."*

*"Our friends want our son to be up when they come over because they come to see him, too. After they have spent some time with him, we put him to bed."*

*"Our children usually go to bed very early. Unless my friends ask specifically to see them, I put them in bed before my friends arrive."*

*"My children go to bed around seven, so I don't invite anybody to come over until after eight o'clock. By that time, the children are asleep. Sometimes my daughter gets the sense that someone is coming and she won't go to bed until she has visited with them a little. We all just accept this. Sometimes she even has a bite of our refreshments, then goes willingly to bed. I find it's easier if I relax and don't use pressure."*

### Helping Child to Socialize

You've learned something valuable. Children let you know when they are ready and need to socialize. It's good for them to learn to socialize with other adults. Sometimes children take to this quite naturally, and other times they need some help and reassurance. Sometimes adults need to be guided in relating to your child. They may be too overwhelming in their greeting, or indifferent, so the parent has to be the child's advocate and guide the situation. In any case, it is a valuable experience for the child.

*"One of the big hassles with company and the baby is the food. He will want a little bit of this, a taste of that, or he will take a bite of something and leave it on someone's lap. I'm afraid we will alienate our friends!"*

As you progress through life, you will notice that many people you thought were your friends are less friendly because they do not like children. You will get to see more and more of the people who are really friends of yours *and* of your children. Some old friendships continue, but many new ones are made.

*"We are trying very hard now to renew some of our old friendships. My husband expects me to be able to entertain with silver and candlelight and gourmet food, just as we used to. I'd like to do that, too, but it's just too much. I get worn out and don't enjoy the whole thing as I used to. Then we both feel let down."*

Certainly, some of the unnecessary details may have to be omitted. Maybe the silver won't be polished and maybe some of the food will be brought in from outside. In this, your husband can help. Perhaps some of the preparation can be done the night before when the baby is asleep. The menu can be the kind that can be prepared ahead and popped into the oven at the last minute.

*"Well, that's what I do. I shop as much as I can when I take the baby out in the carriage; my husband picks up the rest. Then I attend to everything, even to setting the table, the night before. The next day I'm free, and the baby doesn't seem to get in the way as much as some think. Even if he is up when the company comes, we either wait until he goes to bed to eat or sit him beside us and give him a snack."*

*"We never did entertain formally—never silver or candlesticks; but my husband did expect good pasta or something like that. Now company knows it's potluck. Sometimes they bring most of the food. It's not my husband's style, but he is getting used to it for the time being."*

It sounds as though in some cases the wife is worried more about the husband than the guests—how to please him.

*"Well, I guess I'm lucky. My husband was always the manager of the preparations, and he still is. He likes to be the host and the cook."*

*"Before we had the baby, we entertained out at restaurants a lot. Now we don't do that because we want to stay home with the baby. As you know, I still work full time and I just don't have the energy to entertain at home."*

If you have continued working, it is important for your baby to be a priority *after work.* Working women should *not* feel that they have to be super-women and do everything. It is important to see your friends occasionally, however, and to plan for some activities with your husband without the baby—or with other adults in a social way. Occasionally, you should go out with your friends; perhaps you even have some friends with a young child who would like to go out with you. Perhaps you can have some kind of food service, such as an Italian or Chinese restaurant, deliver a fully cooked meal so you can entertain at home with a minimum of effort. We say this not because entertaining is important, but because parents need some adult life together with their friends.

It is not healthy to feel isolated from one's friends and trapped by the baby. Couples who never see their friends sometimes develop a sense of martyrdom about parenthood that covers a sense of resentment. This is not a feeling to be encouraged. It is much better to find a way to socialize, no matter how casually.

# Moving: How to Reduce the Child's Anxieties

Are any of you thinking of moving?

*"Yes, we are about to move. We only have a small bedroom, and there is almost no room for the crib and our bed in the same room. We've begun to pack, and we noticed that the baby seemed confused as we began to put things in boxes in preparation. Do you think she senses something is going on?"*

She certainly is aware that something different is going on. For a child, consistency is very important. She needs to see her things in the familiar places. At this age, she can't understand very well what is happening. You may say, "We are going to a new home," or, "You are going to have a nice room," and she probably will understand little of it. However, she may enjoy helping to put, or drop, things into packing boxes. In this way she can be involved in the move in a positive way.

*"My friends just moved, and their baby was upset and cranky all during the packing and the first couple of weeks they were in the new apartment. The worst part was the sleeping. He just couldn't get used to his new bed; they bought all new furniture for his room. He just wasn't happy; he just clung to an old blanket and teddy bear. It made my friends miserable."*

## Maintaining Child's Sense of Security

It is very distressing to parents when they plan something they think will be just fine for the child and the child doesn't respond with joy. Since the child is not verbal, the parents couldn't talk the changes over with him. They would have been much better off to move his old furniture, pictures, and toys to the new home and set up the room as nearly as it had been in the old apartment. Then they could get new furniture later when the child could understand and participate. It is always a temptation to redecorate for the child, but the child may not appreciate that at this age. For the child, it is important to have his familiar things: they help him maintain his sense of security and basic trust.

*"For the child, what is the best way to move? Is it best to leave the child at a relative's house and get everything done and then go and get him? Or should the child be included in the move? And what about his toys?"*

If you want to arrange to do what is most helpful to the child, take the child to see the new apartment or house several times before the move. Then, in packing, put his toys in at the last minute. All his furniture should be put on the truck last so it will be first off. Then, the child's things can be unpacked first and his room set up as nearly like his old room as possible. It's best to have him with you so that he can see the process and participate with his family. Instead of separating the child from the family, it is better to have a relative or neighbor with you to keep him amused and out of harm. Then he can see what is going on and have the joy of seeing his things unpacked.

Even with the best of plans, he may be a little upset the first night or two. Change in sleep patterns and clinging are signs of the child's anxiety. Sometimes the child is also harder to comfort and gets irritable more easily, or his eating pattern may be disturbed. These signs of anxiety are to be expected, but they will probably be less intense if he is included in the move. In addition, it's a good idea to carry out the child's usual routines as nearly as possible.

## Children Need Reassurance During Move

*"We have just moved and our baby feels upset. I know that she doesn't get the kind of attention she is used to, because we are busy getting unpacked and settled. To take time just to play with her seems like a waste of time, but I guess you're saying she needs it."*

Yes, she needs her regular play, especially because of the strangeness of the place. When she sees her things in place, she will know that this is a place where she can stay and she will get adjusted. You may have to get *your* things unpacked a little more slowly. You will have much more trouble if you try to get her to stop clinging so you can get things done; that only intensifies the clinging. It's best to allow her to be near you as much as possible. Comfort her and play with her; then take her with you as you do things. She may like to help unpack or to play in some of the big packing boxes. You really can't hope to get settled in the efficient way that you would like. Don't try. If it's your expectation that you should do it, that's frustrating to you.

*"Well, we have an older child of four and the baby. The older one was able to help a little, and he talked about his new house; but the baby was upset at first, even though we kept her toys out to the last minute."*

*"Are all children like that? Aren't there some who take it in their stride? Our child adapted easily, but we took our time moving. Each day or so, we took a few things over to the new house and she would play on the floor there. So when we moved it was less of a change for her. We thought about how to make it easier for her and for us. We remembered some of the things from the first year, when she reacted so badly on the weekends that we went to our summer bungalow. Then it was explained to us that the sudden change to a strange setting upset her sense of security."*

*"Well, then you can't get any work done if there is a baby around."*

As we said before, it is better to delay the work than to needlessly undermine the child's sense of security. The work can always be done a little later; putting up curtains or putting the pots away can wait.

■                                                                                          ■

*"We moved a month ago and are going on vacation for a week, which means another new place for her. Do you think this will be unsettling, too? I want her to feel settled, because I go to school again a week after we get back."*

## Too Much Change Is Unsettling

Sometimes parents plan—or are unable to avoid—too many changes in their lives. These changes are often difficult for adults to cope with, but they are much more difficult for children of this age, because they cannot discuss all the changes. Your baby may certainly show some signs of being unsettled from the move, the vacation, and your return to school. If her behavior seems very strange to you, then you can't deal with it and you become angry. But if you realize that her response to all of these changes is normal for a child of her age, and that what she needs is your reassurance and your presence to help her get adjusted, then you will be able to deal with it. Then you won't get annoyed with her and make matters worse. Understanding the limitations of the child's coping mechanisms will ultimately make it easier for the parents.

*"The discussion has been about moving from one apartment to another, but my husband and I are thinking of moving to the suburbs. We moved into a large apartment before the baby came, but we can see that it's very confining. There is a terrace, but I can't really use it for him to play."*

*"My husband and I had a long discussion weighing the pros and cons of city versus country living. We came to the conclusion that he would spend so much time commuting that the baby would hardly see him. It's bad enough now."*

*"My husband wants to move, but I don't. I have friends here and plan to work part-time soon. There are few part-time jobs in the suburbs."*

Each family will find good reasons *for* and *against* suburban and city living. As in all other situations, each family has to make its decision according to its own priorities. It's wise for parents to carefully consider *together* what their priorities are. We know healthy, happy children have been brought up in *all* surroundings. It is important to consider what will enhance the family's well-being and relationships as a family, as well as what best suits the individual needs of each member. It's hard if one member feels he or she is making a sacrifice for the others. Ultimately, the children will be happy where the parents are happy.

## Parental Anger: How to Express It Appropriately

In earlier sessions, we have talked about children's anger and how to handle their tantrums in the most constructive ways. We have also urged you to try to keep calm yourselves and not add your agitation to theirs. We realize that this is often easier said than done. Children can be exceedingly annoying, often just when parents are tired or preoccupied by other problems. All parents lose their tempers at times and yell at their children. Do you find you are doing that more frequently now that the children are older?

## Counterproductiveness of Yelling

*"I yell a great deal more than I want to. I'm a bug on neatness. When the baby throws things and makes a mess after I've just cleaned up, that gets me and I yell."*

Many of us yell when we are angry. We believe the *louder* we yell the more effect it will have on the other person. At the same time, we are unconsciously releasing *our* anger. Yelling is, in fact, more effective as a method of releasing anger than of teaching the child about the behavior we expect. Speaking quietly and firmly is a much more effective way of teaching. Very often, in fact, yelling does the opposite of what we want it to do. It sets the example for the child to yell in return. Or, if the parent yells constantly, the child may simply tune it out and pay no attention. Either response makes the parent more angry and sets up a vicious cycle. We want to help parents avoid such situations in which anger escalates on both sides.

*"Must parents be sweet and gentle all the time? Don't they have a right to be angry and show it and shout 'No'?"*

Of course that happens, especially when the child is about to do something dangerous. The parent may become excited and shout "No" or "Stop." But, as we have said earlier, shouting gives little guarantee that the child's central nervous system will be able to respond in time.

In addition to times of danger, parents may yell because the child has been exceedingly annoying, doing something the parents do not like at all. We want our children to do the things we approve of and stop doing the things we don't like. The best way to accomplish this is to say "No" quietly and firmly. If the child seems not to understand how serious you are, you may have to add an "Absolutely not," so that he or she knows you mean it. You must let children know *firmly* that you mean what you say. That doesn't mean you need to slap them or yell at them—a firm tone of voice and a stern facial expression are usually enough. You have a right and an obligation to let them know when you do not like what they are doing. And, of course, as we have discussed, each limitation should be accompanied by the offer of a substitute approved activity.

*"I've learned that. Otherwise, you get repercussions from it. I get hit, honest. I tell my son 'No' and he knows I mean it; but if I don't give him a substitute right away, he hits me. He needs an alternate outlet."*

You are perfectly right. There must be a substitute activity offered, because he has the impulse to do something. The message to act has gone into his immature nervous system, and it can't be turned off by the child at this age.

You can help the child by diverting the discharge to an appropriate activity. Accepting alternatives is a sign of maturity—it doesn't come overnight. Parents help children achieve this maturity *not* by yelling at them to stop, but by firmly saying "No" and giving them other outlets. Those children who are forced to stop continually without an alternative outlet build up anger, which they may not express. This can lead to the development of a hostile personality structure that we are trying to help you avoid.

*"I can see that yelling is not a good way to discipline. What effect does parents' yelling at each other have on children?"*

It sets a model. They get the idea that this is the way to communicate and they yell, too. That is one thing that happens, and another thing is that it usually frightens and upsets them.

*"You're right. If we yell at each other, our child looks at us in a frightened way and then smiles a lot and looks as if she wants to be reassured that everything is all right. Or she will just laugh out loud, perhaps to make it lighter, or to stop us."*

Sometimes they laugh when they are really ready to cry. They don't know what to do about your yelling and feel very threatened. They laugh, hoping you will stop and laugh, too, because they know you seem pleased when they laugh. Laughter at a time like that is nervous laughter.

*"Do you think that our yelling makes children nervous and upset even if they don't understand what is going on?"*

## Parents' Arguments Frighten Children

Some people have a habit of discussing things in very loud voices and are really not angry, but the children don't understand that. When parents fight in front of children it is very disconcerting to them. Either they will then yell at you that way and yell at their friends, or it frightens them and they don't know what to do about it.

*"In my family no one ever did yell, so anger was never really expressed."*

You can express anger and you should express anger. You should also express pleasure. It should be clear which is which. It doesn't mean you have to turn off your feelings, or that you always wear a smile. Children will never learn the difference between a pleasant feeling or an unpleasant feeling if you do that. They should learn the difference, but it should be appropriate. If you go into a tremendous outburst because something has spilled and the same outburst when someone is hurt, your anger is not proportionate to the situation or appropriate.

Yelling indicates that you have stored up a lot of anger, perhaps over many different things. It may be mostly against your spouse or another relative or the delivery boy. It is not appropriate, when you have been storing up anger from other incidents, to discharge all of it on the child.

Sometimes people yell when they are frightened. Have you seen that?

■                                                                                           ■

## *What Spanking Teaches*

*"Everyone is talking about yelling at their kids when they are bad. What about a good spanking—that stops them!"*

We discussed our concerns about spanking earlier *(see page 392).* We believe it is better to teach what is acceptable and what is not by saying "No" and offering a substitute. Spanking teaches by inflicting pain. It also sets the example of a physical way of handling differences. In cases of parental anger, physical discipline or spanking can often become excessive and lead to child abuse. No parent wants that to happen. We want to try to help you learn different ways, so that you can avoid that kind of relationship. Besides, neither yelling nor spanking produces the results parents would like.

*"Okay, I can understand all that. But how do you keep from yelling or slapping when you are really angry? When I am angry, all my good intentions seem to disappear—I lose my temper and yell. Once or twice, I've even hit the baby; it makes me feel terrible. But how do you handle anger? How do you express anger appropriately, as you say?"*

Everyone needs to learn how to handle anger—how to release anger and how to express anger. When you become very angry at your child, especially a child of this age, who may not be able to understand the reason even if you were able to explain it, you should try to control your own actions. If you feel that that is difficult for you, it is best to put him in his crib or in his room and call someone, your husband or a friend, and *tell that person* about your anger. If you are the active physical type, you may have to go into another room and jump up and down, run in place, or pound a pillow in order to release the angry energy that seems to be overwhelming you. Everyone needs to find the best way to maintain self-control and to release angry feelings. There will be many different ways, from counting to ten to going for a brisk walk. The important thing is to try not to let out all your angry feelings onto the child.

Once you have regained your self-control, then you can talk to the child in very simple terms about your anger. You can say, for example, "Pulling the leaves off the plant makes Mommy very angry." Even if the child does not quite understand, you are beginning to set the model for *verbally* expressing angry feelings.

Children need to learn that their actions cause anger, that it is normal to get angry every once in a while—and most important, that anger can be handled by talking about it. This example of how you handle and express your anger will help the child to handle and express his or her anger.

For the moment, the children are a little young to understand this fully. The important thing, however, is for the parents to begin to set this kind of pattern now. Gradually, the children will understand it—and in the meantime you will not have upset their sense of trust and growing self-esteem by overly harsh or frightening displays of anger.

■                                                                              ■

# Daily Routines: How Much Time to Spend with Children; Time Off for Parents

As the children get older, parents expect to have more free time. Parents are often annoyed to find that although their children are running around, beginning to say a few words, and, at times, even playing by themselves, the children still need a great deal of attention. The parents, especially the mothers, are disappointed not to have gained the freedom they have been looking forward to. In fact, parents with active toddlers often find they have less time and freedom, because the children are taking much shorter naps and seem to be "into everything." Are you finding your daily routines more difficult now?

*"We have our day pretty well programmed. My son is used to following me from room to room when I'm straightening up. You can believe it gets a quick going-over. But it's neat. Then we go to the park, where we meet friends. When he naps, sometimes I do, too; or I read or prepare something for dinner. When he is up, we go out again if it's nice—maybe do a little shopping. Then it's home for a bath and supper and Daddy's arrival. When Daddy comes, that is the big moment of the day for him and my chance to cook dinner. It's getting him simmered down afterward so he will sleep that takes a little doing. I enjoy the day with him. It gets a little monotonous sometimes, so I try to vary it a little, but not much, because it upsets the baby."*

*"Well, you seem to have it all working well. I wish I could say the same. I have a feeling I never get anything done. Maybe I'm not well organized, but I can't get the house neat, the laundry, shopping, and cooking done. The baby won't let me. He just wants me to play with him, or else he is climbing or doing something that takes my attention. Day after day, it's the same—it's frustrating."*

*"I used to feel that way until I began to involve my little girl in what I was doing. If I'm cooking, I put her in a high chair beside me in the kitchen, which is very small. I give her flour, water, or something so that she can do what I am doing. Sometimes that will keep her happy for quite a while and I get my cooking done."*

*"I try to do that, too. I involve my son in what I'm doing as much as I can. I put him up on the counter, where he can watch me as I work, and I talk to him. But if I try to watch television or read a book or something like that, he pesters me and wants my attention."*

## Alternating Play with Parents' Chores

Most of you seem to be having success in keeping your children occupied by involving them in household chores. However, some of you seem annoyed that you can't keep them happy while you are reading or watching television. There is a big difference: in one case, you are involved with the child; in the other you are absorbed in reading or watching TV and the child feels isolated and excluded. Children can't stand this feeling. It is understandable and reasonable that you want to relax and read or watch TV for a while. Sometimes you can put the child in your arms and say, "Mama is reading about this," and you can read aloud to him, even though he doesn't understand. Since he does not feel excluded, he may get down after a while and play with a toy. Then you can go on reading, but not for long. In another ten minutes, you may have to pick him up again. Sometimes the child may find something that really intrigues him and he may keep at it, but his attention span is very short. Children of this age are just getting to the stage when they can play alone for a short time. Eventually, they will have a longer attention span and you will be able to read longer. Then you can say, "This is reading time and Mama is reading her book. You have your book." That time will come, but it hasn't come yet for most children. Sometimes, even now, children can look at their books while you read, or they can be involved in turning the pages of their books. This is a good activity to encourage if it brings pleasure, for it leads to the enjoyment of books and reading later in life. If it is a hassle and not a pleasure, it may be counterproductive. If the child feels that reading separates him from his parents, he may come to dislike reading. This may pose problems later in school.

*"I have to admit that reading has always been very important to me, and I've been getting annoyed when my little girl interrupts me. I push her away when I'm reading. Then she cries and I can't read. Now I understand why we are both so frustrated. I think she is old enough to play alone, but she is not; she thinks I am neglecting her."*

That is precisely the situation. When one does push a child off, it produces a whining, clinging child. This is the situation we all want to avoid.

*"This business of the baby's need to be in the kitchen when I'm cooking bothers me. I want to concentrate on what I'm doing and get it over quickly. It takes so much longer with the baby there."*

The child's need to be with you is something you have to accept at this age. You can organize the situation and make it consistent by stating, "This is Mother's cooking time to make dinner for us." You may even mention all the things you are going to make. Then give the child something to do in his own space in the kitchen and say, "This is what you can cook." Give him some dough to play with if you are baking or give him a spoon and cup to mix things. The child will feel he is participating in what you are doing. Then you can play a game with him.

## *Varying Activities Within Basic Routine*

*"Most of our time is spent going to the park, and I would like to ask about other activities and the daily routine. We go to the park most of his waking hours. I wonder if he will get bored if we spend most of our time that way, but he seems happier there than anywhere else. Have I made it too much of a habit?"*

■                                                                                            ■

Your son is very active and he probably loves the freedom of the park. If you are feeling somewhat confined, it might be a good idea to vary your daily routine. It might be good to try going to a friend's house occasionally. The routine of having an afternoon activity should be continued, but the activity may be varied—going to the park, or visiting, or marketing. The park is good for at least once a day, because that gives your child a place to play with a lot of freedom and a lot of space that he doesn't have at home.

*"I wasn't sure whether he was so locked into the routine that we couldn't go anyplace else."*

It is probably a good idea to try the other things and see. You certainly could try having a friend come to visit, or you could go visiting.

*"I will do that, and maybe we could go for a bus ride."*

Yes, a bus ride or a visit to the children's zoo, if you are near one.

*"I guess my question is, 'Should I force him in the beginning into doing these things if he doesn't want to?' "*

You could give him a chance. If you do it once and he doesn't like it at first, then you can do it again and see—he may like it the second time. You do want to enlarge on the kinds of things that he likes to do. As he gets older and more verbal, you can explain the kind of outing you are going on.

*"Is it necessary to be so cautious? My child seems to thrive on new things."*

Each parent has to be able to tune in on the level of development of her own child and his or her personality. Some children need repetition of the same routine to feel comfortable and have to be gradually educated to new situations. Other children have more inquisitive personalities and welcome change.

*"This discussion makes me realize that I should be talking to my housekeeper about my child's day while I am away at work. I wonder if she is having some trouble now that he is more active?"*

It is always a good idea to talk with the substitute caretaker about the child's routines. Sometimes a person who is wonderful with little babies doesn't give enough stimulation to older children. Toddlers, as you all know, can be very tiring. Working mothers do need to take the time to find out how the child's day is changing as he or she gets older. Then there can be some continuity between weekday and weekend activities.

*"My husband and I both work full time, but we are finding some of the same difficulties on weekends. Our child seems to be with us every second all weekend long. We have no time for ourselves individually or as a couple."*

*"I am glad you brought that up, because my husband is complaining that our weekends are totally child-oriented, even though I spend all week at home."*

## Parents' Time Together

We are now talking about how much time the child needs and how much time the parents need together. Certainly, if both parents work full time, the child needs a lot of their time when they are not working. The weekends need to combine activities that will make the child feel like an important part of the family. This means spending considerable time on child-oriented activities— going to the park or playing with the child at home. If there are important family chores that need doing, then our advice is the same as for mothers at home: try to involve the child in as many of your household activities as possible. A trip to the supermarket with mother or father can be a "family time" and a learning experience for the child, as well as getting a chore done. At the market, father (or mother) can say, "We need to buy cereal. Here it is!" Often the child will recognize the package he or she is accustomed to and point it out. Or you can say, "Now we will buy applesauce. Show me the applesauce." Children will often be able to pick out the proper jar. Shopping also gives parents the opportunity to point out boxes and jars, colors such as the red or blue package, and so on. A mundane trip can be turned into a casual but effective learning experience for the child. Of course, making an early stop at the cookie section and allowing the child a choice—and an *immediate* taste—can also help to make the adventure appropriately gratifying to a toddler.

Lastly, all parents, whether working outside the home or not, are saying that the children are taking too much time. Children of this age need a lot of time. However, parents also need time for themselves. Arrangements should be made to have relatives or baby-sitters help out, so that both mothers and fathers have some time for themselves. A little time away from the child enables the parents to return to the job refreshed and invigorated, so we advise parents to arrange regular times away from the responsibilities of child rearing. This can make the difference between considering child rearing a burden or a joy.

# More on Language Development

Some of you have been expressing pleasure in your children's ability to communicate, and others seem somewhat disappointed. It is good to talk about your expectations and feelings about your children's learning to talk.

*"My son seems to be saying many things and is often annoyed with me because I don't understand him. He seems to have special sounds for certain things that I sometimes understand but often may not, because they are not clear."*

That can be very frustrating for both of you. How do you speak to him? The same way you speak to me or to another adult? You may be speaking too rapidly and not enunciating clearly. The child must hear the rhythm and the sounds clearly so that he can imitate them.

■                                                                          ■

*"Just what do you mean? I don't understand."*

Do you say, "Your dinner is now ready; come and eat it while it is hot. Mommy fixed some good hamburger and vegetables"? That's a lot of words, delivered in a quick businesslike way. The child understands the message, but he may have trouble deciding what to repeat out of all that. Instead, you could say, "Here's Joey's dinner," with a rhythm and vocal modulation. It may sound rather singsong to you, but that doesn't bother the child. In fact, he may then be able to say, "Hee, din" (meaning, "Here is dinner") or, "Want din," at some other time. Then you reply, "You want your din-ner?" so that he can hear the words clearly again. This is what I mean by not speaking too rapidly, so a child can try to imitate you. You are his model. When he jumbles words together, it may be because he hasn't been able to hear them separately and clearly.

## Encouraging Speech

*"Well, I have especially avoided speaking that way because I consider that baby talk. I was given to understand that baby talk retards speech development."*

To enunciate clearly in good English, or whatever other language is used in the home, and to speak slowly is *not* baby talk. Clear, well-modulated speech helps the child's language development. Baby talk is the repetition of a child's mispronunciations or private words. Sometimes, such talk is very endearing. When a child says "pizetti" for "spaghetti," we are tempted to repeat it. That is encouraging baby talk and it may impede the development of proper speech. It is better to recognize what the child means and then say, "Yes, you want your spaghetti."

*"The way of speaking you suggest sounds so artificial. Doesn't the baby have to get used to our speech just as it is? Before our baby came, I hated so much when I saw my friends with their new babies say, 'My itsy, bitsy, witsy honey' or some such things. I thought it was silly, and I vowed I'd never do that."*

Infants respond well to all words that parents use especially for them as terms of endearment. They recognize when a parent's tone is affectionate and when the parent is indifferent or angry. Every baby needs to hear and feel affection through the parent's tone of voice and rhythm of language. Parents have to do what comes naturally to them. If they use special words of endearment for their baby, that's fine. It is also appropriate to repeat the infants' earliest sounds; in that way, they begin to understand that verbal communication is important and valued by the parents. Repeating their sounds was appropriate for children during the first year of life. Now that they are older, it is appropriate to begin to model correct language. The terms of endearment also have to grow with the children and change to suit their levels of development.

*"What should our child be saying now, and how much does she understand?"*

Most children have vocabularies of about twenty words at twenty-one months. Some of your children have many more words; some don't know quite that many. It depends on their own maturational timetables as well as on how much speech stimulation they have had. It is a combination of the two and varies with each child.

Children of this age comprehend much more than they can express. They understand directions such as "Bring me the teddy bear" and "Where is the light?" Some may even understand a little joke; they find concrete incongruities, such as teddy bear wearing mommy's hat, very funny. They do not understand sarcasm or teasing and are very sensitive to a person's tone of voice for cues to meaning.

*"But what should the parents be doing to help the child?"*

Parents should talk to their children as much as possible and name things for them. In the house, you can name objects and make simple sentences: "The light is on" and "The light is off." You can name the foods they eat: milk, apple, orange, cookie, meat. You enunciate the word slowly and clearly. Parents can also point to parts of the children's bodies or their own bodies and name them. Whenever the child points to anything, the parent names it for her. Pointing and naming can be a wonderful game for children at this age. In that way their curiosity will be satisfied and stimulated while their vocabularies are being increased. Parents can also point to things and have the children name them; it's an occasion for parents to show pleasure and approval.

*"I have tried all that with my little fellow, but he doesn't seem to catch on. I can spend half an hour pointing to the object and say it over and over again. He looks at it but he won't repeat it. It makes me very angry, because we are a verbal family and I am so anxious to have him talk early."*

It is not necessary to sit down and have a lesson in speech. Saying the same word over and over can be tedious and boring for him as well as you. He may not be responding because your anxiety makes him anxious and inhibits him; or he may not be ready yet. A child will begin to speak on his own timetable, provided we give him models to follow in an appropriate and natural way, without pressure.

## *Talking with Toddlers*

*"It is very hard for me to talk to my baby. I'm not much of a talker. I guess I always thought that a baby didn't understand much at this age and that speech would come on its own when she understood more. Is that why my baby says so little?"*

It may be the reason why her expressive speech development has not been as fast as the other children's. Some parents talk less than others—that's their personality. Others don't realize it's important to talk with children. If parents don't speak *with* their children, their speech can be delayed. Many of us speak *to* children. We *tell* them what to do. We say, "Come here," "Stop that," "No," and "Drink your milk," but we don't talk *with* them. Some parents don't realize that "talking with" children means naming things and responding by repeating what they say in correct speech. By this we do not mean correcting their speech. If the child says, "Want pizetti," the parent should not say, "No, say *spaghetti.*" The parent should say, "Yes, I'll give you some spaghetti." In this way, the child knows that the parent has understood and is responding positively to her communication. If one says "No" every time a child mispronounces a word, this discourages speech development and sets up a negative interchange between parent and child.

A good way to talk with children of this age, in addition to the naming game, is to talk about what you are doing and about what the child is doing. For example, as you are fixing dinner you can say, "Mommy is going to cook Susie's supper. She is looking in the refrigerator. She is cooking a hamburger. She is cutting carrots. She is pouring milk into Susie's cup." In the same way, you can talk about the child's actions.

Another game for toddlers that encourages communication skills is the listening game. You can identify sounds you hear from the street: the sirens of fire engines, the honking of cars and trucks, and the sound of airplanes. Then you can encourage the child to listen for such sounds. (This game can become increasingly sophisticated and discriminating as the child gets older.)

## Nursery Rhyme Games

*"Aren't there some nursery rhyme games that would be good for speech stimulation?"*

Yes, one good one is "Here we go round the mulberry bush so early in the morning." This can be infinitely varied with simple language changes: "This is the way we wash our hands, brush our teeth, comb our hair, put on our shoes . . . so early in the morning." Another nursery rhyme game that children may begin to enjoy is "Ring around the rosy, / Pocket full of posy, / Ashes, ashes, / We all fall down." Another opportunity for conversation is while the child is swinging. Instead of standing *behind* the child, push from the front and talk about going "up" and "down," "so high," or about other things you see and hear in the park: birds, airplanes, and the like. When you begin to think of it, there are endless simple ways to engage in appropriate conversations with your children.

Of course, another excellent way to stimulate speech and language development is by looking at books with your child and naming the objects. For this age, books with only several objects on a page, or a simple story line, are best. Too many different objects or a complicated story may be too much for the child's level of concentration. *(Suggested reading for children twelve to thirty-six months can be found on pages 687–89.)* Listening to records of nursery rhymes and simple songs is also a good way of stimulating language and having fun with your child. Many children's libraries have a record section where you can get ideas for appropriate selections.

We all know that speech is important as the basis for reading and academic achievement. We must not forget that it is important for communication. At this age, children's pronunciation of words will not be perfect, but parents must try to understand and encourage their attempts at communication by constant approval. Your pleasure in their achievements is contagious—the more fun you have together with language, the more the child's language development will be enhanced.

## Toilet Training: Signs of Readiness

Now that the children are becoming more competent in using their bodies, are developing speech, and are understanding what is said to them, parents often become more concerned about toilet training.

*"I know from our previous discussion and from reading that one should not begin toilet training before the child is ready. But so many of my friends who have children my child's age are beginning training. One little girl is already trained. It makes me a little uneasy. I wonder if I'm being too lax about it."*

*"That's the attitude my mother has. She says all five of us were potty trained by one year—eighteen months at the latest, if we were slow. She thinks I'm lazy or negligent, since I'm not pushing my son. My pediatrician says the child has to be ready; but I sure am tired of carrying diapers around."*

*"I would like my son to be toilet trained by two, but I'm afraid that if I try too soon and he is not ready I will be disappointed. Then he will understand that I am disappointed and will be upset, too. I know that is not a good interaction to set up."*

Your attitude is very perceptive and sensitive. That is just what happens when parents try too soon. Our expectations in this area are usually not in keeping with the child's readiness. Very often this can be the start of a battle over training: the parents think it is time for training, and the child resists because she is not ready. The parents are disappointed; the child senses their disapproval but can't comply. The child's inability is regarded as resistance by the parents, who become more insistent and angry. The child becomes angry, and an unhappy interaction is set up between parent and child that may interfere with other aspects of their relationship. The child may view the parents as always angry and displeased with him. He may have angry feelings and also develop a sense of failure and poor self-esteem. These feelings may lead to a very unpleasant angry attitude, which the child may carry on into adult life. We want to help parents avoid this. That is why we advise parents to be careful about the way toilet training is instituted.

### Indications of Readiness

*"What are some of the indications that a child is ready for toilet training? What can we, as parents, do to help?"*

First, the child must have the understanding that everything has its proper place. You have all been teaching your children this concept, both consciously and unconsciously, as you put your groceries away or as you put their clothes and toys away. Once children understand the concept that toys go in the toy box, clothes go in the closet, groceries go in the kitchen cupboard, wastepaper goes in the basket, garbage goes in the garbage can, they will get the idea that bowel movements and urine go in the toilet. That's how they begin to be ready. That's the first step.

*"Isn't it also necessary for the parent to notice how long an interval they can stay dry?"*

Yes, that is true. When you notice that they have the ability to stay dry for two to three hours, then you know they are beginning to gain control over their sphincter muscles. That is a second indicator that they are getting ready.

*"Is it better to try to establish bowel or bladder training first?"*

It is easier to train for bowels first, because there are fewer bowel movements a day. Most people train for bowels first when they notice the baby has a regular time for bowel movements. Very few children are ready before two. Some may be ready at two years, some more at two and a half. Some are not ready until they are three years old. Our experience shows that if training is started when children are ready, they learn very quickly without a struggle.

## Appropriate Expectations

*"What should we be expecting of our children at this age?"*

Now the children are all about twenty-one or twenty-two months old. They are just learning where everything belongs. They are just becoming aware of how toilet facilities are used. Some have watched their diapers being emptied into the toilet and enjoy flushing the toilet. Some of them have regular times for their bowel movements and have long intervals with a dry diaper. They are just beginning to gain the necessary control, which depends on the maturity of the central nervous system. This ability varies with each child. There is no one age at which all children can be toilet trained.

*"What else needs to happen before they are ready?"*

A very complicated set of responses is necessary for successful training. In the first place, the child must become aware of and understand the sensation of having a full rectum or bladder. Then he must have enough language to indicate his need to the parent. He must also have the understanding of the appropriate place for depositing his stool or urine. He must have the muscle control to withhold the evacuation until he has been taken to the proper place, has had his clothing removed, and has been placed in the proper position. Then he has to be able to relax his sphincters in order to release his bowel movement or urine. In addition, there is an emotional aspect to this process. The child must *want* to give up his baby ways and follow this new procedure. He needs to have the satisfaction of being in control of his body functions.

Parents often interfere and try to control the child's body, but ultimately they cannot force the child to either eliminate or withhold on command. Such attempts result in a battle of wills between parent and child that may continue into adult life.

*"Then should we be introducing the potty chair into the bathroom yet, or is it too soon?"*

If the potty is introduced now, some children may become used to sitting on it. They may sit on it as on a chair with their clothes on, which may reduce the fear of sitting on it properly later. Other children use the potty chair as a toy and experiment with their dolls. This is also a preparatory stage. However, others push it around and just play with it, with no association as to its proper use. In that case, it is better to put it away for a few months. Then you can bring it out again and see if its proper use is better understood.

## *Fears Connected with Toilet Training*

*"My child watches me empty his diaper into the toilet with a great deal of interest. However, when I flush the toilet he often cries and gets very upset. Why is that?"*

Some children are frightened because they feel their stool is part of them; they may be afraid that they will be flushed down the toilet, too. This may also happen in the bathtub if you pull the plug while the child is still in the tub. The child becomes upset because he or she fears going down the drain, too. Children are very sensitive about their bodies, and all are fearful of bodily harm. We need to tune in to their thoughts and feelings about themselves. We need to understand their thinking, which is rather magical at this age. We need to reassure them and wait for them to take the lead rather than imposing our wishes on them before they are able to comply.

*"It's reassuring to have this discussion. I was beginning to feel like an incompetent parent because my child wasn't toilet trained."*

Your success as a parent should not be measured, by you or anyone else, by how early your child becomes toilet trained. Speech is a much more important indicator of the child's progress; and it is not appropriate to put pressure on the child to control bladder and bowels at the same time that speech is developing. Speech requires that the child be able to "let out" and express himself or herself; toilet training requires "holding in." It is usually too much to expect children of this age to accomplish both at the same time. Toilet training is a complicated physiological, emotional, and neurological process. The maturational level of the child's central nervous system is a critical factor in his or her ability to "get it all together." It is, therefore, important that toilet training be postponed until the child is developmentally ready. You will be pleasantly surprised at how easily it is all accomplished if you have the patience to wait until that time.

■                                                                                      ■

# *Manners: What Is Appropriate at This Age?*

Are you beginning to think that your children have reached the age when they should begin to learn manners?

*"While we were engaged, my husband and I would be with some of our friends who already had children, and one of the things that bothered us most was their lack of manners. It seemed to us their parents were too lax and that the children were being brought up to be brats. We vowed to each other that we would never allow that to happen if we had children. But now I realize it's not so easy, because I can't even get my child to say hello or good-bye. What are we doing wrong?"*

## *Appropriate Expectations*

The chances are that there is nothing "wrong"; your expectations from your child are simply not in keeping with her level of development. You are expecting too much social poise from a child who is not yet two. It is true that children of this age can say "Hi" and "Bye." They may say it to family members, but usually they will not greet strangers in this way on request or command.

*"I guess my expectations are too high, too. Yesterday a neighbor came to visit. The baby seemed to like her, handed her some of his toys, and then took them back. He also played 'Peekaboo' with her. When she left, we went to the door and I said, 'Good-bye,' and turned to him to say good-bye or wave. But he just leaned close to me and looked at her and wouldn't say anything. I felt so embarrassed and surprised, because he seemed to like her. I felt he was naughty and I guess he felt my disappointment, because he clung to me and wanted to be held when he normally is very active."*

It is possible that he was sorry to see her go, since he was enjoying her company. Perhaps he was expressing his feeling of disappointment at her leaving and could not say, "Stay." This is just a supposition. What I am wondering is whether your reaction indicates your concern about what the visitor might think of you as a mother. Perhaps you were more concerned about that than about how your child was feeling. Parents need to try to understand how the child perceives the episode. If they tune in appropriately to their child's level of development, parents will understand whether his or her responses are appropriate. They will feel better about their competence as parents and less dependent on the approval, or lack of approval, of neighbors.

*"Well, what is appropriate at this age? When are children ready to say hello and good-bye without a battle?"*

The age at which each child will be able to respond with what the adult considers the appropriate social grace varies greatly. At this stage, if they are beginning to greet family members or close friends, that is fine. The parent should make some positive recognition of the child's greeting so the other adult will respond to the child's remark. For example, when Johnny says "Hi," or "Bye," the parent should point out with some pleasure, "Johnny is saying 'Hi' (or 'Bye')," so that the adult also shows approval. This encourages the child and gives him a feeling of recognition and achievement. This is the positive approach.

## Parents Model Behavior

*"But what if he doesn't do that?"*

Then the parent says it for the child so that the child feels included in the interchange. He hears his parent saying, "Good-bye, Mrs. Jones," or, "Hello, Mrs. Jones." If he has the appropriate behavior modeled often enough, he will do it on his own without prodding and embarrassment when he matures sufficiently. Children should not be *badgered* about manners. Badgering only sets up resistance or cowed capitulation. Neither of these attitudes is appropriate for healthy personality development. Nor are they appropriate for the development of good manners.

*"Does this hold for thank you and please, too?"*

In general the same approach holds true. The parent models the behavior. The child learns more from good models than from verbal direction and exhortation. Often, parents do not say please, thank you, or you're welcome to each other. They consider it understood, or unnecessary, between themselves; but they do expect it of the child. It is very confusing to children when adults behave in one way but expect them to behave in another. Children are very keen observers and very sensitive to nuances of expression and tone of voice.

*"When can parents expect children to begin to respond to manners?"*

It varies for each child, depending on his or her maturational timetable and the quantity of modeling he or she has experienced. In general, children begin to respond with social manners when they are about three; but the modeling should begin as soon as they are born. Infants recognize the difference between angry and pleasant speech. They can feel the tension of unpleasant feelings when parents speak harshly to each other. Parents who speak gently and lovingly and with consideration for each other are better models. One cannot expect children to behave any better than the example their parents set.

*"Should we be teaching them table manners now? My child makes such a mess when he eats. I don't mind so much, but my husband can't stand it."*

You cannot expect children of this age to be neat eaters. They are able now to drink from a cup with some dexterity, but there still are some spills. They are managing to feed themselves with a spoon and fork, although their grip may still be with the hand fisted. Some still prefer to eat with their fingers. As they grow older and become more dexterous, parents can demonstrate how to hold the spoon or fork more gracefully. They will notice how the adults eat, and their table manners will change. If parents push table manners too early, before the child is able to respond, mealtime becomes a tense, unhappy time instead of a pleasant one.

*"Our child's way of eating doesn't bother us. We draw his high chair up to the table. We understand he doesn't have the ability yet to hold his spoon and fork in the right way. He sometimes drops the fork and picks the food up with his fingers. He always finishes before we do and wants to get down. This bothers us because we feel he should learn to stay until everyone is finished."*

You are right in wanting him to learn to wait until everyone is finished, but that is a goal that is not appropriate *now*. At this age, children should be excused from the table because they can't sit still and wait for the rest of the family to finish. Usually, children are not able to do this until they are very much older—about seven or eight years old. Children's manners and behavior are usually better *while at the table* if they are not *forced* to stay too long. It is therefore good to excuse children from the table when they are finished. When they are about four or five, they can learn to say, "May I be excused?" or "May I leave the table?" These children are still a long way from that stage; however, some parents expect it to be happening now.

*"How about their leaving the table and then coming back and seeing you eating something they want? Should you feed them what they want or tell them they have finished? Should you say, 'If you had stayed, you would have had a share, but now you can't have any'?"*

That concept is really beyond the comprehension of children of this age. It is doubtful whether it is ever appropriate, because it makes mealtime a time of conflict.

*"Should you then seat him back in his chair to eat again?"*

That depends upon what he wants. If he wants a piece of bread or a cookie that he can hold as he stands by the table with you, it's not necessary. If it's something that he wants to eat, it would seem best to seat him again.

*"Well, that approach seems reasonable, but it takes so much patience."*

Learning to eat at the table is achieved by parent repetition and modeling, by positive reinforcement rather than scolding. This is not a time to be punitive. Parental modeling of appropriate eating behavior is the best teacher.

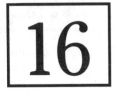

# 16

*Age Twenty-one to
Twenty-four Months*

*Highlights of Development—
Twenty-one Months*

By around twenty-one months, children's motor coordination has developed to the point that they begin to squat when they play; and they can actually kick a large ball. They can also walk up a few steps alone by holding on to the rail, but may still need the support of a parent's hand in walking down stairs. When playing with blocks, most children can make a tower of five or six small blocks before it topples. They can also assemble two or three blocks horizontally as a "train" and push it in imitation of the parent's demonstration. Most children will have become more skillful with puzzles and will be able to place several pieces. At this age, children also can begin to play with a performance box, a box with openings of different shapes in the top. They should be able to place at least the corner of the square shape in the appropriate hole. If it falls in, with or without the parent's help, the child often opens the box to take out the shape, indicating an understanding of where the shape has gone.

Most children's vocabularies have doubled from the ten words that is the average vocabulary at eighteen months. Many children will have considerably larger vocabularies; and some will be combining two or three words in simple phrases. Generally, the children are communicating more verbally. They can now ask for food and toys and other things they want; but they still pull the parents to indicate what they want or to show something of interest. They often echo two or more words that the parents have said.

While eating, the children can now handle a cup well, if they have been given the opportunity to use one. They are still eating most of their food with their fingers, even if they are beginning to master the use of a spoon.

## *Tension Situations in the Family's Day*

When the children were infants, we discussed what periods of the day and what activities caused tension for you. Are these the same now, or have things changed?

### *Late Afternoon; Dinnertime*

*"For me, it is still the late afternoon after we have come indoors and I want to get dinner ready. My son is fussy and wants me to play with him. I feel I've been with him, giving him attention all day. But no, that's not enough—he still wants me to play. That makes me tense and he gets more fussy; then we are in a hassle with each other. I want Daddy to come home and find dinner ready, with us in a good mood; but that isn't the way it usually happens."*

*"That's the time that I'm under most pressure, but not because the baby wants to play. It's because I want to have dinner ready and the baby bathed and in bed before his father comes home. My husband wants peace and quiet when he gets home. He is in no mood to play with the baby on weeknights. He loves our son, but he can only cope in the morning, when they enjoy breakfast together, and on weekends."*

*"We find that time of day bad, too. But I guess we're the cause of it. We're both bushed by then from our jobs. We would love a few minutes to unwind before taking on the children. But they're clinging even before our coats are off."*

It sounds as though late afternoon, just at dinnertime, remains a difficult time for most families. When the children were infants, the late afternoon was a bad time for them. They had difficulty with digestion and falling asleep. Mothers were tired and anxious to get them off to sleep, and the parents' tension made the situation worse. Now that the children are more active and you can be outside more, you may be planning too many afternoon activities. Many of the children are taking shorter naps, so they may be more *fatigued* at the end of the day. The parent's *timing* of the day's activities may be adding to the tension of the predinner period. In the afternoon, there is no need to stay out so long that the mother feels there is a rush to get dinner. It is better to come home a little earlier and not feel pressured.

The child who has been playing with other children in the park all afternoon or riding in his stroller while his mother does errands does not necessarily feel *he* has been with mother "all day." Mother may feel that way because she has been involved in the child's care. The child may want, *and need,* the mother's attention in one-to-one interaction. So if

■                                                                    ■

dinner has to be prepared, the child can be set up with toys or other play materials in the kitchen near mother. She can play with him at intervals, or even involve the child in helping or imitating her cooking.

For those families in which both parents work outside the home, the predinner hour can be very difficult. You have arrived home tired after a day at your jobs. Your inclination may be to put your feet up and talk to no one for twenty minutes. As you have found, this is impossible with a child. The active toddler is at your side or in your lap to *stay*. After a whole day's separation from you, the child really needs your attention and you *must* be prepared to give it. Depending on the hour the parents come home, it is generally a good idea to have the caretaker feed the child earlier. It is often hard for the child to eat in the excitement of the parents' arrival home. Whichever parent gets home first can play with the child. *Then* the other can take over for a while. After some initial attention, the child will be more willing to sit with the parents—perhaps having a snack or dessert—while they eat dinner. After dinner, the child's bedtime routines can be initiated by one parent while the other cleans up. If the parents understand the child's need for their attention, they will be less tense and can enjoy being with the child. The important thing to recognize is the child's need; that is why he or she clings and craves attention. The child is not being naughty; he is behaving appropriately for his age and demonstrating his attachment to the parents. We realize that knowing this may not take away your fatigue, but it may help you to have a more positive attitude. The more cheerfully you respond to the child's need for attention—and the more complete your attention is upon first coming home—the sooner your child will feel reassured and relaxed. As we have said, children sense your tension and become upset; so the more relaxed you can be, the happier the situation will be for all.

*"I know you are right. We try to do that. Sometimes I think I just have to get some chores done before attending to my son. It's a disaster; he cries and whines and makes us both miserable! So now I just sit down and play with him. He gets happy and calmed down and will then play in the kitchen while I fix dinner."*

*"Now I know why we're having trouble: we try to make the baby wait until we are ready to play. It's obvious to me now that he can't wait."*

That's right, he can't wait. If you understand this and willingly fill his need for your attention, you will find that a tense situation does not develop.

## When Parents Are Busy with Their Own Projects

*"What bothers me is not the predinner time, but when I try to do something for myself. Sometimes he won't let me alone when I am doing something such as washing my hair or reading the paper. He just keeps hanging on me and I think, 'Oh, God, when is this going to end?' Sometimes I stop what I am doing and play with him or I put the dryer on low and try to play; but*

*he really wants to sit on my lap and look in the mirror with me. It really throws me off."*

*"My worst time is when I try to polish my nails. My little girl always wants something or begins to putter with the polish. I know I should wait until she is asleep, but she seems to be playing all right alone. Then I think I'll manage to get it done, but it doesn't work."*

By now, we should all be tuned in to the fact that children of this age have difficulty separating from us and want to be included in almost everything we do, especially something as interesting as using bright nail polish. It's just too tempting. If you polish one of the child's nails and let it dry, that sometimes is sufficient for her to allow you to finish your nails; she will then go off to play with something else. Sometimes the noise of hairdryers frightens children and they need reassurance that it is safe for you to use it. The best solution, if one knows the child will interfere, is to postpone that activity to a time when the child is asleep or being taken care of by the father, another relative, or baby-sitter.

## When Company Comes

*"In our family most of the tension comes when we have company. I feel I need to entertain them, but the baby seems to need more attention than usual at that time. Then I find I begin to get angry at the baby and that only makes things worse."*

The children have to be included now, even more than when they were smaller. Having company is a social experience for the child, and it should be managed so that the child feels included. When the child enjoys the company, the guests will also find the child pleasing. We are all afraid that our child will be considered a "brat" and that our child rearing will be criticized. Parents can have the child help them offer cookies or fruit to the visitors. Naturally, the child should be allowed to have some herself. If entertaining takes place in the dining room, a high chair can be pulled up to the table so the child can participate, too. It is useful to set the example of offering something to the guests. It is a learning situation for the child. If parents regard the event in this way, as an opportunity for the child to learn about socialization, then the aspect of being on trial—as a hostess for the visitors—loses its tension-producing potential.

## Shopping

*"My worst moments come when I have to go to the supermarket with my son. He used to sit quietly in the cart. But now that he can walk he is not satisfied to sit in the cart; he squirms and wiggles and reaches for items on the shelf. If we pass something he recognizes or wants, he screams. If he knows the name, he shouts it out at the top of his lungs. Whether I want it or not, I have to get it and put it in the cart to quiet him down, because I hate to have everyone looking at me as though I beat him. Sometimes I'm*

*told to keep him quiet, that I don't know how to raise a child, or that what he needs is a good spanking."*

People who are not the least knowledgeable about child rearing are often the ones who have the most advice to give. Your main concern should be with your child. It can be a learning experience for him to go marketing with you. He can be told you don't need a certain food when he pulls it off the shelf. He can then be encouraged to look for something you *do* need. Soon he will learn to spot some of the items you want, and you can give him approval for that. Often it helps to buy something as a snack for the child when you first enter the store. It is not a good idea, however, to take a baby along for major weekly shopping. It takes too long. Children can't be quiet that long, and they get restless. One should shop for fewer items more often, rather than trying to do all the marketing at one time.

*"My son does fine while I'm shopping. He likes to name the things he knows. He has learned, after several experiences, which things he cannot have. But when we get in the checkout line, he gets very impatient. Then I have to give him a cracker or a piece of orange to keep him quiet."*

You seem to be coping with your son. It might also help to have a toy or two of his with you that he can play with while you are waiting. It is also a good idea to shop when the stores are least crowded, so there won't be a long wait. It takes planning to arrange things so that parents and children do not get caught in tension-producing situations.

## When Parents Are Getting Ready to Go Out

*"The thing that seems to set off problems in our house is planning to go out at night. I try to be calm and not act impatiently, but somehow or other our daughter senses there is something different about my attitude. Then she won't eat her supper as she should or get ready for bed. She senses there is something up, even before the sitter comes. She knows her and likes her, but she also knows that the sitter comes only if I am going away."*

Children are sensitive to any tension the parent feels. Unconsciously, perhaps, you hurry them a little or you've done your hair a little differently. But parents do have to go out and have time for themselves. If you go out on a regular basis, then children usually get used to it. It is a good idea to have the sitter come at times when the mother stays home and does something she wants to, and does not go away. Then the baby-sitter doesn't necessarily mean separation, but can be a friend or playmate and accepted as a good mother substitute when mother is away.

## Visits to the Doctor

*"The worst situation for us is the visit to the doctor. My daughter is very apprehensive when the doctor approaches her, because she's had to have a few shots. When she has a shot, I get upset myself; I hold her, but I can't watch."*

Visits to the doctor can be very traumatic. The parent must be as calm as possible and try to reassure the child. Usually doctors try to get the injections done quickly, and parents should be ready to give the child a big hug when it's over. If you bring a favorite toy along, you can then let the child play. Pediatricians' waiting rooms often have interesting toys and books. It's a good idea to stay for a little while so the child can play there and retain some pleasant memories of the visit.

Different children react differently to injections. We all know they hurt, but some children are more sensitive than others. The important thing is to be honest with the child. Never say, "This won't hurt," because when it does the child loses some trust in you. Instead, say, "This will hurt a little, but then we'll play with the doctor's train (or cars or whatever)." Stay as calm as you can. Your attitude will help to make a tense situation less tense.

## General Health Measures

Parents are always concerned about their children's health. Earlier, we discussed emergencies. We would now like to talk about your children's general health care.

### Infections

*"I'm afraid I'm a health nut. Whenever we are invited anywhere with our son, I try to make sure that no one is going to be there who may be ill. My friends make fun of me, I know, but I am just as careful about their children. If my child isn't well, even if it's only a cold he has had for a week, I let them know so they can decide whether to come or not. Is that being too careful and ridiculous?"*

If more people had that attitude, perhaps it would cut down on the number of infections children have. It's especially important to do that if you know your child is susceptible to colds, particularly if they are frequently accompanied by ear infections. One certainly doesn't want to expose a child needlessly to another child who is ill. However, one needs to try not to overdo this to the point of keeping a child isolated from fun and social experiences.

*"Isn't there a time when children are most contagious? So if you avoid that period, isn't it fairly safe to mingle with the others?"*

Unfortunately, during the twenty-four hours before any physical symptoms of illness appear, the child is probably the most contagious. Therefore, such contact is very difficult to prevent. If a child is doing a great deal of sneezing and coughing, however, it's well to stay at home. This is certainly true when you know that some type of respiratory or intestinal flu is going around. There is no need for a child of this age to be exposed needlessly to a bad case of flu.

■                                                                    ■

*"Speaking of flu, my sister's son just had a terrible bout with intestinal flu. He vomited a lot and had diarrhea as well. Finally, he was so listless that my sister took him to the doctor. He put the child in the hospital for intravenous feeding because he was dehydrated. What should be done to prevent that?"*

Dehydration is a serious problem, especially for children. When a child is vomiting a lot, you should consult your doctor about appropriate treatment. In most cases, doctors suggest that you give the child small quantities of fluid frequently rather than large amounts that may reactivate the vomiting.

*"When I was little, my mother believed in exposing children to all contagious diseases. When I had the measles, she put the three younger children in the same room with me to be sure they all got it, so she wouldn't have to be bothered worrying about anyone getting measles again. Was that an unwise thing to do?"*

Measles can be a serious disease. Many of the childhood diseases can have serious consequences. Not all do, but it can happen; so it is wiser to take precautions. That is why so much money and effort were invested in discovering means of producing immunizations for smallpox, diphtheria, whooping cough, polio, and measles. In fact, immunizations for all these diseases are now a routine part of your child's health care. There has been so much success with smallpox immunization in this country that vaccinations are no longer given in most instances. Although in the old days your mother's attitude was not uncommon, there is some question whether it was entirely wise to force exposure. However, the opposite is not true either: we do not have to "wrap children in cellophane" to keep them away from exposure. We believe that most children develop an increasing immunity to minor infections by the many small natural exposures that occur without anyone realizing it. We know this is an effective way to develop immunity because of the rapid spread of infection in a community that has never been exposed to a specific disease. This is perhaps the proper time to remind every parent to make certain that all immunizations are up-to-date and that you inquire at what age booster shots will be given for each disease. Even though your doctors no doubt keep a record and will remind you, it is important for parents to keep track, too, so no slipups occur.

## *Appetites; Eating*

*"I am concerned about my child's eating, in relation to her general health. I know appetites are poor in the second year compared with the first, but my little girl is approaching two and her appetite is still poor. I'm getting resigned to her small appetite, but my husband gets upset with her picky eating. That gives me the feeling that he thinks I'm a negligent mother if I don't get more food into her. Then I try to put a little pressure, but it never works."*

*"My mother thinks I'm awful because I won't sit for hours trying to get food into my son's mouth. I give him the things I know he likes. If he is hungry, he finger-feeds himself mostly. When he begins to throw his food, I take it away. He takes his milk from a cup and bottle. He gets his vitamins. Isn't that enough? Or should I do what my mother does: sit by the high chair and every time the child opens his mouth shove some food into it?"*

Children vary a great deal in their food consumption from day to day and meal to meal. Most children of this age do not eat, or do not need to eat, the portions or the variety of food offered to them. All of us, as adults, eat more than we need, and we try to make our children do the same. When a child is well, hungry, and offered food he likes, he will eat if it is offered in a pleasant atmosphere without tension and pressure. He should have a regular place that he recognizes as the place where he eats and keeps his utensils and be allowed to feed himself as much as he wants. If children like to feed themselves, this achievement should be recognized and enhanced by offering them food of a consistency that they can manage. Other children still want to be fed. Some may request help as a device to keep the parent close. If that is their *need,* it should be met cheerfully, with gradual encouragement to feed themselves.

*"Well, I just can't resist coaxing the baby to eat when there is just a mouthful or two left on the plate. Then he turns his head away and closes his mouth. That makes me so mad."*

He is telling you he is through. It is much better to remove the food without comment than to put pressure on him. If it bothers you to have food left, serve a little less. Then, when he finishes, you will both be pleased. You can express it by saying, "Good, you finished your dinner." Your comment may stimulate him to finish his dinner the next time in order to evoke that kind of response from you, instead of anger. Everyone will then be happier.

One of the easiest ways to turn a child into a poor eater is to force food on him when he is not hungry.

*"Well, isn't it necessary for children to eat in order to be healthy?"*

If the child's appetite is so poor that you are worried about his health, then the thing to do is to consult your doctor. Let the doctor decide whether the child is malnourished and what ought to be done about it. Usually, the child is gaining weight, growing, is active and happy, and the doctor will find nothing wrong. If he finds that the child's poor appetite is due to something organic, he will prescribe the appropriate measures.

*"Well, suppose there is nothing wrong, but your child is a poor eater and that upsets you?"*

Children who are poor eaters are usually more stimulated to eat if their parents pay little or no attention to what they are eating. It is best to eat your own food and express your enjoyment of it. In this way, you give the child a good model to follow. This procedure gives mealtimes an association with pleasure rather than with an unpleasant badgering to eat. The child, if hungry, is more apt to follow that parental example than to use the mealtime as a means of showing resistance to parental pressure. That is a trap to avoid. One very good way to overcome the situation is to place food on the parents' plates but not on the child's. When the parents begin to eat, obviously enjoying the food, a child will usually notice his empty plate and ask for his food.

*"When that lucky moment happens, should you then fill his plate and show how pleased you are?"*

By no means. The best approach is to give the child a very small amount. If that small amount is finished and he asks for more, pleasantly offer another small amount. Don't overwhelm him with attention and praise; just recognize verbally that he finished. Say, "That's nice," or, "Good," and go on with your own meal. When this procedure is followed, most children begin to eat and enjoy meals with their parents.

*"Our child never has dinner with us because his daddy comes home too late. What can I do instead?"*

Since he doesn't eat with the family at dinner, it might be possible for you to sit with him at breakfast or lunch and follow the same procedure. During the weekend, when his father is home, you can try to do it. Make sure that his daddy understands the attitude you are trying to convey instead of insisting that the child eats.

*"My child won't ever taste anything new. He just sticks to two cereals, chicken and lamp chops, carrots and rice, apples or bananas. He will never touch orange juice or hamburgers or string beans, many things other children like. He drinks his milk; he will take yogurt—but that's it. Is there anything we should do?"*

That sounds like a well-balanced diet. Since he enjoys his food, and his doctor thinks he is progressing well, I would be content. It seems that there are some children who are not venturesome; they do very well and do not tire of the same foods. Children don't need as much variety as we think. Some children are found to be allergic to the very foods that parents are trying to persuade them to eat. The child feels innately that they are not right for him. So it is best to respect the child's food tastes; he *may* really know best.

In general, there is too much fussing and competing between parents about how much and how many things their child will eat. For small children, variety may not be the "spice of life" that it will be when they are adults; yet many of these children will grow up to be gourmet eaters, so there's no need to worry now.

*"Shouldn't children of this age be eating three meals a day?"*

When you say three meals a day, you are thinking of simulating adult habits. There is some question whether even for adults three large meals a day is really healthy. More recent thinking is that five or six small meals are more readily digestible and put less strain on the digestive system and heart. There is also some question whether the custom of eating our largest meal at night is a good custom. So the answer to your question is that eating less at the designated mealtimes and having a small snack in between is more suitable for this age and, perhaps, for all of us.

# *Children's Need for Appropriate Approval and Disapproval*

## *Limits and Approval*

Now that the children are getting older and doing more, are you finding that you are spending more time saying "No" and disapproving of their activities rather than giving approval?

*"My son is into everything. I am afraid most of our comments are 'No' and 'Stop that'—often for his own or others' safety."*

It is very important, of course, to disapprove of the activities that are harmful to the child or another person. The child needs to learn that certain activities are dangerous, and the parents are obligated to teach this. In general, however, parents are often more inclined to dramatize their disapproval than to emphasize their approval. They just accept what the child does that is right, without letting the child know of their approval. The child needs to get a clear message of both what is approved and what is not approved. Unfortunately, many parents are inconsistent about this. One day a parent may feel fine and therefore is not bothered by a particular activity such as the child's loud motor noise when rolling a car along the floor. On another day the mother is under some stress and the sound bothers her, so she scolds the child for making the same sound. The child's activity is actually appropriate, but it just doesn't suit the mother that day.

*"Well, isn't it normal for parents to be able to cope one day and not be so in control another day?"*

It seems to be all too common, but it gives mixed messages to the child. The inconsistency confuses him. He doesn't understand that he is being restricted because of the parent's *mood*—that it is only all right to make that sound when his parent is in a good mood. We cannot expect a child of this age to make that distinction. If such changes in parental mood are occasional and the parent is usually consistent, then a few instances of inconsistency won't create problems. If the usual situation is one of such inconsistency, then problems are created. The child becomes either inhibited and afraid of the parent's changes of mood or confused and irritable, because he doesn't know what to do. He becomes a "spoiled" child who acts like a "brat" or an ingratiating child who tries always to please. None of these responses is desirable, because it does not lead to healthy personality development and good coping mechanisms in the child.

*"Isn't it putting an awful lot of responsibility on the parents to expect them to be consistent all of the time?"*

Of course it is. Being a parent is a big responsibility. Consistency is very difficult to accomplish in any field, but it is especially important in the rearing of children. No one is perfect; we cannot expect parents to be consistent all the time. But we should try to be as consistent as possible with our approval and disapproval because of its importance in the child's personality development. It is from the consistent recognition of what the child does right and consistent limitation of disapproved activities that the child learns the cultural norms of her family and the society in which she is growing up. This learning by outside control is the precursor to the conscience, or control from within (self-control).

## Appropriate Approval Is Not Spoiling

*"But doesn't it spoil children to always show approval?"*

When we are very young, we need to learn what is right and what is not right. We can learn this only if our parents and other caretakers label for us what is approved and what is not. This recognition of appropriate behavior and limitation of inappropriate behavior has to be repeated until the child learns which is which. Since human beings seem to thrive on approval (we all prefer that to disapproval), it is better to emphasize approval. Then the child will get a sense of positive recognition and will strive for that. Such recognition also develops a healthy feeling of self-worth and self-confidence.

*"It seems to me that children don't really care whether you approve of them or not, as long as they get your attention. Don't children act up just for attention? That's what my mother says."*

Children do want recognition. They can't stand to feel excluded. They will demand attention to feel included. If their appropriate behavior gets no response, children may then do something "naughty" to get attention. When a child needs to do something that's disapproved in order to get attention, a very negative cycle of parent-child relations, which we call the "angry alliance," is set up. The responses of parent and child to each other become more and more negative. To get satisfaction and pleasure this way also leads to what has been termed masochism, or getting pleasure from pain. This is not a positive personality pattern. So when people say, "He's only trying to get your attention," indicating that the child should be ignored, they do not understand the real significance of the situation. They do not understand that the child needs *appropriate* attention.

*"Won't paying attention to them all the time make it difficult later on? People outside the family won't pay that much attention. I don't want my child to grow up always seeking attention."*

Most of us *are* annoyed by attention seekers. We must understand how people get that way in order to avoid it in our children. Children need recognition and attention. If they receive appropriate attention *now*, they begin to develop a sense of self-worth and self-confidence. If they are denied appropriate attention now, when they need it, they continue to seek it, sometimes in very unsubtle and annoying ways, as adults.

## Timetable for Learning to Accept Limits

*"It seems that we are expecting too much from them. We want them to accept limitations easily. How much time does it take? When should we be expecting some response to our limit setting and approval?"*

Learning to accept limitations varies with each child. For some it comes earlier; for others, it may take until they are much older. By three years of age most children understand the common limitations of daily life, but parents want it right away. We remember our parents' demands, and our friends and neighbors keep telling us how the children should behave. That is why we expect so much from our children.

*"Just how much is reasonable for us to expect at this age? For instance, my husband has a very complicated and expensive stereo set in the den, where our son plays most of the time. It's a big temptation for him to touch it. That's the one 'No' that he can't seem to grasp. He goes up to it and looks at me, but still fiddles with it. Am I expecting too much from him to leave it alone?"*

At this age, he recognizes that the stereo is "forbidden territory." He looks back to see if you will take him away or keep him from touching it. He does not yet have the control to leave it alone himself. To develop that self-control may take him another six months or a year. So you have to assist him by giving him a substitute activity in which he can discharge the need to turn knobs on and off. His own toy record player or a car that winds may be a successful substitute. He may protest, but that's healthy and normal. Finally, he will accept the limitation. When he does, you must show recognition and approval.

*"Before, you mentioned the stages that children go through as they learn self-control. Could you just go over it again?"*

At first, when they are between eight and twelve months old and you say "No," they stop whatever they are doing momentarily. That gives the parent time to go to them, move them away, and give them something else to do. During the next stage, which may last from twelve months to about two and a half years, they know in advance what is a no-no but they look back for help in stopping. Next, they may go up to a forbidden object, say "No" to themselves, but still touch the object unless they have parental help. Around three years of age, many are able to say "No" to themselves and not touch the forbidden object—unless it is exceedingly tempting. Some children achieve this level even later. Each child has a different maturational timetable for this, too.

## Discipline Versus Punishment

We were talking earlier about getting a child to respond to limitations, about the importance of appropriate approval as well as disapproval. Are you finding that you are saying "No" less and showing more approval? Do some of you feel that you need to use some physical reinforcement to be more effective?

*"I know from my experience with my son that by limiting him consistently he doesn't do the things I minded so much in the park, such as taking toys away from other children. I give back the other child's toy, and he now accepts his own. It is getting much easier. I see other mothers in the same situation hit their children. They think I'm nuts because I don't."*

There are many parents, perhaps most, who were brought up that way. That is their image of appropriate discipline to prevent children from becoming "brats." They feel that they must control the child, or the child will control them. They follow the model set by their own parents.

*"Well, what harm will it do? They seem like nice people, and they seem to get results."*

*"I don't think they get results. I have a neighbor who is always slapping her child. Each day she seems to hit harder, but he still does things to upset her. As a matter of fact, I think he is the kind of child you mean when you say a child is a brat."*

### Slapping

Slapping or spanking may relieve the parent's anger, but it generally does not evoke the kind of response from the child that the parent desires. Most children who are hit do not become sweet and obedient; they become sullen or angry or frightened. When they sulk, hit back, or cry, the parents become even more angry. The next time, the parent uses a little more force—in some instances, the parent may lose control and become abusive. That is one of the dangers of getting this cycle going.

■          ■

*"The baby whom I bring to the center is my second child. I know better now how to cope with him. My daughter is four years older, and I have to admit that I more than scolded her. I am sure that my treatment of her made her afraid of me. When I call her name, she seems to cringe, as though she expects to be hurt. Her expression always seemed to be sullen and sad. Nothing seemed to please her. Even in nursery school, the teachers talked to me about it. Now I understand how I should treat her. We are beginning to get better results—sometimes a smile, but there is still a long way to go. I can't emphasize enough what a difference it makes to treat children with patience and understanding, instead of hitting all the time."*

Here we have a real-life example of what hitting can do in personality development. You have seen one type of outcome: the sullen and depressed child.

*"That was the outcome with one child. Isn't it possible that it would not affect all children in the same way? Maybe that is just the way her daughter was born to be?"*

It is true that each child has a different endowment at birth, so not all would respond in the same way to the same treatment. We don't know the endowment of each child, but we do know that children are very responsive to the care they receive. If they are given consistent, patient, loving care, children have a better chance to develop into caring adults and to develop their maximum potential than if they are beaten. It has been well documented that children brought up without this kind of caring relationship cannot form the caring relations with others that lead to healthy personality development. Without caring for others, these children become the delinquent, socially destructive, addicted, conscienceless population that is now victimizing our society—but they themselves were victims of neglect and/or abuse.

*"Is that the only outcome we can expect? Are there no other consequences?"*

Yes, there are some who, instead of becoming angry, sullen, depressed, or actually destructive, become so inhibited that they lose all ambition and drive to accomplish, even though there is nothing wrong with their intellectual endowment. Their talents are wasted. Because they have always met with negative response and punishment, they give up and don't try. They have never tasted the joy of approval. We have all seen adults like that. They seem to be intelligent and yet they never seem to achieve anything. They never seem to find the thing they want to do. This is not the outcome we want for our children, either.

*"This all sounds so scary. It makes being a parent such a responsibility. When I've seen my son about to do something at the other end of the room, I call to him to stop. When he doesn't, then I become angry and holler very loud. That usually stops him, but I feel myself getting very angry when he repeats the same thing another time. My impulse is to grab him and hit*

*him—not hard, but just so he will know I mean business and remember. That's what my mother tells me to do. She thinks I'm spoiling him unless I hit him."*

Certainly, being a parent is a great responsibility, one of the most important responsibilities of life. No one claims that carrying out our responsibilities is easy; but when one is effective in child rearing, there is no greater reward.

One of you spoke about the inclination to hit your child if he didn't remember to respond appropriately the second time. You are following the model of the way your parents brought you up, thinking that it is the right way. Parents often think slapping or spanking will hasten the child's appreciation of what is right and wrong. We forget that the child's immature nervous system does not respond and store messages with the efficiency of the adult's. There is, instead, a long lag before a message to stop gets to the appropriate centers of control in the child's brain and is translated into action. Slapping the child actually jams the overloaded nervous system and often makes it harder for him to respond promptly and appropriately. In addition, it gives the child a negative model of behavior. At some later time, the child will try to slap the parent or another child.

*"If a child slaps you, shouldn't you slap him back to teach him a lesson?"*

If you do that, you will be teaching the child to *slap* rather than *not to slap*, because you are providing and reinforcing a behavior model. Also, slapping the child back will only aggravate an already tense situation and may seriously damage the parent-child relationship.

## Spanking

While we are talking about slapping, we might as well talk about spanking. Spanking a child to "teach him a lesson" does indeed teach a lesson: that when one is *bigger* and *more powerful,* one can hit another person and get away with it. We have seen in our groups here that the children who were spanked tend to hit others to settle their differences. Those who have been restrained verbally in a way appropriate to their age tend to settle their differences verbally.

We are not saying that an occasional slap will create a violent or overly submissive child. None of us is perfect, and there are times when babies and children can be exceedingly trying, usually just at the times when we as adults are tired or upset ourselves. If we realize the bad effect physical punishment can have, however, we can try to control our own actions. All of us have to learn how to handle and dispel our own anger. No one should feel guilty about having angry feelings. They are a natural part of our human makeup, but we all need to help each other learn how to release our angry feelings appropriately. *(See pages 417–20 for discussion on how to handle anger.)*

■                                                                                              ■

*"That explanation makes a lot of sense. Perhaps, if everyone used this approach, there'd be less violence."*

We believe that it could make a big difference. There is another point that needs clarification. One of you said you *called* across the room to get your child to stop doing something. You expect to control your child's activity from a distance. That does not work with children of this age. Often they are so absorbed that they do not hear, or do not understand, your prohibition. The parent must go to the child as quickly as possible and show disapproval of what he is doing, immediately giving him a substitute activity. Then overtly show your approval and pleasure about the new activity. This is how the child learns to use an approved outlet for his impulse. He learns what he *can* do instead of being hit to a standstill, to put it a little harshly.

All parents get tired and out of sorts at times and occasionally use measures they don't approve of themselves. At these times, parents feel pushed too far. An occasional explosion may upset a child temporarily, but the hurt can be mended by talking about it and finding something pleasant to do together. What we are concerned about is using physical punishment as the usual form of discipline, so that it becomes the pattern of life for that child.

*"Does a child nearly two years old understand when we continue to be angry long after the event? A friend of mine does that. If her child misbehaves, she will not smile at him or answer except in an angry tone for hours after the episode is over."*

A child of this age can't understand the reason for the continued anger after the episode is over. He can't remember the episode and sometimes he doesn't fully understand the reasons for the parent's anger in the first place. That is why it is so important to show disapproval *at the time,* substitute another activity, and show approval for it, repeating the same procedure each time that behavior occurs until the child learns.

## Consistency of Limits

*"What happens if parents do things in different ways? What bothers me may not bother my husband, so I seem to be the strict one and he comes out looking like the lenient one."*

For each child the number of repetitions needed to learn about limits differs. Each parent has to get to know and understand his or her child, and both parents need to apply the same limits for the same behavior. If one is lenient and the other strict, that confuses the child. The results may be a whining, irritable child, the kind that is referred to as a "spoiled child" or a "manipulative child." This child, knowing the parents have differing ways of handling a situation, will try out each one to get something that he wants. But he will not feel secure or happy in that situation, and neither will the parents.

∎                                                                        ∎

*"Isn't agreement between parents very hard to achieve?"*

It is indeed difficult for parents to agree all the time and to be consistent, but this is one of the learning experiences of parenthood. Parents must be able to communicate with each other and agree on their procedures. They should try not to correct each other in front of the child. This, too, leads to confusion and disparagement of one of the parents, which also upsets the child.

# Family Rivalries: Everyone's Need for Attention

Rivalries within the family can cause tension and interfere with the family's functioning in a harmonious and satisfying way. There can be all kinds of rivalries in any one family. We have talked about the rivalry of children with siblings and other children for parental attention and toys. Some of you may have similar feelings regarding the way others in the family relate to the child or to you.

## Rivalries with Grandparents

*"I suppose it is childish of me, but ever since the baby came it has seemed to me that my parents are more concerned about my baby than about me. It seems as though they've sort of forgotten about me. They always seem to be all eyes for the baby. Of course, I'm pleased that they care so much, but I guess I still want to be their child too—and I'm kind of jealous of my own child."*

It is good that you can recognize that feeling. Perhaps it indicates some of your unresolved needs that you could not discuss objectively with your family if you found the suitable moment. If that is not possible, and if you cannot feel that the attention paid to your child is in a way attention to you, perhaps discussing it here will help.

*"It's funny you should say that. My parents give me the feeling that I'm still a child and couldn't know how to take care of the baby. When they come, they compete with me in taking care of the baby. My mother, especially, tries to get the baby to enjoy the way she plays with him and acts as though I just don't throw the ball the right way to him or read the stories with the right expression."*

*"I think my husband's parents do a little of that, too. But what both my husband and I mind most is that when we go to their house, they won't allow us to set limits. They always say, 'Another cookie won't hurt,' or 'Let him stay up a little longer'—things like that. Then when we take him home, he acts as though we are cruel parents and only his grandparents treat him right. Aren't they spoiling him?"*

It seems that grandparents do cause feelings of inadequacy or rivalry in different ways. It seems that you are having feelings about these situations that may be interfering in your relations with them and your child. It is good that you can talk about it. Of course, most grandparents show a lot of concern about their grandchildren, sometimes to the exclusion of their own children. They also have a great deal of difficulty in relinquishing their parenting roles and continue to treat you as children. They show you how to raise your children, just as they showed you what to do when you were little. It is well to remember that many grandparents still see their children as children and have a hard time accepting that they are grown up and now competent to be parents themselves. Grandparents often indulge their grandchildren by giving them extra treats. Children thrive on special treatment like that occasionally. It doesn't really hurt them if it is an occasional treat and not a daily undermining of parental discipline. In a day or two, they "recover" from a visit with grandparents. They eventually get to know that there are some extra treats at grandma's and what is expected in their own home, if the pattern is followed consistently. We must recognize that in some families it is just the opposite: the grandparents are more severe disciplinarians and consider the parents too lenient. So one has to cope with each situation and try to establish some consistency for the child.

## Rivalries Between Parents

*"I have a feeling of need for attention, or recognition, not so much from my parents or in-laws, but from my husband. Ever since the baby came—and he is now almost two—my husband's main concern has been our son. If our son hasn't run to greet him the minute he opens the door at night, he gets sort of tense and wants to know where he is. When he sees the baby, he sweeps him up in his arms and they cuddle. I'm lucky if he turns to me and says hello."*

Many parents have these feelings. Often a parent will wish for recognition but suffer in silence until the issue is magnified out of proportion. It is common for a new baby to take up the interest of the father. However, the mother must not shrink back into the kitchen and just let it go on. She must take some initiative and be at the door to greet her husband and try to reinstate his attention and affection on a new level. She can at least say, "Now it's my turn. I'm glad you're home," after the baby has been greeted. That's usually all it takes in a normal situation.

*"But it's not the same as before. The minute my husband puts his arm around me, the baby tries to butt in. So we include him, too."*

It is normal for the child to want to be included, and that should happen. However, Daddy can say, "First, I'll kiss you, then Mommy, then we'll all have a hug," or something to that effect.

*"You know, I've been listening to all this and thinking about our situation. I'd guess that if my husband were here, he would say that in our family it's*

■                                                                    ■

*just the opposite. I think he feels that I have left him out and that all I seem to be concerned about is the baby. At first, he seemed involved, too; but now he just acts as though the baby is mine, and he has little to do with him unless the baby actively involves him in something. Then my husband seems pleased and gets involved."*

You are probably right: your husband is feeling left out and hasn't been able to discuss it with you. It is not an unusual situation. If the wife recognizes this feeling, it can usually be corrected. Some women need to be reminded that their husbands need attention, too. It is best when parents can enjoy the baby together. When one parent feels left out and this feeling is overlooked, the situation can lead to serious consequences, even to the dissolution of a marriage. This result can usually be prevented by dealing with the problem appropriately. In any situation, it is important to be aware of the other's feelings and try to understand how both parents and children are affected and feel about what is happening in their lives.

## Rivalries with Caretakers

*"One problem that hasn't been mentioned yet is the problem of a working mother who comes home and finds her child so involved with the care-taker—in my case, it's her grandmother—that I feel a little jealous and don't seem to be able to cope with it. If it were a maid, I could change maids and break up this love affair; but it's my mother, and I need her help."*

One is very fortunate when one's mother can take care of the child. It is important for the child to establish an involved, close relationship with one substitute caretaker—in this case, the grandmother. However, that doesn't mean the mother needs to be left out. She must establish her own special role with her child. When she comes home, the mother should not try to take over what the grandmother does, but do something different with the child. She should have special games that only she plays with the child.

Even if one is not lucky enough to have a grandparent act as the substitute caretaker, an employed person can establish a warm relation with the child. Such a person is to be cherished, because she is fulfilling a very important role in helping the child to form a stable, trusting relationship with another. This sense of trust will help the child in adult life to form good relationships with his own family. Constantly shifting caretakers is detrimental to the child, because these interrupted relationships interfere with the process of forming binding relations. This insecurity puts an even greater burden on the working parent than the rivalry that might result if the caretaker forms a close bond with the child.

*"I think I have a different kind of rivalry problem: it is with my husband and the way he plays with our son. I'm with him all day, giving my all. The minute my son hears his father's key in the door, he drops me like a hot potato and I feel rejected. Is there something wrong with me?"*

The situation you describe is quite common. The interpretation of many mothers is that the child prefers the father. The child may prefer the father *at that moment* because he is a new face at the end of the day. The child looks forward to the way he plays with him. This attitude is desirable, because most children in our society see their fathers so little. It does not mean the child prefers father over mother. *Parents are partners.* Each has an important place in the child's life. In each family, parents fulfill their roles according to their own personalities and the family's situation and needs. In no two families will these roles be alike, nor should they be.

## Spoiling Versus Gratification

The older the children get, the more verbal and definite they become in expressing their desires. Parents are generally pleased with this increase in the children's ability to express themselves. The children are now easier to understand; there is less guesswork. What they need, want, or would like to do are often things that parents can easily satisfy. At times, however, children's requests cannot or should not be gratified. Parents often have a great deal of difficulty about responding to their child's requests. Do you feel that you are "spoiling" if you acquiesce more often than you refuse?

*"That's one of the main things my husband and I argue about. He feels that I am too lenient. I say 'Yes' to as many things as I feel are right. My husband thinks that is spoiling. He is strict and has a tendency to say 'No.' If I'm sorting the laundry and my son comes up to me and wants to play ball with me, I'll stop for a minute and play with him. If he goes over to my husband while he is reading the paper or watching a ball game, he'll say, 'No, not now. I'm busy'—and that's that. My husband says I spoil him and am getting him to expect that his every wish will be gratified."*

*"In our house, it is just the opposite: I'm considered the strict one. I'm the one who says to my son, 'No climbing on the sofa,' because I'm afraid he will fall. My husband comes home from work and says, 'Ah, let him be. I'm here.' My husband just doesn't understand that when he's not there and I'm out of the room, the baby may climb and fall. The baby doesn't understand it's okay to climb only if Daddy is there. But my husband thinks I'm inhibiting him by not letting him climb."*

It is evident that there is a great deal of confusion about gratification and spoiling. It seems to cause problems between parents and between generations in many families. Probably the first thing that needs to be taken into account is the child's age and stage of development. Right now, we are discussing children who are not yet two years old. What are their needs? What is their understanding and ability to delay gratification?

At this stage, children should be emerging from the stage when they needed instant gratification of physical needs, such as hunger, to a period in which they are learning to delay gratification for longer periods. Parents should be trying to help the child make this transition. It has to be done in small steps. The mother who understands her child's developing capacity to wait can help the child to delay gratification.

In the case of the child who interrupted his mother to play for a moment, the mother understood the child's need to have some involvement with her. So the mother stopped and responded to his need before going on with her chore. The father, in that case, didn't recognize the legitimate need of a child of this age to feel involved with, and not excluded by, the parent. The mother wasn't spoiling the child; she was being *appropriately* responsive.

In the case of the climber, the mother has a legitimate fear of the child's falling, but she also knows her husband's attitude. These parents should calmly discuss their different opinions. They must come to an agreement either that daddy will uphold the mother's limits or that the child will learn that climbing is something he can do *only* when daddy is there. In fact, it may become an activity that he looks forward to sharing with his father. These children are getting old enough to associate certain activities with each parent. From early infancy, they have been experiencing the differences in the way each parent held them, talked to them, fed them, comforted them, and played with them. At this age, climbing and jumping are motor activities that most children are beginning to practice. The attitudes exhibited by the mother and father, in this case, are both right. These activities should be encouraged and not inhibited; but they must be safely channeled and monitored by the parents.

## What Is a "Spoiled" Child?

*"I now have a clearer understanding of what is meant by age-appropriate gratification. But what is spoiling?"*

A "spoiled child" is one whose needs have not been appropriately met or one whose needs have been inconsistently met. One day the parent will play; the next day, in a similar situation, the parent will refuse. One day, jumping and climbing will be allowed; the next day these activities will be inhibited. Sometimes snacks are allowed before a meal; on another day they are not. This inconsistency confuses the child, because he doesn't know where he stands. He can't learn whether his requests or activities will result in approval or disapproval. This insecurity regarding the parents' responses often causes the child to become cranky and whiny. After much fussing the child may get what he wants. Usually he can't recognize that he has been gratified because such "gratification" often comes from frustrated parents in a grudging way. This child has not had the experience of consistent, appropriate gratification and limitation. When parents learn how to handle these situations consistently, the child will begin to respond better and the whole family atmosphere will be considerably more pleasant and rewarding.

*"What I refer to as spoiling is giving a child everything he asks for. That's what happens when he goes to Grandmother's house: she lets him have as many cookies as he wants and he does not have to nap if he doesn't want to. When he comes home, I have to spend several days getting him back into his regular routine."*

An occasional break in a child's routine doesn't spoil him. He soon gets back to the routine of the standards set at home. If he visits Grandma's home on a regular basis, he will learn what is appropriate behavior there and what is expected at home. Children can learn that different people expect different things—that prepares them, in fact, for the world outside the family. The way parents help children to cope with these differences is by their own consistent support, by their patient teaching of the limits. This support gives the child the sense of security and self-confidence that will enable him or her to cope with the "hard world" outside the family.

## Development of Self-confidence

*"I'm glad you mention that. My husband thinks that we must treat our son tough because it's a tough world, especially for a Hispanic child. You are saying that it is important for the family to be supportive, not tough, so that the child develops self-confidence."*

That's right. The world is tough in different ways for most children. We want our children to become competent adults so they can cope with the different adversities that they encounter in life. Children learn to cope best when they are helped to develop self-confidence. Parents teach this not by being tough and threatening, but by satisfying their reasonable needs and desires, recognizing their achievements, and setting consistent limits. Treating them harshly to toughen them will not enhance their ability to cope and will set the example for hostile, aggressive relations with others.

## Children Need Attention—Not Gifts

*"What about the child whose parents give her every toy or game she wants, plus more? She has so much that she doesn't play with any of it. She just flits from one thing to another, acts bored, and doesn't know what to do."*

Material overindulgence often occurs in families in which parents have little time for children and try to make up by buying them material satisfaction. What children *really need* is more communication with the parents and fewer toys. The child you speak of needs *attention* from her parents; instead, she gets toys.

## Legacies from Parents' Own Upbringing

*"That is one extreme. My experience was the opposite. I was brought up in a household where we did not dare ask for anything. We had to wait until it was offered. My parents were exceedingly strict with all four of us. I think that because of that my tendency is to be very lenient. My husband accuses*

*me of spoiling. I think he is too strict. So we often disagree about giving in to our son."*

In some instances, we unconsciously follow the example of our parents; in other cases, we consciously avoid repeating their pattern. There's quite a difference between gratifying a child's every wish and responding positively when it is appropriate. We should make a conscious effort to respond appropriately to each child instead of responding as though we are still trying to correct our parents' treatment of *us*.

*"I think I've fallen into that trap, but in a somewhat different way. I think I am stricter with my child than I would be if I didn't feel that I had to show my mother, who is a frequent visitor, that I'm in control. I guess I am still reacting to my feelings about my mother. She was very strict; in order to get praise from her, I had to be a perfect child."*

It sounds as though you are still trying to get your mother's approval by acting toward your child as you believe she would consider right. This is a very common situation. Sometimes, when we feel we were unable as children to satisfy our parents, we try as adults to satisfy them by treating our children as they treated us—even though it may not be the best way and will only perpetuate feelings of inadequacy.

In general, we do not have to worry about spoiling our children by fulfilling their dependency needs. They are not yet two years old. By our consistent and appropriate satisfying of those needs and our consistent limitations when they are necessary, our children will develop a sense of trust in us and a sense of security in themselves that will help them become competent, likable children, and not "spoiled brats."

## Appropriate Games and Toys; TV

Are you beginning to find that your children are getting bored with their toys and are no longer interested in the games that you have been playing together? Are you finding new things to do with them?

*"I am so glad that we are going to talk about this. I have completely run out of ideas. My son is happy outside where he can run around, but on a rainy day we both go crazy indoors."*

*"We were having the same problem. Then a week ago, my mother arrived with some rubber figures of animals and people she bought at Childcraft. My daughter loves them. She plays by herself or with us."*

*"I was having a problem with my son banging on the furniture with his blocks, so I got one of those benches with pegs you pound with a hammer. He will spend about ten minutes at a time banging on that. He'll probably get bored soon, he uses it so much; but it's just perfect right now."*

## New Activities and Toys

The children are ready now for new activities and toys. Both of the suggestions that have just been made are good ones. The rubber figures will be a source of entertainment and learning for several years because the child will play more and more sophisticated, imaginary games with them—imitating family situations or situations that take place in school. There are also sets of both farm and zoo animals. Playing with them can be enhanced by using plain cardboard blocks that children can build into houses for themselves or for their toys. Children may also like nesting boxes that they can begin to fit inside one another or stack up like towers. They will soon be ready for the beginning set of (large) Lego pieces as well as jumbo beads for threading and stringing and a shoelacing toy. A performance (shape-sorting) box with pieces of different sizes and shapes is an appropriate toy for this age. There are many variations of this toy, including a postbox and a lockbox. Other good toys are puzzles with a limited number of pieces. Puzzles that have little knobs on the pieces are easier for children of this age to manipulate.

*"All these toys sound great, but they are all so expensive. Aren't there some things one can make at home?"*

There are a number of household items that can double as children's toys and that often amuse children more than expensive toys. Most children enjoy playing with plastic, wood, and metal spoons and pots and pans with lids. An old purse filled with odds and ends such as combs, old compacts, necklaces, and bracelets will often entertain a child for hours. Plastic jars with screw tops are also good for play and for increasing finger coordination. From this age on, children will enjoy cardboard boxes of all sizes. Large boxes can become houses that they play in; smaller ones can become trains and cars that can be set up in a row. Instead of buying pull toys, you can make your own from a shoe box and string.

All children love playing with water. While you are in the kitchen, you can fill the sink, cover your child's clothes with a plastic apron, and let her play with kitchen utensils such as a funnel, measuring cups, muffin tins, empty plastic squeeze bottles, sponges, or plastic containers. The household items that make interesting playthings are endless in number, once you start looking around you; and this manipulation of objects is a great learning experience for your child.

*"One rainy day I amused my son with an empty egg carton. He enjoyed putting small objects such as beads and spools of thread into the compartments. When there was something in every one, he closed the lid. Then he opened it and took them all out."*

*"Another toy that is not expensive and that my daughter loves is a plastic telephone. When I am on the phone, she gets hers. She doesn't talk yet, but she still likes to copy me."*

■           ■

Yes, a plastic telephone is a very good toy, not only to keep the child amused while you are on the phone but to encourage verbal communication. You can begin to have conversations with her as she holds her toy phone.

*"Another good toy is the Busy Box with gears, bells, and bolts to screw. Our son will accept that as a substitute when we take him away from the stereo."*

*"What about music? Can't we begin doing musical activities with the children now?"*

There are a number of good children's records of nursery rhymes and songs. Children will begin to sing along with the record or with the parent's singing. Children enjoy parents' singing, no matter how off-key. You can get some bells for the child's wrists, so that she can make music herself while she listens. Some children like beating on a drum; drums can be made from a coffee can or oatmeal carton. Children also like to bang two metal pot covers together as they listen to music or dance or march around. Some children may also be interested in playing with a xylophone.

## Art Activities

*"Can they do some painting?"*

It may be a little early for some children to handle paints and a paintbrush, but finger painting is appropriate at this age. It is particularly fun for the child when the parent joins in. A less messy art form is drawing with crayons. Many parents don't let their children draw with crayons because they are fearful for their walls or furniture, but these children should be having the experience of drawing *with parental supervision.* Soon the children will be ready to use "play dough," which can easily be made at home. (The recipe is: 3 parts flour, 1 part salt, and 1 part water. Food coloring can be added to make different colors.) Homemade play dough can be kept about ten days in an airtight bag in the refrigerator. Finished products can be dried in the oven or simply out in the air. The children will enjoy creating varieties of lumps. Don't expect fine art at this age!

## Outdoor Activities

*"We're okay indoors, but in the park my child is running, jumping, and climbing so much now, it scares me."*

Children of this age are much more physically active. They are beginning to climb more, and the playground slide suddenly looks very high when one's small child is heading to the top. Each parent must know her own child's capabilities and be available for appropriate assistance without inhibiting the child's motor development and sense of independence. All toddlers need to be held as they slide down until they have learned to slow themselves down by pushing their feet against the sides of the slides. Some children will fearlessly climb up; their parents need to be close by to avert accidents. Children's accomplishments should be acknowledged by the parents; the sense of physical mastery is important to the child's self-confidence and self-esteem.

*"Are there other physical activities that we could be encouraging now?"*

Some of the children may be ready for a riding toy that they can propel with their feet on the ground. Children can be encouraged to gain motor control by walking backward and standing on one foot. They enjoy copying how animals walk or hop or jump. This can be made into a game that other mothers and children can join in.

## Television

*"What about TV? The child of one of our friends loves watching* Sesame Street, *and I am tempted to get that hour of peace and quiet; but I am afraid TV will become a habit. Is that true?"*

There have been many studies and surveys on how much television children watch. We have learned that many children spend more time watching television than going to school and that most watch three to four hours a day. So the answer to your question is, "Yes, TV can become a habit." Television provides easy entertainment; the child (or adult) can sit passively without making the effort that goes into reading a book. At this age, children should spend time being read to and exposed to appropriate books. Many educators think that the decline in national reading scores is the result of too much television and too little reading. It is therefore recommended that the introduction of television be delayed for as long as possible. There are really very few programs that are appropriate for two-year-olds. *Sesame Street,* for example, was designed for four-year-olds as a substitute for nursery or preschool experience. Following the production techniques of advertising, many children's shows use fast-paced, jam-packed formats. Children are therefore bombarded with attention-getting scenes and visual effects. It is true that children can recite letters and numbers earlier after viewing *Sesame Street,* but whether this helps them to learn concepts is still in question. Using television as an educational tool is an important idea. There have been many articles written on the merits and disadvantages of *Sesame Street,* and we encourage parents to read them. We are inclined to think that it is too stimulating, fast-paced, and skills-oriented for children of this age.

In general, we strongly recommend *very limited* viewing for *all* children, both in time spent and programs watched. Television should not be used to keep the child quiet while the parent does chores. Often the quieter the child, the better the parent likes it. But the electronic companion is not a substitute for human contact and stimulation. If the child is exposed to TV for too long, he or she is deprived of the parent's stimulation of speech, touch, and involvement. If the parent leaves the child alone by the TV, she may be away too long. When she returns, she finds that the pleasant, harmless program has ended and the child is watching something frightening, unpleasant, or violent. As yet, there have been no conclusive studies of the effects of violent programs on children, but violent programs clearly are bad models for life and seem to foster aggressive behavior in *some* children. In addition to limiting the time, therefore, we advise you to monitor carefully the kind of shows being watched by your children. To do this effectively, you should watch with your child and make sure that both the overt and the hidden messages of the program are acceptable to you. In addition to violence, there are many stereotypical portrayals of minorities, women, and the elderly that can contribute to children's prejudices. The commercials on children's programs can foster desires for products such as sugar-coated cereals, which are unhealthy, or for expensive, short-lived toys. If parents watch television with their children and discuss the programs with them, it can be a valuable learning experience.

## Cognitive Development: Parents as Teachers

Now that the children are getting to be more verbal, how do you view your role as a parent?

*"We are finally comfortable with the mechanics of child care and we are able to concentrate on the fun of playing with our daughter. Now that she is talking, I am wondering when we should teach her the alphabet. I have friends who are doing that."*

Teaching the alphabet may be possible, but teaching a song or a rhyme is more appropriate now.

*"My surprise at the beginning was how little the baby could do and how much care she needed. She was totally helpless. Now I'm constantly amazed at how much she can do on her own."*

*"My husband and I experienced some of these same feelings. It wasn't till we came here that we began to recognize that playing with the baby in the right way could help her development. That's when we began to feel a new kind of importance in her life and a new kind of involvement with her."*

### Development of Trust and Attachment

You all seem to be well aware of your roles as caretakers. Certainly, that is a primary element in parenting. However, while you were responding to the baby's needs, you were also teaching the baby that you were reliable and that you could be trusted. In addition to being caretakers, therefore, you are the *first* teachers. As the children developed basic trust in you and the world, they became attached to you. That primary feeling of attachment and affection is one of the most important "lessons" to be learned in life. Learning to relate to the parent is the forerunner of being able to be involved with and relate to others: teachers, friends, and, later in life, associates, spouses, and their own children. This ability is also the groundwork that is needed for cognitive development and a drive for learning. It is becoming increasingly recognized that the lack of this early affectional relationship may account for the difficulty many children have in school and for the ineffectiveness of much of the remedial efforts to help them.

*"That was a good period for us when we understood about establishing trust and affection. After he learned to walk and get about, it was difficult— he got into everything. It seemed we were always running after him, trying to show him the right way to use things."*

## Understanding of Environment

That is a large part of the parent's role in the child's early years. The child needs to learn how to manipulate toys and objects around the house: how to open and close doors without getting fingers caught in them, how to open and close boxes and jars, how to eat, how to dress. Parents are teaching all the time, consciously or unconsciously. Each new experience adds to the child's understanding of the world and to his cognitive development.

*"I know that I should be looking at myself as a teacher. But when I'm in a hurry and I have to stop him repeatedly for doing something he is not supposed to, I get angry."*

Of course, there are moments of anger when something is boiling over on the stove or the telephone is ringing. As the mother tries to attend to these, she notices the child doing something he or she should not be doing. She gets irritated at the child—that will certainly happen occasionally. In general, when one becomes a parent, new priorities should be set. Adaptations have to be made so that the first priority is attention to the child's needs; the household chores then come second. Children absorb most of the information about their lives by being around the parents, watching them, and participating in simple things such as setting a table or putting all the teaspoons into their slot in a drawer. Learning where everything belongs and what objects are for is part of cognitive development. Parents often take this aspect of learning for granted. Parents need to discuss what they are doing and allow the child to make comments as well. There is nothing so satisfying to parents as a verbal child. Learning how a child interprets events is a fascinating and enlightening aspect of child rearing.

*"Well, does that mean you have to speak almost every minute with the child? I've been looking forward to his playing by himself so I'd have more time for myself."*

■                                                                              ■

One does not have to spend every minute playing or talking with a child. But one has to be available to help fix a broken toy, or point out an alternate way if a toy is too wide to go through a door, or make suggestions about how to do something *after* the child has exhausted his resources. The child has to have a chance to arrive at his or her own solutions. Parents have to stand back and give children this opportunity—up to the point of frustration. Then they should step in and offer help.

Children also need to learn about time and when it is time for various activities, such as playing, taking a bath, or eating dinner (as well as when it is time for mommy to cook dinner or do her nails or go shopping). These are concepts about everyday life that two-year-olds begin to comprehend when they are discussed and incorporated regularly into their lives.

*"All the things that you are mentioning happen naturally in the course of a day. I don't regard them as enhancing cognitive development. My feeling is that I should be teaching my son the letters of the alphabet, colors, how to count, and maybe even how to read his name and other words. I've even read that someone devised a system of labeling different items in the house, so that when the baby saw the label and named the object he learned to read as well as talk."*

There are all sorts of systems that are advocated for enhancing children's education. There is as yet no proof that learning to read at two is important for intellectual development. A two-year-old has far to go in concept formation, which he learns best from contact with his parent and from everyday situations in his home and its environs. We sing songs about the alphabet that children enjoy, but at this point such learning is mostly rote memory. The association of the sound with the written symbol is perhaps beginning for a few exceptional children; they may respond to learning letters if the parent's approach is casual and unpressured. The danger is that most children are really not ready and parents apply too much pressure. Their impatience at the child's lack of response gives the child a sense of failure and can actually turn the child off reading later on. In general, kindergarten is soon enough for most children to learn the alphabet. Now they should be learning other things that will not be as appropriate later.

## Learning to Talk

*"What special things should we be teaching them now? What is appropriate that we might be missing?"*

A major accomplishment of the two-year-old is language: an increasing vocabulary and the ability to speak in three-word sentences. Some children may use even longer sentences. As we have said before, parents play a very important role in the child's acquisition of language. A child will make sounds but never speak a language unless he or she is spoken to. Language development requires stimulation and modeling by the parents.

They label objects and encourage the child to repeat words. They point out objects and situations in books and describe what they do around the house as they cook, clean, put things in order, and play games. Parents also name and describe more abstract things such as work, play, pleasure, happiness, and sadness. This parental teaching takes place in natural situations and contributes to the child's cognitive development, even though it is not usually labeled in that way.

At this age, the child is also learning how to manipulate toys such as toy cars and trucks, arranging them in various ways. Playing with dolls and stuffed animals also helps the child to work out difficult life situations and to express emotion, both affection and anger. Children mimic what they see, following and internalizing the parental models.

## Games

*"What about games? I understand 'Peekaboo' is an important teaching game."*

That's right. "Peekaboo" is a game that gives both parent and child fun and pleasure. At the same time, it teaches the child that some person or thing that he or she cannot see for a moment continues to exist—that someone or something that goes away can come back. There are also nursery rhyme games like "London Bridge" and "Ring-Around-a-Rosy" that help teach the child words and understanding of language in an entertaining way.

Another skill that parents can appropriately encourage at this age is drawing. Children should be encouraged to draw with crayons: free scribbling and imitations of simple forms such as lines or circles. Parents often prohibit this activity out of fear that the children will scribble on the walls. The answer is that parents must *monitor* this activity, not inhibit it.

## Learning Concepts

Finally, this is the age at which it is appropriate for children to be learning the concepts that will make reading and more formal reasoning meaningful later on. A child has trouble giving meaning to abstract symbols (reading) if he or she doesn't understand what the words mean, even if they have been properly sounded out. Children obviously need to know the names of all the common objects before *reading* them will give much pleasure. Additionally, children need to learn the concepts of up and down, in and out, on top of and under, and in front of and behind. It is really very difficult for a first-grader to progress if he or she, in learning to read, sounds out "behind," for example, but doesn't know what it means. The teaching of these concepts, therefore, is a most appropriate activity for parents of children around two years of age. Children can also begin to learn about shapes, and which shapes belong together, from doing puzzles with three or four simple and complete geometric shapes such as circles, squares, triangles, and rectangles, or puzzles with complete animal shapes of three or four different pieces.

After this discussion, you will understand why children can learn more from their parents during these first formative years at home than they may learn from many academic situations. Additionally, you will realize that it is considerably easier for children to take advantage of school when they have had this kind of appropriate preparation at home. Children who have had recognition for their achievements at home generally continue positive involvement in formal education.

*"This discussion gives me more of an idea about natural teaching and makes me feel more comfortable with what we are doing already. Though I didn't want to, I felt I had to drill the baby to repeat words, and he just turned away. I was afraid there was something wrong with my child's intelligence. I guess I was so anxious that he should progress later in school that I got way ahead of him."*

That is a very common error. Parents' expectations are often beyond their child's capacity. This often happens when they compare their child with friends' children who are older, or even to older siblings. All of us have a way of forgetting at what age we ourselves or an older child actually accomplished a certain activity. Then we expect too much of the younger child, disappointing ourselves and giving the child a feeling of failure. We are trying to help parents avoid this by developing expectations that coincide with the level of the child's development. Appropriate parental expectations combined with appropriate parental guidance and teaching generally lead to accomplishments by the child that are satisfying for both parent and child. The patient helping of children to understand concepts and the fostering of feelings of accomplishment and self-confidence are the best ways parents can give their children a head start for school.

## *Sleep Changes: Nap Patterns; The Move from Crib to Bed*

How are the children sleeping now? Do you have any questions about sleep patterns or naps?

### *When Do Children Give Up Naps?*

*"We are just beginning to have a problem. Our little girl, who used to take naps very easily—a short one in the morning and a really long one in the afternoon—is beginning to resist her afternoon nap. If she doesn't have it, she gets very cranky late in the afternoon; in fact, she is impossible. She is cranky for her bath and hardly eats her supper, but she does sleep at night. It may be a good idea to eliminate the afternoon nap, since she sleeps so well at night. Her morning waking is about 6:00 A.M., which is very early; but my husband gets up early, so it is not such a problem."*

■                                                                          ■

*"My child is trying to eliminate her afternoon nap, too; but she falls asleep at 5:00 or 5:30 from sheer exhaustion and sleeps till 6:00 or so. Then she gets her second wind. We can't get her to bed until 9:00—sometimes 10:00 P.M.—and that cuts into our evening together."*

It is apparent that some of the children are going through a transition period. There is no set time when children should give up their naps. It depends entirely on the child and his need for sleep. Some children nap until they are four or five years of age; others stop around two. The child who has been taking two naps usually consolidates them into one at this age. Parents can tell by experimenting whether a morning nap or an afternoon nap is better for the child.

A child who wakes very early in the morning may need a late-morning nap, or his lunch can be given earlier, followed by an early-afternoon nap. The child who takes only an afternoon nap and tries to eliminate it clearly is not quite ready if she falls asleep just before supper. It may be necessary to shorten her day and give her an early bath and supper and an earlier bedtime. Even if children won't nap, a quiet period should be instituted when they can rest in their cribs or beds and play quietly alone. A quiet time can also consist of sitting quietly with mother and looking at books or listening to records.

Gradually all these changes in sleep patterns emerge into a new pattern; but during the transition one has to experiment and see which solution works best for each child and family.

## Climbing Out of Cribs

*"We are lucky our little girl still naps and sleeps all night. But now when she wakes, she no longer waits for me to come to get her; she climbs right out of her crib. When I come into her room, she is playing on the floor. She hasn't fallen out, but I am afraid she will. Is there something to do about that?"*

It seems that some of the children are not sleeping as long as their parents thought and they may be left waiting in their cribs too long. When they were younger and less mobile, they stayed in their cribs. Now many won't stay, and parents have to be alert and take them out sooner, so they won't fall.

Another problem when children get out of their cribs without the parents' knowledge is that they may get involved in some activity that is harmful. As you well know, children of this age should not be wandering around unsupervised, especially in the kitchen or bathroom or near stairs. You can all imagine the possibilities for trouble without our listing them. Some parents may find that placing a gate in the doorway to the child's room is helpful. Many children will not be content to stay in their rooms, but they will call out. This will alert the parents that they are up. For the child's safety, it is best for a parent to get up when the child is up. If you wake up when she does and then take her out of the crib, she may never have the need to climb out.

*"My child wakes up, climbs out of his crib, comes onto our bed, and wants to play. It may be four in the morning, and we are not ready for that. But we don't want to upset him or scold him. What should we do?"*

It is important for him to know that it is still "sleep time," not "getting up time." Take him back to bed, tuck him in, and assure him everyone is going back to sleep. Tell him you will come and get him in the morning when it is "getting up time."

## Readiness for Big Beds

*"We are having a different situation now. Our little girl takes her naps in her crib. At night, however, she will not fall asleep unless she is put to sleep in 'the big bed,' our bed. Then we move her to her crib."*

*"We were having the same situation with our little boy. Last week, we spent the weekend with friends. They had no crib for him, just a studio couch in the den. We were a little bit worried because of the new place and the big bed with no rail, we put chairs around it. He liked it and slept all night. So we wondered if that was a signal that he is ready for a youth bed."*

Children's enjoyment of sleeping in regular beds is certainly one of the signals that they are ready. In most cases, when the children are a little older, they enjoy selecting a real bed and seeing it installed in their rooms. They feel very grown up then. In many cases, having their own beds eliminates the problem of their getting up and coming into parents' beds. Some children are ready for a bed around two years of age, but most are really not ready until two and a half or three, some even later. If the child is not ready, the change should not be made. Some children are attached to their cribs. They are their havens and castles.

*"We are expecting a new baby in about six months. Our son will be about two and a half then. We were planning to give his crib to the baby and give him a bed, but he seems very attached to his crib. So we are wondering if that's a good idea."*

In general, it is not advisable to give the crib to the baby when the older child is still using it and is attached to it. His sleep pattern may be disturbed. In addition, the older child's loss of his crib may heighten his feelings of loss of his mother's attention when the new baby comes. Because the baby has mother *and* his crib, the older child may feel doubly displaced. This feeling can initiate or intensify sibling rivalry that parents find difficult to cope with. Most of us would like to minimize or avoid this kind of stress if at all possible. Although it may seem like an unnecessary expense to have two cribs, it may turn out to be a valuable investment for the emotional well-being of the family. Some families may be able to borrow a crib for the baby until the older child is ready for a bed.

*"We are expecting a new baby, too. Our son is climbing out of his crib and prefers to sleep on the daybed we already have in his room. We have told him that as soon as the baby comes he can have that bed for himself because he is going to be a big boy by that time. He is looking forward to that."*

Your son sounds ready to make the change. In addition, you have made it a privilege and reward for being the older child, so that any feelings he has of being displaced from his crib will be minimized. In all cases, when a new baby is expected, it is a good idea to emphasize the advantages of being the older child. In the next six months, the child who is attached to his crib may have matured sufficiently to want a big bed and may relinquish the crib easily to the new baby. On the other hand, the child who seems ready may suddenly decide he wants to keep his crib when he actually sees the baby using it. It is therefore important for parents to be sensitive to the child's feelings about his crib and not force him to give it up prematurely.

*"We are not expecting a new baby, but we have a big bed for our child in his room. Luckily, we left the crib up, mainly because we haven't decided where to store it, and we find that sometimes he prefers to sleep in the crib again. Now we will leave it up until he is really ready and doesn't ask to be put into it anymore."*

The move from the crib to a bed is a big event in a child's life. Most of us regard it as just a matter of refurnishing the child's room. To the child it is much more than that—it is a move from infancy to childhood. The move is often accompanied by a mixture of excitement and joy and a little fear and regression, for which parents must be prepared. It is another change in the child's life that is better dealt with on the child's maturational timetable, and not at the parents' convenience.

## *The Second Child: How to Cope*

We want to discuss what happens in the family when a second child is born, especially when the older child is under three. Some of you already have a second child, and some will have one soon. Others may be thinking about it. What are your feelings and experiences?

*"Because of my profession and for medical reasons, I could not wait. There are only twenty months between my boys. I knew from our earlier discussions what some of the difficulties might be. Although I knew there would be great demands on my time, I did not know how difficult it would be to give both children at least some of what they needed. Fortunately, the second is less demanding than the first. To fulfill the needs of my first child, in fact, I may be taking too much advantage of the second baby's placid disposition. Sometimes I feel I actually neglect him."*

■                                                              ■

When the second child is placid, parents frequently tend to exploit his or her good nature. It is important to recognize that this is happening and try to give the baby the attention he needs. Sometimes arrangements have to be made to have some help for a few hours a day. Someone can entertain the older child while mother attends to and stimulates the baby. When father comes home, he can play with the older child, or the parents can take turns, so that both children have special times with each parent. Sometimes, if one is lucky, a grandparent or other relative is available to help.

## Helping Toddler Relate to New Baby

It is also possible to enlist the older child in helping to stimulate the baby. While an older sibling of three or four is very good in this role, it takes thought and ingenuity to help a two-year-old do this. The parent can encourage the toddler to wave a rattle for the baby, or to place a small stuffed toy in his range of vision, or to place something in his hand. (The parent should closely supervise this activity, because the two-year-old is not mature enough to understand which of his activities might be harmful to the baby.) Helping with the baby in this way enhances the older child's feeling of importance while giving the baby appropriate stimulation. At the same time, the older child can be helped in his language development by talking to his sibling and imitating the parent's way of communicating with the baby.

*"We have the opposite situation. We have to give our second child a great deal of attention. She required an operation, and I had to stay with her in the hospital. It was too much for our two-year-old—first to have so much attention centered on the baby, then to have me away. He had to stay with his grandparents. Although he knows their house and likes to be with them, he had never been there alone overnight. He has an adequate vocabulary for his age, but not sufficient for us to explain that I would be back, that we still loved him as much as ever, and that soon he would be home again. From a happy, active boy who could amuse himself, he has become a whining, clinging 'baby.' I know why; but it is so hard to give both of the children the attention they need. How can I get him back to his former state?"*

That was a very difficult situation. You did all you could to make it easier for your son, but it was beyond his experience and level of comprehension. It is good that you understand the cause of his clinging and regression. Now he needs time with you in order to be assured that you are not leaving him. It would be helpful if someone else could care for the baby for a little while each day, so you could have a separate time for him alone. He needs some undivided attention from you to get over his feeling of abandonment and to help him reestablish his former sense of security. If the baby has recovered, he can also be involved in playing with the baby. Then he can experience a sense of pleasure in relation to the baby and have less of a feeling that the baby only keeps you from him. It will take time to accomplish this; but if you are sensitive to his needs, the situation will improve.

*"Since I brought my baby home, my little girl, who is twenty-two months old, has behaved as if she were bereft. When I went to the hospital to have the baby, my mother, whom she adores, came to stay with us. We give our daughter lots of attention, and our friends are very careful to include her, but she still clings and whines. She wakes at night, which she didn't do before, and she doesn't eat as well as she did. Both my husband and I have tried to spend a little extra time with her and keep her away from the baby, but it doesn't seem to help. We want her to love the baby."*

As adults, we often make the mistake of expecting children to "love" the new baby brother or sister right away. We must recognize that the first child feels displaced—and to a certain extent this is an accurate perception. The parents, particularly the mother, who is probably nursing the baby, are no longer able to give the older child *their* undivided attention. Parents can help the older child to begin to verbalize his or her feelings of anger or disappointment (often young children expect a new baby to play with them immediately). The main thing is not to expect too much in the way of affection and not to criticize the child for lack of enthusiasm. In most cases, acceptance of the baby develops gradually if the parents help the older child to feel loved and secure.

*"Of course, I expected some of these reactions and I think we are coping. But we haven't talked yet about the mother! What about her needs when there is a second child? I hardly have had time to put on lipstick since the new baby came!"*

## The Needs of Each Child

Having enough time to give a new baby and a toddler the attention they need is one of the hardest problems to solve at first. The first child is still quite immature and dependent, but very active; the new baby is totally dependent and relatively inactive. Their individual needs at a given moment may be quite conflicting, and the parent, most often the mother, feels torn between them. Some mothers are very easygoing and casual. They have an easier time coping than more tense and exacting parents. A great deal depends on the mother's personality and physical endurance. Much also depends on the assistance she receives from her husband, relatives, friends, or hired helper. Caring for a toddler and a new baby requires a great deal of organization and stamina, perhaps even more than is required in another profession or business. Parents' needs for support are not widely recognized by our society, nor is the value of good parenting. Without support, child rearing can be a lonely and frustrating experience.

One of the ways for a mother to preserve her health and pleasure in her children is to try to have a rest when the children nap. If the children do not nap at the same time, and no relative, friend, or hired helper is available to take care of the children for a short period each day, then the father must give her a breathing time when he comes home.

*"Well, that is usually not the way it works when my husband comes home. He wants dinner, and the children are cranky and hungry. Everyone wants something, and I only have two hands!"*

One cannot expect the children to understand your need for a little rest and relief, but your husband needs to be aware of his responsibility to help. He has the more mature central nervous system and he can wait for his dinner. Or he can help make it, or go out to the deli and get something for your dinner. This period when everyone seems disorganized will not last forever. In a while, a better routine will be established. The baby's schedule will become more predictable and gradually it will be more like the older child's. Dinnertime, as we discussed before, is a particularly difficult period of the day. Parents need to discuss ways of making it easier for themselves and the children.

*"I can cope with the daily juggling of each child's needs, but once in a while I need to get away. Is that unfair to the children?"*

It is absolutely essential that every parent get some time off. As we have said, no one can do a job twenty-four hours a day every day without relief. A mother's job is no different. Some arrangements must be made so she can have some time for herself. It is important for her emotional and physical health. She can then do her job better and enjoy it more.

*"I went back to work after my second child was born, because I just couldn't take it at home. Then when I came home, I was so glad to see the children that I think I was nicer to them and not so irritated. But I noticed that my younger child, who is nearly two, is not speaking as early as my first. Do you think that may be because my housekeeper is not talking to her enough?"*

Your housekeeper is just as busy looking after two children as you were. In addition, she is probably more concerned about the housekeeping. Some housekeepers feel that the employer is more concerned about the state of the house than the children, because that is what the parents notice most when they come home. It is important to emphasize that you are more concerned with the children than with the housework. Some housekeepers may have trouble changing their priorities. If you have noticed a speech lag in your younger child, you can spend time stimulating the baby's speech when you and your husband are home on weekends.

## Problems Regarding Sharing

*"Our problem has been the sharing of toys. Although my older child has an abundance of age-appropriate toys, he seems to want only what the baby*

*is playing with, such as his rattle or squeeze toy—toys he had given up before the baby came. I don't like to push him away from the baby and take the toys from him, but it upsets the baby. I find I am getting angry at my son more often than I should. I feel he is selfish."*

It is very common for the older child to want the baby's toys, especially if they were once his. Sometimes, it is best to give the baby new toys and let the older child play with his own again so that he won't feel displaced by the baby. His old toys revive memories of a pleasant time when all attention was paid to him; he also notices the attention you pay to the baby, helping her manipulate the toys. His behavior isn't "selfishness"; it's immaturity. He still needs to be included. So you can try to include him in the baby's play. Have him dangle the toy for the baby and pick it up when the baby drops it; recognize how well he does it. At such times you can also get one of his new toys and by playing with it show him how much more interesting it is than the rattle he played with when he was a baby. You can also show him how he can roll a car along the floor now because he is a "big boy." Try to make being the older child an asset rather than a privation.

*"In our home we have the opposite problem: the baby wants everything the older one has. He is now able to crawl and get into all of my older child's toys. She resents it. I tell her the baby is too young to know not to touch them, but it doesn't seem to help. I feel an uncomfortable relation is developing between them. Is there any way to deal with that?"*

It is natural for the younger one to want to explore, but the older child has a right to her toys and privacy. You must help her by giving the younger child the toys he can have and by protecting the older child's toys. Some toys they can share and play with together, such as rolling a ball to each other; but special toys belonging to the older child must be guarded from the baby's grasp. When the older child recognizes your protection, she will have a better feeling toward her younger sibling and may be able in time to share some toys with him.

*"All of these issues are important, but the hardest thing for my husband and me is to find time to be together. We always seem to be doing something for the children. Perhaps it is because I have a job outside. When we come home we feel the children need all of our attention. We haven't seen our friends or been out to dinner or a movie in months."*

When both parents work outside the home, they may feel guilty about leaving the children for their own time alone together. This is a situation in which many families find themselves. The family's pattern of living must include time for the parents alone. No matter how much one enjoys one's children, or how seriously one feels the responsibility to gratify the children's legitimate needs, time must be arranged for parents to do things for themselves on a regular basis. It is important for them as individuals and as a couple to have time off from child care. Otherwise, parents may become overtired and resentful of their children. This is a situation that everyone wants to avoid.

## *Weaning: What to Do About Bottles*

Now that the children are approaching two, have you begun to consider them old enough to give up their bottles? Have you been getting pressure from friends or relatives to wean your children?

*"Well, I remember that we discussed weaning earlier. At the time, I was worried because my mother was urging me to take away all the baby's bottles. It was pointed out that doing it abruptly was upsetting to the child because it was like a separation from mother. That made me slow down and think about it. So instead, I have been giving him as much milk as he will drink from a cup after each meal. Some of the time he drinks well without spilling. Now he takes a bottle only early in the morning and at bedtime."*

*"My little girl will take a little milk from a cup at each meal, but she spills most of it. So I'd just as soon have her take bottles. It is so much easier for me that I usually don't bother with a cup."*

### *Drinking from a Cup*

All parents have to satisfy their children's and their own needs, but at some point all children need to learn to drink from a cup. Sometimes parents push children to give up their bottles too soon, and sometimes they don't encourage children to learn to drink from a cup soon enough because they want to avoid a mess. There is, of course, a "happy medium." It is a good idea to start with a cup at one meal a day, perhaps the noon meal. When that is successful, the cup can be introduced at another meal or afternoon snack, whichever is most suitable to the daily routine.

*"When should parents really expect children to give up their bottles entirely? You hear so many varied opinions stated with such authority that it's really confusing and more than a little upsetting. My child enjoys his bottle, even though he is two."*

Most specialists in the field of child development now feel that most children can relinquish their bottles with little trauma by around three years. The age varies with each child—some are ready earlier, some a little later. Each child has his or her own timetable and needs; and parents should be concerned about their own child's needs rather than unsolicited advice, no matter how well-meaning.

*"Well, I don't see what all the fuss is about. My baby takes his milk so much faster from a bottle. He can hold it himself, and I am free to do whatever I want. If I give it to him from a cup, I have to sit with him so he won't throw it or spill it. It takes so much time; I just don't have the patience for it."*

Taking care of a child does take time. Children cannot be hurried, especially in eating or drinking. By the age of two, a child should be learning
to use a cup so that he can gradually give up his bottles. A little patience
*now* pays off well *later.* Sitting with a child to assist him in drinking from a
cup once or twice a day helps him advance to a more mature level of
drinking. It also continues intimacy with the parent at mealtime, which is
important.

Parents seem to like to have their children do things early or fast.
Having the child give up his or her bottle *early* makes parents feel
successful as parents. What *really* is important is that the child be allowed
to relinquish the bottle when the *child* is ready. Pushing the child may be
counterproductive and cause resistance instead of cooperation.

*"Along with weaning, another thing that concerns me is when to begin
toilet training. I'm being criticized by my family because my child isn't
weaned or toilet trained yet."*

It is not advisable to begin toilet training when the child is concentrating
on other areas, especially weaning. Most children are hampered in their
progress if too many tasks are introduced at once. It is best to tune in to
the child's readiness for new development and respond to her cues.

### Toilet Training and Weaning

*"We have a different problem. Our son was giving up his bottles and just
beginning to use the potty. Then our daughter was born, and he refuses to
use the potty and insists on having his bottles."*

Your son is exhibiting a very natural regression. He sees the attention that
his baby sister gets having her diapers changed and being fed. He thinks
that these baby ways are good ways for him to get attention, too. Since he
is still quite young and needs to get adjusted to the baby, it would probably
be best to slow down on the weaning and toilet training.

*"We have the same problem and stopped talking about it altogether. We
did continue giving our daughter milk from her cup (except at night),
however, telling her that the baby was much too young and small to do
that. She seemed to feel proud about that."*

That's good. You have given her an idea that there is some advantage in
being older. Often all the child can see is the attention the baby gets; being
older seems like a disadvantage. Parents have to be careful not to say
constantly, "The baby is so small and helpless, he needs my attention. You
are a big girl so you have to wait for Mommy." Parents sometimes
unconsciously convey the disadvantages of being bigger instead of pointing out any advantages. That is a trap we all fall into. We forget that the
two-year-old is still a baby in many ways. Besides, when children are close
together in age, the demands on a parent are very great. The parents want
the child to act older so she can help, or at least wait her turn. If the older

■                                                                              ■

child is very compliant, we can rob her of her babyhood before it is time. If the child is assertive, the parent often labels the child "spoiled" or "bratty" or "naughty." Because the child wants attention like the baby gets, she regresses. If the child is verbal enough, the parents can help her begin to understand her feelings by saying, "I guess you feel like being a baby again. That is all right. In a little while, maybe you will be my big girl again."

The important point is that two years old is really on the young side for most children to give up their bottles or begin toilet training.

## The Child's Understanding of Family Events: Illness, Death, Separation, Divorce

There are many situations that occur in a family that disrupt the usual routine. Some are happy events such as visiting relatives or friends, celebrating a birthday or anniversary, moving, or going on vacation. There are also unhappy or unpleasant situations such as illness or death in the family as well as separation and divorce. Even though the children are older and are becoming more verbal, they still have difficulty understanding and relating to all the different events that can occur in a family. Parents themselves have difficulty dealing with such situations and often do not know how to help their children handle them. Because such occurrences usually arise unexpectedly, we would like to discuss different ways of handling them so that you may be better prepared.

### Illness

*"Just this week my mother took sick and I had to rush over to her house. I had to take my little girl because I didn't have time to get a baby-sitter. Mother had a heart attack; I had to send for an ambulance. I called my husband, who came from his office; but all the time I was rushing around to help Mother, my little girl was very upset. She is very fond of her grandmother and cried. She couldn't understand why Grandmother was not paying attention to her. I knew that, so I held her in one arm and did things with the other—but was very upset myself. By the time the ambulance came, her father was there. He took her home while I went to the hospital. Mother is still there, and I have to visit her every day and leave the baby with a sitter. She continually asks for her grandmother. Her appetite has fallen off, and she has begun waking during the night. I'm not sure I'm handling things right, because I am so upset about my mother, even though she is improving."*

Situations that are so serious and sudden are very difficult to cope with, even for adults, as you have so clearly stated. It seems as though you were very sensitive to your little girl's needs by holding her close as much as you could. At this age, children can understand if you tell them that

Grandmother is sick and that you have to take care of her. It is important to emphasize that you will be back soon. You can also talk about what you will do together when you get back. Then go as quickly as possible and return as soon as you can manage.

*"What about her not eating and sleeping?"*

Whenever there is a change that causes anxiety, children may respond by not eating or not sleeping—or both. These disruptions are to be expected. All that a parent can do is to be patient and comforting and not get upset. When life gets back to normal, the child's appetite and usual sleeping pattern will return.

## Death

*"We had a similar but less fortunate situation in our family. My husband's father, who was a constant visitor and a great pal to my little son, was hit by a car. He did not recover after being taken to the hospital. Our little boy keeps asking for him, and we keep saying he is away. But we know we can't say that forever. One day, we are going to have to tell him. What should we say? We try not to talk about his grandfather in the hope that he will forget about him."*

If you don't mention his grandfather and your son stops asking, that does not mean that he has forgotten. Furthermore, we won't know what sort of fantasy the child may have about his grandfather's sudden disappearance. He may begin to worry that his parents will vanish that way, too. He may even think *he* has done something wrong. So, difficult as it is, it is best to tell the truth. The truth about his grandfather will be difficult for him to understand but less bewildering than silence or the idea that in some way he is at fault.

*"We would like to, but we just don't seem to be able to begin."*

When your son asks again, say that Grandfather had an accident and was hurt very badly and that's why he can't come over. The next time he asks, or a few days later, it may be easier to say that the doctors and nurses tried their best to help Grandfather, but he just couldn't get well. By this age, children have heard the word *die* in reference to flowers, animals, and insects. So, if you say Grandfather died, he may have some awareness of what you mean. He may ask more questions about where Grandfather is and wonder if he will return. Some children have difficulty understanding and accepting the finality of death, even at seven or eight years, so do not be upset or surprised if you are asked these same questions over and over again. The important thing is not to give the child the feeling that this is a topic that must not be discussed. It is a good idea to talk about his grandfather.

*"What if the child cries?"*

You can say how sad you feel and how much you miss Grandfather, too. Tears of grief do not hurt anyone. They are an appropriate expression and release of emotion.

*"Can't one tell the child that Grandfather has gone to heaven and that he is resting in a nice place?"*

If that is part of the family's belief and a comforting idea, one can explain it to one's child that way, even if the child doesn't yet understand completely. One must do and say what is appropriate to the family's beliefs, whether cultural or religious.

## Mourning

*"Do children mourn? How can one tell?"*

Children do mourn. Some children do so by avoiding the subject—never looking at the dead person's picture. Others want to look at the relative's pictures and talk about him or her all the time. Some lose their appetite or experience a change in their sleep patterns. Some become very irritable or tearful for no apparent reason. Others show a great deal of anxiety about their own health and body parts. Others become very clinging to parents and worried about the parents' health, always wanting to know where they are going and when they will return. Others have difficulty playing with peers. If a parent is sensitive to the child's behavior, subtle changes may be detected. That is why it is best to be open with the child and try to answer his or her questions as simply and directly as possible. It is also important to remember to reassure children that your own health is good and so is theirs.

*"After talking about the death of a grandparent, I hate to bring up the death of a pet—but our son's kitten is very sick. I'm afraid she's going to die. I've been thinking we should find another cat for him so he won't be upset."*

If your son is very fond of his kitten, he *will* be upset by her death. That's only natural. It is better not to try to gloss over his loss and to let him know that you are sad, too. Children have a right to mourn the loss of a pet. It is really better not to get a new pet until the child asks for one. No one pet should be any more replaceable by another than one person is replaceable by another.

## Family Arguments

*"What about angry feelings? Sometimes my husband and I get into a discussion that is very heated; there may even be a quarrel in front of our son. What do we do about that? He often acts frightened."*

It is best not to have a heated argument in front of a child, particularly if it involves some difference of opinion about the handling of discipline. It confuses the child and may make him feel guilty. He may even fear that his parents will come to blows or hurt him.

*"Well, what if you just can't help it? What if it's something that doesn't really involve your child? Do parents always have to wait until the child is out of earshot? That's just not normal to be so controlled!"*

That's true. It may not be the usual way two adults have related to each other. However, one has to bear in mind the child's presence, feelings, and possible misinterpretations. So if you are arguing in front of the child, tone it down if you can't postpone it. Explain to the child that Mommy and Daddy have different ideas about something and that you are not angry at the child.

*"When we argue, my little girl covers her ears and cries. She runs either to me or my husband, depending on who is yelling the loudest, and pulls on my (or his) arm. That always brings us to our senses. We are learning not to discuss things that are apt to start trouble in front of her."*

*"Doesn't it give the child an unreal view of the world if he never experiences any dissension in a family?"*

We are not advocating that families give their children an unreal picture of life, as though there are no difficulties. We are suggesting that you bear in mind how children may interpret and respond to arguments and that you be sensitive to their needs. We also have to remember that parents are models for their children. If children see parents quarreling all the time (sometimes violently), this becomes their model of how adults relate to each other. It is likely to influence their behavior when they grow up. None of us wants to set this kind of example for our children. You may argue like this because that was the model set for you. Now, as you bring up your own children, is a good time to try to find a more constructive, more respectful way of relating.

## Separation and Divorce

*"There is another subject that is bothering me: separation and divorce. I've wanted to discuss it for a long time, because my husband and I contemplated divorce before the baby was born. Then the baby came, and we thought maybe that would make us closer again. Things are a little better, but we still have problems. What would we say to our son, and just how would divorce affect him?"*

One would hope that parents would be able, with appropriate help, to avoid divorce. But if that is not possible, the child should be told that the parents love him and that they will always remain his mommy and daddy but that one of them will not be living with him anymore. (We say "one of them" because some mothers leave their children with the fathers. We can no longer take for granted that children will remain with the mother, although in most cases, especially with young children, that is still so.)

■                                                                                            ■

Explain that the other parent will live in his (or her) own house and will come to visit and play with the child, that they will still have good times together. The exact details of the arrangements should be explained to the child in terms that the child can understand. For example, "Daddy will come and take you to the park every weekend." If at all possible, it is best for the child to remain in his own home, at least until he has adjusted somewhat to the separation.

*"If the separation does go on to divorce, should you tell the child?"*

Usually children try very hard to effect reconciliation between parents. By the time the divorce is final, the children may be old enough to understand that the separation has been made permanent by divorce. However, even with children three or four years old, one needs to take care to explain how they will be affected. The parents need to try to understand how the child interprets and feels about it. Some children think that divorce means some surgical process like cutting someone in two, and they are not sure whether the parents are cut apart in some way. Parents have to allow their children to express their ideas and fantasies in order to be sure the children have no misconceptions that cause them undue anxiety. Most important, the child must be reassured that *both* parents still love her or him.

## Single Parents: Special Problems

We have been discussing how families cope with a variety of child-rearing issues. Usually we discuss the role of the members of the traditional two-parent family, but it is important to recognize that an increasing number of families consist of only one parent and that these families have many special problems. We were wondering whether there were some special issues that those of you who are single parents would like to discuss.

### "Where Is Daddy?"

*"It's no secret to all of you how I've had to struggle to arrange appropriate care for my little girl, since I am not married and have to work. You've all helped in discussing different child-care arrangements and how to cope with all my other chores. I'm managing, but now I have different worries. As my daughter gets more verbal, I imagine she is going to ask me where her father is or why she doesn't have one. What is the best thing to say?"*

There are many questions children ask that are difficult to answer. It's best to try to understand the level of the child's thinking when the question is asked. To help in understanding what the child is thinking the parent can ask, "What were you thinking?" or "I wonder why you're asking?" Then, when you have received a reply, you will be in a better position to answer the question. Any answer you give the child should be as simple, direct, and honest as possible. Often adults make the mistake of giving involved explanations, which the child is not able to comprehend.

*"Well, in my case, I didn't want to be married or to live with the man. I just wanted a child before I was too old. I wanted to be a mother and I thought I could be a good one. It's harder than I thought it would be. But I enjoy my child. How can I tell her about that? Her father moved away and I never even told him of her existence. And that's the way I want to keep it."*

For the present, if your daughter asks where her daddy is, you can answer truthfully that he has gone away to work.

*"Suppose she wants to know whether he knows about her?"*

That is a question *you* are worrying about her asking, but it is probably beyond her level of conceptual thinking to ask that now. At this age, she assumes *everyone* knows about her. She is more likely to ask when he will be back. If she does, you can say that you do not know when he will come back but that you do not think he will come back for a long, long time. After all, it is possible that he might at some future time be in contact with you again. At some future time, she may want to know him and you may make a different decision. For now, you can make it clear that she can rely on your care and love.

When she is older, she may ask why her father does not write her or want to visit her. Then you must tell her that he does not know about her, so that she will not feel rejected or deserted by her father. You will have to explain that he moved away before she was born and that is why he does not know.

*"Well, suppose she asks why I didn't tell him?"*

If you don't know where he is, you can say that. You can also say that you wanted her very much and felt you could bring her up alone and make her very happy by yourself. You may also need to explain that you love her but you did not want to live with her father. It is good to be prepared to answer, so that you will not be taken by surprise.

*"My situation is different, but I've been wrestling with similar questions. After three years of a calm and pleasant marriage, my husband found out that we were going to have a baby. He became very upset. He just couldn't cope with the responsibility of being a father and wanted the pregnancy terminated. I couldn't do that; I wanted the baby. We separated and are now divorced. My husband still lives in the neighborhood. We pass each other occasionally in the street as though we were strangers. He doesn't look at our son if he happens to be with me. He has never inquired how we are or made the slightest gesture of concern. I have resumed my maiden name, which is my son's last name, too. There is no financial problem; I have just continued with my job. My son is a happy, easygoing child. Can I tell him that his father didn't want him? That is the truth. What will it do to his self-image to find out his father didn't want him?"*

In the first situation, the mother didn't want the father as a husband. In this case, the father rejected his role. The problem is how to tell the child the truth when he asks about his father without giving him a sense of personal rejection. You could say that his father didn't understand what to do as a father. He just wasn't ready to be a father. But you were ready to be a mother because you knew how and wanted to be a mother. Therefore, you decided to take care of him yourself without the father. This may satisfy him at first. As he matures and asks more sophisticated questions, more explicit answers will have to be given. It so happens that this is not such a unique situation. As he grows older and goes to school, he will meet other children of one-parent families. Then he will not feel so alone and different as you now worry he will feel.

## Male Role Models

*"There is another problem that bothers me, which I suppose is more serious for a male child, and that is: what does one do when there is no male role model? Isn't it true that boys have to have a man around to establish their masculine identity?"*

*Both* parents are important models for children of *both* sexes. The girl, perhaps, has an easier time because she identifies with her mother, but she needs to be aware of what to expect of a male. In two-parent families, the father is the model for her future heterosexual relationships. While the boy in his earlier years may be close to his mother, and even his father's rival, he eventually needs to identify with a male, which is usually his father. Although they can hardly escape some influence from the parental models, some children identify with other family members. In the case of an absent father, a child may identify with a grandfather, uncle, teacher, or minister. It is good for *both* girls and boys to have some contact with an interested adult male.

*"In my case, I have an aunt and uncle who live near enough so we can visit them often. They have been baby-sitters in many an emergency. My son loves them dearly and plays ball with my uncle. Their children are grown up and live far away, so they are very glad to be surrogate parents. I am very lucky, I know."*

*"I live with my parents. My son has my father as his model. He also has the advantage of having my mother, who takes care of him when I go to school three days a week. I was afraid that he would mistake them for his parents. I've been insisting that he call my mother Grandma and me Mother to avoid that."*

*"You are lucky. I have no family nearby. Though I date occasionally, I do not like to keep introducing my child to different men. I've tried some of those groups for single parents, but they are made up mostly of women and the few men are not particularly compatible. I just don't know how to*

*bring my daughter into contact with appropriate males. She is obviously confused because she calls all men Daddy—and that embarrasses me!"*

## Child's Adjustment to Parent's New Friends/Partners

You are raising a very important issue. It is not good for a child to have to keep adjusting to different friends of the parent. The same thing applies when the child visits with the father and his girlfriends. Sometimes these friends of the mother's or the father's are not interested in the child—or worse, they are jealous of the child who resembles the former spouse. There is obviously a need for groups in which single men and women and their children can come together in a family-like atmosphere. Some groups like this have been established by Ys, community centers, and religious institutions. There will need to be many more of these to satisfy the numbers of single-parent families. Also, you can try to get male baby-sitters; your children can benefit from contact with them.

*"My husband died before our little boy was born. Now I have a friend whom I like very much, but he seems too strict with my baby. My son seems a little afraid of him and clings to me. I'm afraid that if we marry—and I do want to marry again—we'll have problems over discipline and the marriage will be an unhappy one. That I don't want. I haven't said anything to my friend about it because I don't want to offend him. Is there some way to deal with that?"*

Before any marriage, the partners should get to know each other's ideas about how they want to live. Their ideas about rearing children are an important aspect of this. So if you both are interested in marriage, it would be appropriate to discuss your feelings about children and their need for approval as well as discipline. Perhaps you can come to some agreement before you run into trouble.

## Living with Grandparents

*"My problem is a little different from the others because I have to live with my parents. My mother is very good to me and lets me go out and take courses. But I have a feeling that she thinks she knows more about raising the baby than I do—and maybe she does. But I decided to have my baby so I could raise her, and my mother makes me feel left out. The only time I feel like a real mother is when I'm here. Then I can see how well my baby is doing and how good I am as a mother. It's been on my mind to mention this before, but somehow I felt I would seem ungrateful to my mother."*

It is hard for you to be in the same house with your mother and try to be your child's mother when your own mother is still mothering you. She is having a hard time recognizing that you are grown now and a mother in your own right. This often happens between mother and daughter, even when they don't live together. It is very hard for a mother to recognize that her own daughter is grown up and may be very competent to bring up her own child. It is not ingratitude on your part, just your desire to be recognized and respected in your new role.

### Financial Concerns

*"My major worry since my divorce has been financial. The child-support payments aren't adequate with the increase in the cost of living. I work part-time but hardly have anything left after paying the baby-sitter. I've decided to try to find another woman in the same predicament. We could pool our resources and live together. I'm lucky to have an apartment that is large enough to share."*

These ideas for developing your own "extended family" units are good ones. It is interesting that other people—single people without children and elderly people—are also beginning to think of sharing living arrangements. Though compromises may have to be made as one adjusts to these new groupings, they can be a mutually beneficial way to solve some of the problems we have been discussing.

It is quite clear that being a single parent, whether mother or father, poses many problems that complicate parenting. No two single parents have exactly the same problems to solve. Each parent has to use his or her own available resources and ingenuity.

## Nursery Schools and Day-Care Programs: At What Age Are They Appropriate?

Some of you have been asking us about the appropriate time to send children to nursery school or to a day-care center. What are your ideas about this?

*"In my neighborhood, all the parents of children my child's age are madly investigating nursery schools. I'm not doing that because it seems ludicrous to me to take my child to an interview for a prenursery program when he isn't even two. Am I naive? Am I making a mistake? Will his education be impaired if he doesn't enter a group when he is two?"*

In large cities or the suburbs, where appropriately aged playmates may not live nearby, parents are tempted to provide play experiences for their child by enrolling them in a prenursery program. However, there is really no necessity for such a formal experience at this age. You are not depriving your child or hampering his development because he is not attending a formal preschool program. Registering a child in a preschool is often looked upon as a solution when families do not live near other children. Some of you live near parks or playgrounds where playmates are available. All you need to do, then, is to go outdoors to these areas and there will be plenty of opportunity for your child to play with other children. There will also be other mothers available to watch them and to socialize with each other. There you will make friends whom you can visit on rainy days. For those of you who worry that the children are not learning enough, it is important to remember that your children are learning a lot at this age from their contact with you and by going with you on errands around your neighborhood.

## *Informal Play Groups*

*"But what if you don't live near a playground and you can't afford a preschool? Then what alternative is there?"*

We feel the best arrangement for this age, even if you could arrange for a prenursery school experience, is the *informal* play group of about four children and their mothers. This group could meet in each other's homes or at the park two or three times a week for an hour or two. If the same group meets fairly regularly, the children get to know each other. They begin to socialize and form friendships. They will need to have their own mothers present at first, but after a while they will feel secure enough so that the mothers may be able to take turns leaving for a short time. This kind of group is very good preparation for nursery school and should precede a formal school program, if it can be arranged.

*"That sounds like a good idea for mothers who know how to organize play for children. I don't think I could do that. But I realize my child isn't ready yet to go to a school away from me. What can I do so that he is not deprived of interesting activity and stimulation?"*

## *Special Activity Groups*

In many communities, the local Y or religious institution has arranged some activities for young children and their parents. Some groups are organized specifically for large motor activity: climbing, jumping, running, and active games. There are even a few for swimming. Some parents like participating in these programs with their children.

There are also programs for children who would be happier with something quieter, such as pasting, crayoning, and finger painting. Parents often appreciate that kind of group because these activities make a mess at home, or because they do not have the proper equipment or space.

There are also music schools that have groups for young children that meet once or twice a week. The children participate in activities such as rhythm exercises, marching, dancing, or playing simple instruments. Some programs also teach songs that appeal to children, and they learn to enjoy listening to music.

There are many things to do with young children that enhance their experience. You will need to research your own community to find these resources. Then you can spend quality creative time with your child before he or she is really ready for a formal school program. Most parents enjoy these experiences as well, as they enhance their ability to spend quality time at home.

*"I have always thought that a child would get more benefit from trained teachers in a setting designed with age-appropriate play areas and materials and a larger choice of playmates than being with three or four other inexperienced mothers and their children."*

This is a very common attitude for parents to take. Children can certainly benefit from teachers who are well trained and empathic, working in a good physical setting with the appropriate equipment. However, there is still one question that is very important and that we have not yet considered. We must consider whether the child is *ready* for this experience. The parents may overlook the child's lack of readiness in their great desire to enrich the child's experience.

## Signs of Child's Readiness for School

*"What are the developments we should be looking for when we make a decision to send our child to a nursery group?"*

One of the first considerations should be how well the child is able to separate from the mother or other caretaker. Most children of this age are not yet ready to separate from their mothers away from home and need to have the experience of being with other children while their mothers are present. The children are starting to play together here in this group but are just beginning to spend time in the children's area with the play teacher. Most of them still come back and touch base with mother a few times during the session, if only for a moment. Not many of them feel comfortable yet leaving the room for a walk down the hall or for play in the playroom across the hall. Most of them run back quickly to see their mothers or to show them something. It is very important for children that their mothers be available so they can do this. Children who do not need to do this are further along in their ability to separate. Each child has his own maturational timetable for separation, as for every other facet of development. It is very important that each child's need be understood so that a separation problem does not develop. This can be difficult to resolve and can recur at separation situations in adult life.

*"Well, that is a good warning for me. I was thinking of taking a job so that I could afford a nursery school. I noticed that my little girl has great difficulty staying even at her grandmother's without me. She does a bit better without me if Grandma comes to our house. I thought what she needed was to separate from me, that nursery school was just the thing for her. All my friends have told me that I am too close to her."*

It sounds as though the contrary is the case: that she is not ready to separate from you yet. Instituting separation too early would probably be too costly for her emotionally and would actually make her more dependent.

*"I have noticed this about my son, too. My family has given me the same line. My husband has intimated that I'm making a sissy of him."*

That is a very common fear. As we have said, forcing separation prematurely would intensify the clinging that a father interprets as being sissy. Actually, this kind of behavior indicates that the child still needs to be close to the mother and is not ready to separate.

*"Well, I used to think that my son didn't care about my leaving because he is so fond of our sitter. I have noticed lately that he won't let me out of his sight when I come home. He wants me to hold him the minute I come in. That bothered me. Now I understand it. I remember that we had discussed this, but somehow until it happens in your own experience you don't really understand it. I guess he isn't as ready to go off to nursery school as I thought."*

Another important sign of readiness is the ability of the child to communicate verbally. These children are quite advanced in this area; most of them are saying words and phrases, and some are trying three-word sentences. Their pronunciation is not always clear, however, and perhaps only a parent can understand them, so it might be difficult to be in a nursery school, where the teacher may not understand them or where they may not understand her. The level of a child's language development is important—both how much he understands and how well he can express himself.

*"I can understand how that can be a problem. But I know a situation in which the child was late in talking, and nursery school was advised to encourage her speech."*

That may have been good advice for that child. I would suspect, however, that the child was older than these and that there was some deficiency in speech stimulation at home.

*"I'm a working mother or, as you prefer to say, a mother working outside the home. I prefer to leave my child at home with his old nurse, whom he adores. I don't think he is ready for nursery school. But he doesn't talk as much as some of the other children here. Do you think he would be better off in nursery school part of the day?"*

In general, we think that two years old is still young for nursery school. If the child is not ready for nursery school, it is much better to leave him with a devoted caretaker, even if she doesn't stimulate speech sufficiently. The parents can make up for this lack by their own attention to speech when they come home in the evening and on weekends. They can also encourage the housekeeper to spend more time talking and playing with the child and not so much time on housework. Sometimes, parents need to model for the housekeeper what she is to do. If she is non–English-speaking, reading books with simple pictures and words will help her learn the language. She may even be pleased at the attention paid her by the parents. If parents understand the situation, remedial steps can be taken in time to prevent later problems. A speech deficit can be detected early and overcome. The anxiety produced by sending a child to school too soon is harder to overcome.

*"So far, everyone has been approaching this question with the options of doing it or not. I simply do not have any option. I can't afford a baby-sitter. I must find a day-care center. Now that I am separated, I must return to work."*

Each of you must weigh your child's need and the family's needs and then look for the best solution considering your own circumstances. As we have said, there are a growing number of programs for two-year-olds, and, if given sufficient time to feel comfortable in this situation, your child can learn to cope.

*"I have taken my little girl to a music group a few times, just to see how she would respond to other children. She seems to like it, but she only wants to watch the activities from my lap. I haven't urged her to join the group, but I feel that the teacher is making overtures and is trying to entice her into the group. This only makes her cling to me. Do you think she is too young for this experience?"*

It seems to me that she is indicating that she is. This brings up another guideline for judging whether a child is ready for a group experience. If the child has had enough social experiences with small informal groups, as we have mentioned before, she may be ready to participate in a larger group—at first with mother and then alone. There are some children whose personalities are such that they have to observe the activities of the group for a while before they can participate. There are others who bound right into a group and take over. The social behavior of these children indicates an earlier readiness. Even some of these children, after the first rush of enthusiasm, may want to return to mother's side. So the level of social development is important. Each parent has to know her child and try to assess this readiness.

*"Whenever we are in the park and there are more than two or three children, my little boy moves away from them and finds a corner to play in by himself. This upsets me. I thought of sending him to nursery school to get over that."*

Parents often come to that conclusion; but the children will do the same thing at nursery school. They are either not ready for that experience or the encounters they have had with other children have not been pleasant ones. Perhaps their play hasn't been appropriately monitored by the parents, so they respond by isolating themselves. It takes patience and understanding to help overcome this. The child needs time to reach the necessary maturational level *on his own timetable.*

*"Most nursery schools require that a child be toilet trained before they will accept the child. Isn't that another guideline?"*

In many nursery schools that is a requirement. Parents often hurry toilet training in order to meet this requirement and cause themselves a great deal of unnecessary disappointment and conflict with their children. They try to teach bowel and bladder control before the children have the neurological control and psychological readiness for this achievement. So this, too, is a consideration in deciding whether your child is ready for nursery school. In this case, as in many others, parents are ready before the child. Each child, as we have said before, has his own maturational timetable. The best results for all concerned are obtained when this is understood and accepted.

## How to Choose a Nursery School or Day-Care Center

Many of you have expressed concern about how to tell whether a preschool program or day-care center is a good one and will be appropriate for your child.

### Importance of First School Experience

*"Yes, I didn't know anything about young children until my daughter was born. Now I have no idea what to look for in choosing a school, but I want to make sure it's the right one. I don't want her 'turned off' by her first school experience."*

It is appropriate that you should be concerned about that. Children's problems with school often stem from their very first experiences, and we should make every effort to get them off to a good start. We talked about the importance of the child's readiness for the group experience of a preschool and his or her ability to separate from parents and home environment. How the parents and the school handle the separation process will have a major effect on the child's adjustment to school. We have talked earlier in the year about the importance of making the introduction of new caretakers or baby-sitters a gradual process, so that the child may become familiar with the new person within the secure setting of the home. This gradual process is even more important when the child encounters new adults and new children within a *new setting,* the school. Parents should therefore expect to stay at the school with their children for several days to a week, or even longer. Young children, especially those under three years of age, need help in making the transition to school. Trying to hurry their adjustment just makes them less secure and more uncomfortable.

*"A friend of mine was told that she should stay for the first two days, and that was all. Her son screamed for the whole morning on the third day, after she left. Then he cried so much the next day that she took him home. Now she has decided to give up that school."*

## Adjustment to Separation

How the school deals with the separation needs of the child and what provisions are made are important questions to ask. One can learn a lot about the general philosophy of the school and about the administrator's understanding of child development from the answer to these questions. No preschool or day-care program for children under three should expect a child to begin the experience *without* separation anxiety. The parent should be allowed and encouraged to stay until the child, the teacher, and the parent herself feel that the child is ready to stay alone. If the school you are interested in has no particular plans for dealing with separation or says there is a policy allowing parents to stay for only a set number of days, it would be wise to look for a different school.

Many preschool programs facilitate the adjustment of children by having the teachers visit the home first. That way, the child is able to become familiar with the new adult. Conversely, the teacher is able to see how the child behaves in the security of the home environment.

Children's adjustments are also facilitated when the program begins gradually, starting with forty minutes to an hour the first day and working up to the full three-hour program over a period of a week or two. Some arrange to have the children begin coming in groups of three or four instead of meeting with the whole class of ten or twelve at once. We must recognize that having to adjust to two or three new adults, ten or twelve children, and a new environment is quite a large assignment for a two-year-old. Most are simply not ready to do it without a lot of support from the parent. For this reason, we are not recommending school for most children at two. However, some parents find they need to send a child to prenursery school or day care because of their work schedules. They should still take into account the child's needs and capabilities so that the best arrangement is made for both parent(s) and child.

## Signs of Readiness for Separation at School

*"Say you like the school's attitude. How can you tell when the child is ready to make it on his own?"*

The first sign of readiness is the amount of time the child spends away from the mother engaged in the activities available in the classroom. If the child spends most of his time away from you, only checking back occasionally, he may be ready. You can test this by saying that you need to go

■                                                                    ■

on an errand and will come back in ten minutes. Some schools have rooms where parents can go for coffee to be somewhat removed from the children but available if needed. If parents leave for a brief period, they should stick to their promise. A ten-minute errand should take ten minutes, not an hour. If this brief separation goes well, then you could try leaving for half an hour or so the next day, until you are staying away for most of the session.

*"What if your child says 'No' and clings?"*

Then you know that she is not ready and you stay. After a few more days, you can try going to the parents' room for coffee or out to make a quick phone call. If, after several weeks, your child still makes a fuss when you try to leave, or still sits by your side and doesn't engage in activities with other children, it may be best to withdraw from the school. A good school director should be cooperative and consult with the parents about this decision.

*"I can see that the school's policy on this issue indicates an understanding of the child, but also an attitude toward parents: whether they are to be gotten out of the way as soon as possible or treated as partners."*

*"I've heard that schools require that children be toilet trained before they will admit them. Is this possible for two-year-olds?"*

As we have discussed, toilet training should take place when the child is ready—and most children are not ready at two. Good schools should know this and not require that children be trained as a prerequisite to admission. The teachers in prenursery programs should also be willing to accept the child's own maturational timetable regarding this issue. So the school's policy on toilet training is another important matter for parents to ask about.

## What to Look for in Toddler Programs

*"I'd like some guidelines on what to look for when I visit a classroom. Obviously, I will look to see how the children seem: whether they are happy and busy, or crying or withdrawn. I will look at the toys to see if there is a good variety. Are there other things I should look for?"*

One should pay considerable attention to the teacher. Notice whether she looks interested in the children. Is she patient, relaxed, and calm? Does she bend down to talk with them and sit on the floor or on small chairs with them? Listen to the way she speaks to the children. Is she soft-spoken, or does she shout commands? Observe how she handles arguments and aggressive behavior. Two-year-olds, as you know, have not yet learned how to share. Observe whether the teacher protects *each* child's rights. Is she sensitive to the needs of both the aggressor and the victim without being harsh or punitive? Is she warm and comforting to the child in tears? Try to observe how well the teacher(s) and assistant(s) work together on the activities and with the children.

*"You're really saying that the teacher is key to what happens in the classroom."*

Yes, that's right. She and her assistant(s) set the tone for everything that goes on in the classroom; so if you see a school where you think the teacher is great, it is good to make sure that she will be there the following year. If she is replaced by a new, inexperienced teacher, the classroom experience could be quite different, although a good director will certainly try to make sure that all the teachers in the school follow the school's particular philosophy.

Other things you can observe or ask about relate to the curriculum and program. Observe (or ask about) the day's activities. There should be a schedule that alternates active and quiet activities, with a sequence of certain activities to start and end the day. This sequence gives the children a sense of knowing the beginning and end of the day. A certain amount of routine at school gives the children the same sense of security that we have encouraged you to provide at home. The classroom should have equipment for a great variety of activities, which the children can explore on their own or with guidance from the teachers. Try to decide whether the activities seem appropriate for two-year-olds. There should not be too many *group* activities, since they are just beginning to play together. There should not be too much emphasis on sharing or taking turns, especially at the beginning of the year. The children should not be expected to do things neatly or sit quietly for very long, and there certainly should not be any emphasis on letters or numbers. You should be looking for a happy, relaxed atmosphere with some structure—not an environment that is pressured or restrictive or academic. Finally, children generally do best when the atmosphere of the school is not too dissimilar from that of the home.

## All-Day Programs

*"My mother has been taking care of my son while I work, but now he is getting to be too active for her. I feel that I must find a day-care center where I can leave him for most of the day. I guess I should be looking for much the same things. Are there any additional features to all-day programs?"*

Certainly, the schedule is very important in an all-day program. You would want to know what provisions are made for mealtimes and for naptimes. Children of this age should have one or two definite rest periods during the day. You would also want to ask about the consistency of care that the center will provide. For example, will the same teachers and assistants be there for the whole time the child is there, or will there by many changes in personnel? Changing caretakers is difficult for two-year-olds, so programs for this age should have a minimum of staff rotation.

It would probably be a good idea to visit a day-care program a couple of times, once in the morning and again in the afternoon. Observe how the children seem to be faring at each time of day. See whether they appear happy and calm or whether they sit off by themselves, looking sad or bored. Day-care programs for children under three are expensive because of the required ratio of adults to children. A good one may therefore be hard to find and too expensive. Sometimes family day care, in which a woman takes several children into her home, would be another possibility for you. Or you might find a program that runs from nine to three that would relieve your mother for most of the day.

Adequate and appropriate day-care facilities for working parents are greatly needed in our society, but parents should try if at all possible to be selective in choosing a center for their children. A child is not *automatically* better off either at home with a relative or at a day-care center with other children. It depends on the relative (or other caretaker), on the type of center, and on the particular child.

*"I have been looking at two programs. One is three blocks from our apartment and is very nice and simple. The other is a twenty-minute bus ride. It is much better equipped, but I'm concerned about the ride."*

In general, it is better if the school is closer. There are other considerations, of course. We would not advise a nearby school that did not meet your other expectations, but a nice, simple school may be just fine for two-year-olds. Remember, the school that you choose now does not have to be the child's school forever. The kind of school that is appropriate for a two-year-old will not necessarily be appropriate for a five-year-old. The important thing is to try to select the appropriate one now, one in which the child will feel comfortable and secure. In several years, you may decide to select a different school in any case. In fact, you may have to, because there are few schools that combine prenursery and elementary school grades.

## Ratio of Adults to Children

*"What ratio of adults to children is best?"*

For two-year-olds, we think that one adult to three or four children is the best. In New York City, the Health Code requires one adult to five children for two- and three-year-olds. Other cities may have different requirements. Licensed programs are visited regularly to make sure that these requirements as well as those relating to toilet facilities, outdoor play space, and safety measures are all being followed.

Once your child is enrolled in school, it is important to keep in contact with the director and the teacher to be sure that you have made a satisfactory choice. Visit every once in a while and talk with the teacher occasionally to ask how things are going. Encourage the teacher to call you if she sees anything different or puzzling in your child's behavior. It is important for teachers and parents to be supportive of each other in their roles. As one of you mentioned earlier, teachers and parents should be partners.

## Involvement of Working Mothers

*"I work full-time. How am I going to be able to be that involved in my child's school?"*

It is important for working mothers to talk with the director about the availability of teachers for conferences in the early morning before school and work or in the evening. Many schools have been slow to accommodate the needs of working parents, but some are doing it now. Occasionally, working parents should take a couple of hours off from work to visit the school. This is particularly important on the days when other parents will be visiting. Children feel very neglected when other parents come and theirs do not. Some schools require that parents help out occasionally, and that is something that parents should ask about before enrolling the child. Often, working parents can be involved in this way; but if it is impossible, another school should be selected.

All in all, the selection of schools for one's children requires common sense and recognition of the validity of one's intuitive feelings about the general atmosphere and the people involved.

## Highlights of Development— Twenty-four Months

The child's second birthday is another one with special significance for parents. There has been tremendous development over the past year. At the beginning of the year, some of the children were walking with one hand held; a few were toddling on their own. Now, most of them run with little or no falling. They can also negotiate stairs alone, both up and down, some even without holding on to the railing. They can kick a large ball upon request without demonstration. When interested in looking at a book, they can turn the pages singly.

At one year, the children could sometimes make a tower of two blocks after demonstration by the parents. Now the children can build a tower of six or seven blocks without demonstration. They can also align two or more blocks into a "train."

The two-year-old no longer scribbles when clutching a crayon in his hand; he may be able to imitate a V and circular stroke. Now when a puzzle with simple geometric shapes is presented, the child may put all the pieces in place after several attempts, indicating that he has learned to associate shapes. He can also successfully insert the square block into the performance box (instead of just inserting the corner as three months ago).

Most children have progressed from the three or four single words they knew at one year to many phrases and two- and three-word sentences. They may even have discarded jargon, the imitative sounds made before words and meaning become associated. They may even use the pronouns *I, me, you.* In communication, the children may be able to refer to themselves by name and verbalize an immediate experience, as well as ask for "more" or "another."

The children have also made great progress in their social development. They are now able to eat with a spoon without turning it over, although finger feeding may still be preferred and eating may still be quite messy.

While dressing, they may be able to pull on simple garments such as underpants, pants, or an open sweater, often with the arms in backward.

# Review of the Accomplishments of the Second Year

We have reached the end of the second year, and this is quite a milestone. Can you remember a year ago and compare your children's abilities then with their present achievements?

## Motor Development

*"Well, yes, I can remember very well that our boy was just taking his first steps alone, and my wife and I were so proud to report it to the group. Now he seems to run more than walk, so he's a handful to watch; he gets away so fast. I like to see him so energetic, but I can see that a full day of watching him may be trying to his mother sometimes."*

*"I remember at a year our little girl was not walking yet, and we were getting anxious because other children were beginning to totter around. You encouraged us by saying that each child was different and not to worry because she was saying more words than some of the others and that was where her energy was going. Now she, too, runs around instead of walking."*

It's obvious that the children's increase in motor activity has been very marked and that, in general, it has been a joy and a relief to know that their motor ability is not impaired in any way. But this development has also brought a need for more careful watching, which parents may find difficult at times.

*"Our situation seems to be different from most. My husband thinks I have inhibited our son because he is so cautious. He doesn't run helter-skelter*

*everywhere. He sort of sizes up the situation before he climbs up or down anything. He never runs very far away or too fast for us to keep up. My husband thinks there is something wrong with him because he prefers to sit and put his blocks in various arrangements and run his little car up or down a chair."*

Not all children develop at the same rate and not all children's energies go into large motor activities with the same intensity. There are variations in the amounts of energy devoted to different aspects of development. That's what makes for the uniqueness of each child and the differences in personality. There is nothing wrong with a child whose interests lie in fine motor skills. Problems often arise when a parent has a set image of what a child should be like and feels that any variation from that image indicates a deficiency in the child. The child is actually perfectly normal, just different from the parent's expectations.

*"Well, for a long time I've been noticing our child's increased interest in how a toy is put together. He inspects it from all sides, turns and twists each part, takes it apart and tries to reassemble it, and sometimes manages to do it without help. That pleases me a great deal. His favorite toy is his Busy Box, which has all kinds of fasteners and knobs to turn."*

You all recognize how much more your children are doing now than they did a year ago. At that time, they barely could put one block on another, or make a scribble on the paper, or put the round piece in its place on the form board. They have come a long way in fine motor skills. What have you noticed in their speech?

## Language Development

*"Oh! I think that has been the most exciting for us. I remember last year how disappointed we were when our little girl could only say about four words. We wanted so much to have her say more, even though we knew that what she was saying was normal for her age. Her vocabulary has grown so, we have lost count; and she even puts three words together in a sentence, such as 'Daddy go work.' We are thrilled."*

*"Yes, I think talking is the most thrilling for us, too. We seem to have gotten past the stage of his saying things in a tone imitating us, but with no discernible words, to saying words clearly so we can understand them. He can name pictures of animals and other things in a book, too. He loves to sit with us and do it for a long time. I enjoy the half hour we spend doing that while my wife gets dinner ready."*

*"We speak two languages in our house. Our child knows a lot of words in both languages, but she hasn't put more than two words together yet. We have to use both languages because my parents live with us and they always speak in Spanish. Is that delaying her speech?"*

It may be delaying her speech a little; but when she does begin to talk, she will have a command of two languages. It is sometimes necessary to use only one language for children who are very slow in speech, but it seems that your child is making adequate progress. Not all children of two years speak in three-word sentences all of the time.

## Social Development

*"Our little boy seems to understand everything, but he doesn't put words together. He points and names over a hundred things and he understands anything we ask him to do, so we haven't been worried. He can do everything else very well. He can feed himself and even tries to put on some of his clothes. He tries to help around the house. If I sweep, he wants to sweep, too. We are pleased."*

It is good that all of you as parents are noticing your own children's achievements and not expecting them to be exactly alike. Some are more advanced in speech, and some are developing faster in other areas.

The children's social horizons are widening, and that's very nice. They are beginning to make tentative contacts with other children in the park and beginning to visit with children in other homes. That, too, is quite an advance over the first year. Have you been noticing another evidence of growth: their growing need to do things by *themselves* when *they* are ready?

## Personality Development

*"Oh, yes! His favorite words now are 'Me do' when he wants to go up and down stairs or walk to the park. He's never ready when I want him to come for lunch or when I want to leave the park."*

*"We, too, have been noticing many instances of her wanting her own way. We are glad she has a mind of her own. We understand that she needs some autonomy and we try to give it to her wherever it's appropriate. There are times when she objects strenuously to doing something. We just accept the protest and try to give her the scenario of what is coming next. We've learned here to recognize her need for some autonomy and that she wasn't being a bad child if she wanted to decide some things herself."*

*"Well, my husband and I were brought up in the 'obedience school' and we had been warned that this year would be the onset of the 'terrible twos.' We seem to be weathering it all right, because we understand that at this age they begin to try their wings, so to speak, and need some independence— and this is not disobedience."*

Parental recognition of the child's need for some autonomy, as well as his or her need for consistent limits and approval when accepting a suitable alternate activity, is really one of the most crucial contributions to the child's personality development that parents can make. You have all begun to work on this during the past year. That process makes it possible for a child to learn to accept authority without being made to feel that he or she is "bad." While limited in one area, the child learns that there is an alternate acceptable activity. Then, in later adult life, he or she will be able to deal appropriately with authority and with limitations and frustrations. Such an adult won't "fight" his or her boss or sulk if it rains on the day of a picnic; it will be possible to think of an alternate activity, such as going to the movies or a museum.

*"We are concerned about having our child develop self-confidence and self-esteem. If he builds something with his blocks or returns a ball we throw, or just even comes to his meals when called, we recognize it with some positive comment."*

That is a very important process; it helps the child develop a positive self-image. We began to talk about that when the baby was able to reach out and hold a toy. We commented on the importance of recognizing the achievement as appropriate for that age. This process has to be continuous, and it is very gratifying to see that parents are concerned with this aspect of personality. A child needs positive recognition in order to develop a good self-image. This helps him explore the world around him, to be involved in school, and to be self-motivated later in life.

## Toilet Training

*"We have been talking about the children's progress, but in my family the only progress that seems to count is bowel and bladder control. When can we expect our child to be trained?"*

One or two of these children may achieve the ability to control these functions in the next few months; the majority will be closer to three years. Some of these children are beginning to inform the parent only *after* the evacuation of bladder or bowel has occurred and then ask for a change of diaper. That is an important step and should be greeted with approval, *not scolding for soiling.* If children are allowed to follow their own natural timetables, toilet training will be accomplished in just a few days. They will gain a sense of autonomy and responsibility for their own functions as well as a sense of achievement when parents show approval.

*"Our son has reached the stage of telling me. But when we get to the bathroom, most of the time he can't perform until he is off the toilet seat and back in his diaper. My mother thinks I should keep him there until he has performed, but he cries to get off."*

If you just go along with your son's signals and recognize the few successes he may have, making no comment over the failures, he will be able to function more easily. His toilet training will be successful when he is ready. Trying to force him may only impede the progress.

*"That takes a burden off my mind, because that is the stage we are in. On some days we have successes once or twice a day; on other days, only failures."*

Success should be recognized and failure overlooked! Each child is at a different level of maturation of the central nervous system. Some will mature faster than others; but, not pushed, they will all become toilet trained without having been made to feel disapproved of or incompetent over this issue. Child development specialists believe such feelings of inadequacy may lead to long-standing character problems in later life, which all of us wish to avoid.

## Weaning from Bottles

*"Well, now, what about bottles? My son takes most of his liquids from a cup after meals when I hold the cup, and sometimes he holds the cup himself. But first thing in the morning and to go to bed at night, he still wants his bottle. I'm perfectly satisfied with this arrangement, but my friends who have grown children say that it is wrong. They took the bottles away as soon as their children could drink from a cup. Most of them say it was before two years."*

Again, we believe that the child's need should dictate the timing for weaning. It is appropriate for the child to learn to drink from the cup, but the child should give up the bottles when he or she is ready. Most children at two years still need the morning and evening bottles; some may require more. For some, the bottle is not so much a nutritional need as an emotional need: not to feel separated from Mother. This need should be respected for what it is; more time spent with Mother in other activities often cuts down the child's need for bottles.

*"Well, when should a child be expected to give up all bottles?"*

Most children are ready around three years of age; some may need them a little longer. Each child has his or her own timetable and special needs. Parents should relate to each child as an individual, and not to the advice of someone who does not know the child or understand the situation.

## Changes and Developments to Expect in the Third Year

*"Now that we have reviewed some of the accomplishments in the second year, what should we be looking forward to next year? Can you give us a little preview?"*

## Increasing Competence

That's a fair request. As we have just been saying, there will be progress in toilet training. The children will also relinquish most bottles, if not all. They will become more competent at self-feeding, and they will be able to put on some of their clothes.

In the area of motor activity, the children will be able to alternate feet

■                                                              ■

when walking upstairs, and some will be able to pedal a tricycle by three. They will be able to make more complicated structures with their blocks. They may learn to discriminate and name colors.

The children's language development will be very exciting to parents because they will be able to express their ideas better in longer, more complicated sentences. They will begin to learn some nursery rhymes and songs. There will be an increase in their understanding of abstract concepts and ideas.

## Increasing Sociability

Socially, they will begin to play more interactively with other children. They will begin to take turns, a process that will be more fully achieved from three to four years of age.

The children's likes and dislikes may become more pronounced, and they will be more vigorous in their protests, developments that may be annoying to parents at times. They will need the same consistency and firmness when limited, and the same recognition for achievement and approval for appropriate behavior. In this way a desire to achieve rather than rebel will become more appealing.

## Increasing Autonomy

As the third year progresses, the children will be able to separate better from parents, in particular, and from home, in general. They will be able to play longer alone and at a greater distance from mother—sometimes away from home without mother.

It will be an interesting and challenging year. Now that you have all become so much more proficient and self-assured as parents and know and understand your children better, it should be a very good year. During this year, you will be preparing your children for greater independence and more relationships with other adults and peers. We advise you to savor and enjoy it. From age three on, your children will spend more and more time in school and away from home. You will have completed the "good start" that all of us want to give our children so that they may be more competent and caring adults.

# The Third Year of Life

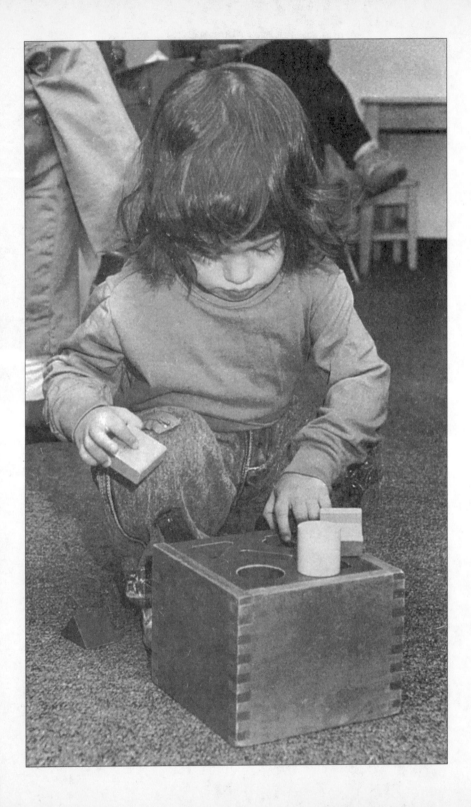

# SECTION I

## Age Twenty-four to Thirty Months

*T*he child's second birthday is one with special significance for parents. There has been tremendous development over the past year. At the beginning of the year, some of the children were walking with one hand held; a few were toddling on their own. Now most of them run with little or no falling. They can also negotiate stairs alone, both up and down, some even without holding on to the railing. They can kick a large ball upon request without demonstration. When interested in looking at a book, they can turn the pages singly.

At one year, the children could sometimes make a tower of two blocks after demonstration by the parents. Now the children can build a tower of six or seven blocks without demonstration. They can also align two or more blocks into a "train."

The two-year-old no longer scribbles when clutching a crayon in his hand; he may be able to imitate a V and circular stroke. Now when a puzzle with simple geometric shapes is presented, the child may put all the pieces in place after several attempts, indicating that he has learned to associate shapes. He can also insert the square block into the performance box, instead of just inserting the corner, as he did three months ago.

Most children have progressed from the three or four single words they knew at one year to many phrases and two- and three-word sentences. They may even have discarded jargon, the imitative sounds made before words and meaning become associated. They may even use the pronouns "I," "me," and "you." The children may be able to refer to themselves by name and verbalize an immediate experience, as well as ask for "more" or "another."

The children have also made great progress in their social development. They are now able to eat with a spoon without turning it over, although finger feeding may still be preferred and eating may still be quite messy.

While dressing, they may be able to pull on simple garments such as underpants, pants, or an open sweater, often with the arms in backward. And they may indicate their preferences for special items of clothing.

All of the above tasks are preparing them for a major step forward—

gaining autonomy. The two-year-old is progressing from being an infant to a separate person. In what ways will they achieve autonomy and how will parents be able to help them? These are some of the questions we will answer in these final chapters.

In the next six months, parents can expect the children to exercise more and more independence. The children may wander away from the parent more frequently, ask a parent to do things their way, demand to sit in a favorite chair, or issue commands for parents to obey. Understanding why and how a child does these things will enable the parent to traverse the treacherous territory often referred to by others as the "terrible twos." If the parent is able to keep in mind that the emerging individual is just practicing and refining his technique, life becomes more amusing and less anxiety-ridden and confrontational.

# 17

# Expectations of the Third Year

## Your Child's Progress

The children have made enormous progress in the last year—they have gone from crawling to walking and now running. They are taking on their own  unique personalities, yet they are still very young and immature. We have noticed that parents' expectations of their children are sometimes beyond the child's level of development. Occasionally, parents are unaware of the progress their child has made and do not enhance it by recognition. Are there some achievements you were expecting by now that haven't occurred? Are you surprised at things your child doesn't do yet?

*"I've been looking forward to conversations with my son, but although he seems to have a pretty big vocabulary and knows the names of most things, he doesn't make sentences yet. I'm getting a little worried. Am I expecting too much too soon?"*

Most children do not speak in sentences until the age of three. They begin to say short phrases by two and a half, such as "Mommy, bye-bye" or "Daddy car" instead of "Mommy is going away," "Daddy is going to the car." Some may be more verbal than that. Each child's development goes at his own maturational pace. Most children, but not all, use short sentences by age three. Some seem to say very little for a long time, and then are able to express themselves well all at once.

*"Being able to talk with our child is the most important area of growth for us. Is there any way to hurry it?"*

We can't change endowment for speech development. However, speaking to the child and modeling clear, modulated speech can help stimulate speech, while a barrage of unmodulated speech may retard it. For example, when giving a child juice one mother may say, "Here is Johnny's juice," emphasizing juice while enunciating clearly and speaking slowly. That is helpful to the child.

Another mother may say quickly in a monotone, "Here's your juice, Johnny. Drink it all up, because it's good for you and Mom wants you to be healthy." This is well-intentioned, but it is too much all at once and makes it difficult for the child to pick out the key word. He may understand his mother's interest, but the individual words do not stand out for him.

*"Is it too much to expect children of this age to put toys back in place? I have tried by showing my daughter, but she doesn't seem to catch on and do it often."*

Parents can show children where things go—the shoe goes here, the block goes there, garbage goes here, and hats go here. When they put something away, parents should recognize the action. When children do something that pleases a parent, they want to do it again and again. And when Daddy comes home, you can say, "Do you know what Amy did today, she put her slippers in the closet."

*"Every time they do it? Even if they have done this particular thing several times and they know that I notice it?"*

After constant recognition and approval from parents, children internalize the recognition and don't need it from anyone else. The adults who need the most recognition are the ones who received the least when they were children. Constant approval of acceptable behavior is what regulates children's motives and develops their self-esteem.

*"I'm expecting my son to accomplish toilet training in the coming year. My mother and husband think that I should have begun toilet training long before this, but I didn't feel my son was ready."*

Children indicate readiness for toilet training. The child has to be able to recognize the sensation of pressure in the rectum or bladder, communicate this to his parent, withhold expulsion until placed on the toilet, and then relax his sphincters. This is a complicated process. Most children demonstrate readiness for it by the end of the third year. Forcing toilet training on a child usually slows down the process and often sets up an angry relationship between parent and child, with disappointment for both. Some experts believe that this relationship may carry over into adult life and affect personality development. Because of the importance of this issue, it will be dealt with in many of our sessions.

*"I would like my daughter to be able to let me out of her sight once in a while and play by herself. She always seems to want to be close to me."*

Children need to be close to their parents, particularly mothers, for much longer than adults think necessary. The child can run off from mother because he knows that he will come back. But when mother leaves, he does not have assurance that she will return. The more parents try to push separation before the child is ready, the more the child will cling.

By the end of the third year children are able to separate from parents more easily. However, in times of stress, such as going to nursery school, they may need their parents' presence until they feel more secure.

■            ■

*"How long do we have to put up with the mess during meals? My husband doesn't want our child to eat at the table with us until he learns to eat properly."*

By age three, most children can use a spoon and a fork adequately, although they may still use a fist grip most of the time. Occasionally, they will still assist their spoon feeding with some hand feeding. Parents should not expect children to be able to eat neatly until they are well past three.

*"My husband, too, gets upset by the messy eating. Because he thinks table manners are very important, he scolds and corrects our child whenever we eat together."*

Table manners are better taught by modeling than by scolding. When children are ready, they need only a little help in holding utensils properly—and approval when this is accomplished—to begin establishing table manners.

*"I'm worried because my child eats so little. I understand that there is a falling off of the appetite in the second year, but when is it regained?"*

By the middle or end of the third year, most children regain their appetites. However, a few children continue to do very well on a small intake. Parents of these children may become anxious and try to force food. This is never productive; it may inhibit a child who, left to his own timetable, would have begun to eat more.

*"I'm still waiting for our daughter to sleep through the night. Of course, she used to wake several times a night. Now she wakes at least once, sometimes twice, and needs a drink of water or just some reassurance. She goes back to sleep quickly, but I haven't learned to do that yet!"*

Some children are always good sleepers. Others are easily aroused during sleep by any number of things, such as a noise, thirst, a gas pain, a dream, fatigue, even anticipation of something pleasant like a promise of a new toy. Wakefulness may become a life-long characteristic, but as children get older, they can cope with it on their own and don't require a parent's presence. Perhaps during this year a better sleeping pattern may be established.

*"My child still needs a nighttime bottle. He drinks well from a cup, but he still wants a bottle before bed. When will he be able to do without it?"*

*"I'm glad my child takes one bottle. That's the only time I'm sure how much milk he has taken. He spills quite a bit down his bib when he drinks from a cup, so I'm not sure how much he consumes."*

Many children require one bottle until they are about three years old. The evening and the early-morning one are usually the last to go. Sometimes it's the child who is not ready to relinquish the bottle, and sometimes it suits the mother's needs. Parental recognition of the accomplishment of drinking from the cup may motivate a child to continue drinking from a cup.

*"My child seems to be making progress in every area except sharing toys. He*

*still clings to his things. Shouldn't he be sharing by this time? I don't like it when people tell me he is selfish and will grow up that way if I don't do something about it."*

Two-year-olds are just beginning to get the idea of thine and mine. Most are not able to fully accept sharing until they are about three years old. However, if the parents continue to indicate what is theirs and what is not, and point out that a toy is still theirs even if another child plays with it, they begin to understand the concept of sharing and taking turns.

## Readiness for Nursery School

Parents are now beginning to think about nursery school and assume their children will be ready. Not all children are ready for nursery school at the same time. Differences in growth, speech, ability to cope with separation, toilet readiness, and socialization all contribute to a child's readiness for nursery school. In addition, parents need to assess early learning groups in their neighborhood to see if they are appropriate for the child. Location, hours, and necessity all need to be considered.

*"I'm glad to be able to discuss nursery school, even though I know my son is not ready for it yet. In my neighborhood, many mothers become frantic about getting their two-year-olds into nursery school. You would think they were competing for admission to Harvard!"*

You might be interested to know that some experts, such as Burton White of Harvard, do not think children should be in formal groups until they are three. White believes that children this age should be in a limited group—ideally, one or two other children—and only if they have no other way of socializing. At three years of age, White feels, children should attend school no more than once or twice a week. He is much more in favor of the informal kind of groups that mothers supervise.

*"Mother-supervised groups worry me. My church has started groups of ten to fifteen children and two mothers. I'm concerned about these mothers' ability. Suppose your child is old enough for such a group but those in charge are not competent. Isn't it better to enter a child in a formal nursery school with trained teachers?"*

We believe small groups are best—for example, three or four mothers and a similar number of children meeting for an hour two or three times a week in each other's homes or at the park. Each mother can supervise part of the activity. One can arrange the motor activities, such as running, riding together, throwing a ball, climbing, and using a slide. Another mother can supervise storytelling or singing games. Another mother can be in charge of snacks. Then the mothers can rotate their roles. This makes it more interesting for both mothers and children; it provides the opportunity to socialize and interact with other mothers and children.

■                                                                    ■

*"Informal groups are fine for mothers who do not work outside the home. But what about the mother who has to work away from home?"*

Mothers who work outside the home have to arrange for competent substitute child care. A nursery school is not a substitute for mother, but a mother may feel more comfortable about leaving her child there than with a housekeeper who is not trained in child care.

*"But a child whose mother works isn't any more ready for nursery school than the child of a mother staying home."*

Readiness for nursery school depends on the child's own maturational time-table—which is a product of his own natural endowment and the effect of the environment in which he has been living. Each parent has to assess her child's development and needs and her own resources and needs, then do what is best for that child in those circumstances.

*"Why are informal play groups recommended over nursery school at this age?"*

Children at this age are not ready to separate from their mothers. They are just learning to interact with one or two children in mother's presence. They are not yet at a level of social and verbal development that will enable them to cope in a large group away from mother. An informal group serves as a natural transition to a larger, more formal group. The group can be disbanded when the children seem fatigued, and an individual child can be removed from the group if need be.

*"When do most children appear to be ready for nursery school?"*

Again, readiness for nursery school varies with each child. In general, children of about three can relate to other children, can express their needs clearly and comprehend simple directions, can separate more easily, are beginning to achieve bowel and bladder control, and have relinquished their bottles. So we suggest that a child should be considered for nursery school when he or she is three years old.

*"I understand that those achievements are important, but I was wondering how often a three-year-old who has accomplished all that should be attending school."*

Most three-year-olds do best when they attend nursery school twice or, at most, three times a week.

*"How long should the nursery-school session be?"*

In most well-run nursery schools, the session for the first weeks are for an hour to an hour and a half, and are then lengthened to two hours as the children's tolerance increases.

### Separation

*"Should we expect the children to separate easily from their mothers at nursery school?"*

The children who are ready will separate easily. Some may even be ready to have mother leave the first day. Others need their mothers to stay for a while—sometimes for several days or for up to two or three weeks. At some schools, mothers spend the whole session with their children for the first few days, then spend the session in a hall outside the classroom or in a room provided for mothers, and then finally leave for the entire session.

*"I think that when the time comes, I'm going to have a harder time leaving my son than he will have leaving me."*

That does happen. Many adults carry vestiges of their own separation problems. Sometimes the mother's reluctance to part is subtly conveyed to the child. The child appears to be having difficulty separating, when in reality it is the mother's problem. Separation is a developmental issue of great significance, and it requires understanding and sensitive handling.

## Teachers' Attitudes About Separation

*"I understand the need to stay with a child at first, but my impression is that teachers frown on mothers' staying. What can I do if a teacher asks me to leave so that she can handle my child?"*

Most nursery-school teachers today have a better understanding of this issue than in the past. Many schools have policies that allow mothers to separate gradually by standing in the back of the room, then in an adjacent room, and finally by leaving when the child appears ready to separate. This usually takes about two weeks. If the child is still unable to separate at the end of that time, the parents and teachers should recognize that he or she is not ready for nursery school.

## Readiness

That doesn't mean the child has to be excluded from other types of social situations. He or she can be entered in an informal play group. Most community libraries have story hours. YMCAs offer exercise and play groups and swim classes that mothers can attend with their children.

Until about age three, children are at their best with only one or two other children. That is why some nursery schools introduce only a few children at a time to the class until the whole class is assembled.

*"Suppose you are a mother working outside the home. It is impossible to spend so much time getting your child adjusted to nursery school."*

Some mothers who work outside the home make arrangements with their employers and make up the time later. Other mothers have the child's caretaker stay with the child at school as long as the child needs to get adjusted.

## Father's Role

*"You talk about mothers staying with the child. Can't the father play a role in this too?"*

We say mother because it is usually the mother who assumes this role. Of course the father can be the one who takes the child to school and stays until the child is able to separate. It depends on the family's situation. In some families, the father's schedule is flexible enough to allow him to spend this time with the child.

*"It seems that until the children are about three, we should not really be expecting them to be ready for nursery school. It's disappointing in a way because I was looking forward to doing some things on my own. But I can see that they need more time to separate, and that the time spent with them now can be very constructive."*

*"I'm very glad I don't have to rush to find a nursery school and that I'll have the better part of a year yet with my daughter. I enjoy being an important part of her development and having fun with her."*

All parents must realize that children need time to reach the stage of development needed for nursery school, and that the time needed is different for each child. The time parents spend with a child of this age can be very important for the child's growth.

## Toilet Training

In the past two years, parents have been advised that most children are not ready for toilet training. Now that the children are in their third year, parents, and sometimes grandparents, are getting more eager for toilet training to be accomplished. It is once again time to assess the children's stage of development—and parents' expectations—in this area.

*"My husband and his mother are trying to pressure me into getting our son toilet trained. I'm not sure he is ready. Could we review just what a child needs to be able to cooperate for toilet training?"*

First, the child needs to be able to understand that things belong in certain places—for example, that dishes belong in one cupboard, groceries in another, garbage goes in the garbage can, and toys have a shelf. The child is then able to understand that urine and stool are deposited in a special place in the bathroom.

*"My child puts everything into the garbage. Would you say that is an indication he is not ready?"*

Yes. He needs more time to be able to understand where things belong.

*"Our son is beginning to observe in the bathroom and announce what he observes. He designates urination as 'wee wee' and a bowel movement as 'poo poo.' Does that signify that he is ready?"*

He may be beginning to understand the purpose of the bathroom. He is closer to being ready for toilet training, because he is verbal enough to label a need, which is the second requirement for toilet training readiness. In addition, a child has to be aware of the sensation of a full bladder or rectum and be able to express this to a parent.

*"My child is beginning to tell me—after she has soiled. That upsets me, and I've been tempted to scold her."*

It's natural for parents to be disappointed at this stage. Your daughter is achieving awareness, but not in time to warn you. That awareness will come if she is reminded that soon she will be able to tell you before she soils. She is in a stage of development that will pass more quickly if she is not intimidated and frightened by parental criticism.

It is best not to make any comment that could be interpreted by the child as criticism. Parents should remember that toilet training is a big step for children. In addition to being able to recognize the need to void and tell a parent in time, children also need to be able to control their sphincter muscles until they are undressed and placed in the proper position at the toilet.

*"My child has sometimes gotten to the point of telling me in time, but when she is put on the toilet seat she can't perform until she is removed and put in a clean diaper. Then she has a bowel movement in a few minutes. That is exasperating, and I'm afraid I have shown my annoyance."*

In addition to being able to hold back until being placed on the toilet, children must also be able to relax the tightened spinchter in order to expel the contents of the bowel or bladder. This ability takes longer to develop. If your child has not achieved this ability yet, there is nothing to be gained by showing annoyance.

Making the child anxious may inhibit the ability to relax the sphincter. The whole process of becoming ready to have bowel and bladder control is a complicated one. Children may accomplish part of it and need more time to achieve it completely. Parents should observe and be aware but not interfere with success by trying to hurry the child.

*"Does bowel control come before bladder control?"*

In most cases, bowel control is achieved before bladder control, because at this age only one or two bowel movements occur during a day. However, there are some children who achieve bladder control first.

*"To achieve bowel control, must a child have a regular time every day to move his bowels?"*

Bowel control is more easily achieved if there is a regular time for bowel movements every day. For one thing, this allows the parents to be on the alert and available for assistance if the child needs it.

*"Should I place a potty seat in the bathroom now so it will be available when my child is ready?"*

First assess how ready your child is to control her toilet activities. If she seems ready, then it may be helpful to have the potty seat available. Some children sit on it clothed for quite a while before they are ready to use it properly.

*"I put a potty seat in our bathroom a few weeks ago. It has not made the impact on my son that I hoped it would. He just pushes it around like a cart. Should I stop him when he does that?"*

You son doesn't seem able to associate defecation and urination with the potty chair. To him it is a toy. It is probably best to put it away until he seems more prepared for it—perhaps for a month or two.

*"Is it better to use a chair that sits on the floor, or a seat that fits the adult seat?"*

Most children adapt more easily to the seat that sits on the floor. If the other type of seat is used, it should firmly attach to the adult seat. It should have back and foot rests, and a strap to keep the child from slipping out. If the seat is unsteady or uncomfortable, the child may become frightened. This may retard progress for many months.

*"My child seems far from being ready for toilet training. He watches me flush the stool from his diaper down the toilet, and he gets so upset that I have to wait till he is busy playing and not watching me before I continue. Is that normal?"*

Some children regard their bowel movements as part of themselves. To see part of themselves flushed down the toilet is very frightening. Until a child is able to deal with this fear verbally, it is best not to expose him to this situation unnecessarily.

*"My daughter is already indicating that she wants to sit on the adult toilet. Twice she has pulled me to the toilet and, suspecting what she was trying to do, I placed her on it. She urinated once and had a bowel movement once, for which I praised her. But she has shown no interest since. I didn't know whether to suggest she use it again or wait till she tells me."*

She is showing that she is developing an awareness of the use of the bathroom. When she is ready, she will let you know. There is no way to predict how soon that will be. It depends on her rate of maturation and perhaps the stimulation she gets by observing others.

*"I have an older daughter. I think I tried to start toilet training long before she was ready, so I'm not going to do that with this one. However, she watches when the older one uses the bathroom; she tries to be just like her big sister. It seems to me she is going to achieve control long before her sister did."*

Many children who are ready to exert control respond to seeing an older sibling or peer use the toilet properly. This is often more effective than any other stimulus—certainly more so than parental coercion.

*"What about nursery schools that require that children have bowel and bladder control? Isn't that a kind of coercion?"*

■                                                                          ■

Not all nursery schools have this requirement. Most nursery-school adminis-trators know that children of this age have either established control or will do so shortly. However, if parents try to force toilet training so that the child can enter nursery school, the child's progress in this area may actually be hindered.

*"When my daughter has a bowel movement while she is napping, she some-times wakes up and smears the stool all over her crib. Of course, I scream 'No, no' when I see her doing it. She seems upset, but she may repeat it in a few days. What should I do?"*

At this stage of development, children like to smear. We've all noted this when they eat cereal or mashed potatoes. We tolerate this form of smearing, but we strongly disapprove of the smearing of stool. Parents can give children an outlet for smearing with playdough or finger paints, in a setting with an apron, and plastic sheets or newspapers, for example. Smearing of stool usually passes when bowel control has been achieved.

*"Throughout these discussions the message has been 'easy does it.' Does that mean we should not be asking our children if they want to use the bathroom, that we should just let them tell us when they are ready?"*

Children between twenty-four and thirty months are at various stages of development and ability. We have observed that when children are ready to exert bowel and bladder control, they make their desires known. The success-ful achievement may take just a few days of child and parent cooperation instead of a few months of struggle. Some children are successful sooner than others, but most will be successful by about age three.

## Communication: Speech and Language Development

When children are between two and two and a half years old, they start to form two- and three-word sentences. Some may even form longer sentences, while a few still have not gone beyond simple phrases. Most children this age understand between a thousand and fifteen hundred words but can express only two or three hundred.

You have been anxiously awaiting the time when your children are able to talk to you. What have you been noticing about the children's speech development? Do you think they are at last acquiring the ability to express themselves?

*"I have noticed a great improvement in our son's speech—three-word sen-tences. But sometimes I don't understand exactly what he is trying to say. I ask him to repeat it, telling him 'Mommy can't understand you,' and I feel so bad that I can't."*

This happens frequently when a child first begins to talk. If you do understand what the child is saying, try saying the words clearly. He will perhaps be able to say them a little bit more clearly himself.

■                                                                                  ■

*"We know what our daughter means. She says 'nackers' for eyeglasses and 'dazu' for diaper. I think it comes from putting together 'diaper you' and 'change you.' "*

You can say, "Yes, diaper." If you say the correct word, she will catch on when she is ready. For now, the point is that she is using language.

## Modeling Correct Speech

*"Should a parent correct a child's mispronunciations?"*

It is best not to correct them, but to simply say the word correctly. For example, if the child says "lelphant" for "elephant" you can say, "Oh, yes, that is the elephant." Don't use the child's pronunciation, but try to speak to him, converse with him, and listen to what he has to say. It's important for children to feel that they are communicating and getting responses.

*"Isn't a parent supposed to correct a child's speech? If not, how does the child learn?"*

The parents' role is to talk with the child and to model correct speech. For example, if the child says "psgetti" or "getti" for spaghetti, the parent should reply clearly "You want spaghetti." The child will be able to adopt this model of speaking when his central nervous system matures sufficiently.

Speech is a complicated process. Think about what it requires. The child has to be able to hear what is said, so his hearing must be intact. To say a word, he must also be able to marshal his vocal chords and the muscles for speech and respiration. Not all parts of this system mature at the same rate. And no two children develop the ability to speak at the same rate.

It is possible to understand how much variability there can be. One can also understand how frustrating it can be for both parent and child to have the parent say over and over again, for example, "say spa-ghe-tti" in trying to correct a child who is not ready to respond at that level and can only manage "psgetti" or just "getti." That is why the parent should model correct speech but not correct the child's pronunciation.

*"I must confess that we are so anxious for our son to speak correctly that I have done just that—sat in front of him and made him look at my mouth as I said a word—'tri-cy-cle,' for instance."*

## Stuttering

Such drilling can inhibit the development of speech. The child may recognize the parent's frustration and therefore seek to avoid such encounters.

*"I've noticed that my son may come up to me and repeat a syllable like 'gu, gu, go' while pushing me. I'll respond, 'Say, go,' but he'll do it again. Can children of this age stutter?"*

Children of this age may hesitate or repeat a syllable. This is a result of their anxiety to communicate coupled with their immaturity. The best approach is to listen patiently to the child without offering a correction—"You want to go. I understand," for example—then matter-of-factly carry out the requested activity. In some cases this occurs when there is too much hurry and tension. The appropriate remedy is to slow down the tempo and rhythm of activity and make no comment about the speech. Given a chance, this will subside without any intervention other than slowing things down.

## Bilingual Families

*"What about speaking more than one language to a child? My mother lives with us, and she speaks only Spanish. My husband and I speak mostly English to each other. Should we speak only one language to the baby? Some people have told us he is slow in talking because we speak two languages in our home."*

Most children brought up in a bilingual family learn to speak both languages and which to speak to whom. These children may initiate speech a little later than others, but usually no lasting difficulty results from the use of two languages. However, children whose speech development is slow—or who have a hearing impairment—should be spoken to in one language.

*"My wife and I work. Our housekeeper takes care of the baby while we are working. Her native tongue is Spanish, and she speaks a broken English. We want her to speak English to our child, but she has difficulty with it and lapses into Spanish. We are satisfied, because we feel that if our housekeeper speaks Spanish and we speak English, our daughter will learn two languages."*

If your child is making progress in both languages, she can only benefit from this situation.

*"I work, too, and I come home late in the evening. Our son spends most of his time with our maid, who can speak both Spanish and English. But she just isn't a communicator, and she doesn't say much. Our son's language acquisition doesn't seem to be as fast as our friends' children of his age. Can this be related to the lack of speech stimulation?*

Your son's timetable for speech development may be slower than that of your friends' children, or it may be that he is not spoken to enough. If a child's caretaker does not stimulate speech development, parents should attempt to make up for this lack by spending as much of their free time as possible speaking with their child.

*"Can a child who isn't stimulated at home and is slow in acquiring speech make up for it when he goes to school?"*

Children can compensate for lost time, but parents should bear in mind that there is a natural timetable for speech development. The best results come when we take advantage of that sensitive period when the children are most receptive to language stimulation. By this age, children should understand about twelve hundred words, understand simple commands and questions, and be able to use about three hundred words. A child needs exposure to language to achieve this level of development.

## Inhibiting Communication

*"Isn't it important how we talk to children, too? I have found that loud voices upset my son. If someone asks him a question in a loud voice, he cringes and can't answer."*

*"I remember feeling that way about one of my uncles when I was little. That tone of voice bothers me even now. So I can see how it may bother a small child."*

Some parents and other adults talk to children the way they talk to adults— loudly, firmly, and emphatically. The tone of voice an adult uses may give a child the impression that the adult is angry. The child may therefore be reluctant to respond.

Another hindrance to effective communication with children is long explanations. At this age, children can't understand or process a lot of detail. They need explanations in short, declarative sentences. For instance, suppose a wheel is locked on your child's toy car. The parent may say, "Your car won't go because the rear axle has picked up a thread that wound around it. It has to be removed before it will go."

The parent could have explained more simply: "The car is stuck. Let's fix it." Then, as the car is repaired: "We unwind the thread. Then the wheel will turn and the car will go." The next time the problem occurs, the child may understand the situation and deal with it on his own.

## Crying

*"My child cries when spoken to firmly, and that upsets us."*

Children want and need to be liked. Your son may believe that if he is spoken to sternly, he is not liked. Or he may interpret the stern words as a scolding.

*"Our child cries whenever he wants something. Sometimes older children give him what he wants when he cries. We don't want him to get into the habit of making requests this way."*

Children of this age are just emerging from a period in which they used crying as a language. Parents should now be patiently and gently encouraging them to be verbal and not cry for things. For example: "Tell Mommy, then Mommy can get it for you. Mommy doesn't understand what you want when you cry." Children have to be dealt with this way repeatedly before they learn that talking is more effective than crying.

Children understand instinctively that there is a change in the way parents respond to them as they get older and become more verbal. They respond well to recognition and approval in simple words they can understand. The resulting boost to their self-esteem brings on a new level of the parent-child relationship that can be most rewarding.

■                                                                              ■

# 18

Now that the children are two and older, their naps are shorter. A few children may even have given up regular naps entirely. This makes the  waking time longer and puts pressure on mother to devise ways of spending time profitability and pleasantly. Although children can play alone a little longer than before, they still demand a great deal of parental attention. How do you spend playtime with your children and how do you feel about it?

*"I've noticed that my son is sleeping less during the day lately. It hasn't caused a problem—in fact, it works out well for us, because we stay outdoors longer. I take him to the park and he plays in the sandbox, or runs around with the other children. When we come home, it's time for bath and supper and then bed. He is quite ready for bed, because he has had such an active afternoon."*

*"We live on a street where there are many children our child's age so we just stay out and play when the weather is warm. We have an earlier bedtime, too."*

*"I work outside the home. Now that our son is awake more, my housekeeper has less time to do the housework. She says it is difficult to find activities to do with him. As a matter of fact, I'm not sure I would either if I were home with him all day."*

Many adults do not know how to spend quality time with a toddler. This is an important period for the child. It's a time when the capacity to learn is very high and curiosity is great. But the child's increasing mobility requires parental intervention for support, for setting limits, and most important, for teaching.
Parents should remember that they are the child's primary teachers—not just guardians or, as some parents seem to view their role, policemen.

*"Could you give an example of what you mean? I've always felt that children learn more in a formal nursery-school setting than they do at home."*

There are many examples. One is the parents' role in teaching the words to name things, people, places, and actions. In other words, parents teach the most important tool a human being has—language. In addition, parents introduce children to abstractions. We teach children number concepts when we point out "two dogs," "three balls," or "one cookie." When we point out the "red" bus or the "yellow" truck, we teach color concepts. When we ask children to get the ball "behind" the chair or "in front of" the table or to pull the block "on" the table or "under" the table, we are teaching spatial relations. When we throw a ball "up" or "down," or to Daddy or Mommy, we teach direction.

*"I never realized how significant even an ordinary daily encounter can be. I think I can pay more attention and do better at it. What about play and games?"*

It is great fun to see children develop interest and understanding of games. At this age they enjoy rolling a ball to a parent or other child and having it rolled back. They may try to throw the ball but usually have little control in direction or force in throwing. They will achieve this later. They enjoy singing games like "Ring-Around-a-Rosey" and "All Around the Mulberry Bush." "Peekaboo" may now advance to hiding objects under a pillow or blanket or even to "Hide-and-Seek" with child and parent. This is a very important game, because children begin to learn from it that things exist even if not visible.

*"I've tried 'Peekaboo' with my daughter, but she becomes frightened if she can't see me. I have to hide so she can see at least part of me. When she hides, she stands so she can be seen. Why does she do that?"*

She is playing the way a child of her age plays. She is still unable to separate fully from you, and she isn't sure that you exist when she can't see you. These are concepts and experiences that she is being helped to understand by playing this game. She is not ready to play by adult rules yet; she plays in a way that makes her comfortable.

*"When can children play this game as adults understand the rules?"*

Children may not be comfortable having themselves, playmates, or parents fully hidden until they are seven or eight years old.

*"I guess this is another example of expectations that a child this age can't meet. What other ways do you suggest for spending time with children this age?"*

You can try activities that improve eye-hand coordination, like stringing large beads, lacing shoes, stacking blocks, placing simple shapes into the openings in a board or box, and doing simple puzzles. In addition, you can try large-muscle activities, like running, riding a kiddie car, climbing small steps, and sliding down a short slide. Some children enjoy crawling through a "tent" made by placing a cloth over a card table.

## Reading

It is good to follow play with quieter activities, such as looking at books and pointing out pictures. The children are beginning to be ready for books containing nursery rhymes and captioned pictures.

*"Are children this age ready to be read fairy tales?"*

Most children of this age are not ready for fairy tales. Learning about reality is more important—for example, understanding that one parent, or both, goes to work and comes back, and that events in their lives occur in a predictable order.

*"My child likes music. We spend quite a lot of time listening to records. She likes to dance to the rhythm."*

Listening to music, moving to a rhythm, and learning to sing songs are very beneficial ways to spend time. Children like to hear their parents sing the same songs over and over. It does not matter to them how well their parents' sing. Children enjoy when parents sing to them, listen to music with them, and demonstrate dancing and clapping movements for them.

*"Sometimes I have to cook or straighten up the house. I can't always spend time just playing with my child, although I enjoy it. When I try to do chores, he calls to me and wants me to play in his room. I don't want to make him unhappy, so I stay with him, but I'm a little irritable and impatient."*

What the child may want is to be in the same room with you. If you're working in the kitchen or laundry room, you can give a toy to the child to play with near you. If you are making a bed or dusting, your child may like to help out.

*"I've tried that with my daughter and it works, but my chores take more time that way."*

But you are not just getting your chores done. You are also teaching your child what is to be done, when, and how. As she learns, she gets a sense of achievement and a sense of pleasure in helping. Parents should remember that it is difficult, if not impossible, for children to hurry.

## Community Resources

*"I don't like to stay in the house so much with my son, but there is just so much outdoor walking and playing we can do. I get bored, and I think it's conveyed to my child. What about organized activities?"*

Most communities have facilities and activities for toddlers. YMCAs offer simple gymnastic groups. Many public pools offer swimming instruction for parents and children. In some communities, there are music activities and basic arts-and-crafts groups for children. One or more of these facilities may be ideal for parents who want a change of scene and stimulation for themselves and their children.

Children can also be taken on short exploratory trips—such as to the post office, grocery store, or local fire station. Most children enjoy zoos, especially petting areas reserved for young children. Many museums have special activities for young children and their parents. Trips to a store should be for specific items; children this age shouldn't be expected to tolerate long shopping trips.

*"I like to visit friends who have children close to my child's age. But these visits often have to be cut short because the children can't get along with each other. Then I feel cheated out of visiting with my friend and am a little cross with my child. Are children of this age too young still for visiting?"*

Children of this age, between two and three years, can manage and even enjoy visiting, but they do best with only one other child. They still need adult supervision and cannot be expected to negotiate sharing toys without supervision. Their visiting behavior improves as they become more familiar with the host child or children, and the host parents' attitudes. The visiting child should bring one or two toys of his own in case the host child has difficulty sharing. It is important for the parent to recognize that the priority is to help the child learn to socialize, not for the adults to socialize. As children become more experienced with interactive play, they may be able to play for as long as a half an hour with a parent nearby.

*"When can children be expected to play together without needing parents to settle squabbles?"*

That varies with each child's ability to socialize and the socializing situations provided. Most children older than three are able to play together reasonably well, and get increasingly better from then on. However, there still may be instances in which parental intervention is needed, even with school-age children.

*"It is nice to hear how other mothers spend time with children. It makes me feel that it's possible to be with a child and not be bored, and at the same time help her develop."*

Spending time with children has gotten poor press from people who do not fully understand the parental role. Many parents who understand that their role is to teach creatively and be supportive get a great deal of satisfaction out of watching the children develop.

## Toys

Toys are important to children. Parents should keep in mind that the attachment a child has for a certain toy may be an important part of the child's emotional development. Loss of a dearly loved toy can cause a child a great deal of needless anguish, and can interfere with the separation process.

Many parents are concerned about the quantity and quality of toys they make available to their children. Have any of you been thinking about this issue?

*"My concern is having too many toys around. When I notice that my child hasn't been playing with certain toys, I put them away. If he later wants anything back, I pull it out again."*

It is good that you don't give away, or throw away the toys, as many mothers do. These toys may be ones the child has become attached to and from which the child has gotten a sense of security. A child whose toy is thrown away may feel as though she has lost a friend. It's much better to save the toys in a box and bring them out again as they are needed. When a toy is reintroduced, the child can be shown a way to play with it more imaginatively.

*"When I was a child, the toys were made of wood and didn't wear out easily. My mother still has some of them."*

*"My husband still has an old stuffed elephant that he had when he was a child, but he can't understand our child's attachment to certain toys."*

Adults sometimes forget the attachments to toys they had when they were children. Recalling these attachments may enable parents to be more in tune with their children.

*"We have a big toy box in which our son settles down and plays. Sometimes he digs deep and pulls out old toys. They are never put away for long."*

Many parents store some less-used toys away so that their children have something stimulating when other toys lose their attractiveness or novelty.

## Mother's Capacity to Play

*"My son is often cranky when he is confined to the house. I didn't realize that he may be tired of his old toys and need something new. I thought it was because I was inept at playing with him."*

Mothers differ in their capacity to play with their children. However, every child has a need to relate to the parent through play. So it is important to notice the kind of toys your child enjoys. It's also important to enhance play by introducing different toys and activities periodically as the child's interests and comprehension increase. Between two and two and a half years of age, children enjoy toys that require them to insert simple shapes into appropriate spaces, although some children may need a little assistance at first. Many mothers make this kind of toy from a milk carton or plastic jar by cutting shapes of cardboard to fit the holes of the same shape in the containers. The shapes may be brightly colored with vegetable dyes.

*"I've done that, and it works well. My daughter sits on the floor and keeps herself busy with this activity for half an hour or more."*

That is a long time for a child to concentrate. Another activity that children now enjoy is putting objects into a wagon or shoe box with a long string, then carting the objects from one part of the room or house to another. This often becomes a delivery-man game later on.

Children this age also like simple puzzles of two or three pieces and one with handles on the pieces. They also like to stack measuring cups and try to arrange the cups in size order, although some may not achieve this until three years of age.

*"I gave my son a few small cardboard boxes of different sizes to play with, and he cherishes them more than store-bought toys. He works at fitting the boxes into each other. Some days it keeps him busy for almost an hour! But some days he gets frustrated and throws the boxes away. Should I give him something else to do then, or show him how he can do it?"*

First assess how upset the child is. If his frustration is great, he may not respond to your efforts to help. If that happens, try removing the toy and introducing another activity. If there is less frustration, show the child how to overcome his difficulty. It is important to do this as unobtrusively as possible so that the child doesn't feel you are taking over. If the toy continues to frustrate the child, possibly he is not ready for it. It would be best to retire the toy for a month or two.

*"I was wondering if big beads strung on a shoelace are all right to introduce now."*

Strung wooden beads that can't be swallowed—about one and a half to two inches in diameter—are appropriate for a child of this age. Sometimes these beads can be purchased with a lacing frame; an old shoe can serve the same purpose.

## Parental Supervision

All of these activities enhance the child's eye-hand coordination and manual dexterity. Many children also enjoy pasting and coloring now.

*"I'm afraid to start my child on activities that involve pasting or coloring. We'll have it all over the house."*

Pasting and coloring should be done under parental supervision, in a suitable place and manner. These activities should be reserved for times when a parent can give undivided attention. If the child pastes or colors in any place other than the one designated for it, the activity should be discontinued.

*"I guess I've been doing the wrong thing. I tell my child to color only on the paper, but when I look again she has been coloring on the chairs, the walls, everywhere. I get angry and scold her."*

Children of this age still need constant supervision when involved in activities that can end destructively.

## Security in Repetition

*"We have been spending a great deal of time indoors looking at books. However, my child sometimes wants to read the same book over and over again. When I try to introduce a different book, he protests. Is that normal?"*

Children may enjoy a familiar book many times in succession. It helps them verify what they know and gives them a sense of security. Some children will explore a new book on their own and finally ask to look at it with a parent.

*"My child just wants to roll a ball or his cars back and forth. He never seems to tire of it. How can I introduce something else?"*

Some children have to be allowed to expand their interests on their own timetable. However, a parent or caretaker can introduce something that accommodates the child's interests, such as building a tunnel, road, or train tracks with blocks. This may arouse interest and start the child on other activities.

*"Our baby wants to hear the same record over and over again. He has a few nursery rhymes and lullaby records. He can tell by the cover which is the one he wants. He can pick it out of a pile even if I try to conceal it."*

Children do become attached to certain songs and rhymes just as they do to toys. However, many children listen to other music when played on the adult cassette player and may increase their repertoire that way. In addition, there are records with action directions and games that are fun and satisfy a child's need to move around as well.

*"My child doesn't have a cassette player, but we sing a lot together and clap and march to music. We enjoy it, and I find visiting children enjoy it too."*

## Sounds

From time immemorial, singing has been part of growing up. Singing is a very good way to relate to a child through music. Children of this age also like musical toys such as drums and xylophones.

*"Someone gave my son a drum, but we had to take it away because we couldn't stand the banging."*

The banging gives him a sense of achievement and power. But if the drum is too noisy for you, the tops of the drumsticks can be covered with sponge. This mutes the sound but allows the child to enjoy the toy and the sound it produces.

*"I made a drum for our child with an empty oatmeal box and two ice cream sticks with sponge at the tips. That rescued a rainy day for us."*

*"This gives me an idea of what to do with the hammer of our daughter's pegboard. I'll paste sponge on the tip so the noise won't bother me so*

*much. Also, there may be less chance of her getting hurt when she misses the peg."*

These are ways to allow a child the freedom to bang, which is one of the activities she may enjoy for the feeling of power it gives and the satisfaction she receives from coordinating hand and eye movements.

## Attachment to Toys

*"My child's favorite toy is a Raggedy Ann doll. She repeats with her doll most of the things I do with her. She changes her, feeds her a bottle, pushes her in her stroller. The doll is a mess. She has other dolls in better shape, but she wants only this one. I've been tempted to replace it with a new one."*

It's best to let your daughter keep the doll. The appearance of the doll may be just what endears the doll to her. Even an exact replica will not be the same for her.

*"My son has an old, ratty stuffed dog that he is so attached to we can't go anywhere without it. When do children give up old toys?"*

Aside from the attachment a child develops for an object, the object may represent to the child a link to parents. That is, the toy may become a transitional object, which helps a child make the transition from total dependence to independence. So these toys must be treated with care and respect in the child's presence. All of children's play should be treated with respect because it is children's "work." The importance of children's play and toys is just beginning to get the attention it should.

## The Effects of Television

There is ongoing discussion and controversy about the effects of television on children. Which programs should they watch, at what age, and for how long? Does violence on the television screen stimulate violence in children? Is television too stimulating before bedtime? Does prolonged television watching affect children's creativity? What does it do to a child's ability to relate to people? What ideas do they get about life from television? Are they confusing reality with fantasy?

The children are older now and more apt to be exposed to television. What are your feelings about the effects of television, and how much television do you let your child watch?

*"I guess I use TV to quiet my child down. When he gets overexcited, I put him on the sofa and turn on the TV. He gets so absorbed that he simmers down almost immediately. Then I can put him down for his nap."*

*"My experience has been just the opposite. My daughter is often scared by things on TV, especially some announcers in commercials. She comes running to me while pointing to the screen and saying, 'Man! Man!'"*

■                                                                              ■

*"I find I have to use the TV as a baby-sitter—sometimes because I don't have anyone else to watch my daughter when I'm doing something that I need to concentrate on, such as preparing a meal, making an important phone call, or even going to the bathroom in privacy."*

We're not concerned about instances when the television is used for a limited time, but rather when it is used for hours on end while a parent or caretaker attends to other matters. This is not at all an uncommon practice.

*"What harm is there in allowing the child to watch television if she is quiet and content, and it allows the mother some time to complete some of her work?"*

A child left in front of a TV set is being deprived of the parent's company. The child is also deprived of learning experiences that he or she gets by observing and participating in what the parent does—for example, making a bed, cooking, putting things away. Any such activity is a learning opportunity for a child and provides a chance for communication that the TV does not.

## Violence

*"I've always worried about the violence that children see on TV. Even children's programs have violent episodes sometimes. What effect does TV violence have on them?"*

Many studies have been and are now being done on this issue. While they are inconclusive, some studies show that violence seen on TV can evoke violence in easily aroused individuals. Certainly the vast amount of violence seen on TV can desensitize a child and make violence seem a normal way of life. The consequences of that attitude are frightening to comtemplate.

*"I've noticed a difference between the games played by children who watch TV and those played by my child, who hasn't watched TV. We don't have a TV set so my child has not been exposed to any of the things you mention, but he is being initiated by others. When I hear this going on, I step in and suggest some other game. It doesn't always work, but I try."*

Children who watch TV a great deal are so influenced by it that it cuts down on their originality and creativity. Some children act out violent scenes or relate to fantasy situations. Others are attracted to lavish displays of cars, clothes, food, and musical styles that are presented on television.

*"I understand what you mean. Children who watch a lot of TV are deprived of the normal spontaneous play that they need and are exposed to situations and concepts that shouldn't be part of their lives. So they don't really have a normal childhood."*

*"I understand that too and it worries me, but what can I do? I set the TV to an appropriate children's program or a nature program and go out of the room for a minute and when I come back there is something violent being shown. You just can't avoid it."*

*"That happens to me too. When I realize that the program is different, I turn the set off. Then my son begins to cry and complain. I try to distract him and get him interested in something else, which usually works. But I don't know what he has seen while I was away and whether it was harmful or not."*

*"I try to get an idea about a program before turning it off so I can figure out what may cause anxiety or confusion for my child. Then I can talk to her about it."*

It is good to try to find out the child's interpretation of what she is watching so that you know her level of thinking and have a clearer sense of what to explain. This approach is better than simply correcting the impression you think the child may have received. Ideally, parents should watch TV with their child so they know what the child has been exposed to and can better help the child deal with her interpretation of a program. This is not possible if the child watches TV alone.

*"Since TV can be such a confusing experience, isn't it best to not have any TV at all?"*

Some parents have used that approach, and it can work with small children. But as children get older, parents cannot always control their TV viewing. TV is apparently here to stay. There *are* some worthwhile educational programs. The sensible approach is to allow your child to view only those programs that meet with your approval. Children learn to accept this just as they do other events in their lives that are arranged for them.

*"In our house, we turn the TV on only at news time. My son usually is in the living room with my husband at the time. Some of the news is pretty terrifying even for me. Should we remove our son from the room, even though he doesn't want to leave Daddy?"*

There is another solution. For example, Daddy can watch the news later at night and read or play with your son when he first gets home. If this is not possible and your son is in the room with Daddy when the news is on, he may not always be watching anyway. Remember, children of this age do not have a long attention span. However, your husband should be aware of when and what your child is watching. He can find out how the child interprets what is being shown on TV, then explain and clarify as necessary.

*"I think the TV has cut off communication in many families. We may sit glued to the set and not exchange a word for an entire evening. I think TV should be monitored for parents, too."*

■                                                                 ■

Judicious use of the TV would help many families, parents, and children alike. Perhaps we could get back to talking more to one another or reading more. Certainly, many children love to be read to. In addition, reading to a child helps to ensure success in school later on.

## Learning to Play with Others

There is now beginning to be more interactive play. As the children socialize more, sharing of toys becomes a pressing issue. Many parents expect children to share toys readily, and the child may be reluctant—in fact, may vigorously protest the suggestion to share. Parents must realize that sharing requires a maturity that a child may not yet have achieved. Children are usually better able to handle sharing at the playground, which is everyone's turf, than at home. In addition, a child recognizes which children play in the manner he enjoys and shuns the ones who don't. Have sharing and play with other children become issues for any of you?

*"There's always a sharing problem when another mother visits with a child my child's age. Shouldn't my child be able to share toys by now?"*

Children between two and two and a half are just beginning to understand what is theirs and what is not. They do not emerge from the "I, my, mine" stage until they are about three. The ease with which children learn to share is also related to the experiences they have had. For example, if a child has been forced to give up a cherished toy before he is ready to do it, he may be reluctant to share other toys.

*"Maybe I've been expecting too much. I've been making my son give his toys to visiting children. I know my friends expect me to see to it that my child shares with their children. If I don't do that, won't he grow up to be selfish?"*

### Parental Fear of Selfishness

Many parents worry that their children will grow up to be selfish adults. However, a child this age who refuses to share is not being selfish in the sense that adults understand the term. The child is only trying to establish his identity, part of this involves claiming what belongs to him.

*"But it is so embarrassing when he refuses to share. What can be done to ease the situation?"*

First, understand the level of your child's development in the area of sharing. Then tell your guest beforehand what behavior is characteristic of him. Until children are comfortable with each other, they may play only with their own toys. Perhaps you can suggest that visitors bring one or two of their own toys so that an exchange can be made.

*"A friend from out of town came to visit with her little girl, who is my daughter's age. My child was holding her doll when we went to the door.*

*The other little girl reached for the doll, and mine drew back and said, 'No!' in a very emphatic, unfriendly tone. My friend was carrying her daughter's favorite Snoopy, so I said, 'Yes, the dolly is yours, but see what a nice Snoopy she has.' As soon as her coat was off, my friend's daughter followed my child into her bedroom, holding her Snoopy, and in no time at all, they warmed up to each other. I can see what unpleasantness there could have been if I had insisted that my child give up her doll to the visitor.''*

*"When other little boys come to play with mine, it seems they all want the same thing—the tricycle. My son will push another child right off the tricycle if he wants it."*

Perhaps you can say, "It's his turn" and hold on to him, then turn to another child and say, "Now it's your turn." If you do it for each child often enough, they will get the idea that each boy gets a chance at it. This is the beginning of learning to take turns.

*"If I did that with my child, he would be kicking and screaming."*

Yes, but if you do not get upset with him and instead help him have his turn and keep repeating the turns, he will begin to wait his turn because he will understand that he will get a chance. Try to arrange the turns so that they come quickly and often.

*"I can arrange these situations better on the playground than at home. Why is that?"*

It may be that because it is not his turf, your son can accept taking turns better. At home the toys are his possessions, so he can't give them up as easily. Parents should remember that when another child takes a toy, the host child may think it has been taken for good.

*"I keep telling him that his toys are not going to be taken away, that they are his. I say, 'You will keep the toy. A friend is just visiting you. When we have a friend visiting, you let him play with your toys for a little while and you play with his. When you visit him, he will let you play with his toys, too.' "*

## Simple Directions

Maybe that's too long an explanation. Instead, you can say, for example, "This is yours. Adam will play with it now, and you will play with Adam's toys." Friendship may be too sophisticated a concept.

*"Is it too sophisticated to say, 'When you are at Derek's house you play with Derek's tricycle, and when Derek is at your house he can ride your tricycle'?"*

Try to offer a direction—not an explanation—and say it in as few words as possible. That's what children understand best at this age.

*"I have noticed that my son can't share certain toys no matter what toy the other child has. That makes for a difficult situation, especially when we invite someone for the first time."*

If you can anticipate the situation, it is certainly wise to tell the other child's parents and suggest that he bring a toy or two of his own. It is also a good idea to put away your child's favorite toys and leave out only the ones that are easy for your child to share. Of course, that does not guarantee that all will run smoothly. Sharing is a difficult concept for children to learn. Parents have to assess how ready their child is for it and not attempt to force the issue.

Parents can model sharing by offering the child something of their own. For example, suppose the parent is eating or drinking something that the child wants. The parent can say, "I will share my sandwich with you." Then the parent can reverse the procedure and ask for something of the child's. Through repetition of such episodes, the child gradually develops a less threatening view of sharing.

*"My child doesn't want to play at all with some children, let alone share a toy. It's very upsetting if the mother of the other child is a good friend. Should I make him play with other children?"*

## Children's Choice of Friends

He may have had a previous unpleasant experience with the other child. Even at this age, children can tell which children play with them in a way they enjoy and which do not. But they may not be verbal enough yet to explain this preference to you.

*"I think I know what bothers my son. This other child, who is in our play group, is a very active, vigorous child. When he wants something, he pushes to get it. He is a nice child—not mean, just aggressive. My son gets very upset if he is pushed. He doesn't like to be touched, let alone pushed."*

*"My daughter is like that. She never grabs something she likes from someone else, but she's always having things grabbed from her. She keeps away from children who do that."*

*"We have a similar problem. My son has two friends who are just like him, but another one is very aggressive. He pushes, bites, fights, and intimidates. My son is terrified of this boy. He'll say, "I hope he's not coming today, and I don't want to go to his house."*

That other boy must have done something that your son didn't like. You shouldn't leave your son in the play group when that boy is there or when it's at that boy's house. That will only intensify his feelings about the other child, and he may develop a fear of being left in any group or at any child's house.

*"We have a neighbor whose child will be two next month. This child and my daughter play constantly and share nicely."*

The gentle children are sometimes the ones who have the problems in groups. The rough, aggressive ones seem to get along better.

*"My son is quite active, and he is shunned by many of the other children and their mothers. There are very few houses that we can visit. When we do visit, I have to be involved with the children every minute."*

As a rule, very active children get along better with other children who are active. These are children whose interest is directed toward large-muscle motor activity. These children should be given appropriate outlets as much as possible. In the suburbs or country, there is room for them to run and chase. In the city, these children can be entered in an activity group that encourages jumping, running, and climbing. These children may then be able to settle down to quieter activity when that is called for.

*"I'm glad to hear that there is nothing wrong with active, assertive children. My son is one of the active ones—'motor oriented,' I've been told. My best friend's little girl is afraid of him, and because of that we don't see each other and it has caused a rift in our relationship."*

This does not have to be a permanent situation. You can continue your friendship and socialize at night when the children are asleep. As the children grow older and mature, they may be able to get along on a verbal level and even enjoy playing together. As children get older, there is growth and change in all areas—social, physical, and intellectual.

*"I'm glad to hear that this sharing problem is just a stage, and that they will later be able to cope with children they steer clear of now. But how long does that take?"*

As we have said, much depends on the child's maturational timetable and how much she is exposed to different situations. In most cases, it takes a few months.

## Playing Alone

As children grow older, parents may become anxious for them to play more by themselves. Children do begin to play alone now, but usually not as long as parents would like. Children of this age are just beginning fantasy play. Some may even have imaginary playmates. While this amuses some parents, others become concerned. Have you been seeing any change in the children's play routines recently?

*"I've noticed recently that my son will play alone on the living-room floor if I'm there too. He doesn't seem to be aware of me at all until I go out of the room. Then he follows me."*

*"The best time with my child is in the kitchen. When I'm cooking, I give him pots and pans. He strews them all over the floor and can enjoy himself and*

*let me work for at least fifteen to twenty minutes. Sometimes he has me taste what he is making, but mostly he just talks to himself."*

The children are more able to play alone in your presence. Some can take on roles—driving a car or cooking, for example—that encourage them to play alone for a limited time.

*"My daughter is interested only in her doll. She doesn't make any effort to play with anything else. She feeds, changes, dresses, and undresses it. She diapers it with facial tissue—loads of it—then takes it for a walk in the doll stroller. Sometimes she sounds as though she is scolding the doll. I get the impression that she is imitating me."*

She is assuming the maternal role, trying to better understand the world around her. Many children imitate their parents, and this gives parents the opportunity to see themselves as their children see them. That can be beneficial for parents; it may help them improve their parenting methods.

## Fantasy Play

*"My daughter is always taking my pocketbook or my shopping bag. She puts it over her arm and pretends to go shopping. She even goes out of the room and comes back with an item or two—a doll or one of her books, for example. She is particularly interested in having a set of keys so she can open the door to come back from the store. She is clearly imitating what we do almost every day."*

She seems to be fantasizing that she is the mother. That makes it possible to separate from you, to go down the hall alone and away from you. Children are now reaching a stage of imaginative play that helps them sort out their experiences. Parents should make an effort to observe a child's play during this stage. It gives a great deal of insight into children's level of development and the way they interpret events in their lives.

## Parental Intrusion

*"I've been doing that. Believe me, it's an eye opener! I was wondering if parents should just watch or get involved. Once in a while I try to get into the act, but my son will say 'No' and wave me away. I guess I'm a little hurt."*

This feeling of rejection is understandable. Now that they have more imagination, children like to feel they can at least control their own play, and they regard parental participation as an intrusion. A more realistic and positive way to regard this attitude on the part of the child is as an advance in development.

*"I guess I've been anticipating the time when my son could play more alone. It seems to have come suddenly and taken me unawares, so I felt rebuffed. Looking at it the way you just put it makes me feel better."*

*"Do you mean that we should never get involved when they are playing alone from now on?"*

A better approach is simply to notice what the child is doing and recognize it—"Oh, you are putting your doll to bed," for example—but not make a gesture to assist if you're not invited to. Children may regard such a gesture as intrusion. At this stage, most children like to have what they are doing recognized and labeled.

## Transitions

*"What if you have to go someplace or dinner is ready and you have to interrupt playtime? When I do that there is usually a scene, with much screaming and crying."*

Children this age have difficulty making transitions from one activity to another. Suppose you have to go out to an appointment. The child can be warned several minutes in advance. After that interval, you can say, "Now, it's time to go." If the child still resists, quietly but firmly tell her that she can finish whatever she is doing when you return home but that now you are going to go out. Name places of interest on the way and what the child will do when she gets there. That is, give her a scenario of what is to come so that she doesn't feel the end of her playtime means the end of all play. If you use this approach consistently, she will get to know that you mean business and that there is a procedure you follow.

## Imaginary Friends

*"My child plays alone pretty well for her age and can change activities fairly easily—with one exception. She has an imaginary friend who goes everywhere with us. I don't know whether to be upset and try to discourage her, or to go along with her."*

*"My son has just begun to have an imaginary dog. At first we thought it was amusing, but he is so serious about it that we are getting a little worried."*

*"My child has many imaginary friends, but they all have the same name— whether it's a teddy bear or a doll or another little girl—so it's sometimes hard to figure out which one she means."*

It is not unusual for a child to have imaginary friends. At this stage of development, children can't fully distinguish between animate and inanimate—the real and the fanciful. They endow everything with the same abilities that they themselves have. For example, it may seem to a child that a doll should talk. The child convinces herself that the doll does talk, and the doll becomes a real companion.

*"My daughter gets so busy with her doll, feeding her and tending to her. When I call for her lunch she brings the doll too, and insists it sit with her at the table. One spoonful of food is for her, the next for the doll. Of course,*

*this procedure slows down our meals. I don't know whether to go along or show my annoyance."*

Children who play alone a good deal are more apt to resort to imaginary playmates. They so want someone to play with that they may invest an available toy with the qualities of the friend they want to have. You should recognize this and say something like "I know you'd like to have a friend to play with, so you are making believe Teddy is your friend and you want him to come to your tea party." Then, you can join in the fantasy.

Children need fantasies. It is the parents' job to help them distinguish what is real from what is fantasy without derogating the fantasy. Fantasy is related to creativity, so it should be dealt with thoughtfully and sensitively.

*"I guess we just assumed that children understand things the way adults do and accept what is real and the way we see it. I must confess I was a little surprised and annoyed when my son wouldn't let his grandfather sit down in a certain chair because that's where the imaginary friend, the toy dog, was sitting. I insisted he let Grandpa sit there. Grandpa just laughed, but I made a scene and my son cried. From now on I'll do better, because I understand what's going on. How long does this stage last?"*

This, too, varies with each child and family situation. In some cases it lasts the better part of a year; in others it remains intense for a much shorter time. It usually disappears as language and means of testing reality becomes a little more advanced. The important thing is not to be angry, show alarm, or make fun of the child.

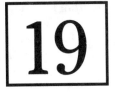

# 19

## *Understanding Your Child's Personality*

### *Your Child as an Individual*

Parents are beginning to recognize the personality characteristics of their children. Some are pleased with the way the child's personality is developing.  Others may find that the child is developing differently than they had hoped or anticipated. Some parents worry that they are trying to mold the child into a replica of themselves; others are actually trying to do this. At one time, infants were thought to be born with a "clean slate" and had no inborn abilities. We know now that infants are born with a specific endowment and a certain capacity for developing that endowment. How well that endowment flourishes is affected by the environment the child encounters.

What have you been noticing about your child's development as a person? Do you think of your child as a person with his own special personality, or as a replica of you or someone else in your family?

*"I've thought a lot about our child's personality. He appears anxious in some situations, such as visiting in an unfamiliar house. I keep wondering if he is going to be an anxious person all his life. He never takes the first step to make friends."*

*"My daughter makes friends with everyone at once. In fact, she seems to take over every situation she is in. Of course, that is cute now, but will that quality make her unpopular when she grows up? I guess I worry because my sister is like that. We never got along, and I'd hate to have my child be like that."*

*"Our child is so different from both of us. We are both very quiet and reserved. He is so outgoing and boisterous that we have said jokingly that there might have been a switch of babies in the hospital."*

We have all seen children who are aggressive, who bound into the room and take in everything in sight and participate immediately. Other children come into a room and simply stand and watch. Likewise, there are some grown-ups who are mixers and back-slappers, and there are others who are friendly in a quiet way. Some like a lot of noise and turmoil, and others like to stay away from that. So it is with our children—each personality is unique.

*"I have to laugh sometimes, because our son seems to be getting so much like his father. He resembles him physically. He seems to be getting his hearty laugh, and he seems to have the same walk. I like that, and I know my husband is thrilled when anyone says, 'He's the spittin' image of you.'"*

Some parents feel uncomfortable with a child whose personality is different from their own, and want their children to resemble themselves as much as possible.

## Parents' Upbringing

*"I have a different attitude. There are things that are part of me that I don't want our boy to have. I don't want him to be so inhibited that he can't express his feelings without a great deal of struggle and the help of therapy."*

It is natural for parents to want to avoid what they interpret as mistakes in their own upbringing. Are there particular issues you have in mind?

*"I want to try to avoid being as critical and demanding as my parents were of me. If I got ninety-five on an exam, for example, they would say, 'You should have gotten one hundred.' So, when my little girl plays with a toy and she doesn't get it quite right, I try not to say, 'That's not right, push this a little bit this way,' because I'm trying to build self-esteem. In that way, I guess I am trying to influence her personality."*

Your recognition of her accomplishments is an appropriate way to influence her development and enhance her self-esteem.

*"I had a big hang-up about food and separation. My two things were that my son should never have separation anxiety and should never be fat. So far, the food issue has worked out very well. But when I see him cling to me so much, I get worried. I think that I may not be handling this issue correctly."*

Apparently, the separation anxiety you experienced has made you more sensitive to it. It may appear to you that your son clings to you more than necessary because of this sensitivity. Most children this age have not yet accomplished separation and may not do so for some time. Try to evaluate behavior in light of what is age appropriate.

*"I want love and encouragement to be present in my home. Now that I'm older, I understand that this was lacking in my mother's home. Also, I want my child to be more aggressive than I was. I was nervous, shy, and stuttered as a child and I want to spare him that. Therefore, I am ultrasensitive when he gets upset, and I try to comfort him. I feel that the emotional aspect of child rearing is very important."*

*"My daughter is just like her grandmother, or at least I think that when she is very determined. That's good, although if she were more like me she would be easier to get along with."*

■                                                                              ■

## *Natural Endowment Versus Parental Influence*

*"How can you tell what is natural endowment and what is parental influence?"*

Some of a child's behavior is modeling after the parent, and some of it is endowment. If the parent hollers, the child will holler; if the parent slaps, the child will slap; if the parent is gentle, the child will be gentle too. There are also patterns in families from generation to generation that seem to indicate a certain genetic endowment—an inclination to athletics, the arts, or the sciences, for example. Even then, we cannot be sure how much is the result of modeling and how much is the result of genetic endowment.

*"My child is developing a very irritating personality. He still wants every-thing, when he wants it. I say, 'Wait a minute' and he bursts into a tantrum. If that's his personality, then I want to influence it. But how?"*

Children don't like to be constantly put off. You don't always say "Wait a minute" to your husband because he wouldn't like it. So you can imagine how being told to wait can affect someone whose frustration tolerance is short. A child is simply not able to wait as long as an adult.

Setting up a battle line when the child is trying for autonomy (the normal age range is eighteen months to two and a half years) establishes a pattern of relating with other people that the child may carry into adult life—a tendency to throw tantrums or to anger easily, for example. This goes on into adult life, so that social contacts have an angry quality and often end in disappointment.

This is a very crucial period; it demands of parents a great deal of patience and understanding of the child's personality.

*"My child always wants to be involved in what I am doing. If I allow that, all goes well."*

The way to deal with this situation is to involve the child. That makes for a more comfortable, happy atmosphere at home. But it takes a lot of time. There has to be a "fit" between mother and child's personality, and the person who can do the adapting isn't the child. Many parents were brought up to think it was the child who had to conform. The outcome of this approach has been adults who cannot manage in life or who are terribly angry every step of the way.

Parents' first job is to form the groundwork for basic trust by being available for children's needs. Now parents are dealing with character building and social responses, how children are going to relate to other people as they grow up. It is important to do it right. Looked at that way, child rearing becomes interesting and exciting and not tedious.

*"Is the way we assess children the way they turn out to be? Do our preconceptions influence them?"*

■      ■

Parental preconceptions do influence children, but the children's endowment will not permit you to mold them in certain ways. They themselves are just now telling you that; this is why this period is so hard. For example, some children rush into a situation and do things immediately, while others stand back and assess the situation. Again, we cannot change these tendencies—they are the result of endowment. What can be influenced is their environment. For example, setting up a parent-child relationship in which everything is a battle leads to a problem-filled pattern of relating with other people. What we are trying to establish are ways of coping with natural endowment. We are not trying to make a retiring person a hail-fellow-well-met, nor a hail-fellow-well-met a retiring person, but rather to recognize fundamental differences and respect them.

## Violence

*"What about violent behavior from boys and its effect on their personalities later?"*

*"I took my son to a three-year-old's group yesterday and the mothers said to me, 'Just wait and see, all boys get locked into climbing. He's going to be Batman and Superman and he's going to want guns.' That made me think. Are these violent tendencies really inevitable?"*

Research has confirmed that boys tend to be more aggressive in their play than girls. But that does not mean that boys are more violent. The violence comes from imitation. A child who has a tendency to be a little more active can be stimulated to be more violent by television, by violence at home or on the street, and by things that are read to him.

Children's play is an indication of how they believe life should be led, or of how it appears to them to be led. If children witness violence, they may internalize it as an acceptable way of life. It is the parents' role to point out nonviolent alternatives. This is a very important area of parent-child interaction.

# Fears and Anxieties

Parents are sometimes surprised and worried when their children develop new fears. In an attempt to allay these fears, many parents make light of them by saying something like "That's silly. There is nothing to be afraid of." Or they may insist, for example, that a dog "won't hurt you," then have the child pat the dog, only increasing the child's fears. If a child is afraid of the dark and claims there are monsters, a parent may turn on the light, look around, and say, "See, there are no monsters. Now go to sleep." To the parent's surprise, the child becomes even more frightened when the light is off again. It may help to ask what the child thinks the monster will do and to agree that it frightens him and then leave a small light on in the room on, so the monster won't reappear.

■                                                                                           ■

Now that the children are getting older and doing more, have you noticed that sometimes they surprise you by suddenly becoming afraid of certain situations?

*"My son loves the zoo. But when we get to the monkey area, he immediately says 'Go now.' He's not scared of small animals like the raccoons and birds, but he is clearly afraid of large animals. Once we had a little girl with us who was the same age as our son, and she wasn't afraid of anything."*

Two children of the same age in the same situation may not react in the same way. Your son was frightened. The little girl was not. How did you feel about that, and what did you do to help him?

*"To tell the truth, I was a little dismayed to find him frightened when the little girl was not. I said, 'You don't have to be scared. Mommy and Daddy will protect you from the animals,' but he wasn't comforted until we left to go to the birdhouse."*

## Parental Response

When children are frightened, it is important to let them know that you understand their feelings, that you are not critical of them, and that you will protect them. When they were smaller, it was sufficient to pick them up and hold them close. Now that they are older, the best thing is to walk away from the frightening scene as quickly as possible to something that is nonthreatening.

*"Later, at home, when I began to tell his grandparents about it, he was upset and put his hand over my mouth to stop me. So I guess he felt that he should not have acted that way."*

He must have picked up some cues that made him unhappy to have the incident reported. It's better not to talk to others about a child's fears in the child's presence.

## Time to Work Through Fears

*"How can you get a child over this feeling? Do you just let it pass and say nothing about it?"*

One of the ways you can handle this situation is by recognizing the fears and avoiding those situations that make the child fearful until the child has had a chance to work through his fear in play. If he is afraid of large animals, he can look at pictures or toy replicas of the animals, talk about the animals with you, and imitate the sounds they make. Sometimes children play the role of the animals themselves and, in that way, discover that they are not threatening. The child can perhaps be told about another child who had the same fear and overcame it.

*"I thought I could just tell my son not be afraid and he'd accept that."*

That's what many parents think, and that's why they become impatient with their children. Children need time to work through fearful situations in their own way and at their own pace.

*"We bought our daughter a toy mouse in a cage. She wouldn't come near it for days. Then it hit us that she was afraid it would get out. When we told her the mouse couldn't get out of the cage, she was able to play with it and enjoy it."*

It is important to allow children to tell you what they are thinking. Parents get used to talking to their children about their own feelings, but neglect to take time to understand the children's interpretation of events and circumstances.

## Need for Consistency

*"That happened with us last Halloween. Our daughter was terrified of a mask her father put on."*

Some children become fearful when their parents wear clothes different from those they usually wear. They certainly can't tolerate masquerade costumes on their parents. Many parents are disappointed at Christmas when father puts on a Santa Claus suit and the child becomes fearful and cries. Children have a fixed image of what father and mother are like; dressing in a way counter to that image may shock a child and undermine his or her sense of security. Most children of this age do not take to new situations readily.

## Darkness and Other Fears

*"My child has recently become afraid of the dark. What could have caused the change?"*

There are many explanations. Sometimes a child is awakened by a loud noise, can't distinguish the objects in his room, and becomes frightened. Or a gas pain may awaken him, and subsequently he associates the pain with darkness and becomes upset if put to sleep again in a dark room. Sometimes this fear develops after a difficulty in a play situation with another child. Or a disturbing dream may awaken the child, and the unpleasantness of the dream becomes associated with the dark. To understand the cause of a fear, a parent has to be aware of the child's experiences.

*"My child insists on having the light on at night."*

A night-light usually helps a child overcome fear of the dark.

*"My son insists on having the whole room lit up. He goes to sleep only if I leave the overhead light on."*

It is a good idea to ask why he needs it on. A dimmer can be attached to the light switch. This allows you to lower the light little by little until your child is comfortable with less light.

■                                                                        ■

*"I think my child is upset by anything that makes a loud noise. The vacuum cleaner, the electric mixer, and even the toaster upset him. When I use any of these appliances, I have to put him several rooms away and close the door. Then he gets upset because I'm separated from him."*

He may learn to cope with the appliances if he is allowed to inspect and play with them when not in use. He may imitate the sounds of the appliances and then be able to tolerate them when they are being used. If there are toy replicas available, play with them may help, too. However, overcoming anxiety over separation from you is not so easily accomplished. Fear of separation—from mother particularly—is a very important issue. It is best, therefore, not to intensify this fear by separating from him while he's trying to cope with a more easily resolved fear.

*"Our son has recently begun to fear going down the slide in the park. He used to love it, and we can't understand why he is now afraid of it."*

It is possible that he is now aware of how high the slide is. So his fear may indicate an advance in his understanding.

*"I think that explains why my daughter suddenly no longer likes to swing high on the park swings. She is just content to sit there and sway back and forth a little. As far as we know, she was never pushed off or swung so high that she was frightened."*

*"Certain tapes upset our daughter. For example, when we come to parts of* Hansel and Gretel, *she covers her ears and runs away till the dance part comes on. So we decided not to play tapes like that anymore."*

*"My son is afraid of a certain man in TV ads. Whenever he comes on, I simply turn the TV to another channel. I don't understand why this man upsets him."*

Many things may frighten children of this age. The child is immature, inexperienced, and unable to explain why certain things bother him. Parents should convey to the child that they understand his fears and that they are there to protect and help him. It may take a long time before the child can verbalize the reason for these fears.

## Separation

The process of separation and individuation is understood by researchers and students in the field of child development, but parents may not realize how long it takes for a child to separate comfortably from them. The child may cry, refuse to play or be consoled, or become quiet, sad, or angry. This may even happen when the parent tries to move the child from one activity to a new one, or put the child to bed. What separation issues are you encountering now, and how do you handle them?

### Child's Response to Separation

*"We are still having difficulty with this, usually when our daughter is over-tired and my husband and I go off in the car. She feels that she should go*

*too, and she cries at the door and throws herself on the floor. It is so upsetting to us."*

Your daughter can't understand why she can't go with you. Knowing that this is the way she reacts when overtired, you may be able to anticipate and avoid it to some extent. It may also be helpful to point out to her that, just as in the course of her day there are times when she goes out and comes back, so also mommies and daddies must sometimes go out and come back—emphasizing the coming back. Also, let her know what she can be doing when you are away. She may still protest, but the misery is usually somewhat diminished.

*"Our son, too, becomes extremely upset when we go out together."*

Children of this age still may become very anxious when their parents leave them, even when they are left with someone they know and like. When children first begin to walk, they move away from mother without realizing what they are doing. They may be so pleased with their new accomplishment that they don't immediately notice the temporary separation. When they realize they are away from mother, they run back to her. If parents try to push children away at this age, they may cling even more. If mother is in the kitchen, an area may have to be set aside from which the child can see her. Similarly, many children have difficulty starting nursery school. For most children, separation is not accomplished until around three years of age.

## Early Day Care

Early day care can be a difficult time for children because they are being made to separate before they are ready. There is less of a problem over separation if the mother understands this and gives her child undivided attention for a while when the day-care session is over.

*"It is more difficult for a child to be left in a different environment? Is it different from leaving the child with a baby-sitter in your own home?"*

Leaving the child with a familiar baby-sitter in the child's home is the best arrangement. Another solution is to leave the child at a neighbor's house that is familiar. Familiar surroundings and routines make separation less upsetting for a child.

## Separating Gradually

*"I have an opportunity to put my son in a play group with four other children. At first I will be staying with him, but eventually I want to leave him the two hours of the session. I am worried that he may not be ready."*

At this stage your child may be ready to spend time in a new setting—as long as you are there too. Perhaps when he becomes more secure there you can try leaving for ten minutes, then half an hour, then for the entire session.

*"What is the danger in not 'weaning' a child gradually from mother?"*

If the child is forced to separate prematurely—before she is ready to cope with it—separation anxiety may set in. The effects of separation anxiety can interfere with her ability to cope throughout her lifetime. For example, some young married adults live in the same apartment house with, or next door to, one set of parents. Sometimes we refer to this as a close-knit family, but it may instead be the consequence of an inability to separate. We often hear of children away at college who get extremely homesick. That, too, may be related to separation anxiety.

Some children are able to separate at two and a half, some not until three and a half or even later. It is different for each child.

*"We are beginning to have a better appreciation of the effects of separation issues. When we came back from California our daughter never wanted her daddy out of her sight, and she wanted us both to bathe her. We thought it was strange, but now we understand."*

We all know that a child has to learn how to sit up, crawl, and stand before he or she can walk. But some parents do not understand that separation is a process as well. Some get stuck in the middle longer than others, some make it through very rapidly, and some need longer for the final transition. Every child achieves separation on his or her own time schedule.

*"Our son has not been sleeping since we came back from Florida about two weeks ago. Shouldn't he have gotten over our being away?"*

He apparently needs more experience with your being home. He may have missed you most when he was put to bed.

*"Well, to tell the truth we left at night when he was asleep, so he may be afraid we will leave again when he is asleep."*

Your child needs assurance that you will stay. It may help to tell him that you and Daddy are home now and that you are going to stay. Perhaps if he realizes that you understand his worry he will feel more comfortable and be able to sleep. Parents sometimes prolong the effects of traumatic events through their inability to understand what is troubling the child.

*"My son has been very upset because his daddy has been away, but he is talking about it, saying, 'I want Daddy to come back.' He says it even when he knows Daddy is at work during the day."*

He is probably saying it because he needs reassurance.

*"He got a big reaction from me when his father went away, and I com-plained over the phone to my husband about his being away, telling him how much our son missed him."*

■                                                                                                              ■

Your being upset only made it harder for your son. Children easily pick up the mood of parents. It can signify to them that something is indeed wrong—in this case, that perhaps Daddy is away forever.

In addition, when Daddy now leaves to go to work for the day, the child is worried that Daddy will stay away. It's important to tell him that Daddy will be home in a little while. He is at work and will be home before the child goes to bed.

It is a good idea to have children visit a parent's place of work so they can picture where the parent goes after leaving home. This may make the parent's daily departure less frightening.

## Nighttime Separation

*"Our child puts up a fuss even when we are going out to a friend's, to dinner, or to a movie. He's usually all right a few minutes later. Can we expect him to understand an explanation like 'You're a big boy now. Mommy and Daddy are going out and we will be back soon, so don't cry'?"*

It is normal for children of this age to protest. But the protest need not be protracted. A competent baby-sitter can engage the child in some pleasant activity. Repeated experience with parents' leaving and returning will enable the child to cope eventually.

*"Our daughter cries hardest when we put her to bed. She clings and seems afraid to be left alone. We tried leaving a light on in her room, but nothing seems to work except sitting with her until she falls asleep."*

Many children find bedtime separation the most difficult, especially if it interrupts play with parents. Children need a simmering-down period and a fixed routine each night that leads to bedtime. Some children may still need parent's presence until falling asleep.

*"My child used to have a difficult time separating at bedtime. Now she puts her dolls to bed first and tells them to go to sleep. Then, when we tell her it is her bedtime, she seems to accept it."*

Parents can help a child with bedtime separation. For example, the child can be told a story about another child who spends the day as your child does, then goes to bed and, on waking in the morning, finds Daddy and Mommy have been sleeping in their bed and are happy and healthy and ready to get up.

*"When I leave my son at Grandma's or a friend's, he protests but then quickly gets involved in some activity. But when I come back to get him, he puts up an even louder protest because he doesn't want to be taken away from whatever he is doing. He seems glad to see me, but he doesn't want to leave. It seems he has a problem separating from everything."*

Many children have difficulty making a transition from one situation to another. It is hard for them to separate from friends and pleasant situations, or to separate at bedtime if they are in the midst of pleasant play with Daddy and Mommy. It sometimes helps to let them know what they will be doing next, such as going home for lunch or to play with their dolls or to meet Daddy. In that way, it doesn't seem like an ending but a beginning of something else.

There are more aspects to separation. We have discussed some of them here, but this is an issue that will continue to come up.

# Sexual Identification and Curiosity

Most parents find it difficult to deal with children's curiosity about sex, gender and sexual identification, and nudity. Many parents are very anxious to learn how to deal with these issues and have many questions. They want to know how much a child needs to know and what to say to satisfy their curiosity.

*"My son has been aware of his body for quite a few months, but now it seems he is noticing more than just his anatomy. It seems he is noticing the difference in sex. When do children begin to do that?"*

At around eighteen months, children become aware of—and start naming—their body parts. You probably have seen that recently. Now, when they are between two and three, they are becoming aware of their genital organs and of the difference between the sexes.

## Naming Body Parts

*"My son ran into the bathroom when my husband was bathing, looked his father over, and then pointed to his genitals, saying, 'That, that.' I guess wanting to know the name. My husband said, 'That's Daddy's penis.' Our son said 'Peen?' and ran out of the bathroom. My husband wasn't sure he had done the right thing."*

The first time that happens, no matter how intellectually prepared we are to respond appropriately, parents may be taken by surprise and fumble for the right reply. When children point to genital organs, parents should name this part of the anatomy just as they would name the knee, eye, or any other part of the anatomy. We don't want children to feel that genitals have some special significance.

*"Should children be given the proper anatomical names or special names? My sister's children refer to their private parts as 'wee wees.' Of course, they will have to learn the real names later in life. I want my child to learn and use the proper name at the start. Is that okay?"*

It is now considered better to give the proper anatomical name. You can tell your child that a male organ is a penis. The female has a vulva, which is an external part of her anatomy, and a vagina, which is an internal part. However, often the female genitalia is simply referred to as the vagina. The child can also be told that the female also has breasts.

*"When do children begin to know what sex they are?"*

They are beginning now to recognize themselves as boys and girls. With most children, gender identity is firmly established by three years of age.

## Nudity

*"In order for children to observe the difference between male and female anatomies, they have to see their parents nude. I've talked to several mothers about that and there seems to be quite a difference of opinion about it. In some primitive tribes, everyone goes around nude. Is that harmful?"*

It depends upon the customs of the people and what is accepted in their culture. In ours, we tend not to expose our bodies.

To little children, the standing adult may seem very large and threatening. Consider the view a small child has when he stands next to a nude parent. His eye level is at about the level of the parents' genitals. For some children such a view may be too stimulating; for others it may be upsetting. They may want their private parts to be the same size. They may question why they do not have pubic hair. Girls often question why their breasts are not as large as mother's. Size is very important to children; they view many situations in terms of size. Since we are not certain at what age and how a child will react, it is best to limit unnecessary exposure to nudity.

*"What if my child comes in when I am taking a shower or about to get dressed? What should I do?"*

Finish the shower quickly and cover up in a robe or towel without making a fuss. If you are undressed, get into your clothes quickly and casually. If you draw too much attention to the situation, the child can be given a sense that there is something wrong with the human body and, by association, something wrong with his own body. Of course, we don't want to foster this impression.

*"My husband and I did not pay much attention to our daughter's presence when we were dressing until she was about eighteen months old and began to point to parts of our bodies. We named the parts for her—breast, penis, and so on. I told my mother, and she had a fit. She said our daughter was too young and that we'd make a sex maniac of her."*

*"My parents reacted the same way. As a result, we began to feel uncomfortable, so we were careful to be dressed or covered when our child was around. But shouldn't children be learning the difference between the sexes about now?"*

The children are getting to the stage when they do have to know the difference between the sexes. But they shouldn't be threatened by differences in the anatomy, or be overstimulated by it. Responding to children's questions about sex frankly and naturally is the best approach parents can take.

## Noticing Sexual Differences

*"What about seeing other children nude?"*

That should be treated in the same way as adult nudity. If a child sees another child of the opposite sex undressed and is curious, anatomical parts—including genitals—should be named matter-of-factly.

*"That situation came up a few weeks ago. My best friend, her husband, and their son came to spend a weekend. When we undressed the children to put them to bed, we gave them baths. My daughter watched the boy, a few months younger than she is, in the tub and she was very curious about his penis and lifted her nightie and looked at herself. We said, 'That is his penis. He is a boy. This is your vulva. You are a girl.' She seemed to accept that explanation. Was that right?"*

That is exactly how a parent should respond in such a situation. Children come to accept sexual differences when they are presented honestly and matter-of-factly.

*"Should children be allowed to play with each other in the nude—say, for an afternoon?"*

That is not a good idea, because children compare their bodies. For some, differences in size may cause concern. Girls may worry that they don't have a penis. Some children may be stimulated to do more touching of themselves or others than is appropriate, and this may arouse sensations with which they are not able to cope.

*"But we don't want them to develop hang-ups about their genitals."*

Nor do we want them to be sexually stimulated before they are emotionally prepared for it. Many adolescents today become sexually active much too early, and it may be partly due to too early exposure to sexual situations. On the other hand, we don't want children to become prudish or afraid of sex. It's not an easy issue to handle, and it's not something that can be decided for every child in the same way.

The important thing is for a boy to be aware that he is a boy and for a girl to be aware that she is a girl, *and* that it's very good for a boy to be a boy, and very good for a girl to be a girl, so that they get the sense that each one is good in his or her own way.

*"But I thought the idea was that it shouldn't be that boys do only this and girls do only that?"*

There will always be a difference in anatomy, sexual capacity, and sex roles. That is all that this early lesson—boys are boys and girls are girls— is suggesting.

■                                                                                                    ■

Of course, we should not limit the experience of girls just because they are girls or that of boys just because they are boys.

It's good for boys to play with dolls because they are getting a sense of taking care of babies. It encourages a sense of gentleness. Similarly, girls should play baseball. Sports and games encourage girls to gain a sense of sturdiness and physical competence. We want each sex to have access to all the opportunities that help make them complete people.

*"Most of my friends have girls. Does it matter that my son plays mostly with girls his age?"*

Children should be encouraged to play with other children of both sexes, and parents should try to arrange such situations.

*"What could happen if a boy played only with girls?"*

The boy may experience pleasure in playing with girls and their doll play to the exclusion of other experiences. He may think it's much nicer to play with girls because girls have everything, since he doesn't have the experience of having the things and doing things that boys do. Such situations, while unusual, are not a cause of concern now because children are just establishing their gender identity and parents can arrange to have appropriate play situations for both sexes. The opposite situation can operate in a similar fashion for a girl exposed only to boys. She may then prefer only boys' activities. So it is important for boys and girls to have playmates of both sexes.

*"I sometimes see my son rubbing his genitals. Why does he do that?"*

Some children do a lot of touching of their genital area. It may be simply an act of discovery and exploration. But if it is done to excess, there may be another reason. For example, the child may have an irritation or clothing may be rough or too small. For some children, such touching is comforting. Others simply need to know that they are still intact.

## Masturbation

*"When does masturbation start?"*

Some children start very early. It is typical of children who are left alone a great deal, or who are put into their cribs for a long time alone. Children who are kept busy and stimulated masturbate much less. It often occurs that when children first discover their genitals, they need to touch them frequently. Some then begin to get a sensation of pleasure and use that to comfort themselves and masturbate. When they have other interests, that need disappears.

*"How old do you think children should be before they are told the facts of life? A lot of people think the earlier, the better. But this seems wrong to me."*

■                                                                              ■

It all depends on the child and his or her experiences. At three, children are naturally curious and should be given explanations, but only on the same level as the questions they ask. Don't go into the details of reproduction if all the child wants to know is the name of the hospital he or she was born in.

*"Won't some explanations scare a child this age?"*

No explanation should be made in a way that frightens a child. It should be only as sophisticated as the question—and the child—seem to warrant.

Children interpret everything concretely. If they want an elaboration, they will ask for one.

*"I think you are taking their childhood away somewhat when you tell them too much. But my friend says, 'It's a new world now.'"*

It *is* possible to provide too much sexual information too early. It is best to ask what the child thinks is the answer to his question, then the answer can be on the child's level of understanding, and in direct response to what the child is asking. Right now, most children are asking only about the differences between boys and girls and trying to establish their own sexual identity.

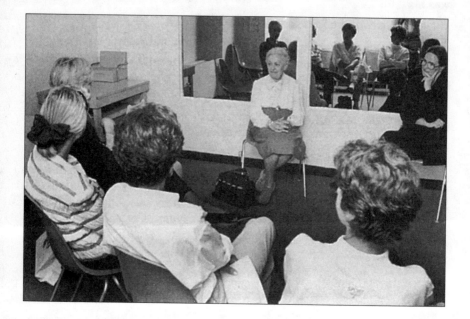

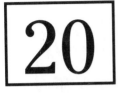

## Setting Limits

Agreement and consistency between parents is very important in establishing discipline. Now that the children are becoming more verbal, a new level of understanding and relating is required. To set discipline priorities, there has to be agreement between parents on what activities are to be limited. If one parent sets certain limits and the other sets different ones, the child may be-  come confused and overburdened. This situation may be further complicated by a housekeeper or grandparents with entirely different ideas about discipline. Are you having any difficulty agreeing with each other on the setting of limits?

### Parental Disagreements

*"Setting limits is the one area where we have the most disagreement. I think my wife is overprotective. I understand that some things are dangerous, and I agree they should be limited, but I want my son to be like a boy."*

*"I understand my husband's fear that I'm undermining our son's masculinity, but he's not with him all the time. For example, I don't allow our son to climb on the sofa, because he can tumble off if I'm not in the room to watch him. But his father allows him to climb, because he is sitting right there."*

Every child needs to exercise and to learn how to climb. However, your child can't distinguish yet that climbing on the sofa is all right when Daddy is there but not when he is home with Mommy. Perhaps you can let him do his climbing in a park that has climbing equipment, or in your yard if there is a place to climb. This way, both parents can permit climbing under supervision and limit it at home.

*"I won't let our daughter walk in the street unless I hold her hand. My husband lets her because he says he can catch her in time."*

Right now, the goal is to have the children accept the limits set by parents as they learn to exercise control themselves. It is dangerous to experiment with a child's judgment on a busy, overcrowded street. If the child cannot accept holding a parent's hand, she should be confined to her carriage until you reach a park or other safe area where she can be allowed to walk alone.

*"Last week, we got into a rowboat with our daughter. Halfway through the ride the child wanted her life jacket off, so I let her, despite my wife's protests. Then our daughter leaned over the edge and nearly fell out. This taught me a lesson. A parent can't always predict what a child this age will do, so it's better to be prepared. I now understand my wife's attitude."*

Of course, each parent has the child's best interests at heart. The important issue is to know the child's level of development, then give her clear messages and set consistent limits. When parents reinforce each other, a child accepts limits more easily and feels more secure as well.

*"I know when our son is going to do something that he should not, so I warn him beforehand. My mother thinks I should let him do it first, then say 'No.'"*

You are right to anticipate and help him not do it, so that you don't have to say 'No' to him afterward. Suppose, for example, that he likes to pick up a certain ashtray. If you see him going toward it, you can give him something else to pick up or distract him in some way. This way, you don't encourage him to do something that you have been trying to teach him not to do. Many parents wait to see if a child has achieved control instead of helping him to achieve it by anticipating the prohibited activity and offering an acceptable substitute. This way is harder—it takes patience and time—but it is most effective. The other way expects control by the child before he has the inner control that comes from appropriate disciplining.

### Threats

*"I'm trying to anticipate, but it is not working. When we are going out and I know my son doesn't want to put on his snowpants, I'll say, 'If you don't put on your snowpants, you can't go with Mommy.' We still have a scene, and I have to force him into the snowpants."*

That is anticipating, but you are threatening him as well. Threats may evoke fear and oppositional behavior in children.

When the child is busy playing and the time comes to go out, give a warning such as "Pretty soon we will be going out to the park to play. When we do, we have to put on our coats and snowpants." A little later announce that it is time to get ready and proceed with the dressing. The child may protest less, because he has not been threatened.

### Protests

*"But what should I do if he still protests?"*

■                                                                                    ■

You can quietly continue dressing him while telling him about all the things he will see and experience when he goes out. The child will begin to accept that snowpants go on before he goes out, and the protests will diminish. It takes patience and persistence on the parent's part, because this is a learning process that takes time.

*"When I take my daughter to another child's house to play, she doesn't want to leave when it's time to come home. So I say, 'If you don't want to come home, I'll go home and leave you here.' She cries and protests, but she still doesn't want to come home. So I take her home crying most of the way."*

If this becomes a pattern—always threatening but never carrying out the threat—you will lose credibility with her. In addition, such threats may frighten the child and thereby interfere with the trust relationship between parent and child. Instead, tell the child that it will soon be time to go home and that you will leave as soon as the activity is finished. This gives a warning, while letting the child know what to expect next.

## Bribes and Bargaining

*"I use a different method. I say, 'If you come home with me I'll give you some cookies.' Or we'll stop for a hamburger or something. It usually works."*

*"I sometimes resort to that approach too. I do it especially if I want him to stop playing and come shopping with me, which he doesn't like. I say, 'If you come shopping, I'll buy some cookies for you.' "*

The way it is stated—"If you do this, I will . . ." makes it a bribe to induce the child to do something. Instead, try mentioning an activity or object you know interests your child: "When we go home we can stop on the way to look at the fire engine" or "When we go to the market you can help push the cart" or "When you stop crying we can go for a ride." This way, you construct a sequence of events, a scenario the child can follow, and you won't be trapped into giving bigger and better bribes.

## Remorse and Apologies

*"I know that a good relationship between parent and child is important. Sometimes I do explode when my child has done something wrong, like throwing her food on the freshly scrubbed kitchen floor. Then I apologize and say, 'Mommy didn't mean to holler but you made me angry.' I don't know if she understands, but I feel better."*

*"Sometimes I lose control too, and then I'm full of remorse and I apologize."*

This can confuse the child. If the child's behavior is not acceptable, she had to know that you disapprove. But if she understands that you are apologizing, she may not understand that you are apologizing for overreacting. She may think you are apologizing for disapproving of what she did. It is best not to apologize until your child can understand this distinction.

*"Do I do irreparable damage if once in a while I explode?"*

Parents are human too. We can't be in control all the time. Sometimes children try our patience beyond our tolerance. Sometimes there are combinations of stresses and the child's behavior is just the last straw. The important thing is that explosive anger should not be the standard way of expressing disapproval. An occasional angry outburst will not do irreparable damage to a child's psyche.

## Discipline Versus Punishment

Setting limits consistently is an important part of parenting. The manner in which this is done is especially important to some parents who experienced harsh disciplining in their own upbringing. Some may feel that it is the only proper way to bring up children. Others go overboard to avoid this method, and may become too lenient or inconsistent. Other parents confuse discipline with punishment, or measure their success as parents by the way their children "mind" them. Do any of you find yourself in these categories?

*"I was brought up by parents who were very strict and didn't believe in 'sparing the rod and spoiling the child.' So I guess I do measure my parenting that way."*

*"I know my parents watch how we bring up our son and how we discipline him. They think we should punish him if he is naughty—a slap on the hand if he touches something he shouldn't, for example. Should we be beginning to punish him?"*

You are equating discipline and punishment. Many people use the words interchangeably. Even some dictionaries offer "discipline" as a synonym for "punishment." But there is a difference between discipline and punishment. Discipline is teaching right and wrong—what is acceptable and what is not—by setting firm and consistent limits. Punishment is teaching limits by inflicting pain and by conditioning a child to behave a certain way through the threat of pain, not through a recognition of what is appropriate behavior and what is not.

*"Is punishment just physical?"*

There is mental or emotional punishment, too. For example, leaving a child home because he is naughty or not giving him something he wants may inflict mental but not physical pain.

*"What if I say, 'You have to put on your coat or we won't go out'?"*

■                                                                          ■

That's a threat of mental punishment.

*"Then how do I let my child know what will happen if he doesn't put on his coat?"*

You can say, "When you put on your coat we will go out." That is a simple statement of a sequence of events. "If you don't put on your coat, I'll spank you" is a threat of physical punishment. "If you don't put on your coat, I'll go without you" is a threat of mental punishment.

*"What's the harm of punishment?"*

That depends on the severity and frequency of the punishment, and the child's endowment. Some children respond by becoming inhibited and unable to show any initiative. Others become angry and lash out at everyone who tries to limit them. Other children become very ingratiating. An angry child can become an adult who can't accept authority in school or on the job and goes about life with a chip on his shoulder.

## Self-discipline

*"I believe in self-discipline. I want our child to achieve self-discipline."*

Self-discipline results when a child has had consistent limit setting for unacceptable activities and recognition for acceptable activities.

*"How far along are our children in achieving this?"*

That brings us back to what we have called the life history of "No." When the children were infants and began to explore things that were dangerous, we said "No," removed them from the object, and gave them something else to explore. Then, when they were beginning to move about and got into things, we said "No" firmly, and the children stopped just long enough for us to reach them.

Then they reached the stage—and some of our children are still in this stage—when they look back to see if the parent or caretaker will help to keep them from doing the prohibited activity. Some parents say the children are teasing—that they know the activity is not allowed. That's true. The children are looking for the parent's reinforcement because they do not yet have sufficient self-control. Some children are now getting beyond this stage. They approach an object, look at it, and say "No, no" to themselves but still touch it. In the next stage they will approach the object, say "No," and move off to another activity on their own. That indicates the achievement of self-discipline.

*"When do they achieve this?"*

That differs with each child, but most children who receive patient and consistent discipline achieve self-discipline at about the age of three.

■                                                                                    ■

## Parental Self-control

*"That means we have a while to go yet. It takes so much patience, which I don't always have. Some days I find I'm saying 'No' constantly."*

Sometimes parents are upset by other things and take out their frustration on the child. The child may be going through a period of transition in which he seems to be doing everything wrong. Parents have to recognize those periods and respond to them appropriately. If the parents are patient and understanding, this stage will pass. As we have said before, limitations should be as few as possible and consistent. The emphasis should be on reinforcement of acceptable behavior.

*"As children, both my husband and I were constantly scolded and punished. We both agree that we don't want to repeat that pattern. But how do we let our child know what behavior we don't approve of?"*

You should be consistent in telling your child what you won't permit and what you will. For example, your child should know that you are displeased or angry with her for drawing on the furniture with lipstick. But she should also know that you approve of her drawing with a red crayon on paper supplied for that purpose.

*"That method worked for my son for the stove and electrical outlets, but now he has taken to running away from me on the street."*

*"My son doesn't put his fingers in light sockets anymore. Instead he tries to connect the appliances with the sockets or unscrew light bulbs and reinsert them. So I have to stop him, but he balks and gets upset."*

*"At the beach, my daughter constantly runs into the water without waiting for me. She loves to have the waves splash over her, but it's not safe and I can't let her do it."*

As children get older they want to explore and try new activities. If these activities are not safe, parents should not allow them, no matter how great a fuss the child makes. For example, if the child will not hold her parent's hand while crossing the street, she should be picked up and carried or put into her carriage. Similarly, a child who runs into the water at a pool or beach should be made to wear a safety device and be taught to wait for the parent to accompany her. Going in the water alone should be allowed neither at the seashore nor at a pool. Children who connect or disconnect electrical appliances need to be taught that this is not allowed; take the appliance or cord away and give the child something else to connect— such as pop beads or toy train tracks. In these cases, parents can't expect children to understand the danger, or to have the judgment to perceive it. Parents teach safety by setting consistent limits. Now that the children are more verbal, they can be told certain things in advance. Parents should use simple statements that the children can understand. For example: "We are going to the park. When we walk to the park we hold Mommy's hand all the way. Children who don't hold Mommy's hand go in the stroller."

*"I'm always afraid my daughter will become as inhibited as I was. Isn't that a danger when a parent is too firm?"*

The danger lies not in being firm but in being harsh and too restrictive. Of course, practices like running into the street, leaning out of a car window, and playing with matches should be limited firmly. But severely limiting less dangerous activities—like banging a toy, riding a scooter around the house, leaving a toy on the floor—may inhibit a child or lead to a very difficult relationship between parent and child. It may also lead to unsatisfactory personality development.

*"If I explode sometimes, do I set back everything I've accomplished?"*

Parents have their moments, too. They may be tired or having difficulty coping, and may "explode" just the way the child sometimes does. But if this is an infrequent event, the effects are not lasting. However, it may be harmful if it becomes the usual manner of relating to a child.

## Expressing Disapproval

Many parents admonish children by issuing sharply worded commands. This method usually does not result in compliance, and sometimes the children respond angrily themselves. How readily do you expect your children to comply with a request or command?

*"I expect my child to come when I call him. He understands what I want, but usually he doesn't come. That makes me angry sometimes."*

*"My child always picks the time I'm busiest—getting dinner ready or getting ready to go out—to get into some mischievous activity. When I call to her to stop, she usually doesn't listen. And if she does listen, she sometimes gets into something else."*

Parents sometimes expect children to listen to their commands, even those issued from across a room. This is an ineffective measure for children of this age. They usually respond only when the parent is physically close.

*"Do you mean if I'm standing at the door ready to go out and my child is dawdling with a toy, and I say, 'Come, we're going out now,' I should go and get him."*

It will save time and energy, and avoid frustration if you warn your child of the next activity, and then take your child's hand and say firmly "It's time for [whatever the activity is]. You can take your toy with you." Or "We'll see your toy when we come back. We are going to . . ." and you recite all the interesting things the child will be experiencing in the next activity.

*"I find my difficulty is when I'm busy with something I can't leave, such as mixing something on the stove or sewing curtains on the machine, so I feel I scream and yell a lot. He doesn't listen and that is exasperating."*

Children this age get very involved in their own activities and explorations. They can't understand that these activities may be dangerous or annoying to adults, so they don't respond. They are not being purposely disobedient, although it may seem that way to parents. If the parent knows she is going to be busy, she should get the child involved with an activity near her.

*"I thought that since my daughter understands what I want I could save myself the trouble of stopping what I'm doing and just tell her."*

She is still too young to respond to that approach. If a parent is consistent with limitations and approval, the child will in time be able to internalize the limitations and then limit herself—usually beginning *after* age three, although a few children begin sooner.

*"I have noticed that the louder I yell to my child, the less response I get. If I use a firm voice and really mean what I say, I get a better response."*

Many parents feel that the child's response will be in proportion to the volume of the request. But children respond better to firmness than loudness.

*"You have to mean business, don't you? You can't be halfhearted about it."*

The parent has to be sure of herself, know what she wants, and convey it to the child by facial expression, tone of voice, and body gesture. Sometimes a parent says something in a stern voice but with a bit of a smile. The child doesn't know whether to respond to the smile, which signifies approval, or to the voice, which signifies disapproval.

*"I'm afraid I do that, because I don't want to seem too harsh. My parents were very stern, and I can still remember how frightened I was when they told me to do something. I guess I'm trying not to do that to my child."*

*"When my child doesn't respond, I get very angry and yell. I have noticed that my husband looks stern, says his say firmly, and gets a much quicker response. Now I understand why. I must have been confusing my child."*

It is important to say what you mean and mean what you say. Children feel more secure when the message is clear.

*"Some children get very angry when they are interrupted. For example, when I stop my child from banging a toy against a table and direct him away from it, he gets angry and tries to knock something over. His angry response bothers me."*

■                                                                                                          ■

*"My son often bites or tries to bite if he is stopped from doing something. Then there are two things to stop. I don't know which is better, to let him go on or stop him and then have him bite!"*

Children don't like to be stopped in the midst of doing something, so they may protest. Biting is a primitive expression of anger. Your child may be able to understand a firm "We don't bite people. Apples and crackers are for biting. Tell mother you don't want to stop. Then we'll see what you can do instead." When this becomes your procedure—to be firm and explicit— this type of behavior gradually lessens.

*"I come prepared with something to bite and I can anticipate it and ward it off and he bites very rarely now."*

Parents have to expect protests, because children do not yet understand restrictions and causality—for example, "If you bang on a glass table, it can break." "If you don't come now, we'll miss the bus."

In addition, parental restrictions interfere with a child's need to establish autonomy and independence. So parents have to anticipate these protests by issuing a warning and then carrying out the accepted activity.

*"What bothers me is that there are so many things that have to be limited. I feel as though I am saying 'No' all day long."*

It is important to make the limits as few as possible. If we are constantly limiting our children, they get to view the parent as only limiting. It is equally, if not more, important for parents to offer approval when that is appropriate, so that the child doesn't develop a negative view of her relationship with her parents.

## Recognition Versus Praise

*"But I can't go around all day praising everything my child does."*

We are not talking about praise, but about recognition for routine activities. Comments such as "You finished your cereal," "You opened the door by yourself," "You held on to the railing," and "You made a picture" all acknowledge little things that children do that parents may notice but don't usually recognize overtly. You don't have to say "How marvelous that you did this," but simply offer positive recognition conveyed by a pleasant tone of voice and expression.

# Coping with Advice from Others

When grandparents and relatives come to visit, they are often critical instead of helpful. Part of the difficulty comes from the conflict between old and new or different beliefs about child rearing. Some grandparents feel that their children are spoiling the baby. Others are overanxious about safety matters and tend to inhibit the children's activity and development. Still others let grandchildren do things that parents don't allow.

Many older parents try to deny their grown children's independent status and need to continue to exert some control. Often they do not have time to see the new parents in action. They come for short visits and the young couple wants to impress their parents with their competence in child rearing. The young parents regress and become anxious as they look again for parental approval . . . or try to avoid parental disapproval. This leads to a very uncomfortable situation that is frustrating for both generations. Do you find your parenting methods are very different from your parents' and friends' methods?

*"I have trouble, not only with my relatives but sometimes with my husband, because he is so influenced by them. They all think I'm spoiling the baby when I respond to his cries."*

New ways of child rearing are often threatening and upsetting to people who have reared children themselves. If you get angry at the advice and just seethe inwardly when your relatives don't view things your way, you don't accomplish much and may hurt your relationships. It may help to say something like "I respect your point of view; I know you've had a lot of experience. Let me try to explain why I am doing it a little differently. I think this way is working out. If it is not successful, then I may try your way."

*"My family says, 'You and your special methods! You think your child is something special.' I tell them that he is something special, and I remind them that they must have felt the same way about their children."*

*"It's very hard for me to speak out like that. I have an aunt who has three grown children, and all are in psychotherapy. Recently, she scolded me unmercifully for letting my little girl hug me. I felt like saying to her, 'Well, if you did more of that with your children, they wouldn't be where they are today.'"*

It is easier to keep quiet. You might be able to handle your aunt by saying "You know, Auntie, everybody has their own way of bringing up their children. You brought up your children your way, the best you knew, and I am trying to bring up my child the best way I know."

*"It is easy when we are talking about it here, but when she is literally screaming at me, I go to pieces. My husband just laughs."*

Your behavior to her revives your whole childhood experience. She's still doing just what she did to her own children and you. It is very hard to escape from your childhood role when it is forced on you. That is one of the reasons why we talk so much about helping our children establish self-awareness early. If they develop self-confidence, they will be better able to cope in such situations.

■                                                                    ■

*"I have the same problem with my in-laws. They do it with their older son, but they are beginning to do it less with me. Maybe I'm beginning to feel more secure and maybe it's because my parents are not that way."*

*"I get the same thing. There is hardly a time that I go to the grocery store that somebody doesn't say something of the same kind to me."*

*"The other day a lady said to me, 'That doesn't seem to be a very good toy.' The baby was busy chewing my keys and enjoying herself. It was keeping her quiet and contented while I was doing my shopping. I simply said, 'I think she will be all right.'"*

*"My father has the same ability to put me in a state of panic."*

Yes, and then it's hard for you to remember that you are a grown-up. You are an adult; and you are really on a par with him now. You are a parent. He has a great deal of interest in you, he has a right to have an opinion and to express it, but he really has no right to direct you. It is perfectly all right to listen to him and then say, "Yes, I see you would have liked that better."

*"It is so easy to say it here, but so difficult to do at home."*

After a while, you will learn to make use of what seems helpful. It is like a music lesson. It seems so easy when your teacher explains it. The hard part is to go home and use what you learned. But practice makes it easier each time.

*"I have trouble with my older brother. My son often wants to be carried after we've walked a short distance outside. Sometimes he is tired, and sometimes I think the traffic frightens him, so I pick him up. My brother says, 'Put him down. Do you want him to be a mama's boy?' I get upset. What makes me so insecure?"*

That is not a sign of insecurity as a mother. You know what to do as a mother and you know what you expect of your child. You are not reacting to your brother as your child's mother, but rather as his little sister. He is putting you back in the mold of little sister, and not allowing you to emerge into your role as mother.

*"I have had similar problems, although I think I am getting more confidence in myself. But sometimes the old feelings seep through when I'm with older members of the family."*

That is not surprising. Look at how many years you were under your family's influence and how short your experience as a mother is. Mothering isn't as familiar a role yet. Your family is probably having a hard time seeing you as a mother. They don't allow you to assert yourself as a mother, and they bring back old insecurities. You have to teach them that you are becoming secure in your role as a mother.

■                                                                              ■

Conflicts also arise over different attitudes toward child rearing. We spoke earlier of spoiling. Are there other areas that cause disagreement?

## Induced Anxiety

*"I'm in trouble with my mother most of the time now that the baby is getting around on her own, especially if the baby tries to climb up into a chair or run down the hall. My mother is always saying, 'Be careful.'"*

*"I have a similar problem. How can you cope with a grandmother who is extremely nervous about everything the child does? If she sees him start to walk, she says, 'Pick him up; he is going to fall,' and she makes us all nervous."*

The overanxiety can influence the child's development. This is another instance in which the parent has to stand up for the child's freedom to explore. It is not easy, but the parent has to patiently assure the anxious relative that the child is capable. You can stand close to the child and show the grandmother how well the child does and overtly recognize the child's achievement. Say that you know children do fall and that you watch to see that the child does not injure himself.

*"I try to do that with an aunt who just dotes on the baby, but I find myself getting angry at her. She acts as though I am not aware or don't care—that only she has the baby's interests at heart."*

Try to stay calm and collected, and don't compete with her to demonstrate who cares more for the child. Calmly show her what the baby can do now. She may then be able to appreciate the baby's achievement, too, instead of worrying everyone about it.

*"I've tried that with my family. It seems to work while I'm in the room, but if I go out, they start fussing again. Now I either take the baby with me or get them started looking at a book with my child."*

## Inhibiting Children

*"My father-in-law thinks children should be seen and not heard. He expects them to sit still and be quiet even at this age. He keeps saying 'Shhh, shhh,' with his finger to his lips, whenever the baby begins to make a sound. Now the baby just clings to me and won't go to him at all."*

Children should be free to express themselves in an age-appropriate manner. Such constant disapproval is not good for the child's self-esteem. Perhaps you can explain this to your father-in-law. Try having him go out with you to the park so that your baby can run around and make noise without disturbing him. Back inside, perhaps he will be ready to look at a book quietly with grandfather.

*"What if your child is shy with everybody and cries when he sees strange people?"*

Such a child needs support from the parent. You have to tell the strangers that he'll get used to them in a few minutes, that he needs time to "look them over." Hold him very close when you are with new people; this will give him a feeling of security. As he grows older, he will begin to feel more secure with new people.

*"Our child is also shy. We know a lady who always asks us, 'What is the matter with your daughter?' Then she pounces on her!"*

Tell this woman there is nothing wrong with your child. She is at the stage in which she is wary of strangers but, if given time to get used to them, she will be friendly. Don't be intimidated by such questions. Stand up for your child.

*"I have a different kind of problem. When my father comes, he always brings candy. I really don't want my child to have it. Then my father and I have a big argument."*

Perhaps you can explain to your father that your doctor and dentist don't think candy is good for the child at this age, and that fruit or crackers would be more appropriate.

*"When my parents come to look after the baby, they skip her bath and let her stay up an hour later. Then she seems cranky the next day. When I suggest that they follow my routine, they say, 'Oh, it won't hurt her every once in a while.' It makes me not want to have them again."*

Life is much easier when parents, grandparents, and baby-sitters all follow about the same routines with a child. On the other hand, if it is only occasional, and if the child really enjoys her grandparents, it may not be so bad. Having a good time with the grandparents is very important in building a relationship with them. Parents should try not to be disapproving of grandparents' care. Within reasonable limits, children can accommodate some variations in routines. If the baby gets back to her schedule after a day or two, there may be no harm done. Children derive security from following routines, but there should be some flexibility.

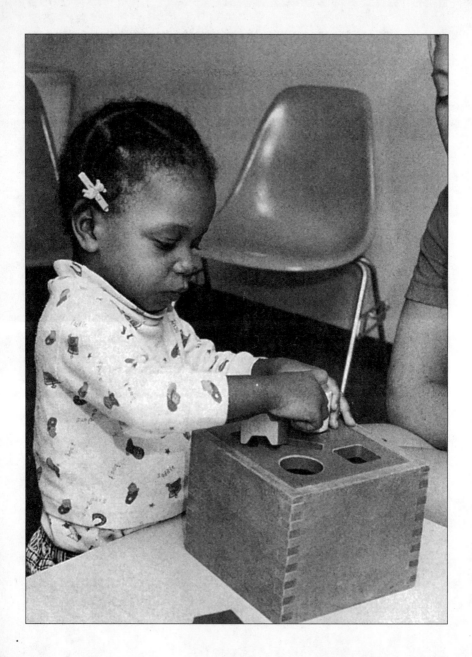

# 21

# The Changing Family Structure

## A Father's Involvement

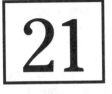

The father's role is undergoing many changes. In some families, the mother works outside the home and the father assumes a bigger share of parenting. Some fathers look forward to coming home to their children and assisting in their care. Other fathers are too busy working long hours to be able to participate, or may feel this is not the father's role, and leave all of the child rearing to the mother.

Some mothers welcome having little assistance in child rearing and with their daily decisions. Other mothers become upset over their husband's refusal to participate in the care of the children. They may be concerned not so much for themselves but because they feel children need a relationship with their father in order to be able to establish their own identity. Many fathers do not realize how important their role is and how much they can contribute to the child's development.

Now that the children are entering their third year, have you fathers noticed any difference in your relationships with them and how you spend time with them?

*"I travel a lot and don't have much time at home, but I have noticed a remarkable change in my daughter. She's more of a person. She can say more. I find I can relate to her better now, and I feel we are more of a family."*

*"I don't travel but I have long hours, so I see my son mostly on weekends. He can now tell me more and do more. We can throw a ball to each other. If we take a walk, he points to things on the way and listens to what I tell him."*

You are noticing advances in the children's competence that are making it easier for you to relate to them. Some mothers are concerned that the children are not getting to know their fathers and that both father and child are missing something valuable.

*"I used to tell my wife that she could have our son until he was five. Then he would be mine and I would take him over and lead him to be a man.*

*But now I'm glad I didn't wait. When I come home, we all have dinner together. My wife gets him ready for bed, then I tell him a story. On Saturdays, he helps me wash the car or some other job."*

Many fathers believe that small children are a mother's concern, that it is not the father's role to tend to the needs of infants. If they are tired when they come home, they feel, the children should be in bed so they can have dinner in peace.

Times have changed. We have learned how important it is for parents to be available for their children's sense of security and trust. Children of both sexes need the experience of relating to both parents, because parents serve as models of what it is like to be an adult man or woman. In some instances, mothers have to go to work while children are very young. Fathers are needed to help in child care and share in household chores. That is changing the family situation.

*"We both work, and we have a housekeeper during the day. My wife comes home before I do, so she has her time with our son before I get home. When I come home, he has his time with me. Our time together is spent in having a bath and getting ready for bed. While I do that, my wife is getting our dinner ready. Then we take turns reading to him and putting him to bed."*

*"I work a late shift and my wife goes to classes in the morning. We've shared in our child's care and the house chores from the start. It's been hard at times, but a good experience."*

## Importance of Play

*"We aren't able to arrange our lives so equally or have help at home, so we take our child to a neighbor, who cares for her till one of us can come for her. We find we haven't been spending time in play, just in the business of making a living, eating, sleeping. Is it important to play?"*

All parents need some form of relaxation. Play is also very important to children. It is their work. They learn about the world through play.

*"How do you find time in a busy day for play? How much time should you spend at play?"*

Every child needs time during which he or she gets undivided attention. The physical care that a child needs takes a great deal of time, and some parents feel that it takes up all of their available time. However, the time spent in relating to a child in meaningful play can be effective even if it is no more than fifteen or twenty minutes a day.

*"What is regarded as 'meaningful' time with a child?"*

Meaningful time is time the child spends doing something special with you, whether it's playing with you or helping you, going to see something with you or being read to by you. Some parents and children enjoy doing something active; others enjoy a quiet activity, such as listening to music or drawing. These times spent together form lifelong memories and shape attitudes toward parents.

*"My contact with my son is just play. We race, play ball, or play hide-and-go-seek. My wife says that I am simply a playmate, that I don't involve myself in anything serious like discipline or teaching."*

While it is important to have a friendly, playful relationship with your child, that should not be the full extent of contact. A father is a model of what a man is and does and should at least participate in establishing the same standards of discipline as the mother. He should also view himself as the child's teacher, advocate, comforter, supporter, and caretaker. He, too, can feed, dress, bathe, and put the child to bed when he is available to do that.

*"In our family that is just what we have to do. We both work. We discussed this arrangement thoroughly before we had our child. Although I agreed intellectually that that was best for us, it seemed a little awkward and unnatural at first. I was raised in a very traditional family. My father was waited on by my mother, and he had little to do with us. I resented that as a child and missed my father's attention, so I was determined not to be the same. When I got used to taking care of the baby, I got over that awkwardness and felt closer and closer to him."*

We are beginning to understand that parents exert more influence on character development by the example they set than by admonition. Studies show that the father who is kind, loving, and involved is more apt to have children who are well motivated than is the cold, distant, autocratic father. A father who can bathe and feed his child does not lose his masculine identity; nor does he lose it if he vacuums the floor, does the laundry, or shops for food. What he shows is that he cares about his child and can take care of him. Does the mother lose her identity if she works outside the home to help support the family?

*"I fully agree. I do what needs to be done when I'm there and my wife does it when she is there. I think our child knows who is his mother and who is his father, and I think he trusts both of us."*

A child observes not only what parents do and say to him, but what they do and say to others as well—particularly each other. The way his parents talk to each other teaches him how a man and woman relate to each other. These are important steps in socialization for a child.

In more and more families, the mother has to work outside the home while the children are still very young. Consequently, parental roles are being redefined and the family structure is changing. Each family has to make accommodations that suit its individual personalities, cultural standards, priorities, and economic situations.

*"This discussion has forced me to look more closely at the role of fathers. It has made me recognize more fully what my role is and what it can mean to my family if I don't assume all aspects of the role. It makes me feel more important than just a checkbook or a live-in baby-sitter."*

That's a very good conclusion to this discussion. As your child grows and matures, your role will enlarge and become even more challenging and interesting.

## *The Single Parent*

We have been discussing issues that are of concern to all families. However, because of special circumstances the very same issues may affect a family more intensely or differently. Specifically, I am referring to the single-parent family. Does anyone have concerns on this subject that they'd like to share?

*"I'm a single parent by choice, and I work part-time. I've enjoyed being a parent, but it has been hard. I have two worries. One is to find the right caretaker for my child when I am working. The other is that I am doing my job in addition to that of being two parents. Am I shortchanging my child?"*

Having proper child care is a concern for most working women.

*"My real worry is what my child is missing without a father. Can I do the job of both parents?"*

A boy needs a male role model to develop his identification as male. A girl needs to know what an adult male is like, so that she can later choose an appropriate mate. It is important for both sexes to have models of how a man and a woman relate to each other and how they fulfill their roles as parents.

*"In order to supply a male image, would having male baby-sitters be appropriate?"*

Some mothers of boys have used male baby-sitters. However, these baby-sitters are usually of high school or college age and are not available for long stretches of time; thus, it's difficult to establish a real relationship. An alternative solution is a male relative, like a grandfather or uncle who lives close by and can be in contact regularly. Male teachers in nursery schools and preschool programs can also serve as role models, as can a neighbor, a family friend, even the family doctor.

*"It is hard to be divorced and a single parent, but I have done it. The problem comes at visiting time. I try to avoid conflict with my ex and to present him in as favorable a light as I can, because I don't want my daughter to grow up being afraid of men. From some of the remarks my child makes after a visit with him, I suspect that he may not be as careful in what he says about me."*

This issue takes on significance no matter which is the custodial parent. Both parents have to keep the welfare of the child in mind and not use the child as a vehicle for hostility.

*"As a divorced woman, I am no longer invited to participate with my married friends in the dinner and theater parties. My social life, except for family affairs, is nil. I don't have money to throw parties myself or go to the theater. Or to pay baby-sitters either, for that matter, if I should go out."*

All single parents find they need to reorganize their lives on less money. This is often difficult. Many communities have recognized the difficulty and have established social and self-help organizations, such as "Parents Without Partners" and "Kindred Spirits." Some churches have also taken steps to alleviate this problem, and many single parents form less formal associations on their own.

## Separation

*"Since I am the only parent, my son doesn't like it when I have to leave him. He accepts staying with the sitter when I go to work, but he hates it when my mother comes over on the rare evening when I go out. When he sees her coming, he cries and clings to me and says 'No Grandma,' but he likes to go to her house. He makes me feel so guilty for leaving him."*

We have to remember that all children of this age are still learning to cope with separation and the fear that a parent may not return. Their ability to separate waxes and wanes. Even so, parents are entitled to have some time for themselves and need not feel guilty for taking it. You should assure the child that you'll be back in a little while. You can say that when you return, you will come in and kiss her good-night. Or you can remind her what you will be doing together the next day.

## Dating

*"What happens if I start dating again? The child of one of my friends was very unpleasant to her dates, interrupted their conversations, and wouldn't go to bed. I wonder if it is best not to meet a date at home."*

It is not a good idea to meet a new date at home. A parade of dates can be upsetting and confusing to a child. The child may feel threatened by this person who seems to be taking mother away each time he comes. However, if it is to be a relationship of some duration, the person can be introduced to the child gradually. Perhaps you can take the child on a short outing to the park or to an ice cream parlor. Perhaps you can arrange a visit at home and introduce the person to the child's toys.

*"What about having a date spend the night?"*

That is something the parent has to decide. It depends on how comfortable you feel with the situation and how accepting the other person seems to be with your child. If it is to be a permanent relationship and the person is going to live with you, a child should be told that and whatever questions the child may have on the subject should be addressed. For example, the child may ask where Daddy will sleep when he comes home. The child should be reminded that Daddy is not coming back, that he is living elsewhere, but that he is still the child's daddy. Then the child should be told just what the new friend's role will be. This explanation may have to be repeated many times before the child gets accustomed to the new arrangement.

*"If I ever find myself in that situation, I would like it to be without any feelings of jealousy on anyone's part."*

That is the ideal situation. It helps if the parent and new partner can remember not to exclude the child, and at the same time not allow the child to dominate the situation so that the new relationship is not jeopardized. This is not easy; it requires understanding of the issues and good communication.

## The Death of a Spouse

*"I am a single parent for a different reason. My wife died a few weeks ago after a long illness. Since then I've been home with my son trying to do all the things his mother and I used to do with him. Now I have to go back to work, but in view of the big loss he has suffered, I am worried."*

He may have more reaction than usual to your leaving for work now. It would help if you could work part-time for the first few days or weeks before returning to work full-time. It is important that the person who takes care of your child be someone he knows, likes, and trusts.

*"We are lucky, because our old housekeeper will be coming back. She knows his routine well, and I will come home as early as I can to be with him for dinner and to put him to bed. But he has been wanting to come into my bed during the night. Is that all right?"*

Coming into your bed is part of his needing to be sure you are really there. He may need to do that until he feels more secure. You can return him to his bed and reassure him that everything is all right and that you will see him in the morning. Eventually he will sleep through the night again.

*"I don't have any urge to socialize except with members of my family and close friends. I want to be with my son now as much as possible. Friends call and invite me out, but I have no desire to go unless my son is included. I suppose that's natural."*

It is natural to feel that way so soon after a bereavement. However, you should try to return to as normal an existence as possible. This is important so that you don't unwittingly become dependent on the child's company and actually keep the child from developing his autonomy. This sometimes happens when a father dies and the son is told he is the man of the house and should take care of his mother, or when a little girl is left with her father and told to take care of him.

Whenever one parent has to assume a double role, a reorganization of life is called for. Single parents have to marshal all their resources and support systems in order to cope. The increase in the number of such situations is making the issue of single parenting one society will have to address and meet with trained homemakers, good day-care and after-school programs, recreational facilities, and flexible work arrangements.

## Preserving the Mother's Mental Health

Many mothers report that the constant demands of child care, the inability on most days to have just a few minutes to themselves, is an overwhelming strain. Many of these mothers have the added pressure of keeping house, as well as trying to continue a meaningful relation with their husbands and maintaining a social life. Some mothers complain that fathers do not understand how pressure-packed their days may be.

We have been discussing children's needs, mothers' quality time with them, and fathers' time with them. Now it's time to discuss a mother's feelings—and how she feels she is getting along, what things bother her, and what can be done to help her.

### Demands on Mothers

*"Do I ever feel that things need improvement! I try to keep in mind that I shouldn't shout, but our son comes into our room so early in the morning that I yell 'Get back to bed.' That starts the day off wrong. I need all my sleep."*

*"Sleep—that's my biggest issue too. Our daughter is so active now that I can't wait till her nap time. I use it to lie down and read a book for twenty minutes. That is my time. It revives me, and I can get through the rest of the day in a good mood."*

*"I've been talking to other mothers, and most feel that this period has been more difficult than the first year. It's a comfort to know it's not just my child; they are all so active and don't nap as long. That bothers me, because we have such a big old Victorian house that I need the nap time to get work done. I can't spare the time for rest. My husband is so proud of the house that I just have to keep it in order. He spent so much time restoring it."*

It is good that the child's nap time is used for mother's rest or reading time. A mother's job doesn't have formal coffee breaks or lunch periods, so she has to take her breaks when the child is asleep. Some mothers make housework a top priority and try to accomplish it at that time. While that may be satisfying for those mothers who find they enjoy cooking or cleaning when not disturbed by the child, most women also need to rest to recoup their energy.

## Maintaining Other Interests

*"It does take a tremendous amount of physical stamina to keep up with my son now, but that doesn't bother me as much as the need to get away and talk to people on another level. I like talking to other mothers about the children, but I also need to talk about politics, art, literature—all the things that interested me before the baby was born. A chance to do that once in a while keeps me sane."*

Every mother should make time to resume some of her former interests. It's a very important health measure.

*"I feel a little guilty doing that. I have no family nearby to take care of my son for a few hours. I don't want to impose on a neighbor, and I hate to spend money on baby-sitters, because money is tight."*

That feeling is understandable. A parent has to make the decisions that fit best with her circumstances. However, many of us put our emotional health last. We have to remember that we can do a better job as parents when we are rested and in a good mood. That contributes to the entire family's well-being. It may make the difference between enjoying the parental role and always feeling deprived of needed rest or stimulating adult activities.

Let's say a mother had a job she liked and had the opportunity to socialize with people she enjoyed. Now she is home caring for the baby and the demands of the household. She often wishes she could see her friends, but she never arranges to do any of the things she used to enjoy. Her child, who is going through the stage of testing autonomy, announces one day that she wants to wear a party dress to play in the sand. Instead of saying firmly, "This is a dress for a party" and putting it away, the mother gets angry and can't think of a way out of the situation. She is tired and stale on the job; she and the child are in an unhappy mood, and the afternoon is a disaster.

*"You've just described my house! That does happen when I'm tired. I've been having a high school girl come in after school for about two hours twice a week. It's a good playtime for the baby and a relief for me. I rest or do something I haven't been able to get to. That little period helps restore my sanity."*

Every mother should make time to converse with another adult occasionally. There are many demands on her; she needs help and some time for a break. In any office there are coffee breaks, which increase the efficiency of the work. Likewise, a mother's efficiency and ability to do things increase if she has a break from her routine. It's mental health insurance for the whole family. If a mother needs relief, it does not mean that she is not a good and loving mother.

## *Fathers' Ideas About Mothers' Role*

*"The thing that bothers me most is that my husband puts a higher priority on a neat, smooth-running house than on the care of our child. He thinks that simply because our son is bigger and can play alone, I can see to the house full-time.*

*"I get the idea that most men think being home is a snap. You go to the park and out to lunch, the baby naps, and you have a ball. Later you go out again and come home, and somehow the shopping is done, the dinner is cooked, the baby is bathed and fed, the laundry is done and sorted, and the house is clean—and all this while spending most of the time just chatting in the park with your friends."*

*"I asked my husband what he thought about my day, and he said, 'Well, both kids arrive in the bedroom about seven A.M. They spend some time with you and some time with me. Then you spend the day playing with the children, taking them out, and feeding them. Then we may meet and all have a hamburger out. Or I come home, and bathe and put the kids to bed while you make dinner.' He left a few things out!"*

*"My husband does spend time with our son, because I take a course. Recently he announced, 'It's hectic, tedious, and boring, but less boring than it was when he was younger. He's now at that age when he's always wanting something different to do. So that's kind of interesting. But he's always at you for something.'"*

If a father spends time alone with his child, he can establish a closer relationship with the child and get a better idea of what a mother's job is like.

*"It certainly worked with my husband. Someone asked him about my being home with our son instead of working, and he said, 'It's very important at this point for her to stay home. Hers is a full-time, very necessary job. I can be replaced much more easily than she can.'"*

*"I think that if I were to characterize my job, I'd say, 'It's all right if you can make the child your sole priority, but when you put another priority in front of him he feels the effect of this.' I have a cleaning woman do the kitchen and the bathroom, and I can enjoy my children while she cleans."*

You have to give the children your high priority, because they need your attention so much of the time. It's the housework that has to be done somewhere in between that interferes.

*"What I find irritating is never getting one thing finished. I start the dishes, then suddenly I am interrupted, so I leave the dishes and go to help the children out. When I have settled them I pass by the beds and get started on that before I get back to the kitchen."*

It is possible to involve your children in helping you to get the housework done. They can help you put some things away. Many children like to be involved in housework this way.

■                                                                              ■

*"I'm beginning to do that more and more, and it really works, although it may take a little longer to get things done. There's less calling me away from what I'm doing."*

## Mothers Working Outside the Home

*"My problem is a little different—and a little harder because I have a nine-to-five job besides my job as a wife and mother. Although my child is taken care of during the day by a sitter, many of the daily chores are left to me. From my point of view, all of the adult contact during the day doesn't make up for the time I'd like to spend with my child, and there is so little time for it."*

*"I have a nine-to-five job too. The only reason I can make a go of things is that my husband helps so much. He helps shop and clean, and takes his turn with the baby. We can't do much socializing, but we figure we'll get to do that when the baby is older."*

Each family has to organize its life in a way that suits its needs. While the mother at home has problems of isolation, the mother on the outside has the problem of having the outside job plus a good part of the home job as well.

Mother's work is never done. Throughout history in many parts of the world, mothers have been required to do more than take care of children. In North America and in most European countries, the mother's function has been to remain at home to care for the children while fathers worked outside the home. Father's job was to support the family, mother's to care for him and the children. In recent years this arrangement has changed. The cost of living has increased to such an extent that two wage earners may be needed in a family. In addition, many women have been educated to engage in the same careers as men and the women's liberation movement has caused many to reassess their needs. More and more of the child care has been left to others than mother. In this country, about 50 percent of mothers of children under the age of three work outside the home. Of course, that does not mean that they are entirely free of the responsibility of child care or home care. How are those of you who are working outside the home getting along? How do you feel about your situation?

*"It is a very mixed situation for me. We both have to work. I like my work, but I feel torn when we leave in the morning and our son cries and doesn't want us to leave. I know he likes our sitter, who has been with us for two years. But it is upsetting to both of us."*

*"I have just the opposite situation. We drop off our daughter at the sitter's and she doesn't give us a backward glance. Although I am glad she isn't unhappy, I find myself wishing she would show some sign of not wanting to part with me. My husband says I should be glad she doesn't cry."*

We have been concentrating on how the children cope with separation. But parents can have trouble dealing with it, too. Many mothers are uncomfortable about leaving their children, even for an occasional night out. Separation is an issue at any age. There is much research being conducted on the effects of separation on children. The effect on parents needs to be studied as well.

## Mother Substitute

*"I am a computer programmer. I felt that if I didn't keep up with all the new developments, I would never be able to reenter the field later. So I made the choice to continue working. My problem isn't separating, but getting help for coverage while I am working. We had our child in a very well-run day-care center with flexible hours, so if I worked late she could stay there. The problem came when she was sick. When that happened, I had to stay home. Naturally, my employer couldn't put up with all these absences, so I had to find someone who would take care of her at home when she gets sick. It took weeks to find someone suitable."*

*"I had the same experience trying to find the right person to take care of our son. I found one who turned out to be fine, but her salary almost equals mine. So, from a financial standpoint, it doesn't make sense. I've been thinking about giving up my job until my son is older and I won't need so much help."*

*"It isn't only the salary that bothers me, but keeping my caretaker happy so that she will stay and I won't be left in the lurch. When I come home, instead of playing with my child I start to make dinner—something the caretaker will like. When she is away weekends, I do things around the house I'm afraid she'll think are not her place to do. I never relax at home with my family."*

Finding satisfactory substitutes to care for children is becoming more and more difficult. In the past, members of the extended family could lend a hand, but the extended family has largely disappeared. There has also been a decrease in the number of people entering the labor market as housekeepers or child-care workers. Although the salaries in this field seem high to many working mothers, they are still not high enough to attract a great many capable people. So when a decent helper is found, a mother can become a slave to the help, in order to keep her happy. A great deal of reorganizing of our social institutions regarding working hours and child care will have to occur before the problem is solved.

*"I don't get a salary. I get a wage. I can't afford hired help. When I take our son back from the baby-sitter, I'm torn between playing with him and getting dinner ready and the house straightened. I usually end up playing. As you pointed out, he doesn't cling so much if I play first. I then get my chores done more easily."*

When a mother comes home from work, children clamor for her attention. No matter how much there is for her to do, it will get done more easily if she tends to the children first. There have to be compromises. In such families it is normal for dinner and bedtime to be later. The schedule has to be different. A well-kept home may no longer be top priority. Perhaps straightening up can be done once a week—after the children are in bed. When they are old enough to help, the children can assist. As more and more mothers work at paid jobs, more fathers are learning to lend a hand with child care.

## Missing Milestones

"What has bothered me is that I missed all of my daughter's 'firsts.' My mother discovered her first tooth, heard her first words, and watched her take her first step. I guess I was jealous of my mother. She had her turn with her children."

"I had the same feeling about missing all the 'firsts.' I sort of wished my sitter would let me make the discoveries and think they were the 'firsts.' "

"That was my feeling too, and then I got hold of myself and said, 'You ought to be glad she is interested enough to notice these things. That shows she is on the ball. It ought to make you more secure and happy about leaving your child with her.' "

Many mothers—and fathers too—find it hard to miss being present at the achievement of their children's developmental milestones, which can be one of the most enjoyable parts of parenthood.

"Because of that I stopped working. I realized that this chance to be there with the baby would only come once. We needed the extra income, but I decided to do some belt tightening and make up for the financial loss later."

## Jealousy of Caretaker

"I don't worry so much about missing the 'firsts.' What bothers me most is that someone else will be winning the baby's love. I worked hard on establishing a bond by holding our daughter in the delivery room and nursing her for six months before I went back to work. When I come home each day, it seems she is just as interested in the baby-sitter's leaving as my coming home. That upsets me, even though I'm glad she likes the baby-sitter."

"I've had that concern, too, but not about the sitter. My husband works at home, so he takes care of our son when I am at work. When I come home, my son seems to be so comfortable with his father that he doesn't relate as much to me as he used to before I worked."

A child establishes a closer relationship with the person who takes care of him most, because that person is fulfilling his daily needs. If that relationship is a happy, affectionate one, the child will develop trust in that parent. However, that does not mean that the bond to the other parent is broken.

*"It is so hard to adjust to the fact that you have to work out a different way of being a mother. Is it different if a child is in day care or at home with a baby-sitter?"*

Whether the child is at home with an individual baby-sitter or in family day care or a more formal day-care setting, when the mother is reunited with her child she needs at first to devote her time exclusively to the child. Household chores can be postponed until the child feels comfortable and assured that she is home to stay. Then she can start a chore in which she can also engage the child. It enhances the relationship if there is some special activity that they do together and that the child can look forward to, such as having a snack together, reading a story, or playing a game. These activities should be repetitive and predictable, so that the child develops a sense of consistency and continuity.

## Time for Parents

*"I gather that consistency and continuity are the key words. But it seems to me that there is no time left for working parents to have any life together on their own."*

*"We waited so long to have a child that we don't mind spending all our free time with him. We take him wherever we go and don't go places he is not welcome. Once in a while, I get the urge to have dinner out with my husband, but he won't hear of it. He is a home person."*

*"At first we felt that way, too. Each of us had to travel frequently for our jobs, so we felt that we were cheating the baby if we took time off for ourselves. But the baby is almost three, and we feel we have given her a good start. Now we are beginning to schedule a little time off for ourselves together."*

All parents need time to be together alone. Everyone needs some refueling time. The job of parenting can be done with much more enthusiasm when such time is arranged. Parents who work outside the home are just as entitled to this time as other parents.

*"The hard part of setting up time for ourselves is that everything is a project. We have to plan and arrange for sitters well in advance, because they are not always easy to get."*

The situation is indeed complex. Our society has not yet begun to make the adjustments necessary to take proper care of the children of working mothers. Perhaps a change like paying mothers to stay home to take care of their own children during the first three years is in order. In addition, parenting groups, where mothers at home with their children could end their isolation and all parents could learn more about child rearing, could be offered.

## The Relationship Between Parents

Most of our discussions have centered on the needs of the child. But the relationship between the parents is also important. Everyone likes to feel that the arrival of a baby enhances the tie between parents. This does happen, but the relationship between parents can become strained if they neglect each other in their concentration on the baby.

Do you feel that your relationship with each other as husband and wife has changed since the arrival of the baby?

*"I think that my husband feels our son is now my top priority. He understands that the baby hasn't taken away my love for him and that my feelings for him are entirely different than those for the baby. But he sulks a little when I have to interrupt what we are doing to attend to the baby."*

### Competing for Attention

*"I know that my wife pays as much attention to me as she can. But I still miss our discussions and the time we spent alone. In that way, yes, I think the baby interferes. Even so, I get a kick out of watching our son and the excitement he shows when he sees me. So I guess it's a trade-off."*

*"It works in a different way with us. In my country, the family revolves around the man absolutely."*

In this country, that is no longer so. Some of us come from different cultures, and this may add to our difficulties. All families have to work out a way in which members show that they cherish each other. That's terribly important to the mental health of the whole family.

There is no doubt that life is different with a baby. A baby's needs are very time- and energy-consuming for parents. Parents can and should arrange to have some private time with each other. It may be possible only once a week, but it is important to arrange for it and then take steps to carry it out. This can be the beginning of drawing parents together in situations they enjoyed before the arrival of the baby. Parents can then enjoy the time spent with the child without feeling that they have been robbed of their time together.

### Father's Expectations

*"I think that the real problem isn't just time together, but what the father's expectations are. My husband comes from a family where the father was top priority, and the children knew it. I think a lot of fathers have that view. But families aren't run that way anymore."*

At one time many families operated like that. In extended families, a grandmother, maiden aunt, or other family member was available to lend a hand with the children so mother could be more attentive to father.

■                                                                                      ■

Hired household help was more available. Even though households today may be smaller and have many labor-saving devices, the need for human assistance is still there.

*"My husband and I are aware of the need to have time together. But baby-sitters are expensive and hard to find. So we sort of leave the issue on the back burner."*

## Mini-Vacations

*"It was getting so bad in our house that we decided to hire an off-duty nurse from the pediatric service of a nearby hospital for one night. We checked into a hotel in the evening, went to dinner with friends we hadn't seen for at least a year, and saw a play. The next morning, both of us slept late for the first time in two years! We had brunch, took a walk, went to the museum for an hour, and came home rested, happy, and as anxious to see our baby as he was to see us."*

Parents do need to have vacations from their children. You are their primary caretakers and shouldn't separate from them at this age for long periods of time, but you can spend a night out away from them. Nobody stays on a job from morning to night and gets up during the nights seven days a week on and on without some kind of respite.

## Changing Roles

It may seem to us that our parents had less difficulty. In some respects, that may be true. The roles of men and women are changing, and that is affecting the family structure. When women viewed being a wife and mother as their primary role and did not have to work outside the home for financial reasons, they were more content to stay home and wait on their husbands and children. When women began to take over men's jobs during the wars, they created new roles for themselves and never could resume the old roles exclusively. Now both men and women are trying to redefine their roles in work, politics, marriage, and child care.

The family structure has to change to adapt to the changing roles. The problem is that children's needs don't change. The number of people devoting time to caring for children is dwindling. Therefore, much of the job falls to the nuclear family, which in many instances is finding it hard to cope. That's why we are so concerned here with helping to improve family relationships. This is a transitional period in society, and we have to help each other find the way that will make for a happy family life, allowing parents as well as children to grow and develop to their maximum potential.

# Realizing Your Child's Capabilities

## 22

## Delaying Gratification

When the children were infants, their parents responded immediately to crying. But now that the children are older they are often expected to wait to have their needs gratified. In fact, parents become impatient with their children because the children's ability to wait is so limited. Parents begin to wonder when they will be free to do simple tasks and activities without interference from their child. Now that the children are older, are you finding that they require the same immediate response to their needs as they did when they were infants?

*"I'm a little disappointed, because I expected that by now my son would be able to wait better than he does."*

At this age, between two and three, children still do not have the ability to wait that adults have. What seem like short delays to us seem like an eternity to a child.

*"As soon as my husband leaves in the morning, my son wants to go out for a walk. But I want to do the dishes and straighten the house first. He just can't wait; he cries. Sometimes, just to get some peace, I do take him out. Other times I just can't and we have a lot of unpleasantness and sometimes even a tantrum."*

*"When I have to wait in a supermarket line with my daughter, she is just impossible."*

*"My worst moments are when I go to my mother's and I have to stay to help her with some task. My son just wants to get out of there and can't wait to go home."*

*"Most of us have had similar experiences. Are we expecting too much of our children too soon? Is there some way we can avoid this conflict?"*

As children get older, their capacity to wait improves. It is the parents' job to help them by prolonging the waiting time gradually. Actually, we've all been doing it to some extent since the children were infants. For example, when the baby cried for food and saw it being prepared, he learned that it was for him and soon began to be able to wait until it was ready. Later, when he threw his toys down and wanted them back, he learned to gesture for that and waited until the toys were returned.

*"Is it possible for a child of this age to wait a half hour until you make the beds, put the dishes in the dishwasher, and put a few things away?"*

It is possible to postpone the child's gratification for as long as a half hour. For example, if the child asks to go for a walk before you are ready, you can say, "Yes, we can go as soon as I make the bed [or put the dishes in the dishwasher]. You can help me and then we will go sooner." This works better than a statement like "No, we can't go now. I have to clean the house." In the first instance, you give the child a positive response and something to do while she is waiting. Most children respond to this approach. In the second instance, your response is negative and frustrating, and the child responds accordingly. In the first case, she learns to postpone her gratification. In the second, she doesn't.

*"This approach has been mentioned in other situations too. My child was very impatient, especially when she asked for a cookie before mealtime. Instead of saying, 'No cookies now,' I've begun to say, 'You can have cookies right after lunch. Help me set the table and we'll have lunch soon.' That seems to work."*

## Telephone Calls

A parent who is talking on the phone is physically present but not in communication with the child or able to attend to the child. To the child this is exclusion, and most children cannot tolerate exclusion.

*"Well, what should be done? A parent does have to talk on the phone sometimes."*

It often helps to include the child by taking him on your lap and telling him with whom you are talking. For example, you might say, "I'm talking to Grandma. I'm telling her what we are going to do today. Do you want to talk to her?" Usually the child will say something and slip off your lap. He has been included, so he is then able to find something to interest him by himself.

*"Suppose it's a business call or something else important."*

You should try to make these calls when the child is napping. If that can't be done, explain the situation to the caller and proceed in the same way: put the child on your lap and tell him who is calling and about what. It doesn't matter whether he understands the subject. The important thing is that he has been included.

■                                                                                                           ■

*"I always try to have everyone call back or leave a number where they can be reached. I tell my family and friends to call after nine P.M., when our child is asleep."*

That approach avoids unnecessary problems. Mothers who are on a telephone squad for an organization should try limiting their calling or responding to times when the child is asleep.

## Talking to Other Adults

*"I have difficulty with our child when I try to talk with my husband or a visitor. Our child can't wait for us to finish a sentence without interrupting."*

As with telephone conversations, the child feels a need to be included. If the child is initially included in the conversation, she will either sit with you and make a remark or two or become interested in a nearby toy which she can play with. The time parents can spend conversing is increased if they direct a remark or two to the child.

*"I like to read, and I especially like to keep abreast of the news every day. When my son seems engrossed in a toy I may pick up the paper and try to read. But that doesn't last long. He spots what I am doing and won't let me finish."*

That is another activity the child interprets as exclusion. Again, if the child is taken onto the parent's lap and told what she is reading about, he may quickly get down and go about his business. Serious reading should be postponed to a time when the child is asleep.

*"I find not reading as much and when I want to to be the hardest part of parenting."*

It is hard even for many adults to postpone gratification. So imagine how hard it is for a young child with an immature central nervous system to postpone gratification. Remember, delay of gratification is a learning process and is achieved slowly.

# Transitional Objects and Self-soothing Behaviors

Many parents find it upsetting to see their child carrying around the remains of a blanket or teddy bear, or sucking their thumbs or reaching for a pacifier. It is important to understand that these are normal activities, the child's way of controlling her environment when she is lonesome, bored, a little anxious, or tired. These activities substitute for the comfort received from mother at an earlier age. Are any of you disturbed by such behavior? How do you deal with it?

*"My son still carries around an old piece of blanket. It seems to satisfy him as much as the whole blanket used to. He won't allow me to replace it with a new blanket."*

How do you feel about it? Aside from washing the blanket, which showed your feeling about its smelly, ragged condition, did you say anything?

*"I've told him he must leave it at home when we go out because he might lose it, and he accepts that. But I dread the scene if we should lose it. Once we left it at his grandmother's house, and we had to drive back to get it. He cried all the way."*

*"When my son finishes a bottle of milk or juice, very often he won't give up the empty bottle. He carries it around, and sometimes goes to bed with it. Friends and family tell me to simply take it away from him, but I don't because he got so upset the one time I tried. When he is busy doing something, he drops the bottle, and I can take it away without any problem."*

A child of this age begins to experience times when every need is not met and tries to satisfy the need himself. He may thrash about and his hand may touch a bottle, a soft blanket, or a soft toy left in the crib. This object may give him a pleasant sensation like he had when mother supplied something that he needed. So instead of crying for mother whenever he feels the need for a pleasant experience, he tries to overcome it in a way he is able to do himself.

*"Can that mean that the mother has failed in some way?"*

Mothers can't be available for every need every minute. There are times when an infant has to wait. Parents may find that holding a certain stuffed animal or edge of a blanket soothes a child and will offer this to the child without realizing that the child may become dependent on it later.

*"Do all children do this? Is it a necessary step in their development?"*

Not all children need to comfort themselves this way. However, it is common. In the literature on child development, favorite toys and objects are referred to as "transitional objects." So they have achieved a place in scientific observation.

*"Should children be allowed to form such attachments?"*

In most cases, it is not a matter of allowing it to happen. These attachments usually happen spontaneously, except when parents initiate or reinforce the attachment because they want to quiet a child.

A parent who sees that a child seems to need the toy or other object only when he is bored or lonesome can engage the child in some diverting activity. Parents can read a book with a child; engage him in playing with a ball, building with blocks, or listening to records together; or even arrange a visit with another child.

There are many things that may upset children or make them anxious—overly enthusiastic visitors, strange places, noises, other children, and animals, for example. It is important for parents to recognize what bothers their child, then be available to him for closeness and comfort, so the child won't feel the need for the soothing objects.

*"Suppose you let a child form an attachment to an object. Will he ever stop on his own?"*

When these objects no longer fulfill a need—as the child becomes more competent and more occupied in play with others and with school activities, for example—these objects are given up. Parents are sometimes impatient to have them relinquished before the child is ready.

*"What about thumb and finger sucking? Shouldn't more strenuous measures be taken about that because of the effect on the teeth?"*

Taking strenuous measures, such as scolding the child, taping the fingers, or painting fingers with a bitter substance to discourage sucking, are all counterproductive. Parents have to remember that being able to put a finger in the mouth is one of the earliest exploratory activities of a baby; it provides her a way of giving herself the first pleasure of which she was aware—sucking at the breast or bottle. Part of the parents' job is to help her find other satisfactions as she grows. In general, the same things that lead to use of a transitional object—fatigue, boredom, loneliness, and anxiety—lead to continued need for satisfaction in thumb sucking, so the same remedial procedures apply.

*"When do children give up these objects without parental encouragement?"*

Most children give up these objects between three and four years of age. However, it may take some children until they are five. Others relinquish these objects by the age of three, or when they enter nursery school.

*"What about the child who continues to use a pacifier?"*

A child who continues to use a pacifier is not attempting to satisfy a sucking need. A child who has had the pacifier stuffed into his mouth to keep him quiet may use it as a transitional object. It is used under the same circumstances—fatigue, boredom, loneliness, and anxiety—and should be dealt with in the same way as any other transitional object.

## Safety Issues

Fearing they will be labeled "overprotective," some parents are reluctant to take safety precautions where such caution is called for—such as at a swimming pool; at a lake or ocean; or on a trafficked street, where children of mixed ages are playing without supervision. There is a difference between setting limits to help ensure safety and inhibiting the child's natural exploratory activities—such as using a slide or swing in the park, riding a tricycle, running, and climbing over an obstacle. Parents deal with these situations differently. Have you ever been called an overprotective parent?

*"My husband is always telling me that I am too anxious—that I see danger in undangerous situations."*

## Water Safety

*"Last weekend, we went rowing on a lake. Before we got into the boat, I put a life belt on our daughter. Later, she wanted to take it off. Her father let her, even though I protested. Then she leaned over the side and almost fell out, but we both caught her and almost fell out ourselves."*

*"We have that all the time with our son. He wants to go in the water without a life jacket or water wings, and I won't let him. His father feels I'm making a 'sissy' out of him, that I should let him take chances."*

*"In the summer we spend a lot of time at a community pool. We stay in the shallow end, but I can't be sure my son won't stray too far away. So I insist on a life jacket, even though I'm one of the few mothers who does. Other mothers tell me I'm overprotective."*

No parent wants to be called anxious or overprotective. However, in certain situations safety precautions must be taken. Most water areas for young children have strict rules—and for a good reason. A parent should not rely on a child's judgment or self-control. It is much better to institute precautions consistently than to be giving children mixed signals about safety.

## Street Safety

*"Now that he can walk, my son doesn't want to hold my hand or be strapped into his stroller. We live on a busy street, and I am afraid that he may run off before I can stop him. So I insist that he hold my hand or else get into the stroller. This sometimes causes a scene, and I wonder if I'm being too cautious."*

*"I let our son walk to the end of each block alone, and he waits for me at the curb. Then I hold his hand and we cross together. I think he knows he has to wait for me."*

*"I can't do that with our daughter. The minute she is out of the stroller, she is off and running and I have to chase after her. I wouldn't dream of trusting her judgment."*

We want to teach our children to respond to our limits and we want to feel we can trust them. However, on a busy street that is quite risky. It is the child who waits who poses the more difficult problem, because a parent can't be certain that the child won't be lured into the street by something like a ball or brightly colored paper, or become so absorbed in walking that he forgets to stop at the curb. At this age, the child still needs close supervision.

■                                                              ■

*"But children have to have someplace where they can be on their own."*

That is true. It can be accomplished best in a park or on a quiet side street. If this is made a regular event, the child learns that when mother says "When we get to the park [or other landmark]," he will be given freedom to walk and explore.

*"When can a parent expect children to understand to be careful of traffic?"*

This varies with the maturational timetable of each child. A general answer is when the child is verbal and can understand the danger involved.

## Playground Safety

*"At the playground, older children sometimes take over where the little ones are playing. Some of these older children are very considerate, but others are very vigorous and boisterous. The little ones may get hit with balls thrown too hard, poked with shovels, or banged with bikes. When that happens, I stand close to my child and ward off these kids. That causes comments such as 'Don't keep him such a baby' or 'Let him grow up.'"*

*"That happens to us too, even when we go visiting and there happen to be older children. Then I'm really in a spot: he doesn't want to leave, and he can't participate safely."*

Parents of children this age have to intercede by organizing turns in activity or by playing with their children in such a way that the older ones will want to participate too. Some children who have been maltreated by older children may themselves become "bullies" when they get older. Others may be inhibited in their social development if they are not protected in these situations.

*"What is the real meaning of the term 'overprotective'?"*

Overprotectiveness is generally understood to mean the inhibition of age-appropriate exploratory behavior. For example, a parent who keeps a child who is just learning to walk strapped in a high chair or stroller and doesn't permit her any freedom on the floor for fear she might fall is being overprotective.

*"Our children are at the stage where they want to climb up and down the slide in the park. I am afraid to let my son do this, so I avoid going to the park as much as possible. Am I being overprotective?"*

Children of this age need to engage in activities that develop large muscles. Climbing is one of these activities. Allow your child to climb, at first while he holds on to you and the rail, and then to be there to catch him when he comes down. Then offer recognition of his accomplishment. As he practices and becomes more proficient, give him less assistance but still be ready to steady him. In time, you will be more at ease when he climbs.

■                                                                                    ■

## Safety in the Home

*"My son wants to climb on everything. He tries to climb the bookshelves. I'm afraid he will pull them over and I stop him. Is that all right? I'm not home during the day, because I work. My housekeeper, who has five children, says boys will be boys and that I should let him."*

Of course, if there is a danger that the shelves will topple over, your son should not be allowed to climb on them. Perhaps the housekeeper can take him to a playground and let him climb there, where safer climbing opportunities are provided.

Some communities have special gym classes for young children that provide activities for large-muscle development. Many rural areas have fences, trees, and hills that are ideal for climbing. Some parents set up climbing areas in the home—ladders fastened safely to walls, for example.

*"My boy loves to run. He's still a little clumsy and he falls, so I'm constantly saying 'Not so fast,' 'Be careful,' or 'You'll get hurt, so slow down.' Once he fell and skinned his chin on the pavement, and it was a long time healing. I guess I have fears of his being permanently disfigured or breaking an arm or a leg. Some of my friends think I am overdoing it a little."*

Perhaps you are conveying some of your anxiety to him, and as a result he is a little inhibited and lacking motor control. If you are so worried about his running on the pavement, perhaps you can have him run in a grassy area where spills won't be so traumatic. Running is part of a child's normal development at this age. Fortunately, the bones of children this age are more pliable and breaks do not occur as often as one might fear.

Certainly, the parents' job of defining limits for safety and allowing enough room for development is not easy. Furthermore, what may be right for one family may not be right for another. However, there are certain guidelines for water safety, traffic precautions, and playground situations that are common sense and can serve for most people.

## Manners

Naturally, parents want their children to have good manners. They want their children to greet and part with people properly, to use utensils instead of their hands, to be perfect hosts, to take turns, to share toys, to sit still through meals, and to refrain from interrupting when adults are conversing. The children are older now, but they are still not mature enough to act this way consistently.

We have discussed manners before. We were wondering if this issue is still a concern and if so, how you are coping.

### Table Manners

*"Our daughter isn't so good on the cup by herself, but she does manage with the spoon now without putting it in her mouth upside down. Once in a*

*while she gets a little impatient. She tries to get food in her mouth with her hands, and winds up smearing it all over herself. I simply wipe the food off and let her try again. She seems to be making progress."*

*"My child eats only food she can hand-feed herself. She has completely given up the spoon and fork, although she was getting the hang of feeding herself pretty well. So I give her just what she can pick up by hand. She is very fastidious; everything has to be dry and neat."*

Most children this age are learning to use a spoon. Some have begun to use a fork, although it is often abandoned temporarily. Some can manage with a cup. In general, the children are more competent with utensils than they were at age two, but they are still a little messy.

## Modeling Manners

*"I can't see fussing about table manners. I'm satisfied if my daughter gets her food down, because she is such a poor eater. Isn't it true that in time all children begin to eat the right way?"*

In general, that is true. If parents and other caretakers model proper handling of utensils, children will follow suit as they become more competent. Many children respond to comments such as "Mommy and Daddy hold our spoons this way" and "You hold your spoon all by yourself very nicely" or a similar expression of approval.

*"Don't you have to correct them each time so they will remember? My husband and I have a tendency to do that."*

*Repeated correction sometimes has the opposite effect. It may make eating too problematic and cause some to lose interest in eating. You have to recognize what helps your child the most and what level she has achieved. Some children are very responsive and have matured enough to want to emulate the parents in this way.*

*"I've been trying for a long time to get my child to say 'please' and 'thank you.' Am I jumping the gun a little?"*

It is good to say "please" and "thank you" to your child and as a model for him when you speak to each other. If sometimes he says either "please" or "thank you" in some form such as "ta" or "tata" first, recognize that he has said it and then say, "That's nice" or a similar comment.

*"My friend's son is the same age as my son. The other day, she was insisting that he say 'please.' After several promptings, he began to cry, so she just gave him the juice. I wouldn't have done that. Am I too lenient or is she too demanding?"*

Simply modeling and providing approval and recognition when success is achieved is a more effective approach. Dissatisfaction felt by a parent may be conveyed to the child, who then has a loss of self-esteem.

■                                                                                        ■

*"Does the same principle apply to greetings and good-byes? Sometimes I try to make my child say good-bye to a visitor. He complies only once in a while. Should I just say it myself in the hope that this will stimulate him to do it when he is ready?"*

That is usually the best approach. If you are not expecting compliance, you do not convey a feeling of disappointment to the child.

*"But what about people who give you the feeling that there is something wrong with your baby or the way you are bringing him up?"*

The important issue to remember is your child's feelings and his relationship with you. Perhaps you can reply for the child while holding his hand. This includes him in the greeting and may encourage him to offer his own greeting.

*"I don't care about strangers, but it bothers me when Grandma says, 'Johnny doesn't say hello to Grandma?'"*

It may help if the reply gives the visitor the idea that you are working on the issue. You can say, for example, "Yes, we're working on it. Pretty soon he'll be saying hello by himself."

*"It isn't just visitors and grandparents. I wonder what methods my sitter is using in this area. When I came home the other day, my sitter was returning with my daughter from a stroll. The sitter was trying to make my daughter say 'good-bye' to a neighbor, and was critical when the baby didn't respond."*

It is difficult but necessary to find out about baby-sitters' methods and have them deal with issues your way. If they are literate, you might provide them with books about child rearing in a tactful way. You can say, "Here is a book that explains our ideas about children. Maybe you'd like to read it sometime and see what you think of it." In some places there are courses for caretakers in which your caretaker may be willing to be enrolled.

## Dining Out

*"My husband and I used to go out for dinner several times a week. Since our baby was born, we've tried to go out at least once a week—primarily to give me a change of scene. But restaurants have become very expensive, and now there is the cost of a baby-sitter. So last week we decided to go with our son to a fast-food place. He wouldn't sit still. Is it too much to expect them to sit through a meal quietly now?"*

*"We've gone through the same thing with our daughter. The first time we went to a very fine French restaurant that we had always liked. It was a disaster. The next week we tried a nearby Chinese restaurant. They welcomed all of us, brought a high chair and a few paper toys for the baby, and served the meal quickly. Between tastes of rice and Chinese cookies for the baby, we managed to enjoy ourselves."*

*"I don't care where we go, as long as it's out! So we've settled for a nearby hamburger joint. It's quick. Our baby chews on a bun, some meat, and even french fries. There is a lot of hustle and bustle, so he doesn't have to be so quiet and we don't get embarrassed if he stands up or climbs into our laps."*

As some of you have found out, children of this age are not ready for a formal slow-service dinner in a restaurant. It is best to pick places where the food is served quickly and children are welcome. Most children are able to manage for as long as they are eating. If given a toy, book, or crayon and paper to amuse her, the child may remain seated twenty minutes to a half hour.

*"What if the child is still restless and wants to walk around?"*

If that happens, the parents can take turns walking with the child to different parts of the restaurant—the lobby, a window, or the cash register, for instance. The child may then be able to sit a little while again back at the table. Perhaps he can be offered some dessert or some milk. A great deal depends on the time of day—whether the child is being kept up past a nap time or bedtime. The lighting in the room can make a difference— what adults consider romantic lighting may seem dark and scary to a small child.

Of course, the child's hunger level is also a factor. If he has just been fed at home, he will certainly show no interest in eating and sitting still. If he is very hungry, he will not be able to wait. It is a good idea to carry a few crackers or some bread for the child to munch on until the meal is served. The parents' attitude also can contribute to the child's response. If they are relaxed and in a good mood, things go better. If they are tense, the child senses it and can become tense and restless too.

## Sharing

*"Our daughter's behavior when we have company is beginning to bother us a little. She doesn't allow anyone to play with her things. If she passes out cookies, she takes a bunch for herself first. It's upsetting, especially if you don't know the visitor well."*

Now that the children are becoming more verbal and sociable, parents may expect them to be good hosts and hostesses too. Sometimes a plate of cookies held by both parent and child can be passed around. The parents should see to it that the child has a chance to partake of the cookies. If this is the usual pattern when company comes, the child begins to learn the sequence of events and gets the idea of a host's role. It is quite natural for your child to grab a bunch for herself if she hasn't had her share.

*"What about when there are guests and you are talking and the child interrupts? Should you make the child wait?"*

■   ■

*"Parents just can't just talk to their guests—at least, not in our house. So my husband and I take turns talking to guests."*

Taking turns talking to guests is one solution. Another is to include the child in your conversations. Even if he doesn't understand all that is being said, he may be less demanding. In some cases, it is best to interrupt your conversation to meet a child's need. At this age children are still not able to wait for you to finish, but most can cooperate when the parent says something like "Just a second, dear, and Mommie will get . . . ," then complies with the request. What usually causes problems is that parents exploit the "just a second" and exhaust the limits of a child's tolerance.

## Dealing with Special Events

Most children become upset at the prospect of going to the doctor or dentist, or to the hospital. Parents wonder whether to tell the children in advance or to say nothing until the event is at hand. It is also difficult for many parents to decide how much to tell the child. Some parents find this is a problem even when the event is enjoyable, such as a trip, a visit to grandparents or inlaws, a party, or the arrival of a friend. Children may become very excited and anxious about these events as well, and may experience mood changes, or changes in sleep and eating patterns. Are you experiencing any difficulty in knowing when and how to tell your child about an upcoming event?

*"I have that problem every time a baby-sitter is due to arrive. I know my son is not going to like having me leave, so I don't want him to be anxious too long in advance. At the same time, I don't want it to be a shock when the sitter arrives. But somehow I never hit it right. He always gets upset when I mention going out."*

*"If I say 'I'm going' just twenty minutes before leaving, my daughter is upset the whole time. If I tell her earlier than that, she sometimes forgets and gets interested in something. Then she isn't moping when I actually leave."*

We should be honest and prepare children for things to come, but timing also has to be considered. For instance, if you are going out for dinner that night, you don't have to prepare the child in the morning. After the child has finished her dinner, you can say, "Mommy and Daddy are going out tonight and your sitter [mentioning the name] is coming to be with you. She will play with you, read to you, and put you to bed. Before you know it, Daddy and Mommy will be back."

*"My child always protests no matter what I say."*

We can't expect a child to say, "All right, Mommy, I don't care if you go out. Have a nice time." Children need to show you that they are displeased. It is normal for them to react in a way that shows their attachment to you and to show some concern about your leaving.

*"When my baby-sitter comes in, my daughter is quite unfriendly to her until I leave. My sitter can't understand why the baby isn't happy to see her."*

Of course, your child feels more secure with you. Another reason for your child's mood is that when you go away, she is not sure that you are coming back. You have to emphasize that you are going to be back in a little while, perhaps adding that when you come back, you and she are going to do some fun things. Often, whether you have expressed this or not, the child may get the idea that you are annoyed with her, and she wonders if you are going to go away and not come back. Perhaps she has been a little bit naughty that day and you have been displeased with her for something, so maybe—just maybe—you are not going to come back. She does think that way and we have to be aware of how she may think. If you can explain this to the baby-sitter, the sitter may be less disturbed by the child's mood and may try to be more helpful to the child.

*"What we do is have a special project under way before the baby-sitter arrives. The baby-sitter then continues with the activity until I am out the door. For example, we'll make cookie dough that is to go into the oven after I'm gone. The activity then becomes more important than the separation."*

It's a very good idea to have special games and activities that occur only with the baby-sitter—a record that only the baby-sitter puts on, a toy that is used only when she's there, or refreshments that are enjoyed only by the child and baby-sitter. This makes your leaving a less stressful and more exciting time for your child.

## Visits to the Doctor

*"We can't seem to solve our biggest problem—doctor's visits. My son is afraid he is going to get a shot each time he goes. Sometimes he does, so I can't promise him he won't when I have to tell him we're going."*

Many children get upset at the prospect of seeing a doctor because of the inoculations and testing doctors must do. If you have had this experience with your child, you might try to get him a toy doctor's kit. This allows him to act out a visit to the doctor, and perhaps give "shots" to his teddy bear or doll. He may then begin to feel less fearful of visits to the doctor.

It is important for parents not to convey anxiety to the child. Find out what is going to be done at the visit. Then, about half an hour before leaving the house, tell the child where you are going. If he is to have a shot he should be told. Say that you will hold him, that it may hurt a bit for a moment, then it will all be over. Then tell him some pleasant thing that is going to follow the doctor's visit. On the way, perhaps mention the toys he will find in the waiting room before he sees the doctor and what the doctor will say to him in greeting. You might suggest that he show the doctor how big he has grown since the last visit or ask the doctor to examine one of his toys. In time, the child feels that the parent is not anxious and doesn't deceive him or minimize the hurt the child experiences, and then he gains confidence and may even get to enjoy visiting his doctor.

## Visits to the Dentist

Dental visits should be started after most of the teeth have erupted in the latter part of the second year. It is a good idea to arrange a "get acquainted" visit before the first examination. A child can accompany the parent at his or her visit to the dentist and watch all the fascinating things that happen: the chair that gives a ride up and down; the water that spins around in the little bowl; the little paper cups.

*"We don't have any trouble with that. When I say I'm going to the dentist he can't wait, because he knows the dentist will give him a ride in the chair."*

*"Should I take my child to a special children's dentist or to a family dentist?"*

If you have a family dentist who is willing to take the time to interest the child in proper dental hygiene, that dentist is fine. Many dentists are pleased to do that because this is preventive dentistry. But if your dentist is not comfortable dealing with young children or their special needs you should find a pediodontist.

## Hospitalizations

*"What can you say to a child this age who has to be taken to a hospital? Our daughter has a squint. The doctor feels that she has not responded to the patch, and that surgery is needed. The appointment is for next week. We don't know what to tell her."*

You should explain the process to her in language she can understand. Tell her you know how much she dislikes the patch procedure and that the doctor can make the eye better more quickly if you take her to a special house called a hospital. Tell her that you will go with her (if the hospital you have chosen permits parents to stay). Find out from your doctor what the actual procedure is going to be. When your daughter questions you, explain the steps simply (for example, whether she will be going to the operating room on a stretcher or wheelchair). In the days before her stay in the hospital, she can act this out with her dolls if she wishes to. It is a good idea to describe the way the operating-room nurses and doctors dress and that she will take off her clothes and wear a special gown, too. There are picture books now that show children in hospitals that may be helpful if the real situation cannot be demonstrated. Some hospitals offer a presurgery tour for children. The child should know, too, that she will eat and sleep there and that you will be with her. If she feels assured that you will be with her and she gets a sense of your feeling secure, she will, too. Children are usually made more anxious than they would be by the parents' anxiety.

*"Suppose a child has to go to the hospital for other reasons."*

The principle is the same. Tell the child the reason and procedure in language the child can understand. Don't provide too many details. Try to answer all of the child's questions, and let her know that you will be there all the time.

## Other Exciting Events

*"I find that too much advance preparation for happy things like a birthday party sets my child off. He has spells of crankiness and sleep disturbances. So I don't tell him until just before the event."*

*"When my son knows several days in advance that we are going to visit his grandparents, he whines and wants to know when we are going."*

*"My daughter just can't wait if she knows we are going to have a visitor, even people she sees often. First she seems happy, then she begins to ask when they will be coming and gets very tense at every sound. Then she pouts, mopes around, and gets cranky. I've learned not to tell her too far in advance."*

When you tell children of a visit or other event in advance, it is a good idea to keep them occupied until the event. Children this age have no sense of time, nor do they have the ability to wait for days for an event to occur. They become frustrated and irritable when they have to postpone gratification. They should be provided with an activity while they are waiting. When parents understand this, it is easier to cope with the child's behavior. It is also important that the parent not add to the difficulties by being angry and upset.

*"We're planning a trip to California, and we are taking our son with us. We haven't told him yet, but he has not been himself for the past few days. I wonder if he has noticed our preparations for the trip."*

Children are very keen observers and very sensitive to changes in their environments. Your child may have noticed that you are doing something different. Perhaps you are shopping a little more, or mentioning the trip during telephone conversations. He may have overheard something and misinterpreted it.

It may help to include the child in your plans. For example, let him participate in getting his things together—his teddy bear, favorite books, and other items important to him. He can be told how you will travel, what you will see, and where you will stay when you get there. He may need to be told the details many times and may ask many questions. These questions may indicate what sort of anxieties he is having and what reassurance he may need.

■                                                                              ■

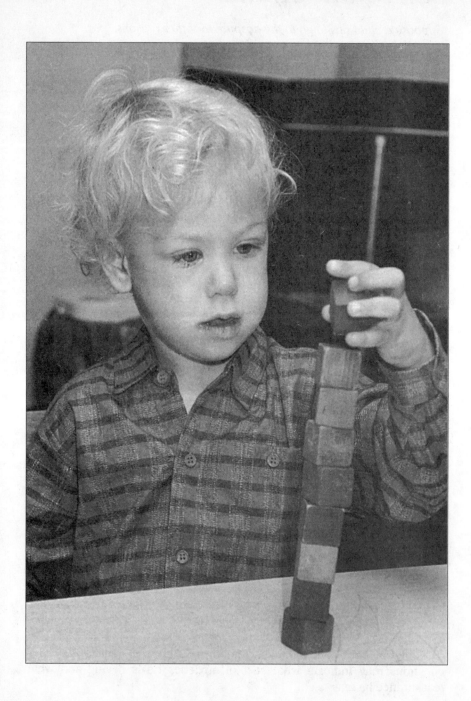

# SECTION II

## Age Thirty to Thirty-six Months

*T*he children have made great strides in their use of language; some of them can communicate and understand quite sophisticated concepts. Their ability to separate from mother has increased; some can even visit Grandma's or a friend's house without her. They are beginning to understand the concept of taking turns and are beginning to engage in interactive play with peers. Some have begun to show interest in toilet training or have already achieved bowel and bladder control.

### *Highlights of Development—Age Thirty to Thirty-six Months*

At age two and a half, your child's development may be progressing rapidly. You may find yourself constantly bombarded with questions or continually running after a very physical toddler, and you are probably tired because your child is so inquisitive and active. A thirty-month-old child can walk on tiptoe, jump with both feet, and stand on one foot. She can run rapidly with little or no falling. She may enjoy small motor tasks such as drawing, coloring, doing puzzles, and playing with toys and dolls. When presented with a puzzle consisting of simple geometric shapes, she is able to fill in most of the puzzle and match one or more of the colors. She may also be able to name items in a book that the parent points out and will be able to give the use of some objects.

A two-and-a-half-year-old may begin to refer to herself by pronoun rather than by name. She is helpful and likes to put things away when her behavior is approved. She can carry breakable objects and likes to steer riding toys in different directions. She often talks at length when given a chance, and she may say "Hello" and "Good-bye" spontaneously but not on command. At some point between thirty and thirty-six months, a child may begin to recount an immediate experience.

Because the year between twenty-four and thirty-six months is a time when children struggle to establish autonomy, parents may get cooperation only part of the time. Children may insist on wearing a particular pair of shoes, or "doing it myself," or staying at home when a parent wants to go out, or ordering a friend or parent to "sit here" when playing. They can dress themselves in simple garments, fastening shoes and unbuttoning easy buttons when given enough time and approval. At the table, they are quite proficient at eating with a fork and spoon and can sit for almost the length of the dinner if included in the conversation and serving.

■                                                                              ■

## Readiness for Nursery School

Some of you have indicated an interest in nursery school programs before children are three. There are many developmental skills children need to acquire before entering nursery school. How ready do you feel your children are for nursery school?

### Language Skills

*"I wanted to enter my son in nursery school last year, but although he was big and well developed physically, his language skills were lacking. I felt a teacher would not be able to understand him. Now he speaks quite clearly and can form short sentences to indicate what he wants."*

*"My daughter is very petite and looks much younger than three. But she spoke early and now can express herself very well, so in that area she is ready for nursery school. But I'm not sure about other areas."*

Of course, being able to communicate verbally is a very important factor in determining readiness for nursery school. A child who cannot make herself understood may feel lost and abandoned no matter how well developed she is physically. In fact, children who are well developed physically or perhaps large for their age are sometimes expected to perform at an older age level. This often leads to disappointment and may interfere with the child's development of a good self-image. Conversely, the petite child, who is able to communicate even above age expectations, may be infantilized.

### Motor Skills

*"My son is a great talker, but he is a little clumsy going up stairs because he doesn't always alternate his feet. And he isn't very good yet at pedaling his tricycle.*

*However, he runs quite well and can throw a ball with pretty good control. Is that unusual?"*

Maturational rates for all areas of development differ for each child. In your son's case, the coordination in his lower extremities is a little slow in developing. It may be due to late maturation of those pathways, or to lack of stimulation. Perhaps he has not had sufficient opportunity for stair climbing or pedaling.

A nursery school should offer space for large-muscle motor activity in a gym or playground for children who are ready.

## Separation

*"I am glad you mention readiness, because although I noticed this before he didn't seem ready in other ways to go to nursery school. So I was comfortable about waiting till he was older."*

In what way did you think he was not ready?

*"He wasn't able to separate from me. He wouldn't play at a neighbor's house with another child he liked and whom we saw every day. If we were visiting somewhere and I went into the next room, he'd follow me no matter how interested he seemed in his play. I was afraid he'd want me to stay at nursery school with him. In the last few weeks, all of that has been changing, so I'm getting to feel he will be ready for nursery in the fall."*

*"My daughter was like that until recently. Now she does quite well in familiar places, like our friend's house or Grandma's, but it takes her quite a while to be comfortable in a new place, so I was wondering about a nursery school."*

Even if the child does not show obvious feelings of being uneasy in a new place, it is a good idea to visit the school ahead of time. He can see children there and what they do; this will give him an idea of what nursery school will be like, and he may feel more comfortable in the first days.

*"I've started walking by the nursery school about the time the children are going home. I tell my child that mothers come to meet their children to go home, and I say 'That's what I will do when you go to school.' Now when we go by the school he says 'My school' and seems pleased. I did that because he had difficulty separating from me to visit anywhere."*

Many parents expect children to be able to separate before they are actually ready. How quickly separation is accomplished depends on the temperament of the child and his maturational timetable, as well as the parents' understanding, support, and patience.

## Adjusting to Many Children

*"I've been wondering how my daughter will react in a group of fifteen or eighteen other children, even though she is doing very well now in her play group of four children."*

■                                                          ■

A small play group is good preparation for nursery school, because a large number of children may intimidate a child at first. Nursery schools are aware of this. Many schools start children on different days, so that children are not confronted by the whole class on the first day.

## Toilet Training

*"While the things we've been talking about are very important, it's toilet training that concerns me most. My worry is that my son won't be toilet trained by three. He shows not the slightest interest in that area."*

Not all children are ready to assume responsibility for bowel and bladder control at the same time. Most children will do it when they are ready—usually, around age three. They can then achieve complete control in a very short time—some in a day, others in two or three days, when allowed to do it on their own.

*"Suppose a child is obviously not ready when nursery school begins, and you have registered the child and paid tuition?"*

You should discuss this with the school officials. Most nursery shools will agree to a release from your commitment or arrange for later admission. The rush to get children into nursery school by a certain date is not always in the child's best interest and puts a strain on the parents as well.

If there are still several months before the start of nursery school, remember that the children may develop a great deal during this time. Development often comes in spurts.

## Selecting a Nursery School

*"I am not sure what to look for in a nursery school and just how to go about evaluating one."*

In selecting a nursery school for their child, parents should find out the teachers' approach to discipline, the ratio of teachers to pupils, and the qualifications of the staff. In addition, they should investigate the physical setup of the classroom—indoor activities, toilet facilities, and outdoor play equipment. They should also look into the specifics of the daily program—whether it is structured or flexible, and whether the school follows a special program such as, for example, the Montessori method. It's helpful if parents see the school in action and observe the class to which their child will be assigned, so that they can become acquainted with their child's future teacher. Watch how the teacher deals with the children, how she settles difficulties between children, how kind and thoughtful she is. Also, listen to her tone of voice, and notice whether she sits close to the children or towers above them, and whether she shows a sense of humor. During the visit, parents should also observe the children.

Do they seem to be happy? Are they busy and involved in their activities? Or are they quiet and sad? Do they wander around aimlessly? Are there many group activities, or are the children allowed to follow their own creative bent?

*"As a child, I was intimidated by teachers and school officials. I want my child to have a better school experience than I had."*

That is understandable. Visiting a few schools, talking to the schools' officials, and asking about programs and approaches may make you less anxious.

*"I asked the first school how they dealt with separation. I was told that the mother is allowed to stay with the child the first day or two, but after that the teacher can handle it better if the mother leaves. I crossed that school off my list."*

A school that has a hard-and-fast rule like this does not allow for the children's different maturational timetables. However, a child that needs more than three or four weeks to separate may not be ready for nursery school.

Many schools have a teacher make a home visit to get acquainted before the child enters school. In this way child and teacher are not complete strangers on the first day.

Other schools have children enter on successive days instead of all at once, so that the class grows gradually. Some start with a short program of one hour the first day or two, then gradually lengthen the school day to two, two and a half, or three hours.

*"Isn't it a little too long to expect them to stay three hours?"*

That is a long stretch for many three-year-olds. The tendency now is to extend the school time not because that is best for the child but because this fits parents' needs (since, more and more often, both parents work). It gives the working mother a sense of security that her child is being cared for while she works, and it reduces her need for child care.

*"I was wondering about school types and philosophies. Is, say, a Montessori approach better than another?"*

Labels don't always tell the story. Parents have to visit the school and see how it operates to determine whether it is the sort of school that suits their ideas and their child. The school's equipment and setup may be adequate, but not the program. Or the teacher may be too casual and not involved enough with the children. The teachers' personalities and methods are more important than any specific label or philosophy.

## Emotional Climate

*"You seem to stress the emotional climate provided by the teachers. But what about the program itself?"*

■

We feel that having a trained, understanding, patient, empathic, friendly teacher who knows child development and can help a child cope and explore a new environment is far more important than the specifics of a program.

*"I am concerned mainly about curriculum—whether there is a set schedule each day or just free play with good and safe equipment. That's important, too, isn't it?"*

Certainly how each day is spent is important. There should be some pattern to the day—ativities that follow one another regularly—just as you pattern events at home. This predictability helps a child develop trust in the school and allays anxiety.

However, structure should never be so rigid that children do not have the opportunity to explore, develop friendships with other children, and experiment with different toys.

*"You mentioned the playground and gym. What about the classroom itself? I've seen some that looked new and fully equipped and others that appeared a little beat up."*

A school should have certain essentials—small chairs, low tables, low shelves stocked with blocks, appropriate dolls and doll furniture, stoves, play dishes, and puzzles. It also should have drawing and painting materials and equipment for motor play. Some schools have dress-up equipment for imaginative role playing, real kitchen setups, tricycles, doll carriages, even roller skates.

A parent should look into how much choice children have in selecting areas of interest. Some children may only want to build with blocks, others to cook all the time, and still others to ride tricycles. How does the teacher encourage them to try other activities? How does she deal with sharing? How does she help the child who is left out by the others? How does she teach respect and care of equipment? How does she model communication? All these aspects of the school and teacher should be considered.

It is also important to notice what kind of group activities there are and how the children participate. Do the children gather willingly for storytime? Is there a time for looking at books individually? Does the teacher sit down with one or two children while some others gather around? Are other children permitted to continue with their own interests?

*"It sounds as if there is a lot for teachers to do. I know in some schools there is a main teacher and some assistants. What should be the proportion of teachers to children?"*

The ideal ratio is one teacher to four children. Most schools manage one teacher to six children and some one to eight. Some states require one teacher to five for this age. Parents should investigate the role of the assistant teachers—how they relate to the main teacher, to each other, and, of course, to the children.

■                                                                                    ■

*"We are musicians, so we are concerned that some form of music appreciation be included in the nursery-school curriculum."*

Music in some form—dancing or clapping to rhythm, playing in a rhythm band or singing, for example—is an essential experience and should be part of any nursery-school day. Listening to records and telling stories to the music is done in some schools.

### Hygiene

One area that we have not yet mentioned is hygiene. How clean and well kept is the school? Are things in their place? Do the bathrooms have low sinks and toilets? Do the children go to the bathroom by turns? Are they accompanied by an adult?

Parents should also look into the question of children attending schools with colds or other infections. What immunizations are required? Is there a nurse available? What first-aid equipment is there? Who is trained in use of this equipment?

*"I'm curious about snack time in nursery school. I don't allow my child to have sweets, so what can I do if sweets are offered at the school?"*

Snack time is an important activity for children of this age. It is a time during which they learn to take turns and to serve others. They may also begin to learn about proper nutrition. If you are encouraging your child to develop certain eating habits, you may be able to arrange with the school to have your child given a certain food during snack time. Of course, you will have to supply this food. The essentials of good nutrition are being given much more attention at nursery schools now.

*"Should only large, formal nursery schools be considered? What about informal groups run in homes for just a few children?"*

These groups have a lot to offer as well. They can give a child more individual attention in a less intimidating environment. There may be less equipment, but there may be more imaginative use of the materials that are provided.

## Nursery School Interviews

Some parents have begun or are soon to begin nursery-school interviews. Some schools request psychological evaluations prior to consideration for admission. Some parents worry that it may be harmful to the child, others are afraid something negative may be discovered. Many parents wonder how valid such a test can be for a child of this age, and whether tests given at this time can foretell the behavior of a child when he or she actually begins nursery school.

*"When we submitted our nursery-school application, we were told we must have our son tested. I was surprised and upset. I thought they must have*

*discovered something wrong. I later found out that some schools routinely require such testing. What do they expect to find out about children who are this age?"*

Many schools that require this testing believe it helps to have some objective standard by which to measure applicants. It has been found that most children of a certain age respond to standardized questions in a particular way. The ones that do respond within the expected range form the groups from which the school makes its selection. This method can help make the selection more uniform.

*"When I asked about these tests, I was told that they are used to avoid the criticism that selections are made on too personal a basis and to avoid favoritism to certain children. That made me feel a little more comfortable."*

## Anxiety

*"Can these tests be harmful to a child in any way? It seems to me that they can be very upsetting at best."*

Of course, no physical harm can come to the children as a result of testing. But some children are made anxious by the unaccustomed situation as well as by the stranger who administers the test.

*"My neighbor's daughter was too upset by the situation to cooperate in the testing. My neighbor said she wouldn't subject her child to it again, even if she lost the money she paid."*

*"I have friends whose children thought it was a game and seemed to enjoy it."*

The tests—and the environment in which they are administered—are designed to minimize adverse responses. Many children, if properly prepared, respond to the testing as a game. Some are fatigued by the length of the procedure, so testing is frequently done in two sessions.

*"Is there any preparation for these tests, like special games or books?"*

There is no special preparation. By this time, the children have been stimulated in motor and language activity. They have had practice with puzzles and building toys, as well as with activities such as riding a tricycle, jumping, and climbing. They can relate to peers and adults appropriately for their age.

*"Aren't there some factors that affect the outcome of the test? I've heard that some children are asked to come back to repeat the test."*

Certain factors can affect a child's performance on the test. One of these is the emotional state of the child at testing time. For example, any disruption of routines—a visit to grandparents, visitors at home, not sleeping well the night before the test, or an angry confrontation with a sibling or parent—can upset a child and influence the child's performance. Parental anxiety or undetected onset of an illness or cold prior to the test can also have an effect.

Another factor is the setting in which the test is given. For example, the building in which the examination takes place may remind the child of going to the doctor's and may upset him. Examiners are aware of this possibility, so most have the test-site offices decorated in pleasing colors with appropriate pictures and children's furniture and a few toys to put the child at ease.

The personality and appearance of the examiner may also affect the child. The examiner should be trained to approach a child pleasantly and to present himself or herself in a way that will entice the child to want to participate.

## Advance Preparation

*"Should a child be told in advance about the test? If so, how?"*

Parents should tell the child less than twenty-four hours before the test that he is going to a special place to meet a person who will talk to him and play games with him. It is important to add that the parent will be there with him.

*"What if your child asks why he has to meet this person?"*

The child should be given an answer that explains the reason as simply and matter-of-factly as possible. The child can be told that he is going to see a person who knows about schools and will be able to determine what kind of school would be best for him.

*"Aren't there some schools that don't require formal evaluation? The school I'm taking my son to makes admissions decisions based on an interview and on observing the child in a classroom situation. What are they observing?"*

There are many good schools that do not require prior testing. A trained person observes the way the child walks, talks, plays with toys, and relates to her. She notes his attention span, his level of anxiety, and how he responds to frustration. She tries to determine the child's grasp of simple spatial and visual concepts. The child may also be invited to a classroom to see how he interacts with other children.

*"Suppose he clings and won't do anything he is asked at that time but would really be ready at three. How would the mother and school know that so long in advance?"*

There is no way to predict how a child will develop. However, interviewers are aware that children can mature a great deal between two and a half and three years of age, and they make certain allowances.

*"Isn't the testing a better prediction?"*

It has been found that no testing done on children younger than three years had predictive value. Admissions decisions based on an interview and detailed history are as reliable as those made after formal testing. No test alone can give a full assessment of a child. Other information—family history, impressions of adults close to the child, observations of the child's behavior at home and play, and interviews with the child—are needed.

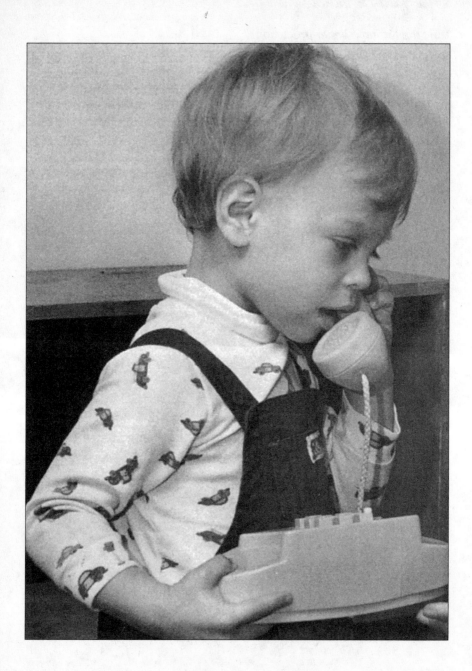

# 24

The children's communication skills are improving. Their sentences are becoming longer and their ability to express complicated concepts is increasing. They are beginning to use more prepositions, adjectives, and adverbs. Some parents are finding that their children are ordering them around and they begin to feel that the children are controlling them. They also notice the way their children talk to other children. They are afraid they will upset their friends and then won't have friends.

What have you been noticing about your child's speech development?

*"We are thrilled because our son is saying so much more. We were worried, because we both work and he was home with a housekeeper who didn't talk much. So we made a point of spending more time talking with him and reading to him when we came home. Maybe that helped, and maybe he was not ready until about a month ago, when words just seemed to pour out and then little phrases like 'Mommy home,' 'Din all gone,' and 'Baby go bye-bye in ca'age.' It's not perfect, but it's coming along and we are so happy with his progress so far."*

You are right, it is hard to say which was the more important factor. As we have said before, it is usually a combination of the child's maturational timetable and environmental stimulation.

## Stages of Speech

Children's acquisition of speech comes in stages. We were all pleased when the children began to name objects and people, and even more so when they began to say phrases and three-word sentences. As their

sentences become more complex, children begin to make announcements: "I came in my car" or "I came in a taxi," for example. Later, they begin to give directions to each other: "Put the doll in the carriage" or "Don't read." They speak to us this way, too, and we may be offended because it sounds like a command. But this is only a stage in speech development—an imitation of the way we speak to them, perhaps—and will gradually give way to a more conversational, interactional form of communication. The children will begin to show concern for one another and for the reactions they receive. They will be asking permission and raising more questions, such as, "I take the shovel, okay?" or "You play with me?"

*"I must have talked a lot to my son, because he is doing a lot of talking. Sometimes he just orders me around. He'll say, 'Let's go home now' in a very commanding way. I don't know whether to laugh or be angry."*

*"My daughter calls to me and says, 'Momma, come here this minute.' Maybe that is the way I sound to her. In a way it's amusing, but I don't want her talking that way to others."*

Of course, the tone of voice a child uses may be an imitation of a parent. Most children go through a stage of commanding. However, they are not as dictatorial as they sound. They are simply expressing themselves, and we are the ones making that interpretation.

*"Sometimes I hear my son talking to himself as he plays with his blocks. He'll say, 'Put the car here. Go slow.' Or he'll say to his car, 'No, no, don't go there.' Is that unusual?"*

That is not at all unusual at this age. The children's language has improved to the point that they talk aloud as they play. They are really thinking out loud.

## Collective Monologue

*"I've begun to notice that when we have one or two children playing together in our house they don't actually talk to or play with each other most of the time. They will each be playing with something, and each will seem to be describing what he or she is doing without the slightest attention to what the others are saying. Once in a while one may glance at what the other one is doing, perhaps making a comment (but usually not), and then going on with his own thing. They don't seem to be really playing with one another. Is this part of this stage too? Should I intervene and try to get them to play together more?"*

*"I've noticed that too, and though it seems an odd way to play I like it because it keeps a group of children quiet when they are playing in the house."*

To an adult this behavior may seem strange, but it is a normal stage. This level of development has been given the name "collective monologue" by language-development experts. Each child seems to be conducting her own monologue in the company of other children, and requires neither an audience nor input from others. Parental involvement here may interfere with the child's fantasy or her way of working through issues of interest to her. It is much better for the parent to be a silent observer.

*"You learn quite a lot about yourself if you listen. The other day I heard my little girl scold her doll: 'Sit down and be quiet! Let Mommy talk on the phone.' That got to me, because I didn't realize I did it so often or that she was upset by it."*

*"I heard my daughter say to her doll as she put it into the doll bed, 'Don't cry, Mommy be back soon' over and over again. I began to think perhaps she was reassuring herself as much as the doll. She doesn't cry now when I go out, but she used to. Maybe that's how she got over it."*

Until now, the children have been observers, taking in everything adults do and say. Now they are becoming more expressive. Parents should observe closely the way their children are expressing themselves now, and use those observations to better understand their children.

## *Cause and Effect*

*"I've been wondering how much they really understand what we say. I try to reason with my son. For example, I explain to him why he has to hold my hand to cross the street or why we mustn't leave the refrigerator door open. But it doesn't seem to register at all."*

*"That's just what I've been wondering about. When I give a careful explanation, either he doesn't understand or he doesn't try. Maybe he simply doesn't listen."*

*"I think they don't listen. I know my son does not. He seems to be too impatient to get on to the next thing. What can I do about that?"*

A child is not yet able to understand cause and consequence unless she has experienced it many times. Remember how many times the children had to throw something off the high-chair tray until they understood the consequences of their actions? Even now they may try to throw things out of windows or down toilets. They can't foresee the consequences.

*"But we tell them, and it doesn't seem to matter. I give a whole lecture about something and it doesn't matter."*

Consider this example: Johnny runs across the street ahead of his mother. She goes after him, grabs him, and says, "You must hold mother's hand. A car might have come along, and the driver might not have been able to stop in time. He might have hurt you, and you would have had to go to the hospital. That would make Mommy and Daddy very sad and you would have to stay in the hospital a long time."

The mother should simply have said, "You must hold mother's hand crossing the street. Cars can hit you." Many parents make the mistake of giving involved explanations before a child is ready for those explanations. Children need a short statement consistently repeated until they have absorbed it.

*"I think I know what you mean. A week or so ago while we were out walking, my daughter pulled her hat off her head. I said, 'It's a cold day.*

*You'll catch cold and be sick and have to go to bed. You won't be able to go out to play and your friends won't be able to come and play with you. You might have to take medicine . . .' and on and on. But she would not keep her hat on. A few days later she did get a cold; whether it had anything to do with the hat I don't know. All I said was, 'You didn't wear your hat. Now you have a cold.' She just gave me a long look, and from then on she hasn't removed her hat when we are outside."*

Because of their limited experience, it is very difficult for children to respond to lengthy admonitions. As parents, we try to protect them from experiences that we know are harmful; that is our job. But it is also our job to try to tune in to their level of communication. They have made great strides this past year; a few have even reached a conversational stage. In a few more months, their conceptual capacity will have made even greater progress.

# Fantasy Versus Reality

Another area of concern to parents of children this age is how to interpret and understand their expressions of fantasy. Parents sometimes mistake fantasy for lying, or worry that the child can't distinguish reality from fantasy. Are your children expressing some of their fantasies to you?

## Lying

*"I have a question about lying. This morning my son said, 'Mommy, I did poo in the potty.' When I asked him to show it to me, he said, 'No, I washed it away.' I didn't know how to react. I quickly changed the subject, because I didn't want to give him the idea that he could get congratulated for something he didn't do. I hadn't started encouraging him to use the toilet, so I don't think I gave him any reason to want to please me."*

This is a common dilemma for parents, and it should be handled very sensitively. It's best to be nonjudgmental, so that you don't give an innocent child the feeling of distrust or one who is telling a story a feeling of not being believed. You can say in a nonconfronting tone, "Oh, you did? Well, next time please let me see, too." Notice that I said "telling a story." Children of this age are not lying in the sense that we use the term. That is, they are not telling a falsehood with the intent to deceive.

Parents have to remember that a child of this age cannot tell the difference between what he would like to have happened and what really did happen. In other words, he has difficulty distinguishing reality from fantasy. Sometimes a child is so eager to have something occur that he begins to believe it really did and reports it that way.

## Imaginary Friends

*"My daughter has an imaginary friend. At times I think she knows that she manufactured him and that it's a game, but at other times I am not sure."*

■                                                                    ■

*"My son also has imaginary friends. He tells me long stories of what they are doing or going to do. Should I go along with him and play up the fantasy, or should I tell him he is making believe?"*

You should accept the child's fantasy and go along with it, while letting the child know that you know his friend is not real, but that it is all right to make believe.

Let's suppose you are sitting down to lunch and your child says, pointing to your chair, "Not there, Tommy is sitting there." You can say, "Oh, let's make believe Tommy is sitting over there," then, pointing to another chair, "He is having lunch with us and I will sit in my chair." Before your child can protest, you can quickly divert his attention by saying, "What do you think Tommy likes for lunch?"

*"When I try that approach, my child always protests that the imaginary friend is 'really real,' and I get nowhere!"*

You should let your child know that you understand how much he would like to believe his friend is real, because you know how much he would like to have a friend playing with him right now. Tell him it's all right to make believe. In that way you make him comfortable with his fantasy, yet aware of it.

*"I'm having a hard time getting my daughter to understand the difference between real and make-believe. How can I help her?"*

Sometimes it helps to switch roles, to make believe you are the child and that your child is the mother. The child may pretend to dress you, comb your hair, or feed you. Then you can revert to your real roles and say, for example, "Now, I'm going to be the real mommy again, because I have to make our dinner so we can have it ready when Daddy comes home and you are his real little girl. No more pretend."

If your child protests, you can assure her that you can play make-believe again. Mention a specific time, so that she understands that you mean it.

*"My son pretends a lot, but I know now when he is pretending. When it's something he wants to do he uses the word 'someday.' 'I'm going on the tramway again someday,' or 'I'm taking a helicopter someday.' "*

*"My daughter is not like that; she is very unpredictable. The other day her grandmother asked where we were going. My child piped up that she was going to a party. Grandma asked, 'What party?' My daughter answered, 'My birthday party.' Annoyed and surprised, Grandma said, 'It's not your birthday.' "*

Children do a lot of wishful thinking. Seeing Grandma may have evoked a wish that she was going to her birthday party. After all, Grandmas are known to give presents for birthdays.

■                                                                              ■

## Dreams

*"What about dreams—a dream that they really believe happened?"*

Children sometimes have dreams that are so vivid they believe they actually happened. A child may wake up at night disturbed by a dream. The parent should reassure the child that it was only a dream, that it didn't really happen, and that you are there to take care of them.

## Tall Tales

*"You seem to be saying that all that a parent need do is gently point out what is real and what isn't. I'm worried that if I take this approach with my son, it will be easy for him to slip into outright lying when he is older."*

*"I get flack from my parents that I'm too accepting of the things my child tells me and that he'll grow up to be a liar. I remember having my mouth washed out with soap for telling a lie, but I don't want to resort to that."*

*"At what age can children tell what is real from what is not? When does a tall tale become a lie?"*

A child may have difficulty distinguishing between reality and fantasy until the age of five or six. Parents have to continue to help children make this distinction. Punitive measures like washing the mouth out with soap or spanking may encourage the very behavior the parent is trying to stop.

*"I can still hear my mother's voice: 'Tell Mother the truth. I'll be able to tell if you are lying, so don't try it.' Or: 'Are you sure you're telling the truth?' I hated that."*

When parents are aware of the level of the child's development, they understand that the child is confusing fantasy with reality and that she has to be given help to understand the difference. These are difficult concepts and the child needs time to be able to learn to deal with them. Most children brought up without accusations of lying do not resort to lying later on. This takes patience and understanding on the part of parents, but it helps in a child's later moral development.

# Whining

Many children go through a period when whining is one of their primary coping mechanisms.

Some of you have recently made comments about whining. Is whining still a concern for any of you?

*"My daughter doesn't whine often, but when she does it upsets me. I used to say that if I ever had a child I wouldn't permit whining."*

*"My daughter whines quite often. I tell her to stop, but that just seems to make things worse."*

■                                            ■

Telling a child to stop whining usually does not work. For some children, whining is a way to deal with situations that are difficult for them. If a child has been told not to cry, whining may be a kind of compromise between a cry and a demand.

## Causes

*"When I have answered what she has asked me for the twentieth time, I explode. At eight o'clock this morning she started saying, 'I want to leave for the park.' I said, 'Not just now, in a few minutes,' and she just stood there whining. It has happened a lot, and I have lost my patience and I'll say, 'I don't want to hear you saying it again and if you are going to keep asking, go in the other room.' I know it's wrong, because it doesn't work."*

It is not unusual for parents to respond in that way to whining. Some parents sometimes add a warning threat, such as "If you don't stop whining right now, we won't go to the park at all." That approach may only worsen the problem.

Children this age have little sense of time, so they may become anxious and impatient when they have to wait. Whining is their way of coping with situations they can't control.

One way of dealing with whining is to reassure the child. You can say, for example, that you know she wants to go to the park and that you will be going very soon. You can suggest that she get her toys ready, or help you with whatever chores you have to finish before you leave. Most children respond well to this approach.

*"My daughter sometimes asks for candy or a treat right before lunch. Instead, I give her something to do and ask her to help me make lunch. She is so busy that she doesn't have a chance to whine. Then, right after lunch, I let her have the candy. Since I've been following this routine, she's cut down on the whining."*

*"My son sometimes wants to be picked up when we are walking. My husband gets annoyed with him and tries to ignore him. So my son begins to whine. I decided to pick him up as soon as he asks and let him know it is okay. That has cut out the whining, and now he asks to be picked up less than before."*

*"I've noticed that my child begins to whine just when I begin to talk to someone on the phone or when I'm busy doing housework. Why does he pick just these times to whine for something?"*

Close examination of the situation may reveal that the whining started only after the child made a request that went unheeded.

## Delaying Too Long

*"Maybe that explains our situation. We've begun remodeling the house we are living in, and we try to get a project done each week. Since we began*

*this schedule, my son's whining seems to have increased. I guess I've been too busy to notice the first time he calls for something."*

*"Does that mean parents should stop whatever they are doing the minute a child wants something?"*

We have been saying that children of this age are *beginning* to be able to delay gratification, and that parents have to help them by increasing delay in small increments. One of the causes of whining is delaying recognition and gratification of the child's needs beyond his level of tolerance.

## Ignoring

*"My mother says that the way to break a child of whining is to ignore him when he whines and to give him attention when he stops. But I just can't ignore my son's whining, so I eventually give in."*

Your mother is following a method that some people in the child-development field advocate. Their theory is that a behavior will be stopped because when it is not noticed, it will be extinguished by lack of reinforcement. This can happen. However, this approach can give a child the message that no one cares, and may cause him to give up easily when faced with a challenge. He may also become angry and demanding, or withdrawn and depressed. Your mother's method can stop the whining but the accompanying responses may be more undesirable. A parent should try to assess the causes of the whining and deal with them as they occur.

## Appropriate Attention

*"Isn't whining just a way of getting attention. If so, should we be encouraging that? My mother says, 'He just wants attention so just leave him alone.'"*

There is nothing unusual or unhealthy about children needing or wanting attention; it is characteristic of this level of development. The parents' job is to try to satisfy the child's needs in a way that is consistent with the child's level of development. As we have said, some children respond to challenging situations by whining. Others cry or have a temper tantrum or just give up. We are not trying to devise methods of punishment for a child's need for attention.

*"I have found that our son whines when he is tired and just doesn't know what he wants. If I'm not tired, too, I can cope with it and do something quiet with him, or even get him in for a nap or to bed early."*

Of course, parents get tired too. They have moments when they can't summon up all the good parental qualities they have when they feel fresh and rested. It's good that you recognize that the child's fatigue, as well as your own, can cause whining.

■                                                                         ■

## *Regression*

The children have been making progress in many areas. However, there may be occasional setbacks that cause parents to feel there is something wrong either with the child or with their child-rearing methods. Has this happened to any of you?

### *Feeding Themselves*

*"My son, who has always been independent and has been able to feed himself very efficiently for many months, suddenly asked me one night to feed him his dinner. At first I didn't know what to do. It was such a switch from his usual way that I did it without saying anything. The next day he was feeding himself again."*

This sort of regression is usually transitory. It often occurs when the child is tired or has recently witnessed a younger child being fed. The child may want some of the attention that is being bestowed on the younger child. He is giving a message that he feels left out. If he is told to feed himself, it may make him feel that being able to feed himself leads to being left out.

One way to handle this situation is to acknowledge that it must seem nice to be a baby and be fed again. Then feed him without further comment, but make favorable remarks when he does something more age appropriate, like helping to put toys away or drinking from a cup.

### *Carrying*

*"My son has been walking since he was eleven months old, but every once in a while he still wants to be carried. I had gotten to the point where we didn't need to take a stroller with us on walks. But I never know when he'll ask to be carried, so I've begun taking the stroller again. Is his behavior unusual?"*

On the contrary, it is quite common. The novelty and wonder of being able to move on his own has worn off. He may realize all of a sudden how large the world is, and feel a need to be safely held and carried, as he was as a baby. Sometimes children are simply unable to keep up with the parents' pace.

*"Should they be picked up? They are older now, and harder to carry. When I try to put my daughter into her stroller, she kicks and screams and won't get in."*

They should be picked up and held to reassure them that you are there for them. Perhaps you can try walking a few steps holding them until they are soothed, then quietly say, "You are such a big boy/girl that I can't hold you anymore. Let's get into the stroller and I'll wheel you." Some children are satisfied when this approach is used.

■                                                                                                    ■

*"At first, I thought there might be something wrong with my child's feet, so I took him to the doctor. Then, when I found there was nothing wrong, I got angry and scolded. That did absolutely no good."*

Scolding is rarely a good response. It is better to try to figure out why the child needs something that he seemed to have outgrown, then respond in an appropriate manner.

## Accidents

*"Is it unusual for a child who has been toilet trained to begin having accidents again? We had no problem training our son. In fact, he was able to control both his bowels and bladder in just a few days. Now he has more accidents than successes, and we don't know what to do."*

This is usually attributable to change in the child's routine, such as an illness, a move, or the arrival of a new baby.

*"We did have a baby, but that was two months ago. It didn't seem to bother him at first. But I have noticed that he constantly watches me change her. I heard this could happen, but I thought it would be sooner."*

When a new baby arrives, an older child may be envious of all the attention lavished on the baby—such as diaper changes. It is a good idea, therefore, to try to notice the older child's more mature accomplishments, so he will continue to feel that it is worthwhile to be the older child.

*"We went on a vacation and were away two weeks. Our daughter seemed to enjoy the overall change, but the change in toilet facilities upset her and she wet herself several times a day. When we got home, she was okay in two or three days."*

*"My child has a bad cold and had to be on medication and forced fluids. He began to have accidents too. As soon as the cold subsided, he got full control again."*

These are both examples of the surprise and anguish parents experience when they aren't aware of the consequences of changes in daily routines.

## Sleeping

*"The change that bothers me most is the change in our son's sleep pattern. He was finally sleeping through the night, and now he gets up again two or three times."*

*"My daughter also did that for a few weeks. Now it's over and she is sleeping again. She cut two molars during that time. I didn't think that teething kept children awake at this age."*

Teething may be a problem for children who are cutting their two-and-a-half-year molars. When this is over, they return to their usual sleep patterns. Children who have had a very active day or whose daytime activity is too tiring may also have difficulty sleeping. Parents who are aware of this can change the child's activites.

*"I know that is our problem. I am on the go all day, but I guess it is too much for our son. I've noticed that when we spend the day quietly at home he seems to go to bed more easily and sleeps better."*

*"My son used to go to bed without any fuss, but lately we can't get him to fall asleep. He calls for us and climbs out of bed. It reminds me of the early months, when we had to rock him to sleep."*

As a child gets older, his sleep pattern may change—including the time he is ready for bed. So if his bedtime is changed accordingly, this problem may be overcome. Some children begin to play more vigorously with their parents before bedtime. Going to bed can therefore become a difficult separation from fun and family activity. Parents should give children a quiet time before bed, so that the separation will not be so difficult. For example, reading or some other routine can make children more receptive to the notion of going to bed.

*"I think playing too vigorously before bed is our problem. Both of us work, so we like to have a good time with our son when we get home. I guess we can't expect to get him to bed as early as we did before without giving him a cooling-off time."*

*"Our child used to be so sociable, always wanting to play at other children's houses. Now she only wants to stay home. Is this unusual?"*

She may have had an unpleasant encounter away from home. She may be unable to express this verbally and is trying to cope with the situation by avoiding it. However, this may be only a stage in the separation process; she is regressing because she needs time to redevelop the ability to separate.

Parents should remember that maturation does not progress steadily but rather by stops and starts—regression and progress.

## *Separation*

We discussed separation early in the year, when the children were just two. When the children pass two years of age, parents may expect them to separate without any protest. But children at this age are not verbal enough to understand that the parents will return; they still have no concept that the parents exist even when they cannot be seen. Some parents have difficulty putting the children to bed and don't realize that removing a child from pleasant play with Daddy or Mommy is an interruption as well as a separation. Children have to cope with separations of varying degrees several times a day—at the end of play time with parents and at bedtime, for example.

Have you noticed any difference in your children's reactions to your leaving them or their leaving you?

*"My son is able to accept his father's leaving every morning, but he is still inconsolable when I leave. Sometimes it gets so bad that I'm tempted to go back."*

Children may get used to one parent leaving on a regular basis, but when the second parent leaves that may be harder to take, because it becomes a separation from both parents.

*"I made the mistake of coming back once or twice. That only made it worse—there was twice the amount of crying. Now I say, 'Good-bye, be back soon.' I leave quickly, and my mother or the baby-sitter quickly gets him involved in some activity. They tell me that he stops crying very quickly and seems happy."*

It is best not to prolong the parting, and to say "good-bye" and "be back soon." The child should be told at what point in his day you will be back— "when you are taking your bath" or "when you come home from your walk," for example.

## Loud Protests

*"As my daughter gets older and bigger, the crying is so much louder and more vigorous and the clinging so much harder to avoid. It has become harder for me. I feel so sorry for her."*

The loudness of the crying at separation is not always in proportion to the child's feelings. The children who cry the loudest may be the easiest to divert, while the children who are less demonstrative may be more affected by separation.

*"Does that mean we really shouldn't leave our children at this stage?"*

Children do need constant physical closeness to their mothers—at least until they are three, and often longer—before they separate comfortably. In our culture that kind of child care is not always possible. Our children are required to accommodate themselves to this situation—and they protest. We are trying to help parents understand children's needs and to deal with them as best as possible, without feeling there is something wrong with the child or with themselves. In some primitive societies, children are always close to their mothers or an assigned mother. Our children are primitive but our society is not. That is the issue.

*"This is such a sensitive issue. What should be done when we do leave a child?"*

One thing is parting quickly without making a big issue and emphasizing your return. Another is to say something like "It is time to . . ." and then say "This is Mommy's time to go to work (or to school, to visit Grandma, etc.)." In addition, it is important to tell the child the time in his day you will return and what you will do together when you return. This reassures him that you really will come back. Also, try to leave him in a comfortable situation in his own home or a familiar setting, with an accepted baby-sitter, relative, or friend.

*"One day I stepped out to get something while my daughter was napping, and she was awake before I got back. She raised such a rumpus in the few minutes before I got back that my mother could not console her. Now she clings and won't let me out of her sight. I realize now that I should have told her before she took her nap."*

Many parents worry that their child won't nap or go to bed if they know the parent is going out. A child *does* accept a parent's leaving more easily if told when you will return. At worst, the child may lose a little sleep, but she will not lose her sense of trust in the parent.

## Bribes and Gifts

*"We tell our son that we will bring him something when we return. This makes it easier for him to let us go, but figuring out what to bring home each time is getting to be a problem."*

*"My sister used that system with her kids and pretty soon they were asking her and everyone who came to visit, 'What did you bring me?'"*

That method has many pitfalls. Material gifts may become a substitute for what should be the real emphasis—the return of the parent.

*"We have a different problem. My son is used to our leaving in the morning as we both work. He likes his baby-sitter. When we get home he climbs all over us, and it's almost impossible even to get our coats off. I'd like to change clothes, and his father needs to relax a little. But our son wants to engage us in play at once. Is that normal now? Shouldn't he know to wait until we are ready?"*

A child this age has no concept of another person's needs. Your child knows only that he has missed you and has been waiting for your return. When you come back, he needs your undivided attention immediately. Of course, you have reasonable needs, too. But if you play with your son first, you can perhaps change your clothes in a more relaxed manner. Daddy may find that playing a few minutes with his son can be relaxing, too. He is tired from doing his work but may have reserve energy to do something different. If he had a gym appointment after work or a tennis game, he would have energy for that.

*"I am home all day with our son. When his father comes home, he is all over him before he takes his coat off. Sometimes my husband hardly has time to greet me. At first I was a little annoyed, but I thought it over and decided I could wait to be greeted. But it does take getting used to."*

*"My child used to behave that way, so my husband worked out a system. He picks our son up, kisses him, kisses me, and then has our son help him get his coat off and walk him to the shower and wait while he showers and changes. Then they play until dinner. Now my son says, 'Shower, daddy, then I play.' "*

When children are very young, parents have to do the adjusting. As they grow and mature, they begin to adapt to some of our patterns. This is the stage they are entering now, although some are more advanced than others.

## Bedtime Separation

*"We don't have a problem leaving our daughter during the day anymore. But at night when we try to put her to bed, she doesn't want to be alone. She wants us to be with her. It doesn't take very long—maybe ten minutes of sitting with her and she's asleep. Why is that still necessary?"*

Leaving the warmth of the family and going to bed is a separation. For some children, it is more difficult than other separations. Perhaps it's the fear of waking and not finding the parents there. All these difficulties will disappear as the child matures.

*"Our daughter can spend a night at Grandma's without us, but she still needs us to stay with her at a birthday party."*

Most children this age can tolerate a parent's leaving a room without following. Some may be able to be left for an hour or two at Grandma's, or at a neighbor's house they have visited frequently with mother. Some may even be able to stay overnight in a familiar place. Most cannot tolerate their parents leaving at night, do not like it, and protest. Some still have difficulty during the day when mother leaves them at home. Some can separate at bedtime easily; others cannot. There's still great variation.

# Gender Identity

Children approaching the age of three are not only interested in anatomical differences but are beginning to be aware of themselves as either male or female and are learning how to fit in these roles.

We have talked before about children's questions concerning anatomical differences between their parents. Have you made any further observations about their discoveries? Do you have questions about this issue?

*"My son has gone from just pointing to his father's penis when he is in the bath and asking, 'What dat?' to pointing to his own penis and comparing himself with his father. I used to bathe him with my four-and-a-half-year-old daughter, and he began pointing to her genital area as though he thought something was missing. So I just said 'That's your penis' when he pointed to it and 'That's her vagina.' I have stopped bathing them together."*

■                                                                              ■

Your son and most children in this age group are establishing their own sexual identity. In a situation such as the one you describe, a parent can say, "You are a boy. You have a penis. Your sister is a girl. She has a vagina." It should be said in a matter-of-fact way that indicates they are of equal importance. This method helps not only in explaining anatomical differences, but in establishing gender identity.

## Homosexuality

*"Can a boy be born with the tendency to behave more like a girl or a girl with the tendency to behave more like a boy? Can a child be born that way, or is it the result of upbringing?"*

There is no absolute answer to that question yet, but there are many theories. Some researchers have evidence that leads to the conclusion that homosexuality is a physiological phenomenon. Most other experts believe that it is a result of childhood experiences.

*"There is so much talk about homosexuality now. I've been wondering how much parents influence a child's sexuality and how much is inborn."*

Each child is born with hormonal and biochemical differences. That is the child's endowment; it can't be changed. However, the experiences to which the child is exposed, as well as the way parents, relatives, friends, caretakers, and others respond to the child, influence the child's self-image and sexual identity. In addition, each culture has certain standards for the feminine and masculine roles.

*"Do you mean that if my son cries, for instance, and we say to him something like 'Be a big boy and don't cry,' we are influencing his sexual identity?"*

Yes, the commonly held view is that boys have to be big and strong and not cry, that crying is for babies and females.

*"What about girls? If I say to a little girl who is being rough in her play that 'little girls don't do that! Be gentle,' am I influencing her to be gentle?"*

Yes. When we make such comments, we are saying that boys can't cry, that it isn't manly, and that only girls are gentle. We are denying that crying is an appropriate expression of sorrow for both boys and girls. Isn't it better to allow boys to cry and girls to be assertive?

*"Even now that women are working outside the home and men are helping with child care, I still feel a little uneasy when my son cries over some disappointment. The thought flashes through my mind, 'Will he be a sissy?'"*

We are in a transition period. Some of the old views still linger.

*"I have no hesitation in letting my daughter play with a truck, but I still feel uneasy when a little boy comes over and gets interested in her dolls, especially when his mother is present and seems to be disturbed by it."*

■

It seems there is a fear that playing with dolls will at best make a "sissy" out of a boy and at worst there is the fear of homosexuality.

*"What kinds of childhood experiences do experts think play a role in determining homosexuality?"*

Remember that these theories were developed by therapists based on case studies. Some have validity and have been useful in therapy. One of the most frequently heard theories is that a very dominant mother may cause her son to fear or distrust females and seek comfort and affection from males. Another theory is that a very dominant father may cause a son to withdraw from a male identification and prefer female activities.

Other explanations have to do with the "family romance" theory, which holds that the child is sexually attracted to the parent of the opposite sex and, frightened by these feelings, defends himself by continuing to prefer relationships with members of the same sex. Most cases of homosexuality are not so simple, but are associated with more than one cause.

## The Family Romance

*"We hear so much about the Oedipal complex. Is that what you are referring to as family romance?"*

At some time when a child is between three and five, the family romance phenomenon begins. For example, a little girl says, "I'm going to marry Daddy," and if Mommy asks what she should do, the girl says, "You can go away" or "You'll marry the mailman" or "Go and live with your mommy." A little boy will want his daddy to go away so that he can take care of Mommy. He wants Mommy to be his girl.

Sigmund Freud found that some people do not get beyond this level of development. For example, a boy may not be able to part from his mother or focus his attention on any other woman. Freud found this in his practice and then related it to the Greek tragedy *Oedipus Rex,* by Sophocles, in which Oedipus unknowingly murdered his own father and then married his own mother. Freud called the situation in which the son's interest remains in the mother the Oedipal complex.

Similarly, a girl may be so attached to her father that she can't form a close attachment to any other male. This is called the Electra complex (again, after Greek legend and a tragedy by Sophocles).

As children grow older and have had good relationships with each parent, they can then attach their affections and attention to other people of the opposite sex. Otherwise the attachment to the parent of the opposite sex may become pathological if a father is consciously or unconsciously seductive to his daughter, or a mother to her son.

Everybody goes through this stage in some form or other for different durations. It's a stage of development during which children are establishing affectional relations. A girl can stay identified with her mother; she does not have to make a change. But a boy has to make a change to identify with his father. This may be difficult—if, for example, the father is stern or not overtly loving.

*"Our daughter recently announced, 'When I grow up I'm going to marry Daddy.' I responded, 'No, you will find your own daddy to marry. You will find the man who will be the daddy to your children.' After much thought she said, 'I'm afraid I may not be able to find him.' Her father said, 'We will help you.' We think that families should help their children in making the right marriage."*

All parents want to help their children make a right choice. This is not always possible. But they can make it possible for them to have contact with what they feel are desirable members of the opposite sex.

By about age five, the Oedipal stage should be disappearing. But parents should continue to offer alternatives, such as "Yes, you do like Daddy a great deal now, but when you grow up you will find a man who is just as nice."

*"Today, girls wear overalls and slacks like boys, and boys have long hair and play with girls' toys. Some fathers perform child care and household chores, while some mothers work and assume some traditionally masculine roles. Aren't sexual distinctions less clear today?"*

It is true that clothes and hairstyles, and household roles and outside work roles, are less distinct sexually. But the most important influence on a child's sexual identity is the way the parents relate to each other. This is the model the child will adopt for behavior as a boy or girl and later as a man or woman.

*"Do you mean that if my wife and I are always arguing with each other, our child will have the same kind of setup when he or she is grown?"*

In most cases, that is so. For example, if a boy's father is always berating his wife, the boy accepts this as the masculine role. He may relate to women in the same way and set up that kind of marriage. If, on the other hand, the wife is always belittling the father, the son may come to believe that males should accept this treatment from females and may later accept that kind of relationship.

## Parental Disagreements

*"I can understand that we don't want to bring up our daughters as shrews or our sons as tyrants, but what should parents do if and when they have disagreements?"*

Disagreements occur in every family. It is important for children to see parents disagree and then resolve the difference. If the relationship between parents is one of basic mutual respect and affection the children have good models to follow, and they are less likely to have confusion in their sexual identity.

# Coping with Anger

## 25

## The Effect of Anger on Children

Anger is an issue that is of concern throughout our lives. Many people have difficulty dealing with anger appropriately. Parents worry about the effect of their displays of anger on a growing child.

Now that the children are approaching age three and are experimenting and exploring more, they are more apt to encounter parental disapproval and anger. Parents may expect children to have better judgment than is realistic, and become upset or angry with the child for her exploratory activities or her failure to respond to limitations. Children may respond by becoming submissive, inhibited, fearful, or withdrawn. Others respond with their own anger. Some children defend against anger by ignoring it.

At this age, children are more verbal and better able to understand, so heated encounters between parents can affect them in ways not anticipated by the parents. The interpretation made by the child may be more devastating than arguing parents realize, and can affect the child's behavior and mood. Overhearing parents discussing a difference of opinion in loud voices can make a child very anxious.

When the children were younger, we discussed how parents deal with anger at their children and toward each other. Now that they are getting to be close to age three, how do you feel about this issue?

*"I find that I get angry more often with my son now than I used to because he is so active now. Sometimes he cries and begs me not to be angry, and then I feel very guilty for being so severe."*

*"When my daughter plays with her doll, she yells at it in the same tone that I use. Although it's amusing, it certainly makes me wish I hadn't used that tone."*

*"It is not so bad when you hear your child imitate you to a doll, but when it's to another child or an adult it sounds just awful. What can be done to cut down on that yelling?"*

It is very hard to change a habitual style of responding. In some cases, it may be the result of the example set by your own parents. In others, it is due to fatigue or the pressures of daily life. When parents become conscious of the reasons they respond with anger, they can, with effort and practice, cut down on angry responses. It is part of the growing a parent has to do.

*"If something has gone wrong and I am angry about it—even if it is not something my son had done—I get angry and impatient with the least little thing that he does and scold him unnecessarily."*

*"I don't scold. I am curt. My voice doesn't go up. I try to be in control as far as the children are concerned, but they sense it and get upset."*

Anger can be misdirected. It often spills over onto innocent and unsuspecting individuals. Children are likely victims of misdirected anger, because they are always exploring and in need of attention that a parent in a state of suppressed anger is unable to give calmly.

*"Yesterday the grocer delivered my order before we got home. A dog, a child, someone had gotten into it and it was strewn in the hall. Of course, I was upset and angry because the delivery boy didn't leave the order with the super, as he was supposed to. My little girl noticed a box of crackers she loves and opened it out in the hall. This was enough to provoke a tirade from me. I know I shouldn't have yelled at her, but I did."*

How else do you think you could have handled the situation?

*"The sensible thing to do was to open the door and let my daughter into the apartment, let her have her cracker, pick the groceries up and put them into the house, and then call the store and give them my tirade if I still felt angry."*

The best way to deal with anger is to confront the one who caused it. However, there may be times when one can't do that. For example, a father has had a bad day at the office because his boss has been unreasonable and demanding. Still upset when he comes home, he opens the door and stumbles over a toy that hasn't been put away. He lets the child have it for every injustice that he has suffered. His anger is out of proportion to the situation and really does not have anything to do with the child.

*"What should be done? Something like this must happen in households every day."*

A single episode like that does not cause irreparable damage. However, if that kind of encounter is a frequent occurrence, children are affected.

Children of this age are aware of their parents' attitudes and moods. Some withdraw from a parent who is always angry, some respond angrily in any encounter, and others become very inhibited. So anger can have serious repercussions for a child.

If a parent can't change his way of relating to his child by recognizing that he is projecting anger onto his child and trying to relate to the child in a more appropriate way, then the parent should perhaps seek professional help.

*"What can a parent do after such an episode if it only happens once in a while?"*

The children are now old enough to understand when a parent says she is sorry. The parent can explain that she was upset about something else and didn't mean to be angry with the child (or was tired, or had a headache, or was in a hurry—whatever the reason), then suggest they share an activity that the child enjoys like reading a book, playing ball, or going for a ride.

*"But won't apologizing undermine a parent's authority?"*

A child approaching the age of three is beginning to be able to understand the concept of an apology—regret for doing something wrong and a promise not to do it again. A parent who can admit a mistake and make amends sets a good example for a child. However, this cannot be exploited, so that the child gets the message that one can make mistakes all the time and all one has to do is apologize. One has to try to emphasize "not doing it again."

*"I work outside of the home. With trying to be a mother, too, I guess I'm always in kind of a rush. I get angry when I'm rushing around the kitchen and my son gets underfoot or wants to play. Then I realize that he needs me for that, too, so I feel guilty and apologize."*

It is difficult to hold down two jobs, inside and outside of the home. A mother in this situation should attend to important tasks and let others go so that there is time to play with a child. Making that adjustment and feeling comfortable with it can help a mother deal with daily frustrations without anger.

*"I've made that adjustment, but sometimes my husband gets upset about the way some chores are neglected. Once in a while we have words about it, which seems to terrify my daughter. She runs to both of us, hugs us, and begs us to 'be nice.' It's never a serious quarrel, just a few loud words, but she stays upset."*

*"What may happen to a child who is exposed to parents who argue a lot? That's our way of relating to each other. We're both very argumentative."*

Children of all ages become very upset when parents are angry with each other. Some children immediately feel that they are the cause of the anger; they cling to parents and may develop a fear of being abandoned. Some exhibit sleep disturbances or have appetite changes. Some are irritable and contrary with peers and parents. When a child shows changes in any of these areas, a stress in the family may be the cause.

*"Are you saying that parents should never show anger to the child or to each other? That just isn't possible, even in the best of homes."*

That is not what we are saying. A child who does something unacceptable has to be told that it is not acceptable—that you are displeased, perhaps even angry. He has to know what makes you angry and what pleases you. One of the parents' jobs is to teach that distinction consistently and patiently.

However, when parents show anger with each other or someone else, children of this age may not be able to cope with it. They may interpret the anger to mean that something awful is going to happen to them. Of course, there are occasional outbursts in any family. Constant exposure to anger can result in personality difficulties which we are trying to prevent or at least minimize. Generally speaking, however, there should be no loud arguments in the presence of children. If parents must argue, they should go out for a walk or argue after the children are sound asleep. The way we express anger is the model that we set for our children. If we always use a loud voice, throw things and slam doors, that is the way our children will express it. If we "clam up" and use the silent treatment and glare at each other, that is what they will do.

*"So our example is important, but it's not fatal if they see us angry occasionally?"*

That's right. However, you need to let your child know that he is not the cause of the anger. That is important because when children think they are the cause of the anger, they may also think that you will leave them. The fear of abandonment is one of the frequent fears of early childhood and remnants of this fear may persist into adult life.

## Resolution of Anger

*"Then it's okay to quarrel in front of a child if we make sure he understands he is not the cause?"*

That is part of it, but not all. The child should also see a resolution of the quarrel. He needs to see a restoration of normal feelings between the parents—a "kiss and make up" ending, if you will.

■                                                                      ■

## Physical Violence

*"What if the parents come to blows?"*

A child must never be a witness to physical violence between parents. For one thing, it is very frightening for the child. The witness to violence is emotionally beaten, too. Your way of showing anger is the model for your child; later in life, this is the way he will behave when angry. This is how family violence becomes sanctioned and perpetuated.

*"So the message seems to be that kids can see us angry, but we better mind how we do it. If we don't want generations of fighting mothers and fathers, we'd better kiss and make up."*

That about sums it up. We want to teach our children that it is okay to be angry, and demonstrate for them how to express and resolve anger.

# Your Child's Anger

We have been discussing your angry feelings and the effects of anger on children. How do you deal with your children when *they* get angry?

*"This is a situation that comes up almost every day, and on some days more than once. When my son was an infant, he would cry and get red in the face. I used to think it was funny for a baby to be angry. But when he gets angry now, it's different. It upsets me. All I want him to do is to stop crying and tell me what is bothering him."*

*"My problem is that whenever my child gets angry, I get frightened. I think she is going to be just like my sister, who is always angry at something. I yell for her to stop, which doesn't help."*

It's quite natural to want a child to stop an angry display, whether he is just crying or doing something more physical, like pounding his mother with his fists. We often hear a parent scold and say, "Stop that crying this minute! I can't help you till you stop." This effort to squelch the anger may inhibit the child, and the child may later be unable to express anger appropriately.

*"What is a better way to handle such a situation?"*

Parents should try to determine what causes an angry response in their child. When the child gets angry, you can say that you know he is upset, but that if he can tell you what is bothering him you will see if you can make the situation better. This way he is given a chance to express his feelings without being scolded, and he is shown that there can be a resolution to the problem.

## Supermarket Outbursts

*"Sometimes my child throws a tantrum in the middle of the supermarket if I won't buy him something he wants. I get embarrassed and want to wring*

*his neck, but I control myself and get him out of the supermarket as fast as possible."*

If you know that your child is apt to get angry in certain situations, you have several options. Either do not take him to the supermarket or, before you go, tell him what he will be able to have at the market (and get his snack first) and that you will not buy candy or gum. However, if the outburst still ensues, you can pick him up, hold him close and tell him you know he is upset because he wants what he cannot have, but he can have whatever you have agreed upon. He will learn what is expected and the outbursts will diminish, although he may still frequently test you. Parents must remember that a tired child cannot respond reasonably. Very little is effective when the child is tired, except getting the child home and to bed as quickly as possible.

*"Both of us work, so on the weekend we try to get most of the week's shopping done. Naturally, we have a lot to buy and we must rush. Our daughter gets upset, because we don't have time to let her pick items off the shelves. Shouldn't she be able to understand that we are in a hurry?"*

Children of this age still cannot hurry. As we have said before, their nervous systems just can't process thoughts, sensations, and experiences rapidly. It is better to allow extra time and shop more slowly.

## Unsolicited Advice

*"Now that my son is almost three, he responds pretty well if I am patient following his angry outbursts. But in a public place there are always people offering advice such as 'What that kid needs is a good spanking,' or 'If he were my kid, I'd give him a whack on the behind and he'd shut up.' "*

The important thing is to concern yourself with your child's feelings, not theirs. You don't want to escalate your child's anger by a demonstration of your own.

*"I have to confess that at first I get upset and feel hurt when my child gets angry at me. Then I realize that he is a person, too, and has a right to express his feelings. I try to find out what is wrong and to comfort him. He has been responding quite well to that approach."*

*"Now that my daughter is almost three, she is able to tell me what is making her angry, and it's a little easier to handle her anger now. This morning in the park, she was screaming furiously because she wanted a little boy's fire engine. I told her that she had her doll and that when the boy was finished playing with his fire engine maybe he would give her a turn. She was able to accept that. But it is not always that easy."*

■                                                                              ■

*"I've noticed that when I stop my daughter from doing something or don't give her what she wants right away, she can accept it if I give her the reason. For instance, if she wants to put on a party dress when we are going for a walk, I may say, 'That's a party dress. We are not going to a party. How about wearing the blue dress?' She accepts that explanation. In the past, she would stamp her feet and cry."*

Some of you are confirming what we have been trying to point out in all our discussions—that as the children become more mature and are able to say more, they are better able to accept limitations without angry outbursts.

## Approval and Disapproval

As the children grow older and become more competent and more venturesome, parents find themselves cautioning and admonishing them more. Parents may fall into the trap of recognizing only the child's misdeeds, neglecting to recognize the child's achievements. Many parents have been brought up by parents who believed that achievements are to be expected and therefore should not be specially recognized. Many children raised this way get the feeling that they can never please their parents and may stop trying. Or they may seek recognition and reassurance constantly.

Are you finding that you spend more time disapproving than approving? Do you think your child is beginning to understand what he is expected to do and what he is not expected to do?

*"I don't know if we just are lucky to have a child who responds, but I find we are not always saying 'No.' There are plenty of times our son does things we approve of, and we let him know we are pleased."*

I notice that you do not know whether to attribute your child's responsiveness to luck or to something you did. In most cases, it is a combination of both. Each child is different. Some need a good deal of repetition before they internalize and accept a particular limit. All children need overt recognition and approval of acceptable behavior.

### Picking Up Toys

*"Our clashes now are mostly over picking up toys. Our daughter is better than she used to be, but it still takes a long time for her to come around. If I say, 'When we pick up the toys, then we can go for a walk,' she may start picking them up right away. But usually I have to start and then she joins in."*

*"We have a similar problem. Sometimes my son says, 'I'm tired, you do it.' I feel like saying, 'You do it this minute,' the way my mother did. Instead, I say, 'We'll do it together. I'll help you.' When it's done I say, 'Look, you*

*helped and we did a wonderful job.' I feel better, and he looks happy."*

*"Sometimes that works for us. Once in a while my son absolutely refuses to pick up his toys. I say, 'We'll go to the park when you've picked them up.' If he doesn't do it, we don't go to the park that day. He knows it, so he starts to put them away, although sometimes he waits awhile."*

Putting away toys is a big issue at this stage of a child's development. In a few months, when they start nursery school, this will be part of the daily routine, so mothers should be beginning this at home now.

However, we can't expect them to comply every time. You are discovering that your child responds if you are patient. When a child does comply, it is important to offer recognition of the accomplishment. This helps the child feel good about himself and his accomplishment.

*"I try to be patient, but I just can't all the time. Some days I yell. Sometimes my daughter gets scared and runs to comfort me. That makes me feel guilty, so I put the toys away and apologize for yelling."*

*"I yell sometimes, too, but I get nowhere. My son just looks bewildered at me, but he doesn't put his toys away."*

An occasional angry outburst is not fatal. Harm comes when this becomes the norm. A child needs parental guidance that is patient, supportive, and approving.

## Noisy Play

*"What bothers me is rough, noisy play in the house. My son likes to throw his ball in the house and hit things with it. He rides his tricycle up and down the hall, and is delighted when he crashes into something. He builds with his blocks and crashes his buildings so he can start a new one. I'm constantly saying, 'No, don't do that anymore. Stop this minute.' He may stop for a minute, but he goes right back to some other noisy activity."*

Many children of this age like to make loud noises and engage in large-muscle activity. It gives them a sense of power and control. However, if the noise upsets you so that you are constantly disapproving of your child's play, you have to set limits. The child should be told that balls and tricycles are for outside. When he plays with his blocks and he takes the structure down without crashing it, you can show him how pleased you are when he does it that way. Then you can encourage indoor play with appropriate toys, like coloring books, puzzles, small cars, and trains. Many children are happy indoors if they are permitted to help with simple chores.

*"We've been talking about a child's need for approval. My parents say that if a child is always shown approval at home, he won't be able to cope with*

*disapproval later in life. They admit that that is why they were so strict with us, and that's the way their parents were with them."*

We are not saying that a child has to be shown approval constantly, but that attention should be given to things that are acceptable and deserve approval. Recognition of achievements, however small, helps a child acquire a positive self-image. Many parents overlook achievements because they expect them from the child.

# 26

## *Fathers' Expectations*

Both a father's involvement and his expectations are very important, because his role is a model for both daughters and sons. Fathers, like  mothers, have concerns and expectations that should be addressed.

The children are now approximately three. I've met with many of you fathers before to discuss the issues of development. Are there any issues that you would like to discuss now?

### *Stages of Conversation*

*"How should I respond when my son is very demanding and commands me to do something? My instinct is to get angry and tell him he can't talk like that. Am I too hard with him?"*

The commanding tone is part of the child's language development. Normal conversation comes later. Remember how they repeated their first words? They learned how to name objects. After that they put words together in phrases, then in sentences. They announced their observations, then they commanded.

*"I think that's what makes it difficult, because sometimes we can talk very nicely together, then suddenly they go into these commands."*

Usually this regression occurs when they are tired.

*"Yes, that's right, at night."*

When they are tired, they fall back to a stage you think is over. By that time you are tired, too, because it's the end of the day, so that makes it even more difficult.

*"Yes, I can see that. It kind of sums up the situation. I guess it will just take a little more time and I don't need to get angry and offended by his tone."*

*"I have the same situation and its upsets me. I really feel hurt because I expected something different in the way of communication. I am upset when I take off a weekend to be with my son*

*and he is so demanding. It's good to know this isn't going to be the way he will behave all the time."*

This is usually a passing phase. Most children go through it successfully if the parents don't take offense and answer in disagreeable tones.

## Interrupting Conversations

*"Is it too much to expect children to keep quiet and let adults talk? I can't remember when I've been able to talk to my wife without being interrupted by our son. I love my son but still I have needs, too."*

*"Our son, is the same way. I could understand that he needed constant attention as an infant, but now he is going on three."*

Children need to feel included. They cannot understand that parents may have to discuss matters that are not the child's concern. For children this age it is best to pick them up and hold them and say, for example, "Daddy is telling Mommy about what happened in the office today." The child may then wiggle away to play on his own for a few minutes, giving you a moment to talk. More lengthy, discussions can be conducted after the child is asleep or when you are out together without your child.

*"When we are in the car, our son doesn't let us converse unless we include him. If we try to talk only to each other, he says, 'Stop talking so much.'"*

That behavior is characteristic of children this age. They interrupt because they cannot accept exclusion. If you have to discuss something that isn't related to the child, save if for when the child is not there.

*"You just can't expect it? We have told him that Mommy and Daddy have to talk, and that he can watch the cars go by while we are talking."*

You can say, "Watch and see if there is a yellow car. Tell me when you see one." Then you do a *little* talking until he interrupts.

They are at a stage when they can delay a little. For instance, if you are finishing a sentence with your wife, you can say "Just a minute dear" and finish the sentence and then turn your attention to the child. This, of course, may not lead to smooth conversation.

## Parental Disappointment

*"I like athletics, and I always thought we would play ball together— baseball or basketball. When I go out to play on Saturday, I take him to watch me. But he isn't interested. He sits in his carriage and calls for me, or if I let him he runs in the way of the ball."*

You are expecting something of him for which he is too young. At this stage of his development, you might be able to get him interested in playing ball if you just throw a light ball to him in a park or yard. He may not be able to catch it, but he may be able to learn to throw to you. At least you'll be playing together regularly.

*"My wife and I both work. On the weekends my wife has lots of chores, so I thought I'd be biking with my daughter on Saturday mornings and give my wife some time on her own. Our child manages a kiddle car well, but she is nowhere near ready to pedal even a tricycle. So I take her out in her carriage and long for the time we'll be able to bike."*

Some parents purchase child seats which sit on the adult bikes, either behind or in front. You may enjoy riding with your child in that way in a safe place.

## Bedtime

*"If our daughter went to bed earlier, we'd have more time for each other. I think my wife has been too lenient and lets her stay up too long."*

Each family has its own daily routine. In some families fathers come home early, so the child gets used to an early bedtime. In other families, the routine is different; perhaps the father comes home later, so the child's bedtime is later. If both parents work, the evening is the only time they can be with the child, so the child's bedtime may be quite late.

*"I think one of the reasons our son won't go to sleep till quite late is that he has a nap around four-thirty. When he gets up, about five-thirty or six, he is rested and ready to go until nine or ten. I think he could skip his nap and go to bed earlier, but my wife says he gets so cranky that he just falls apart."*

There may be other solutions. Perhaps coming indoors earlier from the afternoon's activities and having an earlier and shorter nap would enable him to go to bed earlier. Or perhaps if he came in earlier and had quiet play times, then an early bath and supper, he would be ready to be put to bed by you when you come home. You could institute bedtime rituals, such as tooth brushing, storytelling, or reading while your wife prepares dinner for the two of you. That would give you time with your child and also time alone with your wife.

*"We both work, and we both get home about the same time. Some nights my wife puts our child to bed, I fix the food, and we all eat together. The next night we swap chores. The one who cooked the food puts the baby to bed and the other cleans up."*

*"I don't see why that arrangement couldn't work for us, too. Even though my wife is home, our child is so active that he takes so much out of her and she can use help with dinner. I know because he wears me out, too, if I'm with him all day."*

*"For me some of the fun is being taken out of it because of the way our child behaves. She seems to have a mind of her own. I think it's because my wife is too lenient. She thinks I'm too strict and expect too much. Is it too much to expect our daughter to come home from an outing without putting up a fuss and crying?"*

■                                                                                   ■

It is normal for children this age to have difficulty moving from one activity to another. Adults have to remember that children's activities are as important to them as our activities are to us. We don't like interruptions either. We don't like to be stopped in the middle of a tennis game or a party or while working on a project to do something that we haven't been warned or consulted about. Children feel the same way. Their way of dealing with it is to cry, ours is to discuss it and come to some resolution.

*"Does that mean we should just give in to them?"*

Certainly not. There are better ways to approach the problem. One way is to give the child warning: "In a few minutes it will be time to go home." Then say "it is time" and get the child ready for the next activity. There will still be some protest. The parent can say "I know you would like to stay but now it's time for [whatever]. We'll be back another day" and continue getting the child ready. Another way is by letting the child know what awaits him. "We are going home to supper and we are going to have your favorite————" or "We will stop to look at the fish in the window at the pet shop."

*"But what if they protest anyway?"*

They will protest at first, but if they feel that you are calm, confident, and not ambivalent, and that you know what you are doing, they will respond after a few experiences of this kind of treatment.

The fathers have all expressed reasonable expectations. The important thing is to keep the child's level of development in mind and then be consistent without being angry in helping the child achieve the desired response.

## Manners

Each culture has its own standards of behavior. Most parents want their children to have good manners and they may have their own personal reasons for such concerns. We discussed manners before, but some of your expectations were a little ahead of your children's abilities. How are you dealing with this issue now?

*"Our child has begun to use his spoon and fork more regularly. We let him know that we are pleased when he uses his utensils properly. He smiles and nods his head. I think he tries a little harder."*

*"We're seeing progress too, especially with the spoon, now that our son has the hang of it. But he sometimes shoves too much into his mouth at once and we have to remove the excess."*

Many of you are witnessing improved and more consistent use of the spoon and fork. With practice and positive recognition from parents, the children's dexterity will continue to increase. Sometimes they still use their hands, and many children fill their mouths too full at times and have be to shown how much to take.

It's a good idea to have them watch while you eat. Show them exactly how much you put on a spoon or fork, how you chew with your mouth closed, and then swallow before taking the next bite. Then watch the child do it and acknowledge success.

*"My spontaneous response is 'No, not that way.' I raise my voice, and I guess I'm a little scary, because my daughter begins to cry and the whole meal is ruined."*

Scolding doesn't help matters. Your daughter and most other children learn best when the correct way is modeled for them and their efforts to follow your example are recognized.

*"We are making some progress with 'please' and 'thank you,' but there are many lapses. How much should we expect at this stage?"*

They may not always remember to say "please" and "thank you." When they do lapse, a gentle reminder is useful.

*"You mean if my child asks for a cookie, I should say, 'When you say, "please," I'll give you a cookie'?"*

There are several ways to get your point across without being angry or harsh. You can say, in a pleasant tone "When you say please I'll be glad to give you a cookie," or "I think you mean 'Please may I have a cookie.'" Most children respond to this approach.

*"If he refuses to say 'please,' should I give him the cookie anyway?"*

The first time it happens on any given day, try saying something like "I guess you forgot to say 'please.' Try to remember it next time." The next time, you can say in a pleasant way, "How are we supposed to ask?" or "What is the magic word?" Show approval when he complies, so that his self-esteem is bolstered and he can see that compliance brought emotional rewards.

*"My son does fine with 'please' and 'thank you'—except when Grandma comes, when I want him to be especially nice. I get a little edgy when that happens."*

We always want our children to behave well when we have company. Now that the children are almost three and are able to understand and say so much more, we expect them to perform well as social beings. If this anxiety is conveyed to the child, the child may become anxious, too, and forget some of the things he has learned. Try saying, "I guess we forgot to say 'please.' Let's try to remember it for next time." In that way you let the visitor know you are aware of the lapse. At the same time, you do not embarrass your child and set up a tense situation for the next time company comes.

*"What about saying 'hello' and 'good-bye' now? When we talked about it last time, you told us to say it for them and set the example."*

*"My daughter still hides behind me and still can't say 'good-bye.' She is a little better at 'hello' and 'hi.' "*

For some reason, most children have more difficulty with greetings and partings than with "please" and "thank you." Some children may not accomplish this until they are four or five, and may need to be reminded even at that age.

*"So we shouldn't force the issue?"*

That's right. Set an example for the child. Give the other person and the child the feeling that he is included by saying "hello" and "good-bye." Before the visit, you can remind the child of the appropriate things to say. You can say, for instance, "We are going to visit Grandma. Let's remember to say, 'Hello, Grandma.' And when we leave, let's remember to say, 'Good-bye, Grandma.' " That sometimes may help.

*"When visitors come, we still can't carry on an uninterrupted conversation. Before we were married and had children, that used to annoy me so much that I vowed I'd never let my children do it."*

At three years of age, children may find it difficult to be excluded. They simply can't understand why a parent is unavailable to them when a visitor comes. But if you make an attempt to include the children in your conversation, they are more likely to leave you alone and continue with their own play. They may still interrupt, but they may be able to wait until you finish a sentence.

*"Our child still doesn't sit through a whole meal; she has to get up and run around. That's okay at home, but not in a restaurant. And we do like to eat out once in a while."*

A child this age who can sit through a meal is still the exception. Most children of this age can't be expected to sit through more than about twenty minutes of a meal. By that time they have usually finished all that they are going to eat anyway. They are still not ready to go to a restaurant where service takes time and where an active or young child is not welcome. As they get older, they learn to sit longer at the table.

*"Our daughter recently sat through a full-course holiday dinner at a family gathering. We were very proud. But she doesn't do that every day at home, and we accept that. We tell her that when she is a big girl she'll be able to sit at the table and talk with Daddy and Mommy. Is that right?"*

That is right. You are simply letting her know what her goals should be, and that what she does now is acceptable.

■ ■

## Unacceptable Language

*"Our son regularly goes to the park, where some of the children are older. He comes back with a few words we don't use at home. I don't know where those children pick up this vocabulary, but it's shocking. Should we explain why we don't want him to use these words?"*

At this age he isn't likely to understand your explanation. You can simply tell him that you don't like those words and that you don't use them. If there are appropriate substitutes for the words, supply them. If he continues to use the words calmly restate your position and then be unresponsive when he uses them. The words will probably disappear from his vocabulary from lack of reinforcement.

*"My son said 'shut up' to me the other day. I was so shocked that I laughed, so he repeated it."*

If you laugh when a child does something surprising or cute for this age, the child may try to evoke that response again. It may take time for him to then accept no response and to stop.

## Sharing

*"What about sharing? Last week, we had friends over. They brought their son, who is almost four. For the first half hour, my son made a fuss every time this boy touched a toy of his. We gave them some snacks and after that it was much better, but we were a little embarrassed."*

The children's ability to share is still erratic. They are better able to share with children they know and see often. In nursery school next year, they will learn to take turns and to share. They will also be more verbal and better able to negotiate with other children. Now, however, they still need to be reassured that a visiting child will only play with a toy and not take it home.

## Shopping

*"When we go into a store, my child touches objects that she shouldn't. Once she squeezed an egg and broke it. I'm trying to get her to understand that she must ask me first if she may touch an object."*

*"I can't go into a toy store with my son without holding on to him, because he gets into everything. I've stopped taking him to stores."*

Children this age are curious and constantly want to touch and explore. It is very difficult for them to understand that it is wrong to touch something that is very tempting. Parents should try to steer clear of such temptations whenever possible until the children are a little older and their self-control is stronger. If parents are patient, they can teach children the concept that certain things are off limits—Mommy's perfume and lipstick, for example.

They can be told that certain things belong to other people and are not to be touched without asking.

## *Weaning*

One important indicator of development is the ability to relinquish the bottle. Most of the children have been drinking from a cup successfully for several months. Many children have already given up the bottle, although some still need the first morning and the last evening bottle. Are any of you concerned about your children's progress with weaning?

*"My son still needs a morning and evening bottle, and I've been wondering just when and how I should go about getting him to give them up."*

Although most children give up the bottle around three, three is not a magical number. Some children are ready earlier than age three; others need a little longer. By this time most of their milk consumption should be from a cup, even if assistance is necessary. A child may give up the night bottle more easily if she is held on mother's lap while drinking the last cup of milk. This simulates the position and security of an earlier stage.

*"We've been continually reminded that any changes in the child's routine should be in keeping with the child's own readiness timetable. Is encouraging the child to get rid of the bottle consistent with that principle?"*

Under no circumstances should a parent take the bottle away abruptly. It should be done in a way that helps the child accept the cup without feeling that he is being separated from a source of comfort. In addition, the child should be given extra attention and recognition for his accomplishment. The parent's job is to help children move to a more mature stage when they are ready.

*"My daughter was slow in reaching all her developmental milestones, and I'm not expecting her to be any different with this one. I think I understand her timetable now, and I am comfortable with it, even though I get flak from family."*

It can be difficult to cope with the opinions of people who are not with a child all the time and may not be aware of her readiness. You can remind these people that every child has his or her own maturational timetable and that you certainly intend to stop the late-evening bottle as soon as you feel your daughter is ready.

*"I went through that with my mother. Finally I said, 'Mom, I assure you he will not be having a bottle when he goes to college, so don't worry.' That worked for me, and maybe it will work for others, too."*

*"I have a different concern: My son isn't a very good eater. He drinks from a cup quite well, but he doesn't get as much as he does from a bottle. So I'm very glad he takes the late-night bottle."*

What does your doctor say about your son's health and nourishment? Does he think he requires the night bottle?

*"He told me months ago to give it up, that he was fine."*

Your anxiety may be making you continue with the last bottle, not your son's readiness. You have to make up your mind when you are ready to try giving him a cup before bedtime.

*"My son has given up the night bottle, but not the early-morning one. It's probably my fault. He wakes up so early that I give him a bottle to get him back to sleep for another hour, so that I can sleep a little longer, too! Is that so terrible?"*

There is nothing wrong with that if it suits your life-style. Allowing bottles until a child is ready to be weaned and doing it gradually in keeping with the child's readiness is a more appropriate way. We are just discussing ways to relinquish the last bottle.

*"What about telling a child that the bottle broke and you have no more, or you lost it?"*

*"I tried that with my child, and she said, 'Go store bottle'!"*

It is never a good idea to tell a child an untruth. Children understand more than we think, and if they sense deceit, it makes them lose trust in what you tell them.

*"Last weekend we stayed at a friend's overnight. In the hurry of packing, I forgot my son's bottle. When I put him to bed, I said, 'Mommy forgot your bottle, but you can have a cup of milk like a big boy.' He accepted the cup and went to sleep without a protest. I was sure he'd want the bottle when we got back home, but he hasn't asked for one."*

*"We recently had overnight guests. We put their daughter on the sofa in our daughter's room. The guest's child had a cup of milk before bed, so I asked our daughter if she would like one. She agreed, and has asked for a cup ever since. She had been so attached to her night bottle—or so I thought— that I was afraid to suggest a cup."*

In each case there were two factors that led to success—a situation that presented itself at a time when the child was ready, and a mother who was able to seize the opportunity.

*"Maybe I'm the one holding on. My daughter takes a few sips and then drops the bottle or gives it back to me. But I'm afraid to stop offering it to her."*

It sounds as though she is trying to tell you she doesn't need the bottle anymore. She might be content with just a sip of water from a cup as part of the bedtime routine.

*"My son doesn't drink from a bottle anymore, but he wants to carry one around. Sometimes he keeps the nipple in his mouth for a while and chews on it, but he never seems to suck at it."*

He is using the bottle as a transitional object. Perhaps in time he will choose a different object.

*"We went through that, too. So I said, 'We won't take it outside, just in the house.' My child accepted that, and soon latched on to a truck, which he carries everywhere now."*

*"What about pacifiers? Don't children have to be weaned from them too?"*

A pacifier satisfies the sucking needs of a child who may take bottles too quickly. It is unwise to offer a pacifier as a substitute for the bottle. The child may continue to use it as a means of comfort when it is no longer appropriate.

*"What if he does continue to use it all the time? I've seen some children of three and even four who always seem to be sucking on their pacifiers."*

Some children seek the comfort of a pacifier when they are anxious, tired, lonesome, or bored. Others use it as a transitional object, much as they become attached to teddy bears, for example. The parent should observe the child and try to correct those situations that cause the child to seek the comfort of the pacifier. For example, if the child is lonesome or bored, a more interesting or stimulating environment should be provided.

*"My son gave up the pacifier months ago. But recently we visited friends whose child was using a pacifier. When we got home, he found his pacifier in a box of toys and began to use it, but he didn't keep it up because the rubber was a little stiff and I guess it didn't fill a need."*

*"I have noticed that when I have my child with me instead of at the baby-sitter's she doesn't use her pacifier. She is an only child, and we are always doing something together at home. But at the baby-sitter's she is one of four children, and she doesn't get all the attention she needs. I understand that, so I try to create a different environment for her at home."*

Parents should try to eliminate use of the pacifier without giving the child the feeling that what he is doing is wrong. Perhaps the child can be kept occupied with a more satisfying or constructive activity. This may take consistent effort on the parents' part, like playing more with him, getting him involved in more household chores, and giving him a sense of achievement.

## Toilet Training

As the children grow, parents feel increasing pressure to toilet train. Some parents are made to feel as though the speed with which they toilet train the child is a measure of their qualifications as parents. There is also the temptation to compare a child's achievement in this area with that of a neighbor's or friend's child. In addition, many nursery schools require that all children be toilet trained.

Some children have achieved bowel and bladder control by this age; others are in various stages of accomplishing this step. How are your children doing in this area?

## Readiness for Toilet Training

*"My son knows where things go and helps to put them away. He tells me when he has soiled or wet himself and wants to be changed. He seems to understand what we use the toilet for, and what the little seat in the bathroom is for, because he puts his teddy bear on it. He just doesn't connect it with himself yet. Is there anything I can do to encourage him?"*

It sounds as though your son is almost ready to be toilet trained. When he puts his teddy bear on the seat, perhaps you can simply point out that someday he is going to be big enough to use the toilet too.

*"Mine is entirely oblivious of the issue. I know there is no use forcing him to sit on the toilet. I did that with my first child, and it was a battle all the time. I would not go through that again, because I feel we developed some unpleasant attitudes toward each other that are present to some extent even today."*

The anger and resistance a child feels during toilet training can indeed linger. We are trying to avoid such an "angry alliance" between parent and child. It takes patience and understanding on the parents' side to avoid this trap.

*"My mother thinks a little clear suggestion doesn't hurt. The other day, after she had been baby-sitting and had to change a soiled diaper, she said to my daughter, 'You are a big girl now, so you can use the toilet the way big girls do.' My daughter looked at her, shook her head, and said, 'Me not big, me little.' "*

Children of this age can be quite astute. They have more of a sense of themselves than we give them credit for. They know when they are ready to move ahead, then they have a natural urge to do so.

*"My daughter has been using the bathroom successfully for almost two months. She simply announced one day that she wanted to use the toilet, pulled off her Pamper, and pulled me to the bathroom to put her on the potty chair. Now she manages it herself, although she calls me to help her get dressed again. I didn't believe it could happen so easily."*

*"My daughter asked to use the toilet last week after watching a cousin who had come to visit, and she has been using the toilet since then."*

Did she just use it without any help from you? What did she do before that?

*"For a few days before that she would ask us to use the toilet. She was rarely successful with urinating, although more often with bowel move-*

*ments. I praised her when she was successful and said nothing when she wasn't. Then, after her cousin's visit, she seemed to be trained."*

*"My son bypassed the potty chair and insisted on being lifted to the regular toilet seat. I was afraid he would fall in, but he carefully braces himself on his hands and holds himself up. That's for bowel movements. He steps to the toilet and urinates standing up. That came first, after watching his father."*

These are success stories that should encourage everyone. Children let their parents know when they are ready.

*"I noticed that my daughter was waking dry from her nap, so I suggested that she try to use the bathroom before getting dressed. She accepted the idea and was successful, and since then she has been responding when it is suggested."*

## Accidents

*"My daughter seemed to train herself. When she is left on her own, she doesn't have accidents. But if I want her to use the bathroom before we go out, she balks. Then, once we are outside, she may announce that she needs to use the bathroom. If we are near one we manage, but if not, she may wet herself a little. Is there any way to overcome this?"*

She's trying to control herself. Perhaps if you model going to the bathroom as all "big" girls do, she may want to use it, too, when not coerced.

*"My daughter can't seem to use an unfamiliar bathroom, so we have accidents when she won't use the bathroom at home before we leave. I was wondering if I should put her back in diapers whenever we go out."*

That may confuse your child. She may find it difficult to know when to exert control and when she can revert to an earlier level. The best approach is to leave the house with a change of clean clothes so that the child can be changed if necessary.

*"What can you say to a child when he has an accident? When this happens, my son acts as though he has committed a crime and expects me to do something terrible to him."*

Each child responds differently to such incidents. Much depends on the child's temperament, how much he wants to win your approval, and what he believes will be the retribution for his failure. The best approach is to be as calm and casual as possible, then say something reassuring, like "It was just an accident. I know you did your best. I brought some clean clothes, and we will change into them as soon as we can."

*"Once a child is toilet trained, is it a good idea to take her to the bathroom before going out, so an accident is less apt to happen?"*

*"I tried that, and I think it caused more problems. Now when I ask my son to use the bathroom before we go out, he insists that he doesn't have to. He*

*runs away and can't go even if I do take him. Now I just take a change of pants with us."*

Sometimes a better approach is to prepare the child by saying, "In a little while, or in five minutes, it will be time for the bathroom." Of course, this works especially well if the child is accustomed to respond to "It is time for dinner [or a bath, etc]." For others it may work better to say, "When you finish your block house [or bathing your doll], it will be time to go to the bathroom."

*"I use that method, and usually it works. But once in a while my child just can't make herself go. Then, when we are outside, she has an accident."*

When this happens, try not to be angry or lose your temper. Instead, say in a quiet voice, "Maybe if we used the bathroom before going out this wouldn't happen. Let's try next time." This approach usually works better than lecturing the children in a threatening tone.

*"Does it make any difference if a child is toilet trained first for bowel movements, then for urinating?"*

That depends on the individual child. Sometimes bowel control is accomplished first because bowel movements are less frequent than urination. Some boys achieve urination control first because their anatomy makes urinating a less complicated procedure. In most cases, both types of control are achieved at once if children are allowed to respond on their own timetable.

## Fears of Flushing

*"My son responded early to bladder training, but he refuses to have a bowel movement on the toilet. So I let him do it in his diaper. When he is ready, he asks me to put his diaper on him. So I do."*

*"My daughter watched me empty her diaper into the toilet and then flush it away. She asked me where it went, and I explained that it went into the sewer and out to the sea. That frightened her, and she would not let me empty her diaper after that. I had to do it when she was asleep."*

This is not uncommon. Some children feel that their bowel movement is part of them and are afraid to have it flushed away. They may fear that they may be flushed away, too.

## Night Wetting

*"My son is completely trained during the day. When should we expect him to be dry at night, too?"*

*"What if I pick up my son before I go to bed and take him to the bathroom? Will that help him keep dry?"*

Most children this age achieve nighttime control on their own. Those who wet generally do so shortly after falling asleep, perhaps because they are too tired or tense to empty their bladders at bedtime. Parents can help these children achieve nighttime control by awakening them and taking them to the toilet. Other children wet early in the morning, because they wake up before the parents do. These children are usually helped when the parents rise early enough to take them to the bathroom before they wet.

### Accidents at Nursey School

*"I have been thinking of nursery school next year. Although most of the schools require children to be toilet trained, they also ask that several changes of clothes be left in case of accidents. Are accidents to be expected?"*

Accidents do occur frequently. The child who has an accident may have been hurried at home and resisted using the bathroom. However, nursery-school teachers have to be prepared for these accidents. Some children get so engrossed in play that they resist going to the bathroom until it's too late. Many teachers are aware of this and set up regular bathroom times. But accidents continue to happen until the children achieve control. Some children do not achieve full control until they are five or six years old.

*"I guess we have to remember that they are still babies even if they are three."*

That is something parents are inclined to forget, especially if the child is verbal and bright. The children have made much progress since we last discussed toilet training, and most of them will have good control of bowel and bladder functions by age three or shortly thereafter.

## Independence: Learning to Help Themselves

We have discussed weaning children from the bottle and pacifer. Other issues can be approached in the same way. For example, the children should be encouraged to do things for themselves, such as dressing, eating and putting away toys. This helps them experience a gradual increase in delay of gratification. Another is helping them experience the sequence of events that lead to a specific conclusion, so that they can finally accept consequences. They are able to do this as their capacity for language increases and concept formation develops. Are you seeing that the children are trying to take care of some of their needs by themselves? How do you respond?

■                                  ■

*"I've noticed that my son tries to dress himself. He can get on his shirt and his underpants. But sometimes he does it backward. I let him do it anyway, because he seems so pleased with himself."*

*"My son tries that too, but he is slow and I have work to do, so I just dress him. It's faster and easier for me."*

Children this age should be given a chance to dress themselves. Success enhances their sense of themselves as achievers. Mothers who work outside the home may need to start at an earlier hour to accommodate the child's level of ability in dressing. Each family should decide what works best for them.

*"I don't work outside the home, but I can't stand waiting while my daughter gets herself dressed. I just don't have the patience."*

As we've said many times before, patience is something parents need to cultivate. It's an important ingredient in many situations, but particularly so in parenting.

*"I envy all parents whose children try to do things on their own. Whenever I suggest to my child that she can dress herself, she says, 'No, you, Mommy.' "*

Your child may not be quite ready to try on her own, and your urging threatens her. By the time children reach nursery school, at about three, most show an interest in dressing themselves. At nursery school, teachers may show them ways of helping themselves into their outer clothes.

*"My child has been eating by herself for quite a while. Although she is sometimes messy and resorts to using her hands to get the food into her mouth, I don't interfere. But when she insists on trying to pour juice or milk she usually spills some. When should children be allowed to pour?"*

Most children love to pour. When they were younger they may have been allowed to practice pouring in the bathtub. Now that most of them have better coordination, they can be allowed to pour from a small pitcher to help water plants or to pour a little milk into a cup. Of course, there may be spills. They should not be emphasized. But the successes should be recognized.

## Delaying Gratification

*"What I'm having a problem with is my son's impatience. He wants everything 'this minute.' "*

*"My daughter used to be that way, but she is getting to be more patient. I say, 'Just a minute' and then do whatever it is she wants. She is more able to wait—not a long time, but enough so I don't feel as pressured."*

Children of this age are beginning to be able to wait a little longer to have their requests satisfied. If parents have been consistent and reliable, a child develops a feeling of basic trust. Since he knows that his parents will see to his needs, he gradually becomes able to wait longer.

*"My son is getting pretty good about waiting for things—except going out. I usually have things to do around the house before we go out, but he just can't wait. It becomes like a tug-of-war."*

One of the ways to deal with impatient children is to involve them in what you are doing. You can ask your child to help you make the bed, dust, or anything else, so that you will be able to get out faster. Children learn quickly the order of events that lead up to a pleasurable activity.

*"I have my son do things for his toy animals—feed them, put them to bed, tell them a story. This cuts down on any pressure that I may feel."*

## Putting Things Away

*"Is it too soon to expect children to put away toys? My daughter's toys are strewn all over by the end of the day."*

When children go to nursery school, one of their activities is "putting away time." They get a certain pride in doing it because of the teacher's approval and manner of sharing in the activity. But they can also begin to learn at home now.

*"I don't allow my son to take out a new set of toys until we put the first group away, so most of the time we don't have such a big mess. My parents think I'm too strict about it."*

Parents all have their own way of dealing with this matter. A child can learn readily if parents are firm and offer recognition of approval when the task is done. Other parents prefer a single clean-up, with cooperation from the child.

## Breaking Toys

*"When is a child old enough to understand that if he breaks a toy, it may not be possible to repair it?"*

A child of this age may not be able to understand cause and effect in this context. If she breaks a toy, she can be shown the damage that is the result of her action. She can be given a simple explanation as well—"When you pull the wheels off your toy car, the car won't go anymore," for example. She may remember this lesson the next time she is playing.

*"When my child breaks a toy, he gets extremely upset. If I can't repair it right away, I promise him I will buy him another one. This calms him down, but is it the right thing to do?"*

This is a difficult part of parenting, but a very essential one. Children learn to help themselves and to delay gratification if they understand that their actions have consequences. Replacing the toy immediately does not help him learn the consequences.

■                                                                    ■

A child who is verbal may be able to understand the consequences of certain actions. A parent is the best judge of when a child is able to comprehend this concept, and should be prepared to help the child learn it at the appropriate time.

## Holidays

Most parents remember the things they enjoyed about holidays when they were children or how they wished they had celebrated them and want to impart tradition to their children. However, children at this age may not be prepared for everything that holidays entail. For example, at Halloween they may enjoy the treats but be frightened by masks, costumes, and jack-o'-lanterns. At Christmastime they may enjoy the tree and its bright lights but be frightened by a large and jovial Santa Claus who takes a child on his lap in a store and greets him too heartily.

How have your children been reacting to holiday festivities? How have you been responding to their excitement and tears?

### Halloween

*"This will be the third Halloween for my son. Last year he was frightened by the masks on kids who came for trick-or-treat. He had trouble getting to sleep that night and for a few nights after that. How much do you think he will understand this year?"*

Children younger than three can grasp neither the religious significance nor the fantasy associated with a holiday. However, parents can prepare a child for certain holiday occurrences. On Halloween, for example, the child can be told that there will be visitors in masks and costumes to whom he will give a treat.

*"Last Halloween we made a small jack-o-lantern. Our daughter was thrilled and asked us to turn out the lights over and over again so she could see it in the dark. It became a game, and she wasn't upset when children came around with lighted pumpkins. But she was excited and had a hard time getting to sleep that night."*

Even something pleasurable can upset a child's sleep routine. Allowing the child a longer time to relax before going to bed usually helps him or her overcome the excitement.

### Christmas

*"Last year I didn't take my daughter near the department-store Santas. She just watched from a distance. I could tell she was interested, but I didn't think she was ready. I felt she may have been too frightened by the experience. I wonder if it would be fun for her this year."*

Christmas can have frightening and fun aspects for children this age. For example, being held by a large and unusually dressed individual in a strange place may be more frightening than pleasant. Most of the children are not yet able to grasp the meaning of Santa Clause anyway. Many parents recall fondly their own childhood Christmasses and are anxious for their children to have similar joyful experiences. But parents must first make certain that their children are ready for the holiday event or activity.

*"Should parents tell children they'll get presents only if they behave? I remember the agony I went through caused by threats from my mother and father: 'If you want Santa to bring you that doll, you'd better remember how to behave.' That still rings in my ears around Christmastime."*

A child this age can be made anxious by the repeated threat of not being visited by Santa. This method is not in keeping with our view of the correct way to teach discipline: to recognize approved behavior, set limits on disapproved behavior, offer appropriate recognition, and refrain from using threats and bribes.

## Anticipation

*"My child gets so excited in anticipation of holidays that I try not to say anything until the day before. But preparations for Christmas begin so far in advance that I just can't use that method at Christmastime."*

*"Christmas is a big event in our family. We all exchange presents. We all bake cookies and make special foods for the big family feast. We try to soft-pedal talk of presents, so as not to get the children overexcited. Still, I hope this year my son will understand more and enjoy the season, if he is a little too excited."*

It is hard to make preparations for a big holiday without getting young children excited and anxious. Children this age cannot understand that all these activities are leading to a happy event. Nor are they able to postpone gratification for very long. Children respond differently in this situation. Some become irritable, others have difficulty sleeping or experience loss of appetite. Parents should keep to usual routines as much as possible, and keep festivities as simple as possible.

## Disillusionment

*"We are troubled by the prospect of having to disillusion our child about Santa Claus. I remember how upset I was when I found out my parents put the presents under the tree. I felt terribly cheated and deceived."*

Each family has to decide for itself how to present holiday rituals to the children. Remember, however, that most children of this age don't comprehend the concept of Santa Claus, so disillusionment should not be a concern yet. However, at this age they can enjoy the bright lights of a tree, the presents (whose wrappings may be more enjoyable than the contents), some of the special holiday foods, and the music.

## Different Cultures and Customs

*"We are members of the Pentecostal Church. We do not tell our children about Santa Claus. Nor do we give gifts on Christmas. It is a religious occasion."*

*"We, too, do not celebrate Christmas with a tree and Santa Claus. We have a piñata, which is full of small presents. On Christmas we crack it, and all the presents come out. The children enjoy that."*

*"We are Jewish. Our holiday is Hanukkah, the festival of lights, which comes around the same time of year as Christmas and lasts eight days. Our custom is to give children a small present each night, although some families give only one large present the first night. Our children know the presents are from their parents and grandparents, but there is still a lot of excitement and preparation."*

*"In a community like ours, where Christmas with Santa Claus is the dominant custom, it is very hard to tell your child that he can't share in the fun because his family doesn't believe in that. So we celebrate our traditions and Santa Claus. That works for us."*

Try not to emphasize what the child can't do. Emphasize what he does instead—such as breaking a piñata or exchanging Hanukkah presents. This helps the child establish cultural identity, and to see that having different traditions and beliefs is not bad. Children should be encouraged to learn to understand and enjoy the rituals of people of different religions.

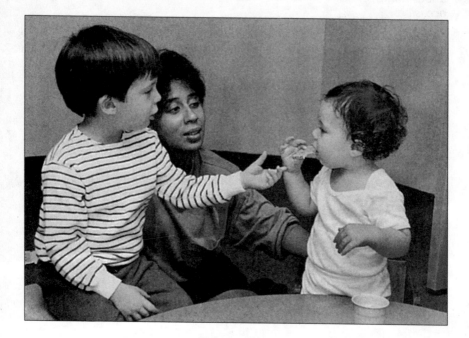

# 27

# *Understanding Your Child's World*

## *New Experiences and Interests*

We have been discussing the relationship of parents and children in their immediate families and occasionally in relation to a neighbor or friend. The children are now beginning to take more interest in the world around them—that is, they observe people and what they do and the relationships between people. They want to know who does what and who relates to whom, as well as the function of many inanimate things like trains, cars, and planes. Have you been aware of your child's interest in things outside himself?

*"I find that I take my son more places with me and that he wants to know who people are and what they do. We pass a police station on our way to the supermarket. If it is time for a shift change, there may be several police officers entering or leaving. He points and says, 'Who's that? What's his name? Where he go? That his home?' I explain that I don't know his name but that he must have one, that he is going to work or home from work, and that the building is not his house where he lives but the office where he has to go. Then he wants to know where the policeman lives. I often make up a story about his home and family, and that quiets him down and satisfies him."*

That seems to be the answer he wants and needs. He seems to need to place this person in uniform, which he doesn't quite understand, in a context of home and family, which he can understand.

*"We went through something similar with my son. Whenever he saw a fire truck go by with sirens shrieking, my son was frightened. He wanted to know who they were and where they were going. I explained the firemen*  *were going to help someone put out a fire. Then I decided maybe it would help him if I took him to a firehouse so he could see the men on the truck when all was quiet and there was no loud action. He loved the experience. The firemen were very kind and let him sit in the truck. It was a great day. Now he considers them his friends, and he is not so afraid of the siren now."*

That was the kind of experience that helps a child understand what is going on around him and takes away some of the fear of things unknown. This is part of many nursery-school programs. How many of you have taken such excursions?

*"I take my daughter to the library with me. She enjoys going there because there is a children's room where she can pick out books. She decides which ones she wants to borrow and she goes to the counter to check them out with me while I check out mine. She now understands that we keep them a little while and that we can get others when we bring these back. Once in a while there is a story hour for three-year-olds. I have taken her and she seems to enjoy it. Now she knows what a library is and what she can do there."*

That not only increases her knowledge about a library, but also gives her an interest in books and reading that may remain with her all her life.

*"Our great adventure recently has been the post office. My daughter watches for the postman each morning to see if he will bring a letter from Grandma. I thought it would be a good idea for us to write a letter to Grandma and stamp it and then take it to the post office to mail so Grandma's mailman could bring her a letter. This she found very exciting, and now she knows what Grandma must do to send a letter."*

*"When I go shopping, I take my daughter. Now she knows that the bakery is where we buy bread and rolls and, occasionally, cookies. She knows the supermarket and where she gets a piece of fruit if she wants something. She is getting to know many of the regular clerks and regards them as friends. Some are pleasant to her and recognize her. I am just wondering what will happen if we meet up with a cross one."*

## Unpleasant Experiences

*"Our routine is somewhat the same. But we did have an unpleasant experience. There was a new clerk in the bakery, and she was quite disorganized and rushed on her first day and didn't say 'hello' to my son or offer a cookie. He began to cry, so I told her the usual procedure and she thrust a cookie in his hand gruffly. On the way home, he kept asking why she didn't want to give him a cookie. I just couldn't think of a good answer so I said maybe next time she would remember—or the old clerk would be back."*

It is too bad that not all people treat children—particularly small children—nicely. We would like to protect our children for as long as possible from such experiences. However, when they do occur we should help the child cope with the situation. We can say, for instance, "The clerk was new. She didn't know just what to do. I think next time she will know. We will remind her if she doesn't remember."

*"It isn't just grown-ups who can be unpleasant. My daughter plays in the same park playground almost every day. Most of the children are getting*

■                                                        ■

to know each other, but the other day there were two new boys in the sandbox. When she approached enthusiastically, expecting to play as usual, one looked up and said, 'Go away.' Then the other one chimed in 'Go away.' She was upset, and she came running to me crying. I tried to comfort her and looked around for their mother, but there was just a maid who was reading and not paying attention. I went up to the boys and said, 'This sandbox is for everyone to share. It is not your sandbox. She plays here every day, and she can play today. There is room for all of you.' They simply picked up some sand and threw it in my face. I turned to the maid. She looked up in a surly way and said, 'Let them fight it out themselves.' I simply kept still, plunked myself down at the edge of the sandbox, and told my child to play in it all she wanted to. They got the idea; soon they were watching my daughter and trying to help her. Do you think I should have let them 'fight it out' among themselves?"*

Children of this age are not ready to advocate for themselves. It is still the parents' job to do it and model for the children the kinds of things to say, as you did.

*"One thing I enjoy is the fact that my son can actually converse with me. He makes such surprising comments and asks so many questions. I don't always know how to answer him."*

*"My daughter does that too. Sometimes she asks a question in a high-pitched voice so everyone can hear on the street. The other day we saw a man walking with the help of a cane in one hand and a kind of crutch in the other. She pointed and said in what seemed to me a very loud voice, 'Mommy, look at the man. Why does he walk like that?' She was very insistent, and I was embarrassed. I explained that he must have hurt his leg and had to walk that way. The first thing she said to her father that night was 'the man must have hurt his leg.' Her father went into more detail and said he must have had an accident and fallen down. That satisfied her more."*

Children are often startled by someone who seems strange to them. They will make comments and ask questions, as your daughter did. Before offering an explanation, it may help to ask the child what she thinks or imagines may have happened. In that way you may find out what the child really wants to know. In this instance, your child may have worried whether such a thing could happen to her or anyone she knew and wanted reassurance.

## Understanding Family Relationships

*"My son is confused by the relationship of one person to another. He is having difficulty understanding that my mother is his grandmother and also the grandmother of my sister's little girl, his cousin. He says, 'No, no, my grandma.' A week ago, when we went to a family gathering, there was a cousin there he had never seen before. My mother had to hold each one on her lap and say, 'I am your grandmother and I am Sally's grandmother.*

*And you are Sally's cousin and she is your cousin and you are both my grandchildren.' Is it unusual for a child to act that way?"*

This is the time that children begin to become aware of relationships. They may need to have these relationships explained to them over and over again. For example, they do not realize until told that Grandma or Grandpa is also Daddy's or Mommy's mother or father. This is indeed a great discovery for children.

*"My daughter is going through that now. She understands that Daddy's mother is her grandmother, but she thinks that her friend's grandmother is her grandmother, too."*

*"My child seems to be trying to get straight who everybody is. He wants to know who their mommy and daddy are, and where they are. At first I thought this strange. Now I can see that it is not just curiosity but trying to understand about people."*

These examples show how the children's worlds are expanding. All of the experiences that they have with policemen, postmen, firemen, and grocery clerks help them become better acquainted with the world outside their homes. Helping them to understand is one of the exciting and pleasant aspects of being a parent.

# Protecting Your Child

Most parents grew up in an era when children were shielded from learning about unpleasant or dangerous events—especially kidnappings and sexual abuse. Childhood was the age of innocence. Now we are living in a different era. There is an increase in violent crimes. Kidnappings and sexual abuse are frequent events and come very close to many of us. For many children all this horror is as close as the TV set. Parents do not want their children to accept violence as the usual way of life, and at the same time they don't want them to be alarmed and believe that they may become victims. But parents do want to prepare their children to cope if confronted by the threat of harm. With the recent discovery of child abuse in some day-care centers, this is a more pressing issue than ever before.

There has been much discussion recently about the rise of violence, particularly in our own communities. No doubt this has caused you some concern. Have you been thinking how best to protect your children from violence?

*"This is a topic that I always tried to avoid. I was brought up to think little children should not have to know about such things. But now I'm not sure. It's happening too often and getting into our own neighborhood."*

*"You don't have to go outside your house. Violence comes right into your living room on TV. You put on what you think is going to be a benign, safe*

*program, and before you know it there are fights, bloodshed, and all kinds of frightening things that you don't want your child to see."*

This is true. But it is possible to control which programs a child watches. A parent should be watching TV with the child to know what she is exposed to and to be able to turn it off or change channels when necessary.

*"What do I do if my child is inadvertently exposed to something that I don't think is right for her? Do I tell her how bad it was, that it was just make-believe, or what?"*

The best approach is to try to find out what the child thought about the program, how the child interpreted it, and how real it seemed to her. Then you may have a better idea of what to say to the child.

*"Recently, I turned on what I thought was a nice story about a mother and her children. I went to the kitchen to put the dinner in the oven, and when I came back the mother had been shot by an intruder. My child was crying and wanted the TV off. He still doesn't want it on, his sleep pattern has been disturbed, and he clings to me. What should be done?"*

How did you handle the situation? What did you say or do?

*"I picked him up and held him and turned off the set as soon as I got an idea of what had happened. I said they were just playing, that is wasn't for real, and I took him into the kitchen with me. When he went back into the living room, he looked at the set and stayed close to me and said 'No, no' to the set."*

It was good that you picked him up and held him and took him to do something with you. It might have been helpful, too, to ask him what he thought happened and then to be able to tell him it was just a story and not real. He also needed to be reassured that it wasn't happening in his own home, and that you were all right and he was all right. For a few days after an episode in which a child is afraid something may happen to a parent or other member of the family or even himself, it is a good idea to reassure the child. For example, you can mention how well you feel, how well he looks, what a nice day it is, and what good things you are going to do. At bedtime, say what fun the day has been and speak of a pleasant event that will happen the next day.

*"What about protecting them from real things that can happen? What I have in mind is kidnapping. How do you prepare a child for such a thing without scaring them to death or even just confusing them?"*

Usually, until children are about three, they are very closely watched by the parent or caretaker and are not accessible to strangers. However, children can wander away in parks, shopping centers, or department stores if not strapped in their carriages. So it is necessary, unpleasant as it may seem, to try to warn them not to talk to strangers when mother or another caretaker is not with them. We must remember the level of their language development—how much they can understand and how much they can say—and not give them a lecture. For example, it is sufficient to say, "When Mommy is not with you, don't talk to somebody you don't know."

*"I used to think that was okay—until the janitor in a building where a friend lives was accused of kidnapping a child in the building. Nothing bad happened; he was found giving her candy. But it is scary. So now I say, 'Don't talk to anybody if Mommy is not there.' "*

*"Isn't that interfering with children's socialization? I can just visualize my child sitting in a room with one of my friends while I'm out getting some refreshments and refusing to speak."*

Of course it is not an ideal situation, and it does hinder socialization. It also requires much anticipation of events on the part of the parent or other caretaker. To avoid antisocial behavior in the situation you described, you would have to take your child, and perhaps even the guest, to get the refreshments ready so the child would not be confronted with a strange visitor.

*"I am glad you always refer to the 'parent or other caretaker,' because I am working outside the home and it is important for me to instruct the caretaker, too."*

We are fully aware that many mothers now work outside the home full- or part-time. They do have to depend in these crucial years on other caretakers, and they need to know how to instruct the caretakers about many issues. With reference to the incident of the janitor giving the child candy, another admonition to children is, for example, "We must not take anything from anybody—not candy, a lollipop, a cookie, not anything—unless Mommy [or name the child's caretaker] says you may."

*"That is one of the big issues for my child and it worries me. I wonder what I should do if she asks me why? I don't want to say because it may be a bad person who may want to hurt you. I don't think she'd buy it anyway."*

At this age, children are beginning to ask "Why?" But an involved explanation may be too much for them to comprehend and result in another "Why?" It is better to say simply but firmly, "That's the way to do it" or "That's the way everyone does it. No one takes things from someone we don't know if Mommy [or the caretaker] doesn't say it is all right to take it." When they are older—say, four or five—they may be able to understand "Because it is dangerous" or "Because they may give you something that isn't for you" or even "Because they may give you something that isn't good for you."

*"I'm always afraid that someone will entice my child to go with them to kidnap her for ransom, or to sexually abuse her. I want to protect her but not scare her."*

■                                                          ■

We want to shield our children and not make them anxious. We have the impulse to "tell it like it is" in order to protect them, but they are too young to understand. However, they can understand an explanation like "Never go anywhere with anyone even if they give you candy and are nice unless Mommy [or the caretaker] says you may. You must always ask Mommy [or the caretaker] first. All children must do that." It is important to emphasize that this is what all children must do, so it doesn't appear to your child that it applies only to her.

*"Recently there have been reports that children have been molested by baby-sitters in their own homes and in day-care centers. What about this problem?"*

These are very grave situations. To counter them, parents need first to have the kind of relationship with their children in which they feel free to confide in the parent—and feel the parent will listen and not disbelieve them. In addition, they have to know that they have a right not to let anyone touch their bodies where they do not want to be touched. That means family members and friends as well. Children seem to have a gut feeling when something's not right, but it helps them to know they have parental support. You can say, for example "Remember, you can tell anyone who touches you that you don't want them to touch you and that you don't like it and to stop it. Then you must tell me about it, even if they tell you not to. I'm your mommy, and I need to know all about what you do. That's the best way."

This is certainly a distasteful situation, but in these times precautions need to be taken as sensitively and appropriately as we know how.

*"Another situation that bothers me is robbers and burglars entering the house in the guise of a serviceperson. My son likes to run to the door now and can reach the knob to open it. I feel I have to tell him not to open the door for anyone. But how can I tell him that it may be someone who has come to rob us?"*

This is another situation that requires a set of precautions, restrictions, and admonitions that are unpleasant for the child. Fortunately, there are some physical precautions that may be taken, such as putting chains on outside doors and installing peepholes. You can also offer a brief explanation, such as "Remember, Mommy has to see who it is before we open the door, for we never open the door unless Mommy [or the caretaker] is there to look out and see who is there. Sometimes we have to ask who it is and what they want."

*"I have noticed that you say 'we have to' instead of 'you must.' Why is that?"*

"You must . . ." sounds like a command. Children do not respond to commands well. "We . . ." connotes a cooperative effort that children can respond to more easily. All of these efforts we are making to help children protect themselves require unpleasant limitations, and we want as much cooperation and compliance from the children as possible.

## *The Second Child*

Some parents may be planning to have another child now. They may feel that the first child is now more ready to accept a sibling, but they may still not know just what to expect. When the children were not quite two, we discussed the issues involved in having a second child before the first was old enough to be able to express feelings verbally. The children were still too young to have achieved bowel and bladder control, to begin to accept separation, and to socialize with peers and some adults. What are your expectations now that the children are almost three and have achieved some of these goals?

*"We waited until now to have our second child because we thought it would be easier for our son to understand what was happening and what to expect when a new baby arrives. He is saying much more and is beginning to tell us how he feels—that he is tired or hungry or wants to play, for example. He understands so much more of what we tell him, so we think we will be able to prepare him for a brother or sister."*

*"We had our second child when our son was just twenty months old. He was very confused when the new baby came home and he had to wait sometimes for attention. That is my one regret over not waiting longer. I think at times he still has feelings of disbelief that the baby is here to stay."*

It is realistic to expect that the children can now understand explanations about the arrival of a new baby. Even more important, they can ask questions that indicate just what their views and expectations are, so parents can help them understand about the baby.

### *Expectations*

*"How much can we expect them to tell us?"*

For example, if you tell your child that soon you will be going to a hospital and you will bring back a baby, your child may say, "Mommy don't go to hospital." His response indicates that he is troubled by your going away. You can then allay his anxiety about what he is going to be doing while you are away and who is going to take care of him. You can tell him that he can talk to you on the telephone and just when you will be coming home. Some hospitals now allow siblings to visit, so you may be able to tell him that he can come to see you. If this is not possible, just showing him the hospital may take some of the mystery away. If the hospital offers a tour for siblings prior to delivery, he can participate in that. He may come to feel he is a participant in the baby's arrival and not an outsider.

■                                                                            ■

*"We are going to have a baby in a little over two months. Our daughter will be three and one month. I tried to emphasize the playmate aspect of having a brother or sister. But recently I heard her tell her playmates that she was going to have a brother and that he would play ball with her. Now I know how big she expects the baby to be and that I have to help her understand that it will be a while before they play ball together."*

While you are explaining what the baby will be able to do, you can also explain just what she will be able to do with the baby. For example, you can tell her that she can shake a rattle to get his attention and to divert him when crying; that she can help wheel his carriage, sing and talk to him, or assist with the bath by handing you soap, powder, or a towel. This will add to her feeling of importance and belonging. It is better not to list all of these items at once, but to mention them from time to time as the opportunity arises.

## Sharing Mother

*"One of my friends has a new baby. Her first child is a girl of three. Every time my friend tries to tend to the baby, the girl claims she needs something desperately—anything to take the mother's attention away from the baby. Whatever toy the baby holds or looks at, she wants. I was quite surprised to see such rivalry. I thought that by three children were better able to share."*

Children around three years of age are beginning to be able to share toys, usually by taking turns. Sometimes they may be able to share spontaneously with children they know. At other times, they share less readily. However, sharing a parent, particularly the mother, is more difficult and may take a great deal of adjustment on both the parents' and the child's part. One way to deal with this issue is to have the older child involved in the care of the baby in ways that are appropriate for her. When the child's efforts are recognized, she gets a sense of achievement that raises her self-esteem and gives her a sense of accomplishment.

## Relating to Baby

*"When I was about three and my younger brother was a baby, I told my mother to send him back. I've heard that other children do it too. Is it because they don't know they are related to the baby?"*

Most children this age are beginning to understand how members of a family are related to each other. They can recognize grandparents, whom they may see often and for whom they may have developed affection early, and they can understand that aunts and uncles are sisters and brothers of their parents. For most children it is around this same age that they can begin to understand that the new baby is a member of the family and here to stay. A child can be told, for example, that the baby is a sister just as

Aunt Jane is mother's sister. Helping a child unravel these relationships is one of the enjoyable parts of being a parent.

## Regression

*"My sister's son is a little over three years old. She had a baby girl about a month ago. Her son has been completely toilet trained for about six months, but he began to wet and soil himself a week after the baby came. Is that just to get his mother's attention?"*

*"A friend of mine has had a problem with her three-and-a-half-year-old daughter ever since she brought her new baby home. Her daughter was completely weaned from the bottle at around two, but now she refuses to drink from a cup. Is it normal for children to go back a step when a new baby comes into the picture? We're expecting a new baby in about six months, and I'd like to be prepared."*

Regressions happen frequently when a new baby is brought home. The older child may see the parent shower so much attention upon the baby and feel that he would like to have that attention, too. He is not so far past the time when he was a baby—wearing diapers, using a bottle—and he remembers the comfort and attention that he received. But it is a transitory reaction.

*"What do you do to get over it? My sister was very upset and scolded her son and said he was too big a boy for that, but he hasn't stopped. There are scenes each day over this situation."*

It is better not to scold the child. That simply adds insult to the injury he feels over having so much attention paid to the baby. He can't understand why it is acceptable for the baby to wet and soil, but it is not acceptable for him to do it. It may help to say something like "I guess you wanted to be a baby again. You used to use a diaper when you were a baby. Now you are a big boy and can use the toilet. The baby can't do that." Then list some of the other things he can do that the baby can't do yet—playing ball or anything else that the child enjoys doing. Then say no more about the incident. If it happens again, change him without reproving or comforting him. When he does use the toilet, acknowledge it and let him know you are pleased that he is your big boy again. Throughout the day, continue to recognize other mature things he can do that the baby cannot. The regression will be overcome more quickly if this approach is used.

*"Is it the same with bottles? I'd hate to have to go back to them once my child was weaned."*

It is much the same situation. The child may watch the baby being held and cuddled by mother while being fed. That scene may bring back memories for her of being in that blissful state. If the child refuses her cup and requests a bottle, the best approach is to give it to her without comment or cuddling. The child may find that milk doesn't taste so good

■                                                                              ■

coming through the rubber nipple and relinquish it after one or two tastes. It may also help to sit with the child, even hold her on the lap, while she drinks from the cup, then refuse to hold her when she drinks from the bottle. Some children want to be breast-fed when observing the baby nurse but when allowed to try it find it is not as pleasant as they remembered and soon give it up. In general, the less fuss made the sooner the regression is overcome.

*"I know it is not possible to manage your life so that the older child feels no displacement by the younger child. But what about giving the baby over to the care of a helper and trying to spend as much time as before with the older child? Or is it better to give up the care of the older child to the helper so he will get undivided attention while the mother takes care of the baby?"*

Of course, both children need their mother and her consistent care. However, if you have a choice it is probably better for you to spend as much time as you can with the older child and try to keep her routine as normal as possible. If the older child is in a nursery school for part of the day, the mother has exclusive time with the baby then. When the older child is home, the mother can arrange to have some exclusive time with her if there is someone to help with the baby. Each family has to work out an approach that is best for that family. A grandmother or aunt may be glad to mind the baby while the parent spends time with the older child. Or parents can spell each other. Working parents especially need to plan special times which each will devote to the children.

## Becoming a Family

*"It sounds as though each child needs so much individual attention. How do they ever get to be a family?"*

Perhaps we have been focusing too much on how to help the older child after a baby has arrived. One of the ways to achieve that is to involve the older child in play with and care of the baby. Parents have to be careful to present play with the baby and its care as a privilege and a bonus—not an obligation. Presented that way, involvement with the baby's care is more likely to be assumed with pleasure and a sense of heightened self-esteem. That helps draw the family together. Of course, there will be days when everything goes smoothly, and those when they do not.

# Grandparents and In-laws

Grandparents play varying roles in the lives of their grandchildren. Some are an important part of the grandchildren's life; others hardly see their grandchildren—because of physical distance or work commitments, for example. What is the relationship between your children and their grandparents?

■                                                                                          ■

*"My parents are dead, and my husband's parents live three thousand miles away. They are too old to travel, and we have not been able to go to visit them. But we talk to them on the phone often and exchange pictures and presents. So my son knows he has grandparents, but that is about it."*

*"My parents live down the street, and we are in each other's houses part of each day. So the relationship is a close one. My husband's parents live quite far away, so they can visit only once every other week. Our son knows both sets of grandparents and has good relationships with all of them. I suppose that is an unusual situation."*

We have hit on two extremes all at once. It is difficult to help a child feel related to grandparents who are so far away, but parents can remind their child that grandparents do exist and care about the child deeply. In the other situation, the child has the good fortune to have two sets of grandparents, and he can spend a lot of time with one set. This gives him the advantages of having an extended family.

*"How important is it for a child to have grandparents and to be close to them? I'm asking this because I feel my parents only interfere with the way I want to bring up my child."*

*"My mother lives with us and is a constant companion and baby-sitter for our child. So no matter how much we differ on some things, the good she does outweighs any occasional disagreement we may have. She gives me a great deal of freedom."*

## Grandparents Who Baby-sit

*"My mother isn't working, but she has six grown children. She says she has done all the baby-sitting she is going to do. No one helped her when her children were little, she says, and all her children will have to do their own baby-sitting just as she did."*

*"In our case, our son is the only grandchild. My parents and my husband's parents have sort of a rivalry to see who can be the baby-sitter. They urge us to leave our son with them if we want to go away. They are also willing to come to our house. Our son likes them all and has certain things he prefers to do with each. One set are entertainers, so they like to sing and play singing and dancing games. The other set likes to do things such as visit the park and the zoo."*

As you have all been saying, families have different needs and ways of doing things. The role of grandparents as baby-sitters is a very important one, especially since good baby-sitters are hard to find and are too expensive for some families. However, grandparents should be permitted other roles with respect to their grandchildren. It is good for children to have other individuals to relate to, with whom they feel secure, whose presence they enjoy, and from whom they can learn. Some grandparents can be models and teachers.

## Financial Support

*"We needed some financial help after the baby came and I stopped working. Our parents came to our rescue, and we didn't have to ask them. They*

*knew there would be an increase in expenses so they offered to help. They don't baby-sit, but they do care."*

*"We've been talking here about grandparents who help in some way. What about when it's the other way round—when you have to help them because they are sick or can't afford to take care of themselves, or both?"*

These are both difficult issues—needing either to accept from, or give to, grandparents time, effort, or financial help. These are realities of life, and the way you handle them sets an example for your children. If the parent has to give up too much time and effort to care for a grandparent, the child may come to resent the grandparent. But if the child has established a good relationship with that grandparent, the child may learn compassion for other human beings.

## Children's Feelings Toward Grandparents

Let's discuss your children's feelings about their grandparents.

*"I hate to say this, but my son is afraid of his grandfather, who is a big, jolly, hearty man with a loud voice. When he comes to visit us, my son cries and clings to me and will not go to him at all. At first that was a disappointment to my father. Now my son is fearful and stands back from him for about an hour. Finally he begins to play with him. Is that an unusual situation?"*

Some children need time to size up a visitor, to see if he is friendly and safe to get close to. Large people with loud voices intimidate some children. A grandfather who is an infrequent visitor may be a virtual stranger to the child, and the child must get used to him. The child needs to know that he is not considered to be behaving strangely and that he will not be forced to make contact with grandfather. In time, grandfather and grandson will be friends if the child is supported by understanding parents and the grandfather is helped to understand the child's needs.

*"My husband's mother recently had a stroke. She gets around now with the help of a cane, and her speech is not clear. When she comes into a room she makes quite a commotion, and my daughter is afraid of her. My mother-in-law was a very pleasant person before the stroke, and my daughter can't understand what has happened. I hold her hand while I try to help Grandma, and she is beginning to help too. She is beginning to understand that Grandma had a 'boo boo' and we are helping her get better."*

How parents deal with a situation sets an example for the child. You showed your child how you helped her disabled grandmother, giving your child support by holding her hand until she followed suit. You helped your daughter overcome her fear by explaining Grandma's condition. It is important that you did not seem upset by Grandma and did not try to avoid having her around. Children's fear is allayed more by the parents' behavior than by any explanation.

## Interfering with Routine

*"My father loves to stop by at night on his way home and play with our son. He gets our son all excited and then leaves. So when Daddy comes home our son is all keyed up and can't settle down for his dinner and bedtime."*

*"Our daughter can't wait to have her grandparents come. They enjoy each other so much. But when they come, all my discipline goes out the window. With them there are no limits to cookies or candy. No toy is too expensive. There is no limit to her running, and no bedtime. When they leave, it takes her several days to get back to normal."*

*"We have the same situation. I'm afraid that my child is going to prefer her grandparents to me because I set limits and they don't."*

*"That is better than a grandparent who is so wrapped up in herself that when she comes to visit she hardly pays attention to the child. My mother-in-law seems to be jealous of the attention we pay our son. She pouts if I have to attend to my son and she has to wait for something."*

Indulgent grandparents do not harm the children. The children will not love them more than their parents—just differently. The extra cookie or later bedtime or excited play all make for good memories of childhood and grandparents. However, if it is too upsetting to the parents, it is always possible to talk it over with grandparents in a kindly way and to set up the kind of things and the manner of play they can find acceptable. Most children learn what to expect from grandparents and parents, and they accept the difference.

A grandparent who seems uninterested in her grandchild may change her ways if she is shown how. She may not know how to assume her role as a grandparent. We tend to think grandparents should naturally know how to be grandparents, and we are annoyed if they don't. Some need to be helped to accept and enjoy the role.

*"My child loves to have his grandmother tell him stories about what it was like when his father was a little boy and how he behaved. During these sessions, my son is quiet and attentive, and he asks questions. He also wants to know about his aunts and uncles and cousins."*

That is a wonderful way for children to learn about their families and family relationships. It is a good experience for the child, and a good way for a grandparent to establish a strong relationship with the child.

## Learning About Their Roots

*"My father-in-law is quite European in his ways, and he likes to tell our children about how it was 'in the old country.' He tells them stories about different family events, how holidays were celebrated . . . things like that. I think they are learning a lot from him."*

■                                                                                     ■

I am sure you are right. Grandparents make a valuable contribution when they teach children about their cultural heritage and family history.

## *Religion and Spirituality*

Now that the children are becoming more active and participating in more activities with you, have some of you been wondering about the introduction of religion and ethics?

*"We've been attending religious services since our daughter was an infant. We had no one to leave her with and since we always attended church we just took her and one of us held her. If she cried, one of us just stepped outside with her."*

*"We've been doing the same with our son, but now that he is older and active it's difficult to keep him quiet during a whole service. One of us may have to go outside with him."*

*"At our church there is a baby-sitting service that we use. Once in a while they call on us to come to help, but most of the time it works."*

*"Our church has set up a play group. The children color books with religious pictures, and around special holidays they learn to sing religious songs. It's geared for young children and is not high pressure at all. The children seem to enjoy it, so we were intending to enter our son as soon as he is three."*

*"Our church offers a program like that, but it starts with two-year-olds. We tried to have our daughter attend, but she would have none of it. She sometimes stands at the door and watches, but only if one of us is with her. We don't want to leave her there crying, because then she'd probably fuss about going to church with us."*

*"My husband and I had very little formal religious instruction. We see the pleasure and comfort some of our peers and their families derive from religion. We feel we'd like our child to have that experience. Is it too soon to begin?"*

The children are still a little too young for formal religious training. They are not verbal enough; nor do they have the necessary conceptual ability. However, some children may be able to separate from parents long enough to spend time in a play group while the parents are attending service.

*"I don't think such young children need formal religious teaching. I think they should be set an example of love and kindness at home, in the way family members talk and act to each other. I wasn't born in this country. In my country the church was mostly for christenings, marriages, and funerals. The real teaching was in the home. That's the way we want it for our son."*

*"Doesn't each family have to do what they think is right according to the way they were brought up?"*

In our country that is the accepted way. However, we are talking about formal religions as they are practiced by different denominations. We are also concerned with ethical issues that are introduced in the home when children are very young and that become the foundation for belief systems.

## Belief Systems

*"Could you explain belief systems?"*

Let's use the example of a mother doing everything in the same order each day for an infant. The infant gets a sense that his day follows a predictable sequence. This helps him develop trust in his mother. When parents are consistently available to fill an infant's needs, the infant establishes trust in them. He has faith that his mother will be there for him. That faith can be the basis for religious faith.

## Trust

*"Do you mean that the baby's ability to trust his parents makes it possible for him to later have faith in God?"*

A child has to be able to trust his parents before he can then trust others. To small children, parents are all-knowing, all-loving, all-powerful beings whom they trust to satisfy their needs. When they grow older they can extend that feeling to a higher power, depending on the religious practices the family embraces.

*"This aspect of being a parent was never part of my thinking. Are there other ways that we influence our children in the area of religion?"*

Let's take setting limits. From the time a child learns to reach out and touch objects, we stop her if the act is harmful and substitute an approved activity. In other words, we set firm limits on disapproved activities and enthusiastically offer approved ones. The child gradually internalizes a whole catalog of do's and don'ts. In this way she learns to distinguish between the approved and disapproved activities of her society. This experience readies her for later acceptance of religious sanctions.

*"We were brought up in a very strict religious denomination. It put fear in our hearts about the least little transgression. Almost everything seemed to be a sin. We don't want that for our child."*

If that was your experience and you were not happy with it, you have every right to make a different choice for your child.

## Sharing and Caring

*"How else do we influence our children's preparation for religious activities? I have in mind spiritual qualities such as loving, sharing, and caring."*

Sharing is something that our children are just beginning to achieve. We help them by teaching them to take turns. At this age, they may be able to take turns with a tricycle in the park or share a cookie with friends. If sharing is not forced on them prematurely, it may come easily to them for the rest of their lives.

Parents teach caring by modeling it for their child—by showing love and care for each other and the child, and by demonstrating concern for each other, other members of the family, and friends.

*"I can see that all the time when my daughter plays with her dolls. She sets up an exact copy of the way we sound, what we say, and how we react. So I guess that is the way she will treat people when she grows up."*

*"What about Bible stories? At our church children are told Bible stories during nursery sessions. We aren't sure our child is ready for them yet."*

Some children this age are able to listen to longer stories, depending on how much the story is simplified conceptually and how much participation and action is supplied in the telling. Some Bible stories can be frightening to children. Or the stories may be too removed from the children's range of experience to be appreciated. Parents should decide about their own child's readiness and whether the manner of presentation is appropriate for the child.

## Belonging to a Group

*"Why should a child be burdened with all the trappings of organized religion when the parents can teach them so many fundamentals at home?"*

It is true that parents can teach the fundamentals of a belief system at home. However, belonging to a particular religious group also helps a child establish group identity. As she grows, this ability can give her a sense of belonging and of being accepted in a social institution. Some of you have expressed a certain remorse over having missed out on this. Each family must make a decision on this issue in view of family members' background, culture, personalities, and experiences. Each family needs to bear in mind that their decision is right for them and that another family's solution is right for that family. Religion is an emotional and social experience that can remain important throughout the child's life.

# Feelings Parenting Evokes

We've spent much time these past months discussing patience, consistency, firmness, creativity, and the many other demands made of parents. So this may be a good time to look at the feelings that parents experience. Some parents may be so busy that they have not even had time to give this subject any thought.

*"I was raised in a large family. Children were considered part of the obligation of marriage; raising them was a job like any other. Love meant*

taking care of us. When my son was born, I stayed home while my wife worked. It was then that my views on child rearing changed. I got such a sense of satisfaction from making him comfortable and seeing him contented after a burp or a little play. That feeling has continued. I suppose my parents felt that way too, but I didn't understand then."

Being a parent can make one more understanding of one's own parents and upbringing.

"I think at first I was scared. The first day my husband went to work and my mother left, there I was a parent, responsible for a human being. Gradually that scared feeling began to lessen, and I began to learn how to notice all the little things the baby did in response to what I did. That got to be fun. I felt I was really learning to be a mother instead of a scared little girl. Now I like the role. I like the job."

"My feelings are very simple. I got my first kick when our baby smiled for the first time. Then I knew I was 'in' as a parent; and ever since, the laughs and hugs make my day. Even if a dozen other things go wrong in the day, that smile makes up for everything."

"I guess I've been what is called a doting father. I can't wait to get home to have my child come running to greet me. We exchange a big hug, and then he wants to play. Finally I get to say hello to my wife, but it seems he comes first now."

"That's the part that used to get to me. When my husband came home and seemed not to pay any attention to me, I felt very jealous. One day we discussed it, and it suddenly dawned on me that I was feeling left out the way I did as a kid when my father paid attention to the new baby after me. Now I enjoy the pleasure my husband and son get from each other."

That experience is common among young mothers, but more often it happens to fathers.

## Fathers' Feelings

"I come from a family which by present standards is very old-fashioned. My father got the red-carpet treatment when he came home, and we kids knew it. So I was quite upset after our baby came to see what a back seat I took. The boys at the office who were fathers kidded me about it and set me straight. Then I began to notice more about the baby, and my wife pointed out things about him. He began to be 'our baby,' not just hers, and that makes me feel good. I realize that I no longer feel the need to be waited on by my wife. I get my attention from her and the baby in a different way, because they are so glad to see me when I get home."

"I sometimes try to think back over the three years to what has given me the most joy. I think of the baby's first smile, of course, and the excitement over the first tooth. But the baby's first steps was the most exciting moment by far."

A child's early advances and accomplishments are exciting moments for parents. All parents feel differently about different "firsts."

*"The most thrilling part for us now is the talking. We are a very verbal family, and it means so much to have our child able to talk with us. It has been such fun to watch her speech develop. The first word, 'Da, Da,' was such a thrill. Then came 'Mama,' and then so many more words in quick succession. Now she speaks in full sentences, and we feel we have a real person."*

*"Ever since our baby began to talk, I felt he was more of a person. Now that he can speak in sentences, he is getting to be a real companion. I don't feel so lonesome anymore when we are together."*

*"Besides the talking, there's the sprouting of ideas. Our child now seems to be making so many more connections. We noticed a while back when he asked where the mailman lived. Before that he knew where we lived and that his grandparents and his little friend lived in different places. Then he became interested in knowing the relationship of one person to another. It was very exciting to watch his mind develop and to help him."*

Language and communication are a very important part of a child's development, something that most parents look forward to eagerly. Language is what differentiates man from other animals. It would not happen if parents did not speak to their children and model language. It is one of the important parts of a parent's job and one that can give a parent much pleasure, as some of you have pointed out.

*"I think I enjoy most the advances our child is making in talking. I feel we are getting to know and understand him better, and he seems to be learning more about us and the world. I feel now there is more of an opportunity to teach him things and that gives me a feeling of being important and having a real purpose."*

## The Parent as Teacher

Parents are the child's first teachers, although the role of the parent as a teacher is one that some parents are not always conscious of. The child can learn more from her parents in her first three years than she learns in the rest of her life. Her initial understanding of the world is through her parents.

*"I used to worry that I might not be doing the right things as a role model for our child. But as our child reached each milestone—smiling, walking, talking, playing, discovering the world and mostly enjoying it—I began to feel more secure and good about being a parent."*

It is interesting to hear you say "mostly enjoying it," because a child's level of happiness is a measure of his development and of how well he is doing overall.

A child is generally thought to be secure and comfortable with himself and his surroundings if he can express joy at his achievements and when, in response to the support of his parents and other aspects of his environment, he is stimulated to explore and achieve more.

*"But we can't all be happy with our children all the time. There are times when they need a little discipline, and they are not happy about that."*

A child may not be happy at the time that she has to accept some limit to her activity. But in the long run a child whose parents have set consistent limits feels secure and comfortable, because she knows that there are boundaries that she can count on. Usually, a secure child is happy and content.

*"Since very early in our son's life we've heard it said that consistent limits lead to a better parent-child relationship and a happier family. In fact, watching him learn to accept limits—beginning with not touching a hot radiator, then not pulling the cat's tail, then holding my hand crossing streets—has given me more satisfaction as a parent than almost anything else."*

*"I used to think that when I became a parent my children would behave. I thought you just had to order a child severely once and that took care of it. Well, I've learned otherwise. It took a lot of patience and perseverance on our part, but we think our child is pretty well behaved and likable, and that's a pleasure and satisfaction that's very special to us."*

Teaching discipline by setting consistent limits while being firm and patient is one of the hardest parts of parenting. Once parents realize that they can achieve this without being police officers to their children, the role becomes very rewarding.

## Enjoying New Things

*"I've had to become interested in so many new things for my child's sake. I've taken her swimming, taught her arts and crafts, and given her an appreciation for music—all things I've never had time for myself. Although it's still on a very primary level, it's added a different dimension to my life."*

*"Having a child has made us think harder about the world we are bringing her up in. We've become more involved in what goes on in our community and the political situation. I think we've grown a lot. Maybe it would have come anyway, but having a child seemed to give us an added incentive."*

*"I have noticed that having my own child has made me more tolerant of and interested in children in general. I care now what happens to children—what kind of world they are inheriting, whether they are happy or not, et cetera. I think I'm a better person for it. It makes life more interesting too."*

These are some of the more subtle themes of having children, and I'm glad you are recognizing them. You all seem to be realizing that you play an important role as advocates for children.

■          ■

*"For me the most satisfying part of being a parent is knowing that there is someone who needs me and loves me and whom I love."*

*"I'm a single parent. It hasn't been easy for me to be breadwinner, teacher, and both parents to my child, but it makes me feel very important and needed, and that makes it all worthwhile for me."*

The affectional aspects of being a parent are important for most parents. It is good for a parent to feel needed and for a child to feel secure that there is someone who will always be available to fulfill his or her needs.

It is obvious that different aspects of parenting affect each parent differently. All in all, it is clear from our discussions that being a parent is an important and diverse role that has many rewards.

# 28

We have come to the end of the three years of the parenting program. We have had many discussions and made many discoveries. What do you view as the major developments in these three years?

*"As a father who can't spend too much time with his son, I notice most the way he gets around now—how active he is on his tricycle, how much better he runs. He can even throw a ball and sometimes he catches it if you can place it right. Come to think of it, that's the way we have fun together."*

*"My wife and I both work, so we look forward to our child's exuberant greeting when we come home. She is so happy to see us and follows us around chattering as we change clothes. She's getting to be a friend and companion."*

*"I'm home most of the time, and I also notice the terrific exuberance about everything. Our daughter is now able to play quite a while, and she is so busy all the time. She moves about so fast that I just can't keep up with her."*

*"Our son is also exuberant and active. He's a lot of fun, but he is a handful. He has to be watched every minute, I don't know how my wife does it all day. I'm pooped after the weekend."*

Some of the children are beginning to be much more active and more exuberant. Although they can play a little longer on their own, they need to be watched carefully, because they are very curious and want to explore new objects and places that may be dangerous.

### Judgment

*"When can I begin to rely on my child's judgment? I guess what I mean is: How long do I have to be so watchful?"*

That question can't be answered specifically. Good judgment comes with maturity and experience, so children acquire it at different stages of development.

## Language

"The advance that I find most astonishing and pleasing is the acquisition of language. My child is actually beginning to converse. She picks up everything she hears. The other day she said to our sitter, 'That is not necessary' when the sitter wanted to help her with a toy. I nearly fell over."

"Picking up new words is great, but it has its drawbacks. My daughter was watching her father hammering a nail into the wall. He missed the nail and hit his finger, and he came out with a 'damn.' She has been repeating it every occasion she gets."

Children imitate what they see and hear. As you have discovered, this can result in amusing or embarrassing situations.

"What should a parent do in a situation like that? The first time we were taken by surprise and laughed, but after that it didn't seem very funny."

Sometimes it is helpful to say something like "Daddy didn't mean to say that. It is not a word to say every day." If the child continues to use the offensive word, ignore it. Use of the word will gradually disappear through lack of reinforcement.

## New Interests

"Along with the increasing conversation, I like the interest my daughter shows in looking at books and wanting to tell what is in the pictures. We spend a lot of time doing that."

"I find the interest my son has in exploring new situations—the bank, the post office, and, of course, the children's room at the library—has increased. He wants to know what is going on everywhere and who is doing what."

Talking with children, listening to them, reading to them, and taking them on small excursions give them experiences that stimulate their concept formation and increase their interest in and understanding of the world around them. That's a part of parenting that many people find exciting.

"I'm not so involved in areas like bathing and dressing our child, but I can't wait to get home some nights just to hear his new discoveries and ideas."

## Socializing

"One thing that is making life a little easier and pleasanter for me is the way my daughter is beginning to behave in her play with other children. She doesn't grab everything the other child has. She is more willing to share or even exchange a toy than she was before. I sometimes hear her say, 'I play with the doll, okay?'"

"I've noticed that too. My son can play amicably with some children for a much longer time. But sometimes it doesn't work that way, and we can't figure it out."

■                                                                    ■

Children have good days and bad days. But you may be noticing that your child plays better with children she knows—a child that she regards as a friend. Problems are more likely to arise with new playmates—children whose ways are not familiar to your child. These situations require a lot of parental involvement and monitoring.

## Manners

"I've noticed that my child is beginning to be better about manners. He more often uses a spoon and fork instead of his hands. He sometimes even says 'Hello' and 'Good-bye.'"

"My child is getting better with 'Thank you' and sometimes even 'Please.'"

"I just can't say we are making much progress with manners. I can't seem to make a dent in that area."

"I'm not impatient with my son's lack of manners, but his grandmother reminds me about it and that gets me on edge."

It's natural to want children to make their grandparents happy about their behavior. But we have to bear in mind that grandparents sometimes forget when certain behavior develops. You can say to the grandparent, "We're working on that. He will be doing that pretty soon."

## Separation

"I'm so glad to report that, for the past two months, my son has been able to stay overnight at his grandmother's without crying for us or waking in the night."

"Even though we both work, we are now able to come home, play a little with our daughter, and go out for dinner or a movie or just visit without the wailing and tears from her. She doesn't like it, and wants to know when we will be home, but it is usually much easier. We do it quite regularly now, and she is getting used to the routine."

Most of the children are showing a great deal of progress with separation, but some may not be able to separate easily and comfortably even at three. Even children age five or six and older are reluctant to separate at times. They need support and reassurance, not disapproval.

## Toilet Training

"My child is now toilet trained. He just decided he was ready and asked to be taken to the bathroom. He had good control in just a couple of days. I was so surprised and pleased."

"My child has achieved control during the day, but occasionally at night she has an accident. So we still use diapers at night."

Achieving bowel and bladder control is a big concern for most parents. In this area, as in others, children have their own timetables of readiness.

Most are ready around age three—but that is not a magic number. Control is achieved by some children well before three and by others well after. Parents should never try to force toilet training on a child.

## Sleep

*"My son used to wake several times a night and come into our room, but that has stopped almost entirely. When it does happen, it is usually when there is some change in routine coming up—a business trip or a vacation, for instance."*

## The Final Bottle

*"My daughter still has a bottle at bedtime. I'll be so glad when she gives it up. She drinks perfectly well from a cup."*

*"My son had given up bottles on his own by the time he was two and a half. But when our daughter was born three months ago, he watched her having one and decided he needed bottles, too. I had been warned, so it didn't upset me. It lasted about a week; now he is back to cups for his milk and juice."*

Giving up the bottle is harder for some children than it is for others. When they are ready, most children give up bottles on their own; others need a little more support. Some give them up when they start nursery school and become busy with more mature activities. A few may be made anxious by nursery school or another change in routine and may cling to a bottle for a sense of security. As we have said so often, the speed with which your child achieves bowel and bladder control and relinquishes bottles are not the achievements by which you should measure success as a parent.

## Accepting Limits

*"Our biggest achievement is that our child has learned to accept some limits when we set them consistently. We are no longer always saying, 'No, don't do that. Let's do it this way.' We have gotten him to close the refrigerator door, not slam doors, and not run across the street. Just that has made life so much more comfortable."*

*"Achieving discipline without having to yell has been the hardest part for us."*

*"Setting limits by being firm and consistent without losing my temper— that's the hardest part of parenting for me. My husband manages better— or at least it seems to me that it is easier for him to be consistent."*

I agree that it is hard. But it is also one of the most important issues of parenting. As we have pointed out before, it is an important part of the process of learning what is and is not acceptable behavior in our society. It is the basis for the development of a conscience later on. It is an ongoing issue for parents, because new and different limits are needed as the child grows. Parents who have achieved the ability to be firm and consistent without being harsh will find that this approach continues to be useful.

## *Preview of the Fourth Year*

Let's preview what is in store in the coming year. The children will be able to play longer and share better, but not always. They will continue to be exuberant, at times even boisterous. There will be a big jump in their attention span and their cognitive ability. Some of their questions will be probing and difficult to answer. Their imaginations will flourish. It should be a very exciting and enjoyable time for all of you.

Coming to the end of these parenting sessions has its rewards. You can all look back on days when comforting, changing, feeding, and burping a baby were your main concerns and you felt so inadequate. But look at your children now. They can walk, run, jump, and climb. They can now communicate, express ideas, and socialize. They are learning to accept limits. They are beginning to tell right from wrong, and beginning to have manners. They are able to separate better. They are more aware of the needs and views of others. Many are toilet trained or about to be. They are happy and competent children. This progress is due in great part to your ability to care for them. You can all be very proud of your achievement.

You have a good foundation in parenting. You will be able to use the policies of dealing with physical activity, discipline, judgment, socialization, separation, communication, and support throughout your children's lives.

# Suggested Reading

The verbal ability and concentration of children expand greatly between twelve and thirty-six months. The books on the following list vary from cloth and cardboard books with few or no words to paper books with simple story lines. If a child shows impatience or restlessness while looking at a particular book, the parent should try a different one. Children may have quite different interests, even at this early age, and the age at which each will enjoy a particular book will vary as well.

Parents and children can make their own books of pictures cut from magazines and pasted on cardboard. Children also enjoy looking at albums of photographs of themselves and hearing stories about themselves.

Adams, George, and Henning, Paul. *First Things*. New York: Platt and Munk.
*At the Table; Going for a Ride; In the House; Trucks*. 1981. Los Angeles: Price/Stern/Sloan *(cardboard)*.
*Baby's First Book*. New York: Platt and Munk *(cardboard or cloth)*.
Barton, Byron. 1986. *Trucks; Boats*. New York: Thomas Y. Crowell.
Battagna. Aurelius. 1976. *Come Walk with Me; I Look Out My Window; This Is My House; Let's Go Shopping; A Trip to the Zoo*. New York: Playskool Manufacturing Company (recommended by Pushaw, 1976).
*The Bear; The Crane; The Train*. 1979. Copenhagen: Carlsen *(cardboard, no words)*.
Bonforte, Lisa. *Baby Animals*. New York: Golden Press *(cardboard)*.
Boynton, Sandra. 1982. *The Going to Bed Book*. New York: Little Simon.
Bridewell, Norman. 1963. *Clifford, the Big Red Dog*. New York: Scholastic.
Brown, Margaret Wise. 1947. *Good Night Moon*. New York: Harper & Row.
———. 1950. *A Child's Good Night Book*. New York: Scott
———. 1952. *The Duck*. Photographs by Ylla. New York: Harper & Row.
Bruna, Dick. *Dick Bruna's Animal Book*. London: Methuen Books *(cardboard)*.
———. *Miffy at the Zoo; Miffy's Birthday*. London: Methuen Books.
———. *My Meals*. A Dick Bruna Zig Zag Book. London: Methuen Books *(cardboard)*.
Burningham, John. 1974. *The Rabbit*. New York: Thomas Y. Crowell.
———. 1975. *The Baby*. New York: Thomas Y. Crowell.
———. 1975. *The Blanket*. New York: Thomas Y. Crowell.
———. 1976. *The Cupboard*. New York: Thomas Y. Crowell.
Cellini, Joseph. 1958. *ABC*. New York: Grosset and Dunlap *(cardboard)*.

Crews, Donald. 1978. *Freight Train.* New York: Morrow.

———. 1980. *Truck.* New York: Greenwillow Books.

Dunn, Phoebe. 1987. *Busy, Busy Toddlers.* New York: Random House.

Ets, Marie Hall. *Play with Me; Just Like Me.* New York: Viking.

Federico, Helen. 1960. *ABC.* New York: Golden *(cardboard).*

*A First Book in My Garden; A First Book in My Kitchen.* 1980. "Object Lesson" series. England: Brimax Books *(cardboard).*

Flack, Marjorie. *Angus and the Cat; Angus and the Ducks.* New York: Doubleday.

Fujikama, Gyo. 1963. *Babies.* New York: Grosset and Dunlap *(cardboard).*

Gay, Zhenya. *Look!* New York: Viking.

*The Golden Fire Engine Book.* New York: Golden Press *(cardboard).*

Johnson, John E. *The Sky Is Blue; The Grass Is Green.* New York: Random House *(cloth).*

Kalan, Robert. 1979. *Blue Sea.* New York: Morrow.

Kessler, Ethel and Leonard. *Do Baby Bears Sit on Chairs?* New York: Doubleday.

Krauss, Ruth. 1945. *The Carrot Seed.* New York: Harper & Row.

———. 1948. *Bears.* New York: Harper & Row.

———. 1949. *The Happy Day.* New York: Harper & Row.

Kunhardt, Dorothy. *Pat the Bunny.* New York: Western.

———. *Tickle the Pig.* New York: Golden.

———. 1984. *Pat the Cat.* New York: Golden.

Lenski, Lois. *Davy's Day.* Henry Z. Walck.

———. *Now It's Fall.* Henry Z. Walck.

———. *I Like Winter.* Henry Z. Walck.

McNaught, Harry. 1976. *Baby Animals.* New York: Random House *(cardboard).*

———. 1976. *Trucks.* New York: Random House.

———. 1979. *Trucks.* New York: Random House.

Matthiesen, Thomas. 1968. *Things to See.* New York: Platt and Munk.

Miller, J. P. 1976. *Big and Little.* New York: Random House *(cardboard).*

———. *Farmer John's Animals.* New York: Random House *(cardboard).*

*My First Toys.* New York: Platt and Munk.

Najaka, Marlies Merk. 1980. *City Cat; Country Cat.* New York: McGraw-Hill *(cardboard).*

*Nursery Rhymes.* 1979. New York: Random House *(cardboard).*

Oxenbury, Helen. 1982. *Beach Day; Good Night, Good Morning; Monkey See, Monkey Do; Mother's Helper; Shopping Trip.* New York: Dial Press *(cardboard, no words).*

———. 1981. *Friends.* New York: Simon and Schuster.

Pfloog, Jan. 1977. *Kittens.* New York: Random House *(cardboard).*

———. 1979. *Puppies.* New York: Random House *(cardboard).*

Pickett, Barbara, and Kovacs, D. 1981. *The Baby Strawberry Book of Pets.* New York: McGraw-Hill *(cardboard).*

———. 1981. *The Baby Strawberry Book of Baby Farm Animals.* New York: McGraw-Hill *(cardboard).*

Rey, H. A. *Anybody at Home?; Feed the Animals; See the Circus; Where's My Baby?* Boston: Houghton-Mifflin.

Rice, Eve. 1977. *Sam Who Never Forgets*. New York: Morrow.

Richter, Mischa. 1978. *Quack?* New York: Harper & Row.

Risom, Ole. 1963. *I Am a Bunny*. New York: Golden Press *(cardboard)*.

Scarry, Patsy. *My Teddy Bear Book*. New York: Golden Press.

Scarry, Richard. 1976. *Early Words*. New York: Random House.

———. 1967. *Egg in the Hole Book*. Racine, Wis.: Western.

———. 1990. *Just Right Word Book*. New York: Random House.

Schlesinger, Alice. 1959. *Baby's Mother Goose*. New York: Grosset and Dunlap *(cardboard)*.

Seiden, Art. 1962. *Kittens; Puppies*. New York: Grosset and Dunlap *(cardboard)*.

"Show Baby" Series: *Bathtime; Bedtime; Mealtime; Playtime*. 1973. New York: Random House *(cardboard)*.

Skarr, Grace. 1968. *What Do the Animals Say?* New York: Young Scott Books.

Steiner, Charlotte. *My Bunny Feels Soft*. New York: Alfred A. Knopf.

*The Tall Book of Mother Goose*. New York: Harper & Row.

Tensen, Ruth M. *Come to the Farm*. Chicago: Reilly and Lee.

*Things That Go*. New York: Platt and Munk *(cloth)*.

Walley, Dean. *Pet Parade*. Kansas City: Hallmark Cards *(cardboard)*.

———, and Cunningham, Edward. *Zoo Parade*. Kansas City: Hallmark Cards *(cardboard)*.

Wells, Rosemary. *Max's First Word; Max's Ride; Max's Toys*. New York: Dial *(cardboard)*.

———. 1985. *Max's Birthday; Max's Breakfast; Max's Bath*. New York: Dial *(cardboard)*.

Wikland, Ilon. *See What I Can Do*. New York: Random House.

Wilkin, Eloise. 1981. *Rock-A-Bye, Baby*. New York: Random House. *(Simple games with rhymes to play with toddlers.)*

Williams, Garth. *Baby Animals*. New York: Western.

———. *Baby's First Book*. New York: Platt and Munk *(cardboard or cloth)*.

———. *The Chicken Book*. New York: Delacorte.

Witte, Pat, and Witte, Eve. *The Touch Me Book*. New York: Western.

———. *Who Lives Here?* New York: Western.

Wolde, Gunilla. *This Is Betsy*. New York: Random House *(series)*.

Woodcock, Louise. *This Is the Way Animals Walk*. W. R. Scott.

Wynne, Patricia. 1977. *The Animal ABC*. New York: Random House *(cardboard)*.

Zaffo, George. *The Giant Nursery Book of Things That Go*. Garden City, N.Y.: Doubleday.

# Bibliography

*Note:* Titles preceded by an asterisk (\*) are especially recommended for parents.

Abrahamson, David. 1969. *Emotional Care of Your Child.* New York: Trident Press.

Ainsworth, Mary D. Salter. 1965. Further research into the adverse effects of maternal deprivation. In *Child Care and Growth of Love,* 2d ed., ed. John Bowlby, 191–241. Harmondsworth, England: Penguin Books.

———. 1967. *Infancy in Uganda: Infant Care and the Growth of Attachment.* Baltimore: The Johns Hopkins University Press.

———. 1969. Object relations, dependency, and attachment: A theoretical review of the infant-mother relationship. *Child Development* 40:969–1025.

Ainsworth, Mary D. Salter, and Bell, Sylvia M. 1972. Attachment, exploration, and separation: Illustrated by behavior of one-year-olds in a strange situation. In *Readings in Child Development,* eds. Irving B. Weiner and David Elkind. New York: John Wiley & Sons.

\*Ames, Louise Bates, and Chase, Joan Ames. 1973. *Don't Push Your Preschooler.* New York: Harper & Row.

Anglund, Sandra. 1968. Here, even infants go to school. *Today's Health.* March, 52–57.

Auerbach, Alice S. 1968. *Parents Learn Through Discussion.* New York: John Wiley & Sons.

Badger, Earladeen D. 1972. A mother's training program. *Children Today* (U.S. Department of Health, Education and Welfare) 1/3:7–11, 35.

Bayley, Nancy. 1940. Mental growth in young children. *Yearbook of the National Society for the Study of Education* 39/2:11–47.

———. 1969. *Bayley Scales of Infant Development.* New York: Psychological Corporation.

Beadle, Muriel. 1970. *A Child's Mind.* New York: Doubleday.

Bel Geddes, Joan. 1974. *How to Parent Alone: A Guide for Single Parents.* Somers, Conn.: Seabury Press.

Bell, Richard Q. 1971. Stimulus control of parent or caretaker behavior by infant. *Developmental Psychology* 4:63–72.

Bell, Sylvia M., and Ainsworth, Mary D. Salter. 1972. Infant crying and maternal responsiveness. *Child Development* 44:1171–90.

Bernstein, B. 1964. Aspects of language and learning in the genesis of the social process. In *Language in Culture and Society: A Reader in Linguistics and Anthropology,* ed. D. Hymes, 251–63. New York: Harper & Row.

Bettleheim, Bruno. 1962. *Dialogues with Mothers.* New York: Free Press.

Bijou, S. W. 1970. *Experiences and the Processes of Socialization.* New York: Academic Press.

Birch, Herbert G. 1970. *Disadvantaged Children: Health, Nutrition, and School Failure.* New York: Harcourt, Brace & World.

Blank, M. 1964. Some maternal influences on infants' rate of sensorimotor development. *Journal of the American Academy of Child Psychiatry* 3:668–87.

Bloom, Benjamin S. 1964. *Stability and Chance in Human Characteristics.* New York: John Wiley & Sons.

Bowlby, John. 1951. *Maternal Care and Mental Health: Report to World Health Organization.* New York: Columbia University Press.

———. 1958. Nature of a child's tie to his mother. *International Journal of Psychoanalysis* 39:350–73.

———. 1960. Grief and mourning in infancy and early childhood. In *The Psychoanalytic Study of the Child.* New York: International Universities Press.

———. 1969–1980. *Attachment and Loss.* 3 vols. (*Attachment; Separation, Anxiety and Anger;* and *Loss, Sadness and Depression*). New York: Basic Books.

*Brazelton, T. Berry. 1969. *Infants and Mothers.* New York: Delacorte.

*———. 1974. *Toddlers and Parents.* New York: Delacorte.

———. 1984. *To Listen to a Child.* Reading, Mass.: Addison-Wesley.

Bresnahan, Jean L., and Blum, William. 1971. Chaotic reinforcement: A socioeconomic leveler. *Developmental Psychology* 4:89–92.

Brim, Orville G., Jr. 1961. Methods of educating parents and their evaluation. In *Prevention of Mental Disorders in Children,* ed. G. Caplan, 122–41. New York: Basic Books.

———. 1965. *Education for Child Rearing.* Reprint. New York: Free Press.

Brody, Grace F. 1969. Maternal childrearing attitudes and child behavior. *Developmental Psychology* 1:66.

Brody, Sylvia, 1956. *Patterns of Mothering.* New York: International Universities Press.

Bronfenbrenner, Urie. 1970. *Two Worlds of Childhood.* New York: Russell Sage Foundation.

Bruner, Jerome S. 1968. *Processes of Cognitive Growth: Infancy.* Worcester, Mass.: Clark University Press.

*Calderone, Mary S. M.D., and Ramsay, James W., M.D. 1982. *Talking with Your Child About Sex: Questions and Answers for Children from Birth to Puberty.* New York: Random House.

Caldwell, Bettye M. 1972. What does research teach us about day care for children under three? *Children Today* (U.S. Department of Health, Education and Welfare) 1/1:6–11.

Caldwell, Bettye M., and Ricciuti, N. N., eds. 1973. *Review of Child Development Research.* Vol. 3 of *Child Development and Social Policy.* Chicago: University of Chicago Press.

Call, Justin; Galenson, Eleanor; and Tyson, Robert L. 1984. *Basic Books.* Vol. 2. New York: Brunner/ Mazel.

■                                                                    ■

*Caplan, Frank, ed. 1971. *The First Twelve Months of Life.* Princeton, N.J.: Edcom Systems, Inc.

Caplan, Gerald, ed. 1961. *Prevention of Mental Disorders in Children.* New York: Basic Books.

Chess, Stella, M.D., and Thomas, Alexander, M.D. 1984. *Origins of Evolution of Behavior Direction.* New York: Brunner/ Mazel.

_____. 1980. *Dynamics of Psychological Development.* New York: Brunner/ Mazel.

*Church, Joseph. 1973. *Understanding Your Child from Birth to Three: A Guide to Your Child's Psychological Development.* New York: Random House.

Clausen, John A., ed. 1968. *Socialization and Society.* Boston: Little, Brown.

*Comer, James, and Poussaint, Alvin. 1975. *Black Child Care.* New York: Stratford Press.

Cook, Thomas, D., et al. 1975. *"Sesame Street" Revisited.* New York: Russell Sage Foundation.

Crandall, Virginia. 1972. Achievement behavior in your children. In *Readings in Child Development,* eds. Irving B. Weiner and David Elkind. New York: John Wiley & Sons.

Danziger, Kurt. 1971. *Socialization.* Reprint. Harmondsworth, England: Penguin Books.

Deutsch, Martin. 1960. *Minority Group and Class Status as Related to Social and Personality Factors in Scholastic Achievement.* Ithaca, N.Y.: Society for Applied Anthropology.

_____. 1964. Facilitating development in the preschool child: Social and psychological perspectives. *Merrill-Palmer Quarterly* 10:249–63.

_____. 1965. The role of social class in language development and cognition. *American Journal of Orthopsychiatry* 35/1:78–88.

Dittman, Laura, ed. 1968. *Early Child Care.* New York: Atherton Press.

*Dodson, Fitzhugh. 1974. *How to Father.* New York: New American Library.

Ende, Robert N. 1983. *Rene A. Spitz: Ideologies from Infancy.* Selected Papers. New York: International Universities Press, Inc.

Erikson, Erik H. 1963. *Childhood and Society.* 2d ed. Reprint. New York: W. W. Norton.

Escalona, Sibylle. 1968. *Roots of Individuality.* Chicago: Aldine Publishing.

Fantz, R. 1963. Pattern vision in newborn infants. *Science* 140:296–97.

Foss, B. N., ed. 1968. *Determinants of Infant Behavior IV.* New York: John Wiley & Sons.

*Fraiberg, Selma H. 1959. *The Magic Years.* New York: Charles Scribner & Sons.

_____. 1977. *Every Child's Birthright: In Defense of Mothering.* New York: Basic Books.

*Galinsky, Ellen, and Hooks, William H. 1977. *The New Extended Family: Day Care That Works.* Boston: Houghton-Mifflin.

Garmezy, Norma, and Ritter, Michael. 1985. *Stress of Coping and Development in Children.* New York: McGraw-Hill.

Garvey, Catherine. 1977. *Play.* Cambridge: Harvard University Press.

*Gesell, Arnold L. 1940. *The First Five Years of Life.* New York: Harper & Row.

_____. 1943. *Infant and Child Care in the Culture of Today.* New York: Harper & Row.

Gesell, Arnold L., and Amatruda, Catherine. 1947. *Developmental Diagnosis.* 2d ed. New York: Paul B. Hoeber.

*Glickman, Beatrice M., and Springer, Nesha B. 1978. *Who Cares for the Baby? Choices in Child Care.* New York: Schocken Books.

Goldstein, Joseph; Freud, Anna; and Solnit, Albert J. 1973. *Beyond the Best Interests of the Child.* Reprint. New York: Free Press.

Goslin, D. A., ed. 1969. *Handbook of Socialization Theory and Research.* New York: Rand-McNally.

*Green, Martin I. 1976. *A Sigh of Relief: The First-Aid Handbook for Childhood Emergencies.* New York: Bantam Books.

Greenspan, Stanley I., M.D. 1981. *Psychopathology and Adaptation in Infancy and Early Childhood.* New York: International Universities Press.

Greenspan, Stanley I., M.D., and Pollock, George H., eds. 1989, 1990. *The Course of Life.* Vols. 1 and 2. of *Infancy.* Madison, Conn.: International Universities Press.

Harlow, H. 1949. The formation of learning sets. *Psychological Review* 56:51–65.

Hawke, Sharryl, and Knox, David. 1977. *One Child by Choice.* Englewood Cliffs, N.J.: Prentice-Hall.

Healy, Jane M. 1987. *You Child's Growing Mind.* New York: Doubleday.

Hellmuth, Jerome, ed. 1970. *Cognitive Studies.* Vol. 1. New York: Brunner/Mazel.

Hess, R., and Shipman, V. 1965. Early experience and cognitive modes. *Child Development* 36:869.

*Hoffman, Dale. 1979. A guide to pre-nursery schools. *New York* magazine, October 15.

Hunt, J. McV. 1961. *Intelligence and Experience.* New York: Ronald Press.

_____. 1971. Parent and child centers: Their basis in the behavioral and educational sciences. *American Journal of Orthopsychiatry* 41/1:13–38.

Johnson, Dale L., et al. 1974. The Houston parent-child development center: A parent education program for Mexican-American families. *American Journal of Orthopsychiatry* 44/1:121–28.

Kagan, Jerome. 1971. *Change and Continuity in Infancy.* New York: John Wiley & Sons.

Kagan, Jerome. 1984. *The Nature of the Child.* New York: Basic Books.

Kagan, Jerome; Kearsley, Richard B.; and Zelazo, Phillip R. 1978. *Infancy: Its Place in Human Development.* Cambridge: Harvard University Press.

Katz, I. 1967. The socialization of academic motivation in minority group children. In *Nebraska Symposium in Motivation,* ed. D. Levine, 133–91. Lincoln, Neb.: University of Nebraska Press.

Kessler, Jane W. 1970. Contributions of the mentally retarded toward a theory of cognitive development. In *Cognitive Studies,* ed. J. Hellmuth, vol. 1, 111–209. New York: Brunner/Mazel.

_____. 1966. *Psychopathology of Childhood.* Englewood Cliffs, N.J.: Prentice-Hall.

Knobloch, Hilda, and Pasamanic, Benjamin, eds. 1974. *Gesell and Amatruda's Developmental Diagnosis.* 3d ed. Hagerstown, MD.: Harper & Row Medical.

Levy, David M. 1956. *Maternal Overprotection.* Reprint. New York: W. W. Norton.

Lewis, M. M. 1963. *Language, Thought, and Personality in Infancy and Childhood.* New York: Basic Books.

————. 1976. *Origins of Intelligence: Infancy and Early Childhood.* New York: Plenum Press.

*Lidz, Theodore, 1968. *The Person: His Development Through the Life Cycle.* New York: Basic Books.

Lief, Nina R., and Zarin-Ackerman, Judith. 1976. The effectiveness of a curriculum of parent education on a group of risk and non-risk mothers and infants. Paper presented at meeting of the American Association of Psychiatric Services for Children, 11 November 1976, San Francisco, California.

Lipsitt, L. 1966. Learning process of human newborns. *Merrill-Palmer Quarterly* 12:45–71.

Litman, Frances. 1969. Environmental influences on the development of abilities. Excerpted from a Harvard Graduate School of Education Pre-School Project Paper presented at the Biennial Meeting of the Society for Research in Child Development, Santa Monica, California.

McClelland, D., et al. 1953. *The Achievement Motive.* New York: Appleton-Century-Crofts, Inc.

McGurk, Harry, 1974. Visual perception in young infants. In *New Perspectives in Child Development,* ed. Brian Foss. Baltimore, Md.: Penguin Books.

Madden, John; Levenstein, Phyllis; and Levenstein, Sidney. 1976. Longitudinal I.Q. outcomes of the mother-child home program—Verbal Interaction Project. *Child Development* 47/4:1015–25.

Mahler, Margaret S., and La Perriere, K. 1965. Mother-child interaction during separation. *Psychoanalytical Quarterly* 34:483–98.

Mahler, Margaret S.; Pine, Fred; and Bergman, Ami. 1975. *The Psychological Birth of the Human Infant—Symbiosis and Individuation.* New York: Basic Books.

Malone, Charles A. 1967. Psychosocial characteristics of the children from a development viewpoint. In *The Drifters,* ed. E. Pavenstedt, 105–24. Boston: Little, Brown.

*Marzollo, Jean. 1977. *Supertot: Creative Learning Activities for Children One to Three and Sympathetic Advice for their Parents.* New York: Harper Colophon Books.

Morris, Ann G., 1974. Conducting a parent education program in a pediatric clinic playroom. *Children Today* 3/6:11–14.

Murphy, Lois B. 1962. *The Widening World of Childhood.* New York: Basic Books.

————. 1963. Problems in recognizing emotional disturbances in children. *Child Welfare,* Dec., 473–87.

Neubauer, Peter B. 1968, The third year: The two-year-old. In *Early Child Care,* ed. L. Dittman, 57–67. New York: Atherton Press.

Newson, Elizabeth, and Newsom, John. 1968. *Four-Year-Olds in an Urban Community.* Chicago: Aldine Publishing.

*Parke, Ross D. 1981. *Fathers.* Cambridge: Harvard University Press.

Pavenstedt, Eleanor. 1965. A comparison of childrearing environments of upper lower and very-low lower class families. *American Journal of Orthopsychiatry* 35:89.

———. 1967. *The Drifters.* Boston: Little, Brown.

Piaget, Jean. 1950. *The Psychology of Intelligence.* New York: Harcourt, Brace.

———. 1970. The stages of the intellectual development of the child. In *Readings in Child Development and Personality,* 2d ed., eds. Paul H. Mussen, John J. Conger, and Jerome Kagan, 291–98. New York: Harper & Row.

Pine, Fred. 1971. On the separation process: Universal trends and individual differences. In *Separation-Individuation: Essays in Honor of Margaret S. Mahler,* eds. John B. McDivitt and Calvin F. Settlage, 113–30. New York: International Universities Press.

*Price, Jane. 1980. *How to Have a Child and Keep Your Job: A Candid Guide for Working Parents.* New York: Penguin Books.

Pringle, M. L. Kellmer, et al. 1967. *11,000 Seven-Year-Olds.* New York: Humanities Press.

Provence, S., and Litman, R. C. 1962. *Infants in Institutions.* New York: International Universities Press.

*Pulaski, Mary Ann Spencer. 1978. *Your Baby's Mind and How It Grows: Piaget's Theory for Parents.* New York: Harper & Row.

*Pushaw, David R. 1976. *Teach Your Child to Talk.* Fairfield, N.J.: CEBCO Standard Publishing.

Rice, Phillip. 1979. *The Working Mother's Guide to Child Development.* Englewood Cliffs, N.J.: Prentice-Hall.

Rowland, L. W. 1948. A first evaluation of Pierre the Pelican. Health Pamphlets, Louisiana Mental Health Studies, no. 1. New Orleans: Louisiana Society for Mental Health.

*Salk, Lee. 1971. *What Every Child Would Like His Parents to Know.* New York: David McKay Co.

Sarbin, Theodore R., and Allen, Vernon L. 1968. Role theory. In *Handbook of Social Psychology.,* 2d ed., eds. Gardner Lindzey and Elliot Aronson, vol. 1, 488–567. Reading, Mass.: Addison-Wesley.

Schaefer, Earl S. 1970. Need for early and continuing education. In *Education of the Infant and Young Child,* ed. V. H. Denenberg. New York: Academic Press.

Sears, Robert R.; Maccoby, E. E.; and Levin, H. 1975. *Patterns of Childrearing.* New York and Evanston, Ill.: Row, Peterson.

Shapiro, David. 1981. *Autonomy and Rigid Character.* New York: Basic Books.

*Singer, Dorothy; Singer, Jerome; and Zuckerman, Diana M. 1981. *Teaching Television: How to Use TV to Your Child's Advantage.* New York: The Dial Press.

Skinner, B. F. 1953. *Science and Human Behavior.* New York: Macmillan.

Smith, M. Brewster. 1968. Competence and socialization. In *Socialization and Society,* ed. J. A. Clausen, 270–320. Boston: Little, Brown.

Spitz, Rene A. 1945. Hospitalism and inquiry into the genesis of psychiatric conditions of early childhood. *Psychoanalytic Study of the Child* 1:53–74.

_____. 1965. *The First Year of Life.* New York: International Universities Press.

*Spock, Benjamin. 1981. *Baby and Child Care.* New York: Pocket Books.

Steinfels, Margaret O'Brien. 1973. *Who's Minding the Children? The History and Politics of Day Care in America.* New York: Simon & Schuster.

Stern, Daniel. 1988. *The Interpersonal World of the Infant.* New York: Basic Books.

*Stone, Joseph, and Church, Joseph. 1968. *Childhood and Adolescence.* New York: Random House.

Talbot, Nathan B.; Kagan, Jerome; and Eisenberg, Leon. 1971. *Behavioral Science in Pediatric Medicine.* Philadelphia: Saunders.

Terman, Lewis M., and Merrill, M. 1972. *Stanford-Binet Intelligence Scale. Form L-M.* 3d revision. Boston: Houghton-Mifflin.

*Thomas, Alexander; Chess, Stella; and Birch, Herbert G. 1968. *Temperament and Behavior Disorders in Children.* New York: New York University Press.

_____. 1977. *Temperament and Development.* New York: Brunner/Mazel.

Weinraub, Marsha, and Lewis, Michael. 1977. *The Determinants of Children's Responses to Separation.* Monographs of the Society for Research in Child Development, no. 172.

*Weiss, Robert S. 1979. *Going It Alone: The Family Life and Social Situation of the Single Parent.* New York: Basic Books.

White, Burton L. 1970. Child development research: An edifice without foundation. In *Readings in Child Development and Personality,* 2d ed., eds. P. H. Mussen et al., 97–117. New York: Harper & Row.

*_____. 1975. *The First Three Years of Life.* Englewood Cliffs, N.J.: Prentice-Hall.

White, Burton L., and Watts, Jean Carew. 1973. *Experience and Environment,* Vol. 1. Englewood Cliffs, N.J.: Prentice-Hall.

Wilson, Ronald S. 1972. Twins: early mental development. *Science* 175/4024:914–17.

Winnicott, D. W. 1951. *Transitional Objects and Transitional Phenomena: A Study of the First Not-Me Possession.* In *Collected Papers.* New York: Basic Books.

Work, Henry H. 1972. Parent-child centers: a working reappraisal. *American Journal of Orthopsychiatry* 42/4:582–95.

Yarrow, Leon J. 1968. Conceptualizing the early environment. In *Early Child Care,* ed. L. Dittman. New York: Atherton Press.

Zambrana, Ruth E.; Hurst, Martha; and Hite, Rodney. 1979. The working mother in contemporary perspective: A review of the literature. *Pediatrics* 64/6:862–70.

Zigler, Edward, and Child, Irvin L. 1969. Socialization. In *Handbook of Social Psychology,* 2d ed., eds. Gardner Lindzey and Elliott Aronson, vol. 3, 450–589. Reading, Mass.: Addison-Wesley.

# Index